Essentials

‎✓ W9-CCC-777

of **Psychological Assessment** Series

Everything you need to know to administer, score, and interpret the major psychological tests.

I'd like to order the following *Essentials of Psychological Assessment*:

- ❑ WAIS®-IV Assessment (w/CD-ROM) / 978-0-471-73846-6 • $46.95
- ❑ WJ III™ Cognitive Abilities Assessment / 978-0-471-34466-7 • $36.95
- ❑ Cross-Battery Assessment, Second Edition (w/CD-ROM) / 978-0-471-75771-9 • $46.95
- ❑ Nonverbal Assessment / 978-0-471-38318-5 • $36.95
- ❑ PAI® Assessment / 978-0-471-08463-1 • $36.95
- ❑ CAS Assessment / 978-0-471-29015-5 • $36.95
- ❑ MMPI-2™ Assessment / 978-0-471-34533-6 • $36.95
- ❑ Myers-Briggs Type Indicator® Assessment, Second Edition 978-0-470-34390-6 • $36.95
- ❑ Rorschach® Assessment / 978-0-471-33146-9 • $36.95
- ❑ Millon™ Inventories Assessment, Third Edition / 978-0-470-16862-2 • $36.95
- ❑ TAT and Other Storytelling Techniques / 978-0-471-39469-3 • $36.95
- ❑ MMPI-A™ Assessment / 978-0-471-39815-8 • $36.95
- ❑ NEPSY® Assessment / 978-0-471-32690-8 • $36.95
- ❑ Neuropsychological Assessment, Second Edition / 978-0-470-43747-6 • $36.95
- ❑ WJ III™ Tests of Achievement Assessment / 978-0-471-33059-2 • $36.95
- ❑ Evidence-Based Academic Interventions / 978-0-470-20632-4 • $36.95
- ❑ WRAML2 and TOMAL-2 Assessment / 978-0-470-17911-6 • $36.95
- ❑ WMS®-III Assessment / 978-0-471-38080-1 • $36.95
- ❑ Behavioral Assessment / 978-0-471-35367-6 • $36.95
- ❑ Forensic Psychological Assessment / 978-0-471-33186-5 • $36.95
- ❑ Bayley Scales of Infant Development II Assessment / 978-0-471-32651-9 • $36.95
- ❑ Career Interest Assessment / 978-0-471-35365-2 • $36.95
- ❑ WPPSI™-III Assessment / 978-0-471-28895-4 • $36.95
- ❑ 16PF® Assessment / 978-0-471-23424-1 • $36.95
- ❑ Assessment Report Writing / 978-0-471-39487-7 • $36.95
- ❑ Stanford-Binet Intelligence Scales (SB5) Assessment / 978-0-471-22404-4 • $36.95
- ❑ WISC®-IV Assessment, Second Edition (w/CD-ROM) 978-0-470-18915-3 • $46.95
- ❑ KABC-II Assessment / 978-0-471-66733-9 • $36.95
- ❑ WIAT®-II and KTEA-II Assessment / 978-0-471-70706-6 • $36.95
- ❑ Processing Assessment / 978-0-471-71925-0 • $36.95
- ❑ School Neuropsychological Assessment / 978-0-471-78372-5 • $36.95
- ❑ Cognitive Assessment with KAIT & Other Kaufman Measures / 978-0-471-38317-8 • $36.95
- ❑ Assessment with Brief Intelligence Tests / 978-0-471-26412-5 • $36.95
- ❑ Creativity Assessment / 978-0-470-13742-0 • $36.95
- ❑ WNV™ Assessment / 978-0-470-28467-4 • $36.95
- ❑ DAS-II® Assessment (w/CD-ROM) / 978-0-470-22520-2 • $46.95
- ❑ Executive Function Assessment / 978-0-470-42202-1 • $36.95
- ❑ Conners Rating Scales™ Assessment / 978-0-470-34633-4 • $36.95

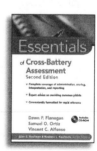

Please complete the order form on the back.
To order by phone, call toll free 1-877-762-2974
To order online: www.wiley.com/essentials
To order by mail: refer to order form on next page

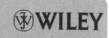

Essentials

of **Psychological Assessment** Series

ORDER FORM

Please send this order form with your payment (credit card or check) to:
John Wiley & Sons, Attn: J. Knott, 111 River Street, Hoboken, NJ 07030-5774

QUANTITY	TITLE	ISBN	PRICE
_____	_____	_____	_____
_____	_____	_____	_____
_____	_____	_____	_____
_____	_____	_____	_____
_____	_____	_____	_____

Shipping Charges:	Surface	2-Day	1-Day
First item	$5.00	$10.50	$17.50
Each additional item	$3.00	$3.00	$4.00

For orders greater than 15 items,
please contact Customer Care at 1-877-762-2974.

ORDER AMOUNT _____

SHIPPING CHARGES _____

SALES TAX _____

TOTAL ENCLOSED _____

NAME_____

AFFILIATION_____

ADDRESS_____

CITY/STATE/ZIP _____

TELEPHONE _____

EMAIL_____

❏ Please add me to your e-mailing list

PAYMENT METHOD:

❏ Check/Money Order   ❏ Visa   ❏ Mastercard   ❏ AmEx

Card Number _____ Exp. Date _____

Cardholder Name *(Please print)* _____

Signature _____

*Make checks payable to **John Wiley & Sons**. Credit card orders invalid if not signed.*
All orders subject to credit approval. • Prices subject to change.

To order by phone, call toll free 1-877-762-2974
To order online: www.wiley.com/essentials

Essentials of
WISC®-IV Assessment
Second Edition

Essentials of Psychological Assessment Series

Series Editors, Alan S. Kaufman and Nadeen L. Kaufman

Essentials of WAIS®-III Assessment
by Alan S. Kaufman and Elizabeth O. Lichtenberger

Essentials of CAS Assessment
by Jack A. Naglieri

Essentials of Forensic Psychological Assessment
by Marc J. Ackerman

Essentials of Bayley Scales of Infant Development–II Assessment
by Maureen M. Black and Kathleen Matula

Essentials of Myers-Briggs Type Indicator® Assessment
by Naomi Quenk

Essentials of WISC-III® and WPPSI-R® Assessment
by Alan S. Kaufman and Elizabeth O. Lichtenberger

Essentials of Rorschach® Assessment
by Tara Rose, Nancy Kaser-Boyd, and Michael P. Maloney

Essentials of Career Interest Assessment
by Jeffrey P. Prince and Lisa J. Heiser

Essentials of Cognitive Assessment with KAIT and Other Kaufman Measures
by Elizabeth O. Lichtenberger, Debra Broadbooks, and Alan S. Kaufman

Essentials of Nonverbal Assessment
by Steve McCallum, Bruce Bracken, and John Wasserman

Essentials of MMPI-2™ Assessment
by David S. Nichols

Essentials of NEPSY® *Assessment*
by Sally L. Kemp, Ursula Kirk, and Marit Korkman

Essentials of Individual Achievement Assessment
by Douglas K. Smith

Essentials of TAT and Other Storytelling Techniques Assessment
by Hedwig Teglasi

Essentials of WJ III™ Tests of Achievement Assessment
by Nancy Mather, Barbara J. Wendling, and Richard W. Woodcock

Essentials of WJ III™ Cognitive Abilities Assessment
by Fredrick A. Schrank, Dawn P. Flanagan, Richard W. Woodcock, and Jennifer T. Mascolo

Essentials of WMS®-III Assessment
by Elizabeth O. Lichtenberger, Alan S. Kaufman, and Zona C. Lai

Essentials of MMPI-A™ Assessment
by Robert P. Archer and Radhika Krishnamurthy

Essentials of Neuropsychological Assessment
by Nancy Hebben and William Milberg

Essentials of Behavioral Assessment
by Michael C. Ramsay, Cecil R. Reynolds, and R. W. Kamphaus

Essentials of PAI® Assessment
by Leslie C. Morey

Essentials of 16 PF® Assessment
by Heather E.-P. Cattell and James M. Schuerger

Essentials of WPPSI™-III Assessment
by Elizabeth O. Lichtenberger and Alan S. Kaufman

Essentials of Assessment Report Writing
by Elizabeth O. Lichtenberger, Nancy Mather, Nadeen L. Kaufman, and Alan S. Kaufman

Essentials of Stanford-Binet Intelligence Scales (SB5) Assessment
by Gale H. Roid and R. Andrew Barram

Essentials of WISC®-IV Assessment, Second Edition
by Dawn P. Flanagan and Alan S. Kaufman

Essentials of KABC-II Assessment
by Alan S. Kaufman, Elizabeth O. Lichtenberger, Elaine Fletcher-Janzen, and Nadeen L. Kaufman

Essentials of Processing Assessment
by Milton J. Dehn

Essentials of WIAT®-II and KTEA-II Assessment
by Elizabeth O. Lichtenberger and Donna R. Smith

Essentials of Assessment with Brief Intelligence Tests
by Susan R. Homack and Cecil R. Reynolds

Essentials of School Neuropsychological Assessment
by Daniel C. Miller

Essentials of Cross-Battery Assessment, Second Edition
by Dawn P. Flanagan, Samuel O. Ortiz, and Vincent C. Alfonso

Essentials of Millon™ Inventories Assessment, Third Edition
by Stephen Strack

Essentials of Creativity Assessment
by James C. Kaufman, Jonathan A. Plucker, and John Baer

Essentials of DAS-II® Assessment
by Ron Dumont, John O. Willis, and Colin D. Elliot

Essentials of WNV™ Assessment
by Kimberly A. Brunnert, Jack A. Naglieri, and Steven T. Hardy-Braz

Essentials of WRAML2 and TOMAL-2 Assessment
by Wayne Adams and Cecil R. Reynolds

Essentials of Evidence-Based Academic Interventions
by Barbara J. Wendling and Nancy Mather

Essentials

of WISC®-IV Assessment

Second Edition

Dawn P. Flanagan

Alan S. Kaufman

 John Wiley & Sons, Inc.

Published by John Wiley & Sons, Inc., Hoboken, New Jersey.
Published simultaneously in Canada.

No part of this publication may be reproduced, stored in a retrieval system, or transmitted in any form or by any means, electronic, mechanical, photocopying, recording, scanning, or otherwise, except as permitted under Section 107 or 108 of the 1976 United States Copyright Act, without either the prior written permission of the Publisher, or authorization through payment of the appropriate per-copy fee to the Copyright Clearance Center, Inc., 222 Rosewood Drive, Danvers, MA 01923, (978) 750-8400 or on the web at www.copyright.com. Requests to the Publisher for permission should be addressed to the Permissions Department, John Wiley & Sons, Inc., 111 River Street, Hoboken, NJ 07030, (201) 748-6011.

Limit of Liability/Disclaimer of Warranty: While the publisher and author have used their best efforts in preparing this book, they make no representations or warranties with respect to the accuracy or completeness of the contents of this book and specifically disclaim any implied warranties of merchantability or fitness for a particular purpose. No warranty may be created or extended by sales representatives or written sales materials. The advice and strategies contained herein may not be suitable for your situation. You should consult with a professional where appropriate. Neither the publisher nor author shall be liable for any loss of profit or any other commercial damages, including but not limited to special, incidental, consequential, or other damages.

This publication is designed to provide accurate and authoritative information in regard to the subject matter covered. It is sold with the understanding that the publisher is not engaged in rendering professional services. If legal, accounting, medical, psychological or any other expert assistance is required, the services of a competent professional person should be sought.

Designations used by companies to distinguish their products are often claimed as trademarks. In all instances where John Wiley & Sons, Inc. is aware of a claim, the product names appear in initial capital or all capital letters. Readers, however, should contact the appropriate companies for more complete information regarding trademarks and registration.

For general information on our other products and services please contact our Customer Care Department within the United States at (800) 762-2974, outside the United States at (317) 572-3993 or fax (317) 572-4002.

Wiley also publishes its books in a variety of electronic formats. Some content that appears in print may not be available in electronic books. For more information about Wiley products, visit our website at www.wiley.com.

Library of Congress Cataloging-in-Publication Data:
Flanagan, Dawn P.
    Essentials of WISC-IV assessment / Dawn P. Flanagan, Alan S. Kaufman.
    —2nd ed.
        p.   cm.
    Includes bibliographical references (p. 516) and indexes.
    ISBN 978-0-470-18915-3 (paper/CD-ROM)
    1. Wechsler Intelligence Scale for Children.   I. Kaufman, Alan S.,
1944-   II. Title.
    BF432.5.W42F58   2009
    155.4'1393—dc22
                                                        2008040280
Printed in the United States of America

10   9   8   7   6   5   4   3   2

For Megan,

Thank you for filling each day with love and joy,
for "working" at the desk beside mine, inspiring me daily
and for reminding me to play.

I love you
— Mom

For Nadeen,

Mon coeur d'ouvre à ta voix	My heart at your dear voice
Comme s'ouvrent les fleurs,	Does unfold and rejoice
Aux baisers de l'aurore!	Like a flower when dawn is smiling!
Mais, ô mon bien ai mé	You can my weeping stay.
Pom mieux secher mes pleurs	My sadness charm away
Avec la voix parle encore!	With your tones so beguiling!
Ainsi qu'on voit des bles	As when a field of grain
Les é pis enduler	Like the waves on the main,
Sous la brise légère,	In the breeze is swaying, bounding,
Ainsi frémit mon coeur.	So all my heart is swayed.

Samson et Dalila, Act II, Scene III
Camille Saint-Saëns (libretto by Ferdinand Lemaire)

With love always,
Alan

CONTENTS

Series Preface   xi

Acknowledgments   xiii

Authors   xiv

Contributors   xv

One   Introduction and Overview   1

Two   How to Administer the WISC-IV   53

Three   How to Score the WISC-IV   106

Four   How to Interpret the WISC-IV   133

Five   Strengths and Weaknesses of the WISC-IV   202

Six   Clinical Applications: A Review of Special Group Studies with the WISC-IV and Assessment of Low-Incidence Populations   216

Seven   Clinical Applications: Assessment of Gifted, Learning Disabled, and Culturally and Linguistically Diverse Populations   262

Eight   The WISC-IV Integrated   310

Nine   Illustrative Case Reports   468

Contents of the CD-ROM:

The *WISC-IV Data Management and Interpretive Assistant* (WISC-IV DMIA) v1.0, an automated program for WISC-IV Interpretation

Norms Tables for WISC-IV Clinical Clusters

Information for Linking WISC-IV Results to Educational Strategies and Instructional Supports

Appendix A   Definitions of CHC Abilities and Processes

Appendix B   CHC Abilities and Processes Measured by Current Intelligence Tests

Appendix C   WISC-IV Subtest *g*-Loadings, by Age Group and Overall Sample

Appendix D   Psychometric, Theoretical, and Qualitative Characteristics of the WISC-IV

Appendix E   WISC-IV Interpretive Worksheet

Appendix F1   General Ability Index (GAI) Conversion Table: U.S. and Canadian Norms

Appendix F2   Cognitive Proficiency Index (CPI) Conversion Table

Appendix G   Summary of Analyses of WISC-IV Indexes

Appendix H   Norms Tables for Clinical Clusters

Appendix I   Linking WISC-IV Assessment Results to Educational Strategies and Instructional Supports

References   516

Annotated Bibliography   532

Index   534

About the CD-ROM   556

SERIES PREFACE

I n the *Essentials of Psychological Assessment* series, we have attempted to provide the reader with books that will deliver key practical information in the most efficient and accessible style. The series features instruments in a variety of domains, such as cognition, personality, education, and neuropsychology. For the experienced clinician, books in the series will offer a concise yet thorough way to master utilization of the continuously evolving supply of new and revised instruments as well as a convenient method for keeping up-to-date on the tried-and-true measures. The novice will find here a prioritized assembly of all the information and techniques that must be at one's fingertips to begin the complicated process of individual psychological diagnosis.

Wherever feasible, visual shortcuts to highlight key points are utilized alongside systematic, step-by-step guidelines. Chapters are focused and succinct. Topics are targeted for an easy understanding of the essentials of administration, scoring, interpretation, and clinical application. Theory and research are continually woven into the fabric of each book but always to enhance clinical inference, never to sidetrack or overwhelm. We have long been advocates of what has been called *intelligent* testing—the notion that a profile of test scores is meaningless unless it is brought to life by the clinical observations and astute detective work of knowledgeable examiners. Test profiles must be used to make a difference in the child's or adult's life, or why bother to test? We want this series to help our readers become the best intelligent testers they can be.

In the first edition of *Essentials of WISC-IV Assessment*, the authors applied a fresh, new, theory-based approach to interpret the latest edition of an old favorite. Just as the publishers of the fourth edition of the WISC departed from Wechsler's traditional Verbal-Performance IQ discrepancy approach, so too did

Dawn Flanagan and Alan Kaufman bring innovation into the crucial task of making test profiles come alive for clinicians in every discipline. But much has happened in the five years since the first edition was published, necessitating a second edition to meet the challenges of assessment in the 2010s. In this revised edition, the authors deal with: (a) the passage of IDEA in 2004 and its ongoing statewide implementation; (b) the emergence of the WISC-IV Integrated on the assessment scene; (c) an expanded research base on the WISC-IV, including new test reviews; (d) and the development of a new, interesting clinical WISC-IV composite, the Cognitive Processing Index. This new edition, fully equipped with a CD-ROM to automate Flanagan and Kaufman's interpretive method, a new case study that demonstrates the use of cognitive assessment within an RTI service delivery model, and a new chapter on the WISC-IV Integrated (guest written by George McCloskey) offers a cutting-edge resource to help practitioners best meet the pressing needs for quality cognitive assessment in today's changing society.

Alan S. Kaufman, PhD, and Nadeen L. Kaufman, EdD, Series Editors
Yale University School of Medicine

ACKNOWLEDGMENTS

W̶e would like to acknowledge several people for their special and extraordinary contributions. We wish to express our deepest appreciation to Alissa Bindiger, whose review of our work significantly enhanced the quality of this book. Alissa's dedication and commitment were truly remarkable. We are also particularly grateful to George McCloskey for providing a chapter on the WISC-IV Integrated; to Brad Hale for providing a case report for inclusion in this book; to Elizabeth Lichtenberger for the countless hours she spent programming the WISC-IV *Data Management and Interpretive Assistant* (DMIA) and for revising her section on clinical applications of the WISC-IV; and to Steven Hardy-Braz, Darielle Greenberg, Nancy Hebben, Jennifer Mascolo, Samuel Ortiz, Martin Volker, and Audrey Smerbeck for graciously revising, updating, and enhancing their sections on the diverse clinical applications of the WISC-IV. We also appreciate the insightful comments and feedback of Marlene Sotelo-Dynega, Thomas Kot, Agnieszka Dynda, Jennifer Kerrigan, and Vincent Alfonso, who dedicated their time and clinical expertise to ensure that this book and the automated *WISC-IV DMIA* would be maximally useful to practitioners.

Finally, the contributions of Isabel Pratt, Sweta Gupta, and the rest of the staff at Wiley are gratefully acknowledged. Their expertise and pleasant and cooperative working style made this book an enjoyable and productive endeavor.

AUTHORS

Dawn P. Flanagan, PhD
St. John's University
Jamaica, NY

Alan S. Kaufman, PhD
Yale Child Study Center
Yale University School of Medicine
New Haven, CT

CONTRIBUTORS

Darielle Greenberg, PsyD
Licensed Psychologist
Private Practice
Richardson, TX

James B. Hale, PhD
Philadelphia College of Osteopathic Medicine
Philadelphia, PA

Steven Hardy-Braz, PsyS, NCSP
U. S. Department of Defense
Fort Bragg, NC

Nancy Hebben, PhD, ABPP-ABCN
Harvard Medical School
Boston, MA

Elizabeth O. Lichtenberger, PhD
Licensed Psychologist
Private Practice
Carlsbad, CA

Jennifer T. Mascolo, PsyD
Columbia University Teacher's College New York, NY

George McCloskey, PhD
Philadelphia College of Osteopathic Medicine
Philadelphia, PA

Samuel O. Ortiz, PhD
St. John's University
Jamaica, NY

Martin A. Volker, PhD
State University of New York at Buffalo
Buffalo, NY

Audrey M. Smerback, AB
University of Rochester
Rochester, NY

One

INTRODUCTION AND OVERVIEW

There are more individually administered tests of intelligence and IQ available today than were available at any other time in the history of psychological assessment and applied measurement. Despite all the innovations and exemplary quantitative and qualitative characteristics of new and recently revised intelligence tests, the Wechsler scales continue to reign supreme. In fact, the Wechsler Intelligence Scale for Children–Fourth Edition (WISC-IV)—like its predecessor, the WISC-III—has quickly become the most widely used measure of intelligence the world over. Because the latest edition of the WISC represented the most substantial revision of any Wechsler scale to date, we developed, in the first edition of this book, an interpretive system for the WISC-IV that was quite different from Wechsler interpretive systems of the past (e.g., Flanagan, McGrew, & Ortiz, 2000; Kaufman & Lichtenberger, 1999). For example, the elimination of the Verbal and Performance IQs required us to reconceptualize previous systems completely. Also, the proliferation of anti-profile research and writing, primarily by Glutting, Watkins, and colleagues, and the anti-profile sentiment that currently characterizes the field, impelled us to deal with the interpretive system not just as an empirical, logical, and theoretical endeavor, but also as a controversial topic. Finally, the nature of the contemporary scene, which has undergone substantial changes in test usage based on the wording of the Individuals with Disabilities Education Act (IDEA) legislation in 2004 and its attendant regulations in 2006, forced us to think outside of the box with an eye toward the future. Thus, the first edition of this book provided a psychometrically and theoretically defensible system of interpreting the WISC-IV and we believe we achieved our goal of anticipating what *best practices* in the use of the Wechsler scales would be in the coming decade (Flanagan, Ortiz, Alfonso, & Dynda, 2008). Our main reasons for this second edition were to update the research that has been conducted with the WISC-IV since the first edition of this book was published in 2004; to provide more detailed information on how to link WISC-IV assessment results to research-based interventions; to extend our interpretive system to include an interesting new cluster, the Cognitive Processing Index or CPI (Weiss, Saklofske,

Schwartz, Prifitera, & Courville, 2006); to demonstrate how the WISC-IV Integrated can complement information gleaned from the WISC-IV; and to include a CD-ROM with a software program that automates our interpretive system. Note that the CD-ROM also contains all the Appendixes to this book. Each appendix may be downloaded for your convenience.

Similar to our previous writings on the Wechsler scales, our main objective was to provide a comprehensive and user-friendly reference for those who use the WISC-IV. This book was developed specifically for those who test children between the ages of 6 and 16 and wish to learn the *essentials* of WISC-IV assessment and interpretation in a direct and systematic manner. The main topics included in this book are administration, scoring, interpretation, and clinical application of the WISC-IV. In addition, this book highlights the most salient strengths and limitations of this instrument. Throughout the book, important information and key points are highlighted in Rapid Reference, Caution, and Don't Forget boxes. In addition, tables and figures are used to summarize critical information and to explain important concepts and procedures, respectively. Finally, each chapter contains a set of Test Yourself questions that are designed to help you consolidate what you have read. We believe you will find the information contained in this book quite useful for the competent practice of WISC-IV administration, scoring, and interpretation.

This chapter provides a brief overview of historical and contemporary views of the Wechsler scales as well as a brief historical account of Wechsler scale interpretation. In addition, the WISC-IV is described and its most salient features are highlighted. Finally, a brief summary of the controversy surrounding profile interpretation with the Wechsler scales is provided, followed by a comprehensive rationale for the interpretive method described in this book.

HISTORICAL AND CONTEMPORARY VIEWS OF THE WECHSLER SCALES

Within the field of psychological assessment, the clinical and psychometric features of the Wechsler intelligence scales have propelled these instruments to positions of dominance and popularity unrivaled in the history of intellectual assessment (Alfonso et al., 2000; Flanagan et al., 2000; Kaufman, 2003; Kaufman, Flanagan, Alfonso, & Mascolo, 2006). The concepts, methods, and procedures inherent in the design of the Wechsler scales have been so influential that they have guided much of the test development and research in the field for more than a half century (Flanagan et al.). Virtually every reviewer of these scales, including those who have voiced significant concerns about them, has acknowledged the monumental impact that they have had on scientific inquiry into the nature of human intelligence and the structure of cognitive abilities. For example, despite the critical content and tone of their "Just Say No" to Wechsler subtest analysis article, McDermott, Fantuzzo, and Glutting (1990) assert their "deep respect for most of the Wechsler heritage" by stating that "were we to say everything we might about the Wechsler scales and their contributions to research and practice, by far our comments would be quite positive" (p. 291).

Likewise, Kamphaus (1993) observed that praise flows from the pages of most reviews that have been written about the Wechsler scales. Kaufman's (1994b) review, entitled "King WISC the Third Assumes the Throne," is a good example of the Wechsler scales' unrivaled position of authority and dominance in the field (Flanagan et al., 2001). Although the strengths of the Wechsler scales have always outweighed their weaknesses, critics have identified some salient limitations of these instruments, particularly as they apply to their adherence to contemporary theory and research (e.g., Braden, 1995; Flanagan et al., 2000, 2008; Little, 1992; Kaufman et al., 2006; McGrew, 1994; Shaw, Swerdlik, & Laurent, 1993; Sternberg, 1993; Witt & Gresham, 1985). Nevertheless, it remains clear that when viewed from an historical perspective, the importance, influence, and contribution of David Wechsler's scales to the science of intellectual assessment can be neither disputed nor diminished. The following paragraphs provide historical information about the nature of the Wechsler scales and summarize important developments that have occurred over several decades in attempts to derive meaning from the Wechsler IQs and scaled scores.

BRIEF HISTORY OF INTELLIGENCE TEST DEVELOPMENT

Interest in testing intelligence developed in the latter half of the 19th century. Sir Francis Galton developed the first comprehensive test of intelligence (Kaufman, 2000b) and is regarded as the father of the testing movement. Galton theorized that because people take in information through their senses, the most intelligent people must have the best developed senses; his interest was in studying gifted people. Galton's scientific background led him to develop tasks that he could measure with accuracy. These were sensory and motor tasks, and although they were highly reliable, they proved ultimately to have limited validity as measures of the complex construct of intelligence.

Alfred Binet and his colleagues developed tasks to measure the intelligence of children within the Paris public schools shortly after the end of the 19th century (Binet & Simon, 1905). In Binet's view, simple tasks like Galton's did not discriminate between adults and children and were not sufficiently complex to measure human intellect. In contrast to Galton's sensorimotor tasks, Binet's were primarily language oriented, emphasizing judgment, memory, comprehension, and reasoning. In the

1908 revision of his scale, Binet (Binet & Simon, 1908) included age levels ranging from 3 to 13 years; in its next revision in 1911, the Binet-Simon scale was extended to age 15 and included five ungraded adult tests (Kaufman, 1990a).

The Binet-Simon scale was adapted and translated for use in the United States by Lewis Terman (1916). Binet's test was also adapted by other Americans (e.g., Goddard, Kuhlmann, Wallin, and Yerkes). Many of the adaptations of Binet's test were of virtual word-for-word translations; however, Terman had both the foresight to adapt the French test to American culture and the insight and patience to obtain a careful standardization sample of American children and adolescents (Kaufman, 2000b). Terman's Stanford-Binet and its revisions (Terman & Merrill, 1937, 1960) led the field as the most popular IQ tests in the United States for nearly 40 years. The latest edition of the Stanford-Binet—the Stanford-Binet Intelligence Scales–Fifth Edition (SB5; Roid, 2003)—is a testament to its continued popularity and longevity in the field of intellectual assessment.

The assessment of children expanded rapidly to the assessment of adults when the United States entered World War I in 1917 (Anastasi & Urbina, 1997). The military needed a method by which to select officers and place recruits, so Arthur Otis (one of Terman's graduate students) helped to develop a group-administered IQ test that had verbal content quite similar to that of Stanford-Binet tasks. This was called the Army Alpha. A group-administered test consisting of nonverbal items (Army Beta) was developed to assess immigrants who spoke little English. Ultimately, army psychologists developed the individually administered Army Performance Scale Examination to assess those who simply could not be tested validly on the group-administered Alpha or Beta tests (or who were suspected of malingering). Many of the nonverbal tasks included in the Beta and the individual examination had names (e.g., Picture Completion, Picture Arrangement, Digit Symbol, Mazes) that may look familiar to psychologists today.

David Wechsler became an important contributor to the field of assessment in the mid-1930s. Wechsler's approach combined his strong clinical skills and statistical training (he studied under Charles Spearman and Karl Pearson in England) with his extensive experience in testing, which he gained as a World War I examiner. The direction that Wechsler took gave equal weight to the Stanford-Binet/Army Alpha system (Verbal Scale) and to the Performance Scale Examination/Army Beta system (Performance Scale). The focus that Wechsler had in creating his battery was one of obtaining dynamic clinical information from a set of tasks. This focus went well beyond the earlier use of tests simply as psychometric tools. The first in the Wechsler series of tests was the Wechsler-Bellevue Intelligence Scale (Wechsler, 1939). In 1946, Form II of the

Wechsler-Bellevue was developed, and the Wechsler Intelligence Scale for Children (WISC; Wechsler, 1949) was a subsequent downward extension of Form II that covered the age range of 5 to 15 years. Ultimately, the WISC became one of the most frequently used tests in the measurement of intellectual functioning (Stott & Ball, 1965). Although the practice of using tests designed for school-age children in assessing preschoolers was criticized because of the level of difficulty for very young children, the downward extension of such tests was not uncommon prior to the development of tests specifically for children under age 5 (Kelley & Surbeck, 1991).

The primary focus of the testing movement until the 1960s was the assessment of children in public school and adults entering the military (Parker, 1981). However, in the 1960s the U.S. federal government's increasing involvement in education spurred growth in the testing of preschool children. The development of government programs such as Head Start focused attention on the need for effective program evaluation and the adequacy of preschool assessment instruments (Kelley & Surbeck, 1991). In 1967, the Wechsler Preschool and Primary Scale of Intelligence (WPPSI) was developed as a downward extension of certain WISC subtests but provided simpler items and an appropriate age-standardization sample. However, because the WPPSI accommodated the narrow 4:0- to 6:5-year age range, it failed to meet the needs of program evaluations because most new programs were for ages 3 to 5 years.

Public Law 94-142, the Education for All Handicapped Children Act of 1975, played an important role in the continued development of cognitive assessment instruments. This law and subsequent legislation (IDEA of 1991, IDEA Amendments in 1997, and IDEA of 2004) included provisions that required an individualized education program (IEP) for each disabled child (Sattler, 2001). A key feature of the development of the IEP is the evaluation and diagnosis of the child's level of functioning. Thus, these laws directly affected the continued development of standardized tests such as the WPPSI and WISC. The WISC has had three revisions (1974, 1991, 2003), and the WPPSI has had two (1989, 2002). The WISC-IV is the great-great-grandchild of the 1946 Wechsler-Bellevue Form II; it is also a cousin of the Wechsler Adult Intelligence Scale–Third Edition (WAIS-III), which traces its lineage to Form I of the Wechsler-Bellevue. Figure 1.1 shows the history of the Wechsler scales.

In addition to the Wechsler scales and SB5, the Woodcock-Johnson Test of Cognitive Ability (originally published in 1977) is in its third edition (WJ III; Woodcock, McGrew, & Mather, 2001); the Kaufman Assessment Battery for Children (K-ABC; published in 1983) is in its second edition (KABC-II; Kaufman & Kaufman, 2004a); and the Differential Abilities Scale (DAS; Elliott,

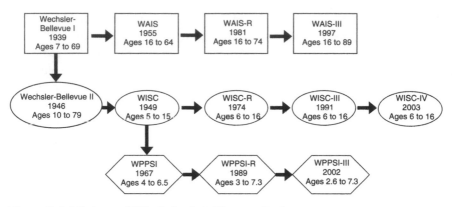

Figure 1.1 History of Wechsler Intelligence Scales

Note: WPPSI = Wechsler Preschool and Primary Scale of Intelligence; WISC = Wechsler Intelligence Scale for Children; WAIS = Wechsler Adult Intelligence Scale. From A. S. Kaufman & E. O. Lichtenberger, *Essentials of WISC-III and WPPSI-R Assessment.* Copyright © 2000. John Wiley & Sons, Inc. This material is used by permission of John Wiley & Sons, Inc.

1991) is in its second edition (DAS-II; Elliott, 2007). Other intelligence tests that have joined the contemporary scene include the Cognitive Assessment System (CAS; Naglieri & Das, 1997), the Universal Nonverbal Intelligence Test (UNIT; Bracken & McCallum, 1997), and the Reynolds Intellectual Ability Scale (RIAS; Reynolds & Kamphaus, 2003). What is most striking about recently revised and new tests of intelligence is their generally close alliance with theory, particularly the Cattell-Horn-Carroll (CHC) theory. (See Appendix A on the CD-ROM for detailed definitions of the CHC abilities and Appendix B on the CD-ROM for a list of major intelligence tests and the CHC abilities they measure.) For a complete discussion of contemporary intelligence tests and their underlying theoretical models, see Flanagan and Harrison (2005).

BRIEF HISTORY OF INTELLIGENCE TEST INTERPRETATION

Randy Kamphaus and his colleagues provided a detailed historical account of the many approaches that have been used to interpret an individual's performance on the Wechsler scales (Kamphaus, Petoskey, & Morgan, 1997; Kamphaus, Winsor, Rowe, & Kim, 2005). These authors describe the history of intelligence test interpretation in terms of four *waves:* (a) quantification of general level; (b) clinical profile analysis; (c) psychometric profile analysis; and (d) application of theory to

DON'T FORGET

Origin of WISC-IV Subtests

Verbal Comprehension Index (VCI)	Historical Source of Subtest
Vocabulary	Stanford-Binet
Similarities	Stanford-Binet
Comprehension	Stanford-Binet/Army Alpha
(Information)	Army Alpha
(Word Reasoning)	Kaplan's Word Context Test (Werner & Kaplan, 1950)

Perceptual Reasoning Index (PRI)	Historical Source of Subtest
Block Design	Kohs (1923)
Matrix Reasoning	Raven's Progressive Matrices (1938)
Picture Concepts	Novel task developed by The Psychological Corporation
(Picture Completion)	Army Beta/Army Performance Scale Examination

Working Memory Index (WMI)	Historical Source of Subtest
Digit Span	Stanford-Binet
Letter-Number Sequencing	Gold, Carpenter, Randolph, Goldberg, and Weinberger (1997)
(Arithmetic)	Stanford-Binet/Army Alpha

Processing Speed Index (PRI)	Historical Source of Subtest
Coding	Army Beta/Army Performance Scale Examination
Symbol Search	Schneider and Shiffrin (1977) and S. Sternberg (1966)
(Cancellation)	Diller et al. (1974), Moran and Mefford (1959), and Talland and Schwab (1964)

Source: From A. S. Kaufman & E. O. Lichtenberger, Essentials of WISC-III and WPPSI-R Assessment. Copyright © 2000 John Wiley & Sons, Inc. This material is used by permission of John Wiley & Sons, Inc.

Note: Supplementary subtests appear in parentheses.

intelligence test interpretation. Kamphaus and colleagues' organizational framework is used here to demonstrate the evolution of Wechsler test interpretation.

The First Wave: Quantification of General Level

Intelligence tests, particularly the Stanford-Binet, were used widely because they offered an objective method of differentiating groups of people on the basis of their general intelligence. According to Kamphaus and colleagues (1997; Kamphaus et al., 2005), this represented the first wave of intelligence test interpretation and was driven by practical considerations regarding the need to classify individuals into separate groups.

During the first wave, the omnibus IQ was the focus of intelligence test interpretation. The prevalent influence of Spearman's *g* theory of intelligence and the age-based Stanford-Binet scale, coupled with the fact that factor-analytic and other psychometric methods were not yet available for investigating multiple cognitive abilities, contributed to the almost exclusive use of global IQ for classification purposes. Hence, a number of classification systems were proposed for organizing individuals according to their global IQs.

Early classification systems included labels that corresponded to medical and legal terms, such as *idiot, imbecile*, and *moron*. Although the Wechsler scales did not contribute to the early classification efforts during most of the first wave of test interpretation, Wechsler eventually made his contribution. Specifically, he proposed a classification system that relied less on evaluative labels (although it still contained the terms *defective* and *borderline*) and more on meaningful deviations from the mean, reflecting the "prevalence of certain intelligence levels in the country at that time" (Kamphaus et al., 1997, p.35). With some refinements over the years, interpretation of intelligence tests continues to be based on this type of classification system. That is, distinctions are still made between individuals who are mentally retarded and gifted, for example. Our classification categories are quite different from earlier classification systems, as you will see in Chapter 4.

It appears that Wechsler accepted the prevailing ideas regarding *g* and the conceptualization of intelligence as a global entity, consistent with those already put forth by Terman, Binet, Spearman, and others (Reynolds & Kaufman, 1990), when he offered his own definition of intelligence. According to Wechsler (1939), *intelligence* is "the aggregate or global capacity of the individual to act purposefully, to think rationally, and to deal effectively with his environment" (p. 3). He concluded that this definition "avoids singling out any ability, however esteemed (e.g., abstract reasoning), as crucial or overwhelmingly important" and implies that any one intelligence subtest is readily interchangeable with another (p. 3).

The Second Wave: Clinical Profile Analysis

Kamphaus and colleagues (1997; Kamphaus et al., 2005) identified the second wave of interpretation as *clinical profile analysis* and stated that the publication of the Wechsler-Bellevue (W-B; Wechsler, 1939) was pivotal in spawning this approach to interpretation. Clinical profile analysis was a method designed to go beyond global IQ and interpret more specific aspects of an individual's cognitive capabilities through the analysis of patterns of subtest scaled scores.

The Wechsler-Bellevue Intelligence Scale, Form I (W-B I), published in 1939 (an alternate form—the W-B II—was published in 1946), represented an approach to intellectual assessment of adults that was clearly differentiated from other instruments available at that time (e.g., the Binet scales). The W-B was composed of 11 separate subtests, including Information, Comprehension, Arithmetic, Digit Span, Similarities, Vocabulary, Picture Completion, Picture Arrangement, Block Design, Digit Symbol, and Coding. (The Vocabulary subtest was an alternate for W-B I.)

Perhaps the most notable feature introduced with the W-B, which advanced interpretation beyond classification of global IQ, was the grouping of subtests into Verbal and Performance composites. The Verbal-Performance dichotomy represented an organizational structure that was based on the notion that intelligence could be expressed and measured through both verbal and nonverbal communication modalities. To clarify the Verbal-Performance distinction, Wechsler asserted that this dichotomy "does not imply that these are the only abilities involved in the tests. Nor does it presume that there are different kinds of intelligence, e.g., verbal, manipulative, etc. It merely implies that these are different ways in which intelligence may manifest itself" (Wechsler, 1958, p. 64).

Another important feature pioneered in the W-B revolved around the construction and organization of subtests. At the time, the Binet scale was ordered and administered sequentially according to developmental age, irrespective of the task. In contrast, Wechsler utilized only 11 subtests, each scored by points rather than age, and each with sufficient range of item difficulties to encompass the entire age range of the scale.

In his writings, Wechsler often shifted between conceptualizing intelligence as either a singular entity (the first wave) or a collection of specific mental abilities. At times he appeared to encourage the practice of subtest-level interpretation, suggesting that each subtest measured a relatively distinct cognitive ability (McDermott et al., 1990). To many, this position appeared to contradict his prior attempts not to equate general intelligence with the sum of separate cognitive or intellectual abilities. This shift in viewpoint may have been responsible, in part, for the development of interpretive methods such as profile analysis (Flanagan et al., 2001).

Without a doubt, the innovations found in the W-B were impressive, practical, and in many ways superior to other intelligence tests available in 1939. More importantly, the structure and organization of the W-B scale provided the impetus for Rapaport, Gill, and Schafer's (1945–1946) innovative approaches to test interpretation, which included an attempt to understand the meaning behind the shape of a person's profile of scores. According to Kamphaus and colleagues (Kamphaus et al., 1997; Kamphaus et al., 2005), a new method of test interpretation had developed under the assumption that "patterns of high and low subtest scores could presumably reveal diagnostic and psychotherapeutic considerations" (Kamphaus et al., 1997, p. 36). Thus, during the second wave of intelligence test interpretation, the W-B (1939) was the focal point from which a variety of interpretive procedures were developed for deriving diagnostic and prescriptive meaning from the shape of subtest profiles and the difference between Verbal and Performance IQs.

In addition to the scope of Rapaport and colleagues' (1945–1946) diagnostic suggestions, their approach to understanding profile shape led to a flurry of investigations that sought to identify the psychological functions underlying an infinite number of profile patterns and their relationships to each other. Perhaps as a consequence of the clinical appeal of Rapaport and colleagues' approach, Wechsler (1944) helped to relegate general-level assessment to the back burner while increasing the heat on clinical profile analysis.

The search for meaning in subtest profiles and IQ differences was applied to the WISC (Wechsler, 1949), a downward extension of the W-B II. The WISC was composed of the same 11 subtests used in the W-B II but was modified to assess intellectual functioning in children within the age range of 5 to 15 years. Subtests were grouped into the verbal and performance categories, as they were in the W-B II, with Information, Comprehension, Arithmetic, Digit Span, Similarities, and Vocabulary composing the Verbal Scale and Picture Completion, Picture Arrangement, Block Design, Digit Symbol, and Coding composing the Performance Scale. The WISC provided scaled scores for each subtest and yielded the same composites as the W-B II: Full Scale IQ (FSIQ), Verbal IQ (VIQ), and Performance IQ (PIQ).

Although the search for diagnostic meaning in subtest profiles and IQ differences was a more sophisticated approach to intelligence test interpretation as compared to the interpretive method of the first wave, it also created methodological problems. For example, with enough practice, just about any astute clinician could provide a seemingly rational interpretation of an obtained profile to fit the known functional patterns of the examinee. Nonetheless, analysis of profile shape and IQ differences did not result in diagnostic validity for the WISC. The next wave in intelligence test interpretation sought to address the methodological flaws in the clinical profile analysis method (Kamphaus et al., 1997; Kamphaus et al., 2005).

The Third Wave: Psychometric Profile Analysis

In 1955, the original W-B was revised and updated and its new name—Wechsler Adult Intelligence Scale (WAIS; Wechsler, 1955)—was aligned with the existing juvenile version (i.e., WISC). Major changes and revisions included (a) incorporating Forms I and II of the W-B into a single scale with a broader range of item difficulties; (b) realigning the target age range to include ages 16 years and older (which eliminated overlap with the WISC, creating a larger and more representative norm sample); and (c) refining the subtests to improve reliability.

Within this general time period, technological developments in the form of computers and readily accessible statistical software packages to assist with intelligence test interpretation provided the impetus for what Kamphaus and colleagues (1997; Kamphaus et al., 2005) called the *third wave* of interpretation—*psychometric profile analysis*. The work of Cohen (1959), which was based primarily on the WISC and the then-new WAIS (Wechsler, 1955), sharply criticized the clinical profile analysis tradition that defined the second wave. For example, Cohen's factor-analytic procedures revealed a viable three-factor solution for the WAIS that challenged the dichotomous Verbal-Performance model and remained the de facto standard for the Wechsler scales for decades and for the WISC, in particular, until its third and fourth editions. The labels used by Cohen for the three Wechsler factors that emerged in his factor analysis of the WISC subtests (i.e., Verbal Comprehension, Perceptual Organization, Freedom from Distractibility) were the names of the Indexes on two subsequent editions of this test (WISC-R and WISC-III), spanning more than 2 decades.

By examining and removing the variance shared between subtests, Cohen demonstrated that the majority of Wechsler subtests had very poor *specificity* (i.e., reliable, specific variance). Thus, the frequent clinical practice of interpreting individual subtests as reliable measures of a *presumed* construct was not supported. Kamphaus and colleagues (1997; Kamphaus et al., 2005) summarize Cohen's significant contributions, which largely defined the third wave of test interpretation, as threefold: (a) empirical support for the FSIQ based on analysis of shared variance between subtests; (b) development of the three-factor solution for interpretation of the Wechsler scales; and (c) revelation of limited subtest specificity, questioning individual subtest interpretation.

The most vigorous and elegant application of psychometric profile analysis to intelligence test interpretation occurred with the revision of the venerable WISC as the Wechsler Intelligence Scale for Children–Revised (WISC-R; Wechsler, 1974). Briefly, the WISC-R utilized a larger, more representative norm sample than its predecessor; included more contemporary-looking graphics and updated items; eliminated content that was differentially familiar to specific groups; and included improved scoring and administration procedures. "Armed with the WISC-R, Kaufman (1979) articulated the essence of the psychometric profile approach to intelligence test interpretation in his seminal book, *Intelligent Testing with the WISC-R* (which was superseded by *Intelligent Testing with the WISC-III;* Kaufman, 1994)" (Flanagan et al., 2000, p. 6).

Kaufman emphasized flexibility in interpretation and provided a logical and systematic approach that utilized principles from measurement theory (Flanagan & Alfonso, 2000). His approach was more complex than previous ones and required the examiner to have a greater level of psychometric expertise than might ordinarily be possessed by the average psychologist (Flanagan et al., 2000). Anastasi (1988) lauded and recognized that "the basic approach described by Kaufman undoubtedly represents a major contribution to the clinical use of intelligence tests. Nevertheless, it should be recognized that its implementation requires a sophisticated clinician who is well informed in several fields of psychology" (p. 484).

In some respects, publication of Kaufman's work can be viewed as an indictment against the poorly reasoned and unsubstantiated interpretation of the Wechsler scales that had sprung up in the second wave (clinical profile analysis; Flanagan et al., 2000). Kaufman's ultimate message centered on the notion that interpretation of Wechsler intelligence test performance must be conducted with a higher than usual degree of psychometric precision and based on credible and dependable evidence, rather than merely the clinical lore that surrounded earlier interpretive methods.

Despite the enormous body of literature that has mounted over the years regarding profile analysis of the Wechsler scales, this form of interpretation, even when upgraded with the rigor of psychometrics, has been regarded as a perilous endeavor primarily because it lacks empirical support and is not grounded in a well-validated theory of intelligence. With over 75 different profile types discussed in a variety of areas, including neuropsychology, personality, learning disabilities, and juvenile delinquency (McDermott et al., 1990), there is considerable temptation to believe that the findings of this type of analysis alone are reliable. Nevertheless, many studies (e.g., Hale, 1979; Hale & Landino, 1981; Hale & Saxe, 1983) have demonstrated consistently that "profile and scatter analysis is not defensible" (Kavale & Forness, 1984, p. 136; also see Glutting, McDermott, Watkins, Kush, & Konold, 1997). In a meta-analysis of 119 studies of the WISC-R subtest data, Mueller, Dennis, and Short (1986) concluded that using profile analysis with the WISC-R in an attempt to differentiate various diagnostic groups is clearly not warranted. More recent evaluations regarding the merits of profile analysis have produced similar results (e.g., Borsuk, Watkins, & Canivez, 2006; Glutting, McDermott, & Konold, 1997; Glutting, McDermott, Watkins, et al., 1997; Kamphaus, 1993; McDermott, Fantuzzo, Glutting, Watkins, & Baggaley, 1992; Watkins & Kush, 1994). The nature of the controversy surrounding clinical profile analysis is discussed later in this chapter.

The Fourth Wave: Application of Theory

Although the third wave of intelligence test interpretation did not meet with great success in terms of establishing validity evidence for profile analysis, the psychometric approach provided the foundation necessary to catapult to the fourth and present wave of intelligence test interpretation, described by Kamphaus and colleagues (1997; Kamphaus et al., 2005) as *application of theory*. The need to integrate theory and research in the intelligence test interpretation process was articulated best by Kaufman (1979). Specifically, Kaufman commented that problems with intelligence test interpretation can be attributed largely to the lack of a specific theoretical base to guide this practice. He suggested that it was possible to enhance interpretation significantly by reorganizing subtests into clusters specified by a particular theory. In essence, the end of the third wave of intelligence test interpretation and the beginning of the fourth wave was marked by Kaufman's pleas for practitioners to ground their interpretations in theory, as well as by his efforts to demonstrate the importance of linking intellectual measurement tools to empirically supported and well-established conceptualizations of human cognitive abilities (Flanagan et al., 2000, 2008).

Despite efforts to meld theory with intelligence test development and interpretation, the WISC-III (Wechsler, 1991), published nearly 2 decades after the WISC-R (Wechsler, 1974), failed to ride the fourth, *theoretical* wave of test interpretation. That is, the third edition of the WISC did not change substantially from its predecessor and was not overtly linked to theory. Changes to the basic structure, item content, and organization of the WISC-III were relatively minimal, with the most obvious changes being cosmetic. However, the WISC-III did introduce one new subtest (Symbol Search) and four new Indexes—namely Verbal Comprehension (VC), Perceptual Organization (PO), Freedom from Distractibility (FD), and Processing Speed (PS)—to supplement the subtest scaled scores and the FSIQ, VIQ, and PIQ. As with the WISC-R, Kaufman provided a systematic approach to interpreting the WISC-III in a manner that emphasized psychometric rigor and theory-based methods (Kaufman, 1994; Kaufman & Lichtenberger, 2000).

Similar to Kaufman's efforts to narrow the theory-practice gap in intelligence test development and interpretation, Flanagan and colleagues (Flanagan & Ortiz, 2001; Flanagan, Ortiz, & Alfonso, 2007; Flanagan, Ortiz, Alfonso, & Mascolo, 2006; Flanagan et al., 2000; McGrew & Flanagan, 1998) developed a method of assessment and interpretation called the *Cross-Battery approach* and applied it to the Wechsler scales and other major intelligence tests. This method is grounded in CHC theory and provides a series of steps and guidelines that are designed to ensure that science and practice are closely linked in the measurement and interpretation of cognitive abilities. According to McGrew (2005), the Cross-Battery approach infused CHC theory into the minds of assessment practitioners and university training programs, regardless of their choice of favorite intelligence battery. Kaufman's (2001) description of the Cross-Battery approach as an interpretive method that (a) has "research as its foundation," (b) "add[ed] theory to psychometrics," and (c) "improve[d] the quality of the psychometric assessment of intelligence" (p. xv) is consistent with Kamphaus's (1997; Kamphaus et al., 2005) fourth wave of intelligence test interpretation (i.e., application to theory).

Despite the availability of theory-based systems for interpreting the WISC-III (and other intelligence tests), the inertia of tradition was strong, leading many practitioners to continue using interpretive methods of the second and third waves (Alfonso et al., 2000). A few critics, however, did not succumb and instead evaluated this latest version of the WISC according to the most current and dependable evidence of science. These reviews were not positive and their conclusions were remarkably similar—the newly published WISC-III was *outdated.* According to Kamphaus (1993), "the Wechsler-III's history is also its greatest liability. Much has been learned about children's cognitive development since the conceptualization of the Wechsler scales, and yet few of these findings have been incorporated into revisions" (p. 156). Similarly, Shaw, Swerdlik, and Laurent (1993) concluded that, "despite more than 50 years of advancement of theories of intelligence, the Wechsler philosophy of intelligence, written in 1939, remains the guiding principle of the WISC-III.... [T]he latest incarnation of David Wechsler's test may be nothing more than a new and improved dinosaur."

Notwithstanding initial criticisms, the several years that followed the publication of the WISC-III can be described as *the calm before the storm.* That is, the WISC-III remained the dominant intelligence test for use with children aged 6 to 16 with little more in the way of critical analysis and review. With the advent of the 21st century, however, the CHC storm hit and has not changed its course to date. In the past 8 years, revisions of four major intelligence tests were published, each one having CHC theory at its base (i.e., WJ III, SB5, KABC-II, DAS-II).

Never before in the history of intelligence testing has a single theory (indeed any theory) played so prominent a role in test development and interpretation. Amidst the publication of these CHC-based instruments was the publication of the WISC-IV. Was it structurally different from the WISC-III? Did it have theory at its base? These questions will be answered in the paragraphs that follow; suffice it to say that the WISC-IV represents the most significant revision of any Wechsler scale in the history of the Wechsler lineage, primarily because of its closer alliance with theory. A brief timeline of the revisions to the Wechsler scales, from the mid-1940s to the present day, and their correspondence to interpretive approaches, is located in Figure 1.2.

Although we have associated our own methods of Wechsler scale interpretation with the fourth wave—application to theory—our methods continue to be criticized because they include an intraindividual analysis component. We believe these criticisms are largely unfounded, primarily because our methods have not been critiqued as a whole; rather Watkins and colleagues have critiqued only one aspect of our systems—intraindividual analysis—and concluded that because their research shows that ipsative subtest scores are less reliable and less stable than normative subtest scores, any conclusions that are drawn from ipsative analysis are unsupported. Notwithstanding the problems with this conclusion, our current interpretive approaches do not involve subtest-level analysis. The intraindividual analysis component of our interpretive approaches focuses on cluster-level, not subtest-level, analysis (Flanagan & Kaufman, 2004; Flanagan & Ortiz, 2001; Kaufman & Kaufman, 2004a). Because there is continued debate about the utility of intraindividual analysis, especially as it applies to Wechsler test interpretation, the following section provides a brief review of the most salient debate issues as well as a justification for the interpretive approach we continue to advocate in this new edition, found in Chapter 4.

THE CONTINUING DEBATE ABOUT THE UTILITY OF INTRAINDIVIDUAL (IPSATIVE) ANALYSIS

Since the early 1990s, Glutting, McDermott, and colleagues "have used their research as an obstacle for clinicians, as purveyors of gloom-and-doom for anyone foolish enough to engage in profile interpretation" (Kaufman, 2000a, p. xv). These researchers have shown that ipsative scores have poor reliability, are not stable over time, and do not add anything to the prediction of achievement after g (or general intelligence) is accounted for. Thus, Glutting and colleagues believe that ipsative analysis has virtually no utility with regard to (a) understanding a child's unique pattern of cognitive strengths and weaknesses or (b) aiding in

Clinical Profile Analysis (Second Wave)

- Interpretation of Verbal/Performance differences
- Interpretation of the shape of the subtest profiles
- Interpretation of both subtest scores and item responses
- Subtest profiles believed to reveal diagnostic information
- Rapaport et al.'s (1945/1946) work had significant impact

Psychometric Profile Analysis (Third Wave)

- Application of psychometric information to interpretation
- Interpretation of empirically based factors
- Incorporation of subtest specificity in interpretation
- Deemphasis on subtest interpretation
- Validity of profile analysis questioned
- Cohen's (1959) work had significant impact
- Matarazzo (1972) related V-P to Crystallized-Fluid
- Bannatyne's (1974) recategorization of subtests
- Sattler's (1974) profile interpretation tables
- Kaufman's (1979) "intelligent" testing approach

Applying Theory to Interpretation (Fourth Wave)

- Theoretical grouping of subtests
- Interpretation based on CHC theory
- Interpretation based on PASS theory (Naglieri & Das, 1997)
- Confirmatory hypothesis validation
- Kaufman (1979, 1994) "intelligent" testing approach
- Kamphaus (1993) confirmatory approach
- McGrew & Flanagan (1998) cross-battery approach
- Flanagan, McGrew, & Ortiz (2000) Wechsler book
- Flanagan & Ortiz (2001) CHC cross-battery approach
- Kaufman & Lichtenberger (2000) *Essentials of WPPSI-R and WISC-III Assessment*

W-B Form I 1939

- Verbal/Performance dichotomy
- Use of subtest scaled scores
- Deviation IQ (FSIQ, VIQ, PIQ)

W-B Form II 1946

- Parallel/alternate form for reliably testing after short time interval

WAIS 1955

- Name consistent with WISC
- Realigned age range to eliminate WISC overlap
- More representative norm sample
- Merged W-B I and II into single scale
- Broader age range
- Improved subtest reliability

WAIS-R 1981

- New norm sample
- Revised graphics
- More durable materials
- Updated item content

WAIS-III 1997

- New and more inclusive norm sample
- Revised graphics
- VC, PO and PS Indexes
- Introduction of WM Index
- Elimination of FD Index
- Decreased time emphasis
- Addition of Matrix Reasoning and Letter-Number Sequencing subtests

Figure I.2 Timeline of Revisions to Wechsler Scales and Corresponding Interpretive Methods

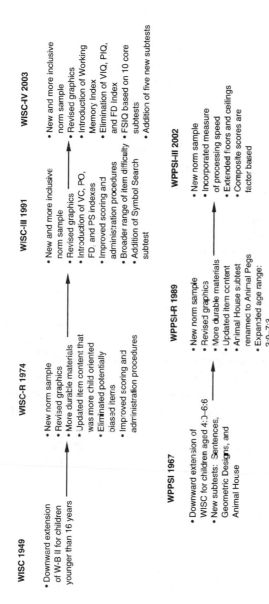

WISC 1949

- Downward extension of W-B II for children younger than 16 years

WISC-R 1974

- New norm sample
- Revised graphics
- More durable materials
- Updated item content that was more child oriented
- Eliminated potentially biased items
- Improved scoring and administration procedures

WISC-III 1991

- New and more inclusive norm sample
- Revised graphics
- Introduction of VC, PO, FD, and PS indexes
- Improved scoring and administration procedures
- Broader range of item difficulty
- Addition of Symbol Search subtest

WISC-IV 2003

- New and more inclusive norm sample
- Revised graphics
- Introduction of Working Memory Index
- Elimination of VIQ, PIQ, and FD Index
- FSIQ based on 10 core subtests
- Addition of five new subtests

WPPSI 1967

- Downward extension of WISC for children aged 4:0–6:6
- New subtests: Sentences, Geometric Designs, and Animal House

WPPSI-R 1989

- New norm sample
- Revised graphics
- More durable materials
- Updated item content
- Animal House subtest renamed to Animal Pegs
- Expanded age range: 3:0–7:3

WPPSI-III 2002

- New norm sample
- Incorporated measure of processing speed
- Extended floors and ceilings
- Composite scores are factor based

Figure 1.2 (Continued)

Note: The first wave of interpretation (quantification of general level) is omitted from this figure due to space limitations and the fact that the publication of the first Wechsler Scale did not occur until near the end of that wave. W-B = Wechsler-Bellevue; FSIQ = Full Scale IQ; VIQ = Verbal IQ; PIQ = Performance IQ; VC = Verbal Comprehension; PO = Perceptual Organization; FD = Freedom from Distractibility; PS = Processing Speed; WMI = Working Memory Index. See Figure 1.1 note for other abbreviations.

developing educational interventions. It is beyond the scope of this chapter to provide a detailed discussion of the numerous arguments that have been made for and against ipsative analysis in the past decade. Therefore, we only comment briefly on the whole of Glutting and colleagues' research and then describe how our interpretive method, which includes (but by no means is defined by) intraindividual analysis, differs substantially from previous interpretive methods.

In much of their writing, Glutting and colleagues have assumed incorrectly that all cognitive abilities represent enduring traits and, therefore, ought to remain stable over time. They further assume that interpretations of test data are made in a vacuum—that data from multiple sources, no matter how compelling, cannot influence the findings generated from an ipsative analysis of scores from a single intelligence battery. Furthermore, the method of test interpretation initially developed by Kaufman (1979) remains the focus of Glutting and colleagues' research, despite the fact that it has changed considerably in recent years (Flanagan & Kaufman, 2004; Flanagan & Ortiz, 2001; Flanagan et al., 2006, 2007; Kaufman & Lichtenberger, 2006 ; Kaufman, Lichtenberger, Fletcher-Janzen, & Kaufman, 2005). Interestingly, these changes reflect, in part, the research of Glutting and colleagues (e.g., McDermott et al., 1992). Perhaps most disturbing is the fact that these researchers continue their cries of "Just Say No" to *any* type of interpretation of test scores beyond a global IQ, and they offer *no* recommendations regarding how clinicians can make sense out of an individual's scaled score profile (e.g., Borsuk et al., 2006; Oh, Glutting, Watkins, Youngstrom, & McDermott, 2004).

We, on the other hand, recognize the onerous task facing clinicians in their daily work of identifying the presumptive cause of a child's learning difficulties. Hence we provide clinicians with guidance in the test interpretation process that is based on theory, research, psychometrics, and clinical experience. What Glutting and colleagues have yet to realize is that our interpretive method extends far beyond the identification of intraindividual (or ipsative) strengths and weaknesses.

Despite its inherent flaws, we believe that intraindividual analysis has not fared well because it historically has not been grounded in contemporary theory and research and it has not been linked to psychometrically defensible procedures for interpretation (Flanagan & Ortiz, 2001). When theory and research are used to guide interpretation and when psychometrically defensible interpretive procedures are employed, *some* of the limitations of the intraindividual approach are circumvented, resulting in the derivation of useful information. Indeed, when an interpretive approach is grounded in contemporary theory and research, practitioners are in a much better position to draw clear and useful conclusions from the data (Carroll, 1998; Daniel, 1997; Flanagan et al., 2006, 2007, 2008; Kamphaus, 1993; Kamphaus et al., 1997; Keith, 1988).

The findings of an intraindividual analysis are not the end of the interpretation process, but only the beginning. We do find many flaws with the purely empirical approach that Glutting and colleagues have used to evaluate the traditional approach to profile interpretation. Nonetheless, we have taken quite seriously many of the criticisms of a purely ipsative method of profile analysis that have appeared in the literature in articles by Watkins, Glutting, and their colleagues (e.g., Borsuk et al., 2006; McDermott et al., 1992; Oh et al., 2004). Indeed, one of us (DPF) has been frankly critical of ipsative analysis that ignores normative analysis (Flanagan & Ortiz, 2002a, 2002b). We have relied on all of these criticisms to modify and enhance our interpretive method. Following are a few of the most salient ways in which we and our colleagues have attempted to improve the practice of ipsative analysis (Flanagan & Kaufman, 2004; Flanagan & Ortiz, 2001; Kaufman & Kaufman, 2004).

First, we recommend interpreting test data within the context of a well-validated theory. Use of the CHC theory of the structure of cognitive abilities is commonplace in test construction and interpretation because it is the best-supported theory within the psychometric tradition (Daniel, 1997; Flanagan & Harrison, 2005; Flanagan & Ortiz, 2001; McGrew, 2005). Without knowledge of theory and an understanding of its research base, there is virtually no information available to inform interpretation.

Second, we recommend using composites or clusters, rather than subtests, in intraindividual analysis. Additionally, the clusters that are used in the analysis must represent *unitary* abilities, meaning that the magnitude of the difference between the highest and lowest scores in the cluster is not statistically significant ($p < .01$; see Chapter 4 for an explanation). Furthermore, the clusters that are included in the interpretive analysis should represent basic primary factors in mental organization (e.g., visual processing, short-term memory). When the variance that is common to all clusters (as opposed to subtests) is removed during ipsatization, *proportionately more reliable variance remains*. And it is precisely this shared, reliable variance that we believe ought to be interpreted because it represents the construct that was intended to be measured by the cluster. For example, when the following clusters are ipsatized—Fluid Reasoning (*Gf*), Crystallized Intelligence (*Gc*), Short-Term Memory (*Gsm*), Visual Processing (*Gv*), and Long-Term Storage and Retrieval (*Glr*)—the variance that is common to all of them (presumably *g*) is removed, leaving the variance that is shared by the two or more tests that compose each cluster. That is, if the *Gf* cluster emerged as a significant relative weakness, then our interpretation would focus on what is common to the *Gf* tests (viz., reasoning). The number of research investigations examining the relationship between broad CHC clusters and various outcome criteria (e.g., academic achievement) provide important validation evidence that may be used to inform the interpretive process (Evans, Floyd, McGrew, & Leforgee, 2002; Flanagan, 2000; Floyd, Evans, & McGrew, 2003; Floyd, Keith, Taub, & McGrew, 2007; McGrew, Flanagan, Keith, & Vanderwood, 1997; Reeve, 2004; Taub, Keith, Floyd, & McGrew, 2008; Vanderwood, McGrew, Flanagan, & Keith, 2002). Much less corresponding validity evidence is available to support traditional ipsative (subtest) analysis.

Third, we believe that a common pitfall in the intraindividual approach to interpretation is the failure to examine the scores associated with an identified *relative weakness* in comparison to most people. That is, if a relative weakness revealed through ipsative analysis falls well within the average range of functioning compared to most people, then its clinical meaningfulness is called into question. For example, despite presumptions of disability, average ability is achieved by most people and most people are not disabled. Therefore, a relative weakness that falls in the average range of ability compared to same-age peers will suggest a different interpretation than a relative weakness that falls in the deficient range of functioning relative to most people.

Fourth, we believe that the lack of stability in an individual's scaled score profile over an extended period of time (e.g., the 3 years spanning initial evaluation and reevaluation) is not unusual, let alone a significant flaw of intraindividual analysis. A great deal happens in 3 years: the effects of intervention. Developmental changes. Regression to the mean. Changes in what some subtests measure at different ages. The group data that have been analyzed by Glutting and colleagues do not have implications for the individual method of profile interpretation that we advocate. The strengths and weaknesses that we believe might have useful applications for developing educational interventions are based on cognitive functioning at a particular point in time. They need to be cross-validated at that time to verify that any supposed cognitive strengths or weaknesses are consistent with the wealth of observational, referral, background, and other-test data that are available for each child who is evaluated. Only then will those data-based findings inform diagnosis and be useful in developing interventions to help the child.

The simple finding that reevaluation data at age 13 do not support the stability of children's data-based strengths and weaknesses at age 10 says *nothing* about the validity of the intraindividual interpretive approach. If one's blood pressure is "high" when assessed in January and is "normal" when assessed 3 months later, does this suggest that the physician's categories (e.g., high, normal, low) are unreliable? Does it suggest that the blood-pressure monitor is unreliable? Or does it suggest that the medication prescribed to reduce the individual's blood pressure was effective?

Despite the pains taken to elevate the use of ipsative analysis to a more respectable level, by linking it to normative analysis and recommending that only unitary, theoretically derived clusters be used, one undeniable fact remains. The intraindividual analysis does not diagnose—clinicians do. Clinicians, like medical doctors, will not cease to compare scores, nor should they:

> Would one want a physician, for example, not to look at patterns of test results just because they in and of themselves do not diagnose a disorder? Would you tell a physician not to take your blood pressure and heart rate and compare them because these two scores in and of themselves do not differentially diagnose kidney disease from heart disease? (Prifitera, Weiss, & Saklofske, 1998, p. 6)

Comparing scores from tests, whether psychological or medical, is a necessary component of any test interpretation process. Why? We believe it is because comparing scores assists in making diagnoses when such comparisons are made using psychometric information (e.g., base-rate data) as well as numerous other sources of data, as mentioned previously (e.g., Ackerman & Dykman, 1995; Flanagan et al., 2007; Hale & Fiorello, 2004; Hale, Fiorello, Kavanagh, Hoeppner, & Gaither, 2001). The learning disability literature appears to support our contention. For example, the *double-deficit hypothesis* states that individuals with reading disability have two main deficits relative to their abilities in other cognitive areas, including phonological processing and rate, or rapid automatized naming (e.g., Wolf & Bowers, 2000). Moreover, in an evaluation of subtypes of reading disability, Morris and colleagues (1998) found that phonological processing, verbal short-term memory and rate (or rapid automatized naming) represented the most common profile, meaning that these three abilities were significantly lower for individuals with reading disability as compared to their performance on other measures of ability. Similarly, other researchers have argued for profile analysis beyond the factor or Index level (e.g., Flanagan et al., 2007; Kramer, 1993; Nyden, Billstedt, Hjelmquist, & Gillberg, 2001), stating that important data would be lost if analysis ceased at the global ability level.

Indeed, this is not the first place that the flaws of the purely empirical approaches advocated by Glutting, McDermott, Watkins, Canivez, and others have been articulated, especially regarding the power of their group-data methodology for dismissing individual-data assessment. Anastasi and Urbina (1997) state,

> One problem with several of the negative reviews of Kaufman's approach is that they seem to assume that clinicians will use it to make decisions based solely on the magnitude of scores and score differences. While it is true that

the mechanical application of profile analysis techniques can be very misleading, this assumption is quite contrary to what Kaufman recommends, as well as to the principles of sound assessment practice. (p. 513)

The next and final section of this chapter provides specific information about the WISC-IV from a qualitative, quantitative, and theoretical perspective.

DESCRIPTION OF THE WISC-IV

Several issues prompted the revision of the WISC-III. These issues are detailed clearly in the *WISC-IV Technical and Interpretive Manual* (The Psychological Corporation, 2003, pp. 5–18). Table 1.1 provides general information about the WISC-IV. In addition, Rapid Reference 1.1 lists the key features of the WISC-IV, and Rapid Reference 1.2 lists the most salient changes from the WISC-III to WISC-IV. Finally, Rapid References 1.3 and 1.4 include the CHC broad and narrow ability classifications of the WISC-IV subtests.

Although you will recognize many traditional WISC subtests on the WISC-IV, you will also find five new ones. The WISC-IV has a total of 15 subtests—10 core-battery subtests and 5 supplemental subtests. Table 1.2 lists and describes each WISC-IV subtest.

Structure of the WISC-IV

The WISC-IV has been modified in terms of its overall structure. Figure 1.3 depicts the theoretical and scoring structure of the WISC-IV as reported in the *WISC-IV Technical and Interpretive Manual* (The Psychological Corporation, 2003). Several structural changes from the WISC-III are noteworthy.

- The VCI is now composed of three subtests rather than four.
- Information is now a supplemental subtest.
- The POI has been renamed the PRI. In addition to Block Design, the PRI is composed of two new subtests, Matrix Reasoning and Picture Concepts, which are primarily measures of fluid reasoning. Fluid reasoning tasks are important as they have little dependence on cultural and educational background (Burns & O'Leary, 2004). Picture Completion is now a supplemental subtest. Object Assembly, Picture Arrangement, and Mazes have been dropped, all of which primarily measured visual processing. Picture Arrangement and Object Assembly were heavily dependent on bonus points for quick responses and presumably were dropped to put less emphasis on response time (Kaufman, Flanagan, Alfonso, & Mascolo, 2006).

Table 1.1 The WISC-IV at a Glance

GENERAL INFORMATION	
Author	David Wechsler (1896–1981)
Publication Date(s)	1949, 1974, 1991, 2003
Age Range	6:0 to 16:11
Administration Time	65 to 80 minutes
Qualification of Examiners	Graduate- or professional-level training in psychological assessment
Publisher	Pearson Assessments/The Psychological Corporation 19500 Bulverde Road San Antonio, TX 78259 Ordering Phone No. 1-800-211-8378 http://pearsonassess.com
Price WISC-IV™ Basic Kit	Includes Administration and Scoring Manual, Technical and Interpretive Manual, Stimulus Book 1, Record Form (pkg. of 25), Response Booklet 1 (Coding and Symbol Search; pkg. of 25), Response Booklet 2 (Cancellation; pkg. of 25), Blocks, Symbol Search Scoring Template, Coding Scoring Template, and Cancellation Scoring Templates. $950.00 (in box) or $1,006.00 (in hard- or soft-sided cases) **WISC-IV™ Scoring Assistant® $228.00** **WISC-IV™ Writer™ $462.00**
COMPOSITE MEASURE INFORMATION	
Global Ability	Full Scale IQ (FSIQ)
Lower Order Composites	Verbal Comprehension Index (VCI) Perceptual Reasoning Index (PRI) Working Memory Index (WMI) Processing Speed Index (PSI)
SCORE INFORMATION	
Available Scores	Standard Scaled Percentile Age Equivalent
Range of Standard Scores for Total Test Composite	40–160 (ages 6:0 to 16:11)

(*continued*)

Table 1.1 (Continued)

NORMING INFORMATION

Standardization Sample Size	2,200
Sample Collection Dates	Aug. 2001–Oct. 2002
Average Number per Age Interval	200
Age Blocks in Norm Table	4 months (ages 6:0 to 16:11)
Demographic Variables	Age Gender (male, female) Geographic region (four regions) Race/ethnicity (White; African American; Hispanic; Asian; other) Socioeconomic status (parental education)
Types of Validity Evidence in Test Manual	Test content Response processes Internal structure Relationships with other variables Consequences of testing

≡ Rapid Reference 1.1

Key Features Listed in the WISC-IV Administration and Scoring Manual (Wechsler, 2003)

- Includes several process scores that may enhance its clinical utility (see Chapters 6 and 7 for a discussion)
- Special group studies designed to improve its clinical utility
- Statistical linkage with measures of achievement (e.g., WIAT-II)
- Includes supplemental tests for core battery tests
- Provides computer scoring and interpretive profiling report
- Ability-Achievement discrepancy analysis available for FSIQ, VCI, and PRI with WIAT-II
- Wechsler Abbreviated Scale of Intelligence (WASI) prediction table (WASI FSIQ-4 and predicted WISC-IV FSIQ range at 68% and 90% confidence interval)
- Twelve subtests on WISC-III yielded four Indexes; 10 subtests on WISC-IV yield four Indexes
- Two manuals included in kit (Administration and Scoring; Technical and Interpretive)

≡ *Rapid Reference 1.2*

Changes from the WISC-III to the WISC-IV

- Structural foundation updated to include measures of *Gf* and additional measures of *Gsm* (i.e., Letter-Number Sequencing) and *Gs* (i.e., Cancellation)
- Scoring criteria modified to be more straightforward
- Picture Arrangement, Object Assembly, and Mazes deleted (to reduce emphasis on time)
- Items added to improve floors and ceilings of subtests
- Instructions to examiners more understandable
- Artwork updated to be more attractive and engaging to children
- Increased developmental appropriateness (instructions modified; teaching, sample, and/or practice items for each subtest)
- Norms updated
- Outdated items replaced
- Manual expanded to include interpretation guidelines and more extensive validity information
- Weight of kit reduced by elimination of most manipulatives
- Arithmetic and Information moved to supplemental status
- Five new subtests added: Word Reasoning, Matrix Reasoning, Picture Concepts, Letter-Number Sequencing, and Cancellation
- VIQ and PIQ dropped
- FSIQ modified substantially to include only 5 of the 10 traditional Full Scale subtests
- Freedom from Distractibility (FD) Index replaced with a Working Memory Index
- Perceptual Organization Index (POI) renamed Perceptual Reasoning Index (PRI)
- Stimulus book has been changed so that the pages are turned toward the child
- Increased use of queries and prompts to improve children's understanding of the task
- WISC-IV record form includes an analysis page that can be used to calculate a child's relative strengths and weaknesses

Source: Information in this table is from the *WISC-IV Technical and Interpretive Manual* (The Psychological Corporation, 2003; Burns et al., 2004; and Kaufman et al., 2006).

≣ Rapid Reference 1.3

WISC-IV Classifications

Subtest	Broad Ability Classifications Based on CFA of WISC-IV Standardization Data[a]		Broad and Narrow Ability Classifications Based on Expert Consensus[b]	
1. Block Design	Gv		Gv	Spatial Relations
2. Similarities	Gc		Gc	Language Development
				Lexical Knowledge
3. Digit Span	Gsm		Gsm	Memory Span
				Working Memory
4. Picture Concepts	Gf		Gf	Induction
			Gc	General Information
5. Coding	Gs		Gs	Rate of Test-Taking
6. Vocabulary	Gc		Gc	Lexical Knowledge
7. Letter-Number Sequencing	Gsm		Gsm	Working Memory
8. Matrix Reasoning	Gf, Gv		Gf	Induction and General Sequential Reasoning

Subtest	CHC Broad Ability	Narrow Ability Classification	Code
9. Comprehension	Gc	General Information	Gc
10. Symbol Search	Gs, Gv	Perceptual Speed	Gs
		Rate of Test-Taking	
11. Picture Completion	Gv, Gc	General Information	Gc
		Flexibility of Closure	Gv
12. Cancellation	Gs	Perceptual Speed	Gs
		Rate of Test-Taking	
13. Information	Gc	General Information	Gc
14. Arithmetic	Gf (especially older children)	Math Achievement	Gq
	Gsm (especially younger children)	Quantitative Reasoning	Gf
		General Information	Gc
15. Word Reasoning	Gc	Lexical Knowledge	Gc
		Induction	Gf

Note: Primary classifications appear in bold type. Secondary classifications appear in regular type. CFA = Confirmatory Factor Analysis.

[a]Keith, Fine, Taub, Reynolds, and Kranzler (2006).

[b]Alfonso, Flanagan, and Radwan (2005).

≋ *Rapid Reference 1.4*

The Psychological Corporation's a Posteriori WISC-IV CHC Classifications

Subtest	Broad Ability Classifications of the WISC-IV Subtests (TPC®)[a]
Block Design	Gv
Similarities	Gf
Digit Span	Gsm
Picture Concepts	Gf
Coding	Gs
Vocabulary	Gc, Glr
Letter-Number Sequencing	Gsm
Matrix Reasoning	Gf
Comprehension	Gc[b]
Symbol Search	Gs
Picture Completion	Gv
Cancellation	Gs
Information	Gc, Glr
Arithmetic	Gq, Gsm
Word Reasoning	Gf

Note: TPC® = The Psychological Corporation.

[a]CHC constructs corresponding to WISC-IV Indexes were provided by The Psychological Corporation® after the publication of the WISC-IV and were obtained from a list of "WISC-IV Frequently Asked Questions (FAQs)" appearing on the Harcourt website.

[b]A classification for the WISC-IV Comprehension subtest was not available from the Harcourt website. The Gc classification denoted for the WISC-IV Comprehension subtest was based on previous classifications (e.g., Flanagan et al., 2000).

- Information and Arithmetic were moved to supplemental status, reducing the emphasis of the WISC-IV on school achievement.
- The FD Index has been renamed the WMI. The WMI is composed of Digit Span and the new Letter-Number Sequencing subtest. Arithmetic, which was formerly part of the FD Index, is now a supplemental subtest, minimizing the influence of math achievement on WMI (Kaufman et al., 2006).
- The PSI remains unchanged. However, a new speed-of-processing test—Cancellation—was added as a supplemental subtest.
- The Verbal IQ (VIQ) and Performance IQ (PIQ) were dropped. This change probably reflects the greatest change in interpretation of Wechsler scales. The VIQ-PIQ discrepancy was overused and its

Table 1.2 WISC-IV Subtest Definitions

Subtest	Description
1. Block Design (BD)	The examinee is required to replicate a set of modeled or printed two-dimensional geometric patterns using red-and-white blocks within a specified time limit.
2. Similarities (SI)	The examinee is required to describe how two words that represent common objects or concepts are similar.
3. Digit Span (DS)	On Digit Span Forward, the examinee is required to repeat numbers verbatim as stated by the examiner. On Digit Span Backward, the examinee is required to repeat numbers in the reverse order as stated by the examiner.
4. Picture Concepts (PCn)	The examinee is required to choose one picture, from among two or three rows of pictures presented, to form a group with a common characteristic.
5. Coding (CD)	The examinee is required to copy symbols that are paired with either geometric shapes or numbers using a key within a specified time limit.
6. Vocabulary (VC)	The examinee is required to name pictures or provide definitions for words.
7. Letter-Number Sequencing (LN)	The examinee is read a number and letter sequence and is required to recall numbers in ascending order and letters in alphabetical order.
8. Matrix Reasoning (MR)	The examinee is required to complete the missing portion of a picture matrix by selecting one of five response options.
9. Comprehension (CO)	The examinee is required to answer a series of questions based on his or her understanding of general principles and social situations.
10. Symbol Search (SS)	The examinee is required to scan a search group and indicate the presence or absence of a target symbol(s) within a specified time limit.

(continued)

Table 1.2 (Continued)

Subtest	Description
11. *Picture Completion (PCm)*	The examinee is required to view a picture and name the essential missing part of the picture within a specified time limit.
12. *Cancellation (CA)*	The examinee is required to scan both a random and a nonrandom arrangement of pictures and mark target pictures within a specified time limit.
13. *Information (IN)*	The examinee is required to answer questions that address a wide range of general-knowledge topics.
14. *Arithmetic (AR)*	The examinee is required to mentally solve a variety of orally presented arithmetic problems within a specified time limit.
15. *Word Reasoning (WR)*	The examinee is required to identify a common concept being described by a series of clues.

Note: Subtests printed in italics are supplemental.

meaningfulness and clinical utility were never made clear in the literature (Kaufman & Lichtenberger, 2006; Kaufman et al., 2006).

- The four Indexes are derived from 10 subtests rather than 12.
- The FSIQ has changed dramatically in content and concept and barely resembles the FSIQ of previous WISCs. It includes only 5 of the traditional 10 subtests: Similarities, Comprehension, Vocabulary, Block Design, and Coding. Among the five new Full Scale subtests, three are from the WMI and PSI.

The *WISC-IV Technical and Interpretive Manual* (The Psychological Corporation, 2003) provides a series of exploratory and confirmatory factor analyses that offer support for the factor structure of the test, depicted in Figure 1.3. Specifically, four factors underlie the WISC-IV—namely Verbal Comprehension, Perceptual Reasoning, Working Memory, and Processing Speed. The structural validity of the WISC-IV is discussed further in the following paragraphs.

Standardization and Psychometric Properties of the WISC-IV

Standardization
The WISC-IV was standardized on a sample of 2,200 children who were chosen to match closely the 2002 U.S. Census data on the variables of age, gender,

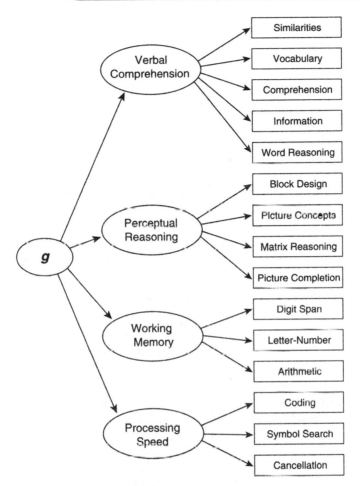

Figure 1.3 The Organization of the WISC-IV

geographic region, ethnicity, and socioeconomic status (SES; parental education). The standardization sample was divided into 11 age groups, each composed of 200 children. The sample was split equally between boys and girls (see Table 1.1).

The WISC-IV has also been adapted and standardized in Canada, the United Kingdom, France, Australia, and Germany; is currently in standardization in Japan (T. Ishikuma, personal communication, July 19, 2008); and will undoubtedly continue to be published throughout the world in many languages and cultures, as was its predecessor, the WISC-III (Georgas, Weiss, van de Vijver, & Saklofske, 2003). The test is the same in Canada as in the United States except for three questions in the Arithmetic subtest that were changed to imperial units of measurements. Standardization norms for Canada can be found on the Harcourt Assessment website.

Reliability

The reliability of the WISC-IV is presented in its *Technical and Interpretive Manual* (The Psychological Corporation, 2003, Table 4.1, p. 34) and is summarized in Rapid Reference 1.5. The average internal consistency coefficients are 0.94 for VCI, 0.92 for PRI, .92 for WMI, .88 for PSI, and 0.97 for FSIQ. Internal consistency values for individual subtests across all ages ranged from 0.72 for Coding (for ages 6 and 7) to .94 for Vocabulary (for age 15). The median internal consistency values for the individual subtests ranged from .79 (Symbol Search, Cancellation) to .90 (Letter-Number Sequencing).

The WISC-IV is a stable instrument with average test–retest coefficients (corrected for variability of the sample) of 0.93, 0.89, 0.89, 0.86, and 0.93 for the VCI, PRI, WMI, PSI, and FSIQ, respectively (The Psychological Corporation, 2003, Table 4.4, p. 40). Rapid Reference 1.6 shows 1-month practice effects (gains from test to retest) for the WISC-IV Indexes and FSIQ for three separate age groups (i.e., 6–7, 8–11, and 12–16) and the overall sample. In general, practice effects are largest for ages 6 to 7 and become smaller with increasing age. As may be seen in Rapid Reference 1.6, average FSIQ gains dropped from about 8 points (ages 6–7) to 6 points (ages 8–11) to 4 points (ages 12–16). Rapid Reference 1.7 shows the WISC-IV subtests that demonstrated relatively large gains from test to retest. For ages 6 to 7, Coding and Symbol Search showed the largest gains, while Picture Completion showed the largest gains at ages 8 to 16. Other interesting facts about 1-month practice effects on the WISC-IV are found in Rapid Reference 1.8.

G-Loadings

G-loadings are an important indicator of the degree to which a subtest measures general intelligence. Additionally, g-loadings aid in determining the extent to which a single subtest score can be expected to vary from other scores within a profile. The WISC-IV subtest g-loadings are provided in Appendix C on the CD at the back of this book. Table C.1 in Appendix C provides WISC-IV subtest g-loadings by age groups and overall sample. These g-loadings represent the unrotated loadings on the first factor using the principle factor-analysis method. This method assumes that g influences the subtests indirectly through its relationship with the four factors. Table C.1 shows that the VCI subtests generally have the highest g-loadings at every age, followed by the PRI, WMI, and PSI subtests. Arithmetic, however, has g-loadings that are more consistent with the VCI subtest loadings as compared to the WMI core battery subtests. Table C.2 in Appendix C includes g-loadings

≣ Rapid Reference 1.5

Average Reliability Coefficients of WISC-IV Subtests, Process Scores, and Composite Scales, Based on Total Sample

	Overall Reliability[a]
Subtest	
Block Design	.86
Similarities	.86
Digit Span	.87
Picture Concepts	.82
Coding	.85
Vocabulary	.89
Letter-Number Sequencing	.90
Matrix Reasoning	.89
Comprehension	.81
Symbol Search	.79
Picture Completion	.84
Cancellation	.79
Information	.86
Arithmetic	.88
Word Reasoning	.80
Process Score	
Block Design No Time Bonus	.84
Digit Span Forward	.83
Digit Span Backward	.80
Cancellation Random	.70
Cancellation Structured	.75
Composite Scale	
Verbal Comprehension Index	.94
Perceptual Reasoning Index	.92
Working Memory Index	.92
Processing Speed Index	.88
Full Scale	.97

Source: Information in this table was reproduced from the *WISC-IV Technical and Interpretive Manual* (The Psychological Corporation, 2003).

[a] Average reliability coefficients were calculated with Fisher's z transformation.

≡ Rapid Reference 1.6

One-Month Practice Effects for the WISC-IV Indexes and Full-Scale IQ (Total N = 243)

Scale	Ages 6–7	Ages 8–11	Ages 12–16	All Ages
VCI	+3.4	+2.2	+1.7	+2.1
	(.31 SD)	(.20 SD)	(.14 SD)	(.18 SD)
PRI	+6.4	+4.2	+5.4	+5.2
	(.46 SD)	(.34 SD)	(.38 SD)	(.39 SD)
WMI	+4.7	+2.8	+1.6	+2.6
	(.33 SD)	(.22 SD)	(.12 SD)	(.20 SD)
PSI	+10.9	+8.2	+4.7	+7.1
	(.72 SD)	(.60 SD)	(.35 SD)	(.51 SD)
FSIQ	+8.3	+5.8	+4.3	+5.6
	(.62 SD)	(.53 SD)	(.34 SD)	(.46 SD)

Source: Data are from WISC-IV Technical and Interpretive Manual (The Psychological Corporation, 2003, Table 4.4).

Note: Intervals ranged from 13 to 63 days, with a mean of 32 days.

for the overall sample from the last column in Table C.1 alongside g-loadings based on confirmatory factor analysis (CFA) using a nested factors model. This latter method assumes that each subtest has a distinct and direct relationship with both g and a broad ability (factor; Keith, 2006). Therefore, the g-loadings in the second column of Table C.2 were derived in a manner more consistent with the factor and scoring structure of the WISC-IV. Table C.2 shows that subtest g-loadings are generally consistent across methods, with two exceptions—both Word Reasoning and Comprehension had high g-loadings (.70 or greater) based on the principal factor-analysis method and medium g-loadings (.51 to .69) based on the CFA (nested factors) method. These g-loadings may be useful in generating hypotheses about fluctuations in a child's scaled score profile.

Floors, Ceilings, and Item Gradients

The floors and ceilings for all WISC-IV subtests are excellent, indicating that scaled scores greater than 2 SDs above and 2 SDs below the mean may be obtained on

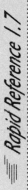

≡ Rapid Reference 1.7

One-Month Practice Effects for the Separate WISC-IV Scaled Scores: Subtests with Relatively Large Gains from Test to Retest

Ages 6–7	Ages 8–11	Ages 12–16
Coding (+0.65 SD)	Picture Completion (+0.68 SD)	Picture Completion (+0.58 SD)
Symbol Search (+0.62 SD)	Symbol Search (+0.52 SD)	Cancellation (+0.44 SD)
Picture Completion (+0.58 SD)	Picture Concepts (+0.52 SD)	Coding (+0.40 SD)
Arithmetic (+0.57 SD)	Cancellation (+0.47 SD)	Block Design (+0.40 SD)
Picture Concepts (+0.50 SD)	Block Design (+0.40 SD)	Picture Concepts (+0.35 SD)
Block Design (+0.45 SD)		
Similarities (+0.45 SD)		
Word Reasoning (+0.42 SD)		
Letter-Number Sequencing (+0.39 SD)		

Source: Data are from *WISC-IV Technical and Interpretive Manual* (The Psychological Corporation, 2003, Table 4.4).

Note: Relatively large gains are defined as at least 0.33 SD (a gain from test to retest of approximately 1.0 scaled score point, depending on the precise SDs at each age). Gains are listed by the magnitude of the gain for each age group. Intervals ranged from 13 to 63 days, with a mean of 32 days.

35

≡ Rapid Reference 1.8

Interesting Facts about One-Month Practice Effects on the WISC-IV

- WISC-IV practice effects (gains from test to retest) are largest for ages 6 to 7 and become smaller with increasing age. Average FSIQ gains dropped from about 8 points (ages 6–7) to 6 points (ages 8–11) to 4 points (ages 12–16). See Rapid Reference 1.6.

- The age-related changes in practice effects held for VCI, WMI, and PSI, but not for PRI. The PRI, which measures the *performance* abilities that traditionally yield the largest practice effects, averaged test–retest gains of about 5 points across the age range (see Rapid Reference 1.6).

- Despite the very large practice effect of 11 points (.72 SD) for ages 6 to 7 on PSI, this age group showed no practice effect at all on Cancellation, the supplemental Processing Speed subtest. In contrast, Cancellation produced among the largest practice effects for ages 8 to 16 (effect sizes of about 0.45 SD; see Rapid Reference 1.7).

- Arithmetic and Letter-Number Sequencing, both measures of Working Memory, had substantial practice effects at ages 6 to 7 (see Rapid Reference 1.7), but yielded little or no gains for all other age groups.

- Picture Completion had by far the largest practice effect for all ages combined (0.60 SD). It joins Picture Concepts and Block Design as the only WISC-IV subtests to yield relatively large test–retest gains for each age group studied: 6 to 7, 8 to 11, and 12 to 16 (see Rapid Reference 1.7).

- Practice effects for Digits Forward and Digits Backward varied as a function of age. For ages 6 to 11, test–retest gains were larger for Digits Backward (effect size of 0.19 SD versus 0.12 SD for Digits Forward). For ages 12 to 13, gains were about equal for Digits Forward and Digits Backward. For ages 14 to 16, test–retest gains were larger for Digits Forward (effect size of 0.29 SD versus 0.11 SD for Digits Backward).

all subtests at all ages. Therefore, the WISC-IV may be used confidently as part of an evaluation for the identification of individuals who are functioning in either the gifted or mentally retarded ranges of functioning, respectively. Item gradients refer to the spacing between items on a subtest. The item gradients for the WISC-IV subtest range from good to excellent across the age range of the test. In fact, the only item gradient violation occurred at age 6. Thus, the spacing between items on the WISC-IV subtests is generally small enough to allow for reliable discrimination between individuals on the latent trait measured by the subtest.

Structural Validity

As stated previously, the structural validity of the WISC-IV is supported by the factor-analytic studies described in the *WISC-IV Technical and Interpretive Manual* (The Psychological Corporation, 2003; see Figure 1.3 in this chapter). However, the manual did not provide information about the stability or invariance of this factor structure across age. In addition, because The Psychological Corporation did not provide factor loadings and factor correlations for the confirmatory factor analyses presented in the manual, additional analyses were needed to clarify the nature of the cognitive constructs measured by the test.

Keith and colleagues (2006) investigated whether the WISC-IV measured the same constructs across its 11-year age span, as well as the nature of those constructs using the WISC-IV standardization data. Results of their analyses indicated that the WISC-IV measures the same constructs across the age range of the test. These constructs are represented by the large ovals in Figure 1.3. However, according to Keith and colleagues, the factor structure of the WISC-IV (depicted in Figure 1.3) is not a good explanation of the constructs measured by the test. Rather, based on a comparison of theory-derived alternative models with the one depicted in Figure 1.3, Keith and colleagues found that a factor structure more consistent with CHC theory provided a better fit to the WISC-IV standardization data. See Appendix A for detailed definitions of the CHC abilities.

According to Keith and colleagues (2006), the WISC-IV measures Crystallized Ability (*Gc*), Visual Processing (*Gv*), Fluid Reasoning (*Gf*), Short-Term Memory (*Gsm*), and Processing Speed (*Gs*). These findings are depicted in Figure 1.4 and are consistent with the results of a recently conducted content-validity study of the WISC-IV, based on CHC theory, that used an expert consensus format (Alfonso, Flanagan, & Radwan, 2005). Rapid Reference 1.3 summarizes the results of the studies conducted by Keith and colleagues (2006) and Alfonso and colleagues (2005). Although The Psychological Corporation identified four factors to describe the constructs underlying the WISC-IV, Rapid Reference 1.3 shows that Keith and colleagues and Alfonso and colleagues found five. In addition, the results of these latter two studies were consistent, with the exception of the CHC abilities presumed to underlie the Arithmetic subtest. Keith and colleagues described this test as *Gf* and *Gsm,* and Alfonso and colleagues classified this test as Quantitative Knowledge *Gq* and *Gf.* Interestingly, following the publication of the WISC-IV and its *WISC-IV Technical and Interpretive Manual* (The Psychological Corporation, 2003), The Psychological Corporation classified all of the WISC-IV subtests according to CHC theory on its website. These classifications are located in Rapid Reference 1.4, which shows that the classifications offered by The Psychological Corporation are similar to those provided in Rapid Reference 1.3, with

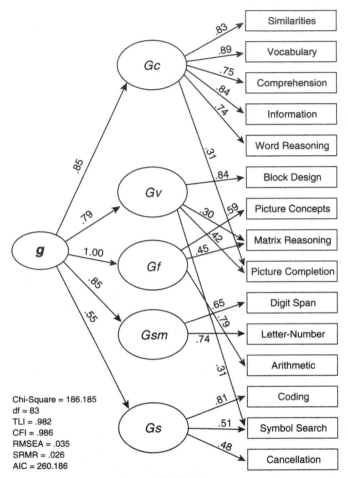

Figure 1.4 CHC Structure of the WISC-IV

Source: Keith et al. (2006). Printed with permission from authors.

Note: df = degrees of freedom; TLI = Tucker Lewis Index; CFI = Comparative Fit Index; RMSEA = Root Mean Square Error of Approximation; SRMR = Standardized Root Mean Square Residual; AIC = Akaike Information Criterion.

only a few exceptions. That is, The Psychological Corporation classified Similarities and Word Reasoning as primarily measures of *Gf* and Arithmetic as primarily a measure of *Gq* and *Gsm*.

Although the factor analyses conducted by The Psychological Corporation and Keith and colleagues (2006) differ, it is important to understand that there is no one *right* method of factor analysis. Indeed, the factor analyses, particularly the exploratory factor analyses, summarized in the *WISC-IV Technical and Interpretive Manual* provide strong support for the WISC-IV four-factor structure; while the confirmatory factor analyses conducted by Keith and colleagues provide strong support for a five-factor structure. Noteworthy is the fact that the five-factor CHC model is more in line with contemporary psychometric theory and research than is the four-factor structure that was used to develop the four WISC-IV Indexes. Nevertheless, our interpretive system permits examiners to interpret the WISC-IV according to either four or five factors. The latter option is made possible by the inclusion of clinical clusters and supplementary norms in our interpretive system (Chapter 4, Step 7).

Briefly, based on the results of independent factor analyses, expert consensus content-validity findings, the CHC classifications of the WISC-IV subtests offered by The Psychological Corporation (see Rapid References 1.3 and 1.4), and our own clinical judgment, we developed eight new clinical clusters:

1. Fluid Reasoning (*Gf*)
2. Visual Processing (*Gv*)
3. Nonverbal Fluid Reasoning (*Gf*-nonverbal)
4. Verbal Fluid Reasoning (*Gf*-verbal)
5. Lexical Knowledge (*Gc*-VL)
6. General Information (*Gc*-KO)
7. Long-Term Memory (*Gc*-LTM)
8. Short-Term Memory (*Gsm*-MW)

These clinical clusters may be used in what we call *Planned Clinical Comparisons* to gain information about a child's cognitive capabilities beyond the four Indexes and FSIQ, as well as to generate hypotheses about cognitive performance to be verified through other data sources. Figure 1.5 provides a *selective testing table* that may be used by the examiner to identify the different combinations of WISC-IV subtests that compose the four Indexes, FSIQ, and new clinical clusters. Use of the clinical clusters in Planned Clinical Comparisons is discussed as an optional interpretive step in Chapter 4.

Relationship to Other Wechsler Scales
In addition to factor analysis and content-validity research, the validity of the WISC-IV is supported by correlations with scores on other comprehensive measures of cognitive ability in normal and special group samples (Wechsler, 2003a; Kaufman & Kaufman, 2004, Table 8.17; Launey, Caroll, & Van Horn, 2007).

Figure I.5 Selective Testing Table

Subtest	Full Scale IQ (FSIQ)	Verbal Comprehension Index (VCI)	Perceptual Reasoning Index (PRI)	Working Memory Index (WMI)	Processing Speed Index (PSI)	Fluid Reasoning (Gf) Cluster	Visual Processing (Gv) Cluster	Verbal Fluid Reasoning (Gf-verbal) Cluster	Nonverbal Fluid Reasoning (Gf-nonverbal) Cluster	Lexical Knowledge (Gc-VL) Cluster	General Information (Gc-K0) Cluster	Long-Term Memory (Gc-LTM) Cluster	Short-Term Memory (Gsm-WM) Cluster [a]
1. Block Design	•		•				•						
2. Similarities	•	•						•					
3. Digit Span	•			•									•
4. Picture Concepts	•		•			•			•				
5. Coding	•				•								
6. Vocabulary	•	•								•		•	
7. Letter-Number Sequencing	•			•									•
8. Matrix Reasoning	•		•			•			•				
9. Comprehension	•	•									•		
10. Symbol Search	•				•								
11. Picture Completion							•						
12. Cancellation													
13. Information											•	•	
14. Arithmetic						•							
15. Word Reasoning								•		•			

[a] The Short-Term Memory (*Gsm*-WM) Cluster is identical to the WISC-IV Working Memory Index.

Correlations with Full Scale IQ

Rapid Reference 1.9 shows the correlations between the WISC-IV FSIQ and the WISC-III FSIQ (.89) as well as the FSIQs from other Wechsler scales that are composed of both verbal and nonverbal subtests (i.e., WPPSI-III, WAIS-III, WAIS-IV, and WASI). Not surprisingly, the WISC-IV FSIQ is highly correlated with the FSIQs of these other Wechsler scales. Data are also included for the new *Wechsler Nonverbal Scale of Ability* (WNV; Wechsler & Naglieri. 2006, Table 5.16) for the Full Scale scores yielded by the WNV four-subtest battery and two-subtest battery. These coefficients (.76 and .58, respectively) are lower than the values for the other Wechsler scales, but that is sensible because the WNV is the only Wechsler scale that excludes verbal tasks.

The correlation of .91 between WISC-IV and WAIS-IV Full Scale IQs is large, and is consistent with the fact that both new Wechsler scales compute Full Scale IQ the same way—namely, based on the 10 subtests that

≡ *Rapid Reference 1.9*

Correlation of Full Scale IQs: WISC-IV and Other Wechsler Scales

	WISC-IV
WISC-III (N = 233)	.89
WPPSI-III (N = 144)	.89
WAIS-III (N = 183)	.89
WAIS-IV (N = 157)	.90
WASI (N = 254)	.86
WNV (N = 102)	
Full Scale Score (four subtests)	.76
Full Scale Score (two subtests)	.58

Note: All values are corrected for the variability of the standardization sample. Coefficients for the WPPSI-III, WISC-III, WAIS-III, and WASI are from *WISC-IV Technical and Interpretive Manual* (The Psychological Corporation, 2003, Tables 5.8, 5.10, 5.12, and 5.14). Coefficients for the Wechsler Nonverbal Scale of Ability are from the WNV Technical and Interpretive Manual (Wechsler & Naglieri, 2006, Table 5.16). Coefficients for the WAIS-IV are from the *WAIS-IV Technical and Interpretive Manual* (Pearson/PsychCorp, 2008, Table 5.9).

compose the four indexes. Even more impressive than the .91 coefficient are the values of .89 between WISC-IV FSIQ and previous FSIQs. These substantial coefficients suggest a continuity of the construct measured by the Full Scale, which is notable because the WISC-IV Full Scale is dramatically different from its predecessors. It shares only five subtests in common with the Full Scales of earlier versions of the WISC and other Wechsler scales.

The substantial correlation between WISC-IV FSIQ and previous FSIQs suggests a continuity of the construct measured by the Full Scale. Nonetheless, it is notable that the WISC-IV Full Scale is dramatically different from its predecessors. It shares only five subtests in common with the Full Scales of earlier versions of the WISC.

The two WMI and two PSI subtests, all of which have relatively "low g–loadings" (.40s to .60s; Tables C.1 and C.2), constitute 40% of the Full Scale. Of these four working-memory and processing speed subtests, only Coding was on previous WISC Full Scales. Excluded from the WISC-IV FSIQ are subtests that have "high g-loadings," like Arithmetic and Information (mid-.70s to low .80s). This different FSIQ better represents the constructs that compose the WISC-IV; however, despite the .89 coefficients with WISC-III FSIQ, it is possible that research findings with previous WISCs do not completely generalize to the WISC-IV (Kaufman, Flanagan, Alfonso, & Mascolo, 2006). For example, FSIQ differences between Whites and African Americans who were matched on SES and other background variables were found to be smaller on the WISC-IV (8.8 points) than on WISC-III (11.0 points) (Prifitera & Saklofske, 1998; Prifitera, Saklofske, & Weiss, 2005). This is a positive finding, discussed later in this chapter. But, as Kaufman and colleagues (2006) note, "clinicians and researchers need to be aware that with the clear-cut improvements in the structure of the major scales that comprise the WISC-IV comes the side effect of bringing into question the generalizability to the WISC-IV of IQ-based research results—even those that are time tested over the past 60 years with the Wechsler-Bellevue II, WISC, WISC-R, and WISC-III" (p. 281).

Convergent–Discriminant Validity Coefficients

The WISC-IV also shows good to excellent convergent–discriminant validity evidence. Rapid Reference 1.10 presents coefficients for the WISC-IV VCI and PRI with verbal and nonverbal scales on other Wechsler batteries. These scales include five Wechsler tests that yield scores on *both* verbal and nonverbal subtests: WPPSI-III, WISC-III, WAIS-III, WAIS-IV, and WASI. For these Wechsler scales, VCI has an average correlation of .84 with other measures of verbal ability, compared to a mean of .60 with measures of perceptual abilities. Similarly, Rapid Reference 1.10 shows that the PRI has an average correlation of .76 with other measures of visual-perceptual ability, compared to a mean of .61 with measures of verbal abilities.

In addition to the more traditional verbal-nonverbal Wechsler batteries, Rapid Reference 1.10 also presents convergent–discriminant coefficients for the WNV, which would be predicted to correlate substantially higher with WISC-IV PRI than VCI. Again, these data support the validity of the WISC-IV Indexes, as the two WNV Full Scale scores (based only on nonverbal subtests) correlated higher with PRI than VCI. The magnitude of the coefficients with the two WISC-IV Indexes is lower than the values for the other Wechsler scales (about .40 with VCI

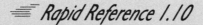

Rapid Reference 1.10

Convergent–Discriminant Validity of the WISC-IV Verbal Comprehension Index (VCI) and Perceptual Reasoning Index(PRI)

	WISC-IV	
	VCI	PRI
WPPSI-III (n = 182, ages 6–7)		
Verbal IQ	**.83**	.63
Performance IQ	.65	**.79**
General Language Composite (GLC)	**.68**	.53
WISC-III (n = 244, ages 6–16)		
Verbal Comprehension Index (VCI)	**.88**	.59
Perceptual Organization Index (POI)	.62	**.72**
Verbal IQ	**.87**	.61
Performance IQ	.61	**.74**
WAIS-III (n = 198, age 16)		
Verbal Comprehension Index (VCI)	**.86**	.64
Perceptual Organization Index (POI)	.57	**.76**
Verbal IQ	**.86**	.69
Performance IQ	.61	**.76**
WASI-4 subtests (n = 260, ages 6–16)		
Verbal IQ	**.85**	.61
Performance IQ	.60	**.78**
WAIS-IV (n = 157, age 16)		
Verbal Comprehension Index	**.88**	.54
Perceptual Reasoning Index	.52	**.77**
WNV (n = 102, ages 7–16)		
Full Scale Score (four subtests)	.47	**.66**
Full Scale Score (two subtests)	.31	**.57**

Source: Convergent and divergent values for the Wechsler Nonverbal Scale of Ability (WNV) are from the *WNV Technical and Interpretive Manual* (Wechsler & Naglieri, 2006, Table 5.16). Convergent values for the WPPSI-III, WISC-III, WAIS-III, and WASI are from the *WISC-IV Technical and Interpretive Manual* (The Psychological Corporation, 2003, Tables 5.8, 5.10, 5.12, and 5.14). The divergent values (VCI with visual-perceptual ability, PRI with verbal ability) were provided by The Psychological Corporation. Convergent values for the WAIS-IV are from the *WAIS IV Technical and Interpretive Manual* (Pearson/PsychCorp, 2008, Table 5.9). Divergent values were provided by The Psychological Corporation. Analysis results from the Wechsler Intelligence Scale for Children—Fourth Edition (WISC-IV).

Note: Correlations of WISC-IV VCI and PRI with other measures of Wechsler's Verbal and Visual-Perceptual ability (average-corrected correlations across two testing orders), respectively, are printed in bold. Coefficients in bold denote convergent validity of WISC-IV VCI and PRI. All values are corrected for the variability of the standardization sample.

and about .60 with PRI) because the content of the WNV is so different from the content of the other Wechsler scales. The reason that the WNV correlated lower with VCI than the other Wechsler scales did is obvious, given the exclusion of verbal tasks from the WNV. The reasons for the lower correlations with PRI are less obvious, but undoubtedly relate to the fact that the WNV includes the novel nonverbal subtests of Recognition for ages 4 through 7 (memory for abstract figures) and Spatial Span for ages 8 though 21 (ability to reproduce the sequence of blocks tapped by the examiner). In addition, the WNV includes familiar Wechsler subtests that were not included in the WISC-IV—Object Assembly (ages 4–7) and Picture Arrangement (8–21). The net result is that the WNV correlates substantially enough with the WISC-IV and a variety of other cognitive batteries (Wechsler & Naglieri, 2006, Chapter 5) to support its construct validity, but it also has its own degree of uniqueness. As Kaufman (2006) notes in the Foreword to the WNV, "its built-in brief form makes it a flexible instrument for a variety of testing purposes within the 4- to 21-year age range, and its clever administrative aids make it a user-friendly instrument whenever it is desirable or essential to test a person's general intelligence nonverbally" (p. iv).

Relationship to WIAT-II

The validity of the WISC-IV was investigated further through an examination of its relationship to academic achievement. Rapid Reference 1.11 includes the

≡ Rapid Reference 1.11

WISC-IV Indexes and Full Scale IQ: Correlations with WIAT-II Achievement Composites

WIAT-II Composite	VCI	PRI	WMI	PSI	FSIQ
Reading	.74	.63	.66	.50	.78
Math	.68	.67	.64	.53	.78
Written Language	.67	.61	.64	.55	.76
Oral Language	.75	.63	.57	.49	.75
Total Achievement	.80	.71	.71	.58	.87

Note: All values are corrected for the variability of the standardization sample. Coefficients are from WISC-IV Technical and Interpretive Manual (The Psychological Corporation, 2003, Table 5.15). Sample sizes range from 538 to 548.

correlations between the WISC-IV Indexes and FSIQ with the WIAT-II Achievement Composites. This Rapid Reference shows that the correlations between the FSIQ and WIAT-II Composites ranged from .75 (Oral Language) to .78 (Reading and Math), indicating that the WISC-IV FSIQ explains 56 to 60% of the variance in these achievement domains. Regardless of whether or not there is significant variability in factor scores, the FSIQ is a robust predictor of academic achievement in normal and clinical samples (Watkins, Glutting, & Lee, 2007; Glutting, Watkins, Konold, & McDermott, 2006; Weiss et al., 2006). The correlation between the FSIQ and WIAT-II Total Achievement Score is .87 (76% of variance explained), which is about as high as the correlation between the WISC-IV FSIQ and the FSIQs of other Wechsler scales (i.e., .89; see Rapid Reference 1.9). These correlations are among the highest ever reported between global IQ and achievement. According to Kenny (1979), "even highly developed causal models do not explain behavior very well. A good rule of thumb is that one is fooling oneself if more than 50% of the variance is predicted" (p. 9). It is likely that either overlapping content or standard deviations greater than 15 or some combination thereof led to spuriously high correlations.

Rapid Reference 1.12 summarizes the WISC-IV subtests that are the best and worst predictors of WIAT-II Achievement Composites. In general, Arithmetic, Vocabulary, and Information are the best predictors of the WIAT-II Composites; and Picture Concepts along with Coding and Cancellation (i.e., the Processing Speed subtests) are the worst predictors of these same composites.

In addition to the validity evidence summarized previously, the *WISC-IV Technical and Interpretive Manual* provides a number of special group studies to investigate the diagnostic utility of the instrument. These studies are discussed in detail in Chapter 6. Overall, the WISC-IV is a reliable and valid measure of a select number of cognitive abilities (viz., Verbal Comprehension [*Gc*], Perceptual Reasoning [*Gf, Gv*], Working Memory [*Gsm*], and Processing Speed [*Gs*]).

Ehnic Differences on the WISC-IV

Historically, Whites have scored about one standard deviation higher than African Americans on Wechsler's scales, with Full Scale IQs differing by 15.9 points on the WISC-R (Kaufman & Doppelt, 1976) and 14.9 points on the WISC-III (Prifitera, Weiss, & Saklofske, 1998, Table 1.1). For the WISC-IV, Full Scale IQ differences are reduced to ¾ SD, or 11.5 points; when SES and other background variables are controlled, that difference reduces to 8.8 points (Prifitera, Weiss, Saklofske, & Rolfhus, 2005, Tables 1.3 & 1.4). As shown in Rapid Reference 1.13, this overall difference in Full Scale IQ is merely an average of wide variations in African American–White

Rapid Reference 1.12

WISC-IV Subtests: The Best and Worst Predictors of WIAT-II Achievement Composites

Reading	Math	Written Language	Oral Language	Total Achievement
BEST				
Vocabulary (.72)	Arithmetic (.74)	Arithmetic (.67)	Vocabulary (.73)	Vocabulary (.76)
Information (.68)	Information (.67)	Vocabulary (.64)	Information (.69)	Information (.75)
Arithmetic (.68)	Vocabulary (.64)	Information (.62)	Similarities (.67)	Arithmetic (.75)
WORST				
Picture Concepts (.42)	Picture Concepts (.42)	Picture Concepts (.41)	Picture Concepts (.41)	Picture Concepts (.47)
Coding (.40)	Coding (.42)	Picture Completion (.40)	Coding (.38)	Coding (.45)
Cancellation (.14)	Cancellation (.11)	Cancellation (.14)	Cancellation (.15)	Cancellation (.15)

Note: Correlations of WISC-IV scaled scores with WIAT-II achievement composite standard scores are repeated in parentheses. All values are corrected for the variability of the standardization sample. Coefficients are from WISC-IV Technical and Interpretive Manual (The Psychological Corporation, 2003, Table 5.15). Sample sizes range from 531 to 548, except for the Arithmetic subtest (n = 301).

≡ Rapid Reference 1.13

Difference in Mean Standard Scores for Whites versus African Americans on the WISC-IV Full Scale IQ and Indexes, Controlling for SES and Other Background Variables

IQ or Index	Difference in Mean Scores (White Minus African American)	
	Ages 6–11	Ages 12–16
Full Scale IQ	6.0	11.8
Verbal Comprehension (VCI)	5.6	12.2
Perceptual Reasoning (PRI)	6.8	10.5
Working Memory (WMI)	1.9	5.9
Processing Speed (PSI)	3.5	5.6

Source: Table 1.6 in Prifitera, A., Weiss, L. G., Saklofske, D. H., & Rolfhus, E. (2005). The WISC-IV in the clinical assessment context. In A. Prifitera, D. H. Saklofske, & L. G. Weiss (Eds.), WISC-IV: Clinical use and interpretation. San Diego, CA: Elsevier Science.

differences based on the specific Index score and age group. With numerous variables controlled (parental education, gender, region, and number of parents living in the household), differences are smallest for the WMI and PSI (3-4 points) and for pre-adolescents than adolescents (6 versus 12 points).

Ethnic differences for Whites versus Hispanics averaged about 10 Full Scale IQ points (2/3 SD), in favor of Whites, on earlier versions of Wechsler's children's scales—11.2 points on the WISC-R (Mercer, 1979), 9.4 points on the WISC-III (Prifitera et al., 1998, Table 1.1)—and that same difference (9.9 points) characterizes the WISC-IV (Prifitera et al., 2005, Table 1.3). Traditionally, the difference in favor of Whites has been much larger on the Verbal than Performance Scale, as would be expected in view of the cultural and, especially, linguistic aspects of the Verbal subtests. Verbal IQ differences were 12 to 14 points on the WISC-R and WISC-III, compared to Performance IQ differences of 5 to 6 points (Mercer, 1979; Prifitera et al., 1998, Table 1.1). On the WISC-IV, that predictable verbal-nonverbal distinction was reflected in the VCI (11.4 points) versus the PRI (7.1 points) (Prifitera et al., 2005, Table 1.3). When controlling for SES and other pertinent variables, all WISC-IV differences are greatly reduced (FSIQ = 4.8; VCI = 6.0; PRI = 2.6) (Prifitera et al., 2005, Table 1.5).

≣ Rapid Reference 1.14

Difference in Mean Standard Scores for Whites versus Hispanics on the WISC-IV Full Scale IQ and Indexes, Controlling for SES and Other Background Variables

IQ or Index	Difference in Mean Scores (White Minus Hispanic)	
	Ages 6–11	Ages 12–16
Full Scale IQ	1.3	8.0
Verbal Comprehension (VCI)	3.7	8.5
Perceptual Reasoning (PRI)	−0.2	3.9
Working Memory (WMI)	2.4	5.5
Processing Speed (PSI)	−1.5	3.4

Source: Table 1.7 in Prifitera, A., Weiss, L. G., Saklofske, D. H., & Rolfhus, E. (2005). The WISC-IV in the clinical assessment context. In A. Prifitera, D. H. Saklofske, & L. G. Weiss (Eds.), WISC-IV: Clinical use and interpretation. San Diego, CA: Elsevier Science.

Furthermore, these differences are merely verbal versus nonverbal; some differences favor Hispanics and age plays a factor as well, as it did for African American–White differences. Rapid Reference 1.14 presents FSIQ and Index differences, by age, for Hispanics versus Whites on the WISC-IV for groups matched on parental education, gender, region, and number of parents living in the household. At ages 6 to 11, the two ethnic groups differed by 1 point on FSIQ and performed about equally well on all scales; differences ranged from a 3.7 advantage for Whites on VCI to a 1.5 discrepancy in favor of Hispanics on PSI. At ages 12 to 16, results were quite different. Whites scored higher on the FSIQ (8 points) and on all scales, with the differences highest on VCI (8.5 points) and lowest on PSI and PRI (3–4 points).

Analogous age-related findings characterized White–Hispanic differences on the Kaufman Brief Intelligence Test (K-BIT; Kaufman & Kaufman, 1990) for global, verbal (Vocabulary), and nonverbal (Matrices) scores adjusted for SES (Kaufman & Wang, 1992). Global IQ differences on the K-BIT favored Hispanics by 1 point at ages 4 to 7 years, whereas Whites scored higher at ages 8 to 12 (2.6 points) and 13 to 19 (6.0 points). Similarly, Vocabulary differences increased with increasing age group (from 3.5 points at ages 4–12 to 6.5 points at 13–19) and the

Matrices difference went from a 5-point advantage for Hispanics at ages 4 to 7 to a 4.4-point edge for Whites at ages 13 to 19.

None of these ethnic differences for Whites relative to African Americans and Hispanics have intuitive explanations; even the age-related findings defy simple understanding. The most insightful discussion that we have read on these complex issues is a chapter written by Weiss and colleagues (2006). They reviewed the often-ignored body of literature on the roles of mental health status, physical health status, education, income, home environment, cognitive stimulation, and individual differences on intellectual development, and they discuss how these variables have a differential impact on different ethnic groups. Weiss and colleagues (2006) emphasize that "children grow up with differing levels of opportunity for cognitive growth and development" (p. 18), that "race/ethnicity are likely to be proxy variables for a set of active mechanisms that have only been partially identified" (p. 32), and that "cognitive growth is malleable, within limits, based on environmental opportunities for cognitive development" (p. 51).

Weiss and colleagues (2006) also conducted an innovative set of multiple-regression analyses using WISC-IV data to demonstrate the mediating effect of SES variables on IQ differences often attributed to race/ethnicity. They showed, for example, that parent education alone accounted for 18.8% of the variance in FSIQ between African American and White samples, much higher than the 4.7% for race alone. Further, controlling for parent education and household income reduced the 4.7% to 1.6%. In their analyses of Hispanic–White differences, the percent of variance due to parental education was 17.5 and the ethnic status percent was 1.4; controlling for SES explained nearly all of the variance attributed to ethnic status. We recommend reading this exceptional chapter in its entirety to fully grasp the role of contextual factors in shaping the IQs earned by individuals from diverse ethnic groups and to be able to give 2-point responses to any questions you may be asked about SES, test bias, or ethnic differences on intelligence tests.

Other Quantitative and Qualitative Characteristics of the WISC-IV

Appendix D on the CD-ROM provides a quick reference to key quantitative and qualitative features of the WISC-IV subtests that may aid in interpretation. Several quantitative characteristics are *evaluated* in Table D.1 according to commonly accepted criteria, including internal consistency and test–retest reliabilities, g-loadings, subtest floors and ceilings, and item gradients. Table D.1 also includes important qualitative characteristics of the WISC-IV subtests. Specifically, each subtest is classified according to degree of cultural loading and linguistic demand.

Also, a list of the most probable factors that influence subtest performance is provided for each subtest. Table D.2 of this appendix provides definitions of the quantitative and qualitative characteristics included in Table D.1 along with an explanation of the criteria used to (a) evaluate the quantitative characteristics and (b) classify the WISC-IV subtests according to select qualitative characteristics. Finally, Table D.2 provides a brief description of the interpretive relevance of each characteristic included in Table D.1. The information included in Appendix D may be used to assist in the generation of hypotheses about a child's unique profile of cognitive capabilities.

CONCLUSION

The contributions to the science of intellectual assessment made by David Wechsler through his intelligence scales are many and substantial, if not landmark. Although he is not recognized as an important theoretician, this neither detracts from his accomplishments nor diminishes his innovations in applied psychometrics. Wechsler was a well-known clinician and, as such, he intentionally placed significant importance on developing tasks that had practical, clinical value, and not merely theoretical value. Thus, the driving force behind the development of the Wechsler scales was no doubt based more on practical considerations rather than theoretical ones. Zachary (1990) stated, "When David Wechsler published the original Wechsler-Bellevue scales in 1939, he said relatively little about the theoretical underpinnings of his new instrument; rather, he followed a pragmatic approach. He selected a set of tasks that were easy to administer and score." (p. 276). Detterman (1985) also attributed much of the popularity of the Wechsler family of tests to their "ease of administration fostered by an organization of subtests that are brief and have long clinical histories" (p. 1715). For better or worse, Wechsler's primary motivation for constructing his tests was to create an efficient, easy-to-use tool for clinical purposes; operationalizing them according to a specific theory of intelligence was not of paramount importance.

Despite these accomplishments and accolades, under the critical eye of subsequent advancements in the field, the failure of the Wechsler scales to keep abreast of contemporary intelligence research cannot be ignored. It is clear that meaningful use and interpretation of the Wechsler scales requires the adoption of a fourth-wave approach in which contemporary theory, research, and measurement principles are integrated.

We believe that clinical judgment and experience alone are insufficient stanchions upon which defensible interpretations can be built. Application of contemporary theory and research to intelligence test use and interpretation is needed.

The interpretive approach offered in this book is an efficient, theoretically and statistically defensible method for assessing and interpreting the array of cognitive abilities underlying the WISC-IV. The subsequent chapters of this book demonstrate how the principles and procedures of both Kaufman's and Flanagan's interpretive methods have been integrated to advance the science of measuring and interpreting cognitive abilities using the WISC-IV.

COMPREHENSIVE REFERENCES ON THE WISC-IV

The *WISC-IV Technical and Interpretive Manual* (The Psychological Corporation, 2003) provides important information about the development of the test and includes descriptions of the subtests and scales, as well as detailed information on standardization, reliability, and validity.

Also see the following resources:

- Prifitera, A., Saklofske, D. H., & Weiss, L. G. (Eds.). (2008). *WISC-IV clinical use and interpretation, Second Edition*. San Diego, CA: Elsevier Science.
- Sattler, J. M. (2008). *Assessment of children: Cognitive foundations* (5th ed.). San Diego, CA: Jerome M. Sattler.
- Weiss, L. G., Saklofske, D. H., Prifitera, A., & Holdnack, J. A. (Eds.). (2006). *WISC-IV advanced clinical interpretation*. San Diego, CA: Elsevier Science.

 TEST YOURSELF

I. Picture Arrangement, Object Assembly, and Mazes were deleted from the WISC-IV battery for which one of the following reasons?

(a) because they are most valid for preschool children

(b) to deemphasize the timed nature of the battery

(c) because surveys regarding WISC-IV development revealed that children did not like these tests

(d) because these tests were deemed unfair to language-impaired children

2. The Block Design subtest is primarily a measure of which of the following CHC abilities?

(a) Visual Processing (*Gv*)

(b) Fluid Reasoning (*Gf*)

(c) Working Memory (*Gsm-MW*)

(d) Processing Speed (*Gs*)

3. **The average reliability of the WISC-IV core battery subtests can be best described as**
   (a) high.
   (b) low.
   (c) medium.
   (d) unacceptable.

4. **Which of the following WISC-IV indexes is the best predictor of written-language achievement?**
   (a) VCI
   (b) PRI
   (c) WMI
   (d) PSI

5. **The WISC-IV represents the most substantial revision of the Wechsler scales to date.**
   True or False?

6. **Cohen's significant contributions that largely defined the third wave of test interpretation included which of the following?**
   (a) empirical support for the FSIQ based on analysis of shared variance between subtests
   (b) development of the three-factor solution for interpretation of the Wechsler scales
   (c) revelation of limited subtest specificity, questioning individual subtest interpretaion
   (d) all of the above

7. **Kaufman's and Flanagan's intraindividual (ipsative) analysis method has improved upon traditional ipsative methods in several ways. One major difference between their approach and traditional approaches is that they recommend using composites or clusters, rather than subtests, in intraindividual analysis.**
   True or False?

8. **When SES is controlled for, the *smallest* differences between Whites and African Americans are found in *processing speed* and**
   (a) verbal comprehension.
   (b) global intelligence.
   (c) working memory.
   (d) perceptual reasoning.

Answers:

1. b; 2. a; 3. c; 4. a; 5. True; 6. d; 7. True; 8. c

Two

HOW TO ADMINISTER THE WISC-IV

Both standardized and nonstandardized procedures should be used together to uncover a child's true abilities. Norm-referenced tests, such as the WISC-IV, provide information to allow the examiner to compare an individual's performance to the performance of a norm group. To obtain accurate scores from a norm-referenced test, standardized procedures need to be followed under a set of standard conditions. When an examiner adheres to these standard procedures and conditions, a fair comparison of the examinee's level of ability can be made to the *normative group*—that is, a representative sample of same-age peers from the general population. As will be discussed throughout this book, however, nonstandardized procedures such as interviews, behavioral observations, and informal assessments should be used alongside standardized tests to provide an integrated and complete picture of a child. Simply taking a snapshot of a child's abilities through a time-limited sample of performance, as is done during the administration of any standardized test, including the WISC-IV, does not provide sufficient information about the child for the purposes of diagnosing and making recommendations.

APPROPRIATE TESTING CONDITIONS

Testing Environment

There are some issues regarding the testing environment that should be considered whether you are testing a child or an adolescent. For a child of any age, it is important to have a testing environment that is relatively bland and free of distractions, both visual and auditory. For example, the surroundings should not have too many toys or windows. However, the surroundings should not be so formal or adult-like that the child or adolescent feels like he or she is in a medical examination room. The testing environment should be comfortable for both you and the examinee. In most situations, only the examiner and the examinee should be in the testing room during the evaluation.

In order to test an examinee with the WISC-IV in a manner consistent with standardized procedures, it is necessary to sit at a table. However, in some cases we have found that when testing a highly energetic young child, it may be advantageous to be prepared to move the testing materials to another location, such as the floor, where the child will best attend to you. With some children, it may be necessary to fluctuate between highly structured testing activities at a table and more informal activities that can be done on the floor. In any case, it is a good idea to use a clipboard, as it provides a smooth writing surface and it can be transported to the floor or other locations, if necessary.

Testing Materials

During testing, we recommend that you sit either opposite the child or at a 90-degree angle from the child in order to most easily view the test-taking behaviors and manipulate the test materials. The testing manual may be propped up on the table and positioned as a shield behind which the Record Form can be placed. This positioning allows the examiner to read the directions easily and prevents the child from being distracted by what the examiner is writing on the Record Form. Only the testing materials that are in immediate use should be visible to the examinee. Stimulus materials can distract young children easily if they are in view. We recommend that you keep other testing materials on the floor or on a chair beside you so that they are readily available to you, but out of the child's view.

Because the WISC-IV contains several materials, including one stimulus book, two pencils, nine blocks, two manuals, two response booklets, three scoring keys, and one Record Form, we recommend that you double-check that all necessary materials are present prior to beginning the testing. A few materials are not contained in the WISC-IV test kit and, therefore, you will need to bring these yourself: a stopwatch, a clipboard, and extra paper for taking notes.

DON'T FORGET
....
Keys to Preparing to Administer the WISC-IV

- Quiet, distraction-free room with table and chairs
- Smooth writing surface
- Stopwatch

Useful materials not in the kit:

- Clipboard
- Extra paper and writing utensils (for recording observations)

Source: From A. S. Kaufman & E. O. Lichtenberger, *Essentials of WISC-III and WPPSI-R Assessment.* Copyright © 2000 John Wiley & Sons, Inc. This material is used by permission of John Wiley & Sons, Inc.

RAPPORT WITH EXAMINEE

Establishing Rapport

When working with children and adolescents, building rapport is crucial to obtaining valid testing results. Even the most experienced examiners may find that it is challenging to juggle the maintenance of rapport with adherence to standardized procedures. When interacting with the child initially, it is important to allow him or her enough time to become accustomed to you before beginning the evaluation. Addressing the child by his or her name, telling the child your name, and spending a reasonable amount of time interacting with the child prior to testing (e.g., discussing the child's interests and hobbies) can aid in establishing rapport (Kaufman & Kaufman, 1993). When conversing with the child, you should remember to be open, honest, and genuine. Any comments that you may make upon initially meeting the child, or throughout testing, should be mildly positive. That is, too much interest in or praise of a child's conversation, appearance, and so on may be viewed suspiciously, especially by adolescents.

In addition to being given time to accustom themselves to you, children must also be given time to become accustomed to the testing situation itself. It is important to note that the manner in which you or, in some cases, a parent or caregiver have introduced the child to the testing situation can have either positive or negative effects throughout the evaluation. Therefore, we encourage examiners and parents to explain to children ahead of time what they should expect during the evaluation. Such explanations can alleviate any anticipatory anxiety that the child may have. For example, it is good to let the child know that the examiner will be showing him or her blocks and books containing pictures and words and will be asking some questions. We advise examiners (and parents) not to use the word *test* when introducing the situation to the child because the word has a negative connotation for many children and can elicit a fear reaction. However, if a child asks directly, "Am I going to take a test?" then it is best not to lie, but rather explain to the child, "Most of the things you are going to be doing are not like the tests you take at school. In fact, lots of kids think that these special kinds of tests are pretty fun." Examiners should also be sure to explain that no one gets all of the questions and problems right, that some questions are easy and some are difficult for everyone, and that what may start off as a fairly easy task could become rather difficult.

Although an examiner should retain control of the testing situation at all times, it is important that the examiner is flexible in structuring the assessment sessions according to the child's needs. Some children may need frequent breaks due to a medical condition (e.g., cerebral palsy), and others may fatigue easily and require several short evaluation sessions (e.g., individuals with Attention-Deficit/Hyperactivity Disorder, or ADHD) and so forth. Examiners should obtain sufficient information about a child's medical and behavioral history prior to evaluating him or her to ensure the validity of the findings. Examiners should also remember not to talk down to children of any age. Rather, they should try to adjust their vocabulary appropriately to the child's age level. Adolescents may become particularly

DON'T FORGET

Keys to Establishing Positive Rapport

- Effectively introduce the child to the testing activities.
- Avoid the word "test."
- Explain the purpose of the assessment following the standardized instructions on page 59 of the *WISC-IV Administration and Scoring Manual* (Wechsler, 2003).
- Allow the child ample time to adjust to the testing situation.
- Achieve a balance between professional (formal) and friendly (informal) demeanor.
- Correct any misperceptions that the child may have about the purpose of testing.
- Describe your role clearly and maintain control of the testing situation at all times.
- Tell examinees that you may use a stopwatch and will record their answers.

Source: From A. S. Kaufman & E. O. Lichtenberger, *Essentials of WISC-III and WPPSI-R Assessment.* Copyright © 2000 John Wiley & Sons, Inc. This material is used by permission of John Wiley & Sons, Inc.

uncooperative if they are treated like younger children. With teenagers, it is important to try to initiate a conversation that is interesting to them but does not appear overly invasive, showing respect for their boundaries. A balance between formality and informality—between being professional and being friendly—should be achieved when testing both children and adolescents. The Don't Forget box above summarizes key points in establishing positive rapport.

Maintaining Rapport

Getting the attention of a child is often not as difficult as keeping his or her attention and motivation. This is when the delicate balance between rapport and adherence to standardized test procedures becomes especially important. Providing frequent praise for a child's efforts is important for maintaining his or her attention and motivation. The examiner should pay close attention to signs of waning attention, frustration, or lack of motivation. Such signs may be verbal (e.g., "How much longer?" or "These are too hard") or nonverbal (e.g., increased fidgeting, sighing, grimacing). These observations are signals to the examiner that it may be necessary to increase encouragement and praise or perhaps to take a break. See the following Caution box for a list of ways to give appropriate feedback and encouragement.

CAUTION

Appropriate Feedback and Encouragement

- Praise frequently but do not be repetitive, which lessens the reinforcement value.
- Be aware that encouragement/feedback may be verbal or nonverbal: Smile, give a pat on the hand, say "Good job," "You sure are working hard," etc.
- Praise and encourage the child's level of effort.
- Be careful *not* to give feedback on whether a particular response is right or wrong.
- Give encouragement *throughout* items, not just when the child is struggling.

Source: From A. S. Kaufman & E. O. Lichtenberger, *Essentials of WISC-III and WPPSI-R Assessment.* Copyright © 2000 John Wiley & Sons, Inc. This material is used by permission of John Wiley & Sons, Inc.

Encouragement and praise may be delivered in many different ways (e.g., an understanding smile, a pat on the hand, saying "We've got a lot more fun things to do," "You're working so hard," "Wow, you're a hard worker"). However, it is important that praise not be overly repetitive, as it will lose its reinforcing effects. Likewise, be careful when praising a child's efforts that you are not giving feedback about whether the child's responses are correct. Encouragement should be given throughout administration of the items, not only when a child is struggling or giving incorrect responses.

Some children may require more than verbal and nonverbal praise to maintain motivation. In these cases, it may be useful to develop a reward system. For example, an agreement may be reached that the child can play with certain toys after a required number of tasks have been completed. Sometimes a small snack may be used as a reward, but you should always discuss this with the parent ahead of time (some parents disapprove of certain types of foods, do not want dinner spoiled, or will need to warn you about their child's food allergies).

Maintaining the child's motivational level requires consistent effort on the examiner's part. It is important to be able to remove materials skillfully and present the next task quickly, which creates a smooth and rapid transition between subtests. It is wise to continue small talk while recording behavioral observations between subtests, as this helps maintain a child's attention, but it is important to limit such conversation to the time between subtests. Frequent eye contact also helps maintain rapport; thus, it is crucial to be familiar enough with the standardized instructions so that you do not have to read them word for word with your head buried in the manual during administration.

Children may occasionally refuse to cooperate, be easily fatigued, or become too nervous to continue. In such situations it is appropriate to give several breaks throughout the testing or to reschedule the testing for another day. However, you should be aware that many children are skilled in "testing" examiners and may try to distract an examiner from the task at hand. Being alert to such behavior helps to keep the testing flowing. When children indicate that they do not want to continue with a subtest (perhaps a challenging subtest), it is advisable to provide encouragement such as "Just try your best" or "Give it your best shot." To prevent undue frustration during timed subtests, it may be useful to allow the child to work past the time limit if he or she is actively involved in the task. Although any response given on timed tests after the time limit has expired is not counted toward the score, allowing extra time under these circumstances may lessen discouragement. The Don't Forget box on this page summarizes various ways to maintain rapport.

TESTING INDIVIDUALS WITH SPECIAL NEEDS

Children with special needs—including those with speech, language, or hearing deficits, visual impairments, Intellectual Disability (formerly Mental Retardation), neurological impairments, physical disabilities, or behavioral disorders—may

DON'T FORGET

Keys to Maintaining Rapport

- Provide frequent praise and encouragement.
- Praise examinees for their effort rather than the correctness of their responses.
- Record all responses, not just incorrect responses.
- Set up a reward system if necessary.
- Give frequent breaks if necessary.
- Reschedule testing if the child is too tired, anxious, or uncooperative.
- Make eye contact; do not bury your head in the manual.
- Make smooth and rapid transitions *between* subtests.
- Use small talk *between* subtests but not *during* subtests.
- Familiarize yourself ahead of time with test directions and test materials.
- Be subtle, not distracting, when using a stopwatch.

Source: From A. S. Kaufman & E. O. Lichtenberger, *Essentials of WISC-III and WPPSI-R Assessment.* Copyright © 2000 John Wiley & Sons, Inc. This material is used by permission of John Wiley & Sons, Inc.

require certain modifications during an evaluation to ensure that the assessment results reflect their abilities accurately. Therefore, it is crucial to obtain thorough information about any disability from the caregiver prior to beginning the assessment. The caregiver may be able to provide suggestions about the best way to elicit a response from the child when he or she is presented with both verbal and nonverbal stimuli. This information is likely to lead to the most appropriate modifications or accommodations during an evaluation for a child with special needs. Examiners should be prepared to be flexible with regard to the types of accommodations that may need to be implemented for children with specific impairments or disabilities, and they should be aware of conditions that may occur earlier than is typical, such as fatigue. In short, the examiner must understand the specific needs of any child, make appropriate modifications or accommodations as necessary, and pay close attention to signs of inattention, disinterest, fatigue, and the like to make sure that the evaluation constitutes a fair assessment of a child's cognitive capabilities.

Notwithstanding, when modifications are made to the standardized testing procedures for any reason, test scores may be altered in an unknown way and use of the test's norms may be invalid. Clinical judgment must be exercised in determining whether modifications to the test or the impact of the specific impairment itself prevents the calculation of standard scores. Modifications may include, but are not limited to, the following:

1. Administer only the VCI and WMI subtests to a child with a visual impairment. However, for Vocabulary (a core VCI subtest) the first four items (pictorial stimuli) cannot be given to visually impaired children who do not earn perfect scores on Items 5 and 6; also, the printed words in the Stimulus Book, which are shown to children aged 9 to 16 as each item is presented, is a procedure that cannot be followed for children with a visual impairment. For Arithmetic (a supplemental WMI subtest), the first five items, which include pictorial stimuli, cannot be administered. Children aged 6 to 7 start the Arithmetic subtest with Item 3, so this supplemental subtest is not recommended for children aged 6 or 7 who have a visual impairment.

2. For children who are deaf or hard of hearing, administer the test in the child's preferred mode of communication (e.g., American Sign Language) or allow the child to lip-read if he or she is able. Examiners who are skilled in testing children who are deaf or hard of hearing are encouraged to study Tables 1.4 and 1.5 and the associated text in the *WISC-IV Administration and Scoring Manual* (Wechsler, 2003, pp. 12–18). Testing this population with the WISC-IV is also discussed in Chapter 6.

3. Provide an appropriate translation for a child who is an English-language learner by using an interpreter, administering the test bilingually or in the child's native language, or using an adapted or translated version of the test.
4. Consider administering only the VCI subtests, WMI subtests, and those PRI subtests that require minimal or no motor skills (i.e., Picture Concepts, Matrix Reasoning, and Picture Completion) to children with motor impairments. Cancellation, which involves less fine motor skill, may serve as a substitute for Coding in deriving the PSI.
5. Extend testing over multiple sessions for children with special needs, as necessary.

It is important to realize that successful evaluation of a child with special needs, indeed of any child, may require the use of supplemental measures or another instrument altogether. Careful consideration of the child's needs, coupled with astute observations of his or her range of verbal and nonverbal capabilities, will help to determine what types of modifications are best.

ADMINISTRATION CONSIDERATIONS

The WISC-IV may be administered to children as young as age 6 years 0 months and as old as age 16 years 11 months. When testing children at these lower and upper limits of the WISC-IV age range, examiners must decide whether this

CAUTION

Modifying Standardized Procedures

- Modification of the standardized procedures to accommodate a child's special needs may invalidate the scores on the test.
- Clinical judgment is key in determining what quantitative and qualitative data are interpretable from the test administration.
- Translating the test into another language through the use of a translator or administering the test bilingually may cause problems in interpreting scores (e.g., word meanings are not equivalent across all languages).

Source: From A. S. Kaufman & E. O. Lichtenberger, Essentials of WISC-III and WPPSI-R Assessment. Copyright © 2000 John Wiley & Sons, Inc. This material is used by permission of John Wiley & Sons, Inc.

Table 2.1 Deciding on the WISC-IV versus Another Battery for 6- and 16-Year-Olds

Age	Estimated Level of Ability	Battery to Administer
6	Below Average	WPPSI-III or an appropriate alternative battery
	Average Range	WISC-IV
	Above Average	WISC-IV
16	Below Average	WISC-IV
	Average Range	WISC-IV
	Above Average	WAIS-IV or an appropriate alternative battery

Source: From A. S. Kaufman & E. O. Lichtenberger, *Essentials of WISC-III and WPPSI-R Assessment*. Copyright © 2000 John Wiley & Sons, Inc. This material is used by permission of John Wiley & Sons, Inc.

Note: WPPSI-III = Wechsler Preschool and Primary Scale of Intelligence–Third Edition; WAIS-IV = Wechsler Adult Intelligence Scale–Fourth Edition.

instrument is the most appropriate or whether, for example, the WPPSI-III or WAIS-III, respectively, may be preferable. When making this determination, it is recommended that you use the WISC-IV with 6-year-olds whom you consider to be of average intelligence (or higher). Otherwise, the WPPSI-III or another instrument with norms for children aged 6 and younger should be used, as deemed appropriate. Likewise, it is recommended that you use the WISC-IV with 16-year-olds whom you consider to be within the average range or below. Otherwise, the WAIS-III or another instrument with norms for adolescents and adults should be used. That is, to ensure the availability of a sufficient number of items to assess a child's ability adequately, the WPPSI-III should be used with 6-year-olds who are below the average range because it provides significantly easier items than the WISC-IV, and the WAIS-III should be used with 16-year-olds who are above the average range because it provides significantly more difficult items than the WISC-IV. These recommendations are summarized in Table 2.1.

RULES FOR STARTING AND DISCONTINUING SUBTESTS

The administration rules of the WISC-IV are detailed in the *WISC-IV Administration and Scoring Manual* (Wechsler, 2003) and are also located on the Record

Form. In this section we highlight the general administration rules. Some of the WISC-IV subtests start at predetermined items according to the child's age, whereas other subtests begin at Item 1 regardless of age. Rapid Reference 2.1

≡ Rapid Reference 2.1

Starting Points and Reverse Rules of Subtests

Subtest	Age-Based Starting Point (reverse rules)	Age and Starting Point
1. Block Design	✓(Yes)	6–7: Item 1 8–16: Item 3
2. Similarities	✓(Yes)	6–8: sample, then Item 1 9–11: sample, then Item 3 12–16: sample, then Item 5
3. Digit Span	(No)	6–16: Forward, Item 1; Backward sample, then Item 1
4. Picture Concepts	✓(Yes)	6–8: Samples A and B, then Item 1 9–11: Samples A and B, then Item 5 12–16: Samples A and B, then Item 7
5. Coding	(No)	6–7: Coding A, sample items, then test items 8–16: Coding B, sample items, then test items
6. Vocabulary	✓(Yes)	6–8: Item 5 9–11: Item 7 12–16: Item 9
7. Letter-Number Sequencing	(No)	6–7: qualifying items, sample item, then Item 1 8–16: sample item, then Item 1
8. Matrix Reasoning	✓(Yes)	6–8: Samples A–C, then Item 4 9–11: Samples A–C, then Item 7 12–16: Samples A–C, then Item 11
9. Comprehension	✓(Yes)	6–8: Item 1 9–11: Item 3 12–16: Item 5
10. Symbol Search	(No)	6–7: Symbol Search A, sample items, practice items, then test items 8–16: Symbol Search B, sample items, practice items, then test items

11. Picture Completion	✓(Yes)	6–8: sample, then Item 1 9–11: sample, then Item 5 12–16: sample, then Item 10
12. Cancellation	(No)	6–16: sample, practice, then Item 1
13. Information	✓(Yes)	6–8: Item 5 9–11: Item 10 12–16: Item 12
14. Arithmetic	✓(Yes)	6–7: Item 3 8–9: Item 9 10–16: Item 12
15. Word Reasoning	✓(Yes)	6–9: Samples A and B, then Item 1 10–16: Samples A and B, then Item 5

Source: From the Administration and Scoring Manual of the Wechsler Intelligence Scale for Children Fourth Edition. Copyright © 2003 The Psychological Corporation. Adapted and reproduced by permission. All rights reserved.

Note: Children suspected of developmental delay or cognitive impairment may begin subtests at earlier items.

identifies which subtests have age-based starting points (denoted by checkmarks) and reverse rules and also provides the starting points for specific age categories throughout the entire age range of the battery.

On subtests with age-based starting points (later than item 1), examinees must establish a *basal* or perfect score on the first two items administered to receive full credit for all previous items (called *reversal items*). When the examinee does not achieve an initial basal on a subtest with an age-based starting point, the examiner must give the reversal items in reverse sequence until perfect scores are achieved on two consecutive items. The *WISC-IV Administration and Scoring Manual* (Wechsler, 2003) includes specific instructions for examiners when the first set of items administered is too difficult for the child. These instructions are referred to as *reverse rules*. Table 2.2 provides the reverse rules for each subtest, and the Don't Forget boxes (at right and on page 65) contain important information relating to these rules.

DON'T FORGET

When the examinee receives full credit on the first item administered but not the second item, on a subtest with age-based starting points, the first item is used to meet the reversal criterion of two consecutive perfect scores.

Table 2.2 Summary of Reverse Rules

Subtest	Reverse Rule
1. Block Design	Ages 8–16: Score of 0 or 1 on *either* of the first two items given, administer preceding items in reverse order until two consecutive perfect scores are obtained.
2. Similarities	Ages 9–16: Score of 0 or 1 on *either* of the first two items given, administer preceding items in reverse order until two consecutive perfect scores are obtained.
3. Digit Span	None
4. Picture Concepts	Ages 9–16: Score of 0 on *either* of the first two items given, administer preceding items in reverse order until two consecutive perfect scores are obtained.
5. Coding	None
6. Vocabulary	Ages 6–16: Score of 0 or 1 on *either* of the first two items given, administer preceding items in reverse order until two consecutive perfect scores are obtained.
7. Letter-Number Sequencing	None
8. Matrix Reasoning	Ages 6–16: Score of 0 on *either* of the first two items given, administer preceding items in reverse order until two consecutive perfect scores are obtained.
9. Comprehension	Ages 9–16: Score of 0 or 1 on *either* of the first two items given, administer preceding items in reverse order until two consecutive perfect scores are obtained.
10. Symbol Search	None
11. Picture Completion	Ages 9–16: Score of 0 on *either* of the first two items given, administer preceding items in reverse order until two consecutive perfect scores are obtained.
12. Cancellation	None
13. Information	Ages 6–16: Score of 0 on *either* of the first two items given, administer preceding items in reverse order until two consecutive perfect scores are obtained.
14. Arithmetic	Ages 6–16: Score of 0 on *either* of the first two items given, administer preceding items in reverse order until two consecutive perfect scores are obtained.
15. Word Reasoning	Ages 10–16: Score of 0 on *either* of the first two items given, administer preceding items in reverse order until two consecutive perfect scores are obtained.

Source: From the Administration and Scoring Manual of the Wechsler Intelligence Scale for Children–Fourth Edition. Copyright © 2003 The Psychological Corporation. Adapted and reproduced by permission. All rights reserved.

At times, an examiner may administer items prior to the recommended start point for a child suspected of developmental delay or cognitive impairment. Although this is an acceptable practice, it is important to

DON'T FORGET

Scores obtained on reverse items are included in the discontinue criteria.

remember that if the child receives full credit on the first two items of his or her age-appropriate start point, full credit must be given to all previous items even when one or more of these items were answered incorrectly. The Caution box on this page lists common general errors in administration.

In addition to starting points and reverse rules, subtests also have *discontinue rules*. Starting and discontinue rules were developed to minimize testing time. Similar to starting rules, discontinue rules differ across subtests. These rules typically

CAUTION

Most Frequently Observed Administration and Scoring Errors Made by Graduate Students

Error	% of Protocols with Error
Failing to query verbal responses	88
Calculating subtest raw scores incorrectly	80
Failing to record verbatim an examinee's response on the test protocol	76
Calculating subtest scaled scores incorrectly	76
Calculating IQ or factor index scores incorrectly	73
Reporting confidence intervals incorrectly	73
Reporting percentile ranks incorrectly	73
Summing subtest scaled scores incorrectly	71
Administering an incorrect number of items	49
Using an incorrect starting point	49
Assigning too many points to a test response	48

Source: Adapted from Loe, Kadlubek, and Marks (2007). The WISC-IV protocols of 17 first-year graduate students, who administered the test for training purposes, were examined for errors by two practicing school psychologists. Each graduate student administered the WISC-IV three times, yielding a total of 51 protocols. Protocols were examined for errors and errors were coded into three categories: administration, computation, and recording. Repeated practice of test administration was not effective in reducing the frequency of the errors.

require that a certain number of consecutive zero-point responses be obtained prior to discontinuing the subtest. Table 2.3 lists the discontinue rules for the WISC-IV subtests.

When administering a subtest, you may occasionally find that you are unsure of how to score a response and, therefore, of whether a subtest should be discontinued. Most often this uncertainty may arise during Verbal Comprehension subtests that have some subjectivity in scoring—most notably Vocabulary, Similarities, and Comprehension. If it is not possible to quickly determine whether a response is correct, it is best to continue administering

Table 2.3 Summary of Discontinue Rules

Subtest	Discontinue Rule
1. Block Design	After 3 consecutive scores of 0
2. Similarities	After 5 consecutive scores of 0
3. Digit Span	Digit Span Forward: After scores of 0 on *both trials* of an item Digit Span Backward: After scores of 0 on *both trials* of an item
4. Picture Concepts	After 5 consecutive scores of 0
5. Coding	Coding A and B: After 120 seconds have elapsed (or sooner if the child finishes in less than 120 seconds)
6. Vocabulary	After 5 consecutive scores of 0
7. Letter-Number Sequencing	If a child aged 6–7 is unable to respond correctly to either qualifying item *or* if a child receives scores of 0 on *all three trials* of an item
8. Matrix Reasoning	After 4 consecutive scores of 0 *or* 4 scores of 0 on *five* consecutive items
9. Comprehension	After 4 consecutive scores of 0
10. Symbol Search	Symbol Search A and B: After 120 seconds have elapsed (or sooner if the child finishes in less than 120 seconds)
11. Picture Completion	After 6 consecutive scores of 0
12. Cancellation	After 45 seconds have elapsed for each item (or sooner if the child finishes in less than 45 seconds)
13. Information	After 5 consecutive scores of 0
14. Arithmetic	After 4 consecutive scores of 0
15. Word Reasoning	After 5 consecutive scores of 0

Source: From the Administration and Scoring Manual of the Wechsler Intelligence Scale for Children–Fourth Edition. Copyright © 2003 The Psychological Corporation. Adapted and reproduced by permission. All rights reserved.

further items until you are certain that the discontinue rule has been met. This procedure is the safest because the scores can always be reviewed later and items that are passed after the discontinue criterion has been met can be excluded from the child's raw score on the subtest. However, the information obtained on the items that were accidentally administered beyond the discontinue criterion may provide valuable *clinical* information. If you do not follow the procedure just described, and note later that you did not administer enough items to meet the discontinue rule, then the subtest should be considered spoiled. You should *not* go back and administer the items in an attempt to meet the discontinue rule. If you need to derive a scaled score based on the subtest raw score on this test, you would need to explain that the score most likely underestimates the child's ability.

RECORDING RESPONSES

The manner in which responses are recorded during administration of the WISC-IV is very important. Examiners should be careful to write down responses verbatim for all items administered or attempted. This recording is especially important for Vocabulary, Similarities, Comprehension, and Information (i.e., subtests that tend to elicit a good amount of verbiage). However, even when only brief verbal responses are given, such as during the Arithmetic and Digit Span subtests, they should be recorded, as they may prove useful in the interpretation process. It is tempting for some examiners to write down only a child's score, rather than the child's exact response, but this practice is discouraged. If only a 0, 1, or 2 is recorded on the Record Form, then irretrievable clinical information may be lost. Recording all responses affords the examiner an opportunity to note patterns in responding that may be useful in interpretation. For these same reasons, it is crucial to attempt to capture most of what is said verbatim. This can be quite a challenge with extremely verbose children. The use of abbreviations can make the process of recording information easier and can also help to balance the maintenance of rapport with the gathering of essential information. Rapid Reference 2.2 shows a list of commonly used abbreviations.

In addition to recording what a child says, you may need to also record your own statements. For example, if you probed to clarify an answer by saying, "Tell me more about it," you should always record the letter Q in parentheses on the Record Form directly after the response that you queried. During the process of interpretation of a child's performance, it may be of clinical interest to note whether many of the child's responses were elicited by querying or whether the child produced most responses spontaneously. Beyond noting the level of

≋ *Rapid Reference 2.2*

Abbreviations for Recording Responses

@	at
B	both
DK	don't know
EO	everyone
INC	incomplete (response wasn't completed within the time limit)
LL	looks like
NR	no response
P	prompt
PC	points correctly
PPL	people
PX	points incorrectly
Q	question or query
R	repeated
Shd	should
SO	someone
ST	something
↓	decrease
↑	increase
U	you
w/	with
w/o	without
W/d	would

Source: From A. S. Kaufman & E. O. Lichtenberger, *Essentials of WISC-III and WPPSI-R Assessment*. Copyright © 2000 John Wiley & Sons, Inc. This material is used by permission of John Wiley & Sons, Inc.

querying typically required for a child, it may be useful to determine whether the quality of response improved after the child was queried. Some children may tend not to add anything to their first responses (e.g., they may respond to most queries with "I don't know"); others may elaborate a great deal after a query but may not necessarily improve their scores; and some children will improve their scores most of the time when queried.

TIMING

Precision is necessary for administration of subtests that require timing. The examiner must be prepared to utilize his or her stopwatch for 6 out of the 15 WISC-IV subtests.

The use of a stopwatch should be unobtrusive so that it is not distracting to the child. If possible, use a stopwatch that does not make beeping sounds. If children ask whether they are being timed, you may want to respond, "Yes, but you don't need to worry about that." The WISC-IV Record Form contains a picture of a clock at the beginning of each timed subtest as a reminder to examiners that a stopwatch is required.

> ## DON'T FORGET
>
> The six timed subtests on the WISC-IV include the following:
> - Block Design
> - Coding
> - Symbol Search
> - Picture Completion
> - Cancellation
> - Arithmetic

As you are giving the directions to the timed subtests, you should already have your stopwatch out and ready for use. This is especially helpful when testing children who are impulsive and may want to begin testing earlier than you expected. Rapid Reference 2.3 lists some important points to remember when timing a child.

≡ Rapid Reference 2.3

Important Points to Remember When Using a Stopwatch on Timed Tests

1. If a child asks for clarification or repetition of an item after timing has begun, continue timing while you repeat the item.

2. When a child appears to have completed a timed item but does not provide you with a clear indication that he or she is finished, ask "Are you done?"

3. If you stop timing because a child appears to have completed an item, restart the stopwatch immediately upon recognizing that the child is still working and record the entire time that he or she worked on that item. Estimate the number of seconds that the stopwatch was off and add that to the total completion time.

QUERYING

Examiner judgment often comes into play during subtests that allow a wide variety of responses, such as many of the Verbal Comprehension subtests. If a child's response appears too vague or ambiguous to score, examiners must decide whether to query or prompt the child for clarification. The administration manual of the WISC-IV lists responses to Vocabulary, Similarities, Comprehension, and Information items that should be queried. However, the responses in the manual are only illustrative, leaving the examiner to decide whether to query other responses that are not presented in the manual's scoring system. The key to deciding whether to query a response is its ambiguity or incompleteness.

> # DON'T FORGET
>
> - Whenever you query a child, place a Q in parentheses on the Record Form next to the response you queried.
> - Do not query a child if he or she spontaneously produced an incorrect or zero-point response, unless a Q appears in parentheses next to the same or a similar response in the manual.

The manner in which children are queried may impact how they respond. Therefore, it is crucial that querying be done with neutral, nonleading questions. Good queries include, "Tell me more about it" or "Explain what you mean." The examiner should avoid providing any hints or clues to the answer and should use only the queries listed in the manual. Be careful not to ask, "Can you tell me more?" because a likely response is "No."

REPEATING ITEMS

Occasionally, a child you are testing may not completely hear the instructions or understand the instructions or a question that was read. In some cases, the child may ask you to repeat the question. Generally, it is okay to repeat a question or set of instructions; however, for the WISC-IV Digit Span and Letter-Number Sequencing subtests, a number or number-and-letter sequence, respectively, may not be repeated. When a child requests to have instructions or an item repeated, you must repeat the entire set of instructions or the entire item, not just a portion of it.

Another situation that may warrant a repetition of items is a pattern of responding in which the child provides correct answers to difficult items and incorrect or "I don't know" responses to easier items. That is, if you believe that a child may have known the answers to earlier, easier items, then it is acceptable and desirable to readminister these items, as responses to these testing-of-the-limits procedures may prove useful in interpretation. A child may have received a zero on initial items due to anxiety or insecurity, leading to an incorrect response. Testing the limits may reveal that the child actually knew the answers to these questions. Although you are not permitted to change 0-point responses to 1- or 2-point responses in this situation, information from the testing-of-the-limits procedure may be used, for example, to support an interpretation of a subtest score's reflecting an underestimate of ability due to anxiety. It is important to note, however, that an incorrect response that is *spontaneously* corrected at any time during the evaluation session should be changed from a raw score of 0 to a raw score of 1 or 2 as appropriate.

SUBTEST-BY-SUBTEST RULES OF ADMINISTRATION OF THE WISC-IV CORE SUBTESTS

1. Block Design (PRI, Core)

The WISC-IV Block Design subtest requires the examinee to replicate a set of modeled or printed two-dimensional geometric patterns using red-and-white blocks within a specified time limit. The stimulus materials for the Block Design subtest include nine cubes, each having two red sides, two white sides, and two red-and-white sides. A stopwatch, the *WISC-IV Administration and Scoring Manual* (Wechsler, 2003), the Stimulus Book, and the Record Form are needed for this subtest.

The WISC-IV Block Design subtest administration is based on age-based starting points. A child aged 6 to 7 begins at Item 1; a child aged 8 to 16 begins at Item 3. If a child aged 8 to 16 does not receive credit on either trial of Item 3, the examiner should administer Items 1 and 2 in reverse sequence until the child obtains a perfect score on two consecutive items. The Block Design subtest is discontinued after three consecutive zero-point responses.

The WISC-IV Block Design subtest, like the WISC-III Block Design subtest, provides two trials for Items 1, 2, and 3. The child works directly from models constructed by the examiner on Items 1 and 2 and constructs the remaining designs based on the pictorial models presented in the Stimulus Book. If the child attempts to duplicate the sides of the model, the examiner should tell the

CAUTION

Seating Arrangement for the Block Design Subtest

When administering the WISC-IV Block Design subtest, the examiner should sit in a position (e.g., directly opposite the child) that maximizes his or her ability to recognize any rotations to the child's designs.

Source: From A. S. Kaufman & E. O. Lichtenberger, *Essentials of WISC-III and WPPSI-R Assessment.* Copyright © 2000. John Wiley & Sons, Inc. This material is used by permission of John Wiley & Sons, Inc.

child to match only the tops of the blocks. Demonstrations are provided by the examiner on both trials of Items 1 through 3. The second trials of each of these three items are administered only if the child is unable to assemble the blocks correctly within the time limit. Item 1 has a 30-second time limit, Items 2 through 5 have a 45-second time limit, Items 6 through 10 have a 75-second time limit, and Items 11 through 14 have a 120-second time limit. Item 1 utilizes two blocks, Items 2 through 10 utilize four blocks, and the remaining items include all nine blocks.

Similar to the rotation rules on the WISC-III Block Design subtest, any rotation of 30 degrees or more is considered a failure. The examiner is allowed to correct only the first rotation. All incorrect responses, including rotations, should be recorded on the Record Form by sketching the design constructed by the child. Correct responses are indicated by placing a checkmark over the grid of stimulus blocks associated with those items on the Record Form. Table 2.4 provides a description of the changes in the administration of the Block Design subtest from WISC-III to WISC-IV. The Don't Forget box on page 73 provides a description of behaviors that the examiner should note during the administration of the Block Design subtest. It is important to note that the behaviors outlined in this Don't Forget box (and in subsequent Don't Forget boxes outlining "behaviors" to note for each WISC-IV subtest) are meant to provide examiners with information that may aid in hypothesis generation. Any hypotheses that are generated from this list, however, must be tested with other methods and data sources. Consistent findings from multiple data sources are necessary to either retain or reject hypotheses.

A noteworthy change from WISC-III to WISC-IV is that the Block Design subtest is administered as the first, as opposed to the seventh, subtest. The changes in

Table 2.4 Changes in Administration: Subtest 1, Block Design (PRI, Core)

WISC-III	WISC-IV
Administered in the middle of the test sequence (Subtest 7)	Administered as the first subtest in the test sequence
Reverse in normal sequence, i.e., Design 1, then Design 2	Reverse in reverse sequence, i.e., Design 2, then Design 1
No diagram explaining setup for right-handed vs. left-handed children	Diagram explaining setup for right-handed vs. left-handed children
12 test designs	14 test designs: 10 retained designs, 4 new designs
All ages begin with Design 1	Aged-based starting points: • Ages 6–7 begin with Design 1 • Ages 8–16 begin with Design 3

DON'T FORGET

Behaviors to Note on Block Design

- Observe problem-solving styles while the child is manipulating the blocks. Some children use a trial-and-error approach, whereas others appear to approach the construction of a design haphazardly, seemingly without learning from earlier errors. Other children develop a strategy and use it consistently throughout the subtest.

- Consider the level of planning involved. Does the child examine the problem systematically and appear to plan carefully before arranging the blocks, or does the child approach the task impulsively?

- Observe how the child arranges the blocks to form a correct response. For example, does the child work from the outside in, constructing the corners first and then the center of the design, or vice versa? Such approaches may provide information about the child's visual analytic style.

- Be aware that motor coordination and hand preference may be apparent during this task. Note whether children seem clumsy in their manipulation of the blocks, have hands that are noticeably trembling, or move very quickly and steadily.

- Look to see whether children refer back to the model while they are working. This could indicate a visual memory difficulty, cautiousness, or other factors.

- Examine whether children tend to be obsessively concerned with details (e.g., lining up the blocks perfectly). Such behaviors may negatively impact the child's speed.

- Observe how well children persist, especially when the task becomes more difficult. Note how well they tolerate frustration. Do they persist past the time limit, or do they give up with time to spare?

- Look to see whether children lose the square shape of some designs (violation of the matrix), even if they have managed to recreate the overall pattern. This kind of response may indicate figure-ground problems.

- Note whether children are noticeably twisting their bodies to obtain a different perspective on the model or are rotating their own designs. Such behaviors may indicate visual-perceptual difficulties.

- Note whether children fail to recognize that their designs look different from the model, as this may indicate visual-perceptual difficulties.

Source: From A. S. Kaufman & E. O. Lichtenberger, *Essentials of WISC-III and WPPSI-R Assessment.* Copyright © 2000 John Wiley & Sons, Inc. This material is used by permission of John Wiley & Sons, Inc.

administration order from WISC-III to WISC-IV may affect examinees' performance. By its being positioned as the first subtest administered, children might perform differently on Block Design than they would have if it remained in the middle of the sequence. Thompson's research (Thompson, 1987; Thompson,

Howard, & Anderson, 1986) suggests that its position is a significant variable in the scores the child earns. Although scores for Block Design on the WISC-IV are normed as the first WISC-IV subtest administered, for the clinician it is important to note that this variable may be important for test interpretation. If a child performs surprisingly low on Block Design (relative to other PRI subtests or to the remainder of subtests in general), that weakness might be related to a slow establishment of rapport, emotional content of the child, metacognitive issues of the child, or cognitive issues of the child. It is also possible that examinees will perform *better* on Block Design, as the first subtest administered (when they are "fresh"), than they would have performed had the subtest been embedded in the middle of the sequence. That finding was supported for a sample of adults tested on the WAIS-R in the research conducted by Thompson and his colleagues.

In working with brain-injured children it is important to note that difficulties with Block Design may be observed. By virtue of its being the first administered subtest, poor performance may have a negative effect on rapport, which may lead to an adverse impact on subsequent subtests. Picture Completion, the first subtest administered on the WISC-III, was, and is, seen as a nonthreatening, low-*Gf*, easy-to-respond-to task. As a result, Picture Completion, rather than Block Design, appears to be a better fit as the first subtest in the battery. WISC-IV Picture Completion is a supplemental subtest and was, therefore, not a legitimate contender to be administered first. However, examiners who are testing brain-injured individuals—or anyone who is believed to need a more gradual introduction to the cognitive assessment—would be wise to administer the supplemental Picture Completion subtest before administering Block Design.

Similarly, whenever a child performs poorly on the last couple of tasks administered during a test session, examiners need to consider factors such as fatigue or boredom. This topic is pertinent for Digit Span, which was moved to the beginning of the WISC-IV, whereas it was administered near the end of the WISC-III. By approaching testing from a clinical perspective, the examiner is advised to be cognizant of the fact that children with attentional problems are likely to do better on WISC-IV Digit Span (administered as Subtest 3) than they would have done on WISC-III Digit Span (Subtest 12).

Given these caveats, the examiner is reminded that the WISC-IV was intended to be administered in the order presented in the manual. Although there are times when this is not advisable (e.g., using a substitution), most times the subtests are administered in the suggested sequence. It is important that rapport be established and maintained throughout the evaluation. To establish rapport, the examiner may wish to give a task that is viewed by most children as mildly interesting, nonthreatening, and without excessive demands prior to administering the first subtest on the WISC-IV (Block Design). As noted, administering Picture Completion first should accomplish that goal.

2. Similarities (VCI, Core)

The WISC-IV Similarities subtest requires the examinee to describe how two words that represent common objects or concepts are similar. Unlike for Block Design and many other WISC-IV subtests, there is no separate stimulus material for the Similarities subtest. The *WISC-IV Administration and Scoring Manual* (Wechsler, 2003) and Record Form are the only items needed for this subtest.

The WISC-IV Similarities subtest item administration is based on age-based starting points. A child aged 6 to 8 begins with the sample item, then Item 1; a child aged 9 to 11 begins with the sample item, then Item 3; and a child aged 12 to 16 begins with the sample item, then Item 5. If a child aged 9 to 16 does not obtain a perfect score on either of the first two administered items, the preceding items should be administered in reverse sequence until a perfect score on two

DON'T FORGET
....
Behaviors to Note on Similarities

- Observe whether the child benefits from feedback (if it is given) on items that allow the examiner to provide an example. Children who learn from the example may have flexibility, whereas those who do not may be more rigid or concrete.

- Be aware that length of verbal responses gives important behavioral clues. Overly elaborate responses *may* suggest obsessiveness. Of course, data from other sources are necessary to support or rule out this hypothesis.

- Be aware that quick responses or abstract responses to easy items *may* indicate overlearned associations rather than higher level abstract reasoning.

- Note how the child handles frustration on this test. For example, some children may give up when faced with frustration by repeatedly responding "I don't know" or stating that the two items are not alike. While these responses may indicate difficulty with conceptualization or categorization, they may also indicate defensiveness or avoidance, especially when seen in older children.

- Note spontaneous corrections during the administration of this test and remember to give credit for them.

Source: From A. S. Kaufman & E. O. Lichtenberger, *Essentials of WISC-III and WPPSI-R Assessment.* Copyright © 2000. John Wiley & Sons, Inc. This material is used by permission of John Wiley & Sons, Inc.

consecutive items is obtained. The Similarities subtest is discontinued after five consecutive zero-point responses.

Items 1 and 2 on the Similarities subtest are teaching items. Thus, if the child does not respond or provides an incorrect response to either Item 1 or Item 2, the examiner provides the correct response. However, if a child fails to provide a correct response on the remaining items (i.e., Items 3–23), no further assistance is provided. Neutral queries may be given throughout the subtest to clarify vague or ambiguous responses.

Table 2.5 provides a description of the changes in the administration of the Similarities subtest from WISC-III to WISC-IV. The Don't Forget box on page 75 provides a description of behaviors that the examiner should note during the administration of the Similarities subtest.

3. Digit Span (WMI, Core)

The WISC-IV Digit Span subtest consists of two parts: Digit Span Forward and Digit Span Backward. Digit Span Forward requires the examinee to repeat numbers verbatim as they were stated by the examiner. Digit Span Backward requires the examinee to repeat numbers in the reverse order as they were stated by the examiner. There are no stimulus materials for the WISC-IV Digit Span subtest. The only materials needed to administer the WISC-IV Digit Span subtest are the *WISC-IV Administration and Scoring Manual* (Wechsler, 2003) and Record Form.

There are no age-based starting points for the WISC-IV Digit Span subtest; all children begin with Digits Forward, Item 1. Each item has two trials. If an examinee

Table 2.5 Changes in Administration: Subtest 2, Similarities (VCI, Core)

WISC-III	WISC-IV
All ages begin with sample item, then Item 1	All ages begin with sample item, then age-based starting points • Ages 6–8 begin with Item 1 • Ages 9–11 begin with Item 3 • Ages 12–16 begin with Item 5
No reverse rules	Reverse rules for ages 9–16 if either of the scores for the first two items is not perfect
Discontinue after 4 consecutive scores of 0	Discontinue after 5 consecutive scores of 0
The examiner is not allowed to repeat the test items	The examiner may repeat the test items as often as necessary
19 test items	23 test items: 11 retained items, 1 modified item, 11 new items

fails both trials of a Digits Forward item, testing is discontinued and the examiner proceeds to the sample of Digits Backward. If the child can correctly complete the first trial of the Digits Backward sample, then the second trial of the sample item is administered. However, if the child does not respond correctly to the first trial of the Digits Backwards sample, then the examiner tells the child the correct answer and readministers the trial before administering the second trial of the Digits Backward sample. If the child responds incorrectly to the second trial of the Digits Backward sample, the examiner tells the child the correct answer and readministers the trial before beginning Trial 1 of the first Digits Backward item. The Digits Backward task should be discontinued after a score of zero is obtained on both trials of an item.

The rate and intonation of the examiner's speech are important during this subtest. Each of the numbers is to be read at a rate of one per second, and at the end of the sequence of numbers, the examiner's voice should drop slightly, indicating the end of a sequence. It is crucial not to inadvertently *chunk* the numbers into small groups while reading them, as this may provide extra help. Table 2.6 provides a description of the changes in the administration of the Digit

Table 2.6 Changes in Administration: Subtest 3, Digit Span (WMI, Core)

WISC-III	WISC-IV
Digits Forward includes 8 items, each with 2 trials	Digits Forward (called Digit Span Forward on the WISC-IV) includes 8 items, each with 2 trials; Trial 1 of Item 7 was slightly modified (an "8" was substituted for a "6")
Digits Backward includes 7 items, each with 2 trials; only Item 1 requires repetition of *two* digits	Digits Backward (called Digit Span Backward on the WISC-IV) includes 8 items, each with 2 trials; Items 1 and 2 *both* require repetition of two digits. Also, there were slight modifications in 4 trials (both trials of Item 2, Trial 1 of Item 7, and Trial 1 of Item 8)
No process scores available	Process scores able to be calculated to more clearly describe the child's Digit Span performance
Feedback was given for only one of the two sample items on Digits Backward	Feedback is given for *both* of the sample items on Digit Span Backward
Administered near the end of the battery (Subtest 12) when children might be bored, tired, or distractible	Administered near the beginning of the battery (Subtest 3) when children are more likely to be attentive

DON'T FORGET

Behaviors to Note on Digit Span

- Note whether children are attempting to use a problem-solving strategy such as *chunking*. Some children use such a strategy from the beginning; others learn a strategy as they progress through the task.

- Note whether errors are due simply to transposing numbers or to completely forgetting numbers.

- Be aware that inattention, a hearing impairment, or anxiety can influence performance on this test; therefore, such difficulties should be noted if present. Clinical judgment must be exercised in determining whether one or more of these factors is responsible for a spuriously low score.

- Interference with the quality of the testing conditions (e.g., noise outside the testing room) should be noted. Such interference may spoil the subtest, rendering it uninterpretable.

- Watch for rapid repetition of digits or beginning to repeat the digits before the examiner has completed the series. Such behavior may indicate impulsivity.

- Observe whether there is a pattern of failing the first trial and then correctly responding to the second trial. Such a pattern may indicate learning or may simply be a warm-up effect.

- Note spontaneous corrections during the administration of this test and remember to give credit for them.

Source: From A. S. Kaufman & E. O. Lichtenberger, *Essentials of WISC-III and WPPSI-R Assessment*. Copyright © 2000 John Wiley & Sons, Inc. This material is used by permission of John Wiley & Sons, Inc.

Span subtest from WISC-III to WISC-IV. The Don't Forget box here provides a description of behaviors that the examiner should note during the administration of the Digit Span subtest.

4. Picture Concepts (PRI, Core)

The new WISC-IV Picture Concepts subtest requires the examinee to choose one picture from each of the two or three rows of pictures presented to form a group with a common characteristic. The materials necessary for the administration of WISC-IV Picture Concepts include the *WISC-IV Administration and Scoring Manual* (Wechsler, 2003), the Stimulus Book, and the Record Form.

The WISC-IV Picture Concepts subtest administration is based on age-based starting points. A child aged 6 to 8 begins with Sample Items A and B and then

Item 1; a child aged 9 to 11 begins with Sample Items A and B and then Item 5; and a child aged 12 to 16 begins with Sample Items A and B and then Item 7. If a child aged 9 to 16 fails to obtain a perfect score on either of the first two items administered, the preceding items should be administered in reverse order until a perfect score on two consecutive items is obtained. The Picture Concepts subtest is discontinued after five consecutive zero-point responses.

For Sample Items A and B, if the child provides a correct response the examiner should inquire as to the reason the child chose the items. If the child fails to provide a response, the examiner provides a reason. If the child provides an incorrect response, the examiner should provide the correct response as well as the reason the items go together. Items 1 through 12 of the WISC-IV Picture Concepts subtest are two-row items; Items 13 through 28 are three-row items. The Don't Forget box below provides a description of behaviors that the examiner should note during the administration of the Picture Concepts subtest.

5. Coding (PSI, Core)

The WISC-IV Coding subtest requires the examinee to copy symbols that are paired with either geometric shapes or numbers using a key within a specified time limit. The stimulus material for the Coding subtest is the Response Booklet. A stopwatch, the *WISC-IV Administration and Scoring Manual* (Wechsler, 2003),

DON'T FORGET

Behaviors to Note on Picture Concepts

- Be aware that quick responses to easy items may indicate overlearned associations rather than higher level abstract reasoning.

- Note how the child handles frustration on this test. For example, the child may respond by saying "Nothing is alike," indicating defensiveness or avoidance. Other children may give up when faced with frustration by repeatedly responding "I don't know."

- Note whether the child studies the pictures for a few seconds prior to answering. Such behavior may indicate a reflective style.

- Observe whether there is verbalization during problem solving.

- Note any behaviors that give clues to whether errors relate to social or cultural misinterpretation, as opposed to visual-perceptual difficulties.

- Note spontaneous corrections during the administration of this test and remember to give credit for them.

the Record Form, and a pencil without an eraser are also needed to administer this subtest.

The WISC-IV has two different Coding forms: Form A for children aged 6 to 7 and Form B for children aged 8 to 16. The different Coding forms have their own separate pages in the Response Booklet. If the child is left-handed, an extra Coding response key should be placed to the right of the child's Response Booklet so that he or she may have an unobstructed view of the Coding key (some left-handers' hand positions obstruct the key on the Record Form). There are no reverse rules for the Coding subtest. The subtest is discontinued after 120 seconds.

The directions for Coding are very lengthy and contain a lot of important detail. Examiners must be prepared to look up from reading the directions to check that the child is following what is being said. Therefore, the directions should be rehearsed and read carefully to each child. During administration of the sample items, if the child makes any mistake it should be corrected immediately. If the child does not appear to understand the task after the sample items have been completed, further instruction should be given until the child clearly understands the task.

Once the subtest has begun, examiners should be astute observers. Children are not permitted to omit any item or to complete all items of one type at a time; if they are observed doing this they need to be told, "Do them in order. Don't skip any." Some children appear to stop midway through the task; the examiner should remind them to continue until told to stop. Occasionally, children appear frustrated at the end of the test because they are able to complete only a few lines. If this behavior is observed, you may want to reassure the child that most children are not able to complete the entire sheet. Any of the previously mentioned behaviors are worthy of noting. Table 2.7 provides a description of the changes in the administration of the Coding subtest from WISC-III to WISC-IV. The following Don't Forget box provides a description of additional behaviors that the examiner should note during the administration of the Coding subtest.

Table 2.7 Changes in Administration: Subtest 5, Coding (PSI, Core)

WISC-III	WISC-IV
Response sheet attached to protocol	Separate Response Booklet
Specific print (i.e., designs to be copied and the word *sample* with the accompanying right angle) appears in teal-colored ink	All print appears in black ink; item content remains unchanged
	Directions to child have been shortened to be more age appropriate and reduce excess verbiage

---

DON'T FORGET

Behaviors to Note on Coding

- Be aware that the eye movements of children taking the subtest can be informative. Frequent use of the Coding key may indicate poor memory or insecurity. In contrast, a child who uses the key infrequently may have a good memory span, visual memory, and/or associative memory. Check to see where on the key the child's eyes focus, especially with older children. Failing to recognize that the key is numerically ordered (i.e., from 1 through 9) not only suggests poor visual memory, but it may also suggest difficulty with number concepts.

- Note whether the child quickly but carelessly fills in symbols across the rows. This behavior may suggest impulsivity.

- Note whether a child attempts to fill in the symbol for the number 1s first, followed by the symbol for the number 2s. This behavior may suggest good planning ability.

- Watch for shaking hands, a tight grip on the pencil, or pressure on the paper when writing. These behaviors may indicate anxiety.

- Observe signs of fatigue, boredom, or inattention as the subtest progresses. Noting the number of symbols copied during 3-second intervals provides helpful behavioral information in this regard.

- Note whether children spend a significant amount of time trying to perfect each of the symbols that are drawn. This behavior may suggest obsessiveness, excessive attention to detail, or perfectionism.

Source: From A. S. Kaufman & E. O. Lichtenberger, *Essentials of WISC-III and WPPSI-R Assessment.* Copyright © 2000 John Wiley & Sons, Inc. This material is used by permission of John Wiley & Sons, Inc.

---

6. Vocabulary (VCI, Core)

The WISC-IV Vocabulary subtest requires the examinee to name pictures or provide definitions for words. Administration of the Vocabulary subtest requires the *WISC-IV Administration and Scoring Manual* (Wechsler, 2003), the Record Form, and the Stimulus Book. Items 1 through 4 are picture items and are administered only if necessary, as reversal items. Items 5 through 36 are verbal items; the examiner reads the word printed in the Stimulus Book aloud and asks the child to provide a definition. The printed words in the Stimulus Book must be used for children aged 9 to 16, with the examiner pointing to each word as the word is pronounced. One exception to this rule is that the Stimulus Book is not presented to nonreaders above age 8 and can be removed from view when the examiner realizes that the child cannot read. The Stimulus Book is not used for children aged 6 to 8.

The WISC-IV Vocabulary subtest administration is based on age-based starting points. A child aged 6 to 8 begins with Item 5, a child aged 9 to 11 begins with Item 7, and a child aged 12 to 16 begins with Item 9. If a child aged 6 to 16 fails to obtain a perfect score on either of the first two items administered, the preceding items should be administered in reverse order until a perfect score on two consecutive items is obtained. It is important to note that the first two verbal items (i.e., Items 5 and 6) on the WISC-IV Vocabulary subtest require the examiner to provide an example of a 2-point response if the child does not spontaneously give a 2-point response. The Vocabulary subtest is discontinued after five consecutive zero-point responses.

Children sometimes respond by defining a homonym of a word, which is not given credit, and the examiner should query the response. Sometimes a child may provide a slang response that is not found in the dictionary, and the examiner should inquire for another response. Children never receive credit for simply

---

DON'T FORGET

Behaviors to Note on Vocabulary

- Note whether children have difficulties pronouncing words or whether they seem uncertain about how to express what they think.
- Some children supplement what they say with gesturing; others rely on verbal expression more than nonverbal communication.
- Make note of "I don't know" responses or the "tip of the tongue" phenomenon, as these responses and behaviors may indicate word retrieval problems. A lack of rapidity and efficiency in retrieving words from the lexicon can influence test performance negatively, leading to an underestimate of the child's actual word knowledge.
- Note that hearing difficulties may be apparent on this test. The Vocabulary words are not presented in a meaningful context. Note behaviors such as leaning forward during administration to hear better, as well as indications of auditory discrimination problems (e.g., defining confine rather than confide).
- Note verbosity in childrens' responses. They may be attempting to compensate for insecurity about their ability, or they may be obsessive or inefficient in their verbal expression.
- Note spontaneous corrections during the administration of this test and remember to give credit for them.

Source: From A. S. Kaufman & E. O. Lichtenberger, Essentials of WISC-III and WPPSI-R Assessment. Copyright © 2000 John Wiley & Sons, Inc. This material is used by permission of John Wiley & Sons, Inc.

Table 2.8 Changes in Administration: Subtest 6, Vocabulary (VCI, Core)

WISC-III	WISC-IV
Four age-based starting points • Ages 6–8 begin with Item 1 • Ages 9–10 begin with Item 3 • Ages 11–13 begin with Item 5 • Ages 14–16 begin with Item 7	Three age-based starting points • Ages 6–8 begin with Item 5 • Ages 9–11 begin with Item 7 • Ages 12–16 begin with Item 9
Discontinue after 4 consecutive scores of 0	Discontinue after 5 consecutive scores of 0
No reverse rules for ages 6–8	Reverse rules for all ages if either of the scores on the first two items is not perfect
Corrective feedback is provided for Item 1	Corrective feedback is provided for Items 5 and 6
No Stimulus Book	Stimulus Book is used for ages 9–16 (Vocabulary words are not shown to nonreaders)
No picture items	Items 1–4 are picture items that are used as reversal items only (e.g., if a child aged 6–8 fails to provide a 2-point response on either of the first two items administered)
30 test items	36 test items: 27 retained items, 4 new picture items, 5 new verbal items

pointing to an object, so if a child responds nonverbally he or she should be encouraged to give a verbal response. Occasionally, it is apparent that children have mishcard the word you asked them to define; in such a case, the examiner should repeat the word. However, the examiner should never spell the word presented to the child. Table 2.8 provides a description of the changes in the administration of the Vocabulary subtest from WISC-III to WISC-IV. The Don't Forget box on page 82 provides a description of behaviors that the examiner should note during the administration of the Vocabulary subtest.

7. Letter-Number Sequencing (WMI, Core)

The new WISC-IV Letter-Number Sequencing subtest requires the examinee to listen to a sequence of numbers and letters presented orally by the examiner and to recall the numbers in ascending order and the letters in alphabetical order. Administration materials include the *WISC-IV Administration and Scoring Manual* (Wechsler, 2003) and the Record Form.

The WISC-IV Letter-Number Sequencing subtest administration is based on age-based starting points. A child aged 6 to 7 is presented with the qualifying items (counting numbers and reciting the alphabet), sample item, and then Item 1. A child aged 8 to 16 is presented with the sample item, then Item 1. If the child provides an incorrect response on either trial of the sample item, the examiner should provide the correct response and readminister the trial. Each item is composed of three trials and each trial is presented only one time. The Letter-Number Sequencing subtest is discontinued if a child aged 6 to 7 is unable to respond correctly to either qualifying item, or if a child obtains three zero-point responses on all three trials of an item. Standard prompts are allowable on Items 1, 4, and 5. If a standard prompt is needed for any of these items, the examiner should provide the

DON'T FORGET

Behaviors to Note on Letter-Number Sequencing

- Note whether children are attempting to use a problem-solving strategy such as *chunking*. Some children use such a strategy from the beginning; others learn a strategy as they progress through the task.
- Note whether errors are due to the failure to reorder the letter-number sequence, with the sequence being repeated verbatim (which is still credited as correct on certain items) versus the sequence's having been forgotten (which is scored "0").
- Be aware that inattention, a hearing impairment, or anxiety can influence performance on this test.
- Interference with the quality of the testing conditions (e.g., noise outside the testing room) should be noted. Such interference may spoil the subtest, rendering it uninterpretable.
- Observe how well children persist, noting how well they tolerate frustration.
- Observe whether there is a pattern of failing the first trial and then correctly responding to the second trial. Such a pattern may indicate learning or may simply be a warm-up effect.
- Note whether the child treats the task as digits forward or digits backward. Approaching the task in such a manner, although not consistent with examiner instructions, may lead to an adequate score, especially at the younger ages. Remember that when a child gives only verbatim responses (as opposed to the appropriate reordered responses), you cannot draw valid inferences about his or her working memory.
- Note spontaneous corrections during the administration of this test and remember to give credit for them.

prompt and place a *P* on the Record Form to indicate that a prompt was given. The Don't Forget box on page 84 provides a description of behaviors that the examiner should note during the administration of the Letter-Number Sequencing subtest.

8. Matrix Reasoning (PRI, Core)

The new WISC-IV Matrix Reasoning subtest requires the child to complete the missing portion of a picture matrix by selecting one of five response options. Administration materials used for the Matrix Reasoning subtest include the *WISC-IV Administration and Scoring Manual* (Wechsler, 2003), the Record Form, and the Stimulus Book.

The WISC-IV Matrix Reasoning subtest administration is based on age-based starting points. A child aged 6 to 8 is administered Samples A through C, then Item 4; a child aged 9 to 11 is administered Samples A through C, then Item 7; and a child aged 12 to 16 is administered Samples A through C, then Item 11. If the child does not obtain a perfect score on either of the first two items, the preceding items should be administered in reverse order until a perfect score on two consecutive items is obtained. The Matrix Reasoning subtest is discontinued after four consecutive zero-point responses or after four zero-point responses on five consecutive items.

The examiner may provide assistance on the sample items only. The child should indicate his or her response by pointing to the picture in the Stimulus Book or by stating the number associated with the desired answer. The following Don't Forget box provides a description of behaviors that the examiner should note during the administration of the Matrix Reasoning subtest.

DON'T FORGET

Behaviors to Note on Matrix Reasoning

- Observe the level of planning involved. Does the child systematically examine the problem and appear to carefully plan before providing an answer, or does the child appear to be impulsive?
- Be aware that the eye movements of children taking the subtest may be informative, providing information about a systematic versus random approach to problem solving.
- Note whether the child appears to give up easily on more difficult items by stating "I don't know" before examining the item. This type of behavior may indicate that the child has become frustrated with the task.
- Note spontaneous corrections during the administration of this test and remember to give credit for them.

9. Comprehension (VCI, Core)

The WISC-IV Comprehension subtest requires the examinee to answer a series of questions based on his or her understanding of general principles and social situations. The *WISC-IV Administration and Scoring Manual* (Wechsler, 2003) and Record Form are the only items needed for the administration of this subtest.

DON'T FORGET
....
Behaviors to Note on Comprehension

- Observe whether unusually long verbal responses are an attempt to cover up for not actually knowing the correct response or an indication that the child tends to be obsessive about details.
- Be aware that Comprehension requires a good amount of verbal expression; therefore word-finding difficulties, articulation problems, circumstantiality, tangentiality, or circumlocutions (e.g., verbal discourse that is overly detailed, irrelevant, or convoluted, respectively) may be apparent during this subtest.
- Be aware that some Comprehension questions have rather long verbal stimuli; note whether inattention is influencing the child's responses to such items. For example, only part of the question may be answered.
- Note whether defensiveness is occurring in responses to some Comprehension items. For example, when asked about seat belts, if the child's response does not really answer the question and is something like, "We shouldn't have to wear seat belts," this may be defensive responding. Although such responses are scored "0," it is recommended that you follow up if you believe that the child knows the answer.
- Note whether children need consistent prompting when a second response is required or whether they spontaneously provide enough information in their initial answer.
- Observe children's responses carefully to determine whether incorrect responses are a result of poor verbal ability or poor social judgment.
- Note how children respond to queries and requests for elaboration (e.g., "Give me another reason"). Some may be threatened or frustrated by the interruptions, and others may seem comfortable with the added structure. Some children, when asked for "another reason," simply restate the first reason in different words or otherwise do not give a second idea.
- Note spontaneous corrections during the administration of this test and remember to give credit for them.

Source: From A. S. Kaufman & E. O. Lichtenberger, *Essentials of WISC-III and WPPSI-R Assessment.* Copyright © 2000 John Wiley & Sons, Inc. This material is used by permission of John Wiley & Sons, Inc.

Unlike the WISC-III, the WISC-IV Comprehension subtest has age-based starting points. A child aged 6 to 8 begins with Item 1; a child aged 9 to 11 begins with Item 3; and a child aged 12 to 16 begins with Item 5. If a child aged 9 to 16 does not obtain a perfect score on either of the first two items, the preceding items should be administered in reverse order until a perfect score on two consecutive items is obtained. The Comprehension subtest is discontinued after four consecutive zero-point responses.

The WISC-IV Comprehension subtest questions should be read at such a pace that children find it easy to follow the examiner but do not become distracted because of the speed. The questions may be repeated as many times as necessary without changing the wording. It is important to note that the first item on the WISC-IV Comprehension subtest requires the examiner to provide an example of a 2-point response if the child does not spontaneously give a 2-point response. This is done in order to teach the child the type of response expected for each item. On Items 4, 9, 11, 13, 14, and 18 through 21, the child is required to give two general concepts in response to the question in order to receive full credit (i.e., 2 points). On these items, the examiner is required to prompt the child for another response if only one general concept is reflected in the child's response. If the child's response replicates the same general concept, the examiner should prompt once more. If the child's first spontaneous response is incorrect, however, examiners should not prompt for a second response. Table 2.9 provides a description of the changes in the administration of the Comprehension subtest from WISC-III to WISC-IV. The

Table 2.9 Changes in Administration: Subtest 9, Comprehension (VCI, Core)

WISC-III	WISC IV
All children begin with Item 1	Age-based starting points • Ages 6–8 begin with Item 1 • Ages 9–11 begin with Item 3 • Ages 12–16 begin with Item 5
No reverse rules	Reverse rules for ages 9–16 if either of the scores on the first two items is not perfect
Examiner may ask for a second response *once* on items requiring the examinee's response to reflect two (or more) general concepts	Examiner may ask for a second response *twice* (not including a query) if the child's response to the examiner's initial requestioning reflects the same general concept as his or her first response
18 test items	21 test items: 10 retained items with few or no wording changes, 11 new items

Don't Forget box on page 86 provides a description of behaviors that the examiner should note during the administration of the Comprehension subtest.

10. Symbol Search (PSI, Core)

The WISC-IV Symbol Search subtest requires the examinee to scan a search group and indicate the presence or absence of a target symbol or symbols within a specified time limit. The stimulus material for the Symbol Search subtest is the Response Booklet. A stopwatch, the *WISC-IV Administration and Scoring Manual* (Wechsler, 2003), the Record Form, and a pencil without an eraser are also needed to administer this subtest.

The Symbol Search subtest has one Response Booklet with two forms: Symbol Search A for children aged 6 to 7 and Symbol Search B for children aged 8 to 16. There are no reverse rules for the Symbol Search subtest. The subtest is discontinued after 120 seconds.

Although the Symbol Search subtest has a time limit of 120 seconds, prior to beginning the subtest children must go through sample items and practice items that are not timed. It is important not to skip any of the demonstration, even if the child appears to readily understand the task. The directions to the sample, practice, and test items are lengthy and require multiple rehearsals in order to be able to communicate them while maintaining rapport with the child. A minimum of paraphrasing is acceptable while reading the directions; however, every attempt should be made to state them verbatim from the manual. The task should not begin until it is clear that the child understands what is required.

The timing of 120 seconds should be exact. Some children may purposefully or inadvertently skip items, and they should be reminded to complete items in order and to not skip any. Other children may appear to stop the task before the 120-second time limit expires and should be reminded to continue. Table 2.10 provides a description of the changes in the administration of the Symbol Search subtest from WISC-III to WISC-IV. The following Don't Forget box provides a

Table 2.10 Changes in Administration: Subtest 10, Symbol Search (PSI, Core)

WISC-III	WISC-IV
Symbol Search B: 45 test items	Symbol Search B: 60 test items—45 retained, 15 new
	Directions to child have been shortened to be more age appropriate and reduce excess verbiage

DON'T FORGET

....

Behaviors to Note on Symbol Search

- Watch for shaking hands, a tight pencil grip, or pressure on the paper when writing. These behaviors may indicate anxiety.

- Observe attention and concentration. Is the child's focus consistent throughout the task, or does it wane as the task progresses?

- Observe whether children check each row of symbols only once, or whether they recheck the row of symbols in an item more than once. Obsessive concern with detail may be noted.

- Note whether the child quickly but carelessly identifies a symbol as present or absent in a row. This behavior may suggest impulsivity.

- Be aware that eye movements of children taking the subtest can be informative. Consistent glancing back and forth between the target and search groups before making a choice may indicate poor memory. In contrast, a child who refers to the target symbol infrequently may have a good memory span and/or visual memory.

- Watch for signs of fatigue, boredom, or inattention as the subtest progresses, as this subtest is one of the last administered. Noting the number of items answered during each of the four 30-second intervals within the 120-second time limit may provide helpful behavioral information in this regard.

Source: From A. S. Kaufman & E. O. Lichtenberger, Essentials of WISC-III and WPPSI-R Assessment. Copyright © 2000 John Wiley & Sons, Inc. This material is used by permission of John Wiley & Sons, Inc.

description of behaviors that the examiner should note during the administration of the Symbol Search subtest.

SUBTEST-BY-SUBTEST RULES OF ADMINISTRATION OF THE WISC-IV SUPPLEMENTAL SUBTESTS

11. Picture Completion (PRI, Supplemental)

The WISC-IV Picture Completion subtest requires the examinee to view a picture and name the essential missing part of the picture within a specified time limit. To administer this subtest, the examiner needs the *WISC-IV Administration and Scoring Manual* (Wechsler, 2003), the Stimulus Book, the Record Form, and a stopwatch.

The WISC-IV Picture Completion subtest administration is based on age-based starting points. A child aged 6 to 8 begins with the sample item, then Item 1; a child aged 9 to 11 begins with the sample item, then Item 5; and a child aged 12 to 16 begins with the sample item, then Item 10. If a child aged 9 to 16 does not obtain a perfect score on either of the first two items administered, the preceding items should be administered in reverse order until a perfect score on two consecutive items is obtained. The Picture Completion subtest is discontinued after six consecutive zero-point responses.

It is important to note that the first two items on the WISC-IV Picture Completion subtest require the examiner to provide corrective feedback if the child provides an incorrect answer. This is done in order to teach the child the type of response expected from each item.

Because each item on the Picture Completion subtest is timed, the examiner should be exact about his or her timing and begin timing immediately after the item is presented to the child. Timing stops when the child provides an answer or when 20 seconds have elapsed.

Most children find this subtest fun, making it easy to administer. Examiners most frequently make errors on the queries that may be given during the subtest (e.g., forgetting to say the queries altogether or using them more frequently than allowed). Other errors may occur when a child produces an unclear verbal response. In some cases, verbal or nonverbal responses are considered acceptable answers. In other cases, a child must provide a nonverbal response to receive credit for an initial verbal response. If a child provides verbal and nonverbal responses that differ (i.e., one is correct and one is not), the response is considered spoiled and no credit is given. It is noteworthy if a child consistently provides only nonverbal responses (e.g., pointing). Table 2.11 provides a description of

Table 2.11   Changes in Administration: Subtest 11, Picture Completion (PRI, Supplemental)

WISC-III	WISC-IV
Four age-based starting points • Ages 6–7 begin with sample, then Item 1 • Ages 8–9 begin with sample, then Item 5 • Ages 10–13 begin with sample, then Item 7 • Ages 14–16 begin with sample, then Item 11	Three age-based starting points • Ages 6–8 begin with sample, then Item 1 • Ages 9–11 begin with sample, then Item 5 • Ages 12–16 begin with sample, then Item 10
Discontinue after 5 consecutive scores of 0	Discontinue after 6 consecutive scores of 0
30 test items	38 test items: 27 modified items, 11 new items

DON'T FORGET

Behaviors to Note on Picture Completion

- Note the speed with which the child responds. A reflective individual may take more time in responding (but most likely can respond within the time limit), whereas an impulsive individual may respond very quickly but incorrectly.

- Note whether the child is persistent in stating that nothing is missing from the picture (rather than responding, "I don't know"), as it may reflect opposition-ality or inflexibility.

- Note that consistent nonverbal responses (e.g., pointing) may be evidence of word retrieval problems in children. Although it is acceptable to give a non-verbal response, it is far more common to give a verbal response.

- Be aware that verbal responses that are imprecise ("the thingy on the door") or overly elaborate ("the small piece of metal that forms a connection be-tween the molding around the door frame and the door itself, allowing it to open easily") are also noteworthy.

- Be aware that after individuals have been redirected (e.g., "Yes, but what is the *most important* part that is missing?") it is important to note whether they continue to respond with the same quality of response. This persistence in approach may indicate inability to understand the task or inflexibility in thinking.

Source: From A. S. Kaufman & E. O. Lichtenberger, *Essentials of WISC-III and WPPSI-R Assessment.* Copyright © 2000 John Wiley & Sons, Inc. This material is used by permission of John Wiley & Sons, Inc.

the changes in the administration of the Picture Completion subtest from WISC-III to WISC-IV. The Don't Forget box on this page provides a description of behaviors that the examiner should note during the administration of the Picture Completion subtest.

12. Cancellation (PSI, Supplemental)

The new WISC-IV Cancellation subtest requires the examinee to scan both a random and a structured arrangement of pictures and mark target pictures within a specified time limit. The stimulus material for the Cancellation subtest is the Response Booklet. A stopwatch, the *WISC-IV Administration and Scoring Manual* (Wechsler, 2003), the Record Form, and a red pencil without an eraser are also needed to administer this subtest.

There are no age-based starting points for the WISC-IV Cancellation subtest; all children begin with the sample item, continue to the practice items, and then

DON'T FORGET

Behaviors to Note on Cancellation

- Watch for shaking hands, a tight grip on the pencil, or pressure on the paper when writing. These behaviors may indicate anxiety.
- Note whether children have difficulty understanding that they are expected to work quickly. This behavior may relate to immaturity.
- Observe attention and concentration. Is the child's focus consistent throughout the task, or does it wane as the task progresses?
- Observe signs of fatigue, boredom, or inattention as the subtest progresses. Noting the number of responses produced during each of the 45-second item intervals may provide helpful behavioral information in this regard.
- Observe whether the child's response rate is consistent throughout the subtest.
- Note whether the child quickly but carelessly circles responses. This behavior may suggest impulsivity.
- Note the effect of distractors on the child's performance. Remember that the target items are identically placed on both the randomized and nonrandomized forms.

begin Item 1. There are no reverse rules on this subtest. The subtest items are discontinued after 45 seconds have elapsed.

There are two types of items contained within the Response Booklet: random (i.e., the distractors are scattered across the page) and structured (i.e., the target items and distractors are arranged in rows). Each target item is an animal. If the child fails to mark a target or marks a distractor item during the practice items, the examiner should provide corrective feedback. It is important not to proceed to Item 1 until the child fully understands the task. Spontaneous corrections should not be discouraged, unless such corrections occur frequently enough to impede performance. The Don't Forget box above provides a description of behaviors that the examiner should note during the administration of the Cancellation subtest.

13. Information (VCI, Supplemental)

The WISC-IV Information subtest requires the examinee to answer questions that address a wide range of general-knowledge topics. To administer this subtest, the examiner needs only the *WISC-IV Administration and Scoring Manual* (Wechsler, 2003) and the Record Form.

The WISC-IV Information subtest administration is based on age-based starting points. A child aged 6 to 8 begins with Item 5, a child aged 9 to 11 begins with Item 10, and a child aged 12 to 16 begins with Item 12. If the child does not obtain a perfect score on either of the first two items administered, the preceding items should be administered in reverse order until a perfect score on two consecutive items is obtained. The Information subtest is discontinued after five consecutive zero-point responses.

It is important to note that the first two items on the WISC-IV Information subtest require the examiner to provide corrective feedback if the child provides an incorrect answer. This is done in order to teach the child the type of response expected from each item. In terms of item repetition, each item may be repeated as often as necessary, as long as the examiner does not reword the original item in any manner. If the child mishears a word and provides an incorrect answer, the examiner should repeat the entire item with emphasis on the misheard word. This pertains especially to Items 4 and 15. Table 2.12 provides a description of the changes in the administration of the Information subtest from WISC-III to WISC-IV. The Don't Forget box on page 94 provides a description of behaviors that the examiner should note during the administration of the Information subtest.

14. Arithmetic (WMI, Supplemental)

The WISC-IV Arithmetic subtest requires the examinee to mentally solve a variety of orally presented arithmetic problems within a specified time limit. The materials necessary for the administration of the WISC-IV Arithmetic subtest include the *WISC-IV Administration and Scoring Manual* (Wechsler, 2003), the Record Form, the Stimulus Book, and a stopwatch.

The WISC-IV Arithmetic subtest administration is based on age-based starting points. A child aged 6 to 7 begins with Item 3, a child aged 8 to 9 begins with

Table 2.12 Changes in Administration: Subtest 13, Information (VCI, Supplemental)

WISC-III	WISC-IV
Four age-based starting points	Three age-based starting points
• Ages 6–7 begin with Item 1	• Ages 6–8 begin with Item 5
• Ages 8–10 begin with Item 5	• Ages 9–11 begin with Item 10
• Ages 11–13 begin with Item 8	• Ages 12–16 begin with Item 12
• Ages 14–16 begin with Item 11	
30 test items	33 test items: 22 retained items with few or no wording changes, 11 new items

DON'T FORGET

Behaviors to Note on Information

- Note any observable patterns in a child's responses. Patterns of responding such as missing early, easy items and having success on harder items may suggest anxiety, poor motivation, or retrieval difficulties.

- Consider whether incorrect responses are related to the child's cultural background (e.g., on questions about a character in U.S. history at a certain time or about the geography of a specific location). Such observations should be incorporated into interpretation.

- Note whether children provide unnecessarily long responses. Long responses filled with excessive detail may be indicative of obsessiveness, a desire to impress the examiner, or an attempt to cover up for not knowing the correct response.

- Note whether the content of failed items consistently owes to lack of knowledge in a specific area (e.g., numerical information, history, geography); an error analysis may be useful in this regard.

- Note spontaneous corrections during the administration of this test and remember to give credit for them.

Source: From A. S. Kaufman & E. O. Lichtenberger, *Essentials of WISC-III and WPPSI-R Assessment.* Copyright © 2000 John Wiley & Sons, Inc. This material is used by permission of John Wiley & Sons, Inc.

Item 9, and a child aged 10 to 16 begins with Item 12. If the child does not obtain a perfect score on either of the first two items administered, the preceding items should be administered in reverse order until a perfect score on two consecutive items is obtained. If a child provides an incorrect answer or does not respond within 30 seconds to Items 1 through 3, the examiner should provide corrective feedback. The Arithmetic subtest is discontinued after four consecutive zero-point responses.

It is important to note that the Arithmetic items are timed. The examiner should begin timing immediately after each item presentation and stop timing immediately after a child responds or 30 seconds have elapsed. In terms of item repetition, the examiner may repeat each item only once under two conditions (i.e., at the child's request or when it is apparent that the child failed to understand the item); however, timing continues throughout the repetition. There are corresponding pictures in the Stimulus Book for Items 1 through 5, while Items 6 through 34 are presented orally to the child. The child should not use a pencil or paper for this subtest. If the child provides a spontaneous second answer within the 30-second time limit, score the second response. Table 2.13 provides a description of the changes in the administration of the Arithmetic subtest from

Table 2.13 Changes in Administration: Subtest 14, Arithmetic (WMI, Supplemental)

WISC-III	WISC-IV
Four age-based starting points • Age 6 begins with Item 1 • Ages 7–8 begin with Item 6 • Ages 9–12 begin with Item 12 • Ages 13–16 begin with Item 14	Three age-based starting points • Ages 6–7 begin with Item 3 • Ages 8–9 begin with Item 9 • Ages 10–16 begin with Item 12
Discontinue after 3 consecutive scores of 0	Discontinue after 4 consecutive scores of 0
No corrective feedback	Corrective feedback is provided for Items 1–3
Time limits vary depending on the item 24 test items	Every item has a 30-second time limit 34 test items: 7 retained items, 16 new items, 11 modified items

DON'T FORGET

Behaviors to Note on Arithmetic

- Observe children for signs of anxiety. Some children who view themselves as "poor at math" may be anxious during this task. Be aware of statements such as, "I was never taught that in school" or "I can't do math in my head."
- Note whether the child appears to be focusing on the stopwatch. This may be a sign of anxiety, distractibility, or competitiveness. Watch for statements such as, "How long did that take me?"
- Watch for signs of distractibility or poor concentration.
- Be aware that finger counting may occur in children of any age. This may be indicative of insecurity about math skills or may be an adaptive problem-solving tool for younger children. Note if the child attempts to hide finger counting from the examiner, is brazen about finger counting, or is nonchalant about finger counting.
- Note when the child asks for repetition of a question, as it may indicate several things, including poor hearing, inattention, or stalling.
- Observe the child's response style. Does he or she respond quickly, or is he or she methodical and careful in his or her responding?

Source: From A. S. Kaufman & E. O. Lichtenberger, *Essentials of WISC-III and WPPSI-R Assessment.* Copyright © 2000 John Wiley & Sons, Inc. This material is used by permission of John Wiley & Sons, Inc.

WISC-III to WISC-IV. The Don't Forget box on page 95 provides a description of behaviors that the examiner should note during the administration of the Arithmetic subtest.

15. Word Reasoning (VCI, Supplemental)

The new WISC-IV Word Reasoning subtest requires the examinee to identify a common concept being described by a series of clues. To administer this subtest, the examiner needs only the *WISC-IV Administration and Scoring Manual* (Wechsler, 2003) and the Record Form.

The WISC-IV Word Reasoning subtest administration is based on two age-based starting points. A child aged 6 to 9 begins with Sample Items A and B, then Item 1; and a child aged 10 to 16 begins with Sample Items A and B, then Item 5. If a child aged 10 to 16 does not obtain a perfect score on either of the first two items administered, the preceding items should be administered in reverse order until a perfect score on two consecutive items is obtained. The Word Reasoning subtest is discontinued after five consecutive zero-point responses.

When administering the Word Reasoning subtest, the examiner reads each item clue verbatim and gives the child 5 seconds to respond. If the child does not respond within the 5-second time limit, or if the child requests repetition, the examiner should repeat the clue only once and wait 5 seconds more. If the child still fails to respond, or provides an incorrect response, the examiner should present the next clue or item as long as the discontinue rule has not been met. Beginning with Item 7, each item has two clues, and beginning with Item 16, each item has

DON'T FORGET

Behaviors to Note on Word Reasoning

- Note when the child asks for repetition of a question, as it may indicate several things, including poor hearing, inattention, or stalling.
- Take note of whether children respond quickly, are impulsive, or are methodical and careful in their processing of the information.
- Be aware that because children will almost always respond incorrectly before subsequent clues are given, they may become frustrated or insecure about responding.
- Note spontaneous corrections during the administration of this test and remember to give credit for them.

three clues. It is important to remember that when presenting items with two or three clues, the examiner must provide any clues that were already stated (e.g., restate the first and second clue before presenting the third and final clue). If the child provides a correct response before all clues for an item have been presented, the examiner should score 1 point for the item and continue to the next item. The examiner may provide assistance only with the sample items. The Don't Forget box on page 96 provides a description of behaviors that the examinee should note during the administration of the Word Reasoning subtest.

CAUTION

Common Errors in WISC-IV Subtest Administration

Verbal Subtests

Common errors on the Similarities subtest

- Forgetting to provide the correct response if the child fails to respond or the response is incorrect on Items 1 and 2
- Forgetting to administer previous items in *reverse sequence* if a child aged 9–16 does not obtain a perfect score on either of the first two items administered
- Overquerying or underquerying vague responses

Common errors on the Vocabulary subtest

- Forgetting to give an example of a 2-point response if the child's response to Item 5 or 6 is not perfect
- Forgetting to administer previous items in *reverse sequence* if the child does not obtain a perfect score on either of the first two items administered
- Not correcting the child if he or she mishears items, especially Items 11, 23, 32, 33
- Not recording verbal responses verbatim
- Not querying vague or incomplete responses as indicated in the *WISC-IV Administration and Scoring Manual* (Wechsler, 2003)
- Forgetting to use the stimulus book for children aged 9–16 (excluding nonreaders)

Common errors on the Comprehension subtest

- Forgetting to give an example of a 2-point response if the child's response to Item 1 is not perfect
- Forgetting to administer previous items in *reverse sequence* if a child aged 9–16 does not obtain a perfect score on either of the first two items administered

(continued)

- Forgetting to query for a second response if necessary on Items 4, 9, 11, 13, 14, and 18–21
- Not recording verbal responses verbatim
- Defining words if asked by child

Common errors on the Information subtest
- Forgetting to provide the correct response if the child fails to respond or responds incorrectly to Items 1 or 2
- Forgetting to administer previous items in *reverse sequence* if the child does not obtain a perfect score on either of the first two items administered
- Not correcting the child if he or she mishears items, especially Items 4 and 15
- Defining words if asked by the child
- Forgetting to query an incomplete answer as indicated in the *WISC-IV Administration and Scoring Manual* (Wechsler, 2003)
- Being unaware that neutral queries may be given to responses that are incomplete or ambiguous

Common errors on the Word Reasoning subtest
- Forgetting to administer previous items in *reverse sequence* if a child aged 9–16 does not obtain a perfect score on either of the first two items administered
- Forgetting to repeat the clue once after the child fails to respond in the first 5 seconds
- Forgetting to restate first clues when presenting second and third clues
- Repeating a clue more than once (each entire clue may be repeated *one time only*)
- Forgetting the 5-second response-time rules, namely, allowing a child approximately 5 seconds to respond, allowing an additional 5 seconds if a child asks for a clue to be repeated, and crediting responses given in more than 5 seconds
- Forgetting to say "Let's try another one" before *every* new item that is administered

Perceptual Reasoning Subtests

Common errors on the Block Design subtest
- Forgetting to time the child
- Forgetting to administer previous items in *reverse sequence* if a child aged 8–16 fails the second trial of Item 3 or provides an incorrect response to Item 4
- Neglecting to make sure that the proper variety of block faces is showing before an item has been started
- Neglecting to give the five extra blocks on Items 11 through 14

- Placing the model or stimulus book in an incorrect position
- Correcting block rotations more than once
- Forgetting to leave the examiner's manual intact when the child constructs his or her designs for Items 1 and 2
- Forgetting to disassemble the examiner's model when the child constructs his or her design for Item 3

Common errors on the Picture Concepts subtest
- Forgetting to provide the correct response and point to the corresponding pictures in Sample Items A and B if the child responds incorrectly
- Forgetting to administer previous items in *reverse sequence* if a child aged 9–16 does not obtain a perfect score on either of the first two items administered
- Forgetting to point across the first and second row of pictures when providing instructions for completing two-row items
- Forgetting to point across the first, second, and third rows of pictures when providing instructions for completing three-row items
- Forgetting to provide the standard prompts listed in the *WISC-IV Administration and Scoring Manual* (Wechsler, 2003) *as often as necessary* when a child does not select a picture in each row or selects more than one picture in a single row

Common errors on the Matrix Reasoning subtest
- Forgetting to provide the correct response and point to the correct corresponding pictures in Sample Items A, B, and C
- Forgetting to administer previous items in *reverse sequence* if the child does not obtain a perfect score on either of the first two items administered
- Forgetting to point to the pictured responses and the box with the question mark as often as needed when presenting test items

Common errors on the Picture Completion subtest
- Forgetting to time the items (i.e., 20 seconds per item)
- Forgetting to give the correct response to Items 1 and 2 if the child does not respond within 20 seconds or responds incorrectly
- Forgetting to administer previous items in *reverse sequence* if a child aged 9–16 does not obtain a perfect score on either of the first two items administered
- Forgetting to query when the child does not spontaneously point when providing a response from the right-hand column items (which require pointing in addition to a verbal response)
- Giving specific queries listed in the *WISC-IV Administration and Scoring Manual* (Wechsler, 2003) more than once

(continued)

- Asking, "Which one is your answer?" when a child points to the correct place in the picture, but provides a verbal elaboration that spoils the response
- Forgetting to query ambiguous or incomplete verbal responses by asking "Show me where you mean" as often as necessary

Working Memory
Common errors on the Digit Span subtest
- Reading the sequence of digits too quickly
- Inadvertently *chunking* the numbers when reading them
- Repeating a digit sequence if asked
- Giving extra help beyond the sample item on Digits Backward
- Forgetting to administer Digits Backward to a child who receives 0 points on Digits Forward
- Forgetting to administer *both* trials of an item

Common errors on the Letter-Number Sequencing subtest
- Administering the subtest if a child aged 6–7 fails the qualifying items
- Forgetting to remind the child of the correct order on Item 1, Trial 1; Item 4, Trial 2; and Item 5, Trial 1
- Forgetting to acknowledge responses repeated verbatim as correct on Items 1.1, 1.2, 1.3, 2.1, 2.2, 2.3, 3.1, 3.2, and 4.1
- Repeating a letter-number sequence if asked
- Forgetting to administer all three trials of an item

Common errors on the Arithmetic subtest
- Forgetting to time the child
- Stopping the stopwatch when a question is repeated
- Repeating an item more than one time
- Allowing paper and pencil to be used
- Forgetting to provide the correct response to Items 1, 2, and 3 if the child does not respond within 30 seconds or responds incorrectly
- Forgetting to administer previous items in *reverse sequence* if the child does not obtain a perfect score on either of the first two items administered
- Forgetting to remove the Stimulus Booklet after administering Item 5
- Forgetting to give credit for spontaneous corrections within the time limit

Processing Speed

Common errors on the Coding subtest
- Forgetting to administer the correct form, based on the examinee's age (e.g., Coding A: 6–7; Coding B: 8–16)

- Forgetting to time the child
- Forgetting to correct errors on sample items immediately
- Not paying attention to the child and allowing him or her to skip over items or complete a row in reverse order

Common errors on the Symbol Search subtest
- Forgetting to administer the correct form, based on the examinee's age (e.g., Symbol Search A: 6–7; Symbol Search B: 8–16)
- Forgetting to time the child
- Proceeding with the task before the child clearly understands what is required
- Burying your head in the manual while reading directions
- Not paying attention to the child and allowing him or her to skip over items

Common errors on the Cancellation subtest
- Forgetting to time the child
- Forgetting to discontinue after a 45-second interval
- Forgetting to provide corrective feedback when the child marks incorrect responses during the practice items
- Forgetting to provide further explanation as needed when presenting Items 1 and 2

Source: From A. S. Kaufman & E. O. Lichtenberger. *Essentials of WISC-III and WPPSI-R Assessment*. Copyright © 2000 John Wiley & Sons, Inc. This material is used by permission of John Wiley & Sons, Inc.

Note: The WISC-IV allows examinees to spontaneously correct responses at *any* time during the administration of the entire test and receive the appropriate credit on any subtest with the exception of memory tasks, processing-speed tasks, and timed tasks (i.e., Block Design, Arithmetic, Coding, Symbol Search, Picture Completion, Cancellation), which allow for spontaneous correction only during the specified time limits of each subtest. The WISC-IV also allows for the examiner to return to a previously given item and readminister it if the examiner believes that the child knows the answer. The only exception to this, of course, is if the answer to that item is addressed elsewhere on the test.

FREQUENTLY ASKED QUESTIONS: SUBTEST ADMINISTRATION

Pearson® provided information on its website to respond to frequently asked questions (FAQs) about the WISC-IV. One category of FAQs was related to subtest administration and is reproduced in Rapid Reference 2.4. (See page 102.)

≣ Rapid Reference 2.4

Frequently Asked Questions: Subtest Administration

Why are some 0 point or 1 point responses on the verbal subtests not queried?

In standardization it was determined that querying certain responses did not result in any additional information. If you feel the child has more knowledge, based on your clinical judgment, the child's performance on surrounding items, and other observations during the administration, you have the option to query. However, clearly wrong responses should not be queried. In addition, the responses marked with a Query in the manual must be queried.

Why are there separate norms for Block Design with and without time bonuses?

Practitioners have suspected that some children who emphasize accuracy over speed of performance may score lower on Block Design because of time bonuses, while others believe that faster performance reflects a higher level of the ability being measured. The separate scores allow practitioners to evaluate these hypotheses with individual children. Practitioners should be aware that most children in the standardization sample achieve very similar scores on Block Design and Block Design Non-Time Bonus. In fact, a difference as small as two points is considered rare.

Why does WISC-IV start with Block Design?

Although Picture Completion has traditionally been the first subtest administered, it is not a core subtest in the WISC–IV. Block Design was chosen as the first subtest because it is an engaging task that gives the examiner the additional opportunity to establish rapport. This is consistent with a recent revision of another Wechsler product, the WPPSI–III, for which the initial subtest of Block Design has been well-received by examiners. When testing children with motor difficulties, examiners may decide to begin with a different subtest in the interest of rapport.

Why is Digit Span placed so early in the subtest order?

In order to avoid interference effects between Digit Span and Letter-Number Sequencing, these subtests were widely separated in the order of administration.

Why have picture items been added to the Vocabulary subtest?

These items were added to improve the floor, providing a more effective way to assess very low functioning children.

On Picture Concepts, why do some children seem to lose track of the task when three rows are first introduced?

Typically, if children lose the instructional set when three rows are introduced, they have reached the upper limit of their ability on this subtest; they lose track of the instructions and are drawn to the distracters included in each row of items. Children should be prompted as instructed each time this loss of set occurs.

What does it mean if a child guesses right on the first clue of Word Reasoning?

Children are more likely to guess correctly on the easier items such as those that appear in the first half of the item set, especially Item 9. The more difficult items found in the second half of the item set show a very low percentage of correct responses to the first clue. In order to respond correctly, even on the first clue, the child must use deductive reasoning; that is, on the first clue the child has to narrow the potential responses to those that fit a search set defined by the clue and then make a reasoned guess from the range of responses within the set. It is possible that a child who consistently guesses correctly on the first clue may have taken the test recently or may have been coached on the correct responses.

Is color blindness a factor in performance on the Cancellation subtest?

Color blindness is not a factor in performance on the Cancellation subtest. The Cancellation task utilizes color as a visual distracter; it is possible that children who are color blind will be less distracted by the bright colors or will have greater difficulty differentiating objects of various colors. However, it is recognition of the shapes of the objects that is required to place them in categories properly.

TEST YOURSELF

1. **Which of the following subtests require the use of a stopwatch?**
   (a) Block Design, Picture Concepts, Coding, Symbol Search, Cancellation
   (b) Cancellation, Coding, Symbol Search
   (c) Block Design, Cancellation, Coding, Symbol Search
   (d) Block Design, Coding, Picture Completion, Symbol Search, Cancellation, Arithmetic

2. **On a subtest with age-based starting points, when the examinee receives full credit on the first item administered but not the second, the first item is used to meet the reversal criteria of two consecutive perfect scores.**
   True or False?

3. **Which of the following subtests listed does not have reverse rules?**

   (a) Digit Span

   (b) Picture Concepts

   (c) Block Design

   (d) Similarities

4. **Which of the following subtests listed requires the use of a separate Response Booklet?**

   (a) Matrix Reasoning

   (b) Coding

   (c) Arithmetic

   (d) Block Design

5. **If a child asks for clarification or repetition of an item after timing has begun, the examiner should discontinue timing.**
   True or False?

6. **When a child requests to have instructions or an item repeated, the examiner must**

   (a) repeat the entire set of instructions or item, not just a portion of it.

   (b) repeat only the portion of instructions that the child requested repetition for.

   (c) tell the examinee that you are unable to repeat any instructions.

   (d) repeat the entire set of instructions or item, with the exception of items on Letter-Number Sequencing and Digit Span.

7. **Which of the following subtests can serve as a substitute for Digit Span?**

   (a) Arithmetic

   (b) Coding

   (c) Symbol Search

   (d) Letter-Number Sequencing

8. **Which of the following subtests can serve as a substitute for Coding?**

   (a) Arithmetic

   (b) Symbol Search

   (c) Information

   (d) Cancellation

9. **When administering the Word Reasoning test, the examiner must repeat preceding clues as more clues are added.**
   True or False?

10. **Block Design, Digit Span, and Cancellation require a modified administration if the examiner wishes to calculate process scores at a later time.**
    True or False?

11. **You are advising a parent how to describe testing to her 6-year-old child; which of the following is a good example of what the parent might say?**

   (a) "You are going to take a test with a lot of questions, just try your best."

   (b) "You are going to play with some blocks, look at books with pictures and words, complete some puzzles, and answer some questions."

   (c) "The doctor is going to test you for about 2 or 3 hours to try to find out why you have problems in school."

   (d) "You are going to play with the doctor for a while; it will be a lot of fun."

12. **When assessing a child with a visual impairment, it may be advisable to administer subtests from the VCI and WMI only.**
   True or False?

13. **In which of the following situations can an examiner query a response?**

   (a) The response is vague.

   (b) The response is ambiguous.

   (c) The response is incomplete.

   (d) All of the above.

14. **If an examiner finds that he or she did not administer enough items to meet the discontinue rule for a subtest, the subtest should be considered spoiled.**
   True or False?

15. **Which of the following can aid in establishing rapport with an examinee?**

   (a) telling the examinee your name

   (b) addressing the examinee by his or her name

   (c) spending a reasonable amount of time interacting with the examinee prior to testing

   (d) all of the above

Answers:

1. d; 2. True; 3. a; 4. b; 5. False; 6. d; 7. a; 8. d; 9. True; 10. False; 11. b; 12. True; 13. d; 14. True; 15. d

Three

HOW TO SCORE THE WISC-IV

TYPES OF SCORES

Administration of the WISC-IV results in three types of scores: raw scores, scaled scores (standard scores with mean = 10 and SD = 3), and Indexes/Full Scale IQ (standard scores with mean = 100 and SD = 15). The first score calculated by the examiner is the *raw score*, which is simply the total number of points earned on a single subtest. The raw score by itself is meaningless because it is not norm referenced. That is, it has no meaning with respect to level of functioning compared to the general population. To interpret an examinee's performance on a subtest, relative to the general population (and more specifically, to same-age peers), raw scores must be converted to *standard scores* (i.e., a scaled score, process score, Index, or IQ). The metrics for the various Wechsler standard scores are listed in Rapid Reference 3.1. Each subtest produces a scaled score (ranging from 1 to 19) having a mean of 10 and a standard deviation of 3. The factor indexes and IQ (also referred to as *Composite Scores*) have a mean of 100 and a standard deviation of 15. The Verbal Comprehension Index (VCI) and the Perceptual Reasoning Index (PRI) have a standard score range of 45 to 155, the Working Memory Index (WMI) and the Processing Speed Index (PSI) have a standard score range of 50 to 150, and the Full Scale IQ (FSIQ) has a standard score range of 40 to 160.

Intellectual abilities are distributed along the normal probability curve in the general population. Most children score within 1 SD below and above the mean on measures of these abilities. That is, about 68 out of every 100 children tested obtain IQ or Index scores between 85 and 115. A greater number of children, about 96%, obtain scores ranging from 70 to 130 (2 SDs below and above the mean, respectively). The number of children earning extremely high scores (i.e., above 130) is about 2%, and the number earning very low scores (i.e., less than 70) is about 2%. With regard to the Index scores, Crawford, Garthwaite, and Gault (2007) found that it is not unusual for members of the normal population to exhibit at least one abnormal Index score (below the 5th percentile)—14.27% of the WISC-IV standardization sample obtained at least one abnormal Index

≡ Rapid Reference 3.1

Metrics for WISC-IV Standard Scores

Type of Standard Score	Mean	Standard Deviation	Range of Values
Scaled score	10	3	1–19
VCI and PRI	100	15	45–155
WMI and PSI	100	15	50–150
FSIQ	100	15	40–160

score. However, the percentage greatly decreases when looking at two or more abnormal scores.

STEP-BY-STEP: HOW THE WISC-IV IS SCORED

Raw Scores

Each of the items of a subtest contributes directly to the raw score. Three subtests (Block Design, Digit Span, and Cancellation) also allow for the calculation of process scores. *Process scores* involve calculating raw scores for specific items or portions of a subtest (process scores will be discussed later in this chapter and in Chapter 6). The scoring of most subtests is not complicated. Simple arithmetic is all that is necessary to calculate the subtests' raw scores. There are a few subtests, however, in which some element of subjectivity presents a challenge to the examiner during the scoring process. Tips for scoring responses that clearly involve subjectivity are discussed later in this chapter. The Caution box at the top of page 108 presents common errors that examiners make in calculating the raw scores.

Scaled Scores

After the raw scores have been transferred from the inside of the Record Form to the front cover, they are converted to scaled scores. To convert the child's raw score to a scaled score the examiner needs the following: (a) the child's chronological age at the time of testing, (b) the child's raw scores on all subtests, and (c) Table A.1 from the *WISC-IV Administration and Scoring Manual* (Wechsler, 2003).

CAUTION

Common Errors in Raw Score Calculation

- Neglecting to include points from the items below the basal (i.e., items that were not administered) to the total raw score
- Neglecting to add the points recorded on one page of the Record Form to the points recorded on the next (e.g., Similarities lists the first 18 items on one page and the last 5 items on the next page; Vocabulary lists the first 17 items on one page and the last 19 items on the next page; Comprehension lists the first 6 items on one page and last 15 items on the next page; and Word Reasoning lists the first 15 items on one page and the last 9 items on the next page)
- Forgetting to subtract the number of incorrect responses from the number of correct responses on Symbol Search and Cancellation
- Transferring total raw scores incorrectly from inside the Record Form to the front page of the Record Form
- Miscalculating the raw score sum
- Including points earned on items that were presented after the discontinue criterion was met
- Forgetting to attend closely to items that are scored 0, 1, or 2 rather than 0 or 1 only

Source: From A. S. Kaufman & E. O. Lichtenberger, *Essentials of WISC-III and WPPSI-R Assessment.* Copyright © 2000 John Wiley & Sons, Inc. This material is used by permission of John Wiley & Sons, Inc.

In the section of Table A.1 that encompasses the child's chronological age, find the child's raw score for each subtest and the corresponding scaled score. Record the scaled score equivalents in the appropriate boxes in two separate places on the front cover of the Record Form—one labeled "Total Raw Score to Scaled Score Conversions" and another labeled "Subtest Scaled Score Profile." The Caution box on page 109 lists the most frequent errors that examiners make in obtaining scaled scores.

Indexes and FSIQ

Converting scaled scores to Indexes and the FSIQ is the next step in the WISC-IV scoring process. The following is a list of steps necessary to convert scaled scores to Index scores and FSIQ. (The Don't Forget box on page 109 lists the subtests that make up the WISC-IV Indexes and FSIQ.)

CAUTION

Most Frequent Errors in Obtaining Scaled Scores

- Using a score conversion table that references the wrong age group
- Misreading across the rows of the score conversion tables
- Transferring scaled scores incorrectly from the conversion table to the Record Form

Note. From A. S. Kaufman & E. O. Lichtenberger, *Essentials of WISC-III and WPPSI-R Assessment.* Copyright © 2000 John Wiley & Sons, Inc. This material is used by permission of John Wiley & Sons, Inc.

1. Calculate the sum of the appropriate subtests' scaled scores for each of the four Indexes and the FSIQ. Note that Information, Word Reasoning, Picture Completion, Arithmetic, and Cancellation are not used in the sum of scaled scores *unless* they are replacing another subtest. Subtest substitutions are discussed later in this chapter and are presented in Table 3.1. It is important to note that only *one* substitution per scale is allowed.
2. Record the "Sums of Scaled Scores" in the appropriate boxes on the front of the Record Form in the sections labeled "Total Raw Score to Scaled Score Conversions" and "Sum of Scaled Scores to Composite

DON'T FORGET

Subtests Making Up WISC-IV Indexes

VCI	PRI	WMI	PSI
Similarities	Block Design	Digit Span	Coding
Vocabulary	Picture Concepts	Letter-Number Sequencing	Symbol Search
Comprehension	Matrix Reasoning		(Cancellation)
(Information) (Word Reasoning)	(Picture Completion)	(Arithmetic)	

Note: Subtests in parentheses are supplemental tests. All other subtests compose the core battery. The FSIQ is made up of the 10 core battery subtests unless a substitution has been made. See Table 3.1 for allowable substitutions of supplemental tests for core battery tests.

Table 3.1 Guidelines for Substituting Supplemental Subtests for Core Battery Subtests

Core Subtest	Acceptable Substitution
Similarities	Information, Word Reasoning
Vocabulary	Information, Word Reasoning
Comprehension	Information, Word Reasoning
Block Design	Picture Completion
Picture Concepts	Picture Completion
Matrix Reasoning	Picture Completion
Digit Span	Arithmetic
Letter-Number Sequencing	Arithmetic
Coding	Cancellation
Symbol Search	Cancellation

Source: From the Administration and Scoring Manual of the Wechsler Intelligence Scale for Children–Fourth Edition. Copyright © 2003 The Psychological Corporation. Adapted and reproduced by permission. All rights reserved.

Score Conversions." In both these sections, the boxes in which the sums of scaled scores are placed are shaded light green.

3. Convert the sum of scaled scores to VCI, PRI, WMI, PSI, and FSIQ using Tables A.2, A.3, A.4, A.5, and A.6, respectively, in the *WISC-IV Administration and Scoring Manual* (Wechsler, 2003).

4. Record the Index scores and FSIQ (referred to as *Composite Scores* on the Record Form) in two places—one labeled "Sum of Scaled Scores to Composite Score Conversions" and another labeled "Composite Score Profile." Note that in the former section examiners should also record the percentile ranks and confidence intervals for the Index scores and FSIQ, which may also be found in Tables A.2 through A.6 in the *WISC-IV Administration and Scoring Manual* (Wechsler, 2003).

5. Plot scaled scores and composite scores on "Subtest Scaled Score Profile" and "Composite Score Profile," respectively.

Special Considerations for Calculating WISC-IV Index Scores and FSIQ Using Supplemental Subtests

According to the *WISC-IV Administration and Scoring Manual* (Wechsler, 2003), supplemental subtests can be substituted for core battery tests under certain conditions. For example, an examiner may choose to substitute the Cancellation subtest for the Coding subtest for an individual with fine motor difficulties because, like the Symbol Search test, Cancellation requires making slash marks rather than drawing specific shapes. Likewise, the examiner may choose to substitute the Picture Completion subtest for Block Design for the same examinee because Picture Completion requires either a verbal or a pointing response rather than the manual manipulation of objects. Another situation in which a substitution may be warranted is when a core battery subtest is spoiled or invalidated for some reason. For example, when a child clearly misunderstands the directions for the Coding subtest, rendering the results uninterpretable, the Cancellation test may be used along with Symbol Search to calculate a PSI.

An examiner may also choose to calculate an Index using a supplemental test, even when no core battery tests have been spoiled, in order to allow for the most meaningful and accurate interpretation of findings. For example, recently one of the authors supervised the evaluation of a student aged 6 years 10 months who was referred because he had not acquired basic reading skills. This student did not know the alphabet and recognized only a few letters of the alphabet (including A, B, and C). Alternatively, he was able to count to 20 and recognized numbers 1 through 10 readily. He earned a Digit Span scaled score of 11, an Arithmetic scaled score of 10, and a Letter-Number Sequencing scaled score of 5. The examiner reasoned that because of this student's lack of facility with letters, his score on the Letter-Number Sequencing subtest and the WMI (88) was an underestimate of his working memory ability. Substituting Arithmetic for Letter-Number Sequencing resulted in a WMI of 102, which was considered a more accurate representation of his working memory ability. Finally, using a supplemental test for a core battery test may be done when the child earns a raw score of zero on one core battery test *only* and earns credit for items on an appropriate supplemental test. Table 3.1 provides a list of acceptable substitutions for the WISC-IV core battery tests.

In general, although there may be many situations in which substitutions of supplemental subtests for core battery subtests is judged appropriate, they should be done cautiously and in accordance with the guidelines established by the test publisher. The following Don't Forget box lists the guidelines that should be followed by examiners who choose to substitute a core battery test with a supplemental test.

It is important to remember that when supplemental subtests are used to replace core battery subtests, the underlying construct intended to be measured by the Index may change. For example, the subtests that compose the VCI (i.e., Similarities, Vocabulary, and Comprehension) measure qualitatively different aspects

DON'T FORGET

1. One substitution is allowed for each Index score.
   a. Information or Word Reasoning may substitute for one core VCI subtest.
   b. Picture Completion may substitute for one core PRI subtest.
   c. Arithmetic may substitute for either WMI subtest.
   d. Cancellation may substitute for either PSI subtest.
2. When deriving the FSIQ, no more than two substitutions from different Indexes may be made.
3. A supplemental subtest may replace only one subtest in an Index, not two. For example, Picture Completion may replace either Block Design or Matrix Reasoning, but it may not replace both Block Design and Matrix Reasoning.
4. The standard subtest administration order should be followed even when substituting supplemental tests for core battery tests. For example, if Cancellation is being used to replace Coding, then Cancellation should be administered in the order in which it is intended to be administered in the battery. That is, if Coding was not administered, then Cancellation would be administered as the 10th subtest in the core battery or as the 11th subtest when all supplemental tests are administered.

of mainly Crystallized Intelligence (*Gc*). That is, Similarities measures Lexical Knowledge (VL), Language Development (LD), and, to some extent, Fluid Reasoning (*Gf*; Induction); Vocabulary measures VL and LD; and Comprehension measures LD and General Information (K0) and may require general sequential reasoning or deductive reasoning (*Gf*-RG) for some items. Despite our belief that *Gf* is involved in responding to VCI items, the common or most robust portion of the variance among the VCI core battery subtests is *Gc*. However, when Word Reasoning is substituted for Vocabulary, for example, the composition of the VCI changes, consisting of items that rely more substantially on *Gf*. The extent to which the underlying constructs of Indexes change as a result of substitutions was discussed in Chapter 1 and will be addressed again in the next chapter.

Special Considerations for Indexes and IQ with Subtest Raw Scores of Zero

Subtest raw scores of zero deserve special consideration when being converted to scaled scores, Index scores, and IQ. The problem with a raw score of zero is that you cannot determine the child's true ability to perform on the test. A zero raw score does not mean that a child lacks a certain ability. Rather, it means that the particular subtest did not have enough low-level or easy items (called *floor items*) to adequately assess the child's skills. The Don't Forget box on this page lists the only situations in which we believe it is appropriate to calculate Index scores and a FSIQ when one or more raw scores of zero are obtained.

DON'T FORGET

Appropriate Situations for Calculating Index Scores and a Full Scale IQ When Raw Scores of Zero Are Obtained

The FSIQ may be calculated when no more than two raw scores of zero are included in its derivation.

Subtest raw scores of zero must be from different Indexes.

The VCI may be calculated when no more than one raw score of zero is included in its derivation.

If a child obtains one or more raw score of zero on the subtests that contribute to the VCI, then the supplemental tests (i.e., Information or Word Reasoning) should be administered. A supplemental test on which the child earns a basal should substitute for the core battery subtest having a raw score of zero. Remember, no more than one substitution is permissible.

The PRI may be calculated when no more than one raw score of zero is included in its derivation.

If a child obtains one or more raw score of zero on the subtests that contribute to the PRI, then the Picture Completion subtest should be administered. If the child earns a basal on Picture Completion, then this subtest should substitute for one of the core battery subtests having a raw score of zero.

The WMI should not be calculated when a raw score of zero is obtained on any subtest that will be included in its derivation.

If a child obtains a raw score of zero on one of the two core subtests that contribute to the WMI, then Arithmetic should be administered. If the child earns a basal on Arithmetic, then this subtest should substitute for the core battery subtest having a raw score of zero.

The PSI should not be calculated when a raw score of zero is obtained on any subtest that will be included in its derivation.

If a child obtains one raw score of zero on one of the two core subtests that contribute to the PSI, then Cancellation should be administered. If the child achieves a basal on Cancellation, then this subtest should substitute for the core battery subtest having a raw score of zero.

Prorating on the WISC-IV

Prorating the sums of scaled scores to derive composites is allowed in specific instances. However, due to the multitude of problems associated with this technique, examiners are advised to avoid it whenever possible (see *WISC-IV Administration and Scoring Manual,* Wechsler, 2003, pp. 49–50). If an examiner determines through his or her sound clinical judgment that prorating is required, the following should be noted:

1. The sum of scaled scores for the Verbal Comprehension and Perceptual Reasoning Indexes may be prorated only when two of the three contributing subtest scaled scores are valid. Table A.7 in the *WISC-IV Administration and Scoring Manual* (Wechsler, 2003) provides prorated sums of scaled scores for deriving the VCI and PRI.
2. The sum of scaled scores for the Working Memory and Processing Speed Indexes cannot be prorated unless an appropriate *and* valid supplemental subtest scaled score is available for either scale (i.e., Arithmetic and Cancellation, respectively).
3. The examiner should always record the term *PRORATED* next to any Index that was prorated. This term should be marked clearly on the front page of the Record Form and explained fully in the psychological report.

Scoring Subtests Requiring Judgment

While administering the WISC-IV you will likely find that the verbal subtests elicit many more responses than listed in the manual. The multitude of responses given by an examinee, although interesting, may cause frustration for the examiner during the scoring process because of the need to rely on one's judgment. The general scoring criteria are found on pages 40 through 44 in the *WISC-IV Administration and Scoring Manual* (Wechsler, 2003).

In addition to these criteria, there are some basic rules to consider when scoring verbal subtests. First, a child must not be penalized for poor grammar or improper pronunciation. Although grammar and pronunciation are important to note for clinical reasons, it is the *content* of what the child says that is most important for scoring a response. Second, long and elaborate answers are not necessarily worth more points than short, concise ones. Some children have a tendency to respond in paragraph form, which may lead to two or three answers' being given within the context of a single response. If this occurs, either spontaneously or after a query, it is the examiner's responsibility to determine two things—namely, (a) which part of the response was intended as the final response and (b) whether the response has been spoiled. If a child's response contains many answers but none that spoil the response, further querying may be necessary. Sometimes it is clear that in a series of responses the last answer is the final response. In that case, the final response should be the one scored. At other times it is unclear whether the second or third response is intended as the actual response. For clarification purposes you may ask, "You said, 'we wear bicycle helmets because our parents want us to wear them, they look cool, and they protect you.' Which one was your answer?" In some instances, children say that their *entire* long response was what they intended the answer to be, and embedded in that long response are 0-, 1-, and 2-point answers. In such a case, if no response spoils part of the long response, then simply score the *best* response (i.e., the response that would allow the maximum number of points to be awarded to the child).

Subtest-by-Subtest Scoring Keys

The following sections provide important points to remember when scoring the respective subtests on the WISC-IV. We do not review all of the nuances of scoring each part of the subtests here, but we do cover areas that commonly cause difficulty for examiners. Additionally, tables outlining the most salient scoring revisions from the WISC-III to the WISC-IV are presented after each subtest, where applicable.

It is important to note that in addition to the subtest raw score calculations, three WISC-IV subtests presented in this section (i.e., Block Design, Digit Span, and Cancellation) allow for the calculation of *process scores*. According to the test authors, "process scores are designed to provide more detailed information on the cognitive abilities that contribute to a child's subtest performance" (*WISC-IV Technical and Interpretive Manual,* Wechsler, 2003, pp. 107–108). The procedures for calculating process scores for the Block Design, Digit Span, and Cancellation subtests appear in the sections that follow.

1. Block Design (PRI, Core)
- For Items 1 through 3, successful completion on Trial 1 earns 2 points, successful completion on Trial 2 earns 1 point.
- For Items 4 through 8, successful completion of the designs (within the time limit) earns 4 points.
- For Items 9 through 14, bonus points (either 4, 5, 6, or 7 bonus points) are awarded for successfully completed designs on the basis of completion time.
- It is possible to calculate a process score for this subtest (Block Design No Time Bonus [BDN]). This may be accomplished by scoring

0, 1, or 2 on Items 1 through 3, and 4 points for *correct* designs completed within the time limit with no rotation errors on Items 4 through 14.

- Rotated designs of 30 degrees or more are scored 0 points. Circle "Y" or "N" in the "Correct Design" column to indicate whether the child constructed the design correctly, irrespective of rotation.
- Partially complete or incorrect designs are scored 0 points. Incorrect or partially complete designs should be drawn in the "Constructed Design" column of the protocol, and the "N" in the "Correct Design" column should be circled.
- If a child correctly completes a design after the time limit has expired, then no points are awarded (although a note should be made of the child's performance by circling "Y" in the "Correct Design" column of the protocol to indicate that the child constructed the design correctly).
- Include early unadministered items (as correct) and reversal items when calculating the total raw score.
- A maximum of 68 raw score points for standard administration (with bonus points) may be obtained.
- The maximum "Block Design No Time Bonus" raw score is 50 points.

See Table 3.2 for Block Design scoring revisions from the WISC-III to the WISC-IV.

2. Similarities (VCI, Core)

- For all Similarities items, use the general 0-, 1-, or 2-point scoring criteria and specific sample responses as a guide (see *WISC-IV Administration and Scoring Manual,* Wechsler, 2003, p. 71).

Table 3.2 Changes in Scoring: Subtest 1, Block Design (PRI, Core)

WISC-III	WISC-IV
Scoring includes the time bonus points for Items 4–12.	Use of time bonus points restricted to last 6 items.
Block Design No Time Bonus process score unavailable.	Block Design No Time Bonus process score available.
Maximum raw score 69 points.	Maximum raw score 68 points.

Table 3.3 Changes in Scoring: Subtest 2, Similarities (VCI, Core)

WISC-III	WISC-IV
Corrective feedback provided on first 2-point item.	Sample item revised to require a creditable response from child before beginning subtest.
Items 1–5 score 0 or 1 point, 6–19 score 0, 1, or 2 points.	Items 1–2 score 0 or 1 point, 3–23 score 0, 1, or 2 points.
Maximum raw score 33 points.	Maximum raw score 44 points
	Spontaneous correction and readministration of item(s) with correct answer achieves a score.

- Responses listed in the manual are not all-inclusive. Give credit for responses that are of the same caliber as those in the manual.
- The key to scoring Similarities items is the *degree of abstraction* evident in the response. Responses that reflect a relevant general categorization earn 2 points, whereas responses that reflect only one or more common properties or functions of the members of an item pair earn 0 or 1 point.
- Items 1 and 2 are scored either 0 or 1 point and Items 3 through 23 are scored either 0, 1, or 2 points.
- For multiple responses, score the best response as long as no portion of the child's answer spoils the response.
- Include early unadministered items (as correct) and reversal items when calculating the total raw score.
- A maximum of 44 raw score points may be obtained.

See Table 3.3 for Similarities scoring revisions from the WISC-III to the WISC-IV.

3. Digit Span (WMI, Core)
- For each trial, score 1 point for correct responses and 0 points for incorrect responses (or no response).
- The item score is the sum of the two *trial scores* for each item.
- The Digit Span raw score is equivalent to the sum of the item scores for Digits Forward and Digits Backward.
- The Digit Span Forward (DSF) process score is obtained by summing all item scores on DSF.
- The Digit Span Backward (DSB) process score is obtained by summing all item scores on DSB, excluding the sample.

Table 3.4 Changes in Scoring: Subtest 3, Digit Span (WMI, Core)

WISC-III	WISC-IV
No score indicating the longest number of digits recalled correctly.	LDSF and LDSB indicate the longest number of digits recalled correctly.
No scaled scores available for Digit Span Forward or Digit Span Backward.	Scaled scores available for Digit Span Forward and Digit Span Backward.
Maximum raw score 30 points.	Maximum raw score 32 points.

- The Longest Digit Span Forward (LDSF) and the Longest Digit Span Backward (LDSB) process scores both indicate the number of digits recalled on the last Digit Span trial (Forward or Backward, respectively) with a score of 1. For instance, if a child correctly recalls five digits forward once and misses both trials of six digits forward, the LDSF is 5.
- A maximum of 32 raw score points may be obtained.

See Table 3.4 for Digit Span scoring revisions from the WISC-III to the WISC-IV.

4. Picture Concepts (PRI, Core)

- Circle the numbers that correspond to the child's responses for each item on the Record Form. Correct answers are printed in color. Circle "DK" if the child does not respond or states that he or she does not know the answer.
- Award 1 point *only* if the child chooses the correct pictures from *all* rows of an item; 0 points are earned for incorrect responses or no response.
- Score 1 point if a child responds correctly after being given one or more of the following three standardized prompts listed in the *WISC-IV Administration and Scoring Manual* (Wechsler, 2003, p. 91):
  - For two-row items: "Pick one picture from each row, one here (point across first row), and one here (point across second row)."
  - For three-row items: "Pick one picture from each row, one here (point across first row), one here (point across second row), and one here (point across third row)."
  - If a child offers more than one combination of selected pictures as a response, say, "You can give only one answer. Just choose the best one."
- Include early unadministered items (as correct) and reversal items when calculating the total raw score.
- A maximum of 28 raw score points may be obtained.

5. Coding (PSI, Core)

- When 120 seconds have elapsed, tell the child to stop working and record the completion time as 120 seconds, even if the child has not completed all of the items. Do not score any items that may have been completed beyond the time limit (e.g., if the child attempts to finish an item after he or she has been told to stop, if an examiner allows a child to continue working on a nearly finished item in the interest of maintaining rapport). If the child completes all of the items before the 120-second time limit, stop timing and record the time in seconds on the Record Form. Award appropriate bonus points for Coding A.
- Careful placement of the Coding template is necessary for accurate scoring. Be sure to use the appropriate side of the scoring key depending on the form (A or B) administered.
- Score 1 point for each symbol drawn correctly within the 120-second time limit.
- Do not penalize a child for an imperfectly drawn symbol. Symbols do not have to be perfectly drawn to obtain credit, but they must be recognizable.
- If a child spontaneously corrects his or her drawing, give credit to the corrected drawing.
- Items that a child did not attempt (e.g., skipped or did not reach before the time limit expired) should not be counted in the total score.
- Do not count sample items toward the final score.
- On Coding A, if a child completed all items correctly before the time limit expired, he or she receives bonus points based on the total completion time.
- On Coding B, there are no time bonus points awarded for items completed correctly before the time limit.
- A maximum of 65 raw score points may be obtained with time bonus for Coding A; a maximum of 119 raw score points for Coding B may be obtained.

6. Vocabulary (VCI, Core)

- Picture Items 1 through 4 are scored either 0 or 1 point and Verbal Items 5 through 36 are scored either 0, 1, or 2 points.
- Responses listed in the manual are not all-inclusive. Give credit for responses that are of the same caliber as those in the manual.

- On Picture Items 1 through 4, score 0 points for the following responses:
  - Inappropriate marginal responses (e.g., saying "engine" for a pictured fire truck)
  - Generalized responses (e.g., saying "drink" for a pictured milk container)
  - Functional responses (e.g., saying "it's a money holder" for a pictured wallet)
  - Hand gestures (e.g., pretending to pedal in response to a pictured bicycle)
  - Personalized responses (e.g., saying "I have one in front of my house" when shown a picture of a tree)
- Do not penalize a child for articulation errors or poor grammar if it is clear that the child knows the correct name of an object or is able to define it.
- In general, any recognized word meaning is acceptable, but a response that lacks significant content should be penalized (e.g., a response that indicates only a vague knowledge of the word's meaning).
- For multiple responses, score the best response as long as no portion of the child's answer spoils the response.
- Include early unadministered items (as correct) and reversal items when calculating the total raw score.
- A maximum of 68 raw score points may be obtained.

See Table 3.5 for Vocabulary scoring revisions from the WISC-III to the WISC-IV.

Table 3.5 Changes in Scoring: Subtest 6, Vocabulary (VCI, Core)

WISC-III	WISC-IV
Items 1–30 score 0, 1, or 2 points.	Items 1–4 (picture items) score 0 or 1 point; items 5–36 (verbal items) score 0, 1, or 2 points.
Maximum raw score 60 points.	Maximum raw score 68 points.
	Spontaneous correction and readministration of item(s) with correct answer achieves a score.

7. Letter-Number Sequencing (WMI, Core)

- For the qualifying items, circle "Y" or "N" on the Record Form to indicate whether the child aged 6 to 7 years correctly counted to *at least* three or recited *at least* the first three letters of the alphabet.
- For each trial, score 1 point if the child recalls all the numbers and letters in their correct sequence, *even if the child recalls the letters before the numbers.* Score 0 points for incorrect items.
- If standardized prompts are given on specific trials of Items 1, 4, or 5 and the child subsequently corrects his or her previous answer, do not award credit. Record a *P* on the Record Form for any prompt given. The *WISC-IV Administration and Scoring Manual* marks with an asterisk those trials that should be prompted (Wechsler, 2003, pp. 129–130). The following prompts should be used:
  - Item 1 (Trial 1): "Remember to say the numbers first, in order. Then say the letters in alphabetical order. Let's try another one."
  - Item 4 (Trial 2): "Remember to say the letters in order."
  - Item 5 (Trial 1): "Remember to say the numbers in order."
- Sum the scores on the three trials for each item to calculate the item score. A child can score up to 3 points (i.e., all three trials correct) on each item.
- A maximum of 30 raw score points may be obtained.

8. Matrix Reasoning (PRI, Core)

- Circle the numbers that correspond to the child's responses for each item on the Record Form. Correct answers are printed in color.
- Score 1 point for a correct response and 0 points for either an incorrect response or no response.
- Circle "DK" on the Record Form when the child does not respond or states that he or she does not know the answer.
- Include early unadministered items (as correct) and reversal items when calculating the total raw score.
- A maximum of 35 raw score points may be obtained.

9. Comprehension (VCI, Core)

- For all Comprehension items, use the general 0-, 1-, or 2-point scoring criteria and specific sample responses as a guide (see *WISC-IV Administration and Scoring Manual,* Wechsler, 2003, pp. 135–136).

- Responses listed in the manual are not all-inclusive. Give credit for responses that are of the same caliber as those in the manual.
- For items that contain more than one general concept, the child's response must reflect at least two different concepts to earn 2 points. If the child's response reflects only one concept, score the item 1 point and prompt for another concept. If the child's second response reflects the same concept as his or her first response, prompt once more. If the initial response is repeated, or a second concept is not provided, the item score remains 1.
- If a child improves an answer spontaneously or after a query, give credit for the improvement (e.g., when asked why children should drink milk, the child responds, "It's good for you" [1-point response requiring a query] and then, when queried, says "It keeps you healthy" [2-point response]).
- If a child provides several responses that vary in quality but nevertheless do not spoil his or her response, then score the best response (i.e., the response that will result in the maximum number of score points' being awarded).
- Include early unadministered items (as correct) and reversal items when calculating the total raw score.
- A maximum of 42 raw score points may be obtained.

See Table 3.6 for Comprehension scoring revisions from the WISC-III to the WISC-IV.

10. Symbol Search (PSI, Core)

- When 120 seconds have elapsed, tell the child to stop working and record the completion time as 120 seconds, even if the child has not completed all of the items. Do not score any items that may have been completed beyond the time limit (e.g., if the child attempts to finish an item after he or she has been told to stop, or if an examiner allows a child to continue working on a nearly finished item in the

Table 3.6 Changes in Scoring: Subtest 9, Comprehension (VCI, Core)

WISC-III	WISC-IV
Maximum raw score 36 points.	Maximum raw score 42 points.
	Spontaneous correction and readministration of item(s) with correct answer achieves a score.

interest of maintaining rapport). If the child completes all of the items before the 120-second time limit, stop timing and record the time on the Record Form.

- Careful placement of the Symbol Search template is necessary for accurate scoring. Be sure to use the appropriate side of the scoring key depending on the form (A or B) administered.
- Score 0 points if a child marks both "Yes" and "No" for the response to one item.
- On items where there is a clear indication of self-correction (e.g., the child crossed out one answer and endorsed another), score the latter response.
- Sum the number of correct items and the number of incorrect items separately.
- Unanswered items (i.e., skipped or not reached before the time limit) do count toward either the correct or the incorrect total.
- Calculate the raw score by subtracting the number of incorrect items from the number correct.
- A maximum of 45 raw score points may be obtained for Symbol Search A; a maximum of 60 raw score points may be obtained for Symbol Search B.

See Table 3.7 for Symbol Search scoring revisions from the WISC III to the WISC-IV.

11. Picture Completion (PRI, Supplemental)

- If the child responds with an appropriate synonym for the missing part of the picture (e.g., says "door opener" for "door knob"), score 1 point.
- If the child points correctly to the missing part of the picture, but then provides a verbal elaboration that spoils the response (e.g., points correctly to a missing part of a car door, but then says "horn"), score 0 points.
- If the child responds correctly within 20 seconds, score 1 point.

Table 3.7 Changes in Scoring: Subtest 10, Symbol Search (PSI, Core)

WISC-III	WISC-IV
Maximum raw score 45 points on Symbol Search B.	Maximum raw score 60 points on Symbol Search B.

- If the child responds incorrectly or fails to respond within 20 seconds, score 0 points.
- Responses found in the left-hand column of the *WISC-IV Administration and Scoring Manual* (Wechsler, 2003, pp. 166–169) are scored 1 regardless of whether the child points; responses in the right-hand column of the manual are scored 1 *only if* the child points correctly in addition to providing the indicated verbal response.
- The sample responses in the manual are not an exhaustive list. Award credit for any response that is of the same caliber as the samples.
- If a child responds by pointing, record *PC* on the Record Form if the child pointed correctly or *PX* if the child pointed incorrectly.
- Include early unadministered items (as correct) and reversal items when calculating the total raw score.
- A maximum of 38 raw score points may be obtained.

See Table 3.8 for Picture Completion scoring revisions from the WISC-III to the WISC-IV.

12. Cancellation (PSI, Supplemental)

- When 45 seconds have elapsed, tell the child to stop working and record the completion time as 45 seconds, even if the child has not completed the item. Do not score any item that may have been completed beyond the time limit (e.g., if the child attempts to finish an item after he or she has been told to stop, or if an examiner allows

Table 3.8 Changes in Scoring: Subtest 11, Picture Completion (PRI, Supplemental)

WISC-III	WISC-IV
No distinctions made between verbal responses that require pointing and those that should be scored 1 point without pointing.	Distinctions are made between verbal sponses that require pointing and those that should be scored 1 point without pointing.
Strict 20-second time limit for each item.	20-second time limit for each item can be flexibly applied, based on the examiner's clinical judgment.
No indication to be made on protocol of whether the child's response was verbal or indicated by pointing.	Indicate *PC* on protocol when child points correctly and *PX* when child points incorrectly.
Maximum raw score 30 points.	Maximum raw score 38 points.

a child to continue working on a nearly finished item in the interest of maintaining rapport). If the child completes the item before the 45-second time limit, stop timing and record the time on the Record Form. Award appropriate bonus points.

- Careful placement of the Cancellation Scoring Template is essential for accurate scoring.
- When using the scoring template, marks on target objects are scored as correct; marks on nontarget objects are scored as incorrect. Consider objects as marked *only* if it is clear that the child intended to mark them (see *WISC-IV Administration and Scoring Manual,* Wechsler, 2003, pp. 171–172).
- Add the total number of correct and incorrect responses separately.
- Calculate the total raw score by subtracting the total number of incorrect responses from the total number of correct responses. The total raw score for Cancellation is the sum of the item raw scores for *both* Items 1 and 2.
- It is also possible to obtain process scores for this subtest. The total raw score for Cancellation Random (CAR) and Cancellation Structured (CAS) are the total raw scores (including any applicable time-bonus points) for Items 1 and 2, respectively.
- A maximum of 136 raw score points may be obtained.

13. Information (VCI, Supplemental)
- Score 1 point for a correct response and score 0 points for either an incorrect response or no response.
- Responses listed in the manual are not all-inclusive. Give credit for responses that are of the same caliber as those in the manual.
- For multiple responses, score the best response as long as no portion of the child's answer spoils the response.
- Include early unadministered items (as correct) and reversal items when calculating the total raw score.
- A maximum of 33 raw score points may be obtained.

See Table 3.9 for Information scoring revisions from the WISC-III to the WISC-IV.

14. Arithmetic (WMI, Supplemental)
- Score 1 point for a correct response given within the 30-second time limit; score 0 points for either an incorrect response, no response, or a response given after the time limit has expired.

**Table 3.9 Changes in Scoring: Subtest 13, Information
(VCI, Supplemental)**

WISC-III	WISC-IV
Maximum raw score 30 points.	Maximum raw score 33 points.
	Spontaneous correction and readministration of item(s) with correct answer achieves a score.

- If the child provides a numerically correct response but leaves out the units (or states the units incorrectly) that appeared in the question (e.g., says "five" rather than "five *crayons*" or "six" rather than "six *minutes*"), score the response correct. The only exception to this is on items where money or time is the unit; on such items, *alternate* numerical responses must be accompanied by the correct unit (e.g., if the answer is "one dollar," saying "one" is correct; however, if the child transforms the units to quarters, they must say "four quarters," rather than just "four" to receive credit).
- If the child spontaneously provides a correct response in place of an incorrect response within the time limit, score 1 point.
- Include early unadministered items (as correct) and reversal items when calculating the total raw score.
- A maximum of 34 raw score points may be obtained.

See Table 3.10 for Arithmetic scoring revisions from the WISC-III to the WISC-IV.

Table 3.10 Changes in Scoring: Subtest 14, Arithmetic (WMI, Supplemental)

WISC-III	WISC-IV
Point bonus awarded if the answer was given within 10 seconds on items 19–24.	No point bonus for answers provided quickly.
Maximum raw score 30 points.	Maximum raw score 34 points.
	Spontaneous correction and readministration of item(s) with correct answer achieves a score.

15. Word Reasoning (VCI, Supplemental)

- For each clue presented, circle the letter "Y" for a correct response or circle the letter "N" for either an incorrect response or no response.
- If a clue is repeated, record *R* on the Record Form.
- Score 1 point for a correct response or score 0 points for an incorrect response.
- The sample responses provided in the manual are not all-inclusive. Score a response as correct if the response provided is of the same caliber as the listed sample responses.
- Include early unadministered items (as correct) and reversal items when calculating the total raw score.
- A maximum of 24 raw score points may be obtained.

FREQUENTLY ASKED QUESTIONS: SCORING

Pearson has provided information on its website to respond to frequently asked questions (FAQs) about the WISC-IV. One category of FAQs was related to WISC-VI scoring and is reproduced in Rapid Reference 3.2.

≡ Rapid Reference 3.2

Frequently Asked Questions: Scoring

Why are there separate norms for Block Design with and without time bonuses?

Practitioners have suspected that children who emphasize accuracy over speed of performance may score lower on Block Design because of time bonuses, and some believe that faster performance reflects a higher level of the ability being measured and is therefore deserving of a higher score. The separate scores allow practitioners to evaluate these hypotheses with individual children. Practitioners should be aware that most children in the standardization sample achieve very similar scores on Block Design and Block Design No Time Bonus. In fact, a difference as small as two points is considered rare.

If you wanted to reduce the effects of speeded performance, why not completely eliminate a time bonus from Block Design?

In general, higher ability children tend to perform the task faster. Without time bonuses, Block Design is not as good of a measure of high ability.

(continued)

On Letter-Number Sequencing, the examinee is instructed to give the numbers in order first and then the letters in order. Why is credit awarded if the examinee gives the letters first in order and then the numbers in order?

There is a distinction between reordering and sequencing: Reordering involves placing the numbers as a group prior to the letters as a group, and sequencing involves placing the numbers in numerical order and the letters in alphabetical order—regardless of which grouping comes first. This distinction is reflected in the prompt given and relates directly to how a trial is scored. If a child states the letter first on Item 1, the child is prompted to reorder the group. However, despite the prompt, the child still receives credit for his or her original answer because the response is one of the two correct responses listed. Items 4 and 5 prompt the child to place the numbers or letters in sequential order. On these items no credit is awarded if the child has to be prompted because, unlike Item 1, the original sequence is not one of the correct responses listed for these items. You may prompt the child once for Items 1, 4, and 5; you cannot prompt a child on any of the other items for this subtest. Regardless of how the child reorders the numbers and letters, he or she is using working memory in order to place the numbers in sequence and the letters in sequence. Data analyses of the standardization sample showed that the task is equally difficult when either numbers or letters are given first. The reason for instructing examinees to give the numbers first is to provide them with a set or structured way of approaching the task, which is especially helpful for young children or children who have difficulty structuring their own work. This is the same scoring method used for Letter-Number Sequencing on WAIS-III.

On Letter-Number Sequencing, a child can simply mimic the examiner and earn credit on the first 10 trials. Is this really working memory?

The early items measure short-term auditory memory, which is a precursor skill to working memory. The 6- to 7-year-old norms demonstrate that children scoring 10 raw score points obtain above-average scaled scores; this reflects the developmentally appropriate use of short-term memory prior to the exhibition of working memory. Thus, for younger children, Letter-Number Sequencing may assess short-term memory, a prerequisite skill for the development of working memory. The item set and norms reflect this change as children develop working memory. This is analogous to the difference between Digit Span Forward and Backward, which assesses short-term memory and working memory, respectively. Performance on the early items of Letter-Number Sequencing in younger children may be related to performance on Digit Span Forward with any differences potentially attributable to automaticity of letters as compared to numbers.

On Letter-Number Sequencing, how do I score a child's response after a prompt is given on Items 1, 4, and 5?

As noted in the third bullet under General Directions on page 126 of the Administration and Scoring Manual, certain responses to specific trials on Items 1, 4, and 5 require a prompt to remind the child of the task. The prompt for Trial 1 of Item 1 is designed to remind the child to say the numbers first and then the letters. If the child forgets to say the numbers first, award credit for the trial as indicated and provide the prompt. Because the child received credit for his or her initial response to this trial, it is not necessary to award additional credit if the child attempts to correct his or her initial response after the prompt. Trial 2 of Item 4 is the first trial in which the child is required to alphabetically sequence the letters to produce a correct response. If the child provides either of the specified incorrect responses by forgetting to alphabetically sequence the letters, provide the prompt as indicated. If the child provides a correct response to the trial after the prompt, do not award credit for the trial. Similarly, Trial 1 of Item 5 is the first trial in which the child is required to sequence the numbers to produce a correct response. If the child forgets to sequence the numbers and provides either of the designated incorrect responses, provide the prompt as indicated. If the child provides a correct response to the trial after the prompt, do not award credit for the trial.

Why do there seem to be multiple responses for some of the items on Picture Concepts?

The Picture Concepts subtest is scored with either 0 or 1 point. The keyed response represents the best single response in terms of the level of reasoning involved. For example, on more difficult items, credit is not given for categories involving color or shape; emphasis is placed on underlying function. The keyed response was determined through years of research in Pilot, Tryout, and Standardization phases of development. The categories children provided, the ability level of children choosing specific responses, and relationships to performance on Similarities and Matrix Reasoning were all used to determine the keyed response.

The answer to Matrix Reasoning item #26 does not appear to be the only possible answer. Why wasn't "2" given credit?

Item #26 is the second 3 X 3 item. On the first 3 X 3 item (#24), children learn to apply the same transformation from cell #1 across to cell #2, and again from cell #2 to cell #3. If the child follows the pattern from #24, they answer correctly (1) on item #26. Children can arrive at a different answer (2) if they use one transformation rule from cell #1 to cell #2, and a different one from cell #2 to cell #3. This is not the most parsimonious solution, and analyses indicated that children who arrived at the correct response (1) had higher ability levels.

Some of the responses I get on Word Reasoning seem correct to me, but are listed as incorrect. What was the rationale for determining correct and incorrect responses?

(continued)

Some of these responses may have been given 1 point in a 0-, 1-, or 2-point scoring rubric. Such responses may be correct, or partially correct, but do not represent a high level of abstract reasoning. They also tended to be given by children with lower ability. Not all possible responses are included in the examples, however, and the examiner may give credit for a response not listed if she or he determines that it is at the same level of abstraction as the credited responses.

What should I do if a child writes too lightly to be seen through the Cancellation scoring template?

You do not need the scoring template to score the subtest. If necessary, remove the template and simply count each animal with a mark through it and each nonanimal with a mark through it, being sure to double-check your work.

Source: From http://pearsonassess.com/HAIWEB/Cultures/en-us/ Productdetail.htm?Pid=015-8979-044&Mode=resource&Leaf=015-8979-044_FAQ. *Wechsler Intelligence Scale for Children: Fourth Edition.* Copyright © 2008 by Pearson. Reproduced by permission. All rights reserved. *Wechsler Intelligence Scale for Children, WISC,* and *WISC-IV* are trademarks of Pearson registered in the United States of America and/or other jurisdictions.

🐟 TEST YOURSELF 🐟

. . . .

1. **Which subtests allow for the calculation of a "process score"?**
   (a) Block Design, Digit Span, and Cancellation
   (b) Block Design, Digit Span, and Symbol Search
   (c) Coding, Symbol Search, and Digit Span
   (d) Arithmetic, Symbol Search, and Coding

2. **On a Similarities subtest item, Jessica, age 7, provides several responses that vary greatly in quality but do not spoil her response. You should**
   (a) score Jessica's best response.
   (b) score the last response given by Jessica.
   (c) score the first response given by Jessica.
   (d) query Jessica for further information.

3. **If a child obtains total raw scores of 0 on two of the three subtests that compose the Verbal Comprehension scale, including potential substitutes, no VCI or FSIQ can be derived.**
   True or False?

4. **Susan, age 12, attempts to self-correct an item on the Coding subtest. You should**

 (a) score the last response given by Susan within the time limit.

 (b) score Susan's first response, ignoring her self-correction attempt.

 (c) query Susan as to which response is her intended response.

 (d) score Susan's best response.

5. **A *poor* response is an elaboration that does not improve the child's spontaneous response, whereas a *spoiled* response is an elaboration that reveals a fundamental misconception about the item.**

 True or False?

6. **If an examiner administered additional items to a child beyond the point at which testing should have discontinued, the examiner should**

 (a) include all additional items in the total raw score.

 (b) include the additional items in the total raw score only if they are correctly answered.

 (c) award no points for items beyond the correct discontinue point.

 (d) include the additional items in the total raw score by deducting points for incorrect responses committed after the discontinue point.

7. **Samuel, age 10, is suspected to have an Intellectual Disability. Hence, you administer him items prior to his age-appropriate start point. Samuel answered these items incorrectly, but obtained perfect scores on his age-appropriate start point and a subsequent item. In this case, you should**

 (a) consider the subtest spoiled and do not calculate a raw score.

 (b) include the incorrect responses in the calculation of the total raw score.

 (c) award partial credit (i.e., _____ point) for each incorrect item that precedes the age-appropriate start point.

 (d) award full credit for all items preceding the age-appropriate start point.

8. **Although prorating sum of scaled scores is allowed in some situations, it should be avoided when possible.**

 True or False?

9. **The Information subtest should be included in the calculation of which WISC-IV Index:**

 (a) VCI

 (b) PRI

 (c) PSI

 (d) WMI

 (e) None of the above, unless it is used to substitute for another test contributing to the VCI.

10. **When scoring the Symbol Search subtest, you notice that Angela, age 9, skipped some items. You should count the items that she skipped in the incorrect total.**

    True or False?

Answers:

1. a; 2. a; 3. True; 4. a; 5. True; 6. c; 7. d; 8. True; 9. e; 10. False

Four

HOW TO INTERPRET THE WISC-IV

This chapter is designed to simplify the daunting task of generating psychometrically sound and clinically meaningful interpretations of performance on the WISC-IV. A series of steps is provided that will allow the practitioner to organize WISC-IV data in meaningful ways and interpret performance within the context of contemporary theory and research. Our systematic method of interpretation begins with an analysis of the WISC-IV Indexes to determine the best way to summarize a child's overall intellectual ability. Next, both Normative and Personal Strengths and Weaknesses among the Indexes are identified. Interpretation of fluctuations in the child's Index profile offers the most reliable and meaningful information about WISC-IV performance because it identifies strong and weak areas of cognitive functioning relative to both same-age peers from the normal population (interindividual or normative approach) and the child's own overall ability level (intraindividual or ipsative approach). We also offer optional interpretive steps involving WISC-IV composites (that we call *Clinical Clusters*) for examiners who choose to go beyond the FSIQ and Index profile in an attempt to uncover additional information about the child's cognitive capabilities as well as generate potentially meaningful hypotheses about areas of integrity or dysfunction. Finally, we provide an optional interpretive step that allows for a comparison between alternative WISC-IV indexes—namely the General Ability Index (GAI) and Cognitive Proficiency Index (CPI).

As discussed in Chapter 1, our interpretive approach reflects numerous modifications of and enhancements to prior methods of Wechsler test interpretation, including our own (Alfonso, Flanagan, & Radwan, 2005; Flanagan et al., 2000; Flanagan & Ortiz, 2001; Flanagan et al., 2002; Kaufman, 1979, 1994; Kaufman & Lichtenberger, 1999, 2000, 2002). Previously, Kaufman (1979, 1994) stressed ipsative methods for identifying areas of strength and weakness, whereas Flanagan and colleagues emphasized normative approaches (e.g., Flanagan & Ortiz, 2001; Flanagan et al., 2002, 2006; Flanagan, Ortiz, & Alfonso, 2008). Our current method links ipsative analysis with normative analysis, rather than focusing exclusively on either one or the other. In addition, our method (a) excludes individual subtest interpretation; (b) uses base rate data to evaluate the clinical meaningfulness of cluster and index score variability; (c) grounds interpretation firmly in the CHC theory of cognitive abilities and processes; and (d) provides guidance on the use of supplemental measures to test hypotheses about significant subtest variation or outlier scores.

In addition to a *quantitative* analysis of WISC-IV data, we also encourage practitioners to consider a variety of *qualitative* factors that may help to explain a child's test performance. This information is discussed in terms of its utility in interpreting WISC-IV performance and in selecting supplemental measures to augment the WISC-IV when deemed necessary. *In the end, any and all interpretations of test performance gain diagnostic meaning when they are corroborated by other data sources and when they are empirically or logically related to the area or areas of difficulty specified in the referral.*

The interpretive steps described here are illustrated using a WISC-IV profile of Ryan S., a 10-year-old boy referred for a possible reading disability (Ryan's full case report is included in Chapter 9). In addition, a comprehensive *WISC-IV Interpretive Worksheet* (included in Appendix E on the CD-ROM and designed to be completed by hand) walks the examiner through our interpretation method step-by-step. A software program, also included on the CD-ROM, called the *WISC-IV Data Management and Interpretive Assistant v1.0* (or WISC-IV DMIA) automates our interpretive system and is described alongside our description of the worksheet. The WISC-IV Interpretive Worksheet and the WISC-IV DMIA have some stylistic differences but yield identical information. It is recommended that users of this book complete a few interpretive worksheets by hand in order to fully understand the interpretive steps prior to using the automated WISC-IV DMIA. Also, while practicing the WISC-IV interpretive steps, the automated program can be used to check the accuracy of the information you filled out by hand on the interpretive worksheet. Note that the WISC-IV Interpretive Worksheet can be downloaded from the CD-ROM.

REQUIRED INTERPRETIVE STEPS: ANALYZE THE FSIQ AND THE INDEX PROFILE WHEN ALL CORE WISC-IV SUBTESTS ARE ADMINISTERED[1]

STEP 1. Report the Child's WISC-IV Standard Scores (FSIQ and Indexes) and Subtest Scaled Scores

Create a table of the child's standard scores (FSIQ and four Indexes) as well as the child's scaled scores from all subtests administered. Report the name of each Index and subtest along with the child's obtained score on each one. For the FSIQ and Indexes *only*, report the confidence interval, percentile rank, and descriptive

---

[1] These steps may also be used when supplemental tests are used to replace core battery tests in a manner consistent with the publisher's guidelines.

≣ *Rapid Reference 4.1*

Location of Information in *WISC-IV Administration and Scoring Manual* and *WISC-IV Technical and Interpretive Manual* Needed for Score Conversions

Conversion Type	Manual	Location	Page(s)
Total Raw Scores to Scaled Scores	A & S	Appendix A, Table A.1	204–236
Sum of Scaled Scores to VCI	A & S	Appendix A, Table A.2	237
Sum of Scaled Scores to PRI	A & S	Appendix A, Table A.3	237
Sum of Scaled Scores to WMI	A & S	Appendix A, Table A.4	238
Sum of Scaled Scores to PSI	A & S	Appendix A, Table A.5	238
Sum of Scaled Scores to FSIQ	A & S	Appendix A, Table A.6	239
Scaled Scores to Percentile Ranks	T & I	Chapter 6, Table 6.1	100

Note: A & S = *WISC-IV Administration and Scoring Manual* (Wechsler, 2003); T & I = *WISC-IV Technical and Interpretive Manual* (The Psychological Corporation, 2003). Percentile ranks and 90% and 95% confidence intervals for the WISC-IV Indexes (VCI, PRI, WMI, PSI, and FSIQ) are provided in Tables A.2 through A.6 (pp. 237–240) in the *WISC-IV Administration and Scoring Manual.*

category associated with the child's obtained standard scores. For subtests, report only the percentile rank associated with the child's obtained scaled scores. Rapid Reference 4.1 provides a handy guide to locate the tables in the *WISC-IV Administration and Scoring Manual* (Wechsler, 2003) and the *WISC-IV Technical and Interpretive Manual* (The Psychological Corporation, 2003) that the examiner will need to convert raw scores to scaled scores and standard scores, to convert sums of scaled scores to the FSIQ and Indexes, and to obtain confidence intervals and percentile ranks.

Examiners need to select either the 90% or the 95% confidence interval for standard scores—namely, the FSIQ and the four Indexes. Note that the confidence intervals reported in Tables A.2 through A.6 in Appendix A of the *WISC-IV Administration and Scoring Manual* (The Psychological Corporation, 2003, pp. 237–240) take regression toward the mean into account and, therefore, are more asymmetrical at the extremes of the distribution than at the center of the distribution. For example, a PRI of 73 is associated with a 95% confidence interval of +10/−5 (i.e., 68–83); a PRI of 100 is associated with a 95% confidence interval of ±8 (i.e., 92–108); and a PRI of 127 is associated with a 95%

≡ Rapid Reference 4.2

Traditional Descriptive System for the WISC-IV

Standard Score Range	Description of Performance
130 and above	Very Superior
120 to 129	Superior
110 to 119	High Average
90 to 109	Average
80 to 89	Low Average
70 to 79	Borderline
69 and below	Extremely Low

Source: This descriptive system is reported in Table 6.3 in the WISC-IV Technical and Interpretive Manual (The Psychological Corporation, 2003, p. 101).

confidence interval of +5/–10 (i.e., 117–132). Examiners should always report standard scores with their associated confidence intervals.

Three descriptive category systems are reported in Rapid References 4.2 through 4.4. The WISC-IV system, located in Rapid Reference 4.2, is the most traditional of the three and is recommended by the test's publisher (see The Psychological Corporation, 2003, Table 6.3, p. 101). The normative descriptive system,

≡ Rapid Reference 4.3

Normative Descriptive System

Standard Score Range	Descriptive Classification	Description of Performance
131+	Upper Extreme	**Normative Strength**
116 to 130	Above Average	> +1 SD (top 16% of the population) ≥ 116 (85th percentile)
85 to 115	Average Range	**Within Normal Limits** ±1 SD, inclusive (68% of the population) 115 (84th percentile)–85 (16th percentile)
70 to 84	Below Average	**Normative Weakness**
≤ 69	Lower Extreme	< –1 SD (bottom 16% of the population) ≤ 84 (15th percentile)

≡ Rapid Reference 4.4

Alternative Descriptive System for the WISC-IV

Standard Score Range	Alternative Description of Performance[a]
131+	Upper Extreme/Normative Strength
116 to 130	Above Average/Normative Strength
85 to 115	Average Range/Within Normal Limits
70 to 84	Below Average/Normative Weakness
≤ 69	Lower Extreme/Normative Weakness

[a]This classification system is preferred by the authors and is used in this book.

reported in Rapid Reference 4.3, is commonly used by neuropsychologists and is becoming more widespread among clinical and school psychologists (Flanagan, Ortiz, & Alfonso 2007; Flanagan et al., 2002, 2006; Kaufman & Kaufman, 2004). Although either system may be used, of the two, we prefer the latter. Nonetheless, some practitioners may prefer using a system with both descriptive categories (similar to the traditional ones presented in Rapid Reference 4.2) *and* normative categories (similar to those presented in Rapid Reference 4.3). An alternative categorical system of this nature is provided in Rapid Reference 4.4. For example, according to the information presented in Rapid Reference 4.4, an obtained score of 119 is both Above Average and a Normative Strength. Therefore, an examiner may choose to describe this score as "Above Average/Normative Strength." This alternative categorical system is used in our interpretive approach.

Figure 4.1 provides a snapshot of the WISC-IV interpretive worksheet that includes the scores for Ryan, who was administered all 15 WISC-IV subtests. Ryan's examiner used the 95% confidence interval. Although most of the information contained in this figure is found on the cover of the WISC-IV Record Form, examiners may choose to create a similar table for inclusion in a psychological report. Figure 4.2 shows the WISC-IV tab of the WISC-IV DMIA—the tab on which you enter all standard scores and scales scores from the WISC-IV protocol. The WISC-IV tab may be printed and included in a psychological report.

STEP 2. Determine the Best Way to Summarize Overall Intellectual Ability

Two composites for summarizing a child's overall intellectual ability are available for the WISC-IV: (a) the FSIQ, composed of the ten subtests that make up the

STEP 1. Report the Child's WISC-IV Standard Scores (FSIQ and Indexes) and Subtest Scaled Scores

For IQ and Indexes, report standard score, confidence interval, percentile rank, and descriptive category. For subtests, report scaled scores and percentile ranks only. (See Rapid Reference 4.1, "Location of Information in *WISC-IV Administration and Scoring Manual* and *WISC-IV Technical and Interpretive Manual* Needed for Score Conversions;" see Rapid Reference 4.4 for descriptive categories.)

Index/Subtest	Score	95% CI	Percentile Rank	Descriptive Category
Verbal Comprehension	98	[91–105]	45th	Average Range/Within Normal Limits
Similarities	9		37th	
Vocabulary	7		16th	
Comprehension	13		84th	
(Information)	12		75th	
(Word Reasoning)	6		9th	
Perceptual Reasoning	90	[83–98]	25th	Average Range/Within Normal Limits
Block Design	6		9th	
Picture Concepts	10		50th	
Matrix Reasoning	9		37th	
(Picture Completion)	8		25th	
Working Memory	83	[77–92]	13th	Below Average/Normative Weakness
Digit Span	7		16th	
Letter-Number Sequencing	7		16th	
(Arithmetic)	11		63rd	
Processing Speed	70	[65–83]	2nd	Below Average/Normative Weakness
Coding	5		5th	
Symbol Search	4		2nd	
(Cancellation)	5		5th	
Full Scale IQ	83	[79–88]	13th	Below Average/Normative Weakness

Note: Tests appearing in parentheses are supplemental measures. CI = Confidence Interval.

Figure 4.1 WISC-IV Interpretive Worksheet: STEP 1, Illustrated for Ryan, Age 10

Examinee Name:	Ryan		Date of Birth: 1/16/1994		
Date of Assessment:	3/1/2004		Age:	10 yr 1 mo	

Enter the scores in cells bordered in red with examinee's scores.
The program will automatically calculate the next steps for you.

Index/IQ Subtest	Score	95% CI	Percentile Rank	Descriptive Category	Is Index/IQ/Cluster Interpretable?
Verbal Comprehension	98	93-103	45	Average Range/Within Normal Limits	No
Similarities	9		37		
Vocabulary	7		16		
Comprehension	13		84		
(Information)	12		75	*Does not contribute to Index or IQ*	
(Word Reasoning)	6		9	*Does not contribute to Index or IQ*	
Perceptual Reasoning	90	85-95	25	Average Range/Within Normal Limits	Yes
Block Design	6		9		
Picture Concepts	10		50		
Matrix Reasoning	9		37		
(Picture Completion)	8		25	*Does not contribute to Index or IQ*	
Working Memory	83	78-88	13	Below Average/Normative Weakness	Yes
Digit Span	7		16		
Letter-Number Sequencing	7		18		
(Arithmetic)	11		63	*Does not contribute to Index or IQ*	
Processing Speed	70	65-75	2	Below Average/Normative Weakness	Yes
Coding	5		5		
Symbol Search	4		2		
(Cancellation)	5		5	*Does not contribute to Index or IQ*	
Full Scale IQ	83	78-88	13	Below Average/Normative Weakness	No
GAI	94	89-100	34	Average Range/Within Normal Limits	Yes
CPI	73	68-82	4	Below Average/Normative Weakness	Yes
Clinical Cluster *(roll cursor over the red triangle to see which subtests comprise each cluster)*					
Gf Cluster	100	92-108	50	Average Range/Within Normal Limits	Yes
Gv Cluster	83	74-92	13	Below Average/Normative Weakness	Yes
Gf-nonverbal Cluster	97	88-106	43	Average Range/Within Normal Limits	Yes
Gf-verbal Cluster	86	76-96	17	Average Range/Within Normal Limits	Yes
Gc-VL Cluster	81	72-90	11	Below Average/Normative Weakness	Yes
Gc-K0 Cluster	114	104-124	83	Average Range/Within Normal Limits	Yes
Gc-LTM Cluster	Not interpretable				No
Gsm-MW Cluster	83	75-91	13	Below Average/Normative Weakness	Yes

Figure 4.2 WISC-IV Tab of the Data Management and Interpretive Assistant v1.0, Illustrated for Ryan

Verbal Comprehension Index (VCI), the Perceptual Reasoning Index, the Working Memory Index (WMI), and the Processing Speed Index (PSI); and (b) the General Ability Index (GAI), composed of the subtests that make up the Verbal Comprehension Index (VCI) and Perceptual Reasoning Index (PRI; Raiford, Weiss, Rolfhus, & Coalson, 2005). The following steps are recommended for determining the best way to summarize overall ability.

Step 2a. Consider the four WISC-IV Indexes. Subtract the lowest Index from the highest Index. Answer the following question: *Is the size of the standard score difference less than 1.5 SDs (< 23 points)?*

- If YES, then the FSIQ may be interpreted as a reliable and valid estimate of a child's global intellectual ability. Rapid Reference 4.5 provides an example of how to describe this finding. Proceed directly to Step 3.

≡ Rapid Reference 4.5

Example of How to Describe an Interpretable FSIQ in a Psychological Report

An interpretable FSIQ means that the size of the difference between the highest and lowest Indexes does not equal or exceed 1.5 SDs (23 points). In the case of Mark (see Table 4.1), the difference between his highest Index (112 on the VCI) and his lowest Index (103 on the PSI) = 9 points. This value is less than 23 points, so his FSIQ is interpretable.

Mark earned a FSIQ of 112, classifying his overall intellectual ability, as measured by the WISC-IV, as Average Range/Within Normal Limits. The chances are good (95%) that Mark's true FSIQ is somewhere within the range of 108 to 115. His FSIQ is ranked at the 79th percentile, indicating that he scored higher than 79% of other children of the same age in the standardization sample.

- If NO, then the variation in the Indexes that compose the FSIQ is considered too great (i.e., ≥ 23 points) for the purpose of summarizing global intellectual ability in a single score (i.e., the FSIQ). Proceed to Step 2b.

Step 2b. When the FSIQ is not interpretable, determine whether an abbreviated GAI may be used to describe overall intellectual ability. Answer the following question: *Is the size of the standard score difference between the VCI and the PRI less than 1.5 SDs (< 23 points)?*

- If YES, then the GAI may be calculated and interpreted as a reliable and valid estimate of a child's global intellectual ability. To compute GAI: (a) sum the child's scaled scores on the three core VCI and three core PRI subtests, and (b) enter this sum into Appendix F (on the CD-ROM) to determine the child's GAI, percentile rank, and confidence interval (select either 90 or 95% confidence). This table is reprinted from Saklofske, Rolfhus, Prifitera, Zhu, and Weiss (2005, pp. 44–45) with permission. The reliability of GAI is .95 for ages 6 to 11 years (SEm = 3.3) and .96 for ages 12 to 16 years (SEm = 3.0), as reported by Saklofske, Weiss, Raiford, and Prifitera (2006, p. 125). These values are high and very similar to those reported for the FSIQ (range = .96–.97; *WISC-IV Technical and Interpretive Manual,* Table 4.1, p. 34). Note that when the FSIQ is not interpretable, the

Table 4.1 Summary of WISC-IV Scores for Mark, Age 7

Index/Subtest	Score	95% CI	Percentile Rank	Descriptive Category
Verbal Comprehension	**112**	**[105–118]**	**79th**	**Average Range/Within Normal Limits**
Similarities	10		50th	
Vocabulary	14		91st	
Comprehension	13		84th	
(Information)	10		50th	
Perceptual Reasoning	**110**	**[102–117]**	**75th**	**Average Range/Within Normal Limits**
Block Design	12		75th	
Picture Concepts	10		50th	
Matrix Reasoning	13		84th	
Working Memory	**107**	**[99–114]**	**68th**	**Average Range/Within Normal Limits**
Digit Span	11		63rd	
Letter-Number Sequencing	12		75th	
(Arithmetic)	11		63rd	
Processing Speed	**103**	**[94–112]**	**58th**	**Average Range/Within Normal Limits**
Coding	9		37th	
Symbol Search	12		75th	
(Cancellation)	8		25th	
Full Scale IQ	**112**	**[107–117]**	**79th**	**Average Range/Within Normal Limits**

Note: Tests appearing in parentheses are supplemental measures. CI = Confidence Interval.

≡ Rapid Reference 4.6

Example of How to Describe the GAI in a Psychological Report

Ryan's WISC-IV Full Scale IQ (FSIQ) could not be interpreted because he demonstrated too much variability in his performance across the four Indexes that make up this score—namely, the Verbal Comprehension, Perceptual Reasoning, Working Memory, and Processing Speed Indexes. However, because Ryan's performance on the Verbal Comprehension (98) and Perceptual Reasoning (90) Indexes was similar, these Indexes can be combined to yield a General Ability Index (GAI). The GAI differs from the FSIQ in that it is not influenced directly by Ryan's performance on working memory and processing-speed tasks.

Ryan earned a GAI of 93, classifying his general level of intellectual ability as Average Range/Within Normal Limits. The chances are good (95%) that Ryan's true GAI is somewhere within the range of 87 to 99. His GAI is ranked at the 33rd percentile, indicating that he scored higher than 33% of other children of the same age in the standardization sample.

WISC-IV DMIA will automatically provide the GAI if it is interpretable. Rapid Reference 4.6 provides an example of how to describe the GAI in a psychological report. Proceed to Step 3.

- If NO, then the variation in the Indexes that compose the GAI is too great (≥ 23 points) for the purpose of summarizing global ability in a single score (i.e., GAI). Rapid Reference 4.7 provides an example of how to describe the finding of both a noninterpretable FSIQ and a noninterpretable GAI. Proceed to Step 3.

Figure 4.3 provides a snapshot of Step 2 of the WISC-IV interpretive worksheet for Ryan. In this step, it was determined that Ryan's overall intellectual ability was best described by the GAI. Figure 4.4 shows Step 2 from the WISC-IV DMIA. Note that the WISC-IV tab of the DMIA (Figure 4.2) showed that the FSIQ was not interpretable and included a GAI of 94 for Ryan.

STEP 3. Determine Whether Each of the Four Indexes Is Unitary and Thus Interpretable

When the variability among subtest scaled scores within an Index is unusually large, then the Index does not provide a good estimate of the ability it is intended to measure and, therefore, is not interpretable. In other words, when a substantial

≡ Rapid Reference 4.7

Example of How to Describe in a Psychological Report the Finding of *Both* a Noninterpretable FSIQ and a Noninterpretable GAI

A noninterpretable FSIQ means that the size of the difference between the highest and lowest Indexes equals or exceeds 1.5 SDs (23 points). A noninterpretable GAI means that the size of the difference between the VCI and PRI equals or exceeds 1.5 SDs (23 points). In the case of Susan, the difference between her highest Index (98 on the VCI) and her lowest Index (70 on the PSI) = 28 points. This value is more than 23 points, so her FSIQ is noninterpretable. In addition, the difference of 25 points between Susan's VCI (98) and PRI (73) equals or exceeds 1.5 SDs (23 points). Consequently, her GAI is also noninterpretable.

Susan earned a Full Scale IQ (FSIQ) of 76, but this estimate of her overall intellectual ability cannot be interpreted meaningfully because she displayed too much variability in the four Indexes that compose this full scale score. Therefore, Susan's intelligence is best understood by her performance on the separate WISC-IV Indexes—namely, Verbal Comprehension, Perceptual Reasoning, Working Memory, and Processing Speed.

Always interpret a child's overall score on the WISC-IV whenever a global score is essential for diagnosis (e.g., of intellectual disability) or placement (e.g., in a gifted program). Even if both the FSIQ and GAI are noninterpretable based on our empirical criteria, select the one that provides the most sensible overview of the child's intelligence for use in the diagnostic or placement process. Use clinical judgment to make this decision. For example, if the child was impulsive or distractible when administered the working memory and/or the processing speed subtests, then select the GAI (which excludes the WMI and PSI).

DON'T FORGET

Definition of a Unitary Ability

A *unitary ability* is an ability (such as Crystallized Intelligence or Processing Speed) that is represented by a cohesive set of scaled scores, each reflecting slightly different or unique aspects of the ability. Thus, when the variability among the subtest scaled scores that compose a WISC-IV Index is not unusually large, then the ability presumed to underlie the Index is considered unitary and may be interpreted. For example, a child obtaining scaled scores of 9, 5, and 8 on Comprehension, Similarities, and Vocabulary, respectively, has a difference score of 4 associated with the VCI (9 − 5 = 4). A difference of less than 1.5 SDs (i.e., less than 5 points) between the highest and lowest subtest scaled score is needed for an Index to be considered as representing a unitary ability. Therefore, in this example, the VCI represents a unitary ability and may be interpreted as a reliable and valid estimate of Crystallized Intelligence (Gc).

STEP 2. Determine the Best Way to Summarize Overall Intellectual Ability

Step 2a. To determine whether the FSIQ is interpretable, subtract the lowest Index from the highest Index.

Index names:	VCI		PSI		
Index standard scores:	98	−	70	=	28
	(Highest)		(Lowest)		(Difference)

Is the size of the difference less than 1.5 SDs (i.e., < 23 points)?　　　Yes　　

- If YES, then the FSIQ may be interpreted as a reliable and valid estimate of a child's overall intellectual ability.
- If NO, then proceed to Step 2b.

See Rapid Reference 4.5 for an example of how to describe the FSIQ in a psychological report.

Step 2b. To determine whether the General Ability Index (GAI) may be used to summarize overall intellectual ability, calculate the difference between the VCI and PRI.

Index standard scores:	98	−	90	=	8
	(VCI)		(PRI)		(Difference)

Is the size of the difference less than 1.5 SDs (i.e., < 23 points)?　　　　No

- If YES, then the GAI can be calculated and interpreted as a reliable and valid estimate of the child's overall intellectual ability.
- If NO, then proceed to Step 3.

To calculate the GAI, sum the child's scaled scores on the three VCI and three PRI subtests and enter this sum into Appendix F1 to determine the GAI.

Scaled scores:								
9 +	7 +	13 +	6 +	16 +	9	=	54	94
SI	VO	CO	BC	PCn	MR		(Sum of Scaled Scores)	(GAI)

See Rapid Reference 4.6 for an example of how to describe the GAI in a psychological report. Proceed to Step 3.

Figure 4.3 WISC-IV Interpretive Worksheet: STEP 2, Illustrated for Ryan, Age 10

difference between the scaled scores composing an Index is found, the Index cannot be interpreted as representing a unitary ability.

Step 3a. Determine whether the size of the difference among subtest scaled scores within the VCI (composed of three subtests) is unusually large. Subtract the lowest subtest scaled score from the highest subtest scaled score. Answer the following question: *Is the size of the difference less than 1.5 SDs (< 5 points)?*

- If YES, then the ability presumed to underlie the VCI is unitary and may be interpreted.

STEP 2. The Best Way to Summarize Overall Intellectual Ability is Determined
THIS STEP IS AUTOMATICALLY CALCULATED BY THE PROGRAM

Step 2a.   To determine whether the FS-IQ is interpretable, the lowest index is subtracted from the highest index .

Index Standard Scores: $\dfrac{98}{\text{Highest}}$ - $\dfrac{70}{\text{Lowest}}$ = $\dfrac{28}{\text{Difference}}$

Is the size of the difference less than 1.5 standard deviations (i.e., < 23 points)?
NO, proceed to step 2b

Step 2b.   To determine whether the General Ability Index (GAI) may be used to summarize overall intellectual ability,
the absolute difference between the VCI and PRI is calculated.

Index Standard Scores: $\dfrac{98}{\text{VCI}}$ - $\dfrac{90}{\text{PRI}}$ = $\dfrac{8}{\substack{\text{Absolute}\\\text{Difference}}}$

Is the size of the difference less than 1.5 standard deviations (i.e., < 23 points)?
YES, GAI may be interpreted as a reliable and valid estimate of a person's overall intellectual ability.

To calculate the GAI, the scaled scores from the core VCI and PRI subtests are summed, and the GAI that corresponds to this sum is located.

Scaled Scores: $\dfrac{7}{\text{VC}}$ + $\dfrac{13}{\text{CO}}$ + $\dfrac{9}{\text{SI}}$ + $\dfrac{6}{\text{BD}}$ + $\dfrac{9}{\text{MR}}$ + $\dfrac{10}{\text{PCn}}$ = $\dfrac{54}{\text{Sum}}$ = $\dfrac{94}{\text{GAI}}$

Figure 4.4 Step 2 of the Data Management and Interpretive Assistant v1.0, Illustrated for Ryan

- If NO, then the difference is too large (5 points or greater) and the VCI cannot be interpreted as representing a unitary ability.

Step 3b. Follow the same procedure as in Step 3a to determine the interpretability of the PRI (also composed of three subtests).

Step 3c. Determine whether the size of the difference between the subtest scaled scores that compose the two-subtest Working Memory Index (WMI) is too large. Subtract the lower scaled score from the higher one. Answer the following question: *Is the size of the difference less than 1.5 SDs (< 5 points)?*

- If YES, then the ability presumed to underlie the WMI is unitary and may be interpreted.
- If NO, then the difference is too large (5 points or greater) and the WMI cannot be interpreted as representing a unitary ability.

Step 3d. Follow this same procedure as in step 3c to determine the interpretability of the Processing Speed Index (PSI, also composed of two subtests).

For example, the difference between Ryan's subtest scaled scores that compose the PSI is 1 point (i.e., a Coding scaled score of 5 minus a Symbol Search scaled score of 4 equals 1; see Figure 4.1). Ryan's 1-point difference between the scaled scores for the PSI is less than the value needed to render the PSI uninterpretable (i.e., it is less than 5). Therefore, Ryan's PSI represents a unitary ability and may be interpreted. Figure 4.5 illustrates the decision process regarding the interpretability of all four of Ryan's Indexes following the interpretive worksheet in Appendix E. Figure 4.6 shows Step 3 from the WISC-IV DMIA. Note that in addition to the Step 3 tab of the DMIA, the WISC-IV tab (Figure 4.2) indicated whether or not each of the four indexes was interpretable. Rapid Reference 4.8 provides an example of how to interpret a unitary (interpretable) Index. Rapid Reference 4.9 provides an example of how to describe a nonunitary (noninterpretable) Index.

It is important to note that we opted to use the critical value of 5 points for determining the interpretability of all four WISC-IV Indexes instead of using the "base rate < 10% criterion." Our rationale for selecting this criterion was based on the results of the base rate analyses, which indicated that 6 or more points (2 SDs or more) were needed to identify a noninterpretable VCI, WMI, or PSI; and 7 or more points were needed to identify a noninterpretable PRI. These differences seemed too extreme, in our clinical judgment. It would mean, for example, that a child who earned a scaled score of 3 on Coding and 8 on Symbol Search would have an interpretable PSI. Therefore, we opted to

STEP 3. Determine Whether Each of the Four Indexes is Unitary and Thus Interpretable

Step 3a. Calculate the difference between the highest and lowest VCI subtest scaled scores.

VCI subtest scaled scores: 13   –   7   =   6
                        (Highest)   (Lowest)   (Difference)

Is the difference between the highest and lowest VCI subtest scaled scores < 5?   Yes   (No)

- If YES, interpret the VCI as representing a unitary Index.
- If NO, do not interpret the VCI as representing a unitary Index.

Proceed to Step 3b.

Step 3b. Calculate the difference between the highest and lowest PRI subtest scaled scores.

PRI subtest scaled scores: 10   –   6   =   4
                       (Highest)   (Lowest)   (Difference)

Is the difference between the highest and lowest PRI subtest scaled scores < 5? (Yes)   No

- If YES, interpret the PRI as representing a unitary Index.
- If NO, do not interpret the PRI as representing a unitary Index.

Proceed to Step 3c.

Step 3c. Calculate the difference between the WMI subtest scaled scores.

WMI subtest scaled scores: 7   –   7   =   0
                       (Highest)   (Lowest)   (Difference)

Is the difference between the highest and lowest WMI subtest scaled scores < 5? (Yes)   No

- If YES, interpret the WMI as representing a unitary Index.
- If NO, do not interpret the WMI as representing a unitary Index.

Proceed to Step 3d.

Step 3d. Calculate the difference between the highest and lowest PSI subtest scaled scores.

PSI subtest scaled scores: 5   –   4   =   1
                       (Highest)   (Lowest)   (Difference)

Is the difference between the highest and lowest PSI subtest scaled scores < 5? (Yes)   No

- If YES, interpret the PSI as representing a unitary Index.
- If NO, do not interpret the PSI as representing a unitary Index.

Proceed to Step 4. If all four Indexes are not interpretable, refer to pages 149–150 and Step 7 for additional interpretive options.

Figure 4.5 WISC-IV Interpretive Worksheet: STEP 3, Illustrated for Ryan, Age 10

STEP 3. The Four Indexes are Examined to Determine Whether they are Unitary
THIS STEP IS AUTOMATICALLY CALCULATED BY THE PROGRAM
Step 3a.   The difference between the highest and lowest core VCI subtest scaled scores is calculated.

VCI Subtest
Scaled Scores: __13__ - __7__ = __6__
                  Highest   Lowest   Difference

Is the size of the difference less than 5 points?
NO, do not interpret the VCI, as it is not a unitary Index

Step 3b.   The difference between the highest and lowest core PRI subtest scaled scores is calculated.

PRI Subtest
Scaled Scores: __10__ - __6__ = __4__
                  Highest   Lowest   Difference

Is the size of the difference less than 5 points?
YES, interpret the PRI as representing a unitary Index

Step 3c.   The difference between the highest and lowest core WMI subtest scaled scores is calculated.

WMI Subtest
Scaled Scores: __7__ - __7__ = __0__
                  Highest   Lowest   Difference

Is the size of the difference less than 5 points?
YES, interpret the WMI as representing a unitary Index

Step 3d.   The difference between the highest and lowest core PSI subtest scaled scores is calculated.

PSI Subtest
Scaled Scores: __5__ - __4__ = __1__
                  Highest   Lowest   Difference

Is the size of the difference less than 5 points?
YES, interpret the PSI as representing a unitary Index

Figure 4.6 Step 3 of the Data Management and Interpretive Assistant v1.0 Illustrated for Ryan

≡ Rapid Reference 4.8

Example of How to Interpret a Unitary Index in a Psychological Report

The Processing Speed Index (PSI), a measure of Processing Speed (Gs), represents Ryan's ability to perform simple, clerical-type tasks quickly. Ryan's Gs ability was assessed with two tasks—one required Ryan to quickly copy symbols that were paired with numbers according to a key (Coding), and the other required him to identify the presence or absence of a target symbol in a row of symbols (Symbol Search). The difference between Ryan's performances on these two tasks (Coding scaled score of 5 minus Symbol Search scaled score of 4 equals 1) was not unusually large (i.e., was not ≥ 5 points), indicating that his PSI is a good estimate of his processing speed. Ryan obtained a PSI of 70 (65–83), which is ranked at the 2nd percentile and is classified as Below Average/Normative Weakness.

≡ *Rapid Reference 4.9*

Example of How to Describe a Nonunitary Index in a Psychological Report

The Verbal Comprehension Index (VCI), a measure of Crystallized Intelligence (Gc), represents Ryan's ability to reason with previously learned information. Gc ability develops largely as a function of both formal and informal educational opportunities and experiences and is highly dependent on exposure to mainstream U.S. culture. Ryan's Gc was assessed by tasks that required him to define words (Vocabulary, scaled score = 7), draw conceptual similarities between words (Similarities, scaled score = 9), and answer questions involving knowledge of general principles and social situations (Comprehension, scaled score = 13). The variability among Ryan's performances on these tasks was unusually large (i.e., the scaled score range was greater than or equal to 5 points), indicating that his overall Gc ability cannot be summarized in a single score (i.e., the VCI).

Note: Subsequent steps (i.e., Steps 4–7) should be used to provide additional information about Ryan's Gc performance.

use 5 or more points to denote a noninterpretable Index. The value of 5 points was not arbitrary, however. It corresponds to 1.5 SDs (4.5 scaled score points, rounded up)—the same rule used to determine interpretability of the FSIQ and GAI.

Although an Index is considered uninterpretable when the variability among the subtests it comprises is unusually large, in some instances it makes sense to look at the normative classifications of the scaled scores to determine whether a general conclusion may be made about a child's range of observed functioning in the ability presumed to underlie the Index. Specifically, when *all* subtest scaled scores within an Index are either ≤ 8 or ≥ 12, we believe that a statement may be made about performance. For example:

1. If the variability among subtest scaled scores composing an Index is unusually large and all scaled scores are ≥ 12, then describe the child's range of observed functioning in the ability presumed to underlie the Index as a notable integrity as follows: *The Perceptual Reasoning Index (PRI), a measure of Fluid Reasoning and Visual Processing (Gf/Gv), represents Amy's ability to reason using visual stimuli. Amy's Gf/ Gv was assessed by tasks that required her to recreate a series of modeled or pictured designs using blocks (Block Design), identify the missing portion of an incomplete visual matrix from one of five response options (Matrix Reasoning), and*

select one picture from each of two or three rows of pictures to form a group with a common characteristic (Picture Concepts). The variability among Amy's performances on these tasks was unusually large, indicating that her overall Gf/ Gv ability cannot be summarized in a single score (i.e., the PRI). However, it is clear that Amy's Gf/Gv ability is a notable integrity for her because her performance on the tasks that compose the PRI ranged from Average Range/ Within Normal Limits to Upper Extreme/Normative Strength.

2. If the variability among subtest scaled scores composing an Index is unusually large and all scaled scores are ≤ 8, then describe the child's range of observed functioning in the ability presumed to underlie the Index as a notable limitation, as follows: *The Working Memory Index (WMI), a measure of Short-Term Memory (Gsm), represents Amy's ability to apprehend and hold information in immediate awareness and to use it within a few seconds. Amy's Gsm was assessed by tasks that required her to repeat numbers verbatim or in reverse order as presented by the examiner (Digit Span); and to listen to a sequence of numbers and letters and repeat the numbers in ascending order, followed by the letters in alphabetical order (Letter-Number Sequencing). The variability among Amy's performances on these tasks was unusually large, indicating that her overall Gsm ability cannot be summarized in a single score (i.e., the WMI). However, Amy's Gsm ability is a notable limitation for her because her performance on the tasks that compose the WMI ranged from the lower end of the Average range to Lower Extreme/Normative Weakness.*

In the rare instance in which all four Indexes are not interpretable, then you should proceed to Step 7.

DON'T FORGET
....

What Do I Do with a Noninterpretable Index?

When an Index is found to be noninterpretable at Step 3, this means that the variability among the subtest scaled scores composing the Index is too large to allow for the interpretation of a single ability. For example, when the variability among the VCI subtest scaled scores is unusually large, then the VCI cannot be interpreted as representing the ability of Crystallized Intelligence (Gc). However, the subtests composing the noninterpretable Index may be combined with other subtests in different ways to allow for meaningful interpretations of more specific abilities at later steps in the interpretive process (e.g., Step 7).

STEP 4. Determine Normative Strengths and Normative Weaknesses in the Index Profile

Only unitary Indexes identified in the previous step are included in this analysis. For example, in the case of Ryan, only his PRI, WMI, and PSI would be considered at this step (see far right column in Fig. 4.2). To determine Normative Strengths and Normative Weaknesses in a child's Index profile, review the child's scores and consider the exact value of the interpretable Indexes. If the Index standard score is greater than 115, then the ability measured by the Index is a *Normative Strength*. If the Index standard score is less than 85, then the ability measured by the Index is a *Normative Weakness*. If the Index standard score is between 85 and 115 (inclusive), then the ability measured by the Index is *Within Normal Limits*. Although Ryan's PRI of 90 is Within Normal Limits, his WMI and PSI of 83 and 70, respectively, are Normative Weaknesses. Figure 4.7 provides a snapshot of Step 4 of the WISC-IV interpretive worksheet for Ryan. Figure 4.8 shows Step 4 from the WISC-IV DMIA. Note that the WISC-IV tab of the DMIA (Fig. 4.2) also indicates whether an index is a normative strength or weakness in the column labeled "Descriptive Category."

STEP 5. Determine Personal Strengths and Personal Weaknesses in the Index Profile

Step 5a. Compute the mean of the child's Index standard scores and round to the nearest tenth of a point. Note that all Indexes (interpretable and noninterpretable) are included in the computation of the mean for practical reasons. Excluding any Index would result in the need for numerous tables for determining both

---

STEP 4. Determine Normative Strengths and Normative Weaknesses in the Index Profile

Enter the name of each interpretable Index in the table below. Record the standard score for each interpretable Index. Place a checkmark in the box corresponding to the appropriate normative category for each Index.

Interpretable Index	Standard Score	Normative Weakness < 85	Within Normal Limits 85–115	Normative Strength > 115
PRI	90		✓	
WMI	83	✓		
PSI	70	✓		

Figure 4.7 WISC-IV Interpretive Worksheet: STEP 4, Illustrated from Ryan, Age 10

Figure 4.8 Step 4 of the Data Management and Interpretive Assistant v1.0, Illustrated for Ryan

statistical significance and uncommon Index variation (i.e., mean Indexes based on two-, three-, and four-Index combinations).

Step 5b. Subtract the mean of all Index standard scores from each *interpretable* Index standard score. Using the values reported in Table 4.2, determine whether the size of the difference between an interpretable Index and the mean of all Indexes is significant. This table includes differences required for statistical significance at both the .05 and .01 levels. We recommend using the values that correspond to the .05 level, which appear in the shaded rows of Table 4.2. To be considered

Table 4.2 Differences Required for Statistical Significance (at $p < .05$ and $p < .01$) between an Index and the Mean of all Four Indexes, by Age and Overall Sample

Age	p value	Verbal Comprehension	Perceptual Reasoning	Working Memory	Processing Speed
6	.05	7.9	7.9	7.6	9.8
	.01	10.4	10.4	10.0	12.9
7	.05	7.7	7.7	8.2	10.3
	.01	10.1	10.1	10.8	13.6
8	.05	7.3	7.1	7.6	8.4
	.01	9.7	9.3	10.0	11.1
9	.05	7.1	10.9	7.7	8.5
	.01	9.4	14.3	10.2	11.2
10	.05	7.1	10.9	7.7	8.2
	.01	9.3	14.3	10.1	10.8

Table 4.2 (Continued)

Age	p value	Verbal Comprehension	Perceptual Reasoning	Working Memory	Processing Speed
11	.05	6.9	6.9	7.2	7.8
	.01	9.1	9.1	9.5	10.2
12	.05	6.1	6.8	6.8	8.0
	.01	8.1	9.0	9.0	10.5
13	.05	6.6	6.9	7.5	8.1
	.01	8.7	9.1	9.9	10.6
14	.05	6.2	7.2	6.9	8.0
	.01	8.1	9.4	9.0	10.5
15	.05	6.2	7.2	7.2	7.7
	.01	8.1	9.4	9.4	10.2
16	.05	6.2	7.5	6.9	8.0
	.01	8.2	9.8	9.1	10.6
All[a]	.05	6.8	7.2	7.3	8.4
	.01	8.9	9.4	9.6	11.0

Source: Naglieri, J. A., & Paolitto, A. W. (2005). Ipsative comparisons of WISC-IV index scores. *Applied Neuropsychology*, 12, 208–211.

Information in this table was provided by Jack A. Naglieri (personal communication, January 28, 2004). The values shown here are smaller than the values reported in the comparable table by Naglieri and Paolitto (2005) because they chose to apply the Bonferroni procedure when computing the size of the differences needed for significance at the .05 and .01 levels. However, consistent with our goal of generating as many viable hypotheses as possible, we prefer a more liberal approach (uncorrected values), rather than applying the conservative Bonferroni correction for multiple comparisons. For that same reason, we prefer the .05 level of significance to the .01 level, and have shaded the .05 values in the table.

Note: Enter this table only with *interpretable* Indexes. To use this table, calculate the mean of all four Indexes (rounded to the nearest tenth). Subtract this mean value from each interpretable Index and obtain difference scores. Select a significance level (.05 or .01). We recommend using .05 (the shaded portions of the table). Compare the difference score to the value in the appropriate row (.01 or .05) and the appropriate Index column. If the difference score is equal to or greater than this value, then the difference is statistically significant. If the difference score is less than this value, then the difference is not statistically significant. For example, if a 7-year-old obtained an interpretable WMI of 85 and the mean of all four Indexes was 93.2, then you would subtract the mean of all four Indexes from the WMI. The difference score of 8.2 (85 − 93.2 = −8.2) is compared to the value for the WMI at the .05 level for a 7-year-old (i.e., 8.2). Because the difference score equals the value listed in the table, you would interpret the difference as statistically significant. Additionally, because the WMI was lower than the mean, it is considered a Personal Weakness.

[a]All = overall WISC-IV standardization sample (ages 6–16).

statistically significant, the difference must be equal to or greater than the value reported in Table 4.2. Because some of the values for specific age levels differ from those reported for the total sample, we recommend using the differences reported by age. Use the following criteria for identifying personal strengths and weaknesses:

1. If the difference is significant and the interpretable Index is higher than the mean, then the Index is a *Personal Strength* for the child.
2. If the difference is significant and the interpretable Index is lower than the mean, then the Index is a *Personal Weakness* for the child.

Step 5c. Determine whether Personal Strengths and Personal Weaknesses are uncommon using the < 10% base rate criterion. Because *statistical significance* means only that an observed difference is "real" (i.e., not due to chance), it is necessary to determine whether the difference is also unusually large or uncommon in the WISC-IV standardization sample. Differences among Indexes that occur infrequently in the standardization sample may be valuable in making diagnoses and generating educational recommendations when corroborated by other data. Table 4.3 includes the information necessary to determine whether the differences between a child's interpretable Indexes and the mean of all Indexes occur less than 10% of the time in the standardization sample. The shaded row in Table 4.3 contains values reflecting differences that occur less than 10% of the time in the WISC-IV standardization sample. Although we recommend a .10 base rate, Table 4.3 also includes base rates of .01, .02, and .05. If the magnitude of the observed difference between an interpretable Index and the mean of all Indexes is equal to or greater than the value reported for the comparison in the shaded row of Table 4.3, then the difference is uncommon; otherwise, the difference is not uncommon.

Step 5d. Identify Key Assets and High-Priority Concerns in the child's profile using the following criteria to identify Personal Strengths and Weaknesses that are of greatest importance, diagnostically and educationally.

1. Personal Strengths that are also uncommon and greater than 115 are labeled *Key Assets.*
2. Personal Weaknesses that are also uncommon and less than 85 are labeled *High-Priority Concerns.*

CAUTION

Interpretation of Scores

No single score, including an interpretable Index, should be used in isolation to make a diagnosis or to develop an individualized education program (IEP).

Table 4.3   The Size of the Difference Between Each Index and the Mean of All Four Indexes that Is Needed to be Considered Unusually Large or Uncommon

Base Rates	Verbal Comprehension	Perceptual Reasoning	Working Memory	Processing Speed
.01	22.3	21.1	25.0	25.6
.02	20.8	19.3	22.5	23.3
.05	16.8	16.3	18.8	20.0
.10	14.0	13.5	15.0	17.0

Source: Wechsler Intelligence Scale for Children–Fourth Edition. Copyright © 2003 by Harcourt Assessment, Inc. Reproduced by permission of the publisher. All rights reserved. *Wechsler Intelligence Scale for Children and WISC* are trademarks of Harcourt Assessment, Inc., registered in the United States of America and/or other jurisdictions.

Note: "Unusually large or uncommon" denotes difference values that occur infrequently within the WISC-IV standardization sample. Enter this table only with interpretable Indexes. To use this table, calculate the mean of all four Indexes (rounded to the nearest tenth). Subtract this mean value from each interpretable Index and obtain difference scores. Select a base rate value (i.e., .01, .02, .05, or .10). We recommend using .10 (the shaded portion of the table). Compare the difference score to the value listed in the table for each interpretable Index. If the difference score is equal to or greater than the value listed in the table, then the difference is uncommon. If the difference score is less than the value listed in the table, then the difference is not uncommon. For example, if the mean of all four Indexes is 90.5 and the VCI standard score is 104, then the difference score for VCI is 13.5 (i.e., 104 − 90.5 = 13.5). A 14-point difference between the VCI and the mean of all Indexes is needed to be considered uncommon using the 10% base rate criterion. Thus, the difference score of 13.5 for VCI is considered common in the normal population. The values provided in this table are based on the overall WISC-IV standardization sample (ages 6–16).

DON'T FORGET

....

Identifying Personal Strengths and Weaknesses

When determining the child's Personal Strengths and Personal Weaknesses, compare only *interpretable* Indexes to the child's mean Index. *Noninterpretable* Indexes *are* included in the computation of the child's mean Index, but they *are not* compared to that mean or interpreted.

Once the previous steps (Steps 5a–5d) have been completed with the aid of the worksheet (see Fig. 4.9) or DMIA (see Figure 4.10), summarize the results of all Index analyses (Steps 3, 4, and 5) using the table provided in Appendix G (located on the CD accompanying this book). An example of a completed table for Ryan is provided in Figure 4.11 (see Figure 4.12 for an example of how this information would appear on the WISC-IV

STEP 5. Determine Personal Strengths and Personal Weaknesses in the Index Profile

Step 5a. Compute the mean of the child's Indexes and round to the nearest 10th of a point. Note that all Indexes (interpretable and noninterpretable) are included in the computation of the mean.

$$\underset{\text{(VCI)}}{98} + \underset{\text{(PRI)}}{90} + \underset{\text{(WMI)}}{83} + \underset{\text{(PSI)}}{70} = \underset{\text{(Sum)}}{341} \div 4 = \underset{\text{(Index Mean)}}{85.25}$$

Step 5b. Fill in the table below as follows:

- Record the name of each interpretable Index in Column (1).
- Record each interpretable Index standard score in Column (2).
- Record the rounded mean of all Indexes (from Step 5a) in Column (3).
- Record the difference score (i.e., standard score minus mean) in Column (4).
- Record the critical value needed for the difference score to be considered significant in Column (5) (these values are included in the "Personal Strength/Weakness Table for Ages 6 through 16").
- If difference score equals or exceeds the critical value, record a "PS" for a postive (+) difference score or a "PW" for a negative (–) difference score.

Interpretable Index (1)	Standard Score (2)	Rounded Mean of All Indexes (3)	Difference Score (4)	Critical Value Needed for Significance (5)	Personal Strength or Personal Weakness (PS or PW) (6)
PRI	90	85.3	+ 4.7	10.9	
WMI	83	85.3	–2.3	7.7	
PSI	70	85.3	–15.3	8.2	PW

Personal Strength/Weakness Table for Ages 6 through 16

	6	7	8	9	10	11	12	13	14	15	16
VCI	7.9	7.7	7.3	7.1	7.1	6.9	6.1	6.6	6.2	6.2	6.2
PRI	7.9	7.7	7.1	10.9	10.9	6.9	6.8	6.9	7.2	7.2	7.5
WMI	7.6	8.2	7.6	7.7	7.7	7.2	6.8	7.5	6.9	7.2	6.9
PSI	9.8	10.3	8.4	8.5	8.2	7.8	8.0	8.1	8.0	7.7	8.0

Note: The critical values listed in this table are at the *p* < .05 level of significance. For critical values at the *p* < .01 level of significance, see Table 4.3.

Figure 4.9 WISC-IV Interpretive Worksheet: STEP 5, Illustrated for Ryan, Age 10

Are there any Personal Strengths or Weaknesses evident in the child's Index profile? No

- If YES, go to Step 5c.
- If NO, proceed directly to Step 6.

Step 5c. **Determine whether the Personal Strength/Weakness is uncommon (base rate < 10%) in the general population.**

Index	Difference Score (from Step 5b)	PS or PW (from Step 5b)	Critical Value	Uncommon (U) or Not Uncommon (NU)
VCI			≥14	
PRI			≥13.5	
WMI			≥15	
PSI	−15.3	PW	≥17	NU

Note: Difference scores are entered into this table only for *unitary* Indexes that were identified as Personal Strengths or Personal Weaknesses in Step 5b. Difference scores that are equal to or exceed the critical value listed in the fourth column of this table should be denoted Uncommon (U). Difference scores that are less than the critical value should be denoted Not Uncommon (NU).

Are there any uncommon personal strengths or weaknesses evident in the child's Index profile?　　　　　　　　　　　　　　　Yes　

- If YES, go to Step 5d.
- If NO, proceed directly to Step 6.

Step 5d. **Determine whether any of the Interpretable Indexes are Key Assets or High-Priority Concerns.**

Review your findings from Steps 4, 5b, and 5c. In the following table, for each relevant Index place a checkmark in the column that accurately describes the findings for that Index. An Index that is both a Normative Strength and an Uncommon Personal Strength should be identified as a "Key Asset." An Index that is both a Normative Weakness and an Uncommon Personal Weakness should be identified as a "High-Priority Concern."

Index	NS (Step 4)	NW (Step 4)	PS (Step 5b)	PW (Step 5b)	Uncommon (Step 5c)	Key Asset	High-Priority Concern
VCI							
PRI							
WMI		✓					
PSI		✓		✓			

Note: NS = Normative Strength; NW = Normative Weakness; PS = Personal Strength; PW = Personal Weakness.

Proceed to Step 6.

Figure 4.9 (Continued)

STEP 5. *Personal Strengths* and *Personal Weaknesses* in the Index Profile Are Determined

THIS STEP IS AUTOMATICALLY CALCULATED BY THE PROGRAM

Step 5a. The mean of the examinee's Indexes is computed and rounded to the nearest 10th of a point. Note that all Indexes (interpretable and noninterpretable) are included in the computation of the mean.

$$\frac{98}{VCI} + \frac{90}{PRI} + \frac{83}{WMI} + \frac{70}{PSI} = \frac{341}{(Sum)} \ / \ 4 = \frac{85.3}{(Index\ Mean)}$$

Step 5b. The program has completed the table as follows:

· The names of the interpretable Indexes are recorded in column (1)

· The interpretable Index standard scores are recorded in column (2)

· The rounded mean of all Indexes is recorded in column (3) (from Step 5a)

· The difference score (i.e., standard score minus mean) is recorded in column (4)

· The critical value needed for the difference score to be considered significant is recorded in column (5)

· If the difference score ≥ the critical value, a "PS" is recorded for a positive (+) difference score & a "PW" is recorded for a negative (-) difference score.

PROGRAM AUTOMATICALLY COMPLETES THE TABLE

PS = Personal Strength
PW = Personal Weakness

Index	Standard Score	Rounded Mean of All Indexes	Difference Score	Critical Value Needed for Significance	Personal Strength or Personal Weakness
PRI	90	85.3	4.75	7.1	
WMI	83	85.3	-2.25	10.9	
PSI	70	85.3	-15.25	7.7	PW
				8.2	

Examinee's Age: 10

Figure 4.10 Steps 5a-d of the Data Management and Interpretive Assistant v1.0

Step 5c. The difference between each interpretable index and the mean of all indexes is examined to determine whether it is uncommonly large (base rate < 10%)

STEPS 5c & 5d ARE AUTOMATICALLY CALCULATED BY THE PROGRAM

Index	Standard Score	Rounded Mean of All Indexes	Difference Score	Critical Value (<10%)	Uncommon (U) or Not Uncommon (NU)
PRI	90	85.25	4.75	≥14.0	NU
WMI	83	85.25	-2.25	≥13.5	NU
PSI	70	85.25	-15.25	≥15	NU
				≥17	

Step 5d. The interpretable indexes are examined to determine Key Assets or high-priority concerns.

- Findings from Steps 4, 5b, and 5c are reviewed.
- For each relevant Index, a checkmark is placed in the column that accurately describes the findings for that Index.
- Indexes that represent normative strengths and uncommon personal strengths are identified as "Key Assets."
- Indexes that represent normative weaknesses and uncommon personal weaknesses are identified as "High Priority Concerns."

Index	NS (Step 4)	NW (Step 4)	PS (Step 5b)	PW (Step 5b)	Uncommon (Step 5c)	Key Asset	High Priority Concern
PRI							
WMI		X					
PSI		X		X			

Note. NS = Normative Strength; NW = Normative Weakness; PS = Personal Strength; PW = Personal Weakness.

Figure 4.10 (Continued)

Name:	Ryan					
Date of testing:	2/26/04		INTERPRETIVE STEP			
Age:	10					
WISC-IV Index	Standard Score	(STEP 3) Is Index Standard Score Interpretable?	(STEP 4) Normative Strength (NS) or Normative Weakness (NW)?	(STEP 5b) Personal Strength (PS) or Personal Weakness (PW)?	(STEP 5c) Is PS or PW Uncommon?	(STEP 5d) Key Asset (KA) or High-Priority Concern (HPC)?
VCI	98	NO	N/A	N/A	N/A	N/A
PRI	90	YES	NO	NO	N/A	N/A
WMI	83	YES	YES-NW	NO	NO	NO
PSI	70	YES	YES-NW	YES-PW	NO	NO

Clinical Impressions and Suggested (Post Hoc) Clinical Comparisons:

1. Although VCI is the highest standard score in the profile, analysis of its components seems warranted. Examination of the influence of Gf on VCI tasks may be informative (e.g., examine the Verbal Fluid Reasoning Cluster vs. Nonverbal Fluid Reasoning Cluster Clinical Comparison). Certain aspects of Gc should play a prominent role in educational planning.

2. Although PRI is Average/Within Normal Limits, analyses of its components and of Gf vs. Gv difference are warranted (e.g., examine the Nonverbal Fluid Reasoning [Gf-nonverbal] Cluster vs. Visual Processing Cluster Clinical Comparison).

3. Comparison of WMI to information stored in Long-Term Memory (LTM) may be informative (e.g., examine the LTM vs. WM Planned Clinical Comparison).

4. Processing Speed is a notable weakness and suggests a disorder in this basic psychological process, a finding that suggests accommodations may be warranted.

Figure 4.11 Summary of Analyses of WISC-IV Indexes for Ryan (Step 6)

		STEP 3	STEP 4	STEP 5c	STEP 5c	STEP 5d
Summary of Analyses of WISC-IV Indexes						
Examinee Name: Ryan			Date of Birth: 1/16/1994			
Date of Assessment: 3/1/2004			Age: 10 yr 1 mo			
Index	Standard Score	Is Index Standard Score Interpretable	Normative Strength or Normative Weakness	Personal Strength or Personal Weakness	Is PS or PW Uncommon?	Key Asset (KA) or High Priority Concern (HPC)?
VCI		NO				
PRI	90	YES			NU	
WMI	83	YES	NW		NU	
PSI	70	YES	NW	PW	NU	
Write your clinical impressions and suggestions for follow up assessment in the space below.						

Figure 4.12 Step 6 of the Data Management and Interpretive Assistant v1.0, Illustrated for Ryan

DMIA). Figure 4.11 includes a section called "Clinical Impressions and Suggested (Post Hoc) Clinical Comparisons." After reflecting on the findings generated from Steps 3 through 5, you should record your clinical impressions. In addition, you should specify whether any Clinical Comparisons might be useful to conduct in order to gain a better understanding of the child's cognitive capabilities. When an Index is uninterpretable due to too much variability among its component scaled scores, and when all the scaled scores within the Index are neither ≤ 8 nor ≥ 12, then it is likely that additional assessment is warranted to gain a better understanding of the ability or abilities that underlie the Index. For example, Jill obtained scaled scores of 5, 10, and 9 on the Block Design, Matrix Reasoning, and Picture Concepts subtests, respectively. The 5-point difference between Jill's highest and lowest scaled scores within this Index (Matrix Reasoning scaled score of 10 minus Block Design scaled score of 5 equals 5) is unusually large, rendering the PRI uninterpretable. However, because the primary ability measured by Block Design is Visual Processing (Gv) and the primary ability measured by Matrix Reasoning and Picture Concepts is Fluid Reasoning (Gf), conducting the Clinical Comparison of Gv (Block Design + Picture Completion) versus Gf (Matrix Reasoning + Picture Concepts) may reveal important information about Jill's abilities. Planned clinical comparisons were described in Chapter 1 and will be discussed in further detail in Step 7.

It is important to note that neither a normative weakness on an Index nor an uncommon strength or weakness in an individual's Index profile is unusual in the general population (Crawford, Garthwaite, & Gault, 2007, Tables 3 and 7). For example, with regard to normative weaknesses, nearly 40% of children and adolescents are expected to exhibit at least one Index below 85. It is, therefore, common for individuals to display at least one normative weakness in their WISC-IV Index profiles. Consequently, when a person earns an Index below 85 on any one of the four Indexes, that finding—*in and of itself*—is not necessarily a cause for concern. However, it is noteworthy when two Indexes fall below 85, as this occurs only about 17% of the time. Note that standard scores below 85 in three or all four Indexes occurs 7.3% of the time and standard scores below 80 on any two Indexes occurs 9.8% of the time (Crawford et al., 2007, Table 3).

The same kind of caution is needed when focusing only on uncommon personal strengths and weaknesses. If a person displays one uncommon personal strength or weakness, that finding does not raise a red flag because it is quite common: On the WISC-IV, 30.5% of children and adolescents are expected to exhibit one uncommon difference (either strength or weakness) between an Index and the mean of all four Indexes, when using our 10% criterion to determine abnormality (Crawford et al., 2007, Table 7). However, *two* or more uncommon fluctuations is noteworthy (whether two weaknesses, two strengths, or one of each) because only 9.0% of the population displayed two or more. Importantly, less than 1% had three or four uncommon personal strengths and/or weaknesses.

These findings demonstrate that a normative weakness on a WISC-IV Index, in and of itself, or an uncommon personal weakness, in and of itself, is not sufficient evidence of a disorder or impairment. In order for an Index to be indicative of a disorder or impairment, it should first meet the criteria for a *High-Priority Concern* (i.e., it should represent both a normative weakness and an uncommon

DON'T FORGET

Size of Difference Needed Between an Interpretable Index and the Mean of All Indexes to Be Considered Statistically Significant ($p < .05$) and Unusually Large or Uncommon

Index	Difference Required for Statistical Significance	Difference Required for an Uncommon Difference
Verbal Comprehension	6.8	14.0
Perceptual Reasoning	7.2	13.5
Working Memory	7.3	15.0
Processing Speed	8.4	17.0

Note: Differences required for statistical significance are reported for the overall WISC-IV sample. "Unusually large or uncommon" denotes difference sizes occurring less than 10% of the time in the WISC-IV standardization sample.

personal weakness). In addition, other data sources should corroborate the finding of a High-Priority Concern. Crawford and colleagues's (2007) analyses provide important data for interpreting deviations in WISC-IV Index profiles. Their overall finding of how common it is to have normative weaknesses, or to display uncommon personal strengths and weaknesses, reinforces the interpretive approach that we established in the first edition of this book—namely, the key to effective WISC-IV interpretation requires examination of unusual personal strengths and weaknesses *alongside* normative strengths and weaknesses.

STEP 6. Interpret Fluctuations in the Child's Index Profile

Interpreting the child's Index profile provides reliable and useful information for making diagnostic and educational decisions. Because many of the descriptions that are used to classify Indexes (e.g., High-Priority Concerns, Key Assets) may be new to the examiner and other professionals and laypersons who read psychological reports, you should include a paragraph in (or appendix to) your report that defines these terms. To avoid confusion, only provide descriptions of the terms that are actually used in your report. For example, if the child did not have any High-Priority Concerns, then you do not need to define this term in your report. Rapid Reference 4.10 provides a description of all the terms that are used to classify Indexes.

Interpret each Index in a separate paragraph. Begin with strengths (including Key Assets), followed by weaknesses (including High-Priority Concerns). Next, indicate the Index or Indexes that are neither strengths nor weaknesses. Finally, describe the Index or Indexes that are noninterpretable. Figure 4.11 (and Figure 4.12 from the WISC-IV DMIA) shows that Ryan has a Personal Weakness that is also a Normative Weakness (PSI); a Normative Weakness (WMI); one Index that is interpretable and Within Normal Limits (PRI); and one Index that is not interpretable (VCI). Rapid Reference 4.11 provides examples of how to interpret fluctuations in a child's Index profile. This Rapid Reference shows that Indexes may be classified in 1 of 12 ways following the analyses outlined in Steps 3 through 5, each having a different interpretation.

OPTIONAL INTERPRETIVE STEPS

There are two optional interpretive steps for the WISC-IV. The first one (Step 7) allows you to conduct clinical comparisons. Specifically, you may choose to conduct one or more comparisons between Clinical Clusters based on your hypotheses generated at Step 6 or prior to administering the WISC-IV. The second optional step (Step 8) allows you to compare two alternative indexes—the General Ability Index (GAI) and the Cognitive Processing Index (CPI).

≣ *Rapid Reference 4.10*

Terms Used to Describe Fluctuations in a Child's WISC-IV Index Profile

Term (Abbreviation)	Definition
Index	A standard score with a mean of 100 and standard deviation of 15.
Normative Strength (NS)	An Index that is above 115.
Normative Weakness (NW)	An Index that is below 85.
Within Normal Limits (WNL)	An Index ranging from 85 to 115 (inclusive).
Personal Strength (PS)	An Index that is significantly higher than the child's own mean Index, using the .05 level of significance.
Personal Weakness (PW)	An Index that is significantly lower than the child's own mean Index, using the .05 level of significance.
Uncommon Personal Strength (PS/Uncommon)	A Personal Strength that is also substantially different from the child's own mean. That is, the size of the difference between the Index and the mean of all four Indexes is unusually large, occurring less than 10% of the time in the WISC-IV standardization sample.
Uncommon Personal Weakness (PW/Uncommon)	A Personal Weakness that is also substantially different from the child's own mean. That is, the size of the difference between the Index and the mean of all four Indexes is unusually large, occurring less than 10% of the time in the WISC-IV standardization sample.
Key Asset (KA)	An Index that is an uncommon Personal Strength and a Normative Strength.
High-Priority Concern (HPC)	An Index that is an uncommon Personal Weakness and a Normative Weakness.

STEP 7. Conduct Clinical Comparisons When Supplemental WISC-IV Subtests Are Administered

Based on our knowledge of the abilities measured by the WISC-IV, CHC theory, and relevant research on the relations between specific cognitive abilities and processes and learning/achievement, we offer a select number of additional comparisons that

≣ Rapid Reference 4.11

Classification and Interpretation of Index Fluctuations Based on the Index Profile Analyses Described in Steps 3–5

INDEX SCORES THAT ARE CLASSIFIED AS A STRENGTH

1. **Key Asset (Normative Strength and Personal Strength/ Uncommon)**
   Interpretation: Jessica's processing speed is considered a significant strength as compared to other individuals her age in the normal population. In addition, her ability in this area is significantly higher than her abilities in other areas. In fact, the difference between Jessica's processing speed and her abilities in other areas is so large that it is not commonly achieved by other children her age in the normal population. Therefore, Jessica's processing speed is a Key Asset and a notable integrity, a finding that should play an essential role in developing educational interventions. Note that the latter part of this interpretive statement may be germane only when other abilities (cognitive or academic) are either in the lower end of the Average range or lower, suggesting that intervention may be warranted.

2. **Normative Strength and Personal Strength/Not Uncommon**
   Interpretation: Jessica's processing speed is considered a significant strength as compared to other individuals her age in the normal population. In addition, her ability in this area is significantly higher than her abilities in other areas. Therefore, Jessica's processing speed is a notable integrity, a finding that may play an essential role in developing educational interventions. Note that the latter part of this interpretive statement may be germane only when other abilities (cognitive or academic) are either in the lower end of the Average range or lower, suggesting that intervention may be warranted.

3. **Normative Strength but not a Personal Strength**
   Interpretation: Jessica's processing speed is considered a significant strength compared to other children her age in the normal population. Her processing speed is a notable integrity, a finding that may play an essential role in developing educational interventions. Note that the latter part of this interpretive statement may be germane only when other abilities (cognitive or academic) are either in the lower end of the Average Range or lower, suggesting that intervention may be warranted.

4. **Personal Strength/Uncommon but not a Normative Strength**
   Interpretation: Jessica's processing speed is considered a significant strength compared to her abilities in other areas. In fact, the difference between her processing speed and her abilities in other areas is so large that it is not commonly achieved by other children her age in the normal population.

(continued)

Therefore, Jessica's processing speed is a notable Personal Strength, a finding that should play an essential role in developing educational interventions. Note that the latter part of this interpretive statement may be germane only when other abilities (cognitive or academic) are either in the lower end of the Average range or lower, suggesting that intervention may be warranted. Also, in this scenario, Jessica's processing speed may be considered a notable integrity, as it was in the first two scenarios, if her Processing Speed standard score is at the upper end of the Average Range (i.e., 110 to 115). Finally, it is also possible for Jessica's processing speed to be a Personal Strength/Uncommon but a Normative Weakness (i.e., if the Personal Strength/Uncommon is associated with a standard score of <85).

5. **Personal Strength/Not Uncommon but not a Normative *Strength***
   Interpretation: *Jessica's processing speed is considered a significant strength compared to her abilities in other areas. Her processing speed is a notable Personal Strength, a finding that should play an essential role in developing educational interventions. Note that the latter part of this interpretive statement may be germane only when other abilities (cognitive or academic) are either in the lower end of the Average Range or lower, suggesting that intervention may be warranted. Also, it is possible for Jessica's processing speed to be a Personal Strength/Not Uncommon but a Normative Weakness (i.e., if the Personal Strength/Not Uncommon is associated with a standard score of <85).*

INDEX SCORES THAT ARE CLASSIFIED AS A WEAKNESS

6. **High-Priority Concern (Normative Weakness and Personal Weakness/Uncommon)**
   Interpretation: *Jessica's processing speed is considered a significant weakness as compared to other individuals her age in the normal population. In addition, her ability in this area is significantly lower than her abilities in other areas. In fact, the difference between her processing speed and her abilities in other areas is so large that it is not commonly found in the normal population. Therefore, Jessica's processing speed is a High-Priority Concern and suggests that she has a disorder in this basic psychological process, a finding that should play an essential role in developing educational interventions.*[1]

7. **Normative Weakness and Personal Weakness/Not Uncommon**
   Interpretation: *Jessica's processing speed is considered a significant weakness as compared to other individuals her age in the normal population. In addition, her ability in this area is significantly lower than her abilities in other areas. Therefore, Jessica's processing speed may be an area of concern and may have significant implications with regard to her ability to perform basic skills/ tasks quickly and automatically. Once basic skills are acquired, Jessica may need*

[1]Note that additional sources of information are necessary to support the finding of a disorder (e.g., slowed and labored reading, inability to complete assignments in a reasonable amount of time).

the accommodation of extended time or shortened assignments to allow her to complete typical academic tasks.

8. **Personal Weakness/Uncommon but not a Normative Weakness**
   Interpretation: Jessica's processing speed is considered a significant weakness compared to her abilities in other areas. In fact, the difference between her processing speed and her abilities in other areas is so large that it is not commonly found in the normal population. Therefore, Jessica's processing speed is a notable Personal Weakness, a finding that may play a role in developing educational interventions. Note that the latter part of this interpretive statement may be germane only when the actual Processing Speed standard score is in the lower end of the Average Range (i.e., 85–90), suggesting that interventions or accommodations may be warranted. The finding of a Personal Weakness that is uncommon in the normal population does not provide de facto evidence of a processing disorder. This is because it is feasible for a child to have a Personal Weakness/Uncommon that is associated with a standard score that falls in either the Average/Within Normal Limits range or the Above Average/Normative Strength Range.

9. **Normative Weakness but not a Personal Weakness**
   Interpretation: Jessica's processing speed is considered a significant weakness compared to other children her age in the normal population. Her processing speed is a notable weakness and suggests that she may have a disorder in this basic psychological process, a finding that should play an essential role in developing educational interventions.[2]

10. **Personal Weakness/Not Uncommon but not a Normative Weakness**
    Interpretation: Jessica's processing speed is considered a significant weakness compared to her abilities in other areas. Her processing speed is a notable Personal Weakness. However, the finding of a Personal Weakness, in and of itself, does not provide de facto evidence of a processing disorder. A Personal Weakness that is associated with a standard score that falls Within Normal Limits or higher does not, in and of itself, provide evidence of a disorder. Also, it is feasible for a child to have a Personal Weakness/Not Uncommon that is associated with a standard score that falls in the Above Average/Normative Strength range.

OTHER

11. **Index is not interpretable as a unitary construct**
    Description: The Processing Speed Index (PSI), a measure of Processing Speed (Gs), represents Jessica's ability to fluently and automatically perform cognitive tasks, especially when under pressure to maintain focused attention and concentration. Jessica's Gs was assessed by tasks that required her to copy a series of symbols that are paired with numbers using a key (Coding)

[2]Ibid.

(continued)

and indicate the presence or absence of a target symbol within a search group (Symbol Search). The variability among Jessica's performances on these tasks was unusually large, indicating that her overall Gs ability cannot be summarized in a single score (i.e., the PSI).

12. Index is unitary but is neither a strength nor a weakness

Interpretation: The Processing Speed Index (PSI), a measure of Processing Speed (Gs), represents Jessica's ability to fluently and automatically perform cognitive tasks, especially when under pressure to maintain focused attention and concentration. Jessica's Gs was assessed by tasks that required her to copy a series of symbols that are paired with numbers using a key (Coding) and indicate the presence or absence of a target symbol within a search group (Symbol Search). Jessica obtained a PSI standard score of 100, which is ranked at the 50th percentile and is classified as Average Range/Within Normal Limits.

we believe may provide potentially meaningful hypotheses about a child's cognitive capabilities—beyond the information generated from the Index Profile Analysis.

In this step, comparisons are made between pairs of *clinical clusters*. Each clinical cluster is comprised of two or three subtests. Examiners may decide a priori to conduct one or more of these comparisons, in which case the comparisons would be referred to as *Planned* Clinical Comparisons. Alternatively, examiners may decide to conduct one or more of these comparisons *after* they have evaluated a child's performance on the core battery, in which case the comparisons would be referred to as *Post Hoc* Clinical Comparisons.

Rapid Reference 4.12 lists the clinical clusters and the subtests they comprise. Table 4.4 provides internal consistency reliability coefficients and SEMs for each clinical cluster by age and overall WISC-IV standardization sample.

Step 7a. Prior to conducting clinical comparisons, you must first determine whether the clusters in the comparison represent unitary abilities or processes. To do this, compute the difference between the highest and lowest scaled scores that make up the clinical cluster. Answer the following question: *Is the size of the scaled score difference less than 5?*

- If YES, then the clinical cluster represents a unitary ability or process and the clinical comparison that includes this cluster may be made *only* if the other cluster in the comparison also represents a unitary ability or process. Proceed to Step 7b.
- If NO, then the clinical cluster does not represent a unitary ability or process and the clinical comparison that includes this cluster should not be made.

≡ *Rapid Reference 4.12*

Composition of CHC Clinical Clusters

Clinical Comparison

Clinical Cluster: Subtests Composing Cluster

1. Fluid Reasoning vs. Visual Processing

Fluid Reasoning (*Gf*) Cluster:
Matrix Reasoning + Picture Concepts + Arithmetic
Definition: The Fluid Reasoning (*Gf*) Cluster consists of three subtests that measure the broad *Gf* ability in CHC theory. *Gf* is defined as encompassing the mental operations that an individual uses when faced with a novel task that cannot be performed automatically. These mental operations include forming and recognizing concepts, perceiving relationships among patterns, drawing inferences, problem solving, and so forth. Matrix Reasoning and Arithmetic primarily measure the narrow *Gf* ability of *General Sequential Reasoning (Deduction)*, which is defined as the ability to start with stated rules, premises, or conditions and to engage in one or more steps to reach a solution to a novel problem. Matrix Reasoning also involves Induction (I). Arithmetic also measures Math Achievement (A3) and Quantitative Reasoning (RQ). Its primary classification as a measure of *Gf* is based on the research of Keith and colleagues (2006). Picture Concepts primarily measures the narrow *Gf* ability of *Induction*, which is defined as the ability to discover the underlying characteristic (e.g., rule, concept, process, trend, class membership) that governs a problem or set of materials. Matrix Reasoning appears to measure both Deduction and Induction about equally. Although the tests this cluster comprises may involve CHC abilities other than *Gf* (e.g., Visual Processing, Crystallized Intelligence, Quantitative Knowledge, Short-Term Memory), the label *Fluid Reasoning* reflects the *primary ability measured by these tests.*

Note that although Keith et al.'s (2006) results demonstrated a robust *Gf* factor consisting of Matrix Resoning, Picture Concepts, and Arithmetic across most of the age range of the WISC-IV, Arithmetic likely only loaded on the *Gf* factor because there were no other measures of Quantitative Knowledge (*Gq*) included in their analysis. The failure for the Arithmetic *Gq* loading to emerge in the Keith and colleagues (2006) analysis is due to this study being a *within-battery* factor-analysis (McGrew & Flanagan, 1998) study with insufficient indicators for all major CHC domains. In ten different joint or *cross-battery* factor analyses (McGrew & Flanagan, 1998) that included adequate indicators of the major CHC domains, Arithmetic has never displayed a salient *Gf* factor loading but, instead, a consistent *Gq* factor loading. Woodcock (1990) reported a median *Gq* loading of .753 across eight samples. McGrew, Woodcock, and Ford (2002) similarly found Arithmetic to load only on *Gq* in a WJ III/WAIS-III/WMS-III

(continued)

cross-battery study (see Kaufman & Licthenberger, 2002). Finally, Arithmetic again failed to load on *Gf* and, instead, loaded .69 on *Gq* and .20 on *Gs* in a joint WJII/WISC-III cross-battery factor-analysis study (Phelps, McGrew, Knopik, & Ford, 2005). As such, when only the WISC-IV tests are administered, it would not be uncommon to find Arithmetic performance to be more consistent with Matrix Reasoning and Picture Concepts as compared to the other subtests included on the battery (which is why the interpretive system included in this book allows for the calculation of a *Gf* clinical cluster based on the aggregate of these three subtests). However, if other *Gq* tests are included in an assessment along with the WISC-IV Arithmetic subtest, then it is likely that Arithmetic performance would be more consistent with other tests of math knowledge and math achievement as compared to tests of *Gf*. Given the complex nature of Arithmetic, however, it is also likely that short-term memory (*Gsm*; e.g., working memory), in particular, and possibly *Gs*, could either facilitate or inhibit performance on this subtest.

Visual Processing (*Gv*) Cluster:
Block Design + Picture Completion

Definition: The Visual Processing (*Gv*) Cluster consists of two subtests that measure the broad *Gv* ability in CHC theory. *Gv* is defined as the ability to generate, perceive, analyze, synthesize, store, retrieve, manipulate, and transform visual patterns and stimuli. Block Design primarily measures the narrow *Gv* ability of *Spatial Relations*, which is defined as the ability to perceive and manipulate visual patterns rapidly or to maintain orientation with respect to objects in space. Picture Completion primarily measures the narrow *Gv* ability of *Flexibility of Closure*, which is defined as the ability to find, apprehend, and identify a visual figure or pattern embedded in a complex visual array *when knowing in advance* what the pattern is. Although Picture Completion may also involve specific *Gc* abilities (e.g., General Information), the label *Visual Processing* reflects the primary ability measured by this test.

2. Nonverbal Fluid Reasoning vs. Visual Processing

Nonverbal Fluid Reasoning (*Gf*-nonverbal) Cluster:
Matrix Reasoning + Picture Concepts

Definition: The Nonverbal Fluid Reasoning (*Gf*-nonverbal) Cluster consists of two subtests that measure the broad *Gf* ability in CHC theory. *Gf* was defined in Comparison 1. The *Gf*-nonverbal Cluster is less broad than the *Gf* Cluster in Comparison 1. Specifically, because this cluster does not include AR, it deemphasizes receptive language and short-term memory demands. Also, because both Matrix Reasoning and Picture Concepts involve the use of visual stimuli and require only a pointing response, the *Gf* ability underlying this cluster was qualified with the term *nonverbal*.

Visual Processing (*Gv*) Cluster:
Block Design + Picture Completion

Definition: The Visual Processing (*Gv*) Cluster was defined in Comparison 1.

3. Nonverbal Fluid Reasoning vs. Verbal Fluid Reasoning

Nonverbal Fluid Reasoning (*Gf*-nonverbal) Cluster:
Matrix Reasoning + Picture Concepts

Definition: The Nonverbal Fluid Reasoning (Gf-nonverbal) Cluster was defined in Comparison 2.

Verbal Fluid Reasoning (*Gf*-verbal) Cluster:
Similarities + Word Reasoning

Definition: The Verbal Fluid Reasoning (*Gf*-verbal) Cluster consists of two subtests that primarily measure the broad *Gc* ability in CHC theory but also involves reasoning (*Gf*). *Gc* is defined as the breadth and depth of a person's accumulated knowledge of a culture and the effective use of that knowledge. Similarities measures the narrow *Gc* ability of *Language Development*, which is defined as the general development of—or the understanding of words, sentences, and paragraphs (*not* requiring reading) in—spoken native language skills. Word Reasoning measures the narrow *Gc* ability of *Lexical Knowledge*, which is defined as the extent of vocabulary that can be understood in terms of correct word meanings. Because Similarities and Word Reasoning (although primarily verbal or *Gc* subtests) both require the ability to reason (inductively) with verbal stimuli, we chose to label this cluster *Verbal* Fluid Reasoning.

4. Lexical Knowledge vs. General Information

Lexical Knowledge (Gc-VL) Cluster:
Word Reasoning + Vocabulary

Definition: The Lexical Knowledge (*Gc*-VL) Cluster consists of two subtests that primarily measure the broad *Gc* ability in CHC theory. *Gc* was defined in Comparison 3. These subtests, Word Reasoning and Vocabulary, measure the narrow *Gc* ability of *Lexical Knowledge*, which is defined as the extent of vocabulary that can be understood in terms of correct word meanings. Therefore, we chose to label this cluster *Lexical Knowledge*.

General Information (Gc-K0) Cluster:
Comprehension + Information

Definition: The General Information (*Gc*-K0) Cluster consists of two subtests that primarily measure the broad *Gc* ability in CHC theory. *Gc* was defined in Comparison 3. These subtests, Comprehension and Information, measure the narrow *Gc* ability of *General Information*, which is defined as an individual's range of general knowledge. Therefore, we chose to label this cluster *General Information*.

5. Long-Term Memory vs. Short-Term Memory

Long-Term Memory (Gc-LTM) Cluster:
Information + Vocabulary

Definition: The Long-Term Memory (*Gc*-LTM) Cluster consists of two subtests that measure the broad *Gc* ability in CHC theory. *Gc* was defined in Comparison

(continued)

3. These subtests, Information and Vocabulary, measure to a greater or lesser extent the narrow *Gc* ability of General Information. Vocabulary also measures the narrow *Gc* ability of Lexical Knowledge. However, because both Information and Vocabulary represent knowledge that is typically stored in long-term memory, we chose to label this cluster *Long-Term Memory*. Note that Long-Term Memory is not a CHC label per se and therefore should not be confused with the broad Long-Term Retrieval (*Glr*) ability in CHC theory.

Short-Term Memory (*Gsm*-WM) Cluster:[1]
Letter-Number Sequencing + Digit Span

Definition: The Short-Term Memory (*Gsm*-WM) Cluster consists of two subtests that measure the broad *Gsm* ability in CHC theory. *Gsm* is defined as the ability to apprehend and hold information in immediate awareness and to use it within a few seconds. Letter-Number Sequencing and Digit Span (Backward) measure the narrow *Gsm* ability of *Working Memory*, which is defined as the ability to temporarily store and perform a set of cognitive operations on information that requires divided attention and the management of the limited capacity of short-term memory. Digit Span also measures the narrow *Gsm* ability of *Memory Span*, which is defined as the ability to attend to and immediately recall temporally ordered elements in the correct order after a single presentation.

6. Long-Term Memory vs. Verbal Fluid Reasoning

Long-Term Memory (*Gc*-LTM) Cluster:
Vocabulary + Information

Definition: The Long-Term Memory (*Gc*-LTM) Cluster was defined in Comparison 5.

Verbal Fluid Reasoning (*Gf*-verbal) Cluster:
Similarities + Word Reasoning

Definition: The Verbal Fluid Reasoning (*Gf*-verbal) Cluster was defined in Comparison 3.

[1]The Short-Term Memory (*Gsm*-WM) Cluster is identical to the WISC-IV Working Memory Index (WMI).

Step 7b. Calculate the clinical cluster by summing the scaled scores for the subtests that compose the clinical cluster and converting the sum to a standard score using Appendix H (which is located on the CD accompanying this book). Note that unitary clinical clusters are computed and reported automatically by the XBA DMIA.

Step 7c. Determine whether the size of the difference between the clusters in the comparison is unusually large or uncommon, occurring less than 10% of the time in the WISC-IV standardization sample. To do this, calculate the difference between the clusters in the comparison. If the size of the

DON'T FORGET

When Can I Compare Clinical Clusters?

Comparisons between clinical clusters can be made only when both clusters in the comparison represent unitary abilities.

Table 4.4 Internal Consistency Reliability Coefficients and SEMs for the WISC-IV Clinical Clusters, by Age and Overall Sample

Cluster	\					Age						All
	6	7	8	9	10	11	12	13	14	15	16	
_Gf_												
Reliability	.92	.94	.93	.94	.94	.93	.93	.92	.92	.92	.92	**.93**
SEM	4.24	3.67	3.97	3.67	3.67	3.97	3.97	4.24	4.24	4.24	4.24	**4.02**
_Gv_												
Reliability	.88	.89	.90	.89	.90	.92	.91	.91	.89	.91	.91	**.90**
SEM	5.20	4.97	4.74	4.97	4.74	4.24	4.50	4.50	4.97	4.50	4.50	**4.72**
_Gf_-nonverbal												
Reliability	.90	.91	.91	.92	.91	.90	.91	.89	.90	.88	.88	**.90**
SEM	4.74	4.50	4.50	4.24	4.50	4.74	4.50	4.97	4.74	5.20	5.20	**4.72**
_Gf_-verbal												
Reliability	.87	.89	.90	.90	.90	.87	.89	.89	.91	.92	.89	**.89**
SEM	5.41	4.97	4.74	4.74	4.74	5.41	4.97	4.97	4.50	4.24	4.97	**4.89**
_Gc_-VL												
Reliability	.88	.89	.91	.91	.91	.90	.90	.91	.92	.94	.91	**.91**
SEM	5.20	4.97	4.50	4.50	4.50	4.74	4.74	4.50	4.24	3.67	4.50	**4.57**

(*continued*)

Table 4.4 (Continued)

Cluster	Age											
	6	7	8	9	10	11	12	13	14	15	16	All
Gc-K0												
Reliability	.88	.85	.87	.89	.88	.89	.92	.90	.91	.92	.93	**.90**
SEM	5.20	5.81	5.41	4.97	5.20	4.97	4.24	4.74	4.50	4.24	3.97	**4.87**
Gc-LTM												
Reliability	.89	.89	.91	.92	.93	.92	.94	.94	.94	.96	.95	**.93**
SEM	4.97	4.97	4.50	4.24	3.97	4.24	3.67	3.67	3.67	3.00	3.35	**4.07**
Gsm-WM												
Reliability	.92	.90	.91	.92	.92	.92	.93	.91	.93	.92	.93	**.92**
SEM	4.24	4.74	4.50	4.24	4.24	4.24	3.97	4.50	3.97	4.24	3.97	**4.27**

Source: Wechsler Intelligence Scale for Children–Fourth Edition. Copyright © 2003 by Harcourt Assessment, Inc. Reproduced by permission of the publisher. All rights reserved. Wechsler Intelligence Scale for Children and WISC are trademarks of Harcourt Assessment, Inc., registered in the United States of America and/or other jurisdictions.

Note: The Short-Term Memory (Gsm-WM) Cluster is identical to the WISC-IV Working Memory Index (WMI). SEM = standard error of measurement; Gf = Fluid Reasoning; Gv = Visual Processing; Gf-nonverbal = Nonverbal Fluid Reasoning; Gf-verbal = Verbal Fluid Reasoning; Gc-VL = Lexical Knowledge; Gc-K0 = General Information; Gc-LTM = Long-Term Memory; and Gsm-WM = Working Memory.

difference is equal to or greater than the value reported for the comparison in Table 4.5, then the difference is uncommon. If the size of the difference between the two clusters in the comparison is less than the table value, then the difference is not uncommon. Rapid Reference 4.13 provides examples of interpretive statements that may be used in psychological reports to describe the findings of Planned and Post Hoc Clinical Comparisons. Specifically, a comparison between two interpretable clinical clusters can have either one of two outcomes:

1. The size of the difference between the two interpretable clinical clusters is uncommon in the normative population.
2. The size of the difference between the two interpretable clinical clusters is not uncommon in the normative population.

Figure 4.13 shows Steps 7a through 7c of the WISC-IV interpretive worksheet from Appendix E, computed by hand, for Ryan. Note that Steps 7a through 7c are computed automatically by the WISC-IV DMIA (see Figure 4.14). The definitions of the eight clinical clusters are provided on the Step 7c tab of the WISC-IV DMIA (although they have been omitted from Figure 4.14).

Table 4.5 Size of Difference between Pairs of Clinical Clusters Needed to Be Considered Unusually Large or Uncommon

Cluster Comparison	Amount of Difference
Fluid Reasoning (*Gf*)—Visual Processing (*Gv*)	21
Nonverbal Fluid Reasoning (*Gf*-nonverbal)—Visual Processing (*Gv*)	24
Verbal Fluid Reasoning (*Gf* verbal)—Nonverbal Fluid Reasoning (*Gf*-nonverbal)	24
Lexical Knowledge (*Gc*-VL)—General Information (*Gc*-K0)	17
Long-Term Memory (*Gc*-LTM)—Short-Term Memory (*Gsm*-WM)[a]	24
Long-Term Memory (*Gc*-LTM)—Verbal Fluid Reasoning (*Gf*-verbal)	17

Source: Wechsler Intelligence Scale for Children–Fourth Edition. Copyright © 2003 by Harcourt Assessment, Inc. Reproduced by permission of the publisher. All rights reserved. *Wechsler Intelligence Scale for Children and WISC* are trademarks of Harcourt Assessment, Inc., registered in the United States of America and/or other jurisdictions.

Note: "Unusually large or uncommon" denotes differences occurring less than 10% of the time in the WISC-IV Standardization Sample.

[a] The Short-Term Memory (*Gsm*-WM) Cluster is identical to the WISC-IV Working Memory Index (WMI).

Examples of How to Describe the Findings of Planned and Post Hoc Clinical Comparisons in a Psychological Report

Planned Clinical Comparison Finding	Both SS ≤ 85	One SS < 85 One SS ≥ 85	Both SS 85–115 (inclusive)	One SS < 115 One SS ≥ 115	Both SS ≥ 115
Difference Not Uncommon	Interpretive Statement 1	Interpretive Statement 2	Interpretive Statement 3	Interpretive Statement 4	Interpretive Statement 5
Difference Uncommon	Interpretive Statement 6	Interpretive Statement 7	Interpretive Statement 8	Interpretive Statement 9	Interpretive Statement 10

Note: SS = Standard Score.

INTERPRETIVE STATEMENT (the following numbers correspond to numbers in table)

1. Example: *Verbal Fluid Reasoning (Gf-verbal) Cluster = 80; Nonverbal Fluid Reasoning (Gf-nonverbal) Cluster = 75. The difference between Bob's Gf-verbal Cluster of 80 (9th percentile) and his Gf-nonverbal Cluster of 75 (5th percentile) was not unusually large, indicating that it is not uncommon to find a difference of this magnitude in the normative population. Nevertheless, it is important to recognize that Bob's abilities to reason with both verbal and nonverbal information are Below Average and therefore represent Normative Weaknesses relative to his age mates.*

2. Example: *Long-Term Memory (Gc-LTM) Cluster = 90; Verbal Fluid Reasoning (Gf-verbal) Cluster = 84. The difference between Bob's Gc-LTM Cluster of 90 (25th percentile) and his Gf-verbal Cluster of 84 (14th percentile) was not unusually large, indicating that it is not uncommon to find a difference of this magnitude in the normative population. Nevertheless, it is important to recognize that Bob's ability to reason with knowledge (Gf-verbal) fell within the Below Average range of functioning and represents a Normative Weakness relative to his age mates.*

3. Example: Long-Term Memory (Gc-LTM) Cluster = 106; Short-Term Memory (Gsm-WM) Cluster = 100. The difference between Bob's Gc-LTM Cluster of 106 (65th percentile) and his Gsm-WM Cluster of 100 (50th percentile) was not unusually large, indicating that it is not uncommon to find a difference of this magnitude in the normative population. Relative to his age mates, Bob's performances in these areas are within the Average Range of functioning or Within Normal Limits.

4. Example: Nonverbal Fluid Reasoning (Gf-nonverbal) Cluster = 118; Visual Processing (Gv) Cluster = 112. The difference between Bob's Gf-nonverbal Cluster of 118 (88th percentile) and his Gv Cluster of 112 (79th percentile) was not unusually large, indicating that it is not uncommon to find a difference of this magnitude in the normative population. Relative to his age mates, Bob's Gv ability is within the Average Range of functioning, and his Gf-nonverbal ability is Above Average and therefore represents a Normative Strength.

5. Example: Lexical Knowledge (Gc-VL) Cluster = 125; General Information (Gc-K0) Cluster = 120. The difference between Bob's Gc-VL Cluster of 125 (95th percentile) and his Gc-K0 Cluster of 120 (91st percentile) was not unusually large, indicating that it is not uncommon to find a difference of this magnitude in the normative population. Relative to his age mates, Bob's lexical knowledge and general information abilities are Above Average (or if scores are >130, then "in the Upper Extreme") and therefore represent Normative Strengths.

6. Example: Visual Processing (Gv) Cluster = 84; Nonverbal Fluid Reasoning (Gf-nonverbal) Cluster = 60. The difference between Bob's Gv Cluster of 84 (14th percentile; Below Average/Normative Weakness) and his Gf-nonverbal Cluster of 60 (≤ 1st percentile; Lower Extreme/Normative Weakness) is unusually large (differences as large as Bob's discrepancy of 24 points occur less than 10% of the time in the normative population). Higher standard scores on Gv than Gf-nonverbal can occur for many reasons. For example, some children might have a better ability to analyze or manipulate isolated aspects of visual stimuli than to reason with such stimuli. Although Bob's visual processing is better developed than his fluid reasoning, it is important to recognize that Bob demonstrated Normative Weaknesses in both domains. Note that Bob's Gf-nonverbal ability, in particular, represents a disorder in a basic psychological process—but only when this Lower Extreme performance is corroborated by other data sources.

7. Example: Verbal Fluid Reasoning (Gf-verbal) Cluster = 110; Nonverbal Fluid Reasoning (Gf-nonverbal) Cluster = 83. The difference between Bob's Gf-verbal Cluster of 110 (75th percentile; Average Range/Within Normal Limits) and h's Gf-nonverbal Cluster of 83 (13th percentile; Below Average/Normative Weakness) is unusually large (differences as large as Bob's discrepancy of 27 points occur less than 10% of the time in the normative population). Higher standard scores on Gf-verbal than Gf-nonverbal can occur for many reasons. For example, some children might have the ability to reason with verbal information but have difficulty applying their reasoning skills in a similar manner when the stimuli are visual in nature. Not only is Bob's nonverbal fluid reasoning ability less well developed than his verbal fluid reasoning ability, it is also Below Average relative to his age mates and therefore is a Normative Weakness.

(continued)

8. Example: Long-Term Memory (Gc-LTM) Cluster = 115; Verbal Fluid Reasoning (Gf-verbal) Cluster = 85. The difference between Bob's Gc-LTM Cluster of 115 (84th percentile; Average Range/Within Normal Limits) and his Gf-verbal Cluster of 85 (16th percentile; Average Range/Within Normal Limits) is unusually large (differences as large as Bob's discrepancy of 30 points occur less than 10% of the time in the normative population). Higher standard scores on Gc-LTM than Gf-verbal can occur for many reasons. For example, some children might have a well-developed fund of information but are unable to reason well with this information. Although Bob's performance in both domains falls Within Normal Limits relative to his age mates, it would not be unusual for Bob to become easily frustrated when required to reason with general information (e.g., drawing inferences from text).

9. Example: Short-Term Memory (Gsm-WM) Cluster = 116; Long-Term Memory (Gc-LTM) Cluster = 86. The difference between Bob's Gsm-WM Cluster of 116 (86th percentile; Above Average/Normative Strength) and his Gc-LTM Cluster of 86 (17th percentile; Average Range/Within Normal Limits) is unusually large (differences as large as Bob's discrepancy of 30 points occur less than 10% of the time in the normative population). Higher standard scores on Gsm-WM than Gc-LTM can occur for many reasons. For example, some children might have the ability to encode information in immediate awareness long enough to manipulate or transform it but have difficulty retrieving this information. Although Bob's performance in long-term memory falls within Normal Limits relative to his age mates, he may benefit from strategies designed to facilitate information storage and retrieval (e.g., use of mnemonics). (Note: When the standard score on the lower cluster in the comparison is < 85, then replace the last sentence with "Not only is Bob's long-term memory ability less well developed than his short-term memory ability, but it is also in the Below Average [or Lower Extreme, depending on the score] range of functioning relative to his age mates and therefore represents a Normative Weakness." Also note that Bob's Below Average [or Lower Extreme] performance in long-term memory represents a disorder in a basic psychological process—but only when such performance is corroborated by other data sources.)

10. Example: Verbal Fluid Reasoning (Gf-verbal) Cluster = 146; Nonverbal Fluid Reasoning (Gf-nonverbal) Cluster = 116. The difference between Bob's Gf-verbal Cluster of 146 (>99th percentile; Upper Extreme/Normative Strength) and his Gf-nonverbal Cluster of 116 (86th percentile; Above Average/ Normative Strength) is unusually large (differences as large as Bob's discrepancy of 30 points occur less than 10% of the time in the normative population). Nevertheless, it is important to recognize that Bob's abilities to reason with both verbal and nonverbal information are very well developed, falling in the Upper Extreme and Above Average ranges, respectively, compared to his age mates and therefore represent Normative Strengths.

STEP 7. (Optional) Conduct Select Clinical Comparisons

There are six possible clinical comparisons. Select which of the six (if any) make sense to compare based on either the referral question(s) or assessment results (see Rapid Reference 4.12).

Step 7a. Determine whether each clinical cluster is unitary. Using the table below (at left), record the scaled score (SS) for each relevant subtest. On the lines to the right of the table, subtract the lowest from the highest scaled scores to compute the differences. If a difference equals or exceeds 5 points (i.e., 1.5 SDs), the related clinical cluster is not unitary and cannot be used to conduct clinical comparisons. If a difference is less than 5 points, then the clinical cluster is unitary. Clinical comparisons may be made *only* when both clusters that make up the comparison are unitary.

Subtest	SS
MR	9
PCn	10
AR	11
BD	6
PCm	8
SI	9
WR	6
VO	7
CO	13
IN	12
LNS	7
DS	7

Fluid Reasoning (*Gf*) Cluster
Matrix Reasoning + Picture Concepts + Arithmetic
11 (Highest) − 9 (Lowest) = 2 (Difference)

Visual Processing (*Gv*) Cluster
Block Design + Picture Completion
8 (Highest) − 6 (Lowest) = 2 (Difference)

Nonverbal Fluid Reasoning (*Gf*-nonverbal) Cluster
Matrix Reasoning + Picture Concepts
10 (Highest) − 9 (Lowest) = 1 (Difference)

Verbal Fluid Reasoning (*Gf*-verbal) Cluster
Similarities + Word Reasoning
9 (Highest) − 6 (Lowest) = 3 (Difference)

Lexical Knowledge (*Gc*-VL) Cluster
Word Reasoning − Vocabulary
7 (Highest) − 6 (Lowest) = 1 (Difference)

General Information (*Gc*-K0) Cluster
Comprehension + Information
13 (Highest) − 12 (Lowest) = 1 (Difference)

Long-Term Memory (*Gc*-LTM) Cluster
Vocabulary + Information
12 (Highest) − 7 (Lowest) = 5 (Difference)

Short-Term Memory (*Gsm*-MW) Cluster
Letter-Number Sequencing + Digit Span
7 (Highest) − 7 (Lowest) = 0 (Difference)

Figure 4.13 WISC-IV Interpretive Worksheet: STEP 7, Illustrated for Ryan, Age 10

Step 7b. For unitary clusters only, sum the scaled scores for the subtests that compose the cluster. Convert the sums of scaled scores to clinical clusters (i.e., standard scores having a mean of 100 and SD of 15) using Appendix H.

Subtest	SS
MR	9
PCn	10
AR	11
BD	6
PCm	8
SI	9
WR	6
VO	7
CO	13
IN	12
LNS	7
DS	7

$$\frac{9}{(MR)} + \frac{10}{(PCn)} + \frac{11}{(AR)} = \frac{30}{(Sum\ of\ Scaled\ Scores)} = 100 \quad Gf\ Cluster$$

$$\frac{6}{(BD)} + \frac{8}{(PCm)} = \frac{14}{(Sum\ of\ Scaled\ Scores)} = 83 \quad Gv\ Cluster$$

$$\frac{9}{(MR)} + \frac{10}{(PCn)} = \frac{19}{(Sum\ of\ Scaled\ Scores)} = 97 \quad Gf\text{-nonverbal Cluster}$$

$$\frac{9}{(SI)} + \frac{6}{(WR)} = \frac{15}{(Sum\ of\ Scaled\ Scores)} = 86 \quad Gf\text{-verbal Cluster}$$

$$\frac{6}{(WR)} + \frac{7}{(VO)} = \frac{13}{(Sum\ of\ Scaled\ Scores)} = 81 \quad Gc\text{-VL Cluster}$$

$$\frac{13}{(CO)} + \frac{12}{(IN)} = \frac{25}{(Sum\ of\ Scaled\ Scores)} = 114 \quad Gc\text{-K0 Cluster}$$

$$\frac{}{(VO)} + \frac{}{(IN)} = \frac{}{(Sum\ of\ Scaled\ Scores)} = \quad Gc\text{-LTM Cluster}$$

$$\frac{7}{(LNS)} + \frac{7}{(DS)} = \frac{14}{(Sum\ of\ Scaled\ Scores)} = 83 \quad Gsm\text{-MW Cluster}$$

Figure 4.13 (Continued)

Note: For Ryan, the Gc-LTM Cluster is not interpretable. Therefore, no standard score is computed for that cluster.

Step 7c. **Conduct Planned Clinical Comparisons.**

Calculate the difference between the clusters in the comparison. If the size of the difference is equal to or greater than the value reported in the following table, then the difference is uncommon. If the size of the difference is less than the table value, then the difference is not uncommon.

Clinical Comparison	Difference Score (use values from Step 7b to calculate difference score)	Critical Value	Uncommon (U) or Not Uncommon (NU)
Gf versus *Gv*	100 − 83 = 17	≥ 21	NU
Gf-nonverbal versus *Gv*	97 − 83 = 14	≥ 24	NU
Gf-nonverbal versus *Gf*-verbal	97 − 86 = 11	≥ 24	NU
Gc-VL versus *Gc*-K0	114 − 81 = 33	≥ 17	U
Gc-LTM versus *Gsm*-MW		≥ 24	
Gc-LTM versus *Gf*-verbal		≥ 17	

Note: Difference scores that are equal to or exceed the critical values listed in the third column of this table should be denoted Uncommon (U). Difference scores that are less than these critical values should be denoted Not Uncommon (NU).

Step 7d. **Describe results of Planned Clinical Comparisons.**

Regardless of the outcome of Step 7c, review Rapid Reference 4.13 to identify an example of an interpretive statement that most appropriately describes the results of the child's clinical cluster comparison. If the child demonstrated a Normative Weakness in any clinical cluster, refer to Rapid Reference 4.14 for hypotheses about the meaning of such findings. Rapid Reference 4.14 also provides suggestions for educational interventions and instructional strategies that may be useful for children who demonstrate uncommon patterns of performance on the WISC-IV clinical clusters.

Note: MR = Matrix Reasoning; PCn = Picture Concepts; AR = Arithmetic; BD = Block Design; PCm = Picture Completion; SI = Similarities; WR = Word Reasoning; VO = Vocabulary; CO = Comprehension; IN = Information; LNS = Letter-Number Sequencing; DS = Digit Span.

Figure 4.13 (Continued)

Step 7 (Optional). Clinical comparisons are conducted. This step determines whether each clinical cluster is unitary and, therefore, interpretable.

There are six possible clinical comparisons.

You can evaluate all 6 comparisons, or select the comparisons that are most appropriate for the examinee based on the referral questions and assessment results.

Step 7a.   The difference between the highest and lowest subtest scaled scores in a cluster is calculated.

If the size of the difference is less than 5 points, then the clinical cluster is unitary.

Cluster	Highest		Lowest		Difference	Result
Fluid Reasoning Gf Cluster	11	-	9	=	2	YES, interpretable
Visual Processing Gv Cluster	8	-	6	=	2	YES, interpretable
Nonverbal Fluid Reasoning Gf-nonverbal Cluster	10	-	9	=	1	YES, interpretable
Verbal Fluid Reasoning Gf-verbal Cluster	9	-	6	=	3	YES, interpretable
Lexical Knowledge Gc-VL Cluster	7	-	6	=	1	YES, interpretable
General Information Gc-K0 Cluster	13	-	12	=	1	YES, interpretable
Long-Term Memory Gc-LTM Cluster	12	-	7	=	5	NO, not interpretable
Short-Term Memory Gsm-MW Cluster	7	-	7	=	0	YES, interpretable

THE PROGRAM AUTOMATICALLY CALCULATES ALL INTERPRETABLE CLINICAL CLUSTERS IN STEP 7b

Figure 4.14 Steps 7a-c of the Data Management and Interpretive Assistant v1.0, Illustrated for Ryan

Step 7b. Clinical clusters that represent unitary abilities or processes are calculated by summing the scaled scores for the subtests that comprise the cluster and converting the sum to clinical cluster standard score.

THE PROGRAM AUTOMATICALLY CALCULATES ALL CLINICAL CLUSTERS

					Score	Conf. Intv.	Percentile
Fluid Reasoning							
Gf Cluster							
9	+	10	+	11	=	30	
MR		PCn		AR		Sum	
					Gf Cluster = **100**	92–108	50
Visual Processing							
Gv Cluster							
6	+	8	=	14			
BD		PCm		Sum			
					Gv Cluster = **83**	74–92	13
Nonverbal Fluid Reasoning							
Gf-nonverbal Cluster							
9	+	10	=	19			
MR		PCn		Sum			
					Gf-nonverbal Cluster = **97**	88–106	43
Verbal Fluid Reasoning							
Gf-verbal Cluster							
9	+	6	=	15			
SI		WR		Sum			
					Gf-verbal Cluster = **86**	76–96	17
Lexical Knowledge							
Gc-VL Cluster							
6	+	7	=	13			
WR		VC		Sum			
					Gc-VL Cluster = **81**	72–90	11
General Information							
Gc-K0 Cluster							
13	+	12	=	25			
CO		IN		Sum			
					Gc-K0 Cluster = **114**	104–124	83
Long-Term Memory							
Gc-LTM Cluster							
7	+	12	=	19			
VC		IN		Sum			
					Gc-LTM Cluster = **Not interpretable**		
Short-Term Memory							
Gsm-MW Cluster							
7	+	7	=	14			
					Gsm-MW Cluster = **83**	75–91	13

Figure 4.14 (Continued)

183

Step 7c. Clinical comparisons are conducted.

The difference between the clusters in the comparison is calculated.

If the size of the difference is equal to or greater than the critical value reported in the table below, then the difference is Uncommon (U).

If the size of the difference is less than the table value, then the difference is Not Uncommon (NU).

THE PROGRAM AUTOMATICALLY DETERMINES IF CLINICAL COMPARISONS ARE INTERPRETABLE

Clinical Comparison	Difference Score (use values from Step 7b)	Critical Value	Uncommon (U) or Not Uncommon (NU)	Is this comparison interpretable?
Gf versus Gv	17	21	NU	YES
Gf-nonverbal versus Gv	14	24	NU	YES
Gf-nonverbal versus Gf-verbal	11	24	NU	YES
Gc-VL versus Gc-K0	-33	17	U	YES
Gc-LTM versus Gsm-MW		24		NO
Gc-LTM versus Gf-verbal		17		NO

Figure 4.14 (Continued) Note: The definition of all clinical clusters are included on this tab (Step 7c) of the WISC-IV DMIA v1.0 but have been omitted from this figure.

Step 7d. Regardless of the outcome of Step 7c, review Rapid Reference 4.13 to identify an example of an interpretive statement that most appropriately describes the results of the child's clinical cluster comparison. If the child demonstrated a Normative Weakness in any clinical cluster, refer to Rapid Reference 4.14 for hypotheses about the meaning of such findings. Rapid Reference 4.14 also provides suggestions for educational interventions and instructional strategies that may be useful for children who demonstrate uncommon patterns of performance on the WISC-IV clinical clusters. An example of how to use Rapid References 4.13 and 4.14 follows.

≡ Rapid Reference 4.14

Hypotheses for Observed Differences Between Clinical Clusters and Suggestions for Intervention

Fluid Reasoning (*Gf*) Cluster > Visual Processing (*Gv*) Cluster or Nonverbal Fluid Reasoning (*Gf*-nonverbal) Cluster

Hypotheses for Observed Difference: This may indicate that the child's overall reasoning ability is good and that, despite difficulty with visual processing, the child can solve problems by focusing on characteristics that are less visual in nature. For example, on Matrix Reasoning, the child may not focus on the spatial aspects of the pattern to arrive at an answer (e.g., the pattern shifts from top to bottom, then left to right, then back to the top), but rather, he or she may focus on the number of dots in a pattern to complete the matrix. Also, a child with a Fluid Reasoning (*Gf*) Cluster higher than his or her Visual Processing (*Gv*) Cluster may do well when he or she uses a strategy such as verbal mediation to solve problems with substantial visual information. That is, a child may be able to solve a problem involving visual stimuli only after translating the visual information into verbal information.

Suggestions for Intervention: Instructional strategies that may be useful for a child with this pattern of performance include (a) avoiding excessive reliance on visual models, diagrams, and demonstrations; (b) accompanying visual demonstrations with oral explanations; and (c) breaking down spatial tasks into component parts (e.g., providing a set of verbal instructions to match each part). Additionally, because the child may have trouble forming a visual representation of a concept in his or her mind (e.g., a mental image), manipulatives or hands-on, concrete learning experiences may be beneficial when learning about an abstract concept that is visual in nature (e.g., the rotation of the planets in the solar system). Concrete or hands-on experiences should also be supplemented with verbal information.

(continued)

Visual Processing (*Gv*) Cluster > Fluid Reasoning (*Gf*) Cluster or Nonverbal Fluid Reasoning (*Gf*-nonverbal) Cluster

Hypotheses for Observed Difference: This may indicate that the child has good concrete visual skills but experiences difficulty when asked to reason with visual information. Implications may include difficulty with mathematical application tasks, such as making predictions based on visual stimuli (e.g., graphs, charts). A child with this pattern of performance may also have difficulty interpreting visual information. That is, a child with higher visual processing skills than visual reasoning skills may be able to see specific details in visual information but may have difficulty integrating visual information to solve problems.

Suggestions for Intervention: Instructional strategies that may be useful for a child with this pattern of performance include (a) providing step-by-step instructions for mathematical applications tasks that include if-then statements (e.g., "First, look at the slope of the line; next, determine the direction of the gradient; if the slope is positive, then interpret as follows"); (b) highlighting key visual information that must be integrated in some way to arrive at a solution to the problem.

Nonverbal Fluid Reasoning (*Gf*-nonverbal) Cluster > Verbal Fluid Reasoning (*Gf*-verbal) Cluster

Hypotheses for Observed Difference: This may indicate that the child can reason better with visually based stimuli as compared to verbal stimuli. A child with this pattern of performance may learn best when new information is presented visually.

Suggestions for Intervention: Instructional strategies that may be useful for a child with this pattern of performance include (a) allowing the child to sketch drawings or diagrams when learning new information or (b) providing visual adjuncts (e.g., graphs, charts, tables) when teaching verbal concepts.

Verbal Fluid Reasoning (*Gf*-verbal) Cluster > Nonverbal Fluid Reasoning (*Gf*-nonverbal) Cluster

Hypotheses for Observed Difference: This may indicate that the child can reason better with verbally based stimuli as compared to visual stimuli. A child with this pattern of performance may learn best when new information is presented verbally. Moreover, a child with this pattern of performance may do well with lecture formats that are primarily verbal in nature but may "get lost" when too many visual aids are used (e.g., graphs, diagrams) to teach a new concept.

Suggestions for Intervention: Instructional strategies that may be useful for a child with this pattern of performance are similar to those used with the Nonverbal Fluid Reasoning (*Gf*-nonverbal) Cluster > Visual Processing (*Gv*) Cluster pattern of performance described previously.

Lexical Knowledge (*Gc*-VL) Cluster > General Information (*Gc*-K0) Cluster

Hypotheses for Observed Difference: This may indicate that the child has facility with words and can reason with words but has minimal knowledge of factual information or has difficulty applying knowledge in specific situations. A child with this pattern of performance may have difficulty with written expression, in terms of breadth and depth of content, despite an appropriate vocabulary. On reading tasks, the child may be able to read (decode) well and generally comprehend what he or she is reading but may not be able to make meaningful connections or draw inferences due to a lack of background knowledge.

Suggestions for Intervention: Instructional strategies that may be useful for a child with this pattern of performance include (a) providing advanced organizers (outline of material to be discussed in a lecture); (b) teaching the student previewing strategies (e.g., skimming, scanning); (c) highlighting key information; (d) using a method of "what we know, what we don't know" to activate prior knowledge in the student before presenting new topics; and (e) having the student engage in prewriting activities (e.g., brainstorming about the ideas, words, and so on that the child plans to use in written work and assisting the child in "fleshing out" these ideas) when completing writing assignments.

General Information (*Gc*-K0) Cluster > Lexical Knowledge (*Gc*-VL) Cluster

Hypotheses for Observed Difference: This may indicate that the child has good knowledge of factual information but lacks facility with words and may have difficulty reasoning with words. On writing assignments, a child with this pattern of performance may have good content but may be unable to communicate his or her thoughts well. That is, the child's writing may appear immature (e.g., writing is bland, lacks variety with regard to adjectives). On reading tasks, a child with this pattern of performance may have good comprehension when reading about familiar topics, but he or she may have poor comprehension when reading about topics that are novel or that contain several unknown words. Thus, it is not unusual for a child with this pattern of performance to be described as having inconsistent comprehension skills.

Suggestions for Intervention: Instructional strategies that may be useful for a child with this pattern of performance include (a) providing a word bank for written expression tasks; (b) providing a glossary of terms that a child can refer to when completing reading assignments; (c) ensuring that test questions do not include vocabulary terms that are unknown; (d) reviewing or teaching vocabulary words when the child is asked to read from content-area texts; (e) writing key words and terms on the board when lecturing on new content areas; (f) ensuring that instructions contain words that the child knows; (g) simplifying instructions by extending upon unknown words with words that are familiar to the child or defining terms when initially presenting them (e.g., "The composition

(continued)

of igneous rock, that is, what it is made up of, is . . . ."); and (h) teaching the child to use a thesaurus when completing writing tasks.

Long-Term Memory (*Gc*-LTM) Cluster > Short-Term Memory (*Gsm*-WM) Cluster

Hypotheses for Observed Difference: This may indicate that the child can retrieve information but has trouble encoding the information. In other words, the child's stores of knowledge are likely the result of repeated practice using a number of meaningful associations. On reading and writing tasks, a child with this pattern of performance may do well with known topics but poorly on new ones. Additionally, due to difficulty with holding information in immediate awareness long enough to use it, a child with this pattern of performance may have difficulty efficiently copying information from written material or recording information from a lecture or from the board. Finally, a child with this pattern of performance may have difficulty with a bottom-up teaching approach in which the component parts of a general concept are presented separately and sequentially. This teaching approach may cause particular difficulty for the child primarily because he or she cannot hold the component parts in memory long enough to be able to synthesize them into the whole concept.

Suggestions for Intervention: Instructional strategies that may be useful for a child with this pattern of performance include (a) providing succinct directions; (b) ensuring that the child has retained sufficient information from a set of instructions to work independently; (c) providing written directions to supplement oral directions; (d) supplementing oral presentations and lectures by writing important information on the board; (e) repeating important information often; (f) using intonation in your voice to emphasize key points or words; (g) allowing for multiple exposures to new material using different instructional techniques; (h) underlining or highlighting key words in text so that the child has a quick visual aid when attempting to locate information that he or she may have forgotten; (i) encouraging the child to immediately record key information, new vocabulary words, and concepts presented in a lecture or in reading materials; (j) encouraging the child to develop a picture dictionary/encyclopedia that can serve as a word and concept bank to be used for completing assignments; (k) providing the child with a lecture outline in a cloze (fill-in-the-blank) format that allows him or her to record key words and concepts; (l) reducing copying tasks; (m) allowing extra time for copying information; (n) breaking instruction into parts; and (o) using a top-down approach for presenting new concepts, in which the entire concept is presented first, followed by the component parts.

Short-Term Memory (*Gsm*-WM Cluster) > Long-Term Memory (*Gc*-LTM) Cluster

Hypotheses for Observed Difference: This may indicate that the child can encode information but has trouble retrieving it. Children with this pattern may do well with new topics in the short term, but if there is a delay between their learning of information and the need to demonstrate their knowledge, they may demonstrate a poor outcome. A classic example of this is when a parent or teacher indicates that the child demonstrated an understanding of a particular topic while it was being presented but did not remember it later in the day. Also, a child with this pattern of performance is often described as knowing information shortly after studying it but not being able to demonstrate that knowledge later (e.g., on a cumulative exam). It is likely that these children are not forgetting information per se; rather, they are not encoding information at a level that is necessary for efficient retrieval.

Suggestions for Intervention: Instructional strategies that may be useful for a child with this pattern of performance include (a) employing test formats that require recognition (multiple choice, matching, true/false, and fill in the blank with an associated word bank) in favor of test formats that require recall (essay, fill in the blank without a word bank, writing definitions); and (b) introducing key words to the child to facilitate learning and retrieval.

Long-Term Memory (Gc-LTM) Cluster > Verbal Fluid Reasoning (Gf-verbal) Cluster

Hypotheses for Observed Difference: This may indicate that the child has an adequate fund of knowledge but cannot reason well with that knowledge.

Suggestions for Intervention: Instructional strategies that may be useful for a child with this pattern of performance include (a) using specific aids that make the reasoning process more concrete—for instance, if asked to make a prediction based on a reading passage, the child may benefit from a guided questions list that aids in the use of inductive strategies for arriving at the answer; (b) when working with math problems that involve reasoning, providing a guided steps list that aids in externalizing the reasoning process for the child (examples of guided steps include: determine known facts; determine what you are being asked to do; identify what operations should be used to solve a problem); (c) demonstrating the deductive reasoning process by providing various examples of how a rule can be applied across situations; (d) using study guides that contain facts and general information about a topic that can aid the child in completing reading and writing tasks; and (e) making abstract concepts more meaningful by using known information to teach the concept.

Verbal Fluid Reasoning (Gf-verbal) Cluster > Long-Term Memory (Gc-LTM) Cluster

Hypotheses for Observed Difference: This may indicate that the child can reason well, but that he or she has an insufficient amount of information to reason with.

Suggestions for Intervention: A general instructional strategy that may be useful for children with this pattern of performance is to ensure that they have

(continued)

the relevant information that is required to complete assignments; this may require providing them with a glossary of terms, study guides containing key facts about a specific topic, and so forth. The general goal is to ensure that a lack of foundational knowledge does not interfere with the student's ability to fully demonstrate his or her ability to reason with information (e.g., make predictions and inferences, draw conclusions).

Source: The interventions recommended above were based primarily on Mather and Jaffe (2002) and Shapiro (1996).

Ryan demonstrated an uncommon difference between his Lexical Knowledge (*Gc*-VL) Cluster of 81 and his General Information (*Gc*-K0) Cluster of 114. An interpretive statement that can be used to describe Ryan's specific performance pattern on the *Gc*-VL and *Gc*-K0 Post Hoc Clinical Comparison is found in Rapid Reference 4.13. This Rapid Reference shows that Ryan's *Gc*-VL versus *Gc*-K0 pattern corresponds to Interpretive Statement 7. This interpretive statement provides an example of how to describe a pattern of performance wherein one Index is < 85 and the other is ≥ 85 and the difference between them is uncommon. Using Ryan's *Gc*-VL versus *Gc*-K0 pattern of performance, the following interpretive statement may be made: *The difference between Ryan's General Information (Gc-K0) Cluster of 114 (83rd percentile; Average Range/Within Normal Limits) and his Lexical Knowledge (Gc-VL) Cluster of 81 (11th percentile; Below Average/Normative Weakness) is unusually large (differences as large as Ryan's discrepancy of 33 points occur less than 10% of the time in the normative population). Higher standard scores on Gc-K0 than Gc-VL can occur for many reasons. For example, some children might have an adequate fund of information but lack a strong vocabulary knowledge base and the ability to reason well with words. Not only is Ryan's lexical knowledge ability less well developed than his general information ability, but it is also in the Below Average range of functioning relative to his age mates and therefore is a Normative Weakness.*

Based on information provided in Rapid Reference 4.14, Ryan's pattern of performance (i.e., *Gc*-K0 > *Gc*-VL) may indicate that he has good knowledge of factual information but may lack facility with words and may have difficulty reasoning with words. Hence, Ryan may demonstrate difficulty communicating his thoughts well in writing, despite good content. More specifically, Ryan's writing may appear immature (e.g., bland, lacking variety with regard to adjectives). Although Ryan may demonstrate adequate comprehension when reading about familiar topics, he may have poor comprehension when reading about topics that are novel or that contain several unknown words. Thus, it would not be unusual for Ryan's reading comprehension skills to appear to be *inconsistent.*

In addition to providing information related to academic implications of specific performance patterns on the WISC-IV clinical clusters, Rapid Reference 4.14 also provides suggestions for intervention based on these patterns. In Ryan's case it may be beneficial to (a) provide him with a word bank for written expression tasks; (b) provide a glossary of terms that he can refer to when completing reading assignments; (c) ensure that test questions do not include vocabulary terms that he does not know; and so forth. See Rapid Reference 4.14 for additional suggestions and Appendix I on the CD-ROM for information about linking WISC-IV results to educational strategies and instructional supports (See Rapid Reference 4.15 for highlights from this appendix).

≡ Rapid Reference 4.15

Sampling of Educational Strategies and Instructional Support Recommendations for Specific Cognitive Weaknesses

Visual Processing

- For students with perceptual-motor difficulties impacting note-taking, (a) provide a note-taker; (b) provide a second set of notes; (c) utilize a guided notes format to reduce the amount of writing required; (d) allow for lectures to be tape-recorded.
- Enlarge print on written handouts and worksheets using a copier or computer and/or commercially available materials (e.g., texts from the Recording for the Blind and Dyslexic; www.rfbd.org).
- Allow for the use of a page magnifier for tasks involving reading.
- Minimize the amount of visual information on a page.
- Use visual devices, such as highlighting, underlining, or color-coding, to focus attention on important visual information (e.g., operational symbols, test directions, key words).
- To help a student keep focus when working with visual material, use a *window* overlay (e.g., an index card with a rectangular cutout) to block out peripheral stimuli that can overwhelm the student. Alternatively, use a ruler for line-by-line reading, or encourage the student to keep his or her place with his or her finger.
- For writing assignments, impose visual structure by darkening lines, using raised line paper (to provide kinesthetic feedback), or folding paper to create large and distinct visual sections.

Short-Term and Long-Term Memory

- Provide written instructions to augment oral instructions.
- Provide frequent repetition and review.

(continued)

- Shorten the number of directions given at any one time.
- Utilize strategies (skimming, scanning, text preview) to increase the student's familiarity with material thereby minimizing the demands on short-term memory.
- Maintain eye contact with the student during the provision of oral instructions.
- Minimize extraneous auditory and visual stimuli to reduce competing demands on attention.
- Record lengthy sequences of information so that the student has time for repetition and adequate opportunity to encode information into long-term memory.
- Require the student to repeat and/or paraphrase directions to facilitate the encoding and storage of information.
- Provide additional time for the student to answer questions and complete assignments.
- Provide prompts or cues to facilitate the student's retrieval of information.
- Provide recognition-type test formats that employ multiple-choice, true-false, or matching formats to minimize the demands on free recall of information.
- Use visual association and mental imagery techniques to support the encoding and retrieval of information.
- Encourage the use of mnemonic devices to facilitate the storage and retrieval of information (e.g., using the acronym HOMES to recall the Great Lakes of Huron, Ontario, Michigan, Eerie, and Superior).
- Allow for specific aids (e.g., multiplication tables) to be utilized during assignments.

Fluid Reasoning/Nonverbal Fluid Reasoning
- Externalize the reasoning process by explaining strategies and steps aloud.
- Provide a guided questions list for recurring procedural steps (e.g., how to approach a word problem, how to answer an inferential question regarding a story character's emotional state).
- Teach abstract concepts by using concrete examples and manipulatives/models.
- For arithmetic difficulties, refer to websites that provide remedial activities, worksheets, and suggestions for accommodating students with math difficulties in the classroom (e.g., www.mathgen.com; www2.ups.edu/community/tofu).
- Provide activities that encourage the student to activate prior knowledge, make predictions, and monitor meaning during learning tasks.
- Provide hands-on, experiential activities that engage the student and actively involve him or her in the process of learning.
- Assess the student's prior knowledge and activate such knowledge before teaching new concepts or presenting novel tasks.

- Teach procedures and concepts concretely and intensely (with frequent repetition) by using manipulatives and visual aids (e.g., figures, diagrams).
- Externalize the reasoning process by verbalizing the relationships between specific concepts and procedures. Help the student to make connections between understood information before focusing on the introduction of new knowledge.
- Use previewing strategies and advanced organizers to facilitate the student's comprehension of material, thereby improving his or her likelihood of success when reasoning with such information.
- Use examples, use modeling, and provide definitions when introducing new conceptual material with which the student must apply his or her reasoning skills.
- Review concepts that were presented and review the importance of such concepts as well as the relationship between newly presented concepts and previously learned information.

Slow Cognitive Processing
- Extended time.
- Reduced number of items to complete, questions to answer, length of writing and reading assignments, and so forth.
- Build in *wait time* when requesting information from a student with a processing speed deficit.
- Utilize strategies appearing in previous "Short-Term Memory" section.
- Pay attention to time of day when assigning tasks requiring rapid mental processing (e.g., end of day or early morning may not be ideal as cognitive resources may be limited and/or *exhausted* at these times).
- Provide opportunities for frequent practice to assist students in acquiring automaticity in specific basic skill areas (e.g., basic math computations, spelling).

Lexical Knowledge, General Information, and Verbal Fluid Reasoning
- For difficulties with word knowledge and general fund of information, refer to websites focused on building vocabulary and general informational knowledge. Some websites include:
  - www.vocabulary.com
  - www.askanexpert.com
  - www.encyclopedia.com
  - www.surfnetkids.com/games
  - www.m-w.com/game (word game of the day)
  - www.randomhouse.com/words
  - www.wordsmith.org/awad/index.html

(continued)

- Provide models and/or for reasoning with verbally based information (e.g., when identifying similarities between objects based on physical characteristics a teacher might state, "we have pictures of a marble, a basketball, and a dime . . . so, we have small, large, small . . . so the two pictures that are most similar are . . .?").
- Ensure that the student understands the words and/or concepts that he or she is being asked to reason with.
- Increase the student's range of word knowledge by using activities that increase synonym knowledge.
- Provide exercises involving verbal analogies and explain the relationship between the words directly and explicitly before requiring the student to solve analogies independently.

It is also possible that uncommon differences between clinical clusters are due to factors other than true differences in ability. A child may demonstrate an uncommon difference between two clinical clusters, *suggesting* a true difference in ability; but further investigation may reveal that the uncommon difference is more appropriately attributable to factors that are external to the child. For example, a child who obtains a Nonverbal Fluid Reasoning (*Gf*-nonverbal) Cluster of 109 and a Visual Processing (*Gv*) Cluster of 80 is considered to have a true (and uncommon) difference between the abilities presumed to underlie these clusters (i.e., Table 4.5 shows that a 24-point difference in the *Gf*-nonverbal > *Gv* comparison is needed to be considered uncommon). Although each cluster in the comparison is unitary, in some cases it makes sense to examine the subtest scaled scores composing each cluster to determine whether external, rather than internal (cognitive), factors are the primary cause for the observed difference. For instance, suppose a child's scores on the subtests that make up the Nonverbal Fluid Reasoning (*Gf*-nonverbal) Cluster were both within the Average Range (e.g., Matrix Reasoning scaled score of 12 and Picture Concepts scaled score of 11), and the child's scores on the subtests making up the Visual Processing *(Gv)* Cluster were in the Below Average to Average Range (e.g., Block Design scaled score of 5 and Picture Completion scaled score of 8). Before concluding that the child's *Gv* ability is a Normative Weakness and less well developed than his or her *Gf*-nonverbal ability, it makes sense to examine the differences between the

DON'T FORGET:

Appendix I on the CD-ROM contains important information on linking WISC-IV results to educational strategies and instructional supports.

task demands of the three subtests on which the child obtained scaled scores in the Average Range and the subtest on which the child earned a Below Average scaled score.

Consider the *response formats* for each subtest in the previous example. Of these four subtests, Block Design is the only one that *requires* a motor response. Although a pointing response, for example, is acceptable on the Matrix Reasoning and Picture Concepts subtests, the primary response format for these subtests is oral. Furthermore, consideration of the *item formats* for each of the four subtests reveals that Block Design is the only test with strict time limits. Based on these qualitative subtest characteristics, the examiner may hypothesize that the nature of the response format and item format of the Block Design subtest—namely, a timed task requiring a motor response—resulted in a low Block Design score, which attenuated the Visual Processing (*Gv*) Cluster, leading to a spurious finding of an uncommon difference between the Visual Processing (*Gv*) and Nonverbal Fluid Reasoning (*Gf*-nonverbal) Clusters. To test this hypothesis, you may identify other WISC-IV tasks that are timed and require a motor response (i.e., Coding, Symbol Search, Cancellation) to determine whether the child's performance on these additional measures is also hindered by the same qualitative characteristics. To test this hypothesis further, you may administer tests from other batteries that measure visual processing in a manner that does not require a motor response under timed conditions. For example, the WJ III includes tests of visual processing (e.g., Spatial Relations, Picture Recognition) that are not timed and that do not require a motor response. If performance on these visual processing tests is within the Average Range or higher, then the hypothesis that the score on Block Design is spuriously low due to qualitative factors and not underlying ability is supported and the uncommon Visual Processing (*Gv*) Cluster < Nonverbal Fluid Reasoning (*Gf*-nonverbal) Cluster difference is best explained using qualitative information regarding task characteristics rather than true differences in ability.

STEP 8. Determine Whether the Difference Between the Child's GAI and Cognitive Proficiency Index (CPI) Is Unusually Large

The Cognitive Proficiency Index (CPI) is a special four-subtest index that combines the core Working Memory and Processing Speed subtests into a single standard score (Dumont & Willis, 2001; Weiss, Saklofske, Schwartz, Prifitera, & Courville, 2006). The CPI reflects the child's proficiency for processing certain types of information. As Weiss and colleagues (2006) indicate, "Proficient processing, through quick visual speed and good mental control, facilitates fluid reasoning and the acquisition of new material by reducing the cognitive demands of novel tasks" (p. 170). In Chapter 6, Nancy Hebben discusses the CPI concerning its psychometric justification and its meaning from the perspective of neuropsychology. She supports its computation from a psychometric perspective but explains that it may not have a neuropsychological basis. The goal of this step, therefore, is to compute the CPI and to compare it to the GAI using sound psychometric procedures. The result of the comparison has practical and clinical benefits, especially for children with learning disabilities, traumatic brain injuries, and Asperger's Disorder (Weiss et al., 2006); however, deficits in specific neurological substrates should not be inferred even when the child's GAI is unusually larger than his or her CPI.

As detailed in Step 2b, the GAI (composed of the core VCI and PRI subtests) sometimes serves as the best estimate of a child's global ability when the FSIQ is not interpretable. Optional Step 8 is an especially useful interpretive step for those children whose global ability is best represented by GAI (based on Step 2a and 2b computations). However, examiners may conduct optional Step 8 for any child (even when FSIQ is interpretable) so long as both the GAI and CPI are found to be interpretable. Figure 4.15 shows steps 8a through 8c of the DMIA interpretive worksheet from Appendix E, computed by hand for Ryan. Figure 4.16 shows the automated output for Steps 8a through 8c from the WISC-IV DMIA.

Step 8a. Prior to conducting the GAI-CPI comparison, you must first determine whether the two indexes represent unitary abilities or processes.

For the GAI, answer the following question: *Is the size of the difference between VCI and PRI less than 1.5 SDs (i.e., < 23 points)?* (If this question has already been answered in Step 2b, then use that result for Step 8a.)

- If YES, then the GAI can be calculated and interpreted as a reliable and valid estimate of the child's overall intellectual ability. Proceed to the next part of this step to determine whether the CPI can be interpreted.
- If NO, then the GAI–CPI comparison cannot be made.

For the CPI, answer the following question: *Is the size of the difference between WMI and PSI less than 1.5 SDs (i.e., < 23 points)?*

- If YES, then the GAI and CPI can both be calculated and interpreted as reliable and valid estimates of the child's functioning. Proceed to Step 8b.
- If NO, then the GAI–CPI comparison cannot be made.

Step 8b. Calculate the GAI and CPI. (If the GAI has already been calculated in Step 2b, use that value for Step 8 and calculate CPI.)

To compute GAI: (a) sum the child's scaled scores on the three core VCI and three core PRI subtests, and (b) enter this sum into Appendix F1 to determine the

Step 8a. Determine whether the GAI and CPI are unitary.

Index standard scores: $\underline{\quad 98 \quad}$ – $\underline{\quad 90 \quad}$ = $\underline{\quad 8 \quad}$

$\qquad\qquad\qquad$ (VCI) $\qquad$ (PRI) $\qquad$ (Difference)

Answer the following question: *Is the size of the difference between the VCI and PRI less than 1.5 SDs (i.e., <23 points)?* (If this question has already been answered in Step 2b, then use that result for Step 8a.) No

- If YES, then the GAI can be calculated and interpreted as a reliable and valid estimate of the child's overall intellectual ability. Proceed to the next part of this step to determine whether the CPI can be interpreted.
- If NO, then the GAI-CPI comparison cannot be made.

Index standard scores: $\underline{\quad 83 \quad}$ – $\underline{\quad 70 \quad}$ = $\underline{\quad 13 \quad}$

$\qquad\qquad\qquad$ (WMI) $\qquad$ (PSI) $\qquad$ (Difference)

For the CPI, answer the following question: *Is the size of the difference between the WMI and PSI less than 1.5 SDs (i.e., <23 points)?* No

- If YES, then the GAI and CPI both be calculated and interpreted as reliable and valid estimates of the child's functioning. Proceed to Step 8b.
- If NO, then the GAI-CPI comparison cannot be made.

Step 8b. Calculate the GAI and CPI. (If the GAI has already been calculated in Step 2b, use that value for this step and calculate the CPI).

To calculate the GAI, sum the child's scaled scores on the three VCI and three PRI subtests and enter this sum into Appendix F1 to determine the GAI.

Scaled scores:

$\underline{9}$ + $\underline{7}$ + $\underline{13}$ + $\underline{6}$ + $\underline{16}$ + $\underline{9}$ – $\underline{\qquad 54 \qquad}$ $\underline{\quad 94 \quad}$

$\text{SI} \quad \text{VO} \quad \text{CO} \quad \text{BC} \quad \text{PCn} \quad \text{MR} \quad$ (Sum of Scaled Scores) (GAI)

To calculate the CPI, sum the child's scaled scores on the two WMI and two PSI subtests and enter this sum into Appendix F2 to determine the CPI.

Scaled scores:

$\underline{7}$ + $\underline{7}$ + $\underline{5}$ + $\underline{4}$ = $\underline{\qquad 23 \qquad}$ $\underline{\quad 73 \quad}$

$\text{DS} \quad \text{LNS} \quad \text{CD} \quad \text{SS} \quad$ (Sum of Scaled Scores) (CPI)

Step 8c. Determine whether the size of the difference between the GAI and CPI (regardless of direction) is unusually large or uncommon, occurring less than 10% of the time in the WISC-IV standardization sample.

$\underline{\quad 94 \quad}$ – $\underline{\quad 73 \quad}$ – $\underline{\quad 21 \quad}$

$\quad$ GAI $\qquad\quad$ CPI $\qquad\quad$ (Difference)

Answer the following question: *Is the size of the difference greater than 20 points?* (Yes) No

- If YES, then the difference is uncommon (Weiss et al., 2006).
- If NO, then the difference is not uncommon.

Figure 4.15 WISC-IV Interpretive Worksheet: Step 8, Illustrated for Ryan, Age 10

STEP 8. The Difference Between GAI and CPI Is Examined to Determine Whether It Is Uncommonly Large

THIS STEP IS AUTOMATICALLY CALCULATED BY THE PROGRAM

Step 8a.   Examine whether the GAI was found interpretable in Step 2b

Yes, the GAI is interpretable

Step 8b.   To determine whether the Cognitive Proficiency Index (CPI) is interpretable,
the absolute difference between the WMI and PSI is calculated.

Index Standard Scores: $\dfrac{83}{\text{WMI}}$ - $\dfrac{70}{\text{PSI}}$ = $\dfrac{13}{\text{Absolute Difference}}$

Is the size of the difference less than 1.5 standard deviations (i.e., < 23 points)?
YES, CPI may be interpreted as a reliable and valid estimate of a person's proficiency in processing information.

To calculate the CPI, the scaled scores from the WMI and PSI subtests are summed, and the CPI that corresponds to this sum is located

Scaled Scores: $\dfrac{7}{\text{DS}}$ + $\dfrac{7}{\text{LN}}$ + $\dfrac{5}{\text{CD}}$ + $\dfrac{4}{\text{SS}}$ = $\dfrac{23}{\text{SUM}}$ = $\dfrac{73}{\text{CPI}}$

Step 8c.   If both the GAI and CPI are interpretable, then determine whether the difference between them is uncommonly large

Index Standard Scores: $\dfrac{94}{\text{GAI}}$ - $\dfrac{73}{\text{CPI}}$ = $\dfrac{21}{\text{Absolute Difference}}$

Are the GAI and CPI both interpretable?	Uncommon (U) or Not Uncommon (NU)
Yes	U

Figure 4.16 Steps 8a-c of the Data Management and Interpretive Assistant v1.0, Illustrated for Ryan

child's GAI, percentile rank, and confidence interval (select either 90% or 95% confidence). This table is reprinted from Saklofske, Rolfhus, Prifitera, Zhu, and Weiss (2005, pp. 44–45) with permission. The reliability of GAI is .95 for ages 6 to 11 years (SEm = 3.3) and .96 for ages 12 to 16 years (SEm = 3.0), as reported by Saklofske, Weiss, Raiford, and Prifitera (2006, p. 125). These values are high and very similar to those reported for the FSIQ (range = .96–.97; *WISC-IV Technical and Interpretive Manual,* Table 4.1, p. 34).

To compute CPI: (a) sum the child's scaled scores on the two core WMI and two core PSI subtests, and (b) enter this sum into Appendix F2 to determine the child's CPI, percentile rank, and confidence interval (select either 90% or 95% confidence). This table is reprinted from Weiss and colleauges (2006, p. 172) with permission. For ages 6 to 16, the reliability of CPI is .93 and the SEm = 3.95 (R. Dumont, Personal Communication, July 15, 2008).

Step 8c. Determine whether the size of the difference between the GAI and CPI (regardless of direction) is unusually large or uncommon, occurring less than 10% of the time in the WISC-IV standardization sample. To be uncommon the discrepancy must be at least 21 points (as indicated in Weiss et al., 2006, Table 2, a total of 9.4% of the standardization sample had GAIs and CPIs that differed by 21 points or more). Based on Weiss and colleagues's table, examiners who wish to use a different level to determine uncommonly large discrepancies between GAI and CPI should use the following values: 5% = 25 or more points; 2% = 30 or more points; and 1% = 34 or more points.

Step 8d. Illustration: Ryan's GAI was found to be interpretable in Step 2b (VCI of 98 and PRI of 90 differed by only 8 points) and was determined in Appendix F1 to be 94. His CPI is also interpretable (WMI = 83 and PSI of 70 differed by only 13 points). Ryan's sum of scaled scores on Digit Span (7), Letter-Number Sequencing (7), Coding (5), and Symbol Search (4) equals 23, which yields a CPI of 73 (Appendix F2). The GAI–CPI discrepancy of 21 points is exactly the size of the difference needed to denote an uncommonly large difference. Therefore, Ryan's global intelligence, as measured by the GAI, is substantially and notably higher than his proficiency at processing cognitive information via quick visual speed and good mental control. As discussed in Ryan's case report, these processing problems relate directly to his academic problems, especially in reading and writing.

☜ TEST YOURSELF ☞

I. John obtained scaled scores of 8 and 9 on the WISC-IV Digit Span and Letter-Number Sequencing tasks, respectively. When interpreting his WMI of 89, you should consider the Index as representing

   (a) a unitary ability.

   (b) a nonunitary ability.

   (c) a normative strength.

   (d) a key asset.

2. The approach to test interpretation presented in this chapter emphasizes the importance of featuring the

   (a) subtest profile.

   (b) Index profile.

   (c) Verbal-Performance discrepancy.

   (d) FSIQ.

3. A noninterpretable Index should be used when calculating the mean of all Indexes for use in person-relative (ipsative) analyses. True or False?

4. Using the normative descriptive system to describe WISC-IV Index scores, a score of 119 should be described as

   (a) a Normative Strength.

   (b) Within Normal Limits.

   (c) a Normative Weakness.

   (d) none of the above.

5. Mary obtained a VCI of 122, which is significantly higher than her other Indexes and is uncommon in the normal population. Mary's VCI is *best* described as a

   (a) Key Asset.

   (b) Personal Strength.

   (c) noninterpretable Index.

   (d) Normative Strength.

6. An Index that is an uncommon Personal Weakness and a Normative Weakness should be considered a High-Priority Concern. True or False?

7. The difference between Joseph's highest and lowest Indexes was 26 standard score points. Therefore, Joseph's FSIQ is

   (a) noninterpretable.

   (b) interpretable.

   (c) interpretable if you have reason to believe that his lowest Index is invalid.

   (d) a High-Priority Concern.

8. **The new WISC-IV Clinical Clusters can be used in Planned Clinical Comparisons only when they represent unitary abilities.**
   True or False?

9. **Which of the following is *not* true of the interpretive method presented in this book?**

   (a) Individual subtest interpretation is featured.

   (b) Base rate data are used to evaluate the clinical meaningfulness of score variability.

   (c) Interpretation is grounded firmly in the CHC theory of cognitive abilities.

   (d) Guidance regarding the use of supplemental measures to test hypotheses about significant subtest variation or outlier scores is provided.

10. **The variability among Anna's subtest scaled scores composing the VCI is uncommon, but all her scaled scores are > 12. Anna's range of observed functioning in the area of Crystallized Intelligence can be described as a notable integrity.**
    True or False?

Answers:

1. a; 2. b; 3. True; 4. a; 5. a; 6. True; 7. a; 8. True; 9. a; 10. True

Five

STRENGTHS AND WEAKNESSES OF THE WISC-IV

M any additions and modifications have been made to the latest version of the WISC. This chapter provides a brief summary of the strengths and weaknesses of the WISC-IV in terms of its development and content, administration and scoring, reliability and validity, interpretation guidelines, and standardization procedures.

The WISC-IV has several strengths and represents the most substantial revision of any Wechsler scale to date. Some of the WISC-IV's most salient strengths include (a) a robust four-factor structure across the age range of the test; (b) increased developmental appropriateness (e.g., via modified instructions, the addition of specific teaching items); (c) a deemphasis on time; (d) improved psychometric properties; and (e) an exemplary standardization sample.

Many of the ways in which the instrument has been altered and restructured are considered strengths, including (a) the addition of fluid reasoning tasks; (b) better representation of short-term memory (viz., Working Memory); (c) elimination of factorially complex composites (i.e., VIQ, PIQ, Freedom from Distractibility); and (d) emphasis on psychological constructs consistent with contemporary psychometric theory and research.

Although the WISC-IV, like all major intelligence batteries, has weaknesses, we do not consider any of them to be major. For example, although we have included several ways in which the validity data reported in the *WISC-IV Technical and Interpretive Manual* (The Psychological Corporation, 2003) do not fully meet some of the criteria set forth in the joint standards for educational and psychological tests (American Educational Research Association, American Psychological Association, National Council on Measurement in Education, 1999), these standards were relatively new when the WISC-IV was in development and other intelligence tests also fall short for the same reasons cited here (for a detailed discussion, see Braden & Niebling, 2005). Rapid References 5.1 through 5.5 include the strengths and weaknesses of the WISC-IV that we consider most important for examiners to know. These strengths and weaknesses are organized into five categories: (a) test development and content (Rapid Reference 5.1), (b) administration and scoring (Rapid Reference 5.2), (c) reliability and validity (Rapid Reference 5.3), (d) interpretation (Rapid Reference 5.4), and (e) standardization (Rapid Reference 5.5).

≡ *Rapid Reference 5.1*

Strengths and Weaknesses of the WISC-IV: Test Development and Content

Strengths	Weaknesses
• The WISC-IV is the first revision of the WISC that represents a *substantial improvement over its predecessors*, mainly because it adheres more closely to theory (Kaufman, Flanagan, Alfonso, & Mascolo, 2006).	• Long-Term Retrieval (*Glr*)[a] and Auditory Processing (*Ga*) are not represented, although *Glr* is measured by the Children's Memory Scale (CMS; Cohen, 1997), for example, and *Ga* is measured to some extent by the Wechsler Individual Achievement Test–Second Edition (WIAT-II; The Psychological Corporation, 2002), both of which are linked to the WISC-IV through a common sample (Kaufman et al., 2006).
• The FSIQ is based on four Indexes that yield a broader representation of general intellectual functioning than the WISC-III FSIQ.	
• The VIQ and PIQ were eliminated, presumably because they were factorially complex and, therefore, difficult to interpret (Kaufman et al., 2006).	• Visuospatial working memory is not assessed (Leffard, Miller, & Bernstein, 2006).
• A Working Memory Index is included. The Index was formerly known as *Freedom from Distractibility* and has been restructured. Digit Span is now paired with Letter-Number Sequencing—a good measure of working memory. The factorially complex Arithmetic subtest has been relegated	• Cancellation has poor psychometric properties; "its inclusion in the WISC-IV detracts from the overall quality of the test" (Sattler, 2008, p. 311).
	• Test items were developed and reviewed by expert panels to ensure that they reflected their intended constructs. However,

[a]*Long-Term Retrieval* is the ability to store information in and fluently retrieve new or previously acquired information from long-term memory. While the WISC-IV measures *what* is stored in long-term memory (e.g., Information, Vocabulary), it does not measure the *efficiency* with which this information is initially stored in and later retrieved from long-term memory.

(continued)

to supplemental status—a good decision by the publisher—and the new scale name (Working Memory Index) corresponds to a well-researched cognitive process. Eliminating the label *Freedom from Distractibility* (FD)—a label first recommended by Cohen (1952) and perpetuated by Kaufman (1975)—was sensible because it had long outlived its usefulness. The FD factor (often composed of Arithmetic, Digit Span, and Coding/Digit Symbol) was an artifact of the factor analyses of a limited battery of subtests (those composing a variety of Wechsler batteries, starting with the Wechsler-Bellevue, and including the WISC-R and WISC-III) and should not be considered a valid psychological construct (Carroll, 1993).

- The VCI, WMI, and PSI include qualitatively different measures of the constructs they are presumed to measure (Crystallized Intelligence [*Gc*], Short-Term Memory [*Gsm*], and Processing Speed [*Gs*], respectively), making interpretation of these broad cognitive abilities psychometrically sound under certain circumstances (e.g., when the construct is considered a *unitary* ability; see Chapter 4 of the present volume, as well as Kaufman et al., 2006).

- Items were added at the lower and upper levels of subtests to increase their floors and ceilings, respectively (see Chapter 1 and Appendix D on the CD-ROM for details).

- Because the WISC-III Information subtest seemed more highly correlated with knowledge acquired in

details regarding the selection and composition of the panels are lacking (Braden & Niebling, 2005).

- Results of item-bias analyses were used to modify or eliminate items that evidenced bias. However, a summary of findings (e.g., item-bias index means, variances) was not provided (Braden & Niebling, 2005).

- Reduction of manipulatives, through the elimination of Picture Arrangement and Object Assembly, seemingly reduces the *engaging* quality of the WISC-IV as compared to the WISC-III, WISC-R, and WISC. Apart from its use of manipulatives, many examiners found Picture Arrangement to be a valuable subtest clinically. Indeed, it was the only WISC-III subtest that depicted interpersonal situations. There are no such subtests on the WISC-IV, a test structure that Wechsler—the consummate clinician—never would have approved. The structure of the WISC-IV would have permitted the inclusion of Picture Arrangement as a supplemental subtest. Nevertheless, both Picture Arrangement and Object Assembly are included on the new Wechsler Nonverbal Scale of Ability (WNV; Wechsler & Naglieri, 2006), which can be used to supplement the information garnered from the WISC-IV.

- The WISC-IV, like its predecessors, does not include controlled learning tests or tests that allow corrective feedback *throughout*. These types of tests are useful because they allow examiners to observe the learning process more directly and determine whether a child benefits from feedback.

school as compared to other VCI tests, its inclusion as a supplemental VCI subtest on the WISC-IV ensures that the core VCI scale has a reduced dependence on exposure to formal schooling.

- Dropping some of the original 11 subtests, moving others to supplemental status, and adding new ones strengthened the factor structure (though some confounds remain; see Chapter 1 as well as Kaufman et al., 2006, and Keith et al., 2006).

- Mixed measures of ability were either dropped (e.g., Picture Arrangement) or moved to supplemental status (e.g., Picture Completion).

- Picture Concepts appears to be a good visual analog to Similarities (a *verbal concepts* test).

- The developmental appropriateness of the instrument was improved through the modification of instructions and addition of sample and practice items.

- Updated artwork makes the instrument more attractive and engaging to children.

- Substituting a supplemental test for a core battery test may alter the underlying cognitive construct intended to be measured by the Index (e.g., when Picture Completion is substituted for Matrix Reasoning, the resultant PRI will represent a Visual Processing/ Crystallized Intelligence [Gv/Gc] blend much more so than a Visual Processing/Fluid Reasoning [Gv/Gf] blend; Kaufman et al., 2006).

- Separate norms tables for Visual Processing (Gv) and Fluid Reasoning (Gf) were not made available in the *WISC-IV Administration and Scoring Manual.* (Wechsler, 2003). However, shortly after the publication of the WISC-IV, The Psychological Corporation provided us with the data necessary to calculate separate Gv and Gf Indexes (see Chapter 4 and Appendix H).

- Some test materials are of poor quality—notably the templates for Coding, Symbol Search, and Cancellation; also pages can come loose from the spiral bindings on the Stimulus book and Manuals (Sattler, 2008).

- Matrix Reasoning appears to be the only relatively pure measure of Fluid Reasoning (Gf), although a combination of Matrix Reasoning (MR) and Picture Concepts (PCn) provides an adequate Gf-nonverbal cluster (see Chapter 4).

- The colors on some Matrix Reasoning items may be distracting and potentially unfair to colorblind individuals.

☰ Rapid Reference 5.2

Strengths and Weaknesses of the WISC-IV: Administration and Scoring

Strengths	Weaknesses
• The WISC-IV places considerably less emphasis on time as compared to its predecessors. With the addition of a "no time bonus" option for Block Design and the allowance of more flexible timing for Picture Completion, the latest edition of the WISC can be administered using time limits only for those tests that were designed to measure speed directly (i.e., Coding, Symbol Search, Cancellation).	• Sections of the protocol or Record Form are confusing. For example, the analysis page includes three subtest-level discrepancy comparisons with no rationale as to why these particular comparisons were selected. Subsequent to the publication of the WISC-IV, however, The Psychological Corporation provided a rationale for the Similarities–Picture Concepts comparison. Specifically, The Psychological Corporation stated that, while the task demands of the two subtests are
• The WISC-IV has good subtest *floors*, meaning that it contains a sufficient number of easy items to reliably distinguish between individuals functioning in the average, below average, and lower extreme ranges of ability.	similar (i.e., understanding the common concept among two or more things), the stimuli and response modalities of the two subtests differ—Similarities uses verbal stimuli and requires a verbal response, whereas the Picture Concepts subtest uses visual stimuli and requires a motor response (see The Psychological Corporation's website). Based on this rationale, it appears that differences in subtest stimuli may also be the rationale for the other subtest comparisons listed on the analysis page (i.e., Coding–Symbol Search and Digit Span–Letter-Number Sequencing).
• The WISC-IV has good subtest *ceilings*, meaning that it contains a sufficient number of difficult items to reliably distinguish between individuals functioning in the average, above average, and upper extreme ranges of ability.	
• The WISC-IV has good *item gradients*, meaning that subtest items are approximately equally spaced in difficulty along the entire subtest scale, and the spacing between items is small enough to allow for reliable discrimination between individuals of different	• Because the reliability of the separate Digit Span Forward and Digit Span Backward scores is lower than the combined score

ability ranges on the construct measured by the subtest.

- The WISC-IV allows for greater use of queries and prompts to improve the child's understanding of the task.
- Scoring criteria were revised to be more straightforward. The scoring systems are especially improved for Similarities, Vocabulary, and Comprehension regarding the rationale behind correct answers (Sattler, 2008).
- Enhanced utility for children with disabilities (e.g., VCI and WMI subtests can be administered to children with visual or motor impairments; Sattler, 2008)
- A Block Design No Time Bonus (BDN) process score can be calculated. This feature may be useful for a child who has physical limitations, lacks problem-solving strategies, or has personality characteristics that are believed to affect performance on timed tasks (e.g., perfectionism).
- Process scores are available for the Cancellation Random (CAR) and Cancellation Structured (CAS) items, which allow the child's visual selective attention and speed of processing to be evaluated using two modes of presentation.
- Digits Forward and Digits Backward may be scored separately, allowing for a comparison between Memory Span (Digits Forward) and Working Memory (Digits Backward).
- The WISC-IV allows for the calculation of two digit span process

(Digit Span), when meaningful differences are found, they should be corroborated with other data sources.

- The directions for the Letter-Number Sequencing subtest indicate that the examinee must first recall the numbers followed by the letters. However, if the opposite occurs, the examinee is given credit. The Psychological Corporation, however, maintains that regardless of how the child reorders the numbers and letters, he or she is using working memory in order to place the numbers in sequence followed by the letters in sequence. Moreover, data analyses of the standardization sample showed that the task is equally difficult when either numbers or letters are given first. The purported reason for instructing examinees to give the numbers first is to provide them with a set or structured way of approaching the task, which is primarily intended to help young children or children who have difficulty structuring their own work.
- Some items on the Letter-Number Sequencing subtest allow credit to be given for verbatim responses. Although this is counterintuitive to the task demands of a working memory task (i.e., transforming information), The Psychological Corporation explained that the early items on the Letter-Number Sequencing subtest measure short-term auditory memory (or memory span), which is a precursor skill to working memory. Thus, for younger children, the Letter-Number Sequencing test may

(continued)

scores—namely Longest Digit Span Forward (LDSF) and Longest Digit Span Backward (LDSB). Evaluation of these process scores may help examiners evaluate a child's memory capacity further when considerable variability in terms of correct and incorrect responses was demonstrated throughout either the Digits Forward or Digits Backward (or both) components of the Digit Span subtest. For example, when variability on the Digit Span subtest leads to a spuriously low Digit Span scaled score (e.g., as a result of a child's tendency to respond impulsively), LDSF and LDSB will likely provide a better estimate of actual memory capacity.

- The WISC-IV requires examiners to record examinees' responses verbatim, which encourages item analysis and, therefore, adds to the clinical utility of the WISC-IV. For example, examiners may review a child's verbal responses and discover certain patterns (e.g., word-finding difficulties, verbosity).

assess memory span only—a prerequisite skill for the development of working memory. According to The Psychological Corporation, item set and norms purportedly reflect this change as children develop working memory.

- Some correct and incorrect responses to items on Matrix Reasoning and Picture Completion are not explained; therefore, it is not clear to many examiners why certain responses are given (or not given) credit. The Psychological Corporation, however, has been quick to respond to inquiries of this nature. For example, on their website, they state that for specific Matrix Reasoning items, children can arrive at correct answers other than those specified in the manual; however, when these answers do not represent the most parsimonious solution, they are not awarded credit.

- Audiotapes are not used for memory tests, which would have provided a more reliable means of administering the Digit Span and Letter-Number Sequencing subtests, in particular.

- Guidelines are occasionally confusing; for example, directions for tests with sample items do not mention that all children should be given the sample items (Sattler, 2008).

- Examiner training activities are not included in the *WISC-IV Administration and Scoring Manual* (Wechsler, 2003).

- Failure to provide conversion tables for computing Indexes and FSIQ when supplemental subtests are substituted for core subtests (Sattler, 2008).

≡ Rapid Reference 5.3

Strengths and Weaknesses of the WISC-IV: Reliability and Validity

Strengths	Weaknesses
• Reliabilities of the FSIQ and four Indexes are generally high (i.e., .90+) across the age range; reliabilities of subtests are generally medium (i.e., .80–.89) across the age range. • Test–retest reliability (mean interval = 32 days) was provided for 243 children and adolescents aged 6–16 years. Coefficients for the FSIQ and the four Indexes were high to medium for each of the five age groups studied (ranging from .96 for the FSIQ at ages 12–13 to .84 for the WMI at ages 8–9). • Construct validity of the four Indexes is supported by *exploratory factor analysis* (EFA). These analyses support the structure for core subtests and for a combination of core and supplemental subtests. Only Picture Concepts, at ages 6–7, fails to load substantially on its designated factor (i.e., PRI). • Construct validity of the four Indexes also appears to be supported by *confirmatory factor analysis* (CFA), although the support is stronger when only core subtests are included in the analyses. In the analyses of core subtests, goodness-of-fit (GFI) statistics ranged from .96 to .98; when supplemental subtests were added to the analyses, GFI values for four factors dropped to .90–.95. Similarly, root	• Invariance of the factor structure across the age range of the WISC-IV was not investigated by The Psychological Corporation. However, Keith and colleagues (2006) found that the four factors that underlie the WISC-IV are stable across the entire age range of the test. This study was summarized in Chapter 1. • Correlational studies are provided between the WISC-IV and nine other instruments, *eight* of which are also published by The Psychological Corporation, including five Wechsler scales. It would have been desirable for The Psychological Corporation to report correlations with a more diverse group of cognitive and achievement tests, including measures from other publishers (such as the Woodcock-Johnson III Tests of Cognitive Abilities and Tests of Achievement [WJ III COG, WJ III ACH; Woodcock, McGrew, & Mather, 2001]; the Stanford-Binet Intelligence Scales–Fifth Edition [SB5; Roid, 2003]; and the Cognitive Assessment System [CAS; Das & Naglieri, 1997]), to name a few. • The WISC-IV FSIQ correlated .87 with Total Achievement on the Wechsler Individual Achievement Test–Second Edition (WIAT-II; The Psychological Corporation, 2001).

(continued)

mean square error of approximation (RMSEA) values were excellent for the core analyses (.03–.05) and good when all subtests were analyzed (.04–.06). Nevertheless, in order to evaluate the CFA studies sufficiently, an examination of factor loadings is necessary. These values were not reported in the *WISC-IV Technical and Interpretive Manual* (The Psychological Corporation, 2003).

- The WISC-IV FSIQ correlated substantially with the FSIQ on the WISC-III (.89), WPPSI-III (.89), WAIS-III (.89), WAIS-IV (.91), and WASI (.86), supporting the criterion-related validity of the WISC-IV global cognitive score. The validity of the VCI was also given strong support because it correlated in the .80s (.83–.88) with verbal measures on the other five Wechsler scales.

- The *WISC-IV Technical and Interpretive Manual* (The Psychological Corporation, 2003) provides initial clinical validity data by offering Index and subtest profiles for 16 clinical groups: Intellectually Gifted; Mild and Moderate Mental Retardation; Learning Disorders (four separate groups with disorders in *reading, reading and written expression, mathematics,* and *reading, written expression, and mathematics*); Attention-Deficit/Hyperactivity Disorder (one ADHD group with learning disorders, one without); Language-Impaired (one group with expressive disorders, one with mixed receptive-expressive); Traumatic Brain Injury (one group

This coefficient is comparable in magnitude to the correlations between the FSIQ on the WISC-IV and the FSIQ on other Wechsler scales (i.e., WPPSI-III, WISC-III, WAIS-III, and WASI; mean = .88). This curious finding suggests that the WISC-IV and WIAT-II may be *measuring constructs that are more similar than they are different.*

- It was assumed that each subtest would correlate highest with subtests on its own scale, but that was not always the case. At least 40% of all intersubtest correlations represented a violation of this assumption (Kaufman et al., 2006).

- No empirical support is provided for specific claims regarding the development of treatment plans and their presumed correlates to neuropsychological foundations (Braden & Niebling, 2005).

- Although g-loadings were used to explain inconsistencies in the expected pattern of intercorrelations among subtests, they were not reported in the *WISC-IV Technical and Interpretive Manual* (The Psychological Corporation, 2003). However, we obtained g-loadings from The Psychological Corporation and independent researchers who derived them through different methods (Keith et al., 2006). Both sets of g-loadings are reported in Chapter 1 (Appendix C).

- Most of the cited evidence that Indexes and subtests elicit specific psychological processes is based on studies with previous versions of the WISC; however, because common item content with open head injuries, one with closed head injuries); Autistic; Asperger's Syndrome; and Motor Impairment.

was subjectively identified and processes that explain interitem correlations were inferred, no direct evidence is currently available to substantiate claims that examinees actually use those processes (Braden & Niebling, 2005).

- Interview evidence regarding examinees' response processes was obtained and analyzed for two new subtests, but not for other subtests, indicating that validity claims with respect to these processes are based on insufficient data (Braden & Niebling, 2005).[a]

- The use of the term *process score* implies that the score reflects a neuropsychological process, but no direct evidence is available to support this implication (Braden & Niebling, 2005).

- Score differences between groups defined by ethnic, gender, and socioeconomic status are not mentioned. This omission is curious, given the debate that was sparked by research on ethnic group differences with previous editions of the WISC (Braden & Niebling, 2005).

- Practice effects are somewhat large for PRI and PSI (Sattler, 2008).

[a]The *response process standard* refers to evidence that supports the contention that examinees use intended psychological processes when responding to test items (e.g., a reasoning test elicits reasoning rather than recall; Braden & Niebling, 2004).

≣ *Rapid Reference 5.4*

Strengths and Weaknesses of the WISC-IV: Interpretation

Strengths	Weaknesses
• Differences between Indexes required for statistical significance (critical values) are available as well as the cumulative percentages of the standardization sample (base rates)[a] obtaining various Index differences.	• The *WISC-IV Technical and Interpretive Manual* (The Psychological Corporation, 2003) provides limited information and guidance on test interpretation (Kaufman et al., 2006). However, some books have been published in the past few years that have extended WISC-IV interpretation far beyond the confines of the manual, including this book as well as *WISC-IV Advanced Clinical Interpretation: Practical Resources for the Mental Health Professional* (Weiss, Saklofske, Prifitera, & Holdnack, 2006) and *WISC-IV Use and Interpretation: Scientist-Practitioner Perspectives* (Prifitera, Saklofske, & Weiss, 2008).
• Critical values and base rates are available for all process score comparisons.	
• Provides useful diagnostic information for children who score within 3 SDs of the mean (e.g., the process scores are useful and the four indexes "are helpful in clinical and psychoeducational evaluations and aid in assessing brain-behavior relationships"; Sattler, 2008, p. 310).'	• The *WISC-IV Technical and Interpretive Manual* continually relies on and emphasizes subtest-level pairwise comparisons (i.e., comparing subtest pairs, such as Block Design and Matrix Reasoning) and subtest-level ipsative analysis (e.g., comparing one subtest to the mean of the 10 core battery subtests).
	• Critical values are provided for 105 subtest-level comparisons in the *WISC-IV Administration and Scoring Manual* (Wechsler, 2003, Appendix B.3), with no guidance on how to use this information and

[a]*Base rate* refers to the prevalence or frequency of an observed score difference in the normal population. Typically, score differences that occur in less than 10% of the population are considered uncommon and therefore may be clinically meaningful.

no consideration for the *statistical significance* errors that occur when many comparisons are made simultaneously.

- Interpretive steps and interpretive tables are not presented sequentially, which detracts from the user friendliness of the manual. For example, early steps correspond to high-numbered tables and later steps correspond to low-numbered tables.

- Although an interpretive step for process analysis of performance on certain subtests was included, there is little to no guidance on how to interpret the findings of this type of analysis.

- Although Chapter 6 of the *WISC-IV Technical and Interpretive Manual* provides a lengthy description of how examiners may use test findings to identify strengths and weaknesses in a child's scaled score profile, implying that there is value in the method with regard to clinical and educational interventions, no evidence is cited in direct support of this claim (Braden & Niebling, 2005).

- Discussion related to the identification of person-relative strengths and weaknesses using Index, subtest, and within-subtest responses does not include mention of the limitations of these methods that have been cited in the literature over the past decade.

≡ *Rapid Reference 5.5*

Strengths and Weaknesses of the WISC-IV: Standardization

Strengths	Weaknesses
• The WISC-IV was stratified according to a broad base of variables closely matching March 2000 U.S. Census data.	• Arithmetic was standardized on only 1,100 individuals instead of 2,200, a poor psychometric practice (Sattler, 2008).
• The WISC-IV is coequated with the WIAT-II, based on a linking sample of 550 participants aged 6–16. However, no information is available regarding the representativeness of the sample.	

 TEST YOURSELF

1. **The WISC-IV is the first revision of the WISC that represents a *substantial improvement over its predecessors*, mainly because it adheres more closely to theory.**
   True or False?

2. **The Block Design No Time Bonus process score can be useful in which of the following situations?**
   (a) when a child has physical limitations
   (b) when a child lacks problem-solving strategies
   (c) when a child has personality characteristics believed to affect performance on timed tests
   (d) all of the above

3. **The WISC-IV requires examiners to record examinees' responses verbatim, which facilitates later item analysis (e.g., error analysis) and, therefore, adds to the clinical utility of the WISC-IV.**
   True or False?

4. **Which of the following statements is true regarding the construct validity of the four WISC-IV Indexes?**
   (a) The construct validity of the four WISC-IV Indexes is supported by confirmatory factor analysis only.
   (b) The construct validity of the four WISC-IV Indexes is supported by exploratory factor analysis only.

(c) The construct validity of the four WISC-IV Indexes has not yet been supported because the battery is too new.

(d) The construct validity of the four WISC-IV indexes is supported by both confirmatory and exploratory factor analysis.

5. Which of the following cognitive abilities is not represented on the WISC-IV?

(a) Crystallized Intelligence (Gc)

(b) Fluid Intelligence (Gf)

(c) Auditory Processing (Ga)

(d) Short-Term Memory (Gsm)

6. Which of the following WISC-III VCI subtests has been dropped to supplemental status on the WISC-IV?

(a) Information

(b) Similarities

(c) Comprehension

(d) Vocabulary

7. Because the reliability of the separate Digit Span Forward and Digit Span Backward scores is lower than that of the combined score (Digit Span), when meaningful differences are found between these scores, they should be corroborated with other data sources.
True or False?

Answers:

1. True; 2. d; 3. True; 4. d; 5. c; 6. a; 7. True

Six

CLINICAL APPLICATIONS
A Review of Special Group Studies with the WISC-IV
and Assessment of Low-Incidence Populations

REVIEW OF SPECIAL GROUP STUDIES AND UTILITY
OF THE PROCESS APPROACH WITH THE WISC-IV

Nancy Hebben

Special Group Studies
WISC-IV test score results for several special groups are included in the *WISC-IV Technical and Interpretive Manual* (The Psychological Corporation, 2003) and the *WISC-IV Integrated Technical and Interpretive Manual* (The Psychological Corporation, 2004) to help provide information about the test's specificity and its clinical utility for diagnostic assessment. For both the WISC-IV and the WISC-IV Integrated, the special groups studied included children with Autistic Disorder, children with Asperger's Disorder, children with Expressive Language Disorder, children with Mixed Receptive-Expressive Language Disorder, children with Moderate Mental Retardation (hereafter referred to as Intellectual Disability),[1] children with Attention-Deficit/Hyperactivity Disorder (ADHD), children with learning disorders, children with learning disorders and ADHD, and children with Traumatic Brain Injury (TBI). In addition, the special groups studied for the WISC-IV included intellectually gifted children, children with mild Intellectual Disability, and children with Motor Impairment. The specific composition of each special group for each test is available in the manual.

---

[1]Intellectual disability is the currently preferred term for the disability historically referred to as mental retardation. Although the preferred name is intellectual disability, the authoritative definition and assumptions promulgated by the American Association on Intellectual and Developmental Disabilities (AAIDD and previously, AAMR) remain the same as those found in the Mental Retardation: Definition, Classification and Systems of Supports manual (Luckasson et al., 2002).

Caution must be exercised when generalizing from these data for several reasons. The samples for these studies did not consist of randomly selected subjects and generally were based on small numbers, ranging from as few as 19 to as many as 89 subjects. In most cases, data are included from a number of independent clinical settings that did not guarantee that the same criteria and procedures were used for diagnosis. In a number of cases, the groups consisted of participants with a heterogeneous and diverse set of diagnoses. For example, the "children with learning disorders" group included children with reading, written expression, and mathematics disorders. The "children with TBI" group included children with both open and closed head injuries as well as those with different causes and severities of brain injury.

It is crucial to remember that these are group data and are not necessarily representative of a whole diagnostic class and, in many cases, are not specific to the diagnostic class. Though these data may be useful in describing individual children in terms of patterns of cognitive performance, they should not be used to make differential diagnoses. As Kaufman and Lichtenberger (2000) point out with regard to learning disability: "Many variables—including performance on standardized measures of achievement, academic history, developmental history, medical history, family history, and behavioral observations—must be combined to properly evaluate a child with a potential learning disability" (p. 205). This caution should be applied to each of the groups listed previously.

Profile Analysis

Since the publication of the WISC-IV, the use of alternatives to the FSIQ and other index scores such as the GAI (Prifitera, Weiss, & Saklofske, 1998) and Cognitive Proficiency Index (CPI) (Dumont & Willis, 2001; Weiss et al., 2006) has been developed and the utility of those alternatives has been studied with the special groups included in the *WISC-IV Integrated Technical and Interpretive Manual* (The Psychological Corporation, 2004). In addition, several studies have suggested that profile analysis both of the index scores and of the subtest scores may be useful in distinguishing among the special groups in meaningful ways (Fiorello et al., 2007; Mayes & Calhoun, 2004). (For a discussion of the controversy surrounding subtest-level profile analysis see *Applied Neuropsychology*, 2007, Vol. 14, No. 1).

The GAI, first introduced for the WISC-III by Prifitera, Weiss, and Saklofske (1998), has been proposed as an alternative to the FSIQ when two conditions are met: (a) the FSIQ is *not* interpretable (the child's highest and lowest indexes differ substantially, i.e, by at least 1.5 *SD*), and (b) the VCI and PRI are fairly comparable in magnitude (i.e., they differ by less than 1.5 *SD*). (See Step 2 of the interpretive system in Chapter 4.) The GAI combines those subtests believed to be more pure representations of crystallized intelligence and eliminates the 40% contribution of the subtests comprising measures of working memory and processing speed that are included in the FSIQ. The GAI is especially useful for individual children in those special groups for whom there are frequently significant and abnormally large discrepancies between the scales that reflect the more traditional Verbal–Performance dichotomy (VCI/PRI) and the scales that measure attentional abilities and processing speed (WMI/PSI). As indicated by Strauss and colleagues (2006), there are multiple special populations of children for whom this is true, including children with intellectual giftedness (VCI and PRI > WMI and PSI), children with Intellectual Disability (WMI and PSI > VCI and PRI), and children sustaining head injuries (lower PSI than other indexes).

Saklofske and colleagues (2006) recommend the use of the GAI for those children for whom the ability–achievement discrepancy (AAD) required for special services in school is diminished by the fact that their FSIQ has been lowered by deficiencies in working memory and processing speed, making them "less likely to be found eligible for special education services in educational systems that do not allow consideration of other methods of eligibility determination" (p. 116). They suggest the GAI be used for any number of index discrepancies and they also suggest examining the difference between the FSIQ and GAI to determine "the impact of reducing the emphasis on working memory and processing speed on the estimate of general cognitive ability for children with difficulty in those areas due to traumatic brain injury or other neuropsychological difficulties" (p. 116). Use of the GAI may be clinically informative in ways that the FSIQ is not. Saklofske and colleagues (2006) provide a table summarizing the distribution of the FSIQ–GAI discrepancies for the special groups included in the *WISC-IV Technical and Interpretive Manual* (The Psychological Corporation, 2003; Table 4, pp. 123–124). Use of this table allows examiners to compare the magnitude of any discrepancy obtained by the child they are evaluating with the percentage of children who obtained similar or greater levels of discrepancies. The table is especially useful because these percentages are provided separately for children in special populations: intellectual giftedness, intellectual disabilities, motor impairment, ADHD, and specific learning disorders. The separate *norms* permit examiners to compare a child's discrepancy directly with the discrepancies obtained by children from a similar special group, Saklofske and colleagues's (2006) analysis reveals that a large percentage of children with intellectual giftedness, learning disorders, ADHD, brain injury, Autism, Asperger's Disorder, and motor impairment have higher GAIs than FSIQs by 5 or more points, whereas a large percentage of children with intellectual disabilities have higher FSIQs than GAIs by 5 or more points. So while the FSIQ–GAI discrepancy cannot establish a diagnosis or distinguish among the children in these special groups, analysis of the discrepancy and its direction can inform the evaluator of whether or not a child is similar to others in the diagnostic group under consideration and of strengths and weaknesses that might be addressed in a treatment program.

A second composite index, this one summarizing the WMI and PSI into a single score, was also proposed by Dumont and Willis (2001). This composite was named the *Cognitive Proficiency Index* (CPI) by Weiss and colleagues (2006) because they believe it "represents a set of functions whose common element is the proficiency with which a person processes certain types of cognitive information," using visual speed and mental control (see WISC-IV Technical Report #6, p. 170, by Weiss and Gabel for more information). Weiss and colleagues (2006) argue the differentiation of the VCI and PRI into the GAI and the WMI and PSI into the CPI is particularly important in the evaluation of children with special learning needs.

There are at least two questions that come to mind in examination of the utility of the CPI. First, is the CPI just a psychometric convenience to group the WMI and PSI together as cognitive operations relevant to general intellectual functions? Second, does this new index have meaning from a neuropsychological perspective because the underlying cognitive operations have common neurobiological or neuropsychological substrates? These are separate issues.

One key issue must be addressed to answer these questions. If working memory (including the operations needed to activate, maintain, and manipulate information) and processing speed are both functions that (a) may vary independently of other indexes of intellectual functioning and (b) serve as functions that may modulate the expression of intellectual functioning, then the answer to both questions is probably yes. Although it is unlikely that either of these abilities varies completely independently of intelligence across the range of abilities in the population, there is evidence that they are at least, in part, independent. It is also the case that limitations in either of these functions may also limit how general intellectual ability is expressed.

Whether it makes sense to use the WMI and PSI (summarized into the CPI) as markers of learning disability or targets for intervention is an empirical question, but it makes sense to think of them as two critical functions that may help or limit general intellectual ability. The data appear to indicate that, because of the restructuring of the WISC-IV into the four indexes and the FSIQ, it makes psychometric sense to look at the GAI versus the CPI in at least some groups, such as children with intellectual giftedness, since large discrepancies often characterize their performances on the WISC-IV. For such groups, the FSIQ is likely an underestimate (or overestimate) of general intellectual ability.

But having a psychometric justification for combining WMI and PSI into a single index does not imply that they have common substrates. The question about whether working memory and processing speed have common neuropsychological or neurobiological underpinnings is more difficult to answer. There is a great deal of evidence linking various aspects of working memory to different parts of the frontal cortex (i.e., prefrontal, dorsomedial, and dorsolateral all seem to make some contribution). This is not the case for processing speed, which involves a wider array of cortical and subcortical areas; though it is possible the frontal cortex has some role in modulating processing speed. Other brain structures that might contribute to processing speed include the entire cortex itself, the basal ganglia, the various brainstem nuclei that factor into arousal, and the cerebellum. Even if both domains were impaired or limited in a single individual, there is no scientific basis to conclude this was caused by a compromise within the same area of the brain, even though this might be the case.

Children with Autistic Disorder and Asperger's Disorder

Rapid Reference 6.1 details the highest and lowest mean WISC-IV subtest scaled scores for children with Autistic Disorder and Asperger's Disorder. Given that children with Asperger's Disorder are unlike children with Autistic Disorder because they do not show clinically significant delays in language, it not surprising that two of three of their highest scores are on tasks dependent on language (i.e., Similarities and Information). In contrast, for children with Autistic Disorder, whose difficulties include language impairments, one of their three lowest scores was on a language-based task (e.g., Comprehension). Picture Completion, which was a high score for the children with Asperger's Disorder, might reflect the fact that this subtest requires attention to detail without any significant language demands. One might speculate that Block Design was the highest score for the children with Autistic Disorder because this task is not related in any substantial way to Crystallized Intelligence and, therefore, has minimal language demands. Like many of the special groups, the lowest performances were on subtests that make up the PSI, which likely reflects the sensitivity of these measures to generalized cognitive impairment. See the section by Elizabeth O. Lichtenberger on pages 242 to for a more thorough treatment of Autistic-Spectrum Disorders.

As noted previously, children with Autistic Disorder and Asperger's Disorder often obtain lower FSIQs than GAIs. According to Saklofske and colleagues (2006), more than 60% of the children in the WISC-IV special group studies with diagnoses of Autistic Disorder or Asperger's Disorder showed GAIs five or more points greater than their FSIQs, indicating that their WMIs and/or PSIs were negatively influencing the expression of their general intellectual abilities measured by their VCIs and PRIs.

≡ *Rapid Reference 6.1*

Highest and Lowest Mean WISC-IV Subtest Scaled Scores of Children with Autistic Disorder and Asperger's Disorder

Autistic Disorder (FSIQ = 76.4) (N = 19)		Asperger's Disorder (FSIQ = 99.2) (N = 27)	
Highest Subtests	**Scaled Score**	**Highest Subtests**	**Scaled Score**
Block Design	7.9	Similarities	12.1
Matrix Reasoning	7.7	Information	12.0
Picture Concepts	7.4	Picture Completion	11.5
Lowest Subtests	**Scaled Score**	**Lowest Subtests**	**Scaled Score**
Comprehension	5.3	Symbol Search	8.2
Symbol Search	5.2	Cancellation	8.0
Coding	4.0	Coding	6.7

Source: Mean FSIQs and scaled scores are from the *WISC-IV Technical and Interpretive Manual* (The Psychological Corporation, 2003, Tables 5.35 and 5.36).

Note: The Arithmetic subtest is excluded because of very small sample sizes.

Preliminary studies based on profile analysis by Mayes and Calhoun (2004) indicate that distinct patterns of subtest scores from the WISC-IV may characterize different diagnostic groups. For children with autism and Asperger's Disorder, Coding and then Symbol Search were the nonverbal subtests on which they received the lowest scores and Block Design is the nonverbal subtest on which the Autistic sample received the highest score. For these children, their lowest verbal subtest score was Comprehension. The profile patterns seen on the WISC-IV for these groups were similar to those also seen on the WISC-III.

Consistent with the findings on the WISC-IV, where children with autism have shown their best performance on Block Design, the findings from special groups studies of the WISC-IV Integrated reveals that children with autism showed the smallest effect sizes on Block Design No Time Bonus. They also showed small effect sizes for Cancellation Random and Cancellation Structured. Large effect sizes, relative to matched controls, were evident for all other scaled process scores, consistent with the rather global deficits seen in this group of children. For children with Asperger's Disorder, however, and probably reflective of better language skills and cognitive development than children with Autistic Disorder, large effect sizes were seen only for Coding Copy (CDC) (effect size = 1.30), Arithmetic with Time Bonus (ART) (1.05), Cancellation Structured (CAS) (0.96), and Spatial Span Backward (SSpB) (0.80).

Children with Expressive Language Disorders and Mixed Receptive-Expressive Language Disorders

As expected, and as can be seen in Rapid Reference 6.2, children with language disorders show their best performances on tasks that make little demand on language and they perform most poorly on tasks reliant on language skills, particularly ones that require complex verbal expression (i.e., Comprehension and Vocabulary). In addition, Coding, though technically a performance test, is a language-like task that requires a written code and the use of symbols, both areas of difficulty for

≡ Rapid Reference 6.2

Highest and Lowest Mean WISC-IV Subtest Scaled Scores of Children with Expressive Language Disorders

Expressive Language Disorder (FSIQ = 83.0) (N = 27)		Mixed Receptive-Expressive Language Disorder (FSIQ = 77.3) (N = 40)	
Highest Subtests	**Scaled Score**	**Highest Subtests**	**Scaled Score**
Block Design	9.6	Cancellation	8.4
Cancellation	9.4	Block Design	8.3
Picture Completion	8.4	Picture Completion	8.0
Matrix Reasoning	8.4		
Lowest Subtests	**Scaled Score**	**Lowest Subtests**	**Scaled Score**
Comprehension	6.8	Vocabulary	6.2
Vocabulary	6.8	Comprehension	6.2
Arithmetic	6.8	Coding	6.0

Source: Mean FSIQs and scaled scores are from the WISC-IV Technical and Interpretive Manual (The Psychological Corporation, 2003, Tables 5.31 and 5.32).

Note: Sample sizes for Arithmetic are 18 (Expressive) and 25 (Mixed).

children with language disorders, and an area of weakness for the children with Mixed Receptive-Expressive Language Disorder.

Rapid Reference 6.3 lists the scaled process scores producing the largest effect sizes when children with language disorders are compared to matched controls. The process scores listed were interpreted by the test authors as those expected given research studies indicating that children with language disorders have persisting difficulties with "visual reasoning, drawing conclusions, and sequential reasoning" (The Psychological Corporation, 2004, p. 89). Research results also demonstrate that even when children with language disorders are presented with tasks less dependent on verbal expression, such as multiple choice, they continue to do less well than their counterparts with intact language skills. Notably, those children with Mixed Receptive-Expressive Language Disorder produced larger effect sizes on all the subtests in the verbal domain and on all Arithmetic-related process subtests, along with additional difficulties on subtests in the working memory domain, likely signaling the additional compromise from receptive language difficulties on understanding task directions.

Children Who Are Intellectually Gifted or Intellectually Disabled

Rapid Reference 6.4 indicates that the intellectually gifted child does best on conceptually based tasks, but interestingly he or she does not show a strength on tasks dependent on speeded processing. This is particularly important because clinicians are sometimes tempted to infer the presence of acquired deficits in bright individuals who do not show Above Average or better performances across all subtest scores. Intellectual giftedness may reflect Superior conceptual ability without Superior performance on speeded tasks. It is possible that this pattern of performance in children who are intellectually gifted reveals a response set reflecting that they are more interested in optimal performance and accuracy than speed. For a more comprehensive discussion of gifted students, see the section by Martin A. Volker and Audrey Smerbeck, in Chapter 7.

It is very difficult to analyze the pattern of strengths and weaknesses for the children with Intellectual Disability because this group combines multiple etiologies. Intellectual Disability may result from acquired brain damage as well as a variety of genetic and congenital conditions, each potentially affecting the brain and the development of intelligence in a different way. The pattern of strengths and weaknesses for children with Mild or Moderate Intellectual Disability appears to be one of best performance on Cancellation, a task that requires simple processing and scanning with minimal reliance on conceptualization. Their poorest performances are generally on those tasks that rely heavily on acquired knowledge (i.e., Vocabulary and Arithmetic). See the section by Elizabeth O. Lichtenberger on pages 250–253 for a more thorough treatment of Intellectual Disability.

≋ Rapid Reference 6.3

WISC-IV Integrated Process Scores with the Largest Effect Size for Discriminating Samples of Children with Expressive Language Disorders from Matched Controls

Expressive Language Disorder (N = 27)		Mixed Receptive-Expressive Language Disorder (N = 39)	
Process Subtest	**Effect Size**	**Process Subtest**	**Effect Size**
Arithmetic with Time Bonus (ART)	1.33	Arithmetic Process Approach—Part A with Time Bonus (ARPA-AT)	1.96
Letter Span Nonrhyming (LSN)	1.02	Arithmetic Process Approach—Part A (ARPA-A)	1.76
Vocabulary Multiple Choice (VCMC)	0.99	Arithmetic Process Approach—Part B (ARPA-B)	1.69
Picture Vocabulary Multiple Choice (PVMC)	0.94	Similarities Multiple Choice (SIMC)	1.41
Coding Copy (CDC)	0.94	Written Arithmetic (WA)	1.39
Visual Digit Span (VDS)	0.93	Information Multiple Choice (INMC)	1.28
Letter-Number Sequencing Process Approach (LNPA)	0.84	Coding Copy (CDC)	1.26
Similarities Multiple Choice (SIMC)	0.82	Arithmetic with Time Bonus (ART)	1.26
Arithmetic Process Approach—Part B (ARPA-B)	0.81	Comprehension Multiple Choice (COMC)	1.25
		Picture Vocabulary Multiple Choice (PVMC)	1.20
		Vocabulary Multiple Choice (VCMC)	1.14
		Letter-Number Sequencing Process Approach (LNPA)	1.05
		Digit Span Backward (DSB)	0.96
		Visual Digit Span (VDS)	0.94

Note: The effect size, according to the test authors, is the Standard Difference or the difference between the two test means divided by the square root of the pooled variance, computed using Cohen's (1996) formula.

≡ Rapid Reference 6.4

Highest and Lowest Mean WISC-IV Subtest Scaled Scores of Children Who Are Intellectually Gifted or Have Intellectual Disability

Intellectually Gifted (FSIQ = 123.5) (N = 63)		Mild Intellectual Disability (FSIQ = 60.5) (N = 63)		Moderate Intellectual Disability (FSIQ = 46.4) (N = 57)	
Highest Subtests	**Scaled Score**	**Highest Subtests**	**Scaled Score**	**Highest Subtests**	**Scaled Score**
Vocabulary	14.6	Cancellation	6.2	Cancellation	4.4
Arithmetic	14.2	Word Reasoning	5.5	Word Reasoning	3.0
Similarities	14.1	Symbol Search	5.2	Similarities	2.7
Comprehension	14.1				
Lowest Subtests	**Scaled Score**	**Lowest Subtests**	**Scaled Score**	**Lowest Subtests**	**Scaled Score**
Digit Span	12.0	Vocabulary	4.1	Arithmetic	1.8
Coding	11.5	Matrix Reasoning	4.0	Comprehension	1.8
Cancellation	11.0	Arithmetic	3.8	Vocabulary	1.7

Source: Mean FSIQs and scaled scores are from the *WISC-IV Technical and Interpretive Manual* (The Psychological Corporation, 2003, Tables 5.22, 5.23, and 5.24).

Note: Sample sizes for Arithmetic are 24 (gifted), 25 (mild Intellectual Disability), and 30 (moderate Intellectual Disability).

The sample of intellectually gifted children cited in the *WISC-IV Integrated Technical and Interpretive Manual* (The Psychological Corporation, 2004) earned an average FSIQ of 123.5, a VCI of 124.7, and a PRI of 120.4. In contrast, their WMI was only 112.5 and their PSI only 110.6. Similar patterns were obtained in a study by Falk, Silverman, and Moran (2004) at the Gifted Development Center, but there the differences between scores was even greater. The mean FSIQ for this sample of 103 children was 127.2. The mean VCI was 131.7 and the mean PRI was 126.4, compared to a mean WMI of 117.7 and a mean PSI of 104.3. Thus, while those indexes believed to measure reasoning were in the Superior or Very Superior ranges, those indexes summarizing short-term memory and speeded processing were only High Average to Average, respectively. In this group of gifted children, the average difference between highest and lowest composite scores was over 27 points and almost 60% showed discrepancies of 23 points (i.e., 1.5 SD) between their VCI and their PSI. The best subtests for the identification of giftedness are those comprising the VCI followed by the PRI; thus, substituting the GAI for the FSIQ for these children is recommended by Psychological Corporation (see WISC-IV Technical Report # 4) and the National Association for Gifted Children (2008). In this book, the decision whether to use FSIQ or GAI as the global score for intellectually gifted children is determined on an individual-by-individual basis, as it is with all children. Following Step 2 in the WISC-IV interpretive system (Chapter 4), FSIQ is the global score of choice so long as it is interpretable (i.e., highest minus lowest index is less than 1.5 SDs); if it is not interpretable, then the GAI is examined to see if it provides an appropriate estimate of the child's overall intellectual functioning.

Of all the special groups studied, the group of children with Intellectual Disability more often shows a higher FSIQ than GAI because they appear to do better on the less complex tasks comprising the PSI and WMI than on the more complex tasks emphasizing reasoning and acquired knowledge comprising the PRI and VCI. Analysis of the FSIQ and GAI discrepancy for children with Intellectual Disability shows that 25% of children with mild Intellectual Disability and > 22% of children with moderate Intellectual Disability obtained FSIQ scores that were 5 or more points greater than their GAI scores.

Children with Attention-Deficit/Hyperactivity Disorder with and without Learning Disorders

Rapid Reference 6.5 shows the highest and lowest scores for a sample of children with ADHD and no Learning Disorder compared with a sample of children with ADHD and Learning Disorder. Though this study contains the largest sample sizes among the special group studies, the data need to be interpreted with special caution because of the heterogeneity of learning disorders included in the sample. It is very likely that children with Mathematics Disorder will have a different pattern of strengths and weaknesses than children with Reading Disorder. In cases in which one group's strength is the other's weakness, the mean score of the collapsed group for these subtests might literally cancel out the appearance of subtest patterns that are group specific.

Children with ADHD would be expected to show strengths in verbal and perceptual reasoning areas (as long as their attentional problems are not so great as to interfere with test taking itself). Poor performance on Arithmetic, Cancellation, and Coding is likely related to the premium these tasks place on attention, concentration, and speed—all critical areas of concern in this population.

Children with ADHD tend to have difficulties with working memory and processing speed, which may result in lower FSIQ scores. The data presented

≣ Rapid Reference 6.5

Highest and Lowest Mean WISC-IV Subtest Scaled Scores of Children with Attention-Deficit/Hyperactivity Disorder(ADHD)

ADHD (FSIQ = 97.6) (N = 89)		Learning Disorder/ADHD (FSIQ = 88.1) (N = 45)	
Highest Subtests	**Scaled Score**	**Highest Subtests**	**Scaled Score**
Picture Concepts	10.5	Picture Completion	10.3
Picture Completion	10.4	Block Design	9.5
Word Reasoning	10.1	Word Reasoning	9.4
Similarities	10.1		
Lowest Subtests	**Scaled Score**	**Lowest Subtests**	**Scaled Score**
Cancellation	9.1	Arithmetic	7.7
Arithmetic	8.7	Letter-Number Sequencing	7.7
Coding	8.3	Coding	7.5

Source: Mean FSIQs and scaled scores are from *WISC-IV Technical and Interpretive Manual* (The Psychological Corporation, 2003, Tables 5.29 and 5.30).

Note: Sample sizes for Arithmetic are 45 (ADHD) and 27 (Learning Disorder/ADHD).

by Saklofske and colleagues (2006) indicate that more than 40% of children with both a learning disability and ADHD, and more than 30% of children with ADHD alone, obtained GAI scores 5 or more points less than their FSIQ scores. Further analysis of each FSIQ and GAI discrepancy must be evaluated to determine whether or not it represents a statistically significant difference (see Table 2 in Saklofske et al., 2006) and then whether or not that difference is rare or common in the general population at similar intellectual levels (See Table 3 in Saklofske et al., 2006). Mayes and Calhoun (2007) collected data to indicate that the WMI and PSI indexes are the most powerful predictors of learning disorders in children with ADHD. Children with ADHD tend to perform relatively poorly on the subtests comprising these measures, accounting for their lower FSIQs than GAIs. Within the PSI, children with ADHD score lower on Coding than Symbol Search.

Mayes and Calhoun (2006) interpret this profile of "strengths in verbal and visual reasoning and weaknesses in attention, processing speed, and graphomotor skills" as suggesting "a neurological basis for the ADHD profile," because this profile is seen in children with ADHD, learning disorders, and Autistic Disorder, but not in children with psychiatric disorders, such as anxiety and depression. In addition, children with both learning disorders and ADHD showed particularly low scores on Letter-Number Sequencing (Prifitera et al., 2005, p. 489).

Rapid Reference 6.6 indicates that when the special groups of children with ADHD (both with and without Learning Disorder) were given the WISC-IV Integrated, they consistently showed larger effect sizes on the various Arithmetic-related process subtests and on Coding Copy. These results are consistent with the difficulties in auditory working memory and processing speed expected from children with ADHD and suggest that the Arithmetic process subtests may be more sensitive to ADHD than Digit Span and Letter-Number Sequencing, perhaps, because it is more cognitively complex than Digit Span and Letter-Number Sequencing.

≡ Rapid Reference 6.6

WISC-IV Integrated Process Scores with the Largest Effect Size for Discriminating Samples of Children with ADHD from Matched Controls

ADHD (N = 41)		Learning Disorder/ADHD (N = 25)	
Process Subtest	**Effect Size**	**Process Subtest**	**Effect Size**
Arithmetic with Time Bonus (ART)	1.20	Arithmetic Process Approach—Part B (ARPA-B)	1.23
Written Arithmetic (WA)	0.95	Written Arithmetic (WA)	1.11
Arithmetic Process Approach—Part A (ARPA-A)	0.84	Arithmetic Process Approach—Part A (ARPA-A)	1.02
Information Multiple Choice (INMC)	0.84	Arithmetic Process Approach—Part A with Time Bonus (ARPA-AT)	0.96
Coding Copy (CDC)	0.80	Coding Copy (CDC)	0.92

Note: The effect size, according to the test authors, is the Standard Difference or the difference between the two test means divided by the square root of the pooled variance, computed using Cohen's (1996) formula.

Children with Reading, Mathematics, and Written Expression Disorders
In Rapid Reference 6.7 the highest and lowest subtest scores for children with
Reading Disorder compared to children with Math Disorder can be seen. These
groups show somewhat different patterns of strengths and weaknesses. The children with Reading Disorder do best on tasks that are not language based (e.g.,
Cancellation), while the children with Math Disorder do poorest on the Arithmetic subtest. The Arithmetic subtest is among the lowest scores for the children
with Reading Disorder as well, suggesting that this subtest measures a wider range
of processes than arithmetic ability alone.

It is interesting that Cancellation is among the strengths for each group, but in
the previous Rapid Reference was among the poorest performances for children
with ADHD with or without learning disorders. This indicates that poor scanning
and motor speed are not necessary prerequisites for learning disorders per se.

Rapid Reference 6.8 displays the patterns of highest and lowest subtest scores
for two somewhat heterogeneous groups: one that included children with reading and written expression disorders and another that included children with

≡ *Rapid Reference 6.7*

Highest and Lowest Mean WISC-IV Subtest Scaled Scores of Children with Reading or Math Disorder

Reading Disorder (FSIQ = 89.1) (N = 56)		Math Disorder (FSIQ = 88.7) (N = 33)	
Highest Subtests	**Scaled Score**	**Highest Subtests**	**Scaled Score**
Cancellation	10.1	Cancellation	8.9
Picture Concepts	9.3	Vocabulary	8.9
Symbol Search	9.2	Digit Span	8.9
Lowest Subtests	**Scaled Score**	**Lowest Subtests**	**Scaled Score**
Digit Span	8.0	Coding	7.8
Letter-Number Sequencing	7.7	Information	7.5
Arithmetic	7.7	Arithmetic	6.5

Source: Mean FSIQs and scaled scores are from the *WISC-IV Technical and Interpretive Manual*
(The Psychological Corporation, 2003, Tables 5.25 and 5.27).

Note: Sample sizes for Arithmetic are 35 (Reading) and 22 (Math).

≡ *Rapid Reference 6.8*

Highest and Lowest Mean WISC-IV Subtest Scaled Scores of Children with Reading and Written Expression Disorders

Reading and Written Expression Disorders (FSIQ = 92.5) (N = 35)		Reading, Written Expression, and Math Disorders (FSIQ = 87.6) (N = 42)	
Highest Subtests	**Scaled Score**	**Highest Subtests**	**Scaled Score**
Block Design	10.3	Cancellation	9.8
Picture Completion	9.7	Word Reasoning	9.0
Word Reasoning	9.7	Picture Concepts	8.7
		Comprehension	8.7
Lowest Subtests	**Scaled Score**	**Lowest Subtests**	**Scaled Score**
Arithmetic	8.5	Similarities	7.9
Digit Span	8.1	Digit Span	7.9
Coding	7.7	Information	7.7
		Arithmetic	7.0

Source: Mean FSIQs and scaled scores are from the *WISC-IV Technical and Interpretive Manual* (The Psychological Corporation, 2003, Tables 5.26 and 5.28).

Note: Sample sizes for Arithmetic are 23 (reading and writing) and 32 (reading, writing, and math).

reading, written expression, and mathematics disorders. Again, results based on such heterogeneous groups must be interpreted cautiously for the reasons previously noted. The *WISC-IV Technical and Interpretive Manual* (The Psychological Corporation, 2003) also points out the need for studies containing more homogeneous clinical groups. Though both groups would be expected to show weaknesses on tasks that are primarily based on language, Word Reasoning was among their strengths. Closer inspection of the data also revealed only small differences between the highest and lowest scores for both groups. Had the children with specific learning disabilities been grouped separately and their data analyzed separately, very different patterns might have emerged.

For those school districts that continue to require an ability–achievement discrepancy (AAD), children with various learning disorders may be denied services if the FSIQ is the measure compared to achievement to establish the necessary discrepancy. This is because a large majority of these children display relative weaknesses in working memory and processing speed, which depress their FSIQs. For these children, the GAI may be the better composite measure to use in comparison to achievement scores, although the WMI and PSI must still be reported and interpreted. Approximately 50% of children with Reading Disorder (including those with Written Expression Disorder) obtained GAI scores that were 5 or more points greater than their FSIQ scores. More than 30% of the following groups displayed that same type of GAI > FSIQ profile: (a) Mathematics Disorder; (b) Reading, Written Expression, and Mathematics Disorder; (c) Expressive Language Disorder; and (d) Mixed Receptive-Expressive Language Disorder (Saklofske et al., 2006).

When tested on the WISC-IV Integrated, children with learning disorders (like children with ADHD) tended to show the largest effect sizes on the process subtests related to Arithmetic and on some subtests from the working memory domain (see Rapid References 6.9 and 6.10). These results are consistent with

≡ Rapid Reference 6.9

WISC-IV Integrated Process Scores with the Largest Effect Size for Discriminating Samples of Children with Reading or Mathematics Disorders from Matched Controls

Reading Disorder (N = 45)		Math Disorder (N = 29)	
Process Subtest	**Effect Size**	**Process Subtest**	**Effect Size**
Written Arithmetic (WA)	0.78	Arithmetic Process Approach—Part B (ARPA-B)	1.13
Arithmetic Process Approach— Part B (ARPA-B)	0.63	Arithmetic Process Approach—Part A w/ Time Bonus (ARPA-AT)	1.10
Arithmetic Process Approach—Part A (ARPA-A)	0.61	Arithmetic with Time Bonus (ART)	1.05
Coding Copy (CDC)	0.60	Written Arithmetic (WA)	1.04
		Information Multiple Choice (INMC)	0.98
		Arithmetic Process Approach—Part A (ARPA-A)	0.91

Note: The effect size, according to the test authors, is the Standard Difference or the difference between the two test means divided by the square root of the pooled variance, computed using Cohen's (1996) formula.

≡ Rapid Reference 6.10

WISC-IV Integrated Process Scores with the Largest Effect Size for Discriminating Samples of Children with Reading and Written Expression Disorders from Matched Controls

Reading and Written Expression Disorders (N = 26)		Reading, Written Expression, and Math Disorders (N = 33)	
Process Subtest	**Effect Size**	**Process Subtest**	**Effect Size**
Written Arithmetic (WA)	1.68	Arithmetic Process Approach—Part A (ARPA-A)	1.40
Vocabulary Multiple Choice (VCMC)	1.31	Written Arithmetic (WA)	1.39
Arithmetic Process Approach—Part B (ARPA-B)	1.26	Arithmetic Process Approach—Part B (ARPA-B)	1.35
Comprehension Multiple Choice (COMC)	1.25	Arithmetic with Time Bonus (ART)	1.33
Visual Digit Span (VDS)	1.22	Arithmetic Process Approach—Part A w/ Time Bonus (ARPA-AT)	1.31
		Digit Span Backward (DSB)	0.92
		Visual Digit Span (VDS)	1.01
		Information Multiple Choice (INMC)	0.76

Note: The effect size, according to the test authors, is the Standard Difference or the difference between the two test means divided by the square root of the pooled variance, computed using Cohen's (1996) formula.

other profile analyses that indicate that children with learning disorders tend, like many of the special groups, to earn higher VCIs and PRIs than WMIs and PSIs.

Children with Traumatic Brain Injury and Motor Impairment

Rapid Reference 6.11 contains the highest and lowest subtest scores for children with Traumatic Brain Injury (TBI) and Motor Impairment. These groups are also heterogeneous with respect to the localization and severity of their brain damage. The highest subtest scores are in areas known to be fairly well preserved in

≣ Rapid Reference 6.11

Highest and Lowest Mean WISC-IV Subtest Scaled Scores of Children with Traumatic Brain Injury and Motor Impairment

Open Head Injury (FSIQ = 92.4) (N = 16)		Closed Head Injury (FSIQ = 90.0) (N = 27)		Motor Impairment (FSIQ = 85.7) (N = 21)	
Highest Subtests	**Scaled Score**	**Highest Subtests**	**Scaled Score**	**Highest Subtests**	**Scaled Score**
Picture Concepts	9.8	Digit Span	9.7	Word Reasoning	9.3
Digit Span	9.8	Picture Concepts	9.4	Vocabulary	9.1
Matrix Reasoning	9.3	Picture Completion	9.4	Digit Span	8.8
		Similarities	9.4		
		Information	9.4		
Lowest Subtests	**Scaled Score**	**Lowest Subtests**	**Scaled Score**	**Lowest Subtests**	**Scaled Score**
Letter-Number Sequencing	7.9	Cancellation	7.9	Symbol Search	6.2
Block Design	7.9	Coding	7.4	Cancellation	5.9
Coding	7.3	Symbol Search	7.2	Coding	5.9
Symbol Search	6.8				

Source: Mean FSIQs and scaled scores are from the *WISC-IV Technical and Interpretive Manual* (The Psychological Corporation, 2003, Tables 5.33, 5.34, and 5.37).

Note: Sample sizes for Arithmetic are 12 (open), 22 (closed), and 11 (Motor).

TBI, while the lowest would be consistent with the conventional wisdom that TBIs impact working memory (i.e., attention and concentration) and speed of processing. This pattern likely reflects the diffuse cortical and subcortical pathology in many TBIs, rather than focal or localized damage. As expected, the lowest subtest scores for children with motor impairment are on paper-and-pencil tasks that are speeded.

On the WISC-IV Integrated, children with traumatic brain injuries, whether open head injuries or closed head injuries, obtained large effect sizes when

≡ *Rapid Reference 6.12*

WISC-IV Integrated Process Scores with the Largest Effect Size for Discriminating Samples of Children with Traumatic Brain Injury from Matched Controls

Open Head Injury (N = 15)		Closed Head Injury (N = 22)	
Process Subtest	**Effect Size**	**Process Subtest**	**Effect Size**
Block Design No Time Bonus (BDN)	1.12	Block Design No Time Bonus (BDN)	1.25
Coding Copy (CDC)	0.93	Similarities Multiple Choice (SIMC)	0.99
Cancellation Structured (CAS)	0.85	Elithorn Mazes No Time Bonus (EMN)	0.96
		Elithorn Mazes (EM)	0.90
		Block Design Multiple Choice (BDMC)	0.81

Note: The effect size, according to the test authors, is the Standard Difference or the difference between the two test means divided by the square root of the pooled variance, computed using Cohen's (1996) formula.

compared to matched control groups on Block Design No Time Bonus. Those with open head injuries also obtained large effect sizes on two tests of processing speed—Coding Copy and Cancellation Structured. In contrast, those with closed head injuries obtained large effect sizes for Similarities Multiple Choice, Elithorn Mazes No Time, Elithorn Mazes, and Block Design Multiple Choice—all tasks in the perceptual domain. These results are summarized in Rapid Reference 6.12.

A Comparison of the Verbal Conceptual Index and the Perceptual Reasoning Index for the Clinical Samples

The *WISC-IV Technical and Interpretive Manual* (The Psychological Corporation, 2003) suggests that the basic profile analysis begins with an evaluation of discrepancies among the Indexes and that this may be used to "help the practitioner identify potentially meaningful patterns of strengths and weaknesses" (pp. 102–103). Rapid Reference 6.13 presents notable differences between the VCI and PRI composite scores for the special study groups. A *notable discrepancy* is defined in the manual as a difference between Indexes that is ≥ 0.20 SDs (i.e., 3 standard score points or greater). The clinician should be careful in drawing conclusions based on this criterion because a 3-point difference between Indexes does not reflect functional or clinically significant differences in individual children. The discrepancies shown in Rapid Reference 6.13 make some intuitive sense. For example, children with language disorders have a higher PRI than VCI, while children with Motor Impairment have a higher VCI than PRI. Nevertheless, it is recommended that you follow the interpretive steps outlined in Chapter 4 of this book.

≡ *Rapid Reference 6.13*

Verbal-Perceptual Discrepancies: Clinical Samples with Notable VCI-PRI Differences

Clinical Sample	Mean VCI	Mean PRI	VCI-PRI Discrepancy
VCI > PRI			
Motor Impairment	95.5	83.8	+11.7
Math Disorder	93.2	87.7	+5.5
Asperger's Disorder	105.6	101.2	+4.4
Intellectually Gifted	124.7	120.4	+4.3
VCI < PRI			
Expressive Language Disorder	82.7	91.6	−8.9
Mixed Receptive-Expressive Language Disorder	78.2	86.7	−8.5
Autistic Disorder	80.2	85.7	−5.5
Reading and Writing Disorders	94.8	98.0	−3.2

Source: Data are from the *WISC-IV Technical and Interpretive Manual* (The Psychological Corporation, 2003, Chapter 5).

Note: Discrepancy = VCI minus PRI. Notable differences are defined in the *WISC-IV Technical and Interpretive Manual* as ≥ 0.20 SD (3 standard score points or greater).

Clinical Samples with Relatively Low Scores on the Processing Speed Index
Rapid Reference 6.14 compares the PSI composite scores relative to the combined mean of the VCI, PRI, and WMI composite scores for the special study groups. As defined previously, a *notable discrepancy* is a difference of ≥ 0.20 SD or 3 standard score points between the two scores. It is important to notice that every group, including the intellectually gifted, show some degree of *deficit* on the PSI relative to the mean index on the VCI, PRI, and WMI. The lack of specificity of this Index, therefore, does not make it suitable for differential diagnosis. These data provide another instance in which children who are intellectually gifted appear to have a deficit in a function—in this case, processing speed—relative to general intellectual abilities. A more parsimonious explanation is that superior intelligence is not necessarily accompanied by superior processing speed.

Utility of the Process Approach
The *WISC-IV Technical and Interpretive Manual* (The Psychological Corporation, 2003) advises the clinician that "the final step in a profile analysis is the qualitative analysis of individual responses" (p. 107). The *process approach* (Kaplan, 1988)—or

≡ *Rapid Reference 6.14*

Processing Speed Deficits: Clinical Samples with Relatively Low Scores on the PSI

Clinical Sample	Mean Index on VCI, PRI, and WMI	Mean PSI	PSI Deficit
Asperger's Disorder	100.7	86.5	−14.2
Autistic Disorder	80.9	70.2	−10.7
Open head injury	93.9	84.1	−9.8
Closed head injury	93.9	85.0	−8.9
Intellectually gifted	119.2	110.6	−8.6
Motor Impairment	90.4	83.8	−6.6
Learning Disorder/ADHD	91.4	88.2	−3.2

Source: Data are from the *WISC-IV Technical and Interpretive Manual* (Chapter 5).

Note: PSI Deficit = mean of VCI, PRI, and WMI minus mean PSI. Notable differences are defined in the *WISC-IV Technical and Interpretive Manual* as ≥ 0.20 SD (3 standard score points or greater).

the *Boston Process Approach*, as it was originally called (Milberg, Hebben, & Kaplan, 1986, 1996)—focuses on the various processes an individual might use to correctly solve a problem and the processes that might lead to the failure to solve a problem (Hebben & Milberg, 2002).

Though the process approach is intellectually and intuitively appealing, with its emphasis on breaking performance down into elements with potential relevance to rehabilitation and education, its empirical basis is not sufficiently well developed to allow for scientifically supportable clinical predictions. Without precise norms and a clearly spelled-out blueprint of how and when these procedures should be used, there is likely to be tremendous variation in the skill and accuracy with which this approach is applied. The process scores provided in the *WISC-IV Administration and Scoring Manual* (Wechsler, 2003) provide a relatively limited but quantitative picture of some of the processes that may be involved in the performance of several subtests, but as with other data derived from the clinical samples, these analyses cannot typically be used for differential diagnosis.

The WISC-IV Integrated is an attempt to integrate traditional and process-oriented measures of cognitive ability (The Psychological Corporation, 2004) by modifying or expanding the content of the original subtests from the WISC-IV or by modifying the presentation of tests or the way in which responses may be given. The usefulness of the WISC-IV for clinical purposes was investigated in two ways: (a) evaluating the WISC-IV Integrated with special groups and (b) evaluating the relationship of the WISC-IV with other tests appropriate to the special group studied (e.g., children with learning disorders were administered the WISC-IV Integrated and the Wechsler Individual Achievement Test–Second Edition [WIAT-II]) (The Psychological Corporation, 2001). Integration of the results from the WISC-IV Integrated into a child's test protocol and history may provide quantitative and qualitative information useful in understanding a child's functioning and contributing to differential diagnosis.

Clinical Samples with Notable Differences Between Scaled Scores on Digits Forward and Digits Backward

The scaled score differences between Digits Forward and Digits Backward shown in Rapid Reference 6.15 range from 0.7 to 2.9. With the exception of the latter difference, obtained by the children with Motor Impairment, the small differences obtained by the other groups are not likely to be clinically significant and may not even be specific to the clinical samples. Table B.9 in

≡ Rapid Reference 6.15

WISC-IV Process Scores: Clinical Samples with Notable Differences Between Scaled Scores on Digits Forward and Digits Backward

Clinical Sample	Mean Digits Forward	Mean Digits Backward	Difference
Forward > Backward			
Motor Impairment	10.3	7.4	+2.9
Learning Disorder/ADHD	9.4	8.0	+1.4
Moderate Intellectual Disability	3.9	2.6	+1.3
Math Disorder	9.6	8.6	+1.0
Reading, Written Expression, and Math Disorders	8.8	7.9	+0.9
Backward > Forward			
Expressive Language Disorder	7.9	8.6	−0.7

Source: Data are from the WISC-IV Technical and Interpretive Manual (The Psychological Corporation, 2003, Chapter 5).

Note: Difference = mean of Digits Forward minus mean of Digits Backward. Notable differences are defined in the WISC-IV Technical and Interpretive Manual as ≥ 0.20 SD (0.6 of a scaled score point or greater).

the *WISC-IV Administration and Scoring Manual* (Wechsler, 2003) indicates that children must show a greater than 3.62 scaled score difference between Digits Forward and Digits Backward for the difference to be statistically significant at the .05 level. Digit Span Backward is more difficult than Digit Span Forward, so it is not surprising that Digits Forward is better than Digits Backward for most groups.

It is difficult to explain why children with expressive language disorders paradoxically seemed to have more difficulty with Digits Forward than Digits Backward, but these data are derived from a single small sample of children and may not be generalizable to other children with similar diagnostic labels. One explanation for this finding is that it is possible that the requirement to actively manipulate numbers in the backward condition may have engaged these children more than passively reciting them in the forward condition, but a hypothesis such as this requires testing before it can be applied to clinical practice.

Clinical Samples with Notable Differences Between Scaled Scores on Cancellation Random and Cancellation Structured

As can be seen in Rapid Reference 6.16, there is a general advantage for performance on the Random versus the Structured Cancellation conditions. This difference is typically less than 1 scaled score point between the two conditions for most of the special study groups, however, with only the children with Intellectual Disability exhibiting greater than 1 scaled score point difference between Random and Structured Cancellation. This finding is probably due, in part, to practice effects because the random condition follows the structured condition. However,

≣ Rapid Reference 6.16

WISC-IV Process Scores: Clinical Samples with Notable Differences Between Scaled Scores on Cancellation Random and Cancellation Structured

Clinical Sample	Mean Cancellation Random	Mean Cancellation Structured	Difference
Random > Structured			
Moderate Intellectual Disability	5.7	4.3	+1.4
Mild Intellectual Disability	7.1	6.0	+1.1
Asperger's Disorder	8.4	7.5	+0.9
Motor Impairment	6.7	5.9	+0.8
Reading Disorder	10.3	9.6	+0.7
Reading and Written Expression Disorders	9.7	9.1	+0.6
Mixed Receptive-Expressive Language Disorder	9.0	8.4	+0.6
Structured > Random			
ADHD	8.7	9.5	−0.8

Source: Data are from the *WISC-IV Technical and Interpretive Manual* (The Psychological Corporation, 2003, Chapter 5).

Note: Difference = mean of Cancellation Random minus mean of Cancellation Structured. Notable differences are defined in the *WISC-IV Technical and Interpretive Manual* as ≥ 0.20 SD (0.6 of a scaled score point or greater).

the matched controls in the majority of these special group studies demonstrated no notable difference between the random and structured conditions.

Rapid Reference 6.16 indicates that the children with ADHD show a slight advantage for the structured condition over the random condition. Though it is not clear how consistent this pattern is for the individuals in this group, the finding suggests that children with ADHD may benefit from the alignment of the stimuli in the structured condition.

Interesting Facts about the WISC-IV Profiles of Select Clinical Samples

Rapid Reference 6.17 summarizes a number of notable characteristics of the performances of the special study groups on the WISC-IV. Some cautions should be observed, however, before using these data clinically.

Children with reading, written expression, and mathematics disorders earned virtually the same mean Index on the VCI, PRI, WMI, and PSI. As noted previously, this grouping is very heterogeneous and collapsing these groups may be obscuring significant differences and meaningful findings between the various subgroups.

None of the 16 clinical samples studied scored very differently on the Block Design process scaled score (i.e., no additional time bonus points for rapid completion) when compared to their Block Design scaled score. This finding suggests that this particular process score does not add any information above and beyond the standard score, although additional studies of the measure are needed to see if this reduced emphasis on speed benefits particular children (e.g., children with physical limitations).

Children with Motor Impairment had great difficulty reversing Digits Backward but scored normally reciting Digits Forward. Motor Impairment in this group is not clearly defined, however. One could speculate that at least some of the motor impairments that were included reflected deficits in frontal lobe functioning, and that Digit Span Backward, a task sensitive to working memory, may also be reflecting deficits in frontal lobe functioning. This does not necessarily mean that the motor impairment and weakness in Digit Span Backward are caused by the same underlying problem, but rather that they are reflections of different functions attributable to the same structure or neural system.

Children classified as intellectually gifted scored in the Superior range on VCI and PRI but in the average range on WMI and PSI. As previously noted, intellectually gifted children who are superior at accumulating and manipulating knowledge do not necessarily show superiority in working memory and motor speed.

Children with Motor Impairment scored in the Average range on VCI and WMI but in the Low Average range on PRI and PSI. Children with Motor Impairment are at a disadvantage on speeded tasks requiring motor movement; thus, it is

≡ Rapid Reference 6.17

Interesting Facts about the WISC-IV Profiles of Select Clinical Samples

- Children with reading, written expression, and math disorders earned virtually the same mean Index on all four scales (89.7 to 90.5).

- None of the 16 clinical samples included in the WISC-IV manual scored very differently on the Block Design process scaled score (no bonus points) when compared to their regular Block Design scaled score (largest difference was 0.3 of a scaled score point, or 0.1 SD).

- Children with Motor Impairment had great difficulty reversing digits even though they performed at an average level on Digits Forward (see Rapid Reference 6.10).

- Intellectually gifted children averaged 122.6 on VCI and PRI but only 111.6 on WMI and PSI.

- Children classified as having Motor Impairment averaged 93.8 on VCI and WMI but only 81.0 on PRI and PSI.

- Children with reading disorders displayed a relative weakness in working memory (their mean WMI of 87 was about 6 points lower than their average Index on the other three scales).

- Children with math disorders (including those who had other learning disorders) displayed a relative weakness in reversing digits (see Rapid Reference 6.10), perhaps because Digits Backward requires manipulation of numbers.

- Children with Traumatic Brain Injury (TBI)—both closed and open head injuries—had a notable relative weakness in processing speed (see Rapid Reference 6.14).

- Children with Autistic Disorder and Asperger's Disorder each had a striking relative weakness in processing speed, even larger than that of children with TBI (see Rapid Reference 6.14).

not surprising that they obtain lower scores on PRI and PSI. Their motor impairments can prevent them from successfully completing tasks within time limits. It appears that reducing the motor demands on the WISC-IV relative to the WISC-III did not entirely eliminate the motor demands from this instrument.

Children with Reading Disorder displayed a relative deficit in working memory. Their mean WMI was about 6 points lower than their average Index on VCI, PRI, and PSI. This pattern is consistent with other evidence that children with reading disorders often have working memory problems (Gathercole, Hitch, Service, & Martin, 1997; Swanson & Howell, 2001). It is by no means clear, though, whether this pattern is due to problems with mental sequencing, auditory processing, mental manipulation, or some other factor.

Children with Mathematics Disorder showed a weakness in their ability to reverse digits for backward recall relative to forward recall. This finding underlines the lack of specificity of this measure. Children with Math Disorder may be hampered on this task because Digit Span Backward requires mental manipulation of numbers. Other groups without specific problems with numbers, however, showed a larger difference between Digits Forward and Digits Backward than did children with Math Disorder.

Children with TBI, whether closed head injury or open head injury (i.e., skull fracture), displayed a notable weakness in processing speed. In adults, TBI is more often associated with lower PSIs and WMIs than VCIs and PRIs. This finding probably reflects the diffuse axonal injury common to those who have sustained TBI. Because so many groups, including the intellectually gifted, show larger VCIs and PRIs than PSIs, this pattern may not be helpful for diagnosis. This pattern may be clinically meaningful, though, because slowed processing speed can affect learning in general.

Children with Autistic Disorder and Asperger's Disorder had a weakness in PSI that was even larger than that seen in children with TBI. The *Diagnostic and Statistical Manual of Mental Disorders–Fourth Edition, Text Revision (DSM-IV-TR;* American Psychiatric Association, 2000) relates that motor clumsiness is an associated feature of Asperger's Syndrome. It also relates that Autistic Disorder is often accompanied by stereotyped body movements, abnormalities of posture, and various nonspecific neurological symptoms, such as delayed hand dominance. Perhaps these factors influence processing speed, or perhaps there is an interaction between the attentional problems associated with Autistic Disorder and Asperger's Disorder and the difficulties that these children have with motor speed and coordination. This finding needs to be replicated to be considered a reliable feature of these disorders. A more detailed discussion of these disorders is found in the next section of this chapter.

AUTISTIC-SPECTRUM DISORDERS

Elizabeth O. Lichtenberger and Darielle Greenberg

Controversy regarding the clinical diagnoses of Autistic and Asperger's Disorders continues to pose problems for researchers, evaluators, and clinicians alike. Before describing the cognitive profiles of children with autistic-spectrum disorders, it is important to first review this ongoing debate. Numerous papers have questioned whether Asperger's Disorder and high-functioning autism are indeed separate and distinct disorders. Some researchers definitively state that the *DSM-IV* diagnosis of Asperger's Disorder is unlikely or impossible (e.g., Eisenmajer et al., 1996; Ghaziuddin, Tsai, & Ghaziuddin, 1992b; Manjiviona & Prior, 1995; Mayes, Calhoun, & Crites, 2001; Miller & Ozonoff, 1997; Szatmari, Archer, Fisman, Streiner, & Wilson, 1995). Many authors agree that the symptoms of Asperger's Disorder differ only in degree from autism, and thereby place Asperger's simply at another point on the autism spectrum (e.g., Attwood, 1998; Eisenmajer et al., 1996; Manjiviona & Prior, 1995; Mayes et al., 2001; Miller & Ozonoff, 1997; Myhr, 1998; Schopler, 1996; Szatmari et al., 1995; Wing, 1998). However, other researchers support differentiating Asperger's syndrome and high-functioning autism as distinct disorders (e.g., Klin, 1994; Klin, Volkmar, Sparrow, Cicchetti, & Rourke, 1995; McLaughlin-Cheng, 1998; Ozonoff, Rogers, & Pennington, 1991).

Asperger's Disorder and Autistic Disorder have similar diagnostic criteria in the *DSM-IV*, but they have key diagnostic differences. According to the *DSM-IV-TR* (American Psychiatric Association, 2000), children with Asperger's do not have communication deficits (including delay of language, inability to initiate or sustain a conversation, repetitive use of language, and lack of symbolic play), and they do not typically show delays in cognitive development. Also, children with Asperger's Disorder are not generally attracted to inanimate objects, as is typical of children with Autism. Table 6.1 reviews the differences between Asperger's Disorder and Autistic Disorder according to *DMS-IV-TR* diagnostic criteria. A final key factor in making a differential diagnosis for autistic-spectrum disorders is that "Asperger's disorder is not diagnosed if the criteria are met for Autistic disorder" (American Psychiatric Association, 2000, p. 74).

Because of the controversy surrounding the diagnosis of Asperger's Disorder and Autistic Disorder, researchers have repeatedly investigated whether specific patterns of performance on cognitive measures are useful in distinguishing the two disorders. However, the large number of research studies on the topic has not allowed a consensus about cognitive patterns to be reached, partly because of methodological issues involved in analyzing the different studies. The following issues exemplify why comparing various studies is difficult:

- Some studies use participants with high-functioning autism, whereas others use individuals with classic autism (who generally have more developmental disabilities and less-intact speech and language skills).
- Some researchers strictly adhere to diagnoses based on *DSM-IV* criteria, but others use modified criteria.
- Age differences between groups exist in many studies, bringing into question whether age is a critical factor affecting the dependent variables.

Table 6.1 Differences Between Asperger's Disorder and Autistic Disorder, According to *DSM-IV-TR* Diagnostic Criteria

DSM-IV-TR characteristic	Asperger's Disorder	Autistic Disorder
Impairment in social interaction		
Impaired nonverbal behavior	Yes	Yes
Impaired ability to develop peer friendships	Yes	Yes
Impaired ability to seek and share interests	Yes	Yes
Impaired ability in social and emotional reciprocity	Yes	Yes
Restricted, repetitive behaviors		
Preoccupation with restricted interests	Yes	Yes
Stereotypic, repetitive motor interests	Yes	Yes
Restricted range of interests	Yes	Yes
Interests in nonfunctional activities	Yes	Yes
Interests in inanimate objects	No	Yes
Impairments in communication		
Delay in or lack of spoken language	No	Yes
Impaired ability to initiate or sustain conversation	No	Yes
Stereotypic, repetitive use of language	No	Yes
Impaired or lack of symbolic play	No	Yes
Onset		
Delays must be present prior to age 3	No	Yes
Comorbidity		
No delay in cognitive development or adaptive functioning (except in social interaction)	Yes	No

- The dependent measures vary across studies, as well (e.g., WISC, WISC-R, WISC-III, WAIS-R).
- Sample sizes are generally small, which limits the conclusions that can be drawn.

Cognitive Performance Patterns of Individuals with Asperger's and Autistic Disorders

Bearing in mind the methodological issues involved in researching autistic-spectrum disorders, some of the key findings in the literature on cognitive functioning in children with these disorders are summarized here. Research has focused mainly on verbal versus nonverbal functioning and patterns of specific high and low subtests.

Wechsler Verbal versus Nonverbal Performance.   For the past decade, research on children with autism has reported a consistent pattern of higher nonverbal (PIQ) than verbal (VIQ) ability (e.g., Lincoln, Courschesne, Kilman, Elmasian, & Allen, 1988; Rumsey, 1992; Yirmiya & Sigman, 1991). However, more recent research indicates that autistic-spectrum disorders vary extensively with regard to Verbal-Performance IQ discrepancies. Most of the available research analyzes the WISC-R and WAIS-R, with a handful of WISC-III studies and one WISC-IV study available. Other research exists that utilizes such instruments as the Kaufman Assessment Battery for Children (K-ABC) or Stanford-Binet Intelligence Scale–Fourth Edition (SB-IV).

A review of the research indicates that studies differ in how discrepancies are reported. Some studies report Verbal-Performance IQ discrepancies based on the mean group performance, whereas others state the percentage of subjects who showed a Verbal > Performance or Performance > Verbal discrepancy. In the various research studies, the discrepancy size needed to be considered significant is often based on normative data from a test's manual, but other times a Verbal-Performance difference of any size is reported simply if one score is larger than another.

The recent literature shows that, in groups of children with autism (most labeled as having high-functioning autism), the greatest proportion of subjects appear to have Verbal and Performance IQs that are not significantly different from one another. For example, Mayes and Calhoun (2003) found no significant differences in WISC-III Verbal and Performance IQs in autistic subjects with either high or low FSIQs. This finding was further supported by studies using mean WISC-III data (Ghaziuddin & Mountain Kimchi, 2004; Goldstein, Allen, Minshew, William, Volkmar, Klin, & Schultz, 2008; Koyama, Tachimori, Osada, Takeda, & Kurita, 2007; Miller & Ozonoff, 2000). Additional studies found that 56% (Manjiviona & Prior, 1995) to 62% (Siegel, Minshew, & Goldstein, 1996) to 77% (Gilchrist, Green, Cox, Burton, Rutter, & Le Couteur, 2001) of autistic samples had nonsignificant Verbal-Performance discrepancies. A Performance > Verbal pattern was the next most commonly reported finding, ranging from 15% to 33% of the subjects with autism (Gilchrist et al., 2001; Manjiviona & Prior, 1995; Siegel et al., 1996).

For children with Asperger's Disorder, the research on the Verbal-Performance differences also remains inconsistent. Some studies report a large percentage (50–67%) of subjects with a nonsignificant discrepancy between their Verbal and Performance IQs (Gilchrist et al., 2001; Manjiviona & Prior, 1995), but others indicate that only a small percentage (3%) of their subjects have this pattern (Barnhill, Hagiwara, Myles, & Simpson, 2000). There are several studies that reveal 17% to 82% of their subjects with Asperger's display a significant Verbal > Performance pattern (Barnhill et al., 2000; Ghaziuddin & Mountain-Kimchi, 2004; Gilchrist et al., 2001; Manjiviona & Prior, 1995). Yet others report some percentage of subjects with Asperger's (17–33%) with the opposite pattern (Performance > Verbal).

A handful of research has focused on performance differences between children with Asperger's and children with high-functioning autism. Ghaziuddin & Mountain-Kimchi (2004) found significant differences in Index and subtest scores. The Asperger's sample scored significantly higher on Verbal IQ, Full Scale IQ, Information, and Arithmetic than the children with autism. However, other studies (Koyama et al., 2007; Klin et al., 2005) have not supported this finding. Koyoma and colleagues (2007) found that children with Asperger's scored significantly higher on Verbal IQ, Vocabulary, and Comprehension than children with autism, but they did not score significantly higher on FSIQ.

Little research has investigated the Wechsler profiles of other autism-spectrum disorders. Koyoma, Tachimoro, Osada, and Kurita (2006) found that children with high-functioning Pervasive Developmental Disorder Not Otherwise Specified (PDDNOS) show a Performance > Verbal pattern. To date, the typical pattern seen with this population has not been fully researched.

High and Low Subtests. Although patterns of verbal and nonverbal performance have not consistently been shown in either Autistic or Asperger's Disorder samples, two Wechsler subtests have repeatedly been shown to be the highest and lowest in the profiles of these populations. Specifically, Block Design has been reported in numerous studies to be the highest for individuals with autism. Barnhill and colleagues (2000) reviewed 20 studies with this population and found high Block Design scores present in 19 of them. The Comprehension subtest is commonly reported as the low subtest in profiles of autistic individuals. Barnhill's review of 20 studies found low Comprehension scores in 18 of them. Subsequent studies have also validated these Wechsler high and low subtests with autistic populations (e.g., Ghaziuddin & Moundtain-Kimchi, 2004; Goldstein, Beers, Siegel, & Minshew, 2001; Goldstein, Minshew, Allen, & Seaton, 2002; Koyama et al., 2007; Mayes & Calhoun, 2004). In addition, Koyoma and colleagues (2006) found that children with high-functioning PDDNOS have a similar pattern of high–low subtests, although their highest verbal subtest was on Digit Span.

To summarize, children with Autistic Disorder and Asperger's Disorder vary extensively with regard to the Verbal-Nonverbal discrepancy (Kaufman & Lichtenberger, 2002). Despite the high Block Design–low Comprehension pattern, Wechsler profiles or other tests measuring verbal and nonverbal ability have not been shown to reliably differentiate autistic-spectrum disorders. However, intellectual evaluations of individuals with autism or Asperger's Disorder are nonetheless valuable for educational planning.

WISC-IV Findings for Individuals with Autism and Asperger's Disorder

The WISC-IV manual reports findings from a sample of 19 children with Autistic Disorder and 27 children with Asperger's Disorder. The mean ages for the autistic and Asperger's groups were 11.7 and 12.5, respectively. The mean WISC-IV composite scores for each of these groups are shown in Figure 6.1. Globally, the cognitive functioning of the Asperger's group was higher than that of the autistic group across all domains. The largest discrepancy (25 points) between the autistic and Asperger's groups was on the VCI, which is consistent with some recent research (e.g., Gilchrist et al., 2001; Miller & Ozonoff, 2000).

Both groups showed their poorest performance on the PSI (70.2 for the autistic group and 86.5 for the Asperger's group). These deficits are also evident from an examination of the lowest WISC-IV subtest scores (refer back to Rapid Reference 6.1). For both the Autistic group and the Asperger's group, Symbol Search and Coding were two of the three lowest scaled scores. Similar findings were

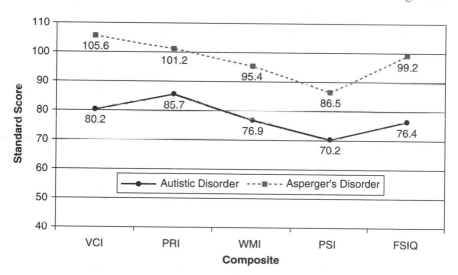

Figure 6.1 Mean WISC-IV Composite Scores for Children with Autistic Disorder (N = 19) and Asperger's Disorder (N = 27)

reported by Mayes and Calhoun (2003), who found a low WISC-III PSI relative to both VCI and POI in children with autism.

In addition to the low PSI subtests, the children with Autistic Disorder also had Comprehension as one of their lowest WISC-IV subtests. This finding is consistent with the vast majority of studies previously cited (e.g., Barnhill et al., 2000). The relatively weaker verbal abilities of the autistic group in comparison to the group with Asperger's Disorder help to explain why Comprehension is one of the three lowest subtests for the autistic group but not for the Asperger's group. Most researchers purport that poor performance of autistic groups on Comprehension is related to poor social judgment and perception as well as poor verbal expression.

Also similar to previously cited research on subtest patterns is the finding that Block Design is the highest subtest for children with Autistic Disorder (see Rapid Reference 6.1). The triad of the highest subtests for the autistic group are from the PRI. In contrast, two of the three highest subtests in the Asperger's group are from the VCI. Picture Completion (a supplemental PRI subtest) is the third-highest subtest for those with Asperger's Disorder. Thus, there are some similarities between WISC-IV findings with the autism-spectrum disorders and findings reported in the literature.

One WISC-IV study tested the validity of the autism data reported in the *WISC-IV Technical and Interpretive Manual* (The Psychological Corporation, 2003). Mayes and Calhoun (2008) administered the WISC-IV to 54 children with *high-functioning autism* (only children with a mean FSIQ of 70 or above were included). Compared to the samples of children with Autistic Disorder and Asperger's disorder described in the WISC-IV Manual, Mayes and Calhoun's sample was about 3 to 4 years younger (mean age of 8.2). An additional methodological difference between the Manual's study and the 2008 study was that Mayes and Calhoun only administered the WISC-IV subtests needed to calculate the index scores (i.e., Cancellation, Information, Arithmetic, and Word Reasoning were not administered).

Mayes and Calhoun's (2008) sample of children with high-functioning autism revealed a similar pattern of performance to the Autistic and Asperger's Disorder samples in the WISC-IV Manual. That is, the lowest mean index scores for the children with high-functioning autism were PSI (85) and WMI (89), whereas the mean VCI was 107. However, the mean PRI (115) for the high-functioning autism group was substantially higher than that achieved by either group in the WISC-IV manual (Autistic Disorder PRI = 86 and Asperger's Disorder PRI = 101). The restricted range of scores that defined the group with high-functioning autism may help explain this seemingly higher score on the PRI. Nonetheless, the general pattern of lower PSI and WMI scores paired with higher VCI and PRI scores reported by Mayes and Calhoun (2008) seems to validate earlier findings on the WISC-IV.

The pattern of highest and lowest subtest scores in the children with high-functioning autism also shared similarities with the Autistic and Asperger's Disorder samples from the WISC-IV manual (despite the fact that four subtests were not administered to the high-functioning autistic group). In the high-functioning autistic group, the Coding (M = 6.6) and Symbol Search (M = 7.9) subtests were the two lowest, followed by Letter-Number Sequencing (8.0). The highest subtest scaled scores were for Matrix Reasoning (M = 13.1), Similarities (M = 12.9), and Picture Concepts (M = 12.5), which were also among the best subtests for the Autistic and Asperger's Disorder groups from the WISC-IV Manual. Block Design is typically among the stronger scores for individuals on the Autism-spectrum, and this was also true for Mayes and Calhoun's (2008) sample with the average Block Design score of 11.6. The overall WISC-IV results from Mayes and Calhoun lend support to the general pattern of earlier findings from samples of children on the autism spectrum. Future studies using the WISC-IV may provide further validation using samples of children who have the commonly occurring diagnoses of autism and Intellectual Disabilities.

Clinical Implications for Testing These Populations

The controversy surrounding differentially diagnosing children with autism from those with Asperger's Disorder may make clinicians and researchers lose sight of what is truly important during assessment: helping individual children. Klin, Sparrow, Marans, Carter, and Volkmar (2000) eloquently state: "Clinicians should also be aware that by simply associating a name to a complex clinical presentation, the understanding of a child's individualized profile of challenges is not necessarily advanced" (p. 310). Thus, although research has not shown a definitive pattern of scores on Wechsler tests to help distinguish children with Asperger's from those with autism, as clinicians, we can certainly use individuals' test data to help develop the most appropriate recommendations for treating the deficits of autism-spectrum disorders.

Evaluators typically use the FSIQ to report overall intelligence or intellectual ability. However, Calhoun and Mayes (2004) reported that when assessing children with autism-spectrum disorders, the FSIQ is not the best predictor of intelligence. A year later, Calhoun and Mayes suggested using the VCI and PRI. Most recently, Mayes and Calhoun (2008) indicate that the General Ability Index (GAI) is the more accurate estimate of intelligence for this population.

Research findings indicate that children with high-functioning autism have weaknesses in attention, graphomotor skills, and processing speed, and strengths in verbal and visual reasoning. These results have implications for educational interventions. Classroom interventions that use strengths to compensate for weaknesses can greatly help children succeed. For example, because of a child's strength in visual reasoning, teachers need to incorporate visual stimuli (such as pictures or videos) into everyday lessons and when teaching new information. Another implication is providing access to word-processing technology, class notes and/or outlines, and allowing more time for written work to alleviate some of the graphomotor and processing speed difficulties (Mayes & Calhoun, 2008). Other interventions include social skills training, adaptations for poor language development (e.g., reducing and simplifying verbal input), and organizational and study skills training.

Intellectual Disability

Unlike the diagnosis of autistic-spectrum disorders, the diagnosis of Intellectual Disability has historically been fairly clear cut. The key criteria for diagnosis of Intellectual Disability are twofold: deficits in overall cognitive functioning and impairment in adaptive functioning. Both the *DSM-IV-TR* (American Psychiatric Association, 2000) and the American Association on Intellectual and Developmental Disabilities (previously the American Association on Mental Retardation or AAMR; Luckasson et al., 2002) require that symptoms of Intellectual Disability be present before age 18. The criterion of subaverage intellectual functioning is defined as an FSIQ (or other global ability score) of approximately 70 or below. The criterion of deficits in adaptive functioning requires impairment in two or more of the following areas: communication, self-care, home living, social interaction, functional academic skills, work, leisure, health, and safety. Both the *DSM-IV-TR* and the American Association on Intellectual and Developmental Disabilities (AAIDD) criteria emphasize that standardized tests include measurement error that should be considered in the diagnostic process, along with using careful clinical judgment.

Research with children who are mentally retarded has generally found equally depressed performance on Wechsler Verbal and Performance scales (Slate, 1995; Spruill, Oakland, & Harrison, 2005; Spruill, 1998; The Psychological Corporation, 2002; Wechsler, 1991). Children assessed with other tests of cognitive ability also typically reveal little variability between scales. For example, the SB-IV Verbal Reasoning and Abstract/Visual Reasoning Area Scores are often equally depressed (Bower & Hayes, 1995), and on the SB5, mean Verbal and Nonverbal IQs were virtually identical for a sample of 119 individuals with documented diagnoses of Intellectual Disabilities (ages 3–25 years, no mean or median age reported; Roid, 2003, Table 4.12). On the second edition of the K-ABC (KABC-II; Kaufman &

Kaufman, 2004a), scores on the composite measuring Visual Processing (Simultaneous/Gv mean of 64.5) were similar to scores on the composite measuring Crystallized Intelligence (Knowledge/Gc mean of 69.1) for 41 children with Intellectual Disabilities. In addition, discrepancies between language and cognitive performance in young children with Intellectual Disabilities do not usually add prognostic information beyond that contained in the global measure of cognitive ability (Vig, Kaminer, & Jedrysek, 1987).

No characteristic Wechsler profiles for children with Intellectual Disabilities have been consistently reported (Spruill, 1998). In an analysis of 10 WISC-R studies, Harrison (1990) reported that children with Intellectual Disabilities have the most difficulty (i.e., score the lowest) on tests of crystallized intelligence, including Vocabulary, Information, Arithmetic, and Similarities. In contrast, these children have their highest scores on Picture Completion and Object Assembly. The occasional slight trend for some groups of children with very low ability to perform better on Performance than Verbal subtests is not something that can be used as a diagnostic characteristic of the population. Indeed, that pattern did not consistently characterize samples of children with Intellectual Disabilities on the WISC-III or WPPSI-III (Bolen, 1998; Canivez & Watkins, 2001; Lichtenberger & Kaufman, 2004; Robinson & Harrison, 2005). Further, although the FSIQ has been shown to be adequately stable in Intellectually Disabled populations, subtest stability and stability of Verbal-Performance discrepancies have been reported as inadequate (Canivez & Watkins, 2001).

WISC-IV Findings on Intellectual Disabilities
To date, the *WISC-IV Technical and Interpretive Manual* (The Psychological Corporation, 2003) contains the only research available on WISC-IV profiles in children with Intellectual Disabilities. The study included a sample of 63 children diagnosed with mild Intellectual Disabilities and 57 diagnosed with moderate Intellectual Disabilities. The mean ages of the groups were 11.9 and 12.2 for the mild and moderate groups, respectively. As is commonly found in intellectually disabled populations, there was very little variability in the subjects' performance. The standard deviations of the composite scores ranged from 9 to 11 points in the mildly retarded group and from 7 to 11 points in the moderately retarded group (a 15-point standard deviation is typical for the nonretarded general population).

The small discrepancies between verbal and nonverbal abilities typically shown on Wechsler tests for samples of children with Intellectual Disabilities was also found in the WISC-IV samples. The mean differences between the WISC-IV VCI and PRI were 1.6 points and 0.2 points for the mild and moderate groups, respectively. Figure 6.2 shows the mean performance of the groups with

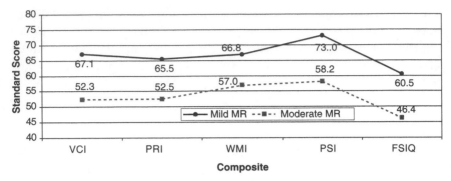

Figure 6.2 Mean WISC-IV Composite Scores for Children with Mild (N = 63) and Moderate (N = 57) Intellectual Disability (formally MR)

Mild and Moderate Retardation on all four of the WISC-IV Indexes. The highest Index scores for both groups were noted on the PSI (73 for the mild group and 58 for the moderate group). These PSI scores were about 6 to 7.5 points higher than the VCI and PRI scores for both the mild and moderate groups, indicating again a rather small amount of variability between the Indexes. The WMI was nearly identical to the PSI in the group with Moderate Retardation, and the WMI was about 6 points lower than the PSI in the group with Mild Retardation.

Although specific subtest patterns on Wechsler tests have not historically been able to characterize the performance of children with Intellectual Disabilities, the highest and lowest WISC-IV subtest scores for these children were examined nonetheless. The patterns of high and low subtests were slightly different for the mild and moderate groups (refer back to Rapid Reference 6.3). Both groups had Cancellation and Word Reasoning among their three highest subtests, and they also had Vocabulary and Arithmetic among their lowest three subtests. For the group with mild Intellectual Disabilities, the third highest subtest was Symbol Search, but for the group with moderate Intellectual Disabilities it was Similarities. Further, Matrix Reasoning was among the three lowest subtests for the mild group, but Comprehension was among the three lowest for the moderate group. Thus, poor acquired knowledge, crystallized abilities, and school-learned knowledge are reflected in the lowest subtests. In contrast, relatively stronger visual attention is one of the skills reflected in the highest subtests. However, these high and low patterns of subtests in and of themselves should not be considered indicative of Intellectual Disabilities.

Finding Subtests with Adequate Floors

Young children with Intellectual Disabilities sometimes have difficulty achieving a floor on tests of cognitive ability. For example, a 6-year-old with moderate

Intellectual Disabilities may not be able to get enough items correct on the WISC-IV to determine where the bottom level of his or her cognitive functioning truly is. Thus, for children with low levels of cognitive functioning from ages 6:0 to 7:3, the WPPSI-III (The Psychological Corporation, 2002) may be a better measure to administer than the WISC-IV. The WPPSI-III has a larger number of low-level items than the WISC-IV, which allows children referred for suspected retardation to achieve a floor if they are functioning at very low levels of ability. For example, consider the scaled scores that children will obtain at ages 6:0 to 6:3 if they earn raw scores of 2 points. On the WISC-IV, raw scores of 2 translate to scaled scores as high as 5 (on Letter-Number Sequencing), with Similarities, Picture Concepts, Matrix Reasoning, and Symbol Search yielding scaled scores of 4. In contrast, at ages 6:0 to 6:3 on the WPPSI-III, raw scores of 2 yield scaled scores as high as 4 only on Comprehension and Similarities.

The findings from the WISC-IV samples of children with Intellectual Disabilities indicate that the test will provide an adequate measure of cognitive ability for most individuals with Intellectual Disabilities (except perhaps for the youngest age). That fact notwithstanding, a diagnosis of Intellectual Disability should be made based only on the results of appropriate measures of both IQ and adaptive functioning. The findings from cognitive testing and measures of adaptive functioning need to be considered within the context of relevant clinical data from a child's background (developmental, educational, medical), history, and behavioral observations before making a differential diagnosis of Intellectual Disabilities.

USING THE WISC-IV WITH DEAF OR HARD-OF-HEARING STUDENTS

Steven T. Hardy-Braz

Historical Overview

The WISC-IV and the WISC-IV Integrated are the latest editions and versions of an intellectual testing instrument with one of the longest and widest traditions of use with deaf and hard-of-hearing populations. This is due primarily to the historical practice of providing a composite that was based on an examinee's ability to manipulate objects in order to solve novel problems or respond with answers that could be communicated with little to no formal language demands (i.e., the Wechsler PIQ). The PIQ, rather than the FSIQ, was considered the best estimate of ability in deaf and hard-of-hearing populations because it did not reflect verbal abilities in any substantial way. Use of the VIQ or FSIQ with these populations often resulted in their being misclassified as Mentally Retarded (now referred to as Intellectually Disabled). Since there were virtually no alternative instruments that assessed intelligence nonverbally or in a reduced-language format back in the days of the original WISC and WISC-R, the Wechsler Performance Scale was the most widely used scale with these populations (Brauer, Braden, Pollard, & Hardy-Braz, 1998). Even today, when alternative nonverbal scales are readily available, Wechsler's nonverbal scales remain the most popular for deaf and hard-of-hearing populations. The primary use of one-half of the instrument provided a safeguard against penalizing deaf and hard-of-hearing examinees for communication difficulties and a lack of access to auditorially imparted information and verbal discourse. This safeguard, however, reduced the construct being measured and made assessments of suspected comorbid developmental or learning disabilities extremely difficult.

WISC-IV Administration Guidelines and Caveats for Deaf and Hard-of-Hearing Populations

The *WISC-IV Administration and Scoring Manual* (Wechsler, 2003, pp. 12–18), the *WISC-IV Integrated Administration and Scoring Manual* (Wechsler, 2004, pp. 19–27), and the *WISC-IV Integrated Technical and Interpretive Manual* (The Psychological Corporation, 2004, Appendix E, pp. 253–259) provide extensive administration guidelines and caveats for using these instruments with deaf and hard-of-hearing populations as compared to the brief description of the results of a clinical study in the WISC-III (Hardy-Braz, 2003b, 2004). These guidelines mention essential variables that are often overlooked in these groups (see Rapid Reference 6.18), discuss the modes of communication often used with members of these groups, and formally rate each subtest and scale on its administration appropriateness for each of four categories of different communication modalities commonly used by members of these populations (see Rapid Reference 6.19). These guidelines were developed as the result of extensive research, feedback, and blind-back translations of every item on every subtest/scale of the WISC-IV and WISC-IV Integrated. Due to publication time constraints, a clinical study was not able to be conducted in time for publication in the manuals. So while the guidelines are very helpful in the selection of subtests and scales that are most appropriate for different individuals, they do not by themselves provide evidence of validity for use of the WISC-IV with members of deaf or hard-of-hearing populations. Therefore, examiners should either wait for such evidence to be published or use professional judgment with regard to the utility of the WISC-IV with deaf and hard-of-hearing populations in accordance with ethical codes. Preliminary evidence for the reliability for the use of the WISC-IV with deaf students is beginning to appear in research projects (see, for example, Krouse, 2008).

≡ Rapid Reference 6.18

Variables to Consider When Assessing Deaf or Hard-of-Hearing Examinees

- Mode(s) of communication
- Age of onset
- Degree of loss
- Type of loss
- Stability of loss
- Age of identification
- Sound frequencies affected
- Educational/communication history
- Historical use of assistive listening devices (ALDs)
- Etiology
- Comorbid conditions
- Parental communication skills

Use of the WISC-IV Verbal Subtests with Deaf and Hard-of-Hearing Populations

The changes and revisions from the WISC-III to the WISC-IV were some of the most extensive undertaken for a Wechsler scale and, therefore, warrant close inspection with regard to the appropriateness of the WISC-IV for deaf and

≡ Rapid Reference 6.19

Communication Modalities/Languages Used by Deaf or Hard-of-Hearing Examinees

- American Sign Language (ASL)
- Simultaneous communication
- Manually coded English
- Signed exact English
- Other native sign languages (e.g., British Sign Language)
- Contact signs or Pidgin signed English
- Cued speech
- Aural/oral

hard-of-hearing populations. The commonly practiced preassessment decision not to administer sections of the full scale (e.g., the Verbal Scale) to these populations was always a compromise that had its own set of consequences. Whereas the Verbal Scale was shown to be a better predictor of academic achievement than the Performance Scale (Kelly & Braden, 1990), the latter scale was most often used. Through the sole use of the PIQ, predictive validity was sacrificed, but the misclassification of deaf and hard-of-hearing individuals as Intellectually Disabled was substantially reduced. This selection also resulted in the narrowing of the construct (i.e., intelligence) to be measured. (Akamatsu, Mayer, & Hardy-Braz, 2008).

Some researchers suggested the careful use of the Verbal Scale with different groups of deaf students with strong warnings about the potential dangers for misuse (see Maller, 2003, for an overview). While this recommendation made sense to specialists with the fluent and direct communication skills needed to translate items into signs and cues, no standard administration guidelines or procedures in American Sign Language (ASL) or other forms of signs (e.g., Signed Exact English) were ever published in any of the previous editions of the WISC, WISC-R, WISC-III, or WISC-III PI manuals; thus, no standardized signed administration procedures with appropriate norms exist. The recommendation to use the Verbal Scale with caution does not work for the vast majority of examiners who are monolingual and untrained either in working with deaf and hard-of-hearing populations or in the proper use of interpreters. Examiners may wish to select another instrument with more empirical support as well as provided translations (e.g., KABC-II, DAS-II, WNV). The subtests on the WNV, for example, are more similar to nonverbal subtests on the WISC-III PIQ than the ones that compose the WISC-IV PRI. The WNV, developed with the assessment of these populations in mind, contains separate validity studies for both deaf and hard-of-hearing populations and collected critical demographic information that is unique to these groups (Brunnert, Naglieri, & Hardy-Braz, 2008).

Use of the WISC-IV Perceptual Reasoning Subtests with Deaf and Hard-of-Hearing Populations

While the publisher of the WISC-IV states that the PRI can be used in situations for which the PIQ formerly was used, examiners should consider the composition of the WISC-III PIQ versus the WISC-IV PRI. The WISC-III PIQ was composed of five core subtests (Picture Completion, Coding, Picture Arrangement, Block Design, and Object Assembly) and two supplemental subtests (Symbol Search and Mazes). The WISC-IV PRI is composed of three subtests (Block Design, Picture Concepts, and Matrix Reasoning), two of which are new. Picture Completion is now a supplemental subtest. Coding and Symbol Search now form the PSI. Picture Arrangement and Object Assembly have been eliminated. Thus, the only core subtest retained from the PIQ on the WISC-III is Block Design. In addition, the cognitive abilities measured by the WISC-III PIQ and the motor skills required to perform the PIQ tasks are different from those measured by the WISC-IV PRI. Therefore, the WISC-IV PRI is not equivalent to the WISC-III PIQ with members of deaf and hard-of-hearing populations. Data are needed before decisions can be made regarding the relationship between the WISC-IV PRI and the WISC-III PIQ with these populations. Preliminary, unstandardized, archival data that were submitted by a variety of examiners from referred cases were analyzed, with results indicating a significantly lower mean PRI (93.21) for a sample of deaf and hard-of-hearing children (n = 128) than the population mean (Krause, 2008). Until more data are available, examiners should consider using other instruments that have been studied more extensively with regard to their use with deaf and hard-of-hearing populations.

Examinee Variables to Consider in the Assessment of Deaf and Hard-of-Hearing Populations

In addition to each examiner evaluating his or her own professional expertise (see Braden, 2005, for a series of recommended steps), the questions an examiner should consider when selecting or planning for an assessment with the WISC-IV, as well as when interpreting results obtained from administration of this instrument, include the following.

- How does the examinee match the characteristics of other individuals with hearing losses?
- How well does the examinee communicate in different modalities?

Deaf and hard-of-hearing individuals vary greatly in terms of developmental history, etiology, presence of comorbid conditions, degree of loss, stability of loss, type of loss, sound frequencies affected, age of onset of the loss, age of identification of the loss, effective use of ALDs, educational placement, and the communication skills of family members (see the annual demographic studies from the Gallaudet Research Institute for more information). Each of these variables should be considered in planning a proper psychological assessment (Sattler & Hardy-Braz, 2002; Sattler, Hardy-Braz, & Willis, 2006). The vast majority (over 96%) have parents who are able to hear and most often unable to communicate fluently in signs. Greater than 40% of the school-aged populations are reported to have an educationally significant comorbid disability. Nevertheless, the most important factor to consider when using the WISC-IV is that of the communication modality or language used by the examinee.

Many deaf or hard-of-hearing examinees need to have the assessment session communicated in different fashions (e.g., via signs or cues, with the aid of an ALD). For example, examinees may communicate in more than one modality and in different modalities depending on whether their communication is receptive or expressive, and they may have different levels of fluency in different modalities or even within the same modality. Each communication modality, however, is an alteration from the standardized administration on which the normative sample information was gathered. Examiners should consider the degree to which each access provision (i.e., alteration from standard procedures) fundamentally alters the intellectual construct that the Index/subtest/item purports to measure. The greater the alteration or modification of the underlying test construct, the greater the need for caution when interpreting results using the normative data provided. For example, the sign-language hand-shape similarities between certain numbers and letters add an additional level of confusion and complexity to the Letter-Number Sequencing subtest.

Even when signs are not used, a hard-of-hearing individual's unique profile of hearing abilities and inabilities (both aided and unaided), as displayed on his or her audiogram, should be examined as an essential component of the test-selection process. Students are often classified in regard to the overall average degree of loss in terms of their ability to perceive pure tone averages (PTAs) across a range of frequencies, and this process results in classifications that can be misleading. Since spoken-language phonemes vary by the frequencies in which they are transmitted and perceived, students with different profiles may perceive different sounds. Students with greater difficulty perceiving high-frequency sounds (relative to low-frequency sounds) may experience more problems with items containing such sounds as *f*, *s*, and *th*, whereas students with greater difficulty perceiving low-frequency sounds may have more trouble with items containing such sounds as *j*, *z*, and *v*. The acoustic environment in which these students are assessed is another variable to consider, especially when assistive listening devices (ALDs) are used.

It is important to remember that a student's ability to speak clearly should not be used as an estimate of his or her intellectual functioning. The administration guidelines published in the WISC-IV manual seek to provide assistance in this decision process. In order to use those guidelines an examiner must know both *how* and *how well* an examinee communicates across modalities prior to administering any or all parts of the WISC-IV. Prior to administering the WISC-IV, examiners should also decide which components of the test (e.g., PRI subtests) can be made administratively accessible to an examinee without altering the underlying construct those components are intended to measure. Examiners should also decide whether WISC-IV test results should be supplemented with tests that permit task access without modifying the test construct, if such tests are available.

Communication Demands of the WISC-IV
Careful consideration of the characteristics of the instrument, the individual, and the examiner is necessary for effective communication and administration. Administration of the WISC-IV to individuals who do not hear clearly, if at all, or

do not communicate via spoken English means that the administration of the test will not be conducted following precise standardization procedures. While there are specialists in the deaf and hard-of-hearing populations as well as examiners who have the skills to communicate fluently, the vast majority of examiners do not. Many examiners will need to utilize the services of a professional sign-language interpreter or cued-speech transliterator. Access through the use of an interpreter/ transliterator can satisfy legal and ethical requirements, but such use can be problematic. Examiners must remain aware that use of an interpreter injects an additional layer of complexity and adds an additional variable into the administration. The clinical rapport between the examiner and examinee can be affected when an interpreter is used. Rapport can also be affected by the manner in which the interpreter relates to both the examiner and the examinee. Examiners should be aware that the demands of communication in a different language directly or via an interpreter can increase the overall test-administration time. Furthermore, as with many other languages, there is not always a one-to-one correspondence between English and ASL signs. It is also important to remember that the signs used in sign language are not used uniformly throughout the country. Many children use signs for basic communication needs that are based on gestures used at home or at school. Both examiner training on the effective use of interpreters *and* interpreter training on the proper interpretation of test directions are highly recommended because they will likely result in an interpreting process that retains the cognitive constructs that underlie the WISC-IV. The *WISC-IV Integrated Technical Manual* (The Psychological Corporation, 2004) has more information regarding suggestions for using sign-language interpreters and cued-speech transliterators.

Examiner Qualifications

The final set of variables to consider when assessing a deaf or hard-of-hearing student concerns the qualifications of the examiner. While a sensitive examiner with adequate resources may be able to meet the communication demands necessary for appropriate administration of the WISC-IV, clinically significant information may be missed, distorted, or lost when the examiner does not understand the examinee's communication needs fully. Therefore, it is recommended that whenever possible examiners consult with fellow professionals and national professional organizations that offer specialized training and support in serving members of these populations. When using the WISC-IV or any other cognitive assessment battery, qualified examiners should possess training and/or background experience in the genetic, developmental, psychological, and sociological aspects of deafness. They should also have formal training and knowledge in assessing cultural, behavioral, motor, visual, and linguistic factors related to deafness. Skills in communicating with deaf and hard-of-hearing students in their primary languages or preferred communication modes, or the use of an interpreter or transliterator according to the student's communication mode so that an effective psychologist-examinee rapport can be developed, are essential but not sufficient. Rapid Reference 6.20 lists several points that examiners should remember when assessing deaf or hard-of-hearing individuals.

Conclusions

While the WISC-IV and WISC-IV Integrated manuals are the first editions to provide administrative guidelines for test selection and use for children who are deaf and hard of hearing, these guidelines should be considered a first critical step toward establishing the usefulness of the WISC-IV with these children. Until validity data are collected in a standardized fashion and made available, these guidelines and the recommendations discussed here should remain preliminary.

=== *Rapid Reference 6.20*

Points to Remember When Assessing Deaf or Hard-of-Hearing Children

- All modifications to the standard WISC-IV administration, especially variations in communication, need to be documented in the interpretive report.
- Depending on the referral question(s), individual characteristics, and communication modality of the assessment administration, subtests from the WISC-IV may need to be supplemented or replaced with other measures.
- ASL, simultaneous communication, signed exact English, cued speech, and other visual communication modalities differ in how they alter WISC-IV test items and their function.
- Examiners should remember that ASL is not universal. Even within the United States there are geographic, ethnic, educational, and generational variations in signs used.
- When interpreting WISC-IV results, an examiner must consider the degree to which an interpreter or transliterator affected the assessment process and should document any findings related to this effect in the interpretive report.
- Interpreters vary in terms of their skill levels as well as their abilities to meet the needs of the examiner and examinee in the assessment situation. Hence, examiners should clarify roles and needs prior to an assessment session.

🦅 TEST YOURSELF 🦅

1. **The GAI, rather than the FSIQ, should be used when the examinee has significantly lower scores in Processing Speed and/or Working Memory as compared to Verbal Comprehension and Perceptual Reasoning.**
   True or False?

2. **Coding, though historically a "Performance" subtest, is a language-like task that requires a written code and the use of symbols, and it may pose difficulty for children with language disorders.**
   True or False?

3. **A child with ADHD would likely perform the best on which of the following subtests?**
   (a) Arithmetic
   (b) Cancellation
   (c) Word Reasoning
   (d) Coding

4. **Children with Asperger's Syndrome and Autism demonstrated their poorest performance on which of the following WISC-IV Indexes?**
   (a) VCI
   (b) PSI
   (c) WMI
   (d) PRI

5. **Historically, specific patterns on Wechsler subtests have not been effective for differentially diagnosing Intellectual Disability.**
   True or False?

6. **The best subtests to administer for the identification of giftedness are those that comprise which of the following WISC-IV indexes?**
   (a) VCI and PRI
   (b) PSI and WMI
   (c) VCI and PSI
   (d) PRI and WMI

7. **Which of the following variables needs to be considered when assessing children who are deaf or hard of hearing?**
   (a) mode(s) of communication
   (b) comorbid conditions
   (c) stability of hearing loss
   (d) all of the above

8. **American Sign Language is universal.**
   True or False?

Answers:

1. True; 2. True; 3. c; 4. b; 5. True; 6. a; 7. d; 8. False

Seven

CLINICAL APPLICATIONS
Assessment of Gifted, Learning Disabled, and
Culturally and Linguistically Diverse Populations

IDENTIFICATION OF GIFTED STUDENTS WITH THE WISC-IV

Martin A. Volker and Audrey M. Smerbeck

In a broad sense, *gifted* is a term applied to productive people who show rare, demonstrable, high-level abilities that are valued within a given cultural context (Sternberg, 1993, 1995). Thus, the nature of giftedness varies across cultures to the extent that different abilities or domains of excellence are valued by different cultures. Within the United States, federal law defines *gifted* and *talented* children as those who demonstrate high performance capability in general intellectual ability, creative or productive thinking, visual or performing arts, leadership, or specific academic areas (Educational Amendment of 1978; Jacob K. Javits Gifted and Talented Students Education Act of 1988; Marland, 1972). These children are assumed to require services not typically provided in schools in order to accommodate their special needs and more fully develop their abilities.

Though all five domains listed under the federal definition are important and valued areas of functioning within our culture (see, for example, J. C. Kaufman, Plucker, & Baer, 2008, concerning the role of creativity in gifted assessment), intelligence tests are most relevant to the identification and assessment of intellectual giftedness. Therefore, the term *gifted* will be used in the rest of this section to refer to intellectually gifted people. Although intelligence tests in general have been criticized on grounds of cultural bias (Tyerman, 1986), low test ceilings (Harrington, 1982; Kaufman, 1993), overemphasis on speed of performance (Kaufman, 1992, 1994; Sternberg, 1982), difficulties evaluating children with more "nontypical" profiles (Sparrow & Gurland, 1998, p. 63), and frequent lack of strong fluid ability measures (Carroll, 1997; McGrew & Flanagan, 1996), each of these issues can be reasonably well addressed by a competent examiner using reliable and valid instruments. Though intelligence tests are not perfect instruments, they are currently the best general predictors of academic achievement (Kaufman & Harrison, 1986; Sparrow & Gurland, 1998), they are the most technically sound psychometric instruments available, and they can potentially identify gifted children who might otherwise go undetected due to behavior problems, learning disabilities, or other issues that might negatively bias those who work with them (Kaufman & Harrison, 1986; Silverman, in press). For example, while teacher nominations and teacher-completed behavior rating scales (e.g., the Gifted Rating Scales [Pfeiffer & Jarosewich, 2003]) are useful for identifying many high-ability children in the initial screening or nomination phase of gifted assessment, these procedures frequently fail to detect those gifted children who are academically unmotivated, misbehaved, disabled, or otherwise inconsistent with the teacher's schema of giftedness. These less visibly gifted children may be identified only by formal psychometric measures that bypass these concerns and directly assess their cognitive abilities. In this sense, formal, psychometric cognitive assessment by a competent examiner may be the most effective method of detecting intellectual giftedness in such school-age children.

The identification of gifted children is often associated with the use of specific cutoff scores. For example, a FSIQ greater than or equal to 2 SDs above the normative mean (The Psychological Corporation, 2003; Winner, 1997, 2000) or a FSIQ greater than 125 (Kaufman & Lichtenberger, 2000) may be among the selection criteria used in some areas for gifted programs. However, what is most important is that the examiner not rigidly adhere to a single cutoff score or criterion. The examiner should be attentive to other sources of information and show special sensitivity to the examinee's cultural background; possible physical, sensory, or learning disabilities; known errors in measurement associated with the test (Kaufman & Harrison, 1986); and known population prevalence of uneven development in different ability areas or expressions of intelligence (e.g., verbal versus nonverbal; Sparrow & Gurland, 1998; Wechsler, 1991).

National surveys of school psychologists have typically shown that the Wechsler scales are the most frequently used individually administered intelligence tests for the identification of gifted students (e.g., Klausmeier, Mishra, & Maker, 1987); the WISC-IV undoubtedly continues that tradition (Sparrow, Pfeiffer, & Newman, 2005), so it is very important that it be thoroughly evaluated for this purpose. To this end, the remainder of this section will evaluate the WISC-IV and its use in terms of testing time and speed-of-performance issues, cultural bias, assessment of fluid reasoning, the nature of gifted profiles, use with gifted and learning disabled examinees, composite scores useful in gifted identification, improved subtest ceilings and extended norms, and dealing effectively with unconventional correct responses.

Testing Time

School psychologists have many responsibilities and need to test efficiently. Long tests can be costly. Ideally, tests need to be comprehensive, yet able to be completed in a reasonable period of time. In the WISC-IV, all 10 subtests needed to calculate the FSIQ and the four Index scores are included in the standard battery. The technical and interpretive manual indicated that although the time required for the administration of the standard battery is similar for the WISC-III and WISC-IV, the WISC-III required the administration of additional supplemental subtests to derive scores for the two smaller factors. Thus, the WISC-IV administration is more efficient, allowing the derivation of all scores in less time. Given that assessments of the intellectually gifted tend to take longer than those of typical children (e.g., 90% of gifted children completed the tests in 104 minutes, versus 90% of the normative sample completing the test in 94 minutes; *WISC-IV Technical and Interpretive Manual,* The Psychological Corporation, 2003, p. 12) and that best practices dictates thorough consideration of scores and other information beyond the FSIQ, this greater efficiency is a decided advantage of the WISC-IV over its predecessor. Furthermore, as will become more apparent in later sections, the WISC-IV's increased emphasis on basic processes in the core battery may actually compromise the FSIQ for many traditionally gifted children. This being the case, taking into account scores beyond the FSIQ should clearly be standard practice in assessing gifted children.

Speed of Performance

The WISC-III has been criticized by those who assess intellectually gifted children because of its perceived overemphasis on speed of performance (Kaufman, 1992, 1994; Sparrow & Gurland, 1998). Among the subtests contributing to the WISC-III FSIQ, scores for Coding, Block Design, Picture Arrangement, Object Assembly, and Arithmetic all included time bonuses. These scores could be adversely impacted by more methodical, reflective, motor-impaired, or otherwise slower response styles, especially for older children for whom the time bonuses were essential for Above Average scores. The fact that the preponderance of these time-laden tasks contributed to the PIQ may have contributed to significant Verbal versus Performance IQ differences in many gifted profiles. The authors of the WISC-IV attempted to address this issue by removing the Object Assembly and Picture Arrangement subtests, making Arithmetic a supplemental subtest without time bonuses, and reducing the time bonus scoring of Block Design. With the exception of Symbol Search, the subtests that were brought into the WISC-IV standard battery to replace those that were removed do not include a significant time component.

Despite these subtest adjustments, slower performance may still affect a gifted child's score; hence, the examiner should attend to the potential involvement of slower response speed on Coding, Symbol Search, and Block Design. For example, the PSI was the lowest average composite score for the group of gifted children tested in the WISC-III validity study (Wechsler, 1991) and a general area of relative weakness for this population (i.e., FSIQ = 128.7 versus PSI = 110.2). The validity study with gifted children reported in the *WISC-IV Technical and Interpretive Manual* shows essentially the same pattern (i.e., FSIQ = 123.5 versus PSI = 110.6; The Psychological Corporation, 2003). Furthermore, a relative weakness in Processing Speed on the WISC-IV has more direct bearing on the interpretation of the FSIQ because Coding and Symbol Search are used in the calculation of both composites.

Though the time bonuses for Block Design on the WISC-IV were reduced relative to the WISC-III, they can still have a significant effect on a child's scores. As a child gets older, time bonuses become essential for Above Average performance on Block Design. Table 7.1 illustrates that, without time bonuses, children above 8 years of age cannot achieve a Block Design score at least 2 SDs above the mean. Children above age 11 cannot achieve a Block Design score even outside the Average range without time bonuses. Thus, examiners should always check for relatively weaker performance on the Processing Speed and Block Design subtests in assessing the impact of speed of performance on the scores of potentially gifted children.

A number of things can be done to examine and offset the possible negative effects of speed of performance. First, if the examiner anticipates a priori that an examinee will have difficulties with speed-oriented subtests, the examiner could specifically select the most appropriate test that minimizes or eliminates such issues for the examinee. Second, the examiner should focus interpretation at the level of the WISC-IV factor-index scores. Be aware that gifted students in the validity study reported in the technical and interpretive manual showed the following mean factor-index profile: VCI = 124.7, PRI = 120.4, WMI = 112.5, and PSI = 110.6 (The Psychological Corporation, 2003, p. 77). Though exact discrepancy

Table 7.1 Highest WISC-IV Block Design Standard Score Possible Without Time Bonuses

	Age in Years:								
	6	7	8	9	10	11	12	13/14	15/16
Block Design Max Std Score:	18	17	16	15	14	13	12	11	10

frequencies were not available, it would not be unusual to find that the PSI and WMI scores were significantly lower than the VCI and PRI scores with these students. As already noted, a lower Block Design score coupled with a relatively lower PSI score could suggest speed-of-performance issues. Fortunately, the WISC-IV has been designed with several process scores that attempt to systematically alter the conditions of testing or scoring in order to give the examiner more interpretive information. A Block Design No Time Bonus (BDN) process score is available to help the examiner assess whether speed of performance made a difference on this subtest, though designs still must be completed within the time limit to receive credit. However, it should be noted that the BDN subtest cannot yield a scaled score of 19 as early as 9 years, 8 months, making this method somewhat less useful for older examinees. Third, the WISC-IV makes several supplemental subtests available that could conceivably be used to replace problematic core subtests. For example, if Block Design is expected to be problematic for a child with motor difficulties, it could be replaced with Picture Completion. The Processing Speed subtests cannot be replaced with nonspeeded subtests because they are designed to measure quick and correct performance. However, focusing on interpretations at the factor-index level allows the examiner to account for and remove their influence, if necessary, in the identification decision. Fourth, testing the limits on time-laden tasks following a complete, standardized administration of the WISC-IV can yield a rough estimate of an examinee's accuracy and problem-solving skills in the absence of time pressure. Finally, if test results lead an examiner to conclude that speed of performance was problematic for the examinee, the WISC-IV results can be supplemented with other measures (see Flanagan & Ortiz, 2001, and Kaufman, 1994, for examples).

The WISC-IV Integrated can provide additional interpretive information regarding the influence of speed on each specific item. A Coding Copy subtest measures how rapidly the examinee can transfer the symbol in the top half of a box to the lower half, thus resembling Coding but with even less cognitive load. Relatively weak scores on Coding Copy are thus strong evidence that the examinee had difficulty producing rapid manual responses and can be used to justify the decision to focus interpretation on untimed tests.

Cultural Bias
It is generally incumbent upon the producer of an intelligence test to demonstrate that it does not significantly favor one group over another for noncognitive reasons, and it is incumbent upon the user of the test to be informed about its appropriate use with various populations (see American Educational Research Association [AERA], 1999). At the item level, the expectation is that a test should

be designed in such a way as to minimize the likelihood that items might be easier or more difficult for individuals from different cultural or subcultural backgrounds. It appears that the authors of the WISC-IV took all reasonable steps to minimize the influence of cultural bias on the test within the general English-speaking population of the United States. The standardization was careful and thorough, matching the 2000 Census numbers across five major demographic variables. A combination of formal expert review and empirical bias analyses were performed to identify and delete or modify problematic items. Experts came from multicultural research and intelligence testing, while empirical analyses included traditional Mantzel-Haenszel and item-response theory bias-analysis techniques. Items were reportedly reviewed on three occasions between the test development and standardization phases (The Psychological Corporation, 2003). Additionally, the Information and Picture Arrangement subtests, which have been criticized for their more culture-laden content, were relegated to supplemental status or deleted from the battery, respectively.

Despite all of the care taken in the standardization and bias analyses, there is no completely culture-free test (Sattler, 2008). Thus, it is up to the examiner to understand when and how it is appropriate to use the WISC-IV. You should be informed and compassionate and use common sense. When you are faced with an examinee for whom the standardization sample is not an appropriate comparison group or for whom certain subtest tasks are not meaningful because of differences related to culture, language, ethnicity, or disability, it behooves the examiner to select an appropriate alternative test, use only appropriate sections of the test, supplement testing with other pieces of information (e.g., other test scores, grades, records, background information from parents and teachers, behavioral observations), and make reasonable accommodations or modifications to ensure that the examinee understands the tasks and is given every reasonable opportunity to respond.

Fluid Reasoning

Three new subtests to the WISC-IV (i.e., Matrix Reasoning, Picture Concepts, Word Reasoning) are purported measures of Fluid Reasoning (*Gf*). *Fluid Reasoning* (or *fluid intelligence*) refers to mental operations or problem-solving approaches a person may use when faced with relatively novel tasks. Both inductive and deductive reasoning are considered to be narrower aspects of this domain (McGrew & Flanagan, 1998). From a CHC perspective, *Gf* bears the strongest relationship to *g* of all the CHC factors at the broad Stratum-II level (Carroll, 1993; McGrew & Flanagan, 1998). Thus, one would expect these subtests to be highly relevant to gifted identification.

The inclusion of *Gf* subtests on the WISC-IV is clearly an attempt to address the criticism that the Wechsler scales have traditionally not measured fluid intelligence well (Carroll, 1997; McGrew & Flanagan, 1996). If one ranks the means for the set of 15 WISC-IV subtests from the gifted group described in the *WISC-IV Technical and Interpretive Manual* (The Psychological Corporation, 2003), the three Fluid Reasoning tasks are among the top 10 subtest means. However, none of them are among the top five subtest means. Assessment of *Gf* using WISC-IV subtests was discussed in Chapter 4, and norms for a *Gf* cluster are provided in Appendix H on the CD-ROM.

Gifted Profiles on the WISC-IV

There were a number of concerns regarding the WISC-IV validity study reported in the *WISC-IV Technical and Interpretive Manual* (The Psychological Corporation, 2003). Although discussed in Chapter 6, these concerns deserve further elaboration here. The study included 63 students previously identified as intellectually gifted by a score ≥ 2 SDs above the mean on a standardized measure of cognitive ability. The specific cognitive measures used to initially identify these children were not reported. The study reported significant differences favoring gifted students over matched controls on all core and supplemental subtests, except the nonsignificant difference for the Cancellation subtest. Gifted students also scored significantly higher on the FSIQ and all Indexes compared to matched controls. However, the WISC-IV FSIQ (M = 123.5) and Indexes (reported earlier) for the gifted sample were lower than expected. It is not unusual for the Flynn effect (Flynn, 1987) and statistical regression to the mean to lead to lower scores for an extreme scoring group upon retesting with a new cognitive measure. As the mean FSIQ in the WISC-III gifted validity study only fell from ≥ 130 to 128.7 (Wechsler, 1991, p. 210), the sharper WISC-IV dropoff requires further explanation.

First, it is possible that statistical regression had an unusually strong effect because the original measure or measures used to identify the children as gifted were excessively varied or less than adequately related to the WISC-IV, such as short-form or group-administered cognitive tests. A second possibility lies with the normalization and smoothing procedures used in the calibration of the FSIQ and Indexes. These procedures, which are only vaguely described in the *WISC-IV Technical and Interpretive Manual* (The Psychological Corporation, 2003), appear to have pulled in the tails of the IQ distribution to some extent. To illustrate, a direct linear transformation of the WISC-IV sum of subtest scores into the deviation quotient distribution would suggest an IQ distribution ranging from approximately 35 to 165. However, the manual reports values ranging from 40 to 160. Thus, it is possible that the normalization and smoothing procedures may have led to more extreme scores' being pulled in closer to the center of the distribution. Finally, the difference may be due to the changes in the WISC-IV core subtest battery relative to the WISC-III. Gifted individuals are unlikely to be equally advanced across all cognitive domains (Winner, 2000) and tend to obtain the highest scores in subtests assessing more *g*-loaded cognitive domains. Of the 10 core subtests on the WISC-III, only one (Coding) primarily assessed the lower level skills—such as memory span or processing speed—that tend to be less remarkable in gifted samples (Rimm, Gilman, & Silverman, 2008). By comparison, the WISC-IV 10 subtest core battery includes four (Digit Span, Letter-Number Sequencing, Coding, and Symbol Search). While the study made it evident that gifted children score significantly higher on the WISC-IV when compared to matched controls, the consistency and degree of the differences may be less than expected.

Given this evidence, it is not surprising that gifted individuals rarely have flat profiles. Rimm, Gilman, and Silverman (2008) reported substantial discrepancies between WISC-IV indexes (i.e., ≥ 23 points) in 74 to 79% of cases in two gifted samples, suggesting that so called *nontypical* profiles appear to be typical of gifted students. Based on the publisher's validity study, it appears that the two smaller factors (i.e., PSI and WMI) are the most likely to stand out with relatively lower scores than the two larger VCI and PRI factors. This was replicated in the two samples described by Rimm and colleagues (2008) and by the National Association of Gifted Children (NAGC) sample reported in WISC-IV Technical Report No. 7 (Zhu, Cayton, Weiss, & Gabel, 2008). In all gifted samples reviewed, the VCI and PRI means were higher than the WMI mean, which was in turn higher than the PSI mean. The precise reasons for this will need to be clarified by further research, but certainly the two larger factors are more psychometrically robust, have stronger construct validity, and are more *g* loaded than the two smaller factors (see Appendix C). From the CHC perspective (McGrew, 1997, 2005), three of the four factor indexes could be ranked according to their theoretical relationship to *g*. The VCI, reflecting Crystallized Ability (*Gc*), would be first; the PRI reflecting, Visual Processing (*Gv*) and Fluid Reasoning (*Gf*), second; and the PSI, reflecting Processing Speed (*Gs*), third. The exact position and status of the WMI are unclear, as Working Memory appears to be a broader construct than CHC theory's Stratum II Short-Term Memory (*Gsm*) factor (see McGrew & Flanagan, 1998, pp. 21–23), and Quantitative Reasoning (*Gq*) is clearly an aspect of Arithmetic, though it is only a supplemental subtest. Nonetheless, the general pattern holds, and gifted children appear best able to demonstrate their skills through VCI and PRI subtests.

The fact that discrepancies among the WISC-IV Indexes do not appear to be unusual in the gifted population lends further credence to the notion that all scores should be considered when evaluating a potentially gifted child. The WISC-IV is well suited to giving useful information beyond the FSIQ, and it is clear that the separate Indexes should not be ignored. In the absence of meaningful discrepancies between Indexes, a FSIQ may reflect an accurate and useful overall estimate of an examinee's ability. However, this should never be assumed to be the case without taking all available scores and other relevant outside information into account.

Giftedness and Learning Disabilities

Individuals with both intellectual giftedness and a specific learning disability (SLD) demonstrate a mixed profile of abilities that will sometimes lead to a failure to identify either concern. Intellectual giftedness is more typically associated with advanced higher order thinking, reasoning, and problem solving. SLDs are characterized by achievement difficulties linked to deficits in basic psychological processes (Individuals with Disabilities Education Improvement Act [IDEIA] of 2004). Due to a phenomenon known as *masking* (McCoach, Kehle, Bray, & Siegle, 2001), average achievement may be observed when a gifted/SLD child applies her/his advanced reasoning skills to overcome or partially compensate for a deficit in a basic processing domain. Another form of masking can occur when examiners fail to look beyond the FSIQ in profiles characterized by large discrepancies between the factor-index scores. In such cases, an average range FSIQ may result when index scores indicative of exceptional ability are averaged in with those reflecting a deficit related to an SLD. In either case, the academic performance of these children would benefit from the supports offered to children with SLDs, while their higher order cognitive abilities could best be developed by programming for the gifted (Volker, Lopata, & Cook-Cottone, 2006).

In cases where the basic processing deficit is related to short-term memory or processing speed, the WISC-IV profile typical of intellectually gifted students may be exaggerated, with the WMI and/or PSI considerably lower than the VCI or PRI. However, when the SLD is more language based, difficulties with language processing could compromise the VCI and/or any of the other Indexes, including the PRI. This phenomenon occurs, in part, because no factor index assesses a psychological construct in a manner completely independent of the influence of other factors. The WISC-IV Indexes are all positively correlated because of their links to general intelligence and other factors that they share. These other factors include the fact that all subtests involve verbal instructions, that both the VCI and WMI subtests require verbal responses, and that the PRI and PSI subtests all involve some degree of visual processing. This means that one or several Indexes could be adversely impacted by the presence of an SLD.

As if the situation were not complicated enough, it is also possible for very bright students to compensate (as in *masking* noted previously) for deficits in one factor through the use of skills from another factor. For example, a student could use her/his strong visual memory (i.e., a narrow aspect of *Gv* theoretically measured by the PRI) to reduce the need to look back at the code key on the coding subtest. This could improve the student's coding score by compensating with a factor theoretically unrelated to processing speed (i.e., through construct-irrelevant variance), which is the factor index to which coding properly belongs. Furthermore, the phenomenon of verbal mediation being used to enhance one's scores on some traditional Wechsler subtests is well known (e.g., see Kaufman, 1994). From a WISC-IV perspective, this could mean using skills measured by the VCI to enhance one's performance on one or more subtests included in the PRI. From a CHC perspective, this could mean using *Gc* skills to enhance one's scores on measures intended to assess *Gv* or *Gf*. This could involve the child talking her/himself through visual-spatial problems or verbally coding visual stimuli to verbally reason through novel visual puzzles.

The diverse assessment needs of a child who is both intellectually gifted and learning disabled requires a comprehensive assessment by a well-trained, sensitive, and flexible examiner. Examiners must pay careful attention to all scores and test behaviors when assessing such children. Use of cross-battery methods, informal testing, and observations of both formal and informal problem solving should be considered in the service of gathering additional information to provide a more detailed picture of the child's strengths and weaknesses. The goal of such an assessment is the creation of an individualized program of accelerated instruction to address intellectual gifts, as well as accommodations, modifications, and remediative interventions to address learning difficulties (Volker, Lopata, & Cook-Cottone, 2006).

Alternative Composites and Subtest Issues

In general, WISC-IV composites that most reflect higher level thinking, reasoning, and problem solving are appropriate for use identifying students for gifted programming. These composites include the FSIQ, General Ability Index (GAI; Raiford, Weiss, Rolfhus, & Coalson, 2005), VCI, and PRI. The fact that the PSI and WMI tend to reflect more basic processing and that they tend to be relatively and substantially lower index scores for gifted students across samples when compared to the VCI and PRI suggests that these indexes should receive less weight in most gifted identification decisions.

The FSIQ is traditionally considered the best overall estimate of general intelligence. Its strength is that it draws on a broad range of subtests reflecting a diverse array of factors. However, the FSIQ has two interrelated weaknesses for the assessment of gifted students. The first is that several subtests on which gifted students have traditionally excelled have been moved out of the core battery (e.g., Arithmetic, Information), while the representation of WMI and PSI subtests (relatively weaker areas for gifted students) has increased in the core battery. The second is that subtests that contribute to the FSIQ are not differentially weighted according to their *g* loading or correlation with the general intelligence factor. The use of differential weighting might have to some extent offset the negative influence of less *g*-loaded subtests on the FSIQ for potentially gifted examinees.

The GAI for the WISC-IV is described in detail with normative tables based on the standardization sample in WISC-IV Technical Report No. 4 (Raiford, Weiss, Rolfhus, & Coalson, 2005). These same tables are also available in Appendix F1 on the CD-ROM that accompanies this book. A GAI is also automatically calculated and reported in the WISC-IV DMIA program on the CD. This index consists of the six core subtests that make up the VCI (Vocabulary, Similarities, and Comprehension) and PRI (Block Design, Matrix Reasoning, and Picture Concepts). It is meant to be used as an alternative estimate of general intelligence when: (a) either the WMI or PSI differs substantially from either the VCI or PRI, and (b) the VCI and PRI do not differ substantially from each other. Given the tendency for the FSIQ to be compromised by the relatively lower scores on the WMI and PSI subtests for gifted students, the GAI is likely to be relevant in many, if not most, gifted evaluations.

Given the higher order nature of the CHC constructs assessed by the VCI (i.e., *Gc*) and PRI (i.e., *Gv* and *Gf*), the fact that these domains tend to be good predictors of academic achievement, and that these Indexes tend to be areas of strength for gifted students, makes these Indexes well suited for gifted identification. Logical situations for their individual use include when a substantive discrepancy exists between them (i.e., making the FSIQ and GAI less meaningful for interpretation), when one is assessing an examinee from a diverse language or cultural background, or when an examinee presents with sensory, speech/language, motor, or neurological issues that may compromise performance on particular subtests.

The recommended use of the FSIQ, GAI, VCI, and PRI in gifted identification is supported by a position paper on the website of the National Association for Gifted Children (NAGC, 2008) as well as a recent chapter on flexible testing of the gifted by Rimm, Gilman, and Silverman (2008). It is consistent with the greater perceived utility of *g*, *Gc*, *Gf*, and *Gv* factors over *Gs*, *Ga*, and *Gsm* factors from a CHC view of intellectual giftedness (see Volker, Lopata, & Cottone, 2006, for more discussion of CHC factors and giftedness).

Consideration should be given to useful WISC-IV supplemental subtests for gifted children. Arithmetic, Information, Word Reasoning, and Picture Completion are all reasonable subtests to consider as supplemental or replacement subtests for potentially gifted students, when necessary. Note that only two subtest substitutions are allowable in the calculation of the FSIQ and only one substitution for each index. Silverman, Gilman, and Falk (2004) from the Gifted Development Center, in Denver, Colorado, report regularly substituting Arithmetic in place of Letter-Number Sequencing in gifted evaluations of children without math phobias. Given the very low *g* loading of the Cancellation subtest and its relatively lower mean score compared to most subtests for gifted students, it is not recommended for use in the identification of gifted examinees.

Improved Standard Subtest Ceilings and Extended Norms

Subtest ceilings are problematic when there are too few difficult items at the top of the subtest and too many examinees are able to respond correctly to all of the items. When this *ceiling effect* occurs, it means that the subtest cannot adequately discriminate among those who score at the top of the subtest. Kaufman (1992) described the subtests of the WISC-III as having excellent ceilings for distinguishing among gifted children between the ages of 6 and 14, with all core subtests allowing standard scores up to 3 SDs above the mean. Though all of the core subtests had ceilings that went at least 2 SDs above the mean even at age 16, it was considered less than optimal that several core subtests could not yield scores 3 SDs out at the top age for the test. In general, Kaufman described the WISC-III subtest ceilings as ranging from excellent to adequate.

In the WISC-IV, subtest ceilings were refined. More-difficult items were added to several subtests in order to expand the range of possible raw scores and push the subtest ceilings further. Now all subtests in the WISC-IV standard battery can yield standard scores up to 3 SDs above the mean at all ages covered by the test. Among the five supplemental subtests, the Word Reasoning subtest begins to show a lower ceiling starting at age 14, but all four other supplemental subtests can yield scores 3 SDs out up through age 16:11. Thus, the WISC-IV has excellent subtest ceilings that allow it to more accurately discriminate among higher functioning examinees.

Additionally, the WISC-IV Technical Report No. 7 (Zhu, Cayton, Weiss, & Gabel, 2008) provides examiners with extended norms for use when assessing highly and profoundly gifted youth. These norms used the existing standardization data to extend the subtest scaled score ceiling from 19 to as high as 28 in certain cases. For example, for a 6 year, 0 month old examinee, raw scores from 34 to 68 on the Vocabulary subtest would typically merit a scaled score of 19. Thus, the examinee who receives a raw score of 35 would receive the same scaled score as one who receives a raw score of 51. Using the extended norms, however, their scaled scores would be 19 and 27, respectively, highlighting the substantive and meaningful difference between them. Expanded tables to derive the four Indexes, the FSIQ, and the GAI are provided as well, so these differences can be reflected in composite scores. However, the item content of the WISC-IV does not encompass a sufficient number of extremely difficult items to provide this degree of differentiation among older adolescents; at age 16, only Digit Span, Coding, Letter-Number Sequencing, and Symbol Search (subtests that are generally less diagnostic of giftedness, regardless) can yield scores beyond 19. Nonetheless, this procedure can help differentiate among different levels of giftedness in elementary-aged examinees, enhancing not only gifted identification but also program planning. Just as a child with an IQ of 130 has markedly different educational needs than those of a child with an IQ of 90, a child with an IQ of 170 has markedly different educational needs than those of a child with an IQ of 130. Appropriate identification is vital as standard gifted programming is thus unlikely to meet the needs of such a child.

Dealing with Unconventional Correct Responses

Although sometimes observed in nongifted youth who are unusually precise, pedantic, literal, creative, or oppositional, unconventional correct responses or *too right* answers are most frequently generated by highly intelligent children. *Too right* answers are those that are technically correct and generally demonstrate more sophisticated knowledge or reasoning than expected for the item level. For example, when asked to provide the inventor of penicillin (often attributed to Alexander Fleming), an exceptionally gifted examinee may respond that Arabian horseback riders deliberately applied the fungus to promote wound healing as far back as the Middle Ages. This would not be similar to any listed response. If the examiner does query, telling the child to, "Explain what you mean," is likely to elicit further discussion of Arabian medicine, rather than an acceptable 1-point response. To further complicate matters, highly gifted examinees may provide answers beyond the examiner's level of knowledge or comprehension. In the previous example, it is reasonable to assume that many psychologists do not recall or were never taught about this innovation and thus would be unable to determine if the examinee's response merits further consideration. These responses are most prevalent on subtests that allow for open-ended verbal responses (i.e., those in the VCI), but they may underlie seemingly incorrect responses to Picture Concepts (e.g., choosing three items that are all exports of Holland) or Matrix Reasoning (e.g., interpreting the matrix through the Fibonacci sequence). As this issue therefore affects five out of the six core subtests that make up the GAI, the composite believed to be most relevant to gifted identification, *too right* answers represent a substantial concern. No specific method of addressing this concern is described in the WISC-IV manual, but a variety of strategies are available for consideration. Table 7.2 lists the various methods for dealing with unconventional responses, along with the pros and cons of using each method.

Table 7.2 Consequences of Different Methods for Dealing with Unconventional Correct Responses

Method	Pros	Cons
Tell the child prior to testing to give *simple* or *textbook* answers.	Reduces the likelihood that difficult-to-score answers will be elicited in the first place.	At times, the child may simplify her/his answer to the point at which he/she receives less credit.
Query possible *too right* answers by asking the child to provide the *simple* or *textbook* response.	Allows the child to give scorable responses when he or she is able to do so.	Permits the child to change her/his answer following nonstandard examiner prompting, leading to an uncertain decrease in reliability.
Give no credit for nonstandard answers. Consider reducing the cutoff score for entry into a gifted program.	Maximizes use of standardized scoring criteria. Makes minimal demands on examiner knowledge and judgment.	Penalizes highly able children and may unfairly underestimate their scores.
Give the child full credit for *too right* answers. In some cases, the examiner may have to delay scoring the item until he or she has the opportunity to research the child's response.	Minimizes the likelihood that the child will be penalized for his or her advanced intelligence. Could apply to PCn and MR if the examinee verbalizes reasons for her or his responses.	Questionably consistent with the standardization, relies heavily on examiner knowledge and judgment regarding which answers are sufficiently advanced to merit full credit.
Administer each subtest in a manner consistent with the standardization, but follow up anomalous answers with a testing of limits procedure. Report the standard scores, as well as how the scores would change with limits testing.	Provides a score fully consistent with the standardization and elucidates the degree to which crediting *too right* answers would alter the child's score.	Time consuming. Examinees may be confused by the procedure. Report of multiple scores may be difficult for parents, teachers, and administrators to interpret.
Follow up VCI subtests that may have been affected by *too right* answers with their WISC-IV Integrated multiple-choice counterparts.	VCI multiple choice tests minimize the potential for *too right* answers to impact the child's score, while maintaining fully standardized administration and scoring.	PCn and MR are not addressed. No extended scoring option (i.e., scaled scores > 19) is available for the WISC-IV Integrated. Additionally, WISC-IV Integrated scaled scores of 19 can only be obtained in all three core VCI subtests through age 13:11, limiting the utility of this procedure for gifted examinees ages 14 and up.

Note: PCn = Picture Concepts and MR = Matrix Reasoning

Of the procedures found in Table 7.2, the latter three seem to be the most defensible and can be integrated based upon the examinee's particular situation. When the examinee gives a small number of unconventional responses that the examiner can determine to be clearly correct, simply crediting these responses appears to be the most valid and efficient method. Qualitative descriptions of the examinee's response style should be included in the report so the reader is aware that these responses received full credit. If substantially more *too right* answers are given, or if the answers are of uncertain quality, the testing-of-limits procedure prevents the examiner from deviating too far from the standardization procedures, but it still provides an opportunity to measure the examinee's performance without the influence of unconventional responses. The WISC-IV Integrated multiple-choice VCI subtests are psychometrically sound and side-step the problem of *too right* answers, but due to ceiling effects, they should be used with caution with adolescent or profoundly gifted examinees.

In conclusion, the WISC-IV has reduced speed-of-performance demands, solid standardization and reasonable minimization of cultural bias, improved coverage of fluid ability, and a variety of scores beyond the FSIQ to assist in the evaluation of uneven abilities frequently seen in gifted profiles (see also Sparrow et al., 2005, for a discussion of how the changes in the WISC-IV impact gifted identification). Several studies of gifted samples using the WISC-IV (e.g., Rimm, Gilman, & Silverman, 2008; Wechsler, 2003; Zhu, Cayton, Weiss, & Gabel, 2008) have shown that the WISC-IV discriminates well between gifted and nongifted matched controls and that uneven WISC-IV index profiles occur frequently in the gifted population. We have made recommendations for dealing with unconventional correct item responses that are more likely to occur when testing gifted examinees. At this time, further research on the WISC-IV with gifted children is still needed to clarify how well they perform on this test relative to other cognitive tests.

USE OF THE WISC-IV AND WIAT-II WITHIN THE CONTEXT OF A CONTEMPORARY OPERATIONAL DEFINITION OF SPECIFIC LEARNING DISABILITY

Jennifer T. Mascolo

The WISC-IV and the Wechsler Individual Achievement Test–Second Edition (WIAT-II) together measure a range of cognitive and academic abilities that are important to assess when evaluating children suspected of having a specific learning disability (SLD). Although these and other major cognitive and academic batteries provide many of the tests necessary for conducting the type of comprehensive evaluation that is required to identify and diagnose SLD, the manner in which these tools are used varies widely. Having reliable and valid tests, such as those that comprise the WISC-IV/WIAT-II, is only part of the SLD evaluation equation. In the field of SLD, it has long been recognized that such tools should be used within the context of an operational definition (see Flanagan et al., 2002; Kavale & Forness, 2000, for a review).

To use the WISC-IV/WIAT-II within the context of an operational definition of SLD, you need to be able to make decisions related to the sufficiency of a WISC-IV/WIAT-II evaluation, identify normative and personal strengths and weaknesses, evaluate potential mitigating factors on test performance, and evaluate underachievement. The information presented here serves as one model for addressing SLD referrals using the WISC-IV and WIAT-II.

Assessing Individuals Referred for Learning Difficulties with the WISC-IV and WIAT-II

Table 7.3 describes the operational definition of SLD developed by Flanagan and colleagues (2002, 2006, 2007). The WISC-IV/WIAT-II may be used within the context of this operational definition for SLD referrals. The essential elements in defining SLD, as illustrated in this table, include (a) interindividual academic ability analysis (Level I-A); (b) evaluation of mitigating and exclusionary factors (Levels I-B and II-B); (c) interindividual cognitive ability and processing analysis (Level II-A); and (d) integrated analysis of abilities and processes (Level III). These elements together form an operational definition of SLD. The WISC-IV/WIAT-II can be used effectively to gather information and test hypotheses at each level of this operational definition. It is only when the criteria at each of these levels of the operational definition are met that you can be reasonably confident that a diagnosis of SLD is appropriate.

It is assumed that the levels of evaluation depicted in Table 7.3 are undertaken after prereferral intervention activities (consistent with a Response to Intervention or RtI approach) have been conducted with little or no success and, therefore, a focused evaluation of specific abilities and processes through standardized testing was deemed necessary. Moreover, prior to beginning an SLD assessment with the WISC-IV/WIAT-II, other significant data sources could have (and probably should have) already been uncovered within the context of intervention implementation. These data may include results from informal testing, direct observation of behaviors, work samples, reports from people familiar with the child's difficulties (e.g., teachers, parents), and perhaps information provided by the child him- or herself. In principle, Level I-A assessment should begin only after the

Table 7.3 Operational Definition of Specific Learning Disability

Essential Element	Focus of Assessment	Examples	Criteria	SLD Determination
Level I-A: Interindividual Analysis of Academic Skills	Performance in academic skills and acquired knowledge	Response to quality instruction and scientifically based intervention via progress monitoring, performance on norm-referenced tests, evaluation of work samples, clinical observations of academic performance	Performance in one or more academic domains falls *outside and below normal limits*	Necessary
Level I-B: Evaluation of Exclusionary Factors	Evaluation of potential primary causes of observed academic skill deficits	Intellectual disability, cultural or linguistic difference, sensory impairment, insufficient instruction or opportunity to learn, organic or physical health factors, emotional or psychological disturbance	Performance cannot be *primarily* attributed to these factors	
Level II-A: Interindividual Analysis of Cognitive Abilities and Processes	Performance in abilities, processes, and learning efficiency	Performance on norm-referenced tests, clinical observations of cognitive performance, task analysis	Performance in one or more cognitive abilities or processes *related to area of academic skill deficiency falls outside and below normal limits*	
Level II-B: Reevaluation of Exclusionary Factors	Evaluation of potential primary causes of observed manifest cognitive ability and processing deficits	Intellectual disability, cultural or linguistic difference, sensory impairment, insufficient instruction or opportunity to learn, organic or physical health factors, emotional or psychological disturbance	Performance cannot be *primarily* attributed to these factors	
Level III: Integrated Ability Analysis	Evaluation of underachievement	Identification of deficits in related academic and cognitive domains along with performance on other abilities within normal limits or higher	Below average aptitude-achievement consistency within an otherwise normal ability profile	Sufficient

Adapted from: Flanagan, Ortiz, Alfonso, and Mascolo (2006).

scope and nature of a child's learning difficulties have been documented. It is beyond the scope of this book to provide a detailed discussion of assessment- and interpretation-related activities for each level of the operational definition. Therefore, only a brief summary of each level follows (see Flanagan et al., 2006, 2007, for a comprehensive description of this SLD model).

Level I-A, Interindividual Academic Ability Analysis with the WIAT-II: Performance in Academic Skills and Acquired Knowledge

Level I-A focuses on the basic concept of SLD: that learning is somehow dis- rupted from its normal course on the basis of some type of internal disorder or dysfunction. Although the specific mechanism that inhibits learning is not directly observable, one can proceed on the assumption that it manifests itself in observable phenomena, particularly academic achievement. Thus, the first component of the operational definition involves documenting that some type of *learning* deficit exists. Accordingly, the process at Level I-A involves compre- hensive measurement of the major areas of academic achievement (e.g., reading, writing, math abilities) or any subset of abilities that form the focus and purpose of the evaluation.

The academic abilities that are generally assessed at this level in the opera- tional definition include the eight areas of achievement specified in the federal definition of SLD as outlined in the Individuals with Disabilities Education Act (IDEA, 2004). These eight areas are math calculation, math reasoning, basic read- ing skill, reading fluency, reading comprehension, written expression, listening comprehension, and oral expression. Most of the abilities measured at Level I-A represent an individual's stores of acquired knowledge. These specific knowledge bases (e.g., Quantitative Knowledge, Reading Ability, Writing Ability) develop largely as a function of formal instruction, schooling, and educationally related experiences. Rapid Reference 7.1 lists the WIAT-II subtests that correspond to the eight achievement areas specified in the federal definition of SLD. This Rapid Reference includes a list of subtests from the Woodcock-Johnson Tests of Achievement–Third Edition (WJ III ACH) and the Kaufman Test of Educational Achievement–Second Edition, Comprehensive Form (KTEA-II; Kaufman & Kaufman, 2004b) that may be used to supplement the WIAT-II, if necessary, via the Cross-Battery method (see Flanagan et al., 2006, 2007, for a detailed review of this approach).

Once you select and administer achievement tests (see Rapid Reference 7.1), evaluate performance to determine whether an academic *Normative Weakness* is present. This is accomplished through an *interindividual academic ability analysis*. This type of analysis involves making normative-based comparisons of the child's

Representation of Academic Abilities by SLD Area on the WIAT-II and Other Comprehensive Achievement Batteries

LD Area Listed in IDEA Definition	WIAT-II	KTEA-II	WJ III ACH
Basic Reading Skills	Word Reading (RD) Pseudoword Decoding (RD)	Letter & Word Recognition (RD) Nonsense Word Decoding (RD, PC:A) Phonological Awareness (PC:A; PC:S) Naming Facility (RAN) (Glr-NA)	L-W Identification (RD) Word Attack (RD, PC:A)
Reading Fluency Skills		Decoding Fluency (RD, RS, PC:A) Word Recognition Fluency (RD, RS)	Reading Fluency (RS)
Reading Comprehension	Reading Comprehension (RC)	Reading Comprehension (RC)	Passage Comprehension (RC, CZ) Reading Vocabulary (V:VL)
Math Calculation	Numerical Operations (A3)	Math Computation (A3)	Math Fluency (N, Gq-A3) Calculation (A3)
Math Problem Solving	Math Reasoning (Gf-RQ)	Math Concepts & Applications (Gf-RQ; Gq-KM, A3)	Applied Problems (A3, KM, Gf-RQ) Quantitative Concepts (KM, Gf-RQ)

	WIAT-II	KTEA-II	WJ III ACH
Written Expression	Spelling (SG) Written Expression (WA)	Spelling (SG) Written Expression (WA, EU)	Spelling (SG) Writing Samples (WA) Editing (EU) Punctuation & Capitalization (EU) Spelling of Sounds (SG, PC:A) Writing Fluency (WA; Gs-R9)
Oral Expression	Oral Expression (CM)	Oral Expression (CM, MY) Associational Fluency (Glr-FA)	Story Recall (LS; Glr-MM) Picture Vocabulary (LD,VL)
Listening Comprehension	Listening Comprehension (LS)	Listening Comprehension (LS)	Understanding Directions (LS, Gsm-MW) Oral Comprehension (LS)

Note. WIAT-II = Wechsler Individual Achievement Test–Second Edition; KTEA-II = Kaufman Test of Educational Achievement–Second Edition; WJ III ACH = Woodcock Johnson Tests of Achievement–Third Edition. See Appendix A for CHC Broad and Narrow ability definitions. Narrow ability classifications are based on expert consensus (Flanagan, Ortiz, Alfonso, & Mascolo, 2006). Story Recall–Delayed (Glr-MM) and Handwriting Legibility Scale are two supplemental measures on the WJ III ACH not included in this table. A3 = Math Achievement; A5 = Geography Achievement; CM = Comunication Ability; CZ = Cloze Ability; EU = English Usage Knowledge; K0 = General (Verbal) Information; KI = General Science Information; K2 = Information about Culture; KM = Math Knowledge; LD = Language Development; LS = Listening Ability; MM = Meaningful Memory; N = Number Fluency; NA = Naming Facility; PC:A = Phonetic Coding:Analysis; PC:S = Phonetic Coding:Synthesis; RC = Reading Comprehension; RD = Reading Decoding; RQ = Quantitative Reasoning; RS = Reading Speed; SG = Spelling Ability; V = Verbal (Printed) Language Comprehension; VL = Lexical Knowledge; WA = Writing Ability; WS = Writing Speed.

WIAT-II (or any other achievement test) performance against a representative sample of same-age or -grade peers from the general population. If Normative Weaknesses in the child's academic achievement profile are not identified, then the issue of SLD may be moot because such weaknesses are a necessary component of the definition, especially in early elementary school years and prior to remedial instruction and intervention. Therefore, the presence of a Normative Weakness established through standardized testing as well as by other means, such as clinical observations of academic performance, work samples, and so forth, is a necessary (but insufficient) condition for SLD determination. By definition, dysfunction in learning as manifest in significant academic difficulties forms the foundation of all prevailing SLD definitions. Therefore, when a Normative Weakness in academic performance or learning is found (irrespective of the particular method by which it is identified), a necessary but not sufficient condition for SLD is established and you can advance to Level I-B.

Level I-B, Evaluation of Exclusionary Factors

The criterion at Level I-B involves evaluating whether any documented Normative Weakness found through Level I-A analysis is or is not *primarily* the result of factors that may be, for example, largely external to the child or noncognitive in nature. Because there can be many reasons for deficient academic performance, you should be careful not to ascribe causal links to SLD prematurely and should develop reasonable hypotheses related to other potential causes. For example, cultural and linguistic differences are two common factors that can affect both test performance and academic skill acquisition adversely and result in achievement data that appear to suggest SLD (this topic is discussed in the next section of this chapter). In addition, lack of motivation, emotional disturbance, performance anxiety, psychiatric disorders, sensory impairments, and medical conditions (e.g., hearing or vision problems) also need to be ruled out as potential explanatory correlates to any Normative Weaknesses identified on WIAT-II (or other) achievement subtests at Level I-A. The crux of the criterion at this level rests on the extent to which any factors other than cognitive impairment can be considered the primary reason for the Normative Weakness in academic performance. If performance cannot be attributed primarily to other factors, then the second criterion necessary for establishing SLD according to the operational definition is met, and assessment may continue to the next level.

It is important to recognize that although factors, such as having English as a second language, may be present and may affect performance adversely, SLD can also be present. Certainly, children who may have vision problems, chronic illnesses, limited English proficiency, and so forth may well possess some type of SLD. Therefore, when these or other factors at Level I-B are present or even when they are determined to be contributing to poor performance, SLD should not be ruled out automatically. Rather, only when such factors are determined to be *primarily* responsible for Normative Weaknesses in learning and academic performance, not merely *contributing* to them, should SLD, as an explanation for dysfunction in performance, be discounted. Examination of exclusionary factors is necessary to ensure fair and equitable interpretation of the data collected for SLD determination and is not intended to rule in SLD but rather to specifically rule out other possible explanations for deficient academic performance. You should remember that the final determination of SLD is made only after all criteria from each and every level are met, irrespective of how dramatic any particular datum or pattern of data may appear initially.

One of the major reasons for placing evaluation of exclusionary factors at this point in the assessment process is to provide a mechanism that is efficient in both time and effort and that may prevent the unnecessary administration of tests or imposition of further invasive and unneeded evaluative procedures. Use of standardized tests, in particular IQ tests, cannot be considered a benign process. The implications and ramifications that can result from their use demands that you carefully and selectively apply them only when necessary. We recognize, of course, that it may not be possible to completely and convincingly rule out all of the numerous potential exclusionary factors at this stage in the assessment process. For example, the data gathered at Levels I-A and I-B may be insufficient to draw conclusions about such conditions as Intellectual Disability, which often requires more thorough and direct cognitive assessment. Therefore, proper assessment must seek to uncover and evaluate as many possibilities as is practical or necessary. When exclusionary factors have been carefully evaluated and eliminated as possible *primary* explanations for poor Level I-A performance—at least those that can be reliably assessed at this level—assessment may advance to the next level.

Level II-A, Interindividual Cognitive Ability Analysis with the WISC-IV: Performance in Cognitive Abilities and Processes

The criterion at this level is similar to the one specified in Level I-A except that it is evaluated with data from an assessment of cognitive abilities and processes (e.g., from the WISC-IV). Analysis of data generated from the administration of standardized tests represents the most common method available by which cognitive functioning in children can be evaluated. However, this does not preclude the use of other types of information and data relevant to cognitive performance. In keeping with good assessment practices, you should actively seek out and gather data from other sources as a means of providing corroborating evidence for whatever conclusions you reach. In general, the assessment process at Level II-A, as with the measurement of abilities at Level I-A, proceeds with the expectation that a child's cognitive performance will be *Within Normal Limits* unless otherwise indicated by careful analysis of all available data. This is true even when actual, verifiable academic Normative Weaknesses are identified at Level I-A. Rapid Reference 7.2 identifies the CHC abilities measured by the WISC-IV as well as by other major intelligence and cognitive batteries.

A particularly salient aspect of any operational definition of SLD is the concept of a neurologically based dysfunction in a cognitive ability or process that presumably underlies the difficulties in academic performance or skill development observed at Level I-A. Because nearly all SLD definitions either specify directly or imply that the relationship between the cognitive dysfunction and the manifest learning problems are not random but rather causal in nature, data analysis at this level should seek to ensure that identified Normative Weaknesses on cognitive tests bear an empirical or logical relationship to those Normative Weaknesses previously identified on achievement tests. It is this very notion that makes it necessary to draw upon cognitive theory and research to inform SLD definitions and increase the reliability and validity of the SLD determination process. Theory and its related research base not only specifies the relevant constructs in SLD determination (e.g., constructs that ought to be measured at Levels I-A and II-A), but it also predicts the manner in which they are related. Therefore, application of current theory and research serves to guide data analysis at all levels, including this one, and provides a substantive empirical foundation from which interpretations and conclusions may be drawn. Table 7.4 provides a summary of the relations between CHC cognitive abilities and processes and reading, math, and written language achievement. This table may assist in organizing assessments at Levels I-A and II-A as well as aid in determining whether the Level II-A criterion has been met.

Meeting the criterion at Level II-A requires the identification of interindividual cognitive ability or processing deficits that are empirically or logically related to the corresponding Normative Weaknesses previously identified in academic performance at Level I-A. When evaluation of cognitive performance is comprehensive and sufficient in terms of measuring the areas of suspected dysfunction and no Normative Weaknesses in cognitive functioning are found, then poor academic performance alone, as identified at Level I-A, is not sufficient to establish the presence of SLD. Likewise, when a Normative Weakness in cognitive functioning is identified at Level II-A but the area of dysfunction is not logically or empirically related to the Normative Weakness at Level I-A, then the presence of SLD is indeterminate.

CHC Abilities and Processes Measured by Current Intelligence Tests

Broad Ability	WISC-IV	KABC-II	WJ III
Gf	Picture Concepts (I; Gc-KO) Matrix Reasoning (I, RG) Arithmetic (RQ, Gq-A3 for ages 11–16 years; Gsm-WM, Gq-A3 for ages 6–10 years)[1]	Pattern Reasoning (I, Gv-Vz) Story Completion (I, RG; Gc-KO; Gv-Vz)	Concept Formation (I) Analysis Synthesis (RG)
Gc	Similarities (LD, V-; Gf-I) Vocabulary (VL) Comprehension (KO) Information (KO) Word Reasoning (VL; Gf-I)	Riddles (VL, LD; Gf-I, RG) Expressive Vocabulary (VL) Verbal Knowledge (VL, KO)	Verbal Comprehension (VL, LD) General Information (KO)
Ga	—	—	Sound Blending (PC:S) Auditory Attention (US/U3, UR)
Gv	Block Design (SR,Vz) Picture Completion (CF; Gc-KO)	Conceptual Thinking (Vz; Gf-I) Block Counting (Vz; Gq-A3) Face Recognition (MV) Triangles (SR;Vz) Rover (SS; Gf-RG) Gestalt Closure (CS)	Spatial Relations (Vz, SR) Picture Recognition (MV)

(continued)

285

Broad Ability	WISC-IV	KABC-II	WJ III
Gsm	Digit Span (MS, WM) Letter-Number Sequencing (WM)	Word Order (MS, WM) Number Recall (MS)	Numbers Reversed (WM) Memory for Words (MS)
Glr	—	Atlantis (MA, LI) Rebus (MA, LI)	Visual-Auditory Learning (MA, LI) Retrieval Fluency (FI)
Gs	Coding (R9) Symbol Search (P, R9) Cancellation (P, R9)	—	Visual Matching (P, R9) Decision Speed (RE, R9)

Source: Narrow ability classifications are based on expert consensus, theory-driven joint factor analyses, and information presented in the test manuals of each cognitive battery (see Flanagan, Ortiz, & Alfonso, 2007).

Note: WISC-IV = Wechsler Intelligence Scale for Children–Fourth Edition; KABC-II = Kaufman Assessment Battery for Children–Second Edition; WJ III = Woodcock-Johnson Tests of Cognitive Abilities–Third Edition. A3 = Math Achievement; I = Inductive Reasoning; K0 = General (Verbal) Information; KM = Math Knowledge; MA = Associative Memory; MM = Meaningful Memory; MS = Memory Span; NA = Naming Facility; P = Perceptual Speed; PC:A = Phonetic Coding: Analysis; PC:S = Phonetic Coding: Synthesis; RG = General Sequential Reasoning; RQ = Quantitative Reasoning; VL = Lexical Knowledge; SR = Spatial Relations; CF = Flexibility of Closure; MV = Visual Memory; WM = Working Memory; R9 = Rate-of-test-taking; Vz = Visualization; SS = Spatial Scanning; CS = Closure Speed; L = Learning Abilities; US/U3 = Speech/General Sound Discrimination; UR = Resistance to Auditory Stimulus Distortion; FI = Ideational Fluency; FA = Associational Fluency. See Appendix A for select CHC broad and narrow ability definitions.

[1]The *primary* classifications of Arithmetic in this table are based on the factor analyses of Keith and colleagues (2006). In most other factor analytic studies, Arithmetic loads primarily on *Gq* (and is considered to be primarily a measure of Math Achievement and Math Knowledge), indicating that specification error may have led to the Keith et al. findings for this subtest.

Table 7.4 Relations Between CHC Cognitive Abilities and Processes and Academic Achievement

CHC Ability	Reading Achievement	Math Achievement	Writing Achievement
Gf	Inductive (I) and general sequential reasoning (RG) abilities play a moderate role in reading comprehension.	**Inductive (I) and general sequential (RG) reasoning abilities are consistently very important at all ages.**	Inductive (I) and general sequential reasoning abilities are related to basic writing skills primarily during the elementary school years (e.g., 6 to 13) and consistently related to written expression at all ages.
Gc	**Language development (LD), lexical knowledge (VL), and listening ability (LS) are important at all ages. These abilities become increasingly more important with age.**	**Language development (LD), lexical knowledge (VL), and listening abilities (LS) are important at all ages. These abilities become increasingly more important with age.**	**Language development (LD), lexical knowledge (VL), and general information (K0) are important primarily after age 7. These abilities become increasingly more important with age.**
Gsm	Memory span (MS) is important especially when evaluated within **the context of working memory.**	Memory span (MS) is important especially when evaluated within the context of working memory.	Memory span (MS) is important to writing, especially spelling skills, whereas working memory has shown relations with advanced writing skills (e.g., written expression).
Gv		May be important primarily for higher level or advanced mathematics (e.g., geometry, calculus).	

(continued)

Table 7.4 (Continued)

CHC Ability	Reading Achievement	Math Achievement	Writing Achievement
Ga	**Phonetic coding (PC) or *phonological awareness/processing* is very important during the elementary school years.**		**Phonetic coding (PC) or *phonological awareness/processing* is very important during the elementary school years for both basic writing skills and written expression (primarily before age 11).**
Glr	**Naming facility (NA) or *rapid automatic naming* is very important during the elementary school years.** Associative memory (MA) may be important.	Important for acquiring basic math skills and in developing automaticity with math facts.	Naming facility (NA) or *rapid automatic naming* has demonstrated relations with written expression, primarily the fluency aspect of writing.
Gs	**Perceptual speed (P) abilities are important during all school years, particularly the elementary school years.**	**Perceptual speed (P) abilities are important during all school years, particularly the elementary school years.**	**Perceptual speed (P) abilities are important during all school years and related to all ages for written expression.**

Note. The absence of comments for a particular CHC ability or process and achievement area (e.g., *Ga* and mathematics) indicates that the research reviewed either did not report any significant relations between the respective CHC construct and the achievement area, or if significant findings were reported, they were weak and were for only a limited number of studies. Also, it may be that research on a particular relationship between a cognitive ability or process and an academic skill has not been conducted to date. Comments in bold represent the CHC constructs that showed the strongest and most consistent relations with the respective achievement domain. Information in this table was reproduced from Flanagan, Ortiz, and Alfonso (2007) with permission from Wiley. All rights reserved.

Level II-B, Reevaluation of Exclusionary Factors

Because new data (e.g., WISC-IV data) were gathered at the previous level, re-evaluation of mitigating or exclusionary factors, as conducted at Level I-B, should be undertaken again at this point. Although establishing the presence of a Normative Weakness in cognitive functioning that is related to an identified Normative Weakness in academic performance (as done in Level II-A) is fundamental to the operational definition of SLD, it should be determined that such a Normative Weakness is not the primary result of exclusionary factors. Reevaluation of mitigating and exclusionary hypotheses at this level illustrates the recursive nature of this component of the SLD determination process. Reliable and valid measurement of SLD depends partly on being able to exclude the many factors that could play a part in affecting cognitive-ability performance adversely. When it can be reasonably determined that the Normative Weaknesses in cognitive functioning identified at Level II-A cannot be ascribed primarily to exclusionary factors, then the necessary criterion at this level is met and advancement to the next level of assessment is appropriate.

Level III, Integrated Ability Analysis with the WISC-IV and WIAT-II: Evaluation of Underachievement

Integrated ability analysis revolves around theory- and research-guided examination of a child's WISC-IV/WIAT-II performance across both cognitive and academic domains in order to establish the condition of underachievement. When the process of evaluating SLD has reached this level, three necessary criteria for SLD determination have already been met: (a) One or more Normative Weaknesses in academic performance have been identified; (b) one or more Normative Weaknesses in cognitive abilities and processes that are related to the area(s) of academic weakness have been identified; and (c) exclusionary factors have been ruled out as the primary causes of the identified Normative Weaknesses in academic and cognitive performance. What has not been determined, however, is whether the pattern of results supports the notion of underachievement in a manner that suggests SLD. The nature of underachievement, within the context of the operational definition presented here, suggests that not only does a child possess specific, circumscribed, and related academic and cognitive Normative Weaknesses—referred to as a below average *aptitude-achievement consistency* in the operational definition of SLD—but that these weaknesses also exist within *an otherwise normal ability profile*. The information in Table 7.4 will assist in evaluating consistencies between cognitive abilities and/or processes and academic achievement.

It is important to understand that discovery of consistencies among cognitive abilities and/or processes and academic skills in the Below Average or lower range could result from intellectual disability or generally low cognitive ability. There-fore, identification of SLD cannot rest on below average aptitude-achievement consistency alone. A child must also demonstrate evidence of intact function-ing (e.g., Within Normal Limits or higher) on WISC-IV and WIAT-II measures, for example, that are less related to the presenting problem. For example, in the case of a child with reading-decoding difficulties, it would be necessary to deter-mine that performance in areas less related to this skill (e.g., *Gf,* math ability) are Within Normal Limits or higher. Such a finding would suggest that the related weaknesses in cognitive and academic domains are not due to a more pervasive form of dysfunction thus supporting the notion of *underachievement*—that the child could in all likelihood perform within normal limits in whatever achieve-ment skill he or she was found to be deficient if not for a specific cognitive defi-cit or disorder. The finding of Normative Weaknesses in a circumscribed set of related or domain-specific, cognitive and academic areas (i.e., below average aptitude-achievement consistency) within an otherwise normal ability profile is, for all intents and purposes, convincing evidence of SLD. In sum, underachieve-ment is established through the aptitude-achievement consistency method only on the basis of two necessary conditions: (a) a consistency between specific cognitive abilities and/or processes as measured by the WISC-IV (and/or other cognitive tests) and one or more academic abilities as measured by the WIAT-II (and/or other achievement tests) that are related and generally confined to the Below Average or lower range of functioning; and (b) performance in some cognitive or achievement areas that is Within Normal Limits or higher. Recently, Flanagan and colleagues (2007) developed a program called the *SLD Assistant* to aid practi-tioners in determining whether an otherwise normal ability profile is evident for individuals who demonstrate below average aptitude-achievement consistencies.

Summary of the Operational Definition of Specific Learning Disability
The preceding paragraphs provided a brief summary of the major components of a contemporary operational definition of SLD that was designed specifically to assist clinicians in the evaluation of SLD. The operational definition presented here provides a common foundation for the practice of SLD determination and will likely be most effective when it is informed by cognitive theory and research that supports (a) the identification and measurement of constructs associated with SLD, (b) the relationship between selected cognitive and academic abilities and processes, and (c) a defensible method of interpreting results. The opera-tional definition is based primarily on the work of Flanagan and colleagues (2002, 2006, 2007) and was adapted here for use with the WISC-IV and WIAT-II. Of the many important components of the definition, the central focus revolved

around specification of criteria at the various levels of assessment that should be met to establish the presence of SLD. These criteria included identification of empirically or logically related academic and cognitive abilities and processes that fell in the Normative Weakness range, evaluation of exclusionary factors, and identification of a pattern of underachievement, including identification of intact functioning.

In keeping with the conclusions of Flanagan and colleagues, when the criteria specified at each level of the operational definition are met (as depicted in Table 7.3), it may be concluded that the data gathered are sufficient to support a diagnosis of SLD in a manner consistent with IDEA (2004) and its attendant regulations. Because the conditions outlined in Table 7.3 are based on current SLD research, the operational definition presented here represents progress toward a more complete and defensible approach to the process of evaluating SLD than previous methods (see also Flanagan, Ortiz, Alfonso, & Dynda, 2007; Hale, Flanagan, & Naglieri, 2008). We believe that an operational definition of this type has the potential to increase agreement among professionals with respect to who does and does not have SLD. Toward that end, Rapid Reference 7.3 lists five questions that guide the SLD assessment activities within the scope of this definition. The questions are phrased in a straightforward manner and together provide an indication of both the type of data that may need to be collected as well as the manner in which the data should be interpreted as being sufficient to meet the respective criteria at each level.

A Comprehensive Framework for Specific Learning Disability Determination

Broadly speaking, *SLD assessment* can be defined as an exercise in decision making. This was evident in the previous discussion of the operational definition of SLD. However, the decision-making process extends beyond the confines of the specifications of the definition to the broader process of assessment as a whole. Whether focusing directly on criteria related to the definition or not, the general process of psychological assessment involves a broader set of questions or conditions that should be attended to in order to establish a firm basis for defending any final interpretations and conclusions. For example, issues related to the degree that the collected data respond appropriately to the specific referral questions, the sufficiency of the evaluation of any abilities or processes that may have been measured, and the nature and type of intervention and remediation that may be required represent components of any comprehensive assessment, particularly those centered on SLD determination.

Attention to the general aspects of SLD assessment is important for several reasons. First, and perhaps most importantly, careful attention to the operational

≡ Rapid Reference 7.3

Summary of Guiding Questions Implied by the Operational Definition of Specific Learning Disability

Question 1   Does the child demonstrate one or more interindividual deficits in one or more academic abilities (e.g., in reading, writing, mathematics)?

Question 2   Can the academic skill deficits be attributed *primarily* to mitigating or exclusionary factors such as sensory impairment, emotional disturbance, inadequate schooling or instruction, limited familiarity with the language used in the test items, low motivation or energy, and so on?

Question 3   Does the child demonstrate interindividual deficits in one or more cognitive abilities or processes that are empirically or logically related to the development or acquisition of the academic ability found to be deficient?

Question 4   Can the cognitive ability or processing deficits be attributed *primarily* to mitigating or exclusionary factors such as sensory impairment, emotional disturbance, intellectual disability, limited familiarity with the language used in the test items, low motivation or energy, and so on?

Question 5   Is there evidence of underachievement as represented by a Below Average aptitude-achievement consistency within an otherwise normal ability profile?

Source: These questions are based on the operational definition presented in Flanagan and colleagues (2002, 2006, 2007).

---

criteria for establishing SLD does not automatically validate the entire assessment process. For example, identifying SLD in reading comprehension serves little purpose if the referral concern centered on difficulties in mathematical computation. Failure to collect data that can be used to answer the questions that precipitated the referral, no matter how meticulously the data were gathered, represents an inefficient use of time and effort. Second, practitioners often take for granted that the abilities and processes they sought to measure were in fact the ones that *were* measured. Unless you carefully evaluate the sufficiency of the data gathered (i.e., the degree to which you actually measured the relevant and precise abilities and processes in question), interpretations may not be valid. Although it is logical to assume that a test of reading comprehension does in fact measure reading comprehension, you should not take for granted that any test will in fact measure what it is purported to measure with equal reliability and validity for every individual and across every age group. Even tests that are presumed to measure the same ability may vary simply as a function of slight differences in task characteristics (e.g., feedback given or not given, verbal responding versus pointing). Accordingly, you should be familiar with the qualitative and quantitative characteristics of any tests used (e.g., task characteristics, reliability at different ages, specificity, validity, floors and ceilings) to further substantiate your impressions (see Appendix D on the CD-ROM). Third, identification of SLD or other problems does not represent an end in and of itself. Rather, it represents the beginning of a new set of assessment activities that seek to link the results of the evaluation to appropriate types of intervention and remediation. Moreover, what might constitute an appropriate remedial strategy or accommodation for a particular type of disability in one child does not imply that the same is true for another child with the same disability. The manner in which SLD manifests in children can vary considerably, even when two children share essentially the same difficulties or diagnosis (e.g., SLD in math or reading).

In sum, defensible evaluation of SLD cannot rest on simply meeting the criteria set forth in the operational definition described here—or in any other definition, for that matter. Careful attention to the issues and questions that make up the activities of the assessment process as a whole, within which the operational definition is embedded, is also required so that proper and defensible decisions can be made. This broader process of SLD assessment is illustrated graphically as a decision-based flowchart and is presented in Figure 7.1. The flowchart is easily navigated via the specification of particular assessment activities and evaluation procedures that proceed on the basis of answers to Yes/No questions. A more comprehensive discussion of the major aspects and decision points involved in the process may be found in Flanagan and colleagues (2006, 2007, 2008). Decisions in the case of Ryan in Chapter 9 of this book were made, in part, following the operational definition presented here.

Conclusion

This section presented an operational definition of SLD that can be used with the WISC-IV and WIAT-II and that was based primarily on the work of Flanagan and colleagues (2002, 2006, 2007). In broad terms, the operational definition described in this section consists of various levels that specify the necessary criteria required for SLD determination. Meeting these particular criteria and evaluating the components of the broader process of assessment (Fig. 7.1) are necessary for making a diagnosis of SLD and constitute a best-practices approach to the assessment of learning difficulties in children (see Flanagan et al., 2008). In

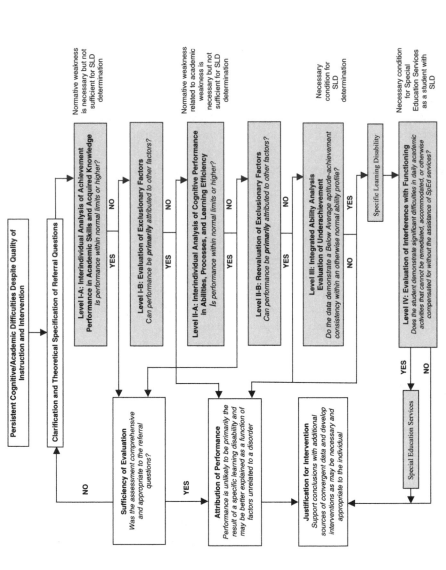

Figure 7.1 Flowchart for SLD Identification Following Flanagan and Colleagues' Operational Definition

sum, the operational definition and comprehensive framework presented here provide practitioners and researchers with an inherently practical method for SLD assessment that is more reliable and defensible than that represented by traditional methods and practices (Hale, Flanagan, & Nagileri, 2008; Kavale, Holdnack, & Mostert, 2005).

BILINGUAL-MULTICULTURAL ASSESSMENT WITH THE WISC-IV

Samuel O. Ortiz

Despite nearly a century of experience and research in testing individuals from diverse cultural and linguistic backgrounds, our understanding regarding what constitutes best practices in this assessment domain remains relatively unclear and uncertain. Perhaps the main reason for this is that few areas in assessment match the range and complexity of variables that characterize the evaluation of culturally and linguistically diverse individuals. For example, when a professional seeks to evaluate an individual who speaks both English and another language, immediate questions are raised regarding whether the evaluation should be conducted in English or the other language, whether the individual has sufficient proficiency to be evaluated in English, whether administration of a nonverbal test would be more appropriate, will any modifications or adaptations to the testing process be necessary, and so forth. Factors that will weigh heavily in making these decisions include age of language exposure and acquisition, degree of acculturation to "mainstream" society, regional location within a country, and support for maintenance of the native language and culture, to name a few (Harris & Llorente, 2005; Ortiz, 2008).

Despite provisions in the latest and prior renditions of IDEA regarding the need to select and administer tests in a manner that is racially, culturally, and linguistically fair (including in the native language where feasible), historically, the vast majority of intelligence testing on non-English–speaking children has been conducted in English (most often with one of the Wechsler Scales, e.g., WISC-IV) and is a common practice that persists to the present day (Ochoa, Powell, & Robles-Piña, 1996). This is not to say that the WISC-IV, given in English, has been popular because it was built upon issues of established fairness or cross-cultural validity. It is more likely that, given the lack of technically adequate tests in languages other than English, the paucity of competent and qualified bilingual-bicultural professionals, and the absence of any systematic framework or guiding principles for addressing bilingual-multicultural issues in assessment, professionals have simply resorted to doing what they know best (Ortiz, 2001). As will be discussed, there are relatively recent theoretically and empirically based methods that allow professionals to account for the manner in which various factors might affect test performance when the WISC-IV (and other tests) are administered in English. In addition, a new wrinkle has been added to the decision-making process by the publication of the WISC-IV Spanish. Professionals with competency in the administration of Spanish-language tests may now wish to consider when this version may be more suitable for use with a particular individual than the English version.

The nature of these types of decisions—that is, the how and why the WISC-IV may be used to assess and evaluate the intelligence and cognitive capabilities of children from diverse cultural and linguistic backgrounds in a fair and equitable manner—as well as the principles on which they should be based constitute the focus and purpose of this section. Readers are cautioned, however, that the procedures described herein are not, in and of themselves, a complete answer to the obstacles extant in assessing diverse children and do not, by themselves, constitute the only—or even a sufficient—solution for establishing definitively the intelligence of such children. It is believed, however, that some of the procedures described in this section represent a significant advancement in the assessment of culturally and linguistically diverse children, particularly as compared to the methods historically and presently employed with the first publication and subsequent revisions of the WISC.

Understanding Bias versus Fairness

Understanding how to approach intellectual assessment with diverse populations using the WISC-IV requires knowledge regarding why certain practices or procedures are or are not equitable or appropriate. Indeed, there are both ethical guidelines (American Psychological Association, 1990, 2002) and professional standards (American Education Research Association, American Psychological Association, & National Council on Measurement in Education, 1999) that require psychologists to adhere to various principles in establishing adequate reliability, validity, and fairness in testing. Whereas the prescriptions for fairness and bias reduction in testing are relatively clear, how such adequacy is actually achieved is significantly more cloudy.

There have been three major procedures used over the years to guide administration of a WISC to children from diverse cultural or linguistic backgrounds. These methods include (a) modifications and adaptations to the standardized administration or scoring of the test; (b) use of selected tests or a battery that is primarily nonverbal; and (c) use of a native-language test, that is, the WISC-IV Spanish (Ortiz & Dynda, in press). Although intended to increase fairness in testing, each of these methods has significant limitations and disadvantages that may not allow professionals to obtain the degree of equity to which they must aspire.

The first method, modifying or adapting the test in terms of administration or scoring, is often seen in procedures in which either extra time is allowed on timed tests (e.g., Block Design) or time constraints are eliminated altogether and the individual is allowed to continue for a reasonable length of time until a correct answer is obtained or it is clear that the solution is not forthcoming. Other adaptations involve accepting responses in either language (irrespective of the language of the test), repeating instructions to ensure comprehension (including explanations in the native language), and mediating task concepts prior to administering items to ensure the individual understands what is required. The most significant difficulty with these procedures is that they violate standardization directly and, in so doing, introduce error to unknown degrees and undermine the reliability and validity of the obtained results. It is difficult enough for professionals to establish validity of scores generated with diverse individuals, but it is virtually impossible to do so if standardization is violated and, therefore, this method is not recommended.

The second method is still perhaps the most common practice for assessing the intelligence of children from culturally and linguistically diverse backgrounds and involves administration of only the subtests that make up the PIQ (Figueroa, 1990) or administration of a nonverbal battery (e.g., Wechsler Nonverbal Scales of Ability). The WISC-IV, including the Spanish version, no longer provides the VIQ or PIQ, but the practice gained popularity in previous versions of the WISC, which utilized this dichotomous organization of subtests segregated into the Verbal and Performance categories. It seemed reasonable and simple enough to suggest that children who had limited English proficiency should be administered the subtests within the Performance category mainly because the Performance subtests relied far less on language development and ability as compared to the Verbal subtests. Thus, the reduction in language demands on the Performance tests should result in an IQ (i.e., the PIQ) that is a fairer estimate of the child's intelligence. In the WISC-IV, one could extend this logic to administration of the subtests that form the Processing Speed Index (PSI; Coding and Symbol Search) and to some extent the Perceptual Reasoning Index (PRI; Block Design, Picture Concepts, and Matrix Reasoning).

In a similar vein, administration of a nonverbal battery has become nearly routine in the evaluation of culturally and linguistically diverse children. As with the logic in using less verbally loaded subtests, the idea here is to eliminate language issues directly. According to Weiss and colleagues (2006), administration of a nonverbal cognitive assessment is "an acceptable answer to this problem"

(p. 49), but this may be an overly optimistic view. Consider for example that in cases in which a child's dysfunction is actually language based or related to verbal abilities, use of nonverbal tests alone will not provide any useful information about possible reasons for language-related dysfunction (e.g., problems in reading or writing). In addition, although nonverbal subtests rely less on language demands than verbal tests, they are not totally devoid of language demands or cultural content nearly to the extent that they may appear. Block Design, for example, requires no verbal expression to provide a response, yet it requires considerable linguistic comprehension to understand the instructions. Likewise, Picture Arrangement does not require any spoken response, but an individual's understanding of the events within the pictures and their sequence is subject to cultural familiarity and knowledge. In point of fact, no test, nonverbal or otherwise, can be administered without some type and form of communication present between the examiner and examinee. Whether that communication occurs verbally or nonverbally (i.e., through gestures), there must necessarily be communication present. Moreover, it is unclear how the nature and demands of the testing situation, such as establishing rapport, explaining the purpose of the testing, teaching the meaning of the pantomime or gestures, instructing when to start, when to stop, what is a right answer, what is a wrong answer, when to work quickly, and so forth, can all be taught and communicated nonverbally.

There are also important theoretical implications to using nonverbal tests. The reduction of language demands afforded by the use of nonverbal tests may appear to yield a fairer estimate of general intelligence but only if one believes in the concept of g, or general intelligence. When examined within the context of CHC theory, nonverbal batteries tend to measure a narrower range of abilities—primarily visual processing and processing speed (Flanagan, Ortiz, & Alfonso, 2007; Flanagan, Ortiz, Alfonso, & Mascolo, 2006) than that which is found on other more comprehensive batteries (e.g., WISC-IV, KABC-II, WJ III, SB-V, DAS-II). If the child's abilities in nonverbal areas are intact, the estimate of intelligence on a nonverbal battery is misleading because it suggests average global intelligence while ignoring a substantial number of other abilities that make up intelligence. Likewise, if the child's abilities in nonverbal areas are deficient, the composite score is again misleading because it will be interpreted as low general ability (similar to low FSIQ) when it may in fact reflect weaknesses in only two areas (i.e., Visual Processing and Processing Speed), but not in areas that were not tested. Weiss and colleagues (2006) note this problem and assert that "the inclusion in WNV of nonverbal tasks that are typically verbally mediated, such as picture arrangement, may further increase construct coverage of the various domains of intelligence measured nonverbally." For some important broad abilities, such as Crystallized Intelligence (*Gc*), Auditory Processing (*Ga*), Reading and Writing (*Grw*), there is simply no way they can be validly measured in a nonverbal manner. A similar theoretical issue arises within the context of evaluation of learning disabilities. For example, IDEA continues to define *learning disability* as a disorder in one or more of the basic psychological processes. The current wording in IDEA 2004 has also included an option for identifying a learning disability on the basis of a pattern of cognitive and academic strengths and weaknesses. Again, CHC theory is ideal in this capacity because it is one of the only intelligence theories that specifies the relations between cognitive and academic abilities and that has been supported by extensive research (Flanagan & Harrison, 2005; Flanagan, Ortiz, & Alfonso, 2007; Flanagan et al., 2006). Use of some nonverbal tests may not allow evaluation of the full range of cognitive processes related to academic performance and might be limited and would not be helpful in identifying specific learning disabilities under this option in IDEA. Thus, professionals concerned with the evaluation of both general intelligence and specific cognitive processes in children from culturally and linguistically diverse backgrounds will need to look beyond nonverbal testing.

As noted previously, the WISC-IV Spanish provides a new tool for professionals who are competent and qualified to use the third option in assessment—administration of native-language tests. On the surface, this option seems ideal and would appear to be a relatively *complete* solution to the problems inherent in the cognitive assessment of culturally and linguistically diverse children. But as with other methods, some problems persist—not the least of which concerns the norm sample. Verbal tests, whether in English or the native language, and nonverbal tests share the same problem relative to norm sample construction—they all fail to construct normative populations that control for two important differences in development among children from diverse populations including level of acculturation and English-language proficiency. According to Harris and Llorente (2005), "in developing norms for a measure such as the WISC or WAIS, it is common practice to exclude individuals from the standardization sample who are not proficient in the English language, although those who speak English as a second language may be included" (p. 392). Children in the United States who are English-language learners (ELLs) may well be proficient enough in English or both languages to be included in the sample but they are not included in any systematic way. As further noted by Harris and Llorente (2005), "these children indeed represent a proportion of U.S. school children who are ELLs. Realistically, however, little is known about the language abilities of these learners and the degree to which they are bilingual" (pp. 392–393). The same can be said for the developmental sample of the WISC-IV Spanish (Braden & Iribarren, 2005). In addition, it should be noted that the actual WISC-IV Spanish norms are *equated* to the WISC-IV norms and thus the Spanish version does not have actual, separate norms (Braden & Iribarren, 2005). Thus, the shortcomings in the English version, with respect to differences in degree, level, and type of bilingual, as well as differences in levels of acculturation, are equally applicable to the Spanish version and raise serious questions about the true representativeness of the norm sample.

In response to these issues, the WISC-IV Spanish utilized additional criteria to help strengthen its representation of diverse Spanish-speaking individuals. For example, the sample was limited to individuals with no more than 5 consecutive years of education in the United States (Braden & Iribarren, 2005; Harris & Llorente, 2006). This criterion attempts to homogenize the bilingualism of the norm sample, at least with respect to Spanish, and the test manual recommends that individuals with more than 5 consecutive years in the U.S. educational system be administered the English version of the WISC-IV (Braden & Iribarren, 2005; Harris & Llorente, 2006; Weiss et al., 2006). This recommendation should be used carefully, however, as it has been shown that comparable scores for ELLs on the WISC-IV, as compared to the largely monolingual English-speaking norm sample, are not achieved until individuals reach the 25th percentile rank (SS > 90) on a standardized test of English-language proficiency (Cathers-Schiffman & Thompson, 2007). A similar result was reported by Harris & Llorente (2005) as well in their examination of the performance of ELLs who spoke primarily Spanish at home, as compared to ELLs who spoke primarily English at home and monolingual English speakers.

The WISC-IV Spanish provides another unique feature designed to help professionals interpret results with more fairness. Whereas the scaled scores are calibrated to reflect the WISC-IV English norm distribution, the WISC-IV Spanish also offers age-based percentile ranks that "are either adjusted for parental education level and years the child has been in U.S. schools (the recommended procedure) or on years in U.S. schools alone" (Braden & Iribarren, 2007, pp. 294–295). The purpose of providing such percentile ranks is obvious in that there are likely to be differences in the experiences of children as a function of length of schooling and parental education level. Unfortunately, the manual does not provide any guidance on when one percentile distribution should be favored over the other and no information is available regarding the bilingualism or acculturation of the individuals comprising the respective groups.

Bilingual Assessment versus Assessment of Bilinguals

When appropriate, use of the WISC-IV Spanish will be limited, of course, to those practitioners who speak Spanish and who are able to meet the ethical guidelines and professionals standards for its use. In an ideal system, every child who needs to be evaluated by a competent and qualified Spanish-speaking practitioner would be so evaluated. Unfortunately, the number of practitioners who possesses both the fluency required for administration as well as the competency in nondiscriminatory assessment that provides the real basis for equitable interpretation is miniscule in comparison to the growing numbers of children who would otherwise benefit from this manner of evaluation. Thus, it is rather ironic that although the Spanish version of the WISC-IV is designed to serve a good portion of that population, its application is limited by the lack of trained and qualified practitioners available to administer it. As a result, many such children will have to be evaluated by monolingual English-speaking practitioners simply because there is no one else to do it. If the lofty goal of fairness in testing is to be reached and maintained, practitioners who speak English only and who will utilize the WISC-IV English version can look toward a recent theoretically and empirically based approach designed to address issues of validity and fairness directly. The remainder of this section outlines this approach.

The Fundamental Objective in Assessment

It should be acknowledged that there is no way in which the WISC-IV (English or Spanish), or any other test for that matter, can be applied in a completely valid and nondiscriminatory manner when evaluating the intelligence of children from diverse backgrounds. Totally unbiased assessment is an illusion, and attempting to remove all the discriminatory components in any evaluation is both an impossible task and an inappropriate professional goal. A more reasonable objective for practitioners engaged in such pursuits is to evaluate the degree to which the results from such assessment have been affected by cultural or linguistic factors. By determining the relative extent to which experiential differences in culture or language may have affected test results, practitioners are in a better position to defend the validity of any conclusions and inferences drawn from the obtained data. For example, in cases in which it can be established that cultural or linguistic factors are not likely to have had a primary or systematic influence on the results, the viability of alternative explanations and hypotheses (including the possibility that a disability exists) is increased and may be pursued with a greater degree of confidence. Conversely, in cases in which cultural or linguistic factors are believed to have had a primary or systematic influence on the test results, the validity of the obtained data remains questionable and further interpretation cannot be defended adequately. Thus, the first step in conducting fairer and more equitable assessments, particularly when using the WISC-IV or similar tests, rests primarily on being able to answer the question, "To what extent are the obtained results a reflection of cultural or linguistic differences or actual measured ability?" Until this determination can be made, the data will be of little, if any, value.

The CHC Culture-Language Matrix and Classifications

The manner in which this fundamental question of bilingual-multicultural assessment can be answered has been formalized in a systematic, research-based approach found in the cultural and linguistic extensions of the CHC Cross-Battery approach (Flanagan, Ortiz, & Alfonso, 2007; Mpofu & Ortiz, in press; Ortiz & Dynda, in press; Ortiz & Ochoa, 2005; Rhodes, Ochoa, & Ortiz, 2005). In general, the approach rests on two interrelated components: the Culture-Language Test Classifications (C-LTC) and the Culture-Language Interpretive Matrix (C-LIM) (see Flanagan et al., 2007).

It has long been established that tests such as the WISC-IV rarely exhibit psychometric forms of bias, particularly in the areas of item content, difficulty sequence, factorial structure, reliability indexes, prediction, or even differential item functioning (Figueroa, 1990; Jensen, 1980; Reynolds, 2000; Sandoval, Frisby, Geisinger, Scheuneman, & Grenier, 1998; Valdes & Figueroa, 1994). However, this does not mean that bias does not exist or is not operating. For example, one area in which tests have consistently been found to evidence bias is with respect to validity (Figueroa & Hernandez, 2000; Jensen, 1976, 1980; Sandoval, 1979; Sandoval et al., 1998). Whether problems with validity constitute *bias* or not, there is no debate regarding the fact that tests are culturally and linguistically *loaded* (Scarr, 1978; Sanchez, 1934; Sattler, 1992). From the very inception of intelligence testing to the present day, research indicates that an individual's familiarity with the content of the test (acculturation) and the degree to which they comprehend the language in which the test is based (proficiency) are directly related to test performance (Aguera, 2006; Brigham, 1923; Cummins, 1984; Dynda, 2008; Goddard, 1913; Jensen, 1976, 1980; Mercer, 1979; Sanchez, 1934; Sotelo-Dynega, 2007; Valdes & Figueroa, 1994; Yerkes, 1921). Taking this body of research into account, both empirical (where data were available) and logical (based on expert consensus) classifications of current tests of intelligence and cognitive abilities were established on the basis of two characteristics: (a) the degree to which a particular test or subtest contains or requires familiarity, specific knowledge, or an understanding of U.S. mainstream culture; and (b) the degree to which a particular test or subtest requires expressive or receptive language skills, either because the ability being measured is language based, the correct response requires verbal competency, or appropriate administration rests upon adequate verbal comprehension by the examinee (McGrew & Flanagan, 1998; Ortiz, 1998). Through the application of a simple, three-level (Low, Moderate, and High) system, tests were thus classified in a matrix according to the degree of cultural loading and degree of linguistic demand, including those from the Wechsler scales. Because of its recent date of publication, research is currently in progress to empirically reestablish classifications for the WISC-IV. However, because some tests were retained from the WISC-III, and because other new tests are similar to existing ones that have already been classified, enough information exists with which to provide preliminary classifications within a new matrix specific to the WISC-IV. Figure 7.2 provides an illustration of the most probable empirically and logically derived Culture-Language Test Classifications for the WISC-IV. Figure 7.2 is reprinted from the WISC-IV tab of the automated Culture-Language Interpretive Matrix available on the CD-ROM that accompanies *Essentials of Cross-Battery Assessment, Second Edition* (Flanagan et al., 2007).

By themselves, the WISC-IV classifications as shown in Figure 7.2 already provide practitioners with one option for reducing some of the potentially discriminatory aspects of assessment. Decades of research on issues related to bias have shown that tests that are lower in cultural content (more abstract or

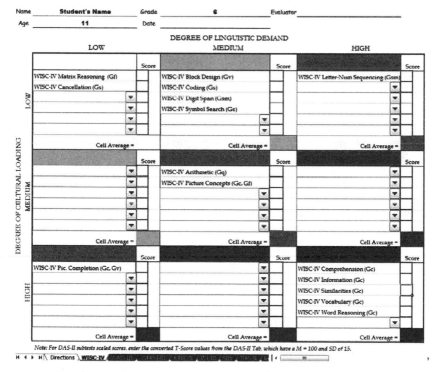

Note: For DAS-II subtests scaled scores. enter the converted T-Score values from the DAS-II Tab. which have a M = 100 and SD of 15.

Figure 7.2 Culture-Language Test Classifications (C-LTC) for the WISC-IV Subtests

Note: This matrix is from the automated Culture-Language Interpretive Matrix (C-LIM) found on the CD-ROM that accompanies *Essentials of Cross-Battery Assessment, Second Edition* (Flanagan, Ortiz, & Alfonso, 2007).

process dominant) and lower in linguistic demands (less verbally laden, with more manipulatives and pictures, etc.) tend to yield results that are more equitable for diverse individuals, although they still are not completely fair (Jensen, 1980; Figueroa, 1990; Rhodes et al., 2005; Sandoval et al., 1998; Valdes & Figueroa, 1994). Thus, users of the WISC-IV may well decide to administer only those tests with the lowest cultural loading and linguistic demands (e.g., Matrix Reasoning and Cancellation). This would be similar to the practice of using only the subtests that made up the old PIQ and is a limited form of nonverbal testing. Unfortunately, while there is some merit to this approach, it suffers from the same flaws as before, including a limited range of abilities being measured, an inability to derive any of the four Indexes (i.e., VCI, PRI, PSI, WMI), and lack of information regarding abilities that may be of importance (e.g., verbal abilities and their relationship to suspected reading difficulties). Thus, such practice is not recommended.

The greatest benefit from use of the WISC-IV classifications listed in Figure 7.2 comes from application of the Culture-Language Interpretive Matrix (Flanagan et al., 2007) in which they are embedded. The C-LIM represents a tool with which practitioners can evaluate the systematic influence of cultural and linguistic differences on test performance—hence addressing the fundamental question regarding the validity of the obtained results. Use of the C-LIM requires that Wechsler scaled scores (and all scores used in the matrix) be converted to the deviation IQ metric (helpful in cases in which subtests from other batteries may be included) prior to calculating an arithmetic average for all tests within each of the nine cells of the matrix. As noted previously, the C-LTC and C-LIM were recently published as computerized software that automates the process of data entry, data conversion, averaging cell scores, and even provides a visual graph to facilitate pattern evaluation (Flanagan et al., 2007). An example illustrating how this is accomplished is presented in Figure 7.3, using hypothetical WISC-IV data. To facilitate identification of the influence of cultural and linguistic differences on test performance, the automated C-LIM also produces a graph to visually represent the obtained data. Figure 7.4 illustrates the same hypothetical data as depicted in Figure 7.3 but in the form of a graph that complements the data as presented in the matrix.

It is important to note that the derivation of the cell averages or means is done only for the purpose of examining *patterns* in the data. The average score in each cell does not represent any particular construct and *must not* be interpreted as such. The score is simply an indication of average performance on a collection of tests (sometimes even just two tests) that share similar characteristics in terms of cultural loading and linguistic demand. Whereas it may be true that when organized in this fashion the cell averages are representing the effect of level of acculturation and English-language proficiency, and are therefore *measuring* these

| Name | Student's Name | Grade | 6 | Evaluator |
| Age | 11 | Date | | |

DEGREE OF LINGUISTIC DEMAND

	LOW	Score	MEDIUM	Score	HIGH	Score
LOW	WISC-IV Matrix Reasoning (Gf)	11	105	WISC-IV Block Design (Gv)	8	90	WISC-IV Letter-Num Sequencing (Gsm)	8	90
	WISC-IV Cancellation (Gs)	9	95	WISC-IV Coding (Gs)	10	100	▼	
	▼		WISC-IV Digit Span (Gsm)	7	85	▼	
	▼		WISC-IV Symbol Search (Gs)	11	105	▼	
	▼		▼		▼	
	▼		▼		▼	
	Cell Average = 100		Cell Average = 95		Cell Average = 90	

		Score		Score		Score
MEDIUM	▼		WISC-IV Arithmetic (Gq)	85	▼	
	▼		WISC-IV Picture Concepts (Gc, Gf)	85	▼	
	▼		▼		▼	
	▼		▼		▼	
	▼		▼		▼	
	Cell Average =		Cell Average = 85		Cell Average =	

		Score		Score		Score
HIGH	WISC-IV Pic. Completion (Gc, Gv)			▼	WISC-IV Comprehension (Gc)	6	80
	▼		▼	WISC-IV Information (Gc)	6	80
	▼		▼	WISC-IV Similarities (Gc)	4	70
	▼		▼	WISC-IV Vocabulary (Gc)	5	75
	▼		▼	WISC-IV Word Reasoning (Gc)	4	70
	▼		▼	▼	
	Cell Average =		Cell Average =		Cell Average = 75	

(Left vertical axis label: DEGREE OF CULTURAL LOADING)

Note: For DAS-II subtests scaled scores, enter the converted T-Score values from the DAS-II Tab, which have a M = 100 and SD of 15.

H ◄ ► H \ Directions \ **WISC-IV** \ WAIS-III / WPPSI-III / KABC-II / WJ III / EBS / DAS-II / C | ◄ | III |

Figure 7.3 Culture-Language Interpretive Matrix (C-LIM) Incorporating Hypothetical WISC-IV Data*

*Note: Scaled scores are automatically converted to the deviation IQ metric (X = 100, SD = 15) in order to facilitate comparison with the Index scores (VCI, POI, PSI, WMI) and allow aggregation with other data.

Note: This matrix is from the automated Culture-Language Interpretive Matrix (C-LIM) found on the CD-ROM that accompanies Essentials of Cross-Battery Assessment, Second Edition (Flanagan, Ortiz, & Alfonso, 2007).

constructs, this is not the purpose of the C-LIM. The averages reported by the C-LIM are important only relative to other averages therein and the pattern they form. No attempt should be made to ascribe meaning to cell averages on an individual basis.

As noted previously, scores for diverse individuals on subtests that are less affected by cultural content or language differences tend to be higher than scores on subtests that are more influenced by these variables. The arrangement of WISC-IV subtests in the matrix—where the cells in the upper left corner are those with the lowest cultural loading and linguistic demand and the cells in the lower right corner are those with the highest—allows for direct examination

Name _____ **Student's Name** _____ Grade _____ 6 _____ Evaluator _____

Age _____ 11 _____ Date _____

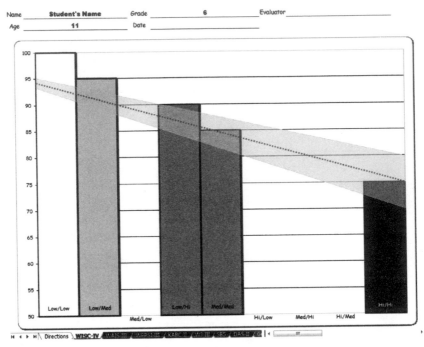

Figure 7.4 Graph Incorporating Hypothetical WISC-IV Data

Note: This graph is from the Culture-Language Interpretive Matrix (C-LIM) found on the CD-ROM that accompanies *Essentials of Cross-Battery Assessment, Second Edition* (Flanagan, Ortiz, & Alfonso, 2007).

of whether, for example, the obtained results follow a declining pattern similar to that predicted by research. Consistent with previous and current studies, if the primary influence on the test results is due to cultural or linguistic factors, then a systematic decline in performance across the matrix from the top-left cells to the bottom-right cells should be evident. Conversely, if the primary influence on the test results is anything other than cultural or linguistic in nature (e.g., fatigue, improper administration), then there is no reason to expect a systematic pattern of degradation in performance across the cells from top left to bottom right. That is, when cultural and linguistic differences are not factors operating systematically upon the data, then any other pattern, or no pattern at all, may emerge. In either of these cases (no decline or no pattern at all) it can be reliably ascertained that test performance was not influenced primarily by the cultural loading or linguistic demand of the WISC-IV tests given, and alternative explanations regarding the obtained results (e.g., measured deficit in processing speed, uncooperative test behavior, inattention and lack of effort) may be reasonably entertained because the validity of the results have been systematically established.

The WISC-IV data presented in matrix form in Figure 7.3 and as a graph in Figure 7.4 illustrate the typical pattern of decline that would be expected of an individual with average ability who comes from a culturally and linguistically diverse background. It should be noted, however, that *typical* does not imply that the pattern is always identical to that which is portrayed in the matrix and graph. Although the same relative pattern of decline from top left to bottom right remains the hallmark of the systematic influence of cultural and linguistic variables on test performance, differences in levels of acculturation and English-language proficiency can alter the resulting averages. This potential variability is the reason for the gray shaded area around the dashed line in the graph depicted Figure 7.4 and is intended to represent the general range of expected decline. The more *different* an individual is relative to the norm sample, in terms of level of acculturation and English-language proficiency, the lower the scores will be. However, the pattern and rate of decline will remain similar and evident in both cases. Unfortunately, it is impossible within the scope of this section to fully detail the manner in which differences in acculturation, language proficiency, and other factors affect the observed pattern of decline and interpretation of results. Readers are referred to Flanagan and colleagues (2007) for a more in-depth treatment of such issues as only a general guide for interpretation can be offered here.

The data contained in Figures 7.3 and 7.4 show a consistent and systematic decline in performance, with the best performance seen on the tests with the lowest cultural loading and linguistic demand (Matrix Reasoning and Cancellation; X = 100) and the worst performance evident on the tests with the highest cultural loading and linguistic demand (Information, Similarities, Vocabulary, Comprehension, and Word Reasoning; X = 75). If standardization in administration was maintained and there is no reason to believe any other attenuating influences were present in the assessment process (e.g., motivation was good, testing was not interrupted, the test was scored correctly), then such a pattern of performance would be unlikely to have occurred as a function of other extraneous factors or influences. Therefore, it can be reasonably concluded that the results are primarily a reflection of cultural and linguistic differences. As such, the temptation to interpret scores in the usual manner, such as through examination of WISC-IV FSIQ or Indexes, should be resisted as there is no defensible basis for drawing inferences from these scores, as they are essentially invalid. On the other hand, had there not been any systematic pattern of decline in the WISC-IV scores, interpretation could have proceeded in a relatively normal manner because cultural and linguistic variables were evaluated systematically and ruled out as the *primary* influence on test performance. Cultural and linguistic influences are likely to always be present and may continue to be contributory causes in such cases. However, as long as they are not seen to be the primary influence on test performance, they do not summarily invalidate the test results and, with minor caveats, valid interpretation may be carried out.

A question often arises regarding use of the C-LTC and C-LIM with the WISC-IV Spanish. In principle, given the issue of norm sample representation discussed previously, the classifications are likely to be the same or quite similar because the issues are the same or similar. Children in the United States may not be receiving native-language instruction and so may show relatively poorer performance in Spanish against the norm group as their native language suffers attrition from limited use and lack of education. This issue becomes particularly salient in light of the differences that exist in the type of schooling and educational program ELLs may receive when starting instruction in U.S. public schools. Whether an individual gets ESL only, a transitional bilingual program, a maintenance bilingual program, a dual-immersion program, or nothing at all will likely have significant implications on test performance on the WISC-IV Spanish (Braden & Iribarren, 2005; Harris & Llorente, 2005; Rhodes et al., 2005). However, because there is very little research on how bilinguals of varying proficiency perform on tests given to them in their native language, no definitive recommendations can be offered regarding expectations of performance. Of course, nothing precludes using the WISC-IV in English in lieu of or in addition to the Spanish version and using the C-LIM to evaluate results obtained in English.

Conclusion

The determination as to whether results obtained from the WISC-IV and the C-LIM indicate the presence of culture or language differences or perhaps something else requires some degree of clinical skill and application of professional judgment. In this way, such determinations are not unlike other clinical decisions that rest on one's level of experience, training, and education. Nonetheless, users of the WISC-IV who cannot use the Spanish version or who have a need to evaluate the intelligence or cognitive abilities of a child from a culturally and linguistically diverse background that is other than Hispanic now have at their disposal a systematic method supported by modern cognitive theory and scientific research that is defensible within the context of nondiscriminatory assessment, meets ethical guidelines, and is consistent with the best standards of practice (Ortiz, 2008). Moreover, the fact that practitioners need not be fluent in another language puts the ability to make crucial determinations regarding the effect of cultural and linguistic variables on test performance within the reach of all professionals, not just those with highly specialized skills. Bilingual-multicultural assessment can be overwhelming and confusing for many practitioners. Through the use of the C-LTC and C-LIM, one of the most critical aspects in such assessment— evaluating the relative influence of cultural and linguistic differences on test performance—is now something that can be readily accomplished using either version of the WISC-IV.

TEST YOURSELF

1. **Gifted children show little variability across the four WISC-IV Indexes and, as such, these Indexes have little meaning for this population.**
   True or False?

2. **Establishing Normative Weaknesses in a child's cognitive functioning is a necessary condition in the operational definition of SLD.**
   True or False?

3. **Which of the following CHC abilities demonstrate(s) a significant relationship with reading achievement?**
   (a) Auditory Processing (*Ga*)
   (b) Short-Term Memory (*Gsm*)
   (c) Processing Speed (*Gs*)
   (d) all of the above

4. **The nature of underachievement, within the context of the operational definition of SLD, suggests that not only does a child possess specific, circumscribed, and related academic and cognitive Normative Weaknesses, but that these weaknesses exist within an otherwise *normal ability profile*.**
   True or False?

5. **Administering only those subtests with the lowest cultural loadings and linguistic demands to culturally and linguistically diverse populations is not recommended because**
   (a) it results in a narrow range of abilities being measured.
   (b) it precludes the calculation of the four Indexes.
   (c) it results in a lack of information regarding other abilities that may be important in understanding the referral concern.
   (d) all of the above.

6. **Which of the following subtests can be described as having a low cultural loading, but a high linguistic demand?**
   (a) Digit Span
   (b) Letter-Number Sequencing
   (c) Arithmetic
   (d) Block Design

Answers:

1. False; 2. True; 3. d; 4. True; 5. d; 6. b

Eight

THE WISC-IV INTEGRATED

George McCloskey

The WISC-IV Integrated is an enhanced version of the WISC-IV resulting from the application of a process-approach conceptual framework to the specific cognitive domains of the WISC-IV. The *integration* of the process approach into the WISC-IV is realized through five major features of the WISC-IV Integrated: (a) additional content in the form of Process Subtests; (b) additional administration and scoring procedures reflecting the process-approach perspective; (c) process standard scores; (d) cumulative percentage base rates for subtest scaled score discrepancy comparisons; and (e) cumulative percentage base rates for process observations. These features add new content to the WISC-IV but also can affect the administration, scoring, and interpretation of some of the core and supplemental WISC-IV Subtests. Incorporation of the WISC-IV Integrated features required changes and additions to the basic WISC-IV manuals and test-kit components. These changes and additions are listed in Rapid Reference 8.1.

The impetus for the development of the WISC-IV Integrated came from Edith Kaplan and colleagues' original applications of the process approach to the Wechsler Scales, beginning with the WAIS-R as a Neuropsychological Instrument (WAIS-R, NI) and continuing with the WISC-III as a Process Instrument (WISC-III, PI). The process approach represents a conceptual framework that informs an examiner's observation of task performance during test administration and the examiner's understanding and interpretation of task performance after test administration. The process approach relative to the WISC-IV embodies several basic conceptions (McCloskey & Maerlender, 2005), including: (a) WISC-IV subtests are complex tasks, with each one requiring the use of multiple cognitive capacities for successful performance; (b) variations in input, processing, and/or output demands can greatly affect performance on tasks involving identical or similar content; and (c) careful, systematic observation of task performance greatly enhances the understanding of task outcome.

≡ Rapid Reference 8.1

Material Changes and Additions Made to the WISC-IV to Create the WISC-IV Integrated

The following components were replaced by components that maintained the WISC-IV information and added the WISC-IV Integrated information:

WISC-IV Administration and Scoring Manual replaced by WISC-IV Integrated Administration and Scoring Manual

WISC-IV Technical and Interpretive Manual replaced by the WISC-IV Integrated Technical and Interpretive Manual

WISC-IV Record Form replaced by the WISC-IV Integrated Record Form

Coding A and B Scoring Key replaced by Coding A and B and Coding Recall Scoring Key

The following WISC-IV components were maintained with no changes and incorporated into the WISC-IV Integrated kit:

WISC-IV Stimulus Book 1

WISC-IV Response Booklet 1

Symbol Search Scoring Key

Cancellation Scoring Template

#2 Pencil without Eraser

Red Pencil without Eraser

The following components were added to the original WISC-IV components to create the WISC-IV Integrated kit:

WISC-IV Integrated Stimulus Book 2

WISC-IV Integrated Stimulus Book 3

WISC-IV Integrated Response Booklet 2

WISC-IV Integrated Response Booklet 3

Block Design Blocks—three blocks added

Block Design Process Approach Grid Overlays

Visual Digit Span Item Card and Sleeve

Spatial Span Board

FEATURES OF THE WISC-IV INTEGRATED

I. Process-Approach Administration and Scoring Procedures

The WISC-IV Integrated includes alterations, enhancements, and additions to the administration and scoring procedures for WISC-IV Core, Supplemental, and Process Subtests. Rapid Reference 8.2 lists the various process-approach procedures employed as a part of the WISC-IV Integrated. These procedures involve altering task formats for Core and Supplemental subtests while using the same item content (e.g., Vocabulary Multiple Choice, Picture Vocabulary Multiple Choice; Arithmetic Process Approach A and B); employing alternate formats with similar item content (e.g., Visual Digit Span, Letter-Number Sequencing Process Approach, Block Design Multiple Choice); completing additional administration procedures for a core subtest (e.g., adding incidental recall tasks to the administration of Coding); completing additional response-recording procedures for timed subtests (e.g., recording performance in 30-second intervals for Coding and Coding Copy); and employing additional scoring procedures with Core, Supplemental, and Process Subtests (e.g., removing the time bonus points from Block Design, assigning bonus points for quick performance for Arithmetic and Multiple Choice Block Design Subtests). The results of these procedures are interpreted in various formats including Process Subtest Scaled Scores (as noted in the previous section), additional Subtest Process Scores, and cumulative frequency base rates (as discussed in sections that follow).

≡ Rapid Reference 8.2

WISC-IV Integrated Process Subtests and Process-Approach Procedures by Content Domain

Verbal Domain

Similarities Multiple Choice (SIMC)

—a Process Subtest that involves administering the items of the Similarities Subtest in a multiple-choice format.

Vocabulary Multiple Choice (VCMC)

—a Process Subtest that involves administering the items of the Vocabulary Subtest in a multiple-choice format.

Picture Vocabulary Multiple Choice (PVMC)

—a Process Subtest that involves administering the items of the Vocabulary Subtest in a multiple-choice format using pictures.

Comprehension Multiple Choice (COMC)

—a Process Subtest that involves administering the items of the Comprehension Subtest in a multiple-choice format.

Information Multiple Choice (INMC)

—a Process Subtest that involves administering the items of the Information Subtest in a multiple-choice format.

Perceptual Domain

Block Design (BD)

—scoring Block Design items without a time bonus (BDN).

Block Design Multiple Choice (BDMC)

—a Process Subtest that uses visual images similar to the design models of the Block Design Subtest.

—recording time for completion of each item to score items with a time bonus.

—scoring items without a time bonus (BDMCN).

Block Design Process Approach (BDPA)

—a Process Subtest that uses an additional set of Block Design items to analyze a child's approach to problem solving; items are administered using modified procedures (Part A and Part B—new Block Design items are administered using 12 blocks instead of 9 for 3 × 3 items; Part B—incorrectly completed items from Part A are readministered using transparent grid overlays).

—scoring Part A and Part B items by counting each correctly placed block.

—observing and recording en route breaks in configuration and breaks in final configuration for Part A and Part B.

—observing and recording extra block construction errors for Part A and Part B.

Elithorn Mazes (EM)

—a Process Subtest that assesses organization and/or planning applied to visual diagrams.

—scoring Elithorn Mazes items without a time bonus (EMN).

—observing and recording instances of motor planning.

—observing and recording latency time (pauses prior to beginning work on an item).

—observing and recording motor imprecision errors.

—observing and recording backward movement errors.

—observing and recording across lane errors.

(continued)

Working Memory Domain

Digit Span (DS)

—obtaining separate scores for Digit Span Forward (DSF) and Digit Span Backward (DSB).

—recording longest span forward and longest span backward.

Letter-Number Sequencing (LN)

—recording the longest letter-number sequence.

Arithmetic (AR)

—scoring items with time bonus added (ART).

Arithmetic Process Approach Part A (ARPA-A) and Part B (ARPA-B)

—a Process Subtest that involves readministration of the Arithmetic Subtest items with modified formats (Part A [ARPA-A]—items are visually and auditorily presented and the visual image remains in view while the child completes work; Part B [ARPA-B]—items are visually and auditorily presented, the visual image remains in view and the child can use paper and pencil while working).

—scoring items with a time bonus for the ARPA-A Subtest and (ARPA-AT).

Written Arithmetic (WA)

—a Process Subtest that presents the items of the Arithmetic Subtests as calculation problems that the child completes using pencil and paper.

Visual Digit Span (VDS)

—a Process Subtest that uses visually presented numbers as stimuli.

—recording longest Visual Digit Span.

Spatial Span (SSp)

—a Process Subtest that uses blocks on a board as stimuli.

—obtaining separate scores for Spatial Span Forward and Spatial Span Backward.

—recording longest span forward and longest span backward.

Letter Span (LS)

—a Process Subtest that uses auditorily presented rhyming (LSR) and nonrhyming (LSN) letters as stimuli.

—obtaining separate scores for Nonrhyming and Rhyming letter spans.

—recording longest Nonrhyming and longest Rhyming spans.

Letter-Number Sequencing Process Approach (LNPA)

—a Process Subtest that employs a modified LNS item type.

—recording longest span.

Processing Speed Domain
Cancellation (CA)
—obtaining separate scores for Cancellation Random (CAR) and Cancellation Structured (CAS).

—recording process observations for each item related to child's search pattern.

Coding (CD)
—administering Coding in a manner that allows for the administration of Coding Recall (CDR).

—recording the number of items completed in each 30-second interval.

Coding Recall (CDR)
—a Process Subtest that requires the child to perform incidental recall tasks after completion of the Coding Subtest.

—recording the Cued Symbol Recall score.

—recording the Free Symbol Recall score.

—recording the Cued Digit Recall score.

Coding Copy (CDC)
 a Process Subtest that involves copying symbols into boxes without code matching.

—recording the number of items completed in each 30-second interval.

These process-approach procedures represent the operationalization of the process approach as applied to the WISC-IV (i.e., they form the basis for obtaining a greater depth of understanding of a child's cognitive strengths and weaknesses in that they enhance the clinician's capacity to identify discrete processes or factors that influence task performance; to observe the effect of altering input, processing, or output demands; to observe in a more focused, systematic manner how children

DON'T FORGET

Although it is a process-approach procedure, when Coding Recall is used in an assessment it must be administered immediately after administration of the Coding subtest during administration of the core subtests. This is the only WISC-IV Integrated process-approach procedure that is administered along with the WISC-IV core subtests.

Note that important directions for how to administer Coding so that Coding Recall can be administered properly are at the end of the directions for Coding on page 125 of the *WISC-IV Administration and Scoring Manual*, and they precede the section titled Coding Recall that starts on page 126.

engage a task and what they do wrong as well as what they do right; and to generate, confirm, or refute clinical hypotheses related to task performance).

2. Process Subtests

The WISC-IV Integrated includes the addition of a number of subtests referred to as *Process Subtests*. These subtests include tasks that are variants of Core and Supplemental Subtests (e.g., multiple-choice Vocabulary, Similarities, Comprehension, and Information Subtests; Visual Digit Span Subtest) as well as unique tasks that expand the pool of cognitive capacities assessed by the WISC-IV (e.g., the Block Design Multiple Choice and Elithorn Mazes Subtests). Table 8.1 shows the Process

---

Table 8.1 WISC-IV Integrated Process Subtests

Verbal Domain

Similarities Multiple Choice (SIMC) —a multiple-choice version of the Similarities Subtest; each item is presented with four or five response options in print form on an easel page; the examiner reads the items and the response options and the child chooses an answer from the response options.

Vocabulary Multiple Choice (VCMC) —a multiple-choice version of the Vocabulary Subtest; each item is presented with four or five response options in print form on an easel page; the examiner reads the items and the response options and the child chooses an answer from the response options.

Picture Vocabulary Multiple Choice (PVMC) —a multiple-choice version of the Vocabulary Subtest; each item is stated orally and the child is shown an easel page with four pictures; the child indicates the picture thought to be the best visual representation of the meaning of the word.

Comprehension Multiple Choice (COMC) —a multiple-choice version of the Comprehension Subtest; each item is presented with four or five response options in print form on an easel page; the examiner reads the items and the response options and the child chooses an answer from the response options.

Information Multiple Choice (INMC) —a multiple-choice version of the Information Subtest; each item is presented with four or five response options in print form on an easel page; the examiner reads the items and the response options and the child chooses an answer from the response options.

Perceptual Domain

Block Design Multiple Choice (BDMC)—a multiple-choice task that uses visual images similar to the design models of the Block Design Subtest; for each item a completed model design is shown at the top of the page and four deconstructed designs appear below it. The child views the completed design and chooses the deconstructed design that would match the model if all of the blocks were pushed together to form a completed design.

(continued)

Table 8.1   (Continued)

Block Design Process Approach (BDPA)—a variant of the Block Design using different designs. Part A requires the child to select the correct number of blocks from a pool of 12 blocks to construct four- and nine-block designs that match a model presented on an easel page. Part B involves readministering items that were scored 0 in Part A. Grid overlays are placed on the models to assist the child in figuring out the placement of blocks.

Elithorn Mazes (EM)—a visual organization and planning task; for each item the child is presented with a triangular maze with multiple interconnected expanding pathways, each containing a strategically placed series of dots; the child must trace a path from the narrow start point to an exit at the broad top of the maze while connecting a specified number of dots along the way.

Working Memory Domain

Visual Digit Span (VDS)—a variant of the Digit Span Subtest that uses visually presented number series. For each item, the child views a series of numbers presented through a window in a card and orally repeats the digit series once it is removed from view.

Spatial Span (SSp)—a variant of the Digit Span Subtest that uses a white board with nine randomly placed blue blocks. For each item, the child watches the examiner touch a series of blocks; the child either touches the block in the same order as the examiner (Spatial Span Forward) or in the reverse of the examiner's order (Spatial Span Backward).

Letter Span (LS)   a variant of the Digit Span Subtest that uses letter series; for each item set, the child listens to a series of nonrhyming letters (LSN) and repeats the letters in the order presented, then listens to a series of rhyming letters (LSR) and repeats the letters in the order presented. For each set, two nonrhyming items of the same length are followed by two rhyming items of the same length.

Letter-Number Sequencing Process Approach (LNPA)—a variant of the Letter-Number Sequencing Subtest; for each item set, the child listens to one item that contains a random series of letters and numbers and two items that contain numbers and a series of letters in an order that spells a word. The child is required to reorder the series, providing numbers first in order of magnitude, and then letters in alphabetical order.

Arithmetic Process Approach (ARPA-A and ARPA-B)—variants of the Arithmetic Subtest that involve readministration of the Arithmetic Subtest items with modified formats; for Part A (ARPA-A) items are visually and auditorily presented and the visual image remains in view while the child completes work; for Part B (ARPA-B) items answered incorrectly in Part A are visually and auditorily presented, the visual image remains in view, and the child can use paper and pencil to help with solving the item.

Written Arithmetic (WA)—a variant of the Arithmetic Subtest that presents the items of the Arithmetic Subtest as calculation problems in a response booklet; the child completes as many calculations as possible using pencil and paper.

(continued)

Table 8.1 (Continued)

Processing Speed Domain

Coding Recall (CDR)—an incidental recall task involving the content of the Coding Subtest; immediately after administration of the Coding Subtest the child is asked to perform three incidental recall tasks: (a) given the numbers one through nine, write the symbol from the code that matches each number; (b) write as many of the nine symbols as possible from memory; and (c) given a row of symbols, write from memory the number that would go with each.

Coding Copy (CDC)—a variant of the Coding Subtest that involves copying symbols into boxes as quickly as possible without any code matching.

Subtests by cognitive domains along with a brief description of each. The directions for administration and scoring of these additional Process Subtests are not in a single location in the WISC-IV Integrated manual; users need to be familiar with the various locations of the administration and scoring directions to avoid confusion while conducting an assessment. Rapid Reference 8.3 indicates the location of the administration and scoring directions for the various Process Subtests and other process-approach procedures. Administration directions for each of the Process Subtests are straightforward and consistent with the procedures employed for the WISC-IV Core and Supplemental subtests. Examiners will need to familiarize themselves with each subtest's specific rules for starting and discontinuing administration. These rules are included in the directions for each subtest and also are included in the WISC-IV Integrated Record Form. All Process Subtest raw scores can be converted to norm-referenced scaled scores for performance interpretation.

≡ *Rapid Reference 8.3*

Location of the Administration and Scoring Directions for the Various Process Subtests and Other Process-Approach Procedures

Administration and Scoring Directions for the following Core, Supplemental, and Process Subtests are included in the WISC-IV Integrated Administration and Scoring Manual *in the following locations:*

Core and Supplemental Subtest Administration Section

Block Design

Similarities

Digit Span

Coding

Process-Approach Procedure for Administering Coding Recall (directly follows Coding Directions)

Vocabulary

Letter-Number Sequencing

Matrix Reasoning

Comprehension

Symbol Search

Picture Completion

Cancellation

Information

Arithmetic

Word Reasoning

Process Subtest Administration Section

Block Design Multiple Choice

Block Design Process Approach

Elithorn Mazes

Visual Digit Span

Spatial Span

Letter Span

Letter-Number Sequencing Process Approach

Arithmetic Process Approach

Written Arithmetic

Coding Copy

Administration and Scoring Directions for the following Process Subtests are included in the WISC-IV Integrated Stimulus Booklet 2:

Similarities Multiple Choice

Vocabulary Multiple Choice

Comprehension Multiple Choice

Information Multiple Choice

Administration and Scoring Directions for the following Process Subtest is included in the WISC-IV Integrated Stimulus Booklet 3:

Picture Vocabulary Multiple Choice

3. Process Scores

In addition to scaled scores for the Process Subtests listed in Table 8.1, the WISC-IV Integrated provides a number of additional norm-referenced Process Scores that are derived from Core, Supplemental, and Process Subtests. These additional process scores reflect the application of the process approach to various subtest tasks, as described in the previous section. Scoring procedures used to obtain Process raw scores are described in various places throughout the *WISC-IV Integrated Administration and Scoring Manual*. Rapid Reference 8.4 provides a list of

≣ *Rapid Reference 8.4*

Process Scores

A quick guide for locating the manual sections that explain how to administer and score subtests in order to obtain Process raw scores that are converted into Process Scaled Scores.

Process Score	WISC-IV Integrated Scoring and Administration Manual Location
Block Design No Time Bonus (BDN)	page 93 (part of Block Design scoring directions)
Digit Span Forward (DSF) Digit Span Backward (DSB) Longest Digit Span Forward (LDSF) Longest Digit Span Backward (LDSB)	page 113 (part of Digit Span scoring directions)
Coding Recall—Cued Symbol Recall Coding Recall—Free Symbol Recall Coding Recall—Cued Digit Recall	pages 128 and 129 (directions for Coding Recall)
Cancellation Random (CAR) Cancellation Structured (CAS)	page 199 (part of Cancellation scoring directions)
Arithmetic with Time Bonus (ART)	pages 218 and 219 (part of Arithmetic scoring directions)
Block Design Multiple Choice No Time Bonus (BDMCN)	page 238 (part of Block Design Multiple Choice scoring directions)
Elithorn Mazes No Time Bonus (EMN)	page 257 (part of Elithorn Mazes scoring directions)
Longest Visual Digit Span (LVDVS)	page 266 (part of Visual Digit Span scoring directions)

Spatial Span Forward (SSpF) Spatial Span Backward (SSpB) Longest Spatial Span Forward (LSSpF) Longest Spatial Span Backward (LSSpB)	page 270 (part of Spatial Span scoring directions)
Letter Span Nonrhyming (LSN) Letter Span Rhyming (LSR) Longest Letter Span Nonrhyming (LLSN) Longest Letter Span Rhyming (LLSR)	page 275 (part of Letter Span scoring directions)
Longest Letter-Number Sequencing Process Approach (LLNPA)	page 278 (part of Letter-Number Sequencing Process Approach scoring directions)
Arithmetic Process Approach Part A (ARPA-A) Arithmetic Process Approach Part A with Time Bonus (ARPA-AT) Arithmetic Process Approach Part B (ARPA-B)	pages 284 and 285 (part of Arithmetic Process Approach scoring directions)
For Subtests: SIMC, VCMC, PVMC, COMC, BDMC, VDS, SSp, LS, LNPA, ARPA-A, ARPA-B Note: While it is clinically relevant to record observations of these behaviors for all subtests, base rates of the frequency of occurrence of these behaviors are available only for the Process Subtests that were administered during the separate WISC-IV Integrated standardization.	For these subtests, process observations are recorded for the following behaviors: Don't Know Responses No Response Self-Corrections Repetitions Prompts

the Process Scores and a quick guide for locating the manual sections that explain how to administer and score subtests in order to obtain process raw scores that are converted into Process Scaled Scores. These additional Process Scores are useful in gaining a greater understanding of the factors contributing to a child's performance on Core, Supplemental, and Process Subtests.

4. Subtest Scaled Score Discrepancy Comparisons

The *WISC-IV Integrated Administration and Scoring Manual* provides tables reporting subtest scaled score differences required for statistical significance and cumulative percentage base rates indicating the frequency of occurrence of subtest scaled score

DON'T FORGET

Clinicians should be aware of the fact that the WISC-IV Integrated normative scores are derived from two distinct standardization samples. Within the WISC-IV Integrated, the Core and Supplemental Subtest scaled scores and the Process Scores derived from Core and Supplemental Subtests (e.g., Block Design No Time Bonus scaled score, Cancellation Random and Cancellation Structured scaled scores) are based on the performance of the original WISC-IV standardization sample containing a total of 2,200 children (see the *WISC-IV Integrated Technical and Interpretive Manual* Chapter 3 for the details regarding the WISC-IV standardization sample). The normative data for the Coding Copy and Coding Recall tasks were also obtained from the WISC-IV standardization sample, but Process Scores for these tasks were not provided in the original WISC-IV manual.

In contrast, the Process Subtest scaled scores and the additional Process Scores derived from the Process Subtests, with the exception of Block Design Process Approach, are based on the performance of a separate WISC-IV Integrated standardization sample of 730 children. These 730 children were administered the WISC-IV Core and Supplemental Subtests (utilizing all of the process-approach administration and scoring procedures) along with all of the WISC-IV Integrated Process Subtests (see the *WISC-IV Integrated Technical Manual* Chapter 8 for the details regarding the separate WISC-IV Integrated standardization sample).

The Block Design Process Approach (BDPA) Subtest that is included as part of the WISC-IV Integrated was not standardized with the rest of the WISC-IV Integrated Process Subtests because of the amount of time required to complete BDPA and its relatively limited applications as a tool for further diagnostic analysis. Although narrow in its focus, the BDPA represents a classic, effective tool for applying the process approach to the analysis of subtest performance and embodies much of the seminal work of Kaplan and colleagues in developing the Boston Processing Approach to neuropsychological test interpretation. Rather than dropping BDPA from the WISC-IV Integrated, the BDPA administration and scoring procedures and norm-referenced scores developed during the standardization of the WISC-III PI were included in the WISC-IV Integrated. The BDPA scores, therefore, are based on the WISC-III PI standardization sample of 550 children. (See the *WISC-III PI Manual*, Chapter 2, for the details regarding the BDPA standardization sample).

discrepancies in the WISC-IV or WISC-IV Integrated standardization samples. These tables are provided for a select set of subtest comparisons and offer an empirical basis for the testing of process-oriented hypotheses about task performance. The discrepancy comparison values and base rates included in the *WISC-IV Integrated Administration and Scoring Manual* and additional discrepancy comparisons and base rates calculated for inclusion in this text appear in Rapid References throughout this chapter.

5. Cumulative Percentages (Base Rates) for Process Observations

Application of the process-approach procedures with some of the WISC-IV subtests involves the coding of specific behaviors observed during the child's performance of a subtest (e.g., frequency of asking for repetition of test items; frequency of use of motor planning when performing Elithorn Mazes items). The relative infrequency of occurrence or the limited range of values for these process observations did not allow for the development of scaled score equivalents. Alternatively, cumulative percentage base rate tables indicating the frequency of occurrence of these behaviors in the WISC-IV Integrated standardization sample were generated to offer clinicians a way of applying a norm-referenced interpretative perspective. Rapid Reference 8.5 provides a list of the specific behavior observations for which cumulative frequency base rate interpretive tables are available.

≡ Rapid Reference 8.5

WISC-IV Integrated Base Rates for Process-Approach Procedures

All Process Base Rate value tables (except Block Design Process Approach) are located in Appendix D of the *WISC-IV Integrated Administration and Scoring Manual*. Block Design Process Approach Base Rate value tables are located in Appendix E.

Perceptual Domain

Elithorn Mazes Process Observation Base Rates

    Motor Planning by Item, Trial, and Response—Table D.5, page 421

    Latency Times by Item, Trial, and Response—Table D.6, pages 422 and 423

    Motor Imprecision Error Scores by Item and Trial—Table D.7, page 424

    Backward Error Scores by Item and Trial—Table D.8, page 425

    Across Error Scores by Item and Trial—Table D.9, page 426

Block Design Process Approach Process Observation Base Rates

    Part A Partial Score—Table E.2, page 461

    Part B Partial Score—Table E.2, page 461

    En Route Breaks in Configuration—Table E.3, page 462

(continued)

Breaks in Final Configuration—Table E.4, page 463

Extra Block Constructions—Table E.5, page 464

Working Memory Domain

Digit Span Process Scores—Base Rate values located in Table D.16, page 436

Longest Digit Span Forward

Longest Digit Span Backward

Visual Digit Span Process Score—Base Rate values located in Table D.17, page 437

Longest Visual Digit Span

Spatial Span Process Scores—Base Rate values located in Table D.18, page 438

Longest Digit Span Forward

Longest Digit Span Backward

Letter Span Process Scores—Base Rate values located in Table D.19, page 439

Longest Letter Span Nonrhyming

Longest Letter Span Rhyming

Letter-Number Sequencing and Letter-Number Sequencing Process Approach Process Scores—Base Rate values located in Table D.20, page 440

Longest Letter-Number Sequence

Longest Letter-Number Process Approach Sequence

Process Score Comparison Base Rate Values

Longest Digit Span Forward versus Longest Digit Span Backward (LDSF–LDSB)—Table D.21, page 441

Longest Spatial Span Forward versus Longest Spatial Span Backward (LSSpF–LSSpB)—Table D.22, page 442

Longest Letter Span Nonrhyming versus Longest Letter Span Rhyming (LLSN–LLSR)—Table D.23, page 443

Longest Letter-Number Sequence versus Longest Letter-Number Process Approach Sequence (LLN–LLNPA)—Table D.24, page 444

Processing Speed Domain

Cancellation Observed Strategies Base Rate—Table D.27, page 447

Coding Recall Process Score Base Rates—Table D.28, page 448

Cued Symbol Recall

Free Symbol Recall

Cued Digit Recall

Coding B Process Score Base Rates—Table D.29, pages 449 and 450

  1–30 seconds

  31–60 seconds

  61–90 seconds

Coding Copy Process Score Base Rates—Table D.30, pages 451–453

  1–30 seconds

  31–60 seconds

  61–90 seconds

Multiple Domains Combined

Process Observation Base Rates

  Don't Know Responses by Subtest for SIMC, VCMC, PVMC, COMC, BDMC, VDS, SSp, LS, LNPA, ARPA-A, ARPA-B—Table D.31, page 454

  No Response by Subtest for SIMC, VCMC, PVMC, COMC, BDMC, VDS, SSp, LS, LNPA, ARPA-A, ARPA-B—Table D.32, page 455

  Self-Corrections by Subtest for SIMC, VCMC, PVMC, COMC, BDMC, VDS, SSp, LS, LNPA, ARPA-A, ARPA-B—Table D.33, page 456

  Repetitions by Subtest for SIMC, VCMC, PVMC, COMC, BDMC, VDS, SSp, LS, LNPA, ARPA-A, ARPA-B—Table D.34, page 457

  Prompts by Subtest for SIMC, VCMC, PVMC, COMC, BDMC, VDS, SSp, LS, LNPA, ARPA-A, ARPA-B—Table D.35, page 458

CLINICAL APPLICATIONS OF THE WISC-IV INTEGRATED

This chapter is intended to familiarize clinicians with the most essential aspects of interpretation of the additional features included in the WISC-IV Integrated. Additional information related to the underlying rationale for, and use and interpretation of, the WISC-IV Integrated is available in sources such as McCloskey and Maerlender (2005) and Holdnak and Weiss (2006a, 2006b). Discussion of interpretation will be organized according to the four content domains of the WISC-IV Integrated: Verbal, Perceptual, Working Memory, and Processing Speed. Rapid Reference 8.6 provides an overview of the interpretive features of the WISC-IV Integrated within these four content domains.

Verbal Domain

The WISC-IV Integrated application of the process approach to the Verbal Domain tasks is accomplished primarily through the use of Process Subtests

≡ Rapid Reference 8.6

Overview of WISC-IV Integrated Interpretive Features for Verbal, Perceptual, Working Memory, and Processing Speed Domains

- Process Subtest Scaled Scores
- Core/Supplemental Subtest versus Process Subtest Scaled Score Discrepancy Comparisons and Base Rates
- Process Subtest versus Process Subtest Scaled Score Discrepancy Comparisons and Base Rates
- Process Observations for Process Subtests
- Additional Process Scaled Scores and Base Rates for Core, Supplemental, and Process Subtests (for all domains except Verbal)

and Subtest Scaled Score discrepancy comparison tables indicating scaled score significant discrepancy comparison values and discrepancy base rates. The WISC-IV Integrated includes five Verbal Domain Process Subtests: Vocabulary Multiple Choice (VCMC), Picture Vocabulary Multiple Choice (PVMC), Similarities Multiple Choice (SIMC), Comprehension Multiple Choice (COMC), and Information Multiple Choice (INMC). All five of these subtests are multiple-choice versions of their similarly named Core and Supplemental Subtest counterparts. As such, they present the same item content as the Core and Supplemental Subtests, but alter presentation format, input processing demands, and response requirements. Rapid Reference 8.7 provides information about the administration and scoring of these Verbal Domain Process Subtests. Scaled Score equivalents for Verbal Domain Process Subtests are located in the *WISC-IV Integrated Administration and Scoring Manual* in Appendix C, Table C.1.

When to Use the Verbal Domain Process Subtests

In many cases, Verbal Domain Process Subtests will offer children who find it difficult to produce adequate answers through a free-recall response format a chance to demonstrate their abilities through a recognition response format. In other cases, these subtests will enable a clinician to see how a child's performance can be adversely affected by altering the format of these tasks. The Verbal Domain Process Subtests are not intended to be used en masse or with every child who is assessed. There are no set rules dictating the specifics of the use of the Process Subtests

≡ Rapid Reference 8.7

Administration and Scoring of the Verbal Domain Process Subtests

Administration and scoring of the Verbal Domain multiple-choice Process Subtests is very straightforward and easy to follow for clinicians experienced with individually administered multiple-choice-format tasks. A few points will help clinicians to get familiar quickly with these tasks:

- Directions for Administering and Scoring the Similarities Multiple Choice (SIMC), Vocabulary Multiple Choice (VCMC), Comprehension Multiple Choice (COMC), and Information Multiple Choice (INMC) Subtests are located in Stimulus Booklet 2.

- Directions for Administering and Scoring the Picture Vocabulary Multiple Choice (PVMC) Subtest are located in Stimulus Booklet 3.

- SIMC, VCMC, and COMC items are scored 0, 1, and 2 and INMC is scored 0 and 1, similar to their Core/Supplemental Subtest counterparts.

- PVMC is scored 0 and 1 unlike its counterparts the VC and VCMC subtests.

- Start, Reverse, and Discontinue rules are printed on the Record Form for easy reference.

- For all five Verbal Domain multiple-choice subtests, testing is discontinued after five consecutive incorrect responses.

other than that administration of any of these subtests must occur after completion of the administration of the Core and Supplemental Subtests of the WISC-IV. Clinicians can select the specific subtests that are most likely to assist in understanding a particular child's test performance. The decision to use one or more process subtests may be based on information that is obtained prior to the administration of the WISC-IV Core and Supplemental Subtests, such as parent and/or teacher input or records review. After administration of the Core and Supplemental Subtests, the clinician may choose to administer one or more of the process subtests based on observations of the child's performance during the assessment or based on the scores earned by the child on one or more of the Core and/or Supplemental Subtests. Rapid Reference 8.8 lists conditions most likely to lead to the use of one or more Verbal Domain Process Subtests. Whatever the reason for choosing to use Verbal Domain Process Subtests, examiners must keep in mind that the administration of these subtests must occur after the administration of the WISC-IV Core and Supplemental subtests. Administration of the standard WISC-IV subtests should not be interrupted in order to complete a process subtest.

≡ Rapid Reference 8.8

When to Use the Verbal Domain Process Subtests

The decision to use process subtests may occur prior to or after administration of the WISC-IV Core and Supplemental Subtests.

Prior to administration of the WISC-IV, information gathered from parents, teachers, and background records can inform the clinician about situations in which the use of Verbal Domain Process Subtests might be warranted. These situations could include:

Background information indicating

• Speech and language delays

• A language disorder

• Traumatic brain injury, including concussions

Concerns expressed by parents or teachers

• Lack of language production (e.g., does not respond to questions; does not volunteers answers; does not start or participate in conversations)

• Poor use of language skills (e.g., speech is hard to understand; verbal expression of thoughts is hard to follow or unusual; grammar and syntax use is poor; finding the right words is difficult)

• Poor performance on tests despite evidence that the child knows the material covered by the test

After administration of the WISC-IV, observations of how the child performed the Core and/or Supplemental verbal subtests and/or the scores earned on these subtests may lead to the decision to administer one or more of the Verbal Domain Process Subtests. In the case of behavior observations, it may be the way in which the child performed the task rather than the score the child obtained that leads to the administration of one or more process subtests. Observations and scores leading to the use of process subtests could include:

Observations during testing

• Minimal engagement in conversation prior to and after the assessment

• Minimal language production during conversation; reliance on single-word responses and short phrases

• Minimal language production to test items

• Poor grammar and syntax

• Circumlocutions (the child "talks around" a specific word or point, providing long narrative descriptions that do not quite hit the mark exactly)

• Paraphasias (the child makes unusual word substitutions)

- Articulation difficulties (speech is hard to understand)
- Excessive production resulting in spoiled responses from conflicting information
- Word-finding difficulties (the child cannot produce the specific word[s] he/she wants to describe an object or situation)
- Problems with information retrieval ("I know that ..." or "Wait ... wait ... um, um, um")
- Vague general responses
- Lack of adequate response despite an apparent understanding (e.g., clearly understands what a bike is, but is not able to provide an adequate response)
- Inconsistent item response pattern (misses easy items, gets harder items right)
- Atypical performance with items (offers atypical responses or attempts to solve problems in very unusual ways)
- Consistent production of only 1-point responses for subtests in which 0, 1, or 2 points are possible
- Never able to provide more than one reason, even after prompting, when two reasons are required

Scores earned on the WISC-IV Core and/or Supplemental Subtests

- When all verbal subtest scores are in the Below Average range or lower
- When one verbal subtest score is significantly lower or higher than the others
- When significant splits between verbal subtest clusters occurs (e.g., Vocabulary and Information Subtest scores are significantly higher than Similarities and Comprehension Subtest scores)
- When the WMI score is significantly greater than the VCI score
- When the VCI score is significantly lower than the PRI score
- When the VCI score is low or lower than expected based on parent and/or teacher input about the child's abilities
- When many or all subtest scores are average or better but parent and/or teacher reports indicate poor performance on standardized group achievement tests or classroom tests

Use and Interpretation of the Verbal Domain Process Subtests

To effectively use and interpret the Verbal Domain Process Subtests, it is necessary to have an understanding of the multifactorial nature of the Verbal Domain Core and Supplemental Subtests in terms of the cognitive capacities they assess. Similarly, clinicians need to understand what cognitive capacities are assessed by the Verbal Domain Process Subtests and how these can be used in tandem with the Core and Supplemental Subtests to obtain a clearer picture of a child's cognitive strengths and weaknesses.

What Do Verbal Domain Core, Supplemental, and Process Subtests Measure?
The Verbal Domain Subtests were designed primarily to assess the use of specific cognitive capacities applied with verbal content. These capacities are the primary focus of interpretation of the Verbal Comprehension Index as well as each individual subtest, and they include retrieval of verbal information from long-term storage and reasoning with verbal information. The roles of these primary cognitive capacities in task performance are described in detail in Rapid Reference 8.9.

≡ *Rapid Reference 8.9*

Cognitive Capacities Assessed with the Verbal Domain Core and Supplemental Subtests

Primary Cognitive Capacities

Retrieval of verbal content from long-term storage—This cognitive capacity is essential for effective performance on the Vocabulary, Information, and Word Reasoning Subtests. In the case of the Similarities and Comprehension subtests, the relative importance of retrieval of information from long-term storage can vary greatly. If a child is not familiar with words that are presented as part of the directions or the items of the subtest, then lack of retrieval of semantic information will have a limiting effect on performance with Similarities (e.g., does not know the word *lumber*) and Comprehension (e.g., does not know the meaning of the word *advantages*).

Beyond understanding of subtest directions and item content, a child may have stored specific knowledge that can be retrieved and expressed as responses to test items. In the case of the Vocabulary, Word Reasoning, and Similarities Subtests, the type of verbal content retrieved is semantic knowledge; for the Information Subtest, specific content-area knowledge is retrieved; for the Comprehension Subtest, the type of content retrieved is specific knowledge of social conventions and rules or the reasons for practical behaviors.

Reasoning with verbal information—This cognitive capacity most often is required for success with the Similarities, Comprehension, and Word Reasoning Subtests. Reasoning capacity is not assessed directly by the Vocabulary and Information Subtests; individuals who have not registered and stored the needed specific word meanings or content-area facts prior to administration of the Vocabulary and Information Subtests cannot apply reasoning ability to *figure out* the meaning of specific vocabulary words or to induce the answer to factual information questions during test administration. Children with extensive semantic and content-area knowledge stores, however, can access these while responding to specific Similarities and Comprehension Subtest items, thereby bypassing the use of reasoning abilities on those items. While the easier items of the Word Reasoning Subtest can be completed with retrieval of semantic knowledge alone, the more difficult items are much more likely to require the use of some degree of inductive reasoning along with the accessing of semantic knowledge.

Secondary Cognitive Capacities

Auditory Acuity—While listening to the directions provided by the examiner, the child must have adequate auditory acuity. If the child cannot hear all of the speech sounds made by the examiner, directions may be misunderstood. Typically, a child's auditory acuity is assessed and verified to be within normal limits with or without the use of assistive devices prior to test administration so that this capacity should not be a factor in performance. If overlooked, however, a deficit in auditory acuity can significantly impact task performance with all verbal subtests.

Auditory Discrimination—Before responding to the items of each Verbal Subtest, the child must be able to listen to and effectively process the language used by the examiner when directions are being provided. If the child is prone to auditory discrimination errors when listening to others speak, specific words may be misunderstood, resulting in incorrect responses or no response at all.

Auditory Comprehension—Not only must the child be able to hear and discriminate the individual sounds of words spoken by the examiner, the child must also grasp the meaning of the sentences that are being spoken as subtest directions or items. Increasing complexity in the grammar and syntax used in subtest directions and items increases the demand for well-developed auditory comprehension capacities. While all of the Verbal Subtests require the use of auditory comprehension capacities to some degree, the Word Reasoning and Comprehension Subtests make greater demands on these capacities than the Similarities, Vocabulary, and Information Subtests.

Auditory Processing Speed—The speed with which a child can register auditory information can greatly affect the child's ability to register all the information that is presented in a short period of time. Although the items of each Verbal Domain Subtest are read to the child at a normal conversational pace, a child with slow auditory processing speed may not be able to register all of the information provided in each item; this is especially true for the Comprehension and Word Reasoning subtests.

Expressive Language—After hearing and comprehending subtest directions and items, the child is required to use expressive language abilities to communicate a response. While all of the Verbal Subtests require a vocal response, the Vocabulary and Comprehension subtests require more in the way of expressive language production than the other subtests in order for a response to be judged correct.

(continued)

Working Memory—When directions are long or make use of complex grammar and syntax and/or the child requires more than a few seconds to retrieve or compose a response, the child may find it necessary to hold in mind and reference the auditorily presented directions and/or item content while attempting to retrieve relevant information and/or compose a response. Although working memory capacity may need to be accessed for any of the Verbal Subtests, it is most likely to be used when attempting the items of the Comprehension and Word Reasoning Subtests.

Executive Functions—As a class of cognitive capacities, Executive Functions are responsible for cueing and directing the use of other mental capacities that are used for the purposes of perceiving, feeling, thinking, and acting. As such, they are intricately involved in the performance of all the tasks of the WISC-IV. The degree of involvement of specific executive functions in the performance of specific subtests, however, is highly variable and dependent on many factors including the directions provided to the child about how to perform the task and the input, processing, and output demands of the task. In the case of the Verbal Domain Subtests, it is important to understand the role of executive functions in cueing and directing the use of reasoning abilities and cueing and directing the retrieval of information from long-term storage. In the case of most WISC-IV subtests, demands for the use of executive functions are minimized through the use of explicit directions and teaching examples that model how to perform a task and/or the kind of response that is desired. For some children, however, even these executive function aids do not help to ameliorate the effects of their severe executive function deficits, and the effects of these deficits often can be observed in the child's efforts to perform tasks.

For the Verbal Domain Subtests, accurate responding depends in part on the effective use of one or more of the following executive function capacities:

- cueing the appropriate considerations of the cognitive demands of a task and the amount of mental effort required to effectively perform the task
- cueing and directing efficient retrieval from long-term storage
- cueing and directing auditory processing speed
- cueing and directing the use of reasoning abilities
- cueing and directing auditory perception and discrimination
- cueing and directing the focusing and sustaining of attention to auditory stimuli
- cueing and directing the initiation and sustaining of on-demand (i.e., at the request of the examiner) use of expressive language capacities
- cueing and directing the flexible shifting of cognitive mindset to consider and respond to the specific demands of the task
- cueing and directing the use of working memory resources
- recognizing that a cue for retrieval of additional information (i.e., examiner saying "tell me more ...") can aid performance
- coordinating the use of reasoning and retrieval capacities, and possibly working memory, to produce a response

Beyond the two primary cognitive capacities targeted for assessment with the Verbal Domain Subtests, the specific formats of each subtest make demands on the child that require the engagement of additional cognitive capacities in order to achieve success. While these capacities are required for effective subtest performance, they are not considered to be the primary target of the assessment (i.e., the intention of the subtest is not to quantitatively assess the child's use of these cognitive capacities). These secondary cognitive capacities include Auditory Discrimination, Auditory Comprehension, Expressive Language, Working Memory applied to verbal content, and multiple Executive Functions applied to cue and direct the mental processing of language and working with verbal content. The roles of these secondary cognitive capacities in subtest performance are described in detail in Rapid Reference 8.9.

Within the field of psychology, there is much debate as to what specific Verbal Domain Subtests assess in terms of these two primary cognitive capacities. While some psychologists prefer to think of all of the Verbal Domain Subtests as measures of general reasoning ability, others choose to recognize that subtests like Vocabulary and Information, while tending to correlate well with measures of reasoning ability, do not directly involve the use of reasoning ability. Other psychologists are willing to acknowledge the difference between reasoning with information and retrieval of information, but they do not recognize that retrieval of semantic knowledge can play a role in the performance of subtests like Similarities and Comprehension, choosing to think of these subtests only as measures of reasoning ability. Some psychologists deny that reasoning ability is required for any of the verbal subtests and view them all strictly as measures of prior knowledge. Still others ignore completely the distinctions between reasoning and retrieval of information from long-term storage, choosing to think of all of the Verbal Domain Subtests simply as measures of a more general, global capacity referred to as *verbal ability*. As is the case with the primary cognitive capacities, there is similar debate about the roles played by secondary capacities in Verbal Domain Subtest performance.

When Verbal Domain Subtest scores are interpreted, either collectively using the VCI or individually, it is often assumed that the subtests are measuring the primary capacities intended to be assessed. The secondary capacities required for effective performance are either ignored or assumed to be intact and functioning as expected, allowing the focus of interpretation to be on the primary capacities. For example, if a child cannot respond effectively to Similarities and Comprehension items, the assumption often is that the child has poor reasoning abilities; if the child cannot provide adequate responses to the Vocabulary and Information subtests, the assumption is that the child does not know the meanings of the words or does not know the specific facts about which they are being asked. In many cases in which low performance is observed, however, such assumptions are not necessarily warranted. To know if these assumptions about the primary capacities are valid, the role of the secondary cognitive capacities in task performance must be understood and explored in detail. When not accessed, or when applied ineffectively, these secondary cognitive capacities can interfere with task performance to a significant degree, making it inappropriate to focus subtest score interpretation exclusively on the primary capacities that are thought to be assessed.

When low scores or scores that are not consistent with what is known about the child are obtained with one or more of the Core or Supplemental Verbal Subtests, the Verbal Domain Process Subtests can be used to test hypotheses about the sources of poor or unusual performance. As indicated in the previous discussion, poor performance on these tasks is thought to reflect a lack of reasoning and/or a lack of stored knowledge (i.e., a lack of verbal intelligence). Clinicians who appreciate that a low score on one or more verbal subtests could be due to many different sources can draw on the Process Subtests to help obtain a better understanding of why the child performed poorly and of the educational implications of such poor performance.

The multiple-choice response format and the examiner's reading of both the question and the multiple-choice response options of each question (for all but PVMC) alters many of the cognitive demands of the standard Verbal Subtests, as detailed in Rapid Reference 8.10. Although the multiple-choice formats greatly reduce the demands placed on some cognitive capacities for most children, they may also increase the need for the use of other cognitive capacities for some children. The specific ways that multiple-choice formats may decrease or increase cognitive demands are detailed in Rapid Reference 8.10.

It should be clear from the information provided in Rapid Reference 8.10 that the Verbal Domain Process Subtests provide the clinician a chance to see how the child performs with the same item content but with a different set of cognitive demands. While the Process Subtest scores are valuable indicators of how effective the child is with the use of these cognitive capacities, their value as an interpretive tool is enhanced when they are compared to the scores earned on their Core and Supplemental Subtest counterparts. Such comparisons enable the clinician to generate or further test hypotheses about the effects of task format and input, processing, and output demands.

As noted previously, there are some situations in which use of the multiple-choice versions of subtests will reduce the child's effectiveness with item content. From a clinical perspective, knowing when an altered format reduces effectiveness is as important as knowing when the altered format increases effectiveness. Rapid Reference 8.11 provides an interpretive summary table that can be used to

≋ Rapid Reference 8.10

How Verbal Domain Multiple-Choice Process Subtests Alter or Reduce Cognitive Demands

The multiple-choice response format and the reading of both the question and the multiple-choice response options of each question (for all but PVMC) alters many of the cognitive demands of the Core and Supplemental Verbal Subtests, making it easier for some children to demonstrate their capacity to handle item content. These include:

- altering the free-recall retrieval from long-term storage demands to recognition recall from long-term storage demands (VCMC and INMC)
- altering open-ended inductive reasoning demands to a demand for recognition of the effective application of inductive reasoning (SIMC and COMC)
- possibly reducing the auditory discrimination demands imposed when questions are only presented orally (i.e., provided the child is able to use the printed forms of words as a check on what was heard in the oral presentation of the items for SIMC, VCMC, COMC, and INMC)
- possibly reducing the auditory comprehension demands imposed when questions are only presented orally (i.e., provided the child is able to read the questions and response options as a check on what was heard in the oral presentation of the items for SIMC, VCMC, COMC, and INMC)
- eliminating the demand for the use of expressive language abilities (all MC subtests)
- reducing the need to use working memory resources when questions are only presented orally (i.e., provided the child is able to read the questions and response options to reduce the need to hold in mind what was heard in the oral presentation of the items; especially for COMC)
- reducing or altering the executive function demands imposed by the oral presentation of free-recall or open-ended reasoning tasks, including:
  - altering the cueing and directing of free-recall retrieval to the cueing and directing of recognition recall (all MC subtests)
  - altering the cueing and directing of open-ended inductive reasoning to the cueing and directing of the recognition of the effective application of inductive reasoning (SIMC and COMC)
  - eliminating the need to initiate and sustain on-demand use of expressive language abilities (all MC subtests, but especially VCMC and COMC)
  - eliminating or reducing the need to cue and direct flexible shifting of cognitive mindset (SIMC)

(continued)

- reducing or eliminating the need to cue and direct the use of working memory resources (provided the child can read the items and responses; especially COMC)
- eliminating the need to recognize that a cue to say more can aid in the retrieval of additional information (all MC subtests)
- reducing or eliminating the need to coordinate the use of retrieval, reasoning, and working memory (most likely for SIMC and COMC)

How Verbal Domain Multiple-Choice Process Subtests May Increase Cognitive Demands

The multiple-choice formats greatly reduce the demands placed on some cognitive capacities for most children, but they may also increase the need for the use of other cognitive capacities for some children. The specific ways that the multiple-choice response formats may increase cognitive demands include:

- increased need for the use of Auditory Discrimination if the child is not able to effectively use words in print as a check on what is heard during the oral and visual presentation of items
- increased need for the use of Auditory Comprehension if the child is not able to use reading skills to read and reread the questions and response options
- increased demand for faster processing of language, especially if the child is unable to use reading skills to read and reread the questions and response options
- elimination of the use of expressive language abilities for a child whose primary strength is in oral communication
- increased need for the use of working memory resources if the child is unable to use reading skills to read and reread the questions and response options
- introduction of the need to retrieve, or evaluate the accuracy of, visual representations of word meanings
- increased executive function demands including:
  - increased need for cueing and directing recognition recall to select the best response option from several choices
  - introduction of the need to cue and direct inhibition of impulsive responding when considering response options
  - introduction of the need to cue and direct monitoring of attention to details to ensure accurate responding
  - increased need for cueing and directing the use of working memory resources if the child is unable to use reading skills to read and reread the questions and response options
  - increased need for coordinating the use of retrieval, reasoning, and working memory resources if the child is unable to use reading skills to read and reread the questions and response options

Rapid Reference 8.11

Cognitive Capacities Likely to Be Assessed by Verbal Domain Tasks and Reflected in Scaled Score Values

Cognitive Capacity	Verbal Domain Tasks									
	SI	SI MC	VC	VC MC	PV MC	CO	CO MC	IN	IN MC	WR
Free-Recall Retrieval of Knowledge	X		XXX					XXX		XX
Recognition Recall of Knowledge		X		XXX					XXX	
Recognition of Visual Representation of Semantic Knowledge					XXX					
Reasoning with Verbal Content	XXX					XXX				XX
Recognition of Effective Reasoning with Verbal Content		XXX					XXX			
Auditory Discrimination	XX	XX	XX	XX		XX	XX		XX	XX
Auditory Comprehension	X	XX	X	XX		XX	XX	X	XX	XX
Auditory Processing Speed		XX		XX		XX	XX	XX	XX	XX
Expressive Language	XX	XX	XXX	XX		XXX	XX	X		X
Working Memory	X	XX		XX		X	XX		XXX	XXX
EF—Cueing appropriate consideration of the cognitive capacities and mental effort required to perform a task	XX	XX	XX	XX	XX	XX	XX	XX	XX	XX

(continued)

Capacity	1	2	3	4	5	6	7	8	9	10	11
EF—Directing Auditory Perception, Discrimination, and Comprehension	XX	XX	XX	XX	XX	XX	XX	XX	XX	XX	XX
EF—Directing Auditory Attention	X	XX	X	XX	X	XX	XX	X	XX	XX	XX
EF—Directing Processing Speed	X	X	XX	X	XX	XX	X	XX	XX	X	XX
EF—Directing Retrieval	X	XX		X	X		X	XX	X		XX
EF—Directing Reasoning	XX	XXX	XX		XX	XX		X			X
EF—Directing Language Expression	XX		XX	XX		XX	XX	X	X		X
EF—Directing Flexible Shifting of Reasoning Mindset	XXX			X	XX		XX	XX			XX
EF—Directing Working Memory	X	X	X	X	X	X	X	X	X	X	XX
EF—Recognizing and Responding to Prompts for More Information	X			X	X	X		X			
EF—Coordinating the Use of Multiple Capacities Simultaneously	XX	XX	XX	XX	XX	XX	XX	XX	XX	XX	X
EF—Cueing the inhibition of impulsive responding		XX	XX	XX	XX		XX			XX	XX
EF—Cueing attention to auditory and visual details		XX	XX	XX	XX	XX	XX	XX		XX	XX

XXX = Primary Capacity targeted for assessment with the task.

XX = Secondary Capacity highly likely to be impacting task performance.

X = Secondary Capacity possibly impacting task performance

assist with the comparison of Verbal Domain Core and Supplemental Subtests with their multiple-choice Process Subtest counterparts in terms of the cognitive capacities that are most likely to be involved in the performance of test items.

Meaningful interpretation of Core, Supplemental, and Process subtest comparisons starts with the determination of whether a statistically significant and clinically meaningful difference exists between the scores earned on the subtests being compared. The *WISC-IV Integrated Administration and Scoring Manual* provides tables for statistically significant scaled score discrepancies and for scaled score discrepancy base rates. These are based on the data obtained from the performance of the WISC-IV Integrated standardization sample of 730 children.

The differences required for statistical significance at the .15 and .05 levels between Core/Supplemental Subtest scaled scores and their Process Subtest counterpart scaled scores are located in Appendix D, Table D.1. These values are also presented in Rapid Reference 8.12. Given the range of the tabled values it is reasonable to use a rounded value of 3 scaled score points to signify a statistically significant difference for any of the comparisons of Core/Supplemental Subtests with their Process Subtest counterparts.

≡ *Rapid Reference 8.12*

Guidelines for Interpreting Comparisons Between Verbal Domain Scaled Scores

Determining a Significant Difference Between Scaled Scores

The scaled score values for significant differences between Core/Supplemental Subtests and their Process Subtest counterparts as provided in Appendix D, Table D.1 of the *WISC-IV Integrated Administration and Scoring Manual* are shown in the table below:

Significance Level	SI vs. SIMC	VC vs. VCMC	VC vs. PVMC	PVMC vs. VCMC	CO vs. COMC	IN vs. INMC
.15	2.66	2.24	2.27	2.45	2.89	2.39
.05	3.62	3.05	3.09	3.34	3.93	3.26

Based on the values in the table, clinicians can feel comfortable using a rounded value of 3 scaled score points to indicate a significant difference between a Core/Supplemental Subtest and its Process Subtest counterpart. Using a

(continued)

difference of 3 scaled score points is equivalent to using a value that is roughly halfway between the .15 and .05 levels.

Degree of Unusualness of Scaled Score Discrepancies

The cumulative percentages of the standardization sample (i.e., base rates) obtaining scaled score discrepancies of a particular magnitude between Core/ Supplemental Subtests and their Process Subtest counterparts as provided in Appendix D, Table D.2 of the *WISC-IV Integrated Administration and Scoring Manual*. A subset of the values at or above the statistically significant difference of 3 scaled score points are summarized in the following tables for comparisons when the Process Subtest score is greater than the Core/Supplemental score and when the Core/Supplemental Subtest score is greater than the Process Subtest score:

Process Subtest Scores Significantly Larger than Core/Supplemental Subtest Scores

Scaled Score Discrepancy	SIMC > SI	VCMC > VC	PVMC > VC	PVMC > VCMC*	COMC > CO	INMC > IN
3	16.1	11.3	12.7	14.7	19.2	11.2
4	8.8	5.7	7.2	7.5	9.9	4.4
5	3.9	2.4	3.3	3.4	5.7	1.7
6	1.4	1.0	1.4	1.8	2.9	0.6
7	0.7	0.8	1.0	0.8	1.1	0.3

*Note that these values represent a comparison between two Process Subtest scores.

Core/Supplemental Subtest Scores Significantly Larger than Process Subtest Scores

Scaled Score Discrepancy	SI > SIMC	VC > VCMC	VC > PVMC	VCMC > PVMC*	CO > COMC	IN > INMC
3	18.9	12.9	13.3	14.9	17.8	10.3
4	9.8	5.7	5.9	7.1	10.7	3.4
5	4.0	2.1	2.2	3.2	6.7	1.2
6	1.4	1.2	1.1	1.0	3.3	0.3
7	0.3	0.4	0.6	0.3	1.5	0.0

*Note that these values represent a comparison between two Process Subtest scores.

Note from the table that the percentage of the standardization sample demonstrating scaled score discrepancies of 3 points or more is roughly equal for both comparison conditions (e.g., SIMC > SI and SI > SIMC). Also note that discrepancies of 4 scaled score points consistently represent differences demonstrated by 10% or less of the standardization sample and discrepancies of 5 scaled score points consistently represent differences demonstrated by 5% or less of the standardization sample. Clinicians can feel comfortable using scaled score discrepancies of 4 and 5 points generally as the values representing differences demonstrated by less than 10% and less than 5% of the standardization sample, respectively.

When attempting to interpret the significance of Verbal Domain scaled score discrepancies between Core/Supplemental and Process Subtests, clinicians using values of 4 or 5 scaled score points as the criteria for clinical significance for all comparisons will be assured of both statistical significance of the obtained discrepancy as well as a relatively high degree of unusualness of the occurrence of the difference among the standardization sample. Although somewhat more frequent in occurrence, a scaled score difference of 3 points also reasonably might be considered both statistically and clinically significant depending on the specific circumstances of the case and the number of significant subtest comparisons demonstrated by a child.

Cumulative percentages (i.e., base rates) of the standardization sample obtaining various scaled score discrepancies between Core/Supplemental Subtests and their Process Subtest counterparts are located in Appendix D, Table D.2 of the *WISC-IV Integrated Administration and Scoring Manual*. Rapid Reference 8.12 provides a discussion of guidelines for interpreting scaled score discrepancies and discrepancy comparison base rates.

To make use of these comparisons in the most effective manner possible, clinicians need to be thoroughly familiar with exactly what standard score differences actually represent when comparing Verbal Domain Core/Supplemental Subtests with their multiple-choice Process Subtest counterparts. Rapid Reference 8.13 provides a detailed explanation of these comparisons to aid clinicians in making meaningful interpretations when statistically significant differences are found. As discussed in detail in Rapid Reference 8.13, the meaning of the results of subtest scaled score comparisons will vary depending on the age of the child and the level of scaled score performance on the two subtests being compared. Tables 8.2 and 8.3 show a sampling of the Verbal Domain Subtest score difference tables that were used to develop the rationale for interpretation of discrepancy comparisons presented in Rapid Reference 8.13.

Figure 8.1 provides a Verbal Domain Subtest interpretive worksheet for comparing Process Subtest and Core/Supplemental Subtest raw and scaled scores.

≡ Rapid Reference 8.13

Interpreting Differences Between Scores for Core/ Supplemental Subtests and Their Process Subtest Counterparts

When comparing Core/Supplemental Subtests to their Process Subtest counterparts, clinicians must be careful to avoid assumptions about what scaled scores differences, or lack of differences, reflect. Consider the following three subtest comparison examples:

Anthony, Age 8-4

	SI Raw Score	SI Scaled Score	SIMC Raw Score	SIMC Scaled Score	Raw Score Increase	Raw Score Percent Increase
SI vs. SIMC	10	7	25	10	15	150%

Lauren, Age 10-4

	VC Raw Score	VC Scaled Score	VCMC Raw Score	VCMC Scaled Score	Raw Score Increase	Raw Score Percent Increase
VC vs. VCMC	34	10	42	10	8	23%

Chris, Age 12-4

	CO Raw Score	CO Scaled Score	COMC Raw Score	COMC Scaled Score	Raw Score Increase	Raw Score Percent Increase
CO vs. COMC	25	10	26	7	1	4%

Note the relationship between the raw scores and scaled scores in each of these examples. Anthony demonstrated a statistically significant scaled score increase of 3 points. He only earned 10 raw score points for his free-recall responses on SI. With the multiple-choice format of SIMC, Anthony was able to earn 25 points on similarities items, representing a raw score increase of 150% over his free-recall performance. Although Lauren earned the same scaled score on the Vocabulary and Vocabulary Multiple Choice Subtests, her VCMC raw score was 8 points greater than her VC raw score and represents a 23% increase with the use of the VCMC multiple-choice format. Despite Chris's statistically significant drop of 3 scaled score points when COMC was administered, his raw score actually increased by 1 point with the use of the multiple-choice format of COMC.

The score comparisons in these examples actually represent a pattern of raw score to scaled score relationships that are typical when the results of Core/ Supplemental Subtests are compared to their Process Subtest counterparts. This pattern can be summarized as follows:

Core/Supplemental Scaled Score = Process Scaled Score: When a Process Subtest scaled score is identical to the obtained Core/Supplemental Subtest scaled score, the child performed better with the multiple-choice format in a manner that was consistent with the increases demonstrated by same-age children in the standardization sample earning Core/Supplemental scaled scores of a similar magnitude.

Process Subtest Scaled Score > Core/Supplemental Scaled Score: When a Process Subtest scaled score is greater than the obtained Core/Supplemental Subtest scaled score, the child performed even better with the multiple-choice format than the increases typically demonstrated by same-age children in the standardization sample earning Core/Supplemental scaled scores of a similar magnitude. When a child's Process Subtest scaled score is significantly greater than the Core/Supplemental Subtest, the gains from the use of the multiple-choice format can be extremely large (see Table 8.2). As the size of the scaled score difference increases in favor of the Process Subtest score, the larger the percent of raw score increase is demonstrated by the child.

Process Subtest Scaled Score < Core/Supplemental Scaled Score: In many cases, when a Process Subtest scaled score is less than the obtained Core/Supplemental Subtest scaled score, the child performed better with the multiple-choice format, but the increase demonstrated was less than the increases typically demonstrated by same-age children in the standardization sample earning Core/Supplemental scaled scores of a similar magnitude. Only in a smaller number of cases does a Process Subtest scaled score that is less than the obtained Core/Supplemental Subtest scaled score reflect poorer performance with the multiple-choice format. When a child's Process Subtest scaled score is significantly lower than the Core/Supplemental Subtest, the raw score change resulting from the multiple-choice format is more likely to be close to 0 and may even move into the negative range as the size of the discrepancy in favor of the Core/Supplemental Subtest scaled score increases into the statistically unusual range.

The magnitude of the scaled score relationships described vary in a consistent manner based on two factors: (a) the level of the Core/Supplemental Subtest Scaled Score, and (b) the age of the child. The effects of these factors can be summarized as follows:

The lower the Scaled Score, the greater the typical percentage of increase in raw score from free response to multiple choice.

As shown in Table 8.2, the percentage of raw score increase realized from the use of the multiple-choice format is greatest for scaled scores in the Below Average range and gradually decreases in magnitude as the scaled score values increase into the Average range and beyond. This effect is partly due to the fact that the more correct responses a child provides by free response, the fewer the number of incorrect responses that can be improved with the multiple-choice format. Additionally, it is likely that children who are not very effective

(continued)

with a free-response format are more likely to benefit from the reduction in cognitive demands that the multiple-choice format represents.

The younger the child, the greater the typical percentage of increase in raw score from free response to multiple choice.

As shown in Table 8.3, the percentage of raw score increase realized from the use of the multiple-choice format is greatest for children at ages 6 and 7 and gradually decreases in magnitude with increase in age. This effect is partly due to the fact that the older the child, the more correct responses provided by free response and the fewer the number of incorrect responses that can be improved with the multiple-choice format. Additionally, younger children are more likely to benefit from the reduction in cognitive demands that the multiple-choice format represents.

These effects hold for all of the Process Core/Supplemental comparisons, but the magnitude of the effect varies by specific pair comparison. As illustrated in Table 8.2 with data from the 10-4:10-7 age group of the standardization sample, the SIMC-SI comparison produced the largest raw score increases; VCMC-VC, PVMC-VC, and COMC-CO comparisons produced somewhat smaller, roughly equivalent increases; and INMC-IN comparison produced the smallest increases. The general pattern of relationships shown in Table .2 for 10-year-olds was consistently maintained across all age groups.

The examples and discussion provided here should make it clear to clinicians that raw score differences are as important as scaled score differences when interpreting discrepancy comparisons. Clinicians can use the worksheet provided in Figure 8.1 to aid in the analysis of the meaning of both raw and scaled score differences.

CAUTION

When interpreting differences between Verbal Domain Process Subtest scaled scores and Core/Supplemental Subtest scaled scores, the following should be remembered:

1. A finding of no difference between Verbal Domain Process Subtest and Core/Supplemental Subtest scaled scores does not mean that the child did not benefit from the use of the multiple-choice format of the Process Subtest; rather the child benefited from the multiple-choice format in a typical manner.

2. A finding of a significant difference in favor of the Verbal Domain Core/Supplemental Subtest scaled score does not mean always that the child did not benefit from the use of the multiple-choice format of the Process Subtest; rather, in many cases, the child did benefit from the multiple-choice format, but did not do so as much as is typically the case.

To avoid erroneous interpretive statements about Verbal Domain Process Core/Supplemental Subtest comparisons, clinicians can use the worksheet in Figure 8.1 to analyze raw score differences as well as scaled score differences.

Table 8.2 Average Raw Score Gain Percentages Corresponding to Process Subtest Minus Core/Supplemental Subtest Scaled Score Differences

Process Subtest - Core/Supplemental Subtest Scaled Score Difference = −3

Age Group 10-4:10-7

Process Scaled Score	Core Scaled Score	SIMC-SI Ave % Gain	VCMC-VC Ave % Gain	COMC-CO Ave % Gain	INMC-IN Ave % Gain	PVMC-VC Ave % Gain	PVMC-VCMC Ave % Gain
1	4	1750%	1318%	971%	634%	1368%	1372%
2	5	1375%	125%	144%	63%	133%	46%
3	6	477%	111%	122%	56%	114%	39%
4	7	244%	95%	92%	50%	94%	33%
5	8	169%	86%	74%	45%	80%	29%
6	9	140%	74%	70%	40%	70%	24%
7	10	108%	64%	67%	39%	66%	27%
8	11	85%	55%	60%	40%	62%	27%
9	12	76%	52%	54%	38%	59%	25%
10	13	66%	49%	47%	38%	53%	22%
11	14	55%	43%	44%	39%	46%	20%
12	15	47%	41%	41%	37%	42%	17%
13	16	42%	38%	35%	35%	41%	17%
14	17	36%	37%	29%	33%	39%	17%
15	18	32%	35%	26%	31%	36%	15%
16	19	32%	34%	28%	33%	35%	16%

(continued)

Table 8.2 (Continued)

Process Subtest - Core/Supplemental Subtest Scaled Score Difference = 0
Age Group 10-4:10-7

Process Scaled Score	Core Scaled Score	SIMC-SI Ave % Gain	VCMC-VC Ave % Gain	COMC-CO Ave % Gain	INMC-IN Ave % Gain	PVMC-VC Ave % Gain	PVMC-VCMC Ave % Gain
1	1	600%	850%	550%	350%	850%	850%
2	2	925%	61%	69%	13%	69%	6%
3	3	317%	54%	64%	17%	61%	5%
4	4	156%	46%	53%	20%	49%	2%
5	5	106%	41%	45%	18%	46%	4%
6	6	88%	37%	40%	12%	39%	2%
7	7	69%	31%	33%	7%	31%	0%
8	8	55%	28%	27%	7%	24%	-3%
9	9	49%	27%	25%	9%	24%	-2%
10	10	42%	25%	22%	15%	27%	1%
11	11	33%	22%	23%	17%	27%	5%
12	12	28%	22%	24%	16%	27%	4%
13	13	24%	20%	20%	18%	24%	3%
14	14	20%	19%	17%	19%	21%	2%
15	15	21%	18%	16%	16%	19%	1%
16	16	20%	17%	16%	13%	19%	2%
17	17	16%	18%	15%	12%	20%	2%
18	18	12%	19%	15%	11%	20%	1%
19	19	6%	10%	8%	6%	10%	1%

Table 8.2 (Continued)

Process Subtest - Core/Supplemental Subtest Scaled Score Difference = 3

Age Group 10-4:10-7

Process Scaled Scaled	Core Scaled Score	SIMC-SI Ave % Gain	VCMC-VC Ave % Gain	COMC-CO Ave % Gain	INMC-IN Ave % Gain	PVMC-VC Ave % Gain	PVMC-VCMC Ave % Gain
4	1	0%	-47%	-45%	-60%	-47%	-64%
5	2	43%	1%	0%	-18%	6%	-25%
6	3	35%	0%	3%	-16%	5%	-24%
7	4	26%	-2%	6%	-14%	0%	-23%
8	5	18%	-3%	6%	-13%	0%	-21%
9	6	16%	0%	3%	-13%	2%	-20%
10	7	15%	0%	-2%	-12%	0%	-20%
11	8	11%	0%	-2%	-11%	-3%	-20%
12	9	8%	1%	0%	-8%	-1%	-19%
13	10	5%	1%	0%	-3%	2%	-15%
14	11	3%	1%	0%	0%	6%	-11%
15	12	5%	2%	2%	-2%	6%	-10%
16	13	5%	2%	3%	-2%	5%	-10%
17	14	3%	3%	5%	0%	5%	-11%
18	15	3%	4%	6%	-2%	5%	-12%
19	16	-4%	-4%	-3%	-11%	-3%	-11%

Table 8.3 Average Percent Process Subtest Raw Score Gain when Core/Supplemental and Process Subtest Scaled Scores are Equal

	Age Group										
Scaled Scores	6	7	8	9	10	11	12	13	14	15	16
SIMC = 4, SI = 4	25%	200%	237%	204%	156%	156%	131%	118%	98%	98%	78%
SIMC = 10, SI = 10	67%	88%	63%	49%	42%	38%	29%	28%	23%	19%	15%
SIMC = 16, SI = 16	34%	40%	31%	25%	20%	16%	14%	9%	9%	6%	4%
	6	7	8	9	10	11	12	13	14	15	16
VCMC = 4, VC = 4	40%	78%	45%	54%	46%	46%	48%	36%	30%	30%	27%
VCMC = 10, VC = 10	42%	44%	32%	31%	25%	29%	26%	20%	14%	18%	15%
VCMC = 16, VC = 16	42%	34%	26%	22%	17%	15%	15%	11%	8%	4%	2%
	6	7	8	9	10	11	12	13	14	15	16
PVMC = 4, VC = 4	148%	125%	76%	61%	49%	46%	37%	34%	36%	34%	27%
PVMC = 10, VC = 10	67%	54%	40%	31%	27%	29%	26%	25%	23%	22%	21%
PVMC = 16, VC = 16	53%	35%	31%	25%	19%	22%	17%	16%	14%	0%	0%
	6	7	8	9	10	11	12	13	14	15	16
PVMC = 4, VCMC = 4	80%	28%	23%	5%	2%	0%	-8%	-2%	5%	3%	0%
PVMC = 10, VCMC = 10	18%	7%	6%	0%	1%	0%	0%	4%	8%	4%	6%
PVMC = 16, VCMC = 16	7%	1%	4%	3%	2%	6%	2%	4%	6%	0%	0%
	6	7	8	9	10	11	12	13	14	15	16
COMC = 4, CO = 4	4%	42%	56%	53%	53%	45%	37%	31%	29%	24%	28%
COMC = 10, CO = 10	16%	30%	33%	36%	22%	27%	20%	15%	14%	12%	16%
COMC = 16, CO = 16	20%	31%	24%	20%	16%	15%	11%	8%	8%	5%	5%
	6	7	8	9	10	11	12	13	14	15	16
INMC = 4, IN = 4	-10%	-14%	6%	11%	20%	18%	17%	15%	23%	21%	20%
INMC = 10, IN = 10	5%	13%	14%	13%	15%	17%	13%	15%	14%	13%	11%
INMC = 16, IN = 16	16%	19%	-10%	16%	13%	12%	7%	7%	7%	0%	0%

Subtest Comparison	Process Subtest Raw Score (a)	Process Subtest Scaled Score (b)	Core/Supplemental Subtest Raw Score (c)	Core/Supplemental Subtest Scaled Score (d)	Raw Score Analysis Raw Score Diff (a−c) (e)	Raw Score Analysis Raw Score % Change (e/c) (f)	Scaled Score Diff (b−d) (g)	Scaled Score Difference Significant? g > 3?	Scaled Score Difference Unusual? g = 4 (10%) or > 5 (5%)?
SIMC vs. SI								Y N	Y < 10% Y < 5% N
VCMC vs. VC								Y N	Y < 10% Y < 5% N
PVMC* vs. VC	* ___ x 2 − 4 = ___							Y N	Y < 10% Y < 5% N
PVMC* vs. VCMC	* ___ x 2 − 4 = ___							Y N	Y < 10% Y < 5% N
COMC vs. CO								Y N	Y < 10% Y < 5% N
INMC vs. IN								Y N	Y < 10% Y < 5% N

*Multiply the Picture Vocabulary Multiple Choice (PVMC) raw score x 2 and subtract 4 to calculate the raw score differences for comparisons with PVMC.

Figure 8.1 Verbal Domain Subtest Interpretive Worksheet for Comparing Process Subtest and Core/Supplemental Subtest Raw and Scaled Scores.

DON'T FORGET

For the purposes of simplifying the discussion of Verbal Domain Subtest discrepancies, comparisons between the two Vocabulary Process Subtests PVMC and VCMC will always be listed in tables with VCMC designated as the *Core* Subtest and PVMC designated as the *Process* Subtest. This order for comparisons is based on the fact that, although both tasks are Process Subtests that reduce cognitive demands relative to the Vocabulary Subtest, PVMC represents a greater reduction in cognitive demands for the retrieval of semantic knowledge from long-term storage than VCMC. In this sense, PVMC represents a process-approach modification of VCMC as well as VC.

Rapid References 8.14 and 8.15 provide case study examples that include completed interpretive worksheets and illustrate the application of WISC-IV Integrated process-approach procedures in the interpretations of Verbal Domain Subtest performance.

The data provided in Tables 8.2 and 8.3 provide empirical support for the kind of analyses of task-related cognitive demands discussed in Rapid References 8.9, 8.10, and 8.11. As shown by the data, most children in the standardization sample were able to earn more raw score points with the multiple-choice format than with the free response format, consistent with the idea that the multiple-choice format reduces cognitive demands on task performance. As illustrated in the case example in Rapid Reference 8.14, for most children, the most relevant clinical question with the use of the Verbal Process Subtests will be: How much did the child benefit from the use of the altered format? When a child maintains the same raw score or actually earns fewer raw score points with the use of the multiple-choice format, as illustrated in the case example in Rapid Reference 8.15, clinicians will want to look more closely at the child's pattern of item responses to try to gain a greater understanding of the likely sources of difficulty.

DON'T FORGET

When performing raw score discrepancy comparisons involving Picture Vocabulary Multiple Choice, do not forget to transform the PVMC raw score by multiplying the obtained raw score by 2 and subtracting 4. This transformation credits each PVMC item with the equivalent of a full-credit, 2-point response on the VC and VCMC Subtests, and then corrects the total for the fact that the first 4 items of VC and VCMC only earn 1 point for full-credit responses.

Verbal Domain Process-Approach Interpretation

Case Example 1: Juan, Age 11-6, Grade 5, Positive Change Profile

Although Juan was born in the United States and speaks English, his parents are not fluent in English. Juan has received speech therapy assistance since Kindergarten. Juan tests in the Below Average range on most tests of reading and writing skills and has received assistance for several years through the school's Language Arts skill-development program—a Tier II intervention that has focused on helping Juan improve reading comprehension and written expression skills. The school-based multidisciplinary team expressed concern that Juan has not demonstrated much improvement in response to the instructional interventions provided to date and requested a comprehensive psychoeducational assessment. Some members of the team suspected that Juan might be cognitively impaired as he seemed to struggle greatly with reading tasks that required him to reason about what he read.

Juan's comprehensive assessment initially included administration of the WISC-IV Core and a few selected Supplemental Subtests. Juan's VCI standard score of 77 seemed to confirm his teachers' beliefs that Juan's poor performance with Language Arts was related to the fact that he was not very intellectually capable. Juan's PRI standard score of 108, however, certainly suggested that Juan possessed greater intellectual capability than many had thought. The extremely large discrepancy between Juan's VCI and PRI standard scores seemed suggestive of a contrast between a fairly well-developed capacity for reasoning with nonverbal visual information and a severe deficit in the ability to reason with verbal information and/or a very deficient store of verbal knowledge. To further understand Juan's poor Verbal Domain performance, all five of the Verbal Domain Process Subtests were administered.

(continued)

Subtest Comparison	Process Subtest		Core/Supplemental Subtest		Raw Score Analysis		Scaled Score Analysis		
	Raw Score	Scaled Score	Raw Score	Scaled Score	Raw Score Diff (a–c)	Raw Score % Change (e/c)	Scaled Score Diff (b–d)	Scaled Score Difference Significant?	Scaled Score Difference Unusual?
	a	b	c	d	e	f	g	g > 3 ?	g > 4 or 5?
SIMC vs. SI	30	9	12	5	18	150%	+4	Y N	Y < 10% Y < 5% N
VCMC vs. VC	36	6	25	6	11	44%	0	Y N	Y < 10% Y < 5% N
PVMC vs. VC*	2 × 24 – 4 = 44	9	25	6	19	76%	+3	Y N	Y < 10% Y < 5% N
PVMC vs. VCMC*	2 × 24 – 4 = 44	9	36	6	8	22%	+3	Y N	Y < 10% Y < 5% N
COMC vs. CO	30	10	18	7	12	67%	+3	Y N	Y < 10% Y < 5% N
INMC vs. IN	16	6	14	6	2	14%	+0	Y N	Y < 10% Y < 5% N

*Multiply the PVMC raw score × 2 and subtract 4 to calculate the raw score differences for comparisons with PVMC.

As shown in the worksheet, Juan demonstrated an average or better percentage of improvement for all comparisons made. Additionally, four of the six comparisons (SIMC versus SI, PVMC versus VC, PVMC versus VCMC, and COMC versus CO) represented statistically significant increases and one of those four increases (SIMC versus SI) was unusually large in that it was obtained by less than 10% of the standardization sample.

During administration of the WISC-IV Core Subtests, Juan struggled in his attempts to produce adequate free-recall responses for the Similarities, Vocabulary, and Comprehension Subtests. His responses tended to be delivered in very short phrases that did not always reflect effective use of grammar and syntax rules. These responses were usually very vague and often concretely oriented, relating to physical features rather than abstract concepts. Juan had to be prompted frequently to elaborate on his initial statements. Such prompts usually did not produce much in the way of additional statements that could improve his score.

For the Similarities Subtest, Juan initially appeared to have a good grasp of the requirements of the task, producing correct single-word responses that reflected an understanding of the semantic representation of conceptual categories for the first four items administered. Beyond this point, however, Juan was unable to effectively express a conceptual understanding of the similarities between word pairs, earning only partial credit for two additional items by noting physically similar features of object pairs.

When administered the Similarities Multiple Choice Subtest, Juan was able to demonstrate his understanding of conceptual categories much more effectively, by recognizing the most accurate descriptions of similarities for an additional eight word pairs and identifying a partially accurate description for another four word pairs. Juan's additional correct responses represented a 150% increase in correct responding over his free-recall efforts on the Similarities Subtest.

When reviewing the list of cognitive demands from Rapid Reference 8.12, Juan's initial effective performance with free response items and his much more effective performance with multiple-choice items offer evidence that Juan did not experience any difficulties with auditory discrimination, auditory comprehension, or working memory with either item type and that his capacity for reasoning with verbal content is at least in the average range. Juan also did not demonstrate any response behaviors that would suggest difficulties with any of the executive functions required to cue and direct effective responding with the exception of directing and cueing expressive language production. Consideration of all of the factors on the list in Rapid Reference 8.12 for SI and SIMC thus suggests that only two factors—Expressive Language and Executive Function Direction of Expressive Language—are most likely to be the source of Juan's poor performance with the Similarities Subtest. It is important to note that Juan's scaled score of 9 on SIMC was much more similar to his performance on Picture Concepts (scaled score 11) than was his Similarities scaled score of 5.

For the Vocabulary Subtest, Juan again seemed to understand what was required in the way of responses but struggled in his efforts to provide answers. Trying to get Juan to provide a sufficient response for the word bike, for example, required several prompts for more information with the result being only a partially correct 1-point response. Initially, Juan seemed frustrated by the question, saying "a bike is a bike!"; then with prompting, saying "a machine"; and with further prompting, saying "ride on it." Juan earned 2-point responses for only six of his explanations and 1-point partial credit for only five other words.

(continued)

When administered the Vocabulary Multiple Choice Subtest, Juan appeared to have no difficulty listening to all of the response options of each item; he was able to increase all five of his 1-point free response answers to 2-point multiple-choice answers and was able to choose the 2-point multiple-choice response for an additional three items. Juan's performance with the multiple-choice format represented a 44% increase in effective responding over the free response format. Juan's gain with the multiple-choice format was as large as the increase typically demonstrated by 11-year-olds in the standardization sample. As a result, Juan's scaled score for VCMC remained the same as his score for VC (6). While Juan was able to demonstrate the average degree of benefit from the use of the multiple-choice format, his consistent scoring at the 9th percentile with both the free response and the multiple-choice format suggests that Juan's store of word knowledge is relatively limited compared to same-age peers. This hypothesis was further tested using the PVMC Subtest.

When administered the Picture Vocabulary Multiple Choice Subtest, Juan was much more effective at identifying the visual representation of word meanings than at attempting to define them either by free response or by multiple-choice recognition. Juan was able to correctly identify the visual representation of an additional seven words that he could not identify fully or partially by free response on VC and an additional five words that he could not identify fully or partially on VCMC. These score improvements on PVMC represented a 76% increase over VC and a 22% increase over VCMC. Considering all of the factors in Rapid Reference 8.12, the resulting PVMC scaled score of 9 strongly suggests that Juan's store of word-meaning knowledge is at least in the average range, but that the expression of that knowledge is heavily dependent on the format chosen to assess competency. When Juan was required to use his language expression skills, he was not able to demonstrate the full extent of his knowledge store, he did not use this format as effectively as he used a visual recognition format. While the use of a recognition format helped Juan to demonstrate a greater amount of his knowledge store, he did not use this format as effectively as he used a visual recognition format.

For the Comprehension Subtest, as with Similarities and Vocabulary, Juan seemed to understand what was required in the way of responses but found it difficult to provide them. Responses were limited to very short phrases and much prompting was required to attempt to get Juan to improve on vague responses. Juan offered 2-point responses for the first three items and for one later item and provided 1-point responses for an additional six items. Juan was able to offer a second reason only once for items requiring at least two reasons for full credit.

When administered the Comprehension Multiple Choice Subtest, Juan was able to improve four of his six 1-point responses to 2-point responses and provide 2-point responses to four items for which he could not offer accurate free responses. Juan's additional correct responses represented a 67% increase in correct responding over his free-recall efforts on the Comprehension Subtest.

When reviewing the list of cognitive demands from Rapid Reference 8.12, Juan's initial effective performance with free response items and his much more effective performance with multiple-choice items offer evidence that Juan did not experience any difficulties with auditory discrimination or auditory comprehension with either item type and that his capacity for reasoning with verbal content is at least in the Average range. Juan also did not demonstrate any response behaviors that would suggest difficulties with any of the executive functions required to cue and direct effective responding with the exception of cueing and directing expressive language production and/or cueing and directing working memory. Consideration of all of the factors for COMC and CO on the list in Rapid Reference 8.12 thus suggests that, as was the case with the Similarities Subtest, two factors—Expressive Language and Executive Function Direction of Expressive Language—are the factors most likely to be the greatest source of influence in Juan's poor performance with the Comprehension Subtest. It is also possible that Juan is less capable with cueing and directing the use of working memory, or has less access to working memory capacity, when involved with this kind of free-recall task.

For the Information Subtest, Juan was able to provide correct responses for the first five questions he was asked. These questions involved basic factual knowledge that can be acquired from many different sources. When the questions focused on knowledge typically obtained in a formal school setting, Juan was not able to provide any correct responses. He seemed reluctant to spend much time attempting to access information, frequently providing "Don't know" responses or simply shook his head to indicate a lack of response.

When administered the Information Multiple Choice Subtest, Juan was able to recognize the correct response for an additional two items, representing the average amount of gain (14%) experienced by 11-year-olds in the standardization sample from the use of the multiple-choice format. While Juan was able to demonstrate the average degree of benefit from the use of the multiple-choice format, his consistent scoring at the 9th percentile with both the free response and the multiple-choice format suggests that Juan's store of factual knowledge about academic content areas is relatively limited compared to same-age peers. Unfortunately, the lack of a Picture Information Multiple Choice Subtest means that this hypothesis cannot be further tested with a visual representation format as was done in the case of Vocabulary. Given the rest of the information obtained about Juan's cognitive functioning, it is not unreasonable to think that he might have a greater store of information about school subjects than he was able to demonstrate using these two verbal formats.

Report Summary of Performance

The previously described analysis could be summarized in a psychological report as follows:

(continued)

The results of the testing with the five Verbal Domain Process Subtests indicate that Juan's ability to reason with verbal content on the Similarities (5) and Comprehension (7) tasks improved significantly more than was typically the case when a multiple-choice format was used to present items (SIMC 9 and COMC 10). His store of verbal content knowledge and his ability to retrieve that information on the Vocabulary (6) and Information (6) tasks was aided as much as expected with the use of the multiple-choice format (VCMC 6 and INMC 6), meaning that his level of performance remained low relative to same-age peers. When a visual representation multiple-choice format (PVMC) was used to test vocabulary knowledge retrieval, however, Juan was able to demonstrate a much higher level of retrieval of word meanings, earning a score in the average range (9) on the PVMC subtest.

Use of the Verbal Domain Process Subtests suggests that Juan's VCI score of 77 is not an accurate portrayal of either his ability to reason with verbal content or the amount of verbal content stored and available for retrieval. It appears most likely that Juan's low VCI score reflects expressive language difficulties or executive function difficulties with directing the use of expressive language much more than reasoning or knowledge retrieval limitations. Specifically targeted neuropsychological assessment of verbal expression capacities could help determine more specifically the nature of Juan's expressive language difficulties.

Case Outcome

Having a clearer understanding of how the format of a verbal content task can impact Juan's performance and the likely source of Juan's difficulties with free response format questions (which are frequently used in classroom and remedial instruction to assess Juan's comprehension of material that he has read), as well as a better understanding of Juan's capacity to reason with both verbal and nonverbal content, Juan's teachers were better able to more effectively differentiate classroom instruction and assessment and have seen noteworthy improvements in his academic achievement and his attitude toward school. The greatest challenge facing teachers in the future will be how to provide Juan with instruction that takes advantage of his more strongly developed capacity for dealing with nonverbal content and that prepares him for taking on work that enables him to use his cognitive strengths effectively. Less directly relevant to Juan's development of employable skills or his potential contribution to society, but most critical to his school district, will be the challenge of getting Juan to a level of performance on state-wide competency tests that will enable him to receive a high school diploma.

≡ Rapid Reference 8.15

Verbal Domain Process-Approach Interpretation

Case Example 2: Alex, Age 13-4, Grade 8, Negative Change Profile

Although seemingly very intellectually capable, Alex has always had difficulty complying with teacher requests and performing in the classroom and on achievement tests at a level consistent with his apparent cognitive capacities. Alex's teachers have always suspected that he has ADHD, but a formal evaluation has never been done, and Alex's parents have always attributed his poor grades and frequently low test scores simply to a lack of motivation on Alex's part. With Alex's failure of three major courses in the first marking period of the eighth grade, Alex's parents, to the surprise of school staff, submitted a written request to have a psychoeducational evaluation completed.

Alex's comprehensive assessment initially included administration of the WISC-IV Core and a few selected Supplemental Subtests. Alex's VCI standard score of 126 seemed to confirm parents' and teachers' beliefs that Alex is an intellectually capable child. Achievement testing indicated that Alex's academic skills are well developed as well. To further understand Alex's poor Verbal Domain performance, all five of the Verbal Domain Process Subtests were administered.

Subtest Comparison	Process Subtest		Core/Supplemental Subtest		Raw Score Analysis		Scaled Score Diff (b–d)	Scaled Score Analysis	
	Raw Score	Scaled Score	Raw Score	Scaled Score	Raw Score Diff (a–c)	Raw Score % Change (e/c)		Scaled Score Difference Significant?	Scaled Score Difference Unusual?
	a	b	c	d	e	f	g	g > 3 ?	g > 4 or 5?
SIMC vs. SI	34	11	36	15	−2	−5%	−4	Y N	Y < 10% Y < 5% N
VCMC vs. VC	52	11	53	14	−1	−2%	−3	Y N	Y < 10% Y < 5% N

(continued)

357

PVMC vs. VC*	2 × 26 − 4 = 48	9	53	14	−5	−9%	−5	Y N	Y < 10% Y < 5% N
PVMC vs. VCMC*	2 × 26 − 4 = 48	9	52	11	−4	−8%	−2	Y N	Y < 10% Y < 5% N
COMC vs. CO	32	11	35	14	−3	−9%	−3	Y N	Y < 10% Y < 5% N
INMC vs. IN	25	12	24	13	+1	4%	−1	Y N	Y < 10% Y < 5% N

*Multiply the PVMC raw score × 2 and subtract 4 to calculate the raw score differences for comparisons with PVMC.

As shown in the worksheet, Alex demonstrated decreases in raw score performance for all but one of the score comparisons tabled. Additionally, all of the scaled score comparisons reflected a negative change; four of the six comparisons represented statistically significant decreases; and two of the decreases (SIMC versus SI, PVMC versus VC) were unusually large.

During administration of the WISC-IV Core Subtests, Alex was quite adept at providing concise, accurate responses. When more detailed responses were needed, Alex tended to move about in his seat quite a bit, often started up conversations between test items, and frequently had to be prompted to return to work on test items. Despite these behaviors, Alex was able to articulately and succinctly express his thoughts, often in very dramatic manner, usually earning full credit for his answers.

When the Process Subtests were administered, Alex delivered many responses that reflected a lack of attention to auditory and/or visual details, a tendency toward impulsive responding, and a seeming tendency to underestimate the difficulty of some items.

When administered the Similarities Multiple Choice Subtest, Alex increased three 1-point responses to 1-point responses, but he then selected 1-point responses for two items that he had answered with 2-point free responses and selected 0-point responses to two items that had earned a 2-point and a 1-point response, respectively. Alex's response choices were typically delivered very quickly after the complete reading of the item and all response options by the examiner. While the examiner was reading the questions, Alex's eyes were quickly scanning the page, appearing to be following along with the examiner's readings, but his quickly delivered responses often suggested that he had not really completely processed all of the information provided to the degree necessary to make well-considered responses. Alex's free responses to the items he got wrong clearly indicated that he had a better grasp of the conceptual relationships of word pairs than what was reflected in his multiple-choice answers. The cumulative effect of Alex's increases and decreases in performance was a net loss of 2 points, representing a 5% decrease in effectiveness. This relatively minor reduction in raw score translated into a statistically significant and relatively unusual 4 scaled score point decrease due to the fact that the 13-year-olds in the standardization sample typically gained several raw score points when responding with the multiple-choice recognition format of SIMC.

When administered the Vocabulary Multiple Choice and the Comprehension Multiple Choice subtests, the SIMC response scenario was repeated with similar results. Score gains were countered by a larger number of score reductions due primarily to Alex's tendency to offer responses quickly and without careful consideration of all the response options provided. The resulting relatively small raw score reductions again resulted in significant scaled score decreases due to the fact that the 13-year-olds in the standardization sample typically gained several raw score points when responding with the multiple-choice recognition formats of both VCMC and COMC.

Alex's largest drop in efficiency (−5 scaled score points) was demonstrated on the Picture Vocabulary Multiple Choice Subtest. Despite his demonstrated knowledge of word meanings, Alex appeared to underestimate the difficulty of selecting an accurate visual representation of a word's meaning, resulting in the delivery of several incorrect responses for words that he had accurately defined with free response answers. Alex's performance on the PVMC Subtest was more consistent with his performance on the Picture Completion Subtest (Scaled Score 9), a task on which he also demonstrated a great deal of inconsistency in his response pattern, missing relatively easy items and getting much more difficult items correct.

Although Alex managed to increase his score by 1 point on the Information Multiple Choice Subtest, and did not demonstrate the inconsistency in responding that was evident on the other four subtests, his gain was not quite equivalent to that typically demonstrated by 13-year-olds in the standardization sample, resulting in a scaled score drop of 1 point.

When reviewing the list of cognitive demands from Rapid Reference 8.12, Alex's highly effective performance with free response format items for all of the Verbal Core/Supplemental Subtests rules out difficulties with all of the primary and secondary capacities on the list with the exception of some of those under the Executive Function heading. The behaviors observed as Alex worked with the multiple-choice Process Subtests strongly suggest that Alex's reduced scores on these tasks were

(continued)

related to difficulties with three specific executive function self-regulation capacities—cueing the inhibition of impulsive responding, cueing attention to auditory and/or visual details, and cueing appropriate consideration of the demands of a task. When the response format minimized the need to utilize these executive capacities, Alex performed quite well. When the response format required the self-regulated engagement of these capacities, Alex's performance suffered greatly relative to that of same-age peers.

Report Summary of Performance

The previously described analysis could be summarized in a psychological report as follows:

Although Alex was able to provide free response answers that earned scores in the Superior range for all of the Verbal Domain Core Subtests administered, the results of testing with the five Verbal Domain Process Subtests indicated that task performance was significantly less effective when he was required to respond to the same items in a multiple-choice format. When this format was engaged, Alex displayed great difficulties with the use of three self-regulation executive function capacities—cueing the inhibition of impulsive responding, cueing attention to auditory and/or visual details, and cueing appropriate consideration of the demands of a task.

When the response format minimized the need to utilize these executive function capacities through examiner direction and prompts, Alex performed in the Superior range (SI 15, VC 14, CO 14) and the Above Average range (IN 13). When the response format required the self-regulated engagement of these capacities to identify correct responses from among multiple choices, Alex's performance suffered greatly relative to that of same-age peers, with scores mostly dropping into the higher end of the Average range (SIMC 11, VCMC 11, INMC 12) or toward the lower end of the Average range (PVMC 9).

Case Outcome

Alex's teachers and parents found it very helpful to know that while Alex demonstrated superior capacities to reason with and retrieve verbal knowledge from long-term storage, these capacities can be adversely affected when self-regulation executive function demands are increased for a task. These and other findings from the comprehensive evaluation indicated that the executive function difficulties Alex exhibited during the evaluation, at home, and in school warranted consideration of a diagnosis of ADHD and possible medical intervention. Alex's parents agreed to have him evaluated by a pediatrician who specialized in ADHD diagnosis and treatment. From the findings of the complete report, an accommodations plan was developed with Alex's classroom teachers designed to help Alex improve his self-regulation capacities and his performance with classroom assignments and tests.

Perceptual Domain

The WISC-IV Integrated application of the process approach to the Perceptual Domain tasks is accomplished through the use of Process Subtests and additional Process Scores, scaled score discrepancy comparisons, and process-approach observation procedures yielding base rates. The WISC-IV Integrated includes three Perceptual Domain Process Subtests: Block Design Multiple Choice (BDMC), Elithorn Mazes (EM), and Block Design Process Approach (BDPA). Elithorn Mazes is a unique subtest that assesses the use of planning abilities with visual material. Additional process-approach procedures for Elithorn Mazes include recording observations during task performance including the occurrence of motor planning, latency time prior to responding, motor imprecision errors, backward movement errors, and across path errors for each item administered. BDMC and BDPA are variants of the Block Design Core Subtest. BDMC involves the representation of two- and three-dimensional red-and-white block designs on two-dimensional easel pages and does not require motor responses. BDPA uses the red-and-white blocks of the Block Design Subtest but involves different block design items and different administration procedures. Additional process-approach procedures for BDPA involve recording observations during task performance including en route breaks in configuration, final breaks in configuration, and extra block use. Rapid Reference 8.16 provides information about the administration and scoring of these Perceptual Domain Process Subtests.

Scaled score equivalents for Perceptual Domain Process Subtests are located in the *WISC-IV Integrated Administration and Scoring Manual* in Appendix C, Table C.2. Table C.2 also includes scaled score equivalents for the additional process scores of Block Design No Time Bonus (BDN), Block Design Multiple Choice No Time Bonus (BDMCN), and Elithorn Mazes No Time Bonus (EMN). Scaled score differences required for statistical significance are provided in Table D.3 and subtest discrepancy comparison base rates are provided in Table D.4. Tables D.5 through D.9 provide base rates for process-approach observations noted during task administrations. All scaled scores and base rates related to performance on BDPA are included in Appendix E, Tables E.1 through E.5.

All of the WISC-IV Integrated Perceptual Domain process-approach procedures and scores involve the Core Subtest Block Design and/or the Process Subtests BDMC, BDPA, and EM. Matrix Reasoning (MR), Picture Concepts (PCn), and Picture Completion (PCm) are not directly addressed in the WISC-IV Integrated, but a process approach can be applied to these subtests in the analysis of the cognitive demands of each task and analyzing clinically relevant behaviors,

≡ Rapid Reference 8.16

Administration and Scoring of the Perceptual Domain Process Subtests

While administration and scoring of the Block Design Multiple Choice Subtest is straightforward and easy to learn quickly, administration and scoring of the Elithorn Mazes and the Block Design Process Approach Subtests can be challenging even for clinicians experienced with many individually administered tests. A few points will help clinicians to quickly get familiar with all three of these tasks:

- Directions for Administering and Scoring BDMC, BDPA, and EM are located in the *WISC-IV Integrated Administration and Scoring Manual* behind the green Process Subtest Administration tab.

- The Elithorn Mazes, Arithmetic Process Approach-Part B, and Written Arithmetic Subtests require the use of Response Booklet 3 for administration of items.

- BDMC and BDPA items are located in Stimulus Booklet 3. EM items are located in Response Booklet 3.

- Elithorn Mazes is not administered to children ages 6:0 to 7:11.

- Precise timing is required for all three of these subtests; for each item of BDMC, an extra point is awarded if the child responds within the first 5 seconds and a time limit of 30 seconds is applied to all items including the three-dimensional items.

- When administering BDMC, keep in mind that subtest administration begins with the first item, not with a sample item; after Item 19, both a Sample Item and a Practice Item are presented to introduce the child to the three-dimensional items.

- When administering BDPA Part A (BDPA-A) and Part B (BDPA-B), provide the child with 12 blocks even though the child will be required to make either 4-block or 9-block designs.

- For BDPA-B, only administer the items that were scored 0 in BDPA-A, and use the Grid Overlays for each BDPA-B item administered.

- For BDPA and EM, detailed directions for completing process-approach observations are included in the administration and scoring directions of each subtest. These directions need to be reviewed carefully before administration of the subtest because process observations must be recorded during task performance rather than afterward.

- Start, Reverse, and Discontinue rules are printed on the Record Form for all three subtests for easy reference.

such as recording item completion times and examining patterns of item response inconsistencies within a subtest, as discussed later in this section.

When to Use the Perceptual Domain Process Subtests

In many cases, Perceptual Domain Process Subtests will offer children who find it difficult to produce adequate responses to the Core Block Design Subtest a chance to demonstrate their abilities through several modified response formats. In other cases, the Process Subtests, Process Scores, and process observations will enable a clinician to see how a child's performance can be adversely affected by altering or adapting the format of Block Design. Elithorn Mazes offers the clinician a unique perspective on a child's visual planning ability and visuomotor coordination. The Perceptual Domain Process Subtests and observation proce-dures are not intended to be used with every child who is assessed. There are no set rules dictating the specifics of the use of any of the Process Subtests other than that administration of these subtests must occur after completion of the administration of the Core and Supplemental Subtests of the WISC-IV. Clini-cians can select the specific subtests that are most likely to assist in understanding a particular child's test performance. The decision to use one or more Perceptual Domain Process Subtest may be based on information that is obtained prior to the administration of the WISC IV Core and Supplemental Subtests, such as parent and/or teacher input or records review. After administration of the Core and Supplemental Subtests, the clinician may choose to administer one or more of the Perceptual Domain Process Subtests based on observation of the child's performance during the assessment or based on the scores earned by the child on one or more of the Core and/or Supplemental Subtests. Rapid Reference 8.17 lists conditions most likely to lead to the use of one or more Perceptual Domain Process Subtests. Whatever the reason for choosing to use Perceptual Domain Process Subtests, examiners must keep in mind that the administration of these subtests must occur after the administration of the WISC-IV Core and Supple-mental Subtests. Administration of the standard WISC-IV subtests should not be interrupted in order to administer a process subtest.

Use and Interpretation of the Perceptual Domain Process Subtests

To effectively use and interpret the Perceptual Domain Process Subtests, it is necessary to have an understanding of the multifactorial nature of the Perceptual Domain Core and Supplemental Subtests in terms of the cognitive capacities they assess. Similarly, clinicians need to understand what cognitive capacities are assessed by the Perceptual Domain Process Subtests and how these can be used in concert with the Core and Supplemental Subtests to obtain a clearer picture of a child's cognitive strengths and weaknesses.

≡ Rapid Reference 8.17

When to Use the Perceptual Domain Process Subtests

The decision to use one or more of the Perceptual Domain Process Subtests may occur prior to or after administration of the WISC-IV Core and Supplemental Subtests.

Prior to administration of the WISC-IV, information gathered from parents, teachers, and background records can inform the clinician about situations in which the use of Perceptual Domain Process Subtests might be warranted. These situations could include:

Background information indicating

• Delays in visual perceptual development
• Delays in motor development, history of poor coordination, or poor fine motor skills
• Traumatic brain injury, including concussions
• Cerebral Palsy or any other condition that might cause motor impairment
• Executive function difficulties
• Processing speed difficulties
• History of ADHD that indicates interference with visual-motor task performance

Concerns expressed by parents or teachers

• Lack of coordination
• Slow rate of task completion
• Poor use of visual-perceptual skills
• Poor handwriting, drawing, or copying skills
• Impulsive or immature behavior

After administration of the WISC-IV, observations of how the child performed on the Core and/or Supplemental Perceptual Domain Subtests and/or the scores earned on these subtests may lead to the decision to administer one or more of the Perceptual Domain Process Subtests. In the case of behavior observations, it may be the way in which the child performed the task rather than the score the child obtained that leads to the administration of one or more process subtests. Observations and scores leading to the use of process subtests could include:

Observations during testing

• motor control problems
• inconsistent performance with items

- failure to check the accuracy of responses
- impulsive responding
- lack of attention to visual details
- haphazard, trial-and-error approach to Block Design
- inordinate amount of time spent on untimed items
- inability to complete one or more Block Design items despite working effectively toward a solution
- final Block Design constructions with a single block misplaced
- broken configurations produced en route to accurate Block Design item solutions
- broken configurations as final Block Design item product

Scores earned on the WISC-IV Core and/or Supplemental Subtests

- when all Perceptual Domain subtest scores are in the Below Average range or lower
- when one Perceptual Domain subtest is significantly lower or higher than the others
- when significant splits between Perceptual Subtest clusters occur (e.g., Picture Concepts and Picture Completion are significantly higher than Block Design and Matrix Reasoning)
- when the PRI score is significantly lower than the VCI score
- when the PRI score is low or lower than expected based on parent and/or teacher input about the child's abilities

What Do Perceptual Domain Core, Supplemental, and Process Subtests Measure?

The Perceptual Domain Core and Supplemental Subtests were designed primarily to assess the application of reasoning capacities with nonverbal, visual stimuli. Assessment of this capacity is the primary focus of interpretation of the Perceptual Reasoning Index as well as the individual Perceptual Domain subtests. The role of this primary cognitive capacity in task performance is described in detail in Rapid Reference 8.18.

Beyond the primary cognitive capacity targeted for assessment with the Perceptual Domain Subtests, the specific formats of each subtest make demands on the child that require the engagement of additional cognitive capacities in order to achieve success. While these capacities typically are required for effective subtest performance, they are not considered to be the primary target of the assessment

≡ *Rapid Reference 8.18*

Cognitive Capacities Assessed with the Perceptual Domain Core and Supplemental Subtests

Primary Cognitive Capacities

Reasoning with Nonverbal Visual Material—This cognitive capacity is essential for effective performance on most of the items of the Picture Concepts and Matrix Reasoning and Block Design Subtests and some of the items of the Picture Completion Subtest.

- *Picture Concepts Subtest*—The child is required to apply reasoning abilities to identify a physical characteristic or a categorical concept that links two or more pictured objects. All of the objects pictured in the items administered are likely to be familiar to the child (i.e., visually concrete representations).

- *Matrix Reasoning Subtest*—The child is required to apply reasoning abilities to select from five options the missing visual element that will complete a 2×2 or 3×3 visual pattern. Ten of the first 14 items use familiar objects as visual elements to complete patterns of physical relationship (e.g., size, color, number, category membership); the other 25 items use geometric visual elements to complete patterns of abstraction of relationship (size, shape, position, order, location, continuation, closure, addition, subtraction, substitution, transformation).

- *Block Design Subtest*—The child is required to *figure out* how to use a specific number of blocks to construct a design that matches a two-dimensional picture model. All of the models are symmetrical or asymmetrical abstract geometric patterns.

- *Picture Completion Subtest*—The child is required to identify the missing visual element in a picture of a common object or scene. All of the items use concrete, mostly familiar objects and scenes. Half of the items (scattered throughout the subtest) can be solved through careful visual inspection of the visual information provided in the picture. The other half of the items require retrieval of visual knowledge (i.e., knowledge of the visual elements of objects, visual relationships, visual consequences of action) from long-term storage and/or the application of reasoning ability to figure out visual relationships or visual consequences of actions.

It is important to keep in mind that reasoning with nonverbal visual stimuli does not necessarily involve nonverbal reasoning. Reasoning with visual stimuli can involve either nonverbal or verbal reasoning, or some combination of the two. Children are often observed providing verbal responses to Picture Concepts items, talking to themselves about Matrix Reasoning items, and occasionally talking themselves through the placement of blocks on the Block Design Subtest.

The type of reasoning abilities that are engaged to perform Perceptual Domain tasks will depend on the individual child and his or her perceptions of what abilities are required to do the task.

Secondary Cognitive Capacities

Visual Acuity—While attempting to perform the Perceptual Domain tasks, visual acuity is necessary to ensure that all of the visual elements of each item can be accurately viewed. If the child cannot see clearly all of the visual information provided in each item, incorrect responses may result. Typically, a child's visual acuity is assessed and verified to be within normal limits with or without the use of corrective lenses prior to test administration so that this capacity should not be a factor in performance. If overlooked, however, visual acuity problems can significantly impact task performance with any of the subtests that use visual stimuli.

Attention to Visual Stimuli—To perform Perceptual Domain tasks, the child must have the capacity for focusing and sustaining attention for the visual stimuli of each item.

Visual Perception/Representation—To perform Perceptual Domain tasks, the child must have the perceptual capacity to form relatively accurate visual representations of the stimuli presented. Some younger children and many severely impaired children might lack this capacity and have difficulty grasping the visual meaning of the information being presented, especially the more abstract geometric representations.

Visual Discrimination—Many of the items of the Perceptual Domain tasks require careful application of visual discrimination abilities (i.e., the ability to see visual similarities and differences in the visual stimuli being presented). As is the case with Visual Perception, some younger children and many severely impaired children might lack this capacity and have difficulty seeing the visual similarities and differences in the visual images being presented, especially the more abstract geometric representations of the Matrix Reasoning and Block Design Subtests.

Visualization and Working Memory Applied to Visual Stimuli—There should be little doubt that being able to generate visual images "in the mind's eye" and hold and manipulate such visual images can enhance greatly a child's performance with many items of all four of the Perceptual Domain Subtests. For some Matrix Reasoning items, solutions can be derived much more quickly if the child can envision how visual elements would look if rotated or repositioned or if the child can hold in mind aspects of the matrix item while examining and comparing response options. For Picture Concepts, a child will benefit from an ability to hold and compare hypotheses and the objects that were included in each hypothetical grouping and keep track of the hypotheses that have been generated and compared. For Block Design, performance can be enhanced when a

(continued)

visual image of the model can be held in mind to guide the placement of blocks in the child's construction or to envision how a block would look when repositioned within a construction. For Picture Completion, the ability to hold in mind a visually detailed impression of an object can aid in identifying the missing element through comparison of the pictured object with the image being held in the mind's eye.

What is open to debate, however, is whether the use of such visualization and working memory capacities are a necessary precondition for successful performance with any or all of the items of the Perceptual Domain Subtests. It is certainly conceivable that a child with very poor visualization and/or very poor working memory capacities can succeed with many of the Matrix Reasoning, Picture Concepts, and Picture Completion items by frequently and repetitively rescanning the visual stimuli of the items. In the case of Block Design, a child with poor visualization and/or working memory use can frequently compare the design model with the construction in progress to judge the accuracy of block placements and guide further performance.

Manual Motor Dexterity—The Block Design Subtest requires the child to handle four to nine blocks and move them about on a flat surface to construct 2 × 2 or 3 × 3 designs. Scoring criteria stipulate the specific placement of blocks required to earn credit for a design. All designs must be completed within a specified amount of time and, for the six most difficult items, bonus points are awarded for speed of performance. Children who may be lacking in motor coordination for a variety of reasons may find it difficult to handle the blocks, resulting in inaccurate block placements, rotated or fragmented designs, slowed production, and disruption of reasoning and other capacities due to an overfocusing on motor coordination difficulties.

Visual, Motor, and Visuomotor Processing Speed—Because all designs must be completed within a specified amount of time and for the six most difficult items bonus points are awarded for speed of correct responding, processing speed is an important component of successful task performance. Slower processing speed with Block Design items can be the result of slow speed of visual processing, slow speed of motor movement, or slow speed only when required to integrate visual processing with motor movement.

Language Representation of Visual Stimuli—The Picture Completion Subtest encourages the child to provide a verbal label for the missing visual element in each picture. While many children retrieve and state the verbal label representing the visual element that is missing, some children struggle greatly in their efforts to do so; some children describe the function of the missing element rather than name it; and some children prefer to point to the location of the missing element rather than access any language in the formulation of a response.

Executive Function—As a class of cognitive capacities, Executive Functions are responsible for cueing and directing the use of other mental capacities that are used for the purposes of perceiving, feeling, thinking, and acting. As such, they are intricately involved in the performance of all the tasks of the WISC-IV. The degree of involvement of specific executive functions in the performance of specific subtests, however, is highly variable and dependent on many factors including the directions provided to the child about how to perform the task and the input, processing, and output demands of the task. In the case of the Perceptual Domain Subtests, it is important to understand the role of executive functions in cueing and directing the use of both primary and secondary cognitive capacities. For most subtests, demands for the use of executive functions are greatly reduced through the use of explicit directions and teaching examples that model how to perform a task and/or the kind of response that is desired. For some children however, even these executive function aids do not help to ameliorate the effects of their severe executive function deficits, and the effects of these deficits often can be observed in the child's efforts to perform tasks.

For the Perceptual Domain subtests, accurate responding depends in part on the effective use of one or more of the following executive function capacities:

- cueing and directing efficient perception of visual stimuli
- cueing the appropriate consideration of the cognitive demands of a task and the amount of mental effort required to effectively perform the task
- cueing and directing the focusing of attention to visual details and task demands
- cueing and directing sustained attention to tasks
- cueing and directing the use of reasoning abilities (generating novel solutions or making associations with prior knowledge that lead to problem solutions)
- cueing and directing the inhibition of impulsive responding
- cueing and directing the flexible shifting of cognitive mindset to consider and respond to the specific demands of the task
- cueing and directing the use of working memory resources
- cueing and directing the organization of information
- cueing and directing the execution of motor routines (BD only)
- cueing and directing visual, motor, and visual-motor processing speed
- cueing and directing the balance between pattern (global) and detail (local) processing
- cueing and directing the monitoring of work and the correcting of errors
- cueing and directing the coordination of the use of multiple mental capacities simultaneously

(i.e., the intention of the subtest is not to quantitatively assess the child's use of these cognitive capacities). These secondary cognitive capacities include Visual Perception and Representation; Visual Discrimination; Visualization; Motor Dexterity; Visual, Motor, and Visuomotor Processing Speed; Working Memory applied to visual, nonverbal content; and multiple Executive Functions applied to cue and direct the mental processing of nonverbal visual stimuli. The roles of these secondary cognitive capacities in subtest performance are described in detail in Rapid Reference 8.18.

The specific changes made to the Perceptual Domain Subtests in the development of the WISC-IV and the selection of Matrix Reasoning, Picture Concepts, and Block Design as the composition of the Perceptual Reasoning Index greatly increased the likelihood that the cognitive capacity of primary concern—reasoning with visual stimuli—would be the cognitive capacity having the greatest impact on variation in task performance among children. Specific modifications to achieve this goal included:

- reduction of the awarding of time bonus points on Block Design
- removal of the Picture Arrangement, Object Assembly Subtests from the test
- removal of the Picture Completion Subtest from the Perceptual Reasoning Index
- adding the Matrix Reasoning Subtest to the test and the Perceptual Reasoning Index

Although these changes make it more likely that the primary source of variability in task performance will be a child's capacity to reason with nonverbal visual stimuli, it is impossible to minimize the impact of many of the secondary cognitive capacities while increasing the level of task complexity needed to effectively assess reasoning capacities. In CHC parlance, while the measurement of *Gf* may be the target of these tasks, it is exceptionally difficult, if not impossible, to measure *Gf* without measuring, to some degree, *Gv*.

It is important also to note the specific wording being used here to describe the primary cognitive capacity that Perceptual Domain tasks are attempting to assess (i.e., reasoning with nonverbal, visual stimuli). Reasoning with nonverbal visual stimuli is not synonymous with the term *nonverbal reasoning*. Placing nonverbal visual materials in front of a child is not a guarantee that the child will reason nonverbally with those materials, especially when clinicians use standardized directions that include verbal explanations of how to perform items when introducing tasks. While it may be advantageous to reason without engaging language abilities when attempting Perceptual Reasoning tasks, it is not necessary to do so. Clinicians are likely to observe children who engage language abilities to *talk themselves through* some or all aspects of specific Matrix Reasoning or Picture Concepts items. Such verbal mediation can be helpful, or even essential, to the success of some children's efforts with these tasks. Less likely to be observed is the child who attempts to verbally mediate most or all of his or her work with the Block Design Subtest, but even such a mismatched allocation of mental capacities, though unusual, is not entirely without occurrence.

No matter what efforts are made to try to ensure that a specific task is assessing a specific cognitive capacity, many children's neural capabilities will enable them to choose for themselves the cognitive capacities they wish to engage in their efforts with a task. This fact will continue to frustrate the efforts of researchers and clinicians who desire to identify and make use of tasks that are *pure* measures of a single mental capacity. This fact also confounds the standard view of subtest reliability in which all sources of unexplained variability in task performance are considered *measurement error*. Unfortunately, such misguided conceptions of reliability are used to support the argument against the use of subtest-level interpretation of test performance and discourage clinicians from attempting to understand the sources causing individual variation in test performance.

In contrast to the previous discussion, when Perceptual Domain subtest scores are interpreted, either collectively using the PRI or individually, it is assumed often that the scores reflect the primary capacity of reasoning with nonverbal, visual material. In such cases, the secondary capacities required for effective performance are either ignored or assumed to be intact and functioning as expected, thereby allowing the focus of interpretation to be on reasoning capacity. From this perspective, if a child cannot respond effectively to Block Design and/or Matrix Reasoning items, the assumption is that the child has poor nonverbal reasoning ability. In many cases in which low performance is observed, however, such an assumption is not necessarily warranted. To know if the assumption about the primary capacity is valid, the role of the secondary cognitive capacities in task performance must be understood and explored in detail. When not accessed, or when applied ineffectively, these secondary cognitive capacities can interfere with task performance to a significant degree, making it inappropriate to focus subtest score interpretation exclusively on the primary capacity thought to be assessed.

When low scores or scores that are not consistent with what is known about the child are obtained with one or more of the Core or Supplemental Perceptual Subtests, the Perceptual Domain Process Subtests can be used to test hypotheses about the sources of poor or unusual performance. As indicated in the previous discussion, poor performance on these tasks is thought to reflect a lack of reasoning with nonverbal visual material (i.e., a lack of nonverbal intelligence). Clinicians who appreciate that a low score on one or more Perceptual Domain Subtests could be due to many different sources can draw on the Process Subtests, Process Scores, and process-approach observations to help obtain a better understanding of why the child performed poorly and of the educational implications of such poor performance.

The Block Design Process Subtests and Process Scores alter many of the cognitive demands of the Core Block Design Subtest, as detailed in Rapid Reference 8.19. The Block Design No Time Bonus Process Score also quantifies performance in a manner that represents a reduction in cognitive demands. Although the Block Design multiple-choice format greatly reduces the demands placed on some cognitive capacities, it also increases the need for the use of other cognitive capacities. The specific ways that the Block Design Process Subtest response format and the Process Scores decrease or increase cognitive demands are detailed in Rapid Reference 8.19.

≡ Rapid Reference 8.19

How Perceptual Domain Process Subtests and Process Scores Reduce or Add Cognitive Demands

The Process Subtests and Process Scores alter the cognitive demands of the Perceptual Domain Tasks in the following ways:

Block Design No Time Bonus (BDN)

- greatly reduces the impact of the demand for visual, motor, and/or visual-motor processing speed

Block Design Multiple Choice (BDMC)

- eliminates the demand for motor dexterity
- eliminates the demand for motor and visual-motor processing speed
- greatly reduces the need for reasoning with nonverbal visual stimuli as the task emphasizes visual comparison using visual discrimination rather than figuring out how to construct designs that match models
- increases the demand for sustained attention to visual details
- increases the demand for rapid discrimination of visual details
- increases the demand for visual processing speed
- increases the demand for visualization and/or the use of working memory to hold and manipulate visual images

- increases executive functions demands, including:
  - the need for cueing and directing visual perception and discrimination
  - the demand for cueing and directing focusing and sustaining of attention
  - the demand for cueing the inhibiting of impulsive responding
  - the demand for cueing and directing rapid visual processing

Block Design Multiple Choice No Time Bonus (BDMCN)

- greatly reduces the impact of the demand for visual processing speed
- eliminates the demand for motor dexterity
- eliminates the demand for motor and visual-motor processing speed
- greatly reduces the need for reasoning with nonverbal visual stimuli as the task emphasizes visual comparison using visual discrimination rather than figuring out how to construct designs that match models
- increases the demand for sustained attention to visual details
- increases the demand for discrimination of visual details
- increases the demand for visualization and/or the use of working memory to hold and manipulate visual images
- increases executive functions demands, including:
  - the need for cueing and directing visual perception and discrimination
  - the need for cueing and directing focusing and sustaining of attention
  - the need for cueing the inhibiting impulsive responding

Elithorn Mazes (EM)

adds the demand for organization and/or planning with nonverbal visual information

- adds the demand for graphomotor production
- adds the demand for graphomotor processing speed
- adds executive function demands, including:
  - cueing and directing organization and/or planning abilities
  - cueing and directing graphomotor control
  - cueing and directing graphomotor speed

Elithorn Mazes No Time Bonus (EMN)

- greatly reduces the impact of the demand for graphomotor processing speed
- adds the demand for planning with nonverbal visual information
- adds the demand for graphomotor production
- adds executive function demands, including:
  - cueing and directing planning abilities
  - cueing and directing graphomotor control
  - cueing and directing graphomotor speed

The Elithorn Mazes Process Subtest introduces a new set of cognitive capacities into the Perceptual Domain mix. Clinicians interested in examining hypotheses about the effects of executive functions on visuomotor task performance may find this task to be helpful in testing various hypotheses. The cognitive capacities that the Elithorn Mazes Subtest adds to the list of capacities already assessed by Perceptual Domain Subtests are shown in Rapid Reference 8.19. Clinicians, however, must be careful not to overinterpret either the scores or the process observations obtained with Elithorn Mazes, as discussed in the Caution box that follows.

It should be clear from the information provided in Rapid Reference 8.19 that the Perceptual Domain Process Subtests and Process Scores provide the clinician with a chance to see how the child performs with similar and different item

CAUTION

Clinicians need to be careful not to overinterpret the meaning of Elithorn Mazes scores. Although the Elithorn Mazes Subtest is a measure of organization and/ or planning ability or skills and the use of executive functions to cue and direct the use of those organization and/or planning ability or skills, these facts do not justify the use of Elithorn Mazes as a global indicator of executive function capacities.

The most appropriate approach to the interpretation of the Elithorn Mazes Subtest is to treat it as a single, narrow measure of organization and/or planning ability and executive function control of organization and/or planning ability as applied to a specific nonverbal visual task. Poor performance indicates poor organization and/or planning ability/skills and/or poor cueing and directing of organization and/or planning abilities/skills in the context of a visual maze task. Poor scores do not indicate poor executive functions in more general terms. A child who performs poorly with the Elithorn Mazes Subtest might be much more effective in applying executive functions to the performance of any of a number of other tasks.

This same caution applies when clinicians choose to combine scaled scores earned on the Elithorn Mazes, Cancellation Random, and Comprehension Subtests with the Spatial Span Forward task to obtain an Executive Function Index (EFI) score (as outlined in Holdnak, Weiss, & Entwistle, 2006). Although the resulting EFI has the illusion of being a more generalized measure of executive function capacities because it is a composite representing performance across four domains of cognitive functioning, the extent to which such a generalization can be considered valid is debatable given the highly specific nature of the executive function capacities involved in successful performance of each of the four tasks selected for inclusion in the composite.

content and with different sets of cognitive demands. Although the Process Subtest Scaled Scores and the Process Scores are valuable indicators of how effective the child is with the use of these cognitive capacities, their value as an interpretive tool is enhanced when they are compared to the scores earned on Core or Supplemental Subtests or their Process Subtest counterparts. Such comparisons enable the clinician to generate or further test hypotheses about the effects of task format and input, processing, and output demands.

As previously noted, there are instances when the Process Subtest formats will reduce the child's effectiveness with item content. From a clinical perspective, knowing when an altered format reduces effectiveness is as important as knowing when an altered format increases effectiveness. Rapid Reference 8.20 provides an interpretive summary table that can be used to assist with the comparison of Core, Supplemental, and Process Subtest Scaled Scores and Process Scaled Scores in terms of the cognitive capacities that are most likely to be involved in the performance of test items.

Meaningful interpretations of scaled score comparisons start with the determination of whether a statistically significant and clinically meaningful difference exists between the scores earned on the subtests being compared. The WISC-IV Integrated manual provides tables for statistically significant scaled score discrepancies and for scaled score discrepancy base rates for the Perceptual Domain tasks. Additional comparison values were calculated using the same procedures as those outlined in the *WISC-IV Integrated Technical and Interpretive Manual* and are included in Rapid Reference 8.21. The values provided here and in the WISC-IV manual are based on the data obtained from the performance of the WISC-IV Integrated standardization sample of 730 children with the exception of the scores provided for the Block Design Process Approach Subtest (based on the WISC-III PI standardization sample) and the Block Design No Time Bonus Process Score (based on the WISC-IV standardization sample).

As noted earlier, the Block Design Process Approach Subtest was not standardized as part of the WISC-IV Integrated; the BDPA score tables were transferred to Appendix E of the WISC-IV Integrated manual directly from the WISC-III PI. Given their external source, scaled scores from the BDPA could not be compared with the other subtests using the common WISC-IV Integrated standardization sample, which explains the absence from the WISC-IV Integrated manual of BDPA comparisons with other Perceptual Domain tasks. Because of its relatively limited scope of applicability, interpretation of the BDPA is not discussed here in detail. Clinicians wishing to learn more about when and how to use the BDPA process approach should consult Holdnak and Weiss (2006b) for details.

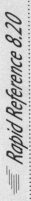

Rapid Reference 8.20

Cognitive Capacities Likely to Be Assessed by Perceptual Domain Tasks and Reflected in Scaled Score Values

Cognitive Capacity	Perceptual Domain Subtests and Process Scores								
	MR	PCn	PCm	BD	BD N	BD MC	BD MCN	EM	EMN
Attention to Visual Details	XX	XX	XX	XX	XX	XXX	XXX	XX	XX
Visual Perception	XX	XX	XX	XX	XX	XXX	XXX	XX	XX
Visual Discrimination	XX	XX	XX	XX	XX	XXX	XXX	XX	XX
Reasoning with Nonverbal Visual Material	XXX	XXX	X	XX	XX	X	X	X	X
Planning Ability/Skills				X	X			XXX	XXX
Organization Ability/Skills	X	XX		X	X			XX	XX
Graphomotor Ability/Skills								XX	XXX
Visualization/Use of Working Memory with Visual Material	X	X	X	X	X	XXX	XXX	XXX	XXX
Motor Dexterity				XX	XX			XX	XX
Visual Processing Speed	XX	XX	XX	XX	X	XXX	X	XX	X
Motor Processing Speed				XX	X			XX	X
Visual-Motor Processing Speed				XX	X			XX	X
Language Representation of Visual Stimuli	X	X	XX						
Executive Functions:									
EF—Cueing and directing efficient perception of visual stimuli	XX	XX	XX	XX	XX	XX	XX	XX	XX
EF—Cueing the appropriate consideration of the cognitive demands of a task and the amount of mental effort required to effectively perform the task	XX	XX	XX	XX	XX	XX	XX	XX	XX

Executive Function (EF)										
EF—Cueing and directing the focusing of attention to visual details and task demands	XX	XX	XX	XXX	XXX	XX	XX	XX	XX	XX
EF—Cueing and directing sustained attention to task	XX	XX	XX	XX	XX	XX	XX	XX	XX	XX
EF—Cueing and directing the use of reasoning abilities (generating novel solutions or making associations with prior knowledge that lead to problem solutions)	XX	X	X	X	X	X	X	X	X	X
EF—Cueing and directing the inhibition of impulsive responding	XX	XX	XX	XX	XX	XX	XX	XX	XX	XX
EF—Cueing and directing the flexible shifting of cognitive mindset to consider and respond to the specific demands of the task	X	X	X	X	X	X	X	X	X	XX
EF—Cueing and directing the use of working memory resources	X	X	X	X	X	X	X	X	X	X
EF—Cueing and directing the organization of information	X	XX		X	X		XX	XX	XX	XX
EF—Cueing and directing the use of planning abilities	X			X	X	X	X		X	X
EF—Cueing and directing the execution of motor routines			XX	XX	XX	XX	XX	XX	XX	XX
EF—Cueing and directing visual, motor and visual-motor processing speed	X	X	X	XX	XX	XX	X	X	XX	X
EF—Cueing and directing the balance between pattern (global) and detail (local) processing	XX	XX	XX	XX	XX	XX	XX	XX	XX	XX
EF—Cueing and directing the monitoring of work and the correcting of errors	XX	XX	XX	XX	XX	XX	XX	XX	XX	XX
EF—Cueing and directing the coordination of the use of multiple mental capacities simultaneously	XX	XX	XX	XX	XX	XX	XX	XX	XX	XX

XXX = Primary Capacity targeted for assessment with the task.

XX = Secondary Capacity highly likely to be impacting task performance.

X = Secondary Capacity possibly impacting task performance.

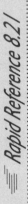

Rapid Reference 8.21

Guidelines for Interpreting Comparisons Involving Perceptual Domain Subtests

Determining a Significant Difference Between Scaled Scores

The scaled score values for significant differences between various Perceptual Domain Subtests and selected subtests from the Verbal and Processing Speed Domains are shown in the following tables. Some of the comparisons tabled here appear in Appendix D, Table D.3 of the *WISC-IV Integrated Administration and Scoring Manual*. Additional comparison values were calculated using the same procedures as those outlined in the WISC-IV Integrated manuals.

Significance Level	MR vs. BD	MR vs. PCn	MR vs. PCm	MR vs. EM*	PCn vs. BD	PCn vs. PCm	PCn vs. EM	BD vs. PCm	BD vs. EM	BD vs. BDMC*	EM vs. BDMC*	EM vs. PCm
.15	2.16	2.34	2.24	2.60	2.47	2.54	2.86	2.37	2.72	2.11	2.55	2.78
.05	2.95	3.19	3.05	3.54	3.36	3.45	3.89	3.23	3.70	2.87	3.48	3.78

*Indicates values that appear in the WISC-IV Integrated manual.

Perceptual Domain Subtests versus Subtests from the Verbal Domain and the Processing Speed Domain

Significance Level	PCn vs. SI	BD vs. SS	EM vs. SS	EM vs. CAS*
.15	2.47	2.55	2.93	3.08
.05	3.36	3.47	3.98	4.19

*Indicates values that appear in the WISC-IV Integrated manual.

Based on the values in the previous table, clinicians can feel comfortable using a rounded value of 3 scaled score points to indicate a significant difference for all of the various subtest comparisons. Using a difference of 3 scaled score points is equivalent to using a value that, in most cases, is roughly halfway between the .15 and .05 levels.

Clinicians familiar with Table D.3 in the *WISC-IV Integrated Administration and Scoring Manual* may notice that the values tabled here for comparisons with the Elithorn Mazes Subtests are different than those in the manual. The values tabled in the WISC-IV manual are in error. Using the SEM values and z values reported in the manual, the values tabled here are accurate.

Comparisons involving No Time Bonus Process Scores represent a different kind of comparison than the Subtest comparisons tabled previously. BDN, BDMCN, and EMN are scores that are derived by applying an alternate scoring structure to their *parent* subtests BD, BDMC, and EM. Because they represent numerical transformations that assign different values to the same test performance, the only source of variance to account for in these transformed scores is due to differences in the amount of time taken to complete items (i.e., there is no source of error variance in these scores independent of the error variance already accounted for in the parent subtest). If you know how many items the child completed correctly, you can predict (i.e., calculate) with 100% accuracy the child's No Time Bonus raw score.

It is therefore not really appropriate to calculate and use a standard error of measurement for these tasks to indicate the amount of possible variation in No Time Bonus scores that is due to unaccounted for sources of variance on repeated administrations *of the parent task*. Likewise, differences between No Time Bonus Process Scaled Scores and their parent Subtest Scaled Score are not influenced equally by independent sources of error variance, making it inappropriate to average SEM values to obtain a statistically significant value for the reliability of a difference between these two scores, as the No Time Bonus score is completely dependent on the parent subtest item scores and cannot vary independent of them.

The transformation of parent subtest scores into No Time Bonus scores, however, does not always produce a perfect correlation between the two sets of scores. This is because the No Time Bonus score distribution has a more restricted range of values, and the less restricted set of values of the parent subtest must be collapsed into ranges to fit the more restricted set of No Time Bonus scores. Tables 8.4, 8.5, and 8.6 show the relationship between Subtest raw and scaled scores and No Time Bonus Process raw and scaled scores at various age ranges for BD/BDN, BDMC/BDMCN, and EM/EMN comparisons, respectively. As shown in Tables 8.4, 8.5, and 8.6, this collapse results in overlapping parent subtest raw score ranges. For example, in Table 8.4, a 12-year-old child

(continued)

379

who correctly completes 11 Block Design items has the chance to earn a total of 9 bonus points from items 9, 10, and 11. If that child earns no bonus points on items 9, 10, and 11, the raw score earned is 38, which is equivalent to a BD Subtest Scaled Score of 9; if another child earned 1 bonus point on each of these items, the BD raw score earned is 41, which is equivalent to a BD Scaled Score of 10; if another child earns 3 bonus points on each of these items, the BD raw score is 47, which is equivalent to a BD scaled score of 11. These three raw score point values all produce different BD scaled scores because they represent different levels of performance in terms of the amount of time required to complete items. When the time differences are eliminated and only the base number of points for completing each design is assigned to produce a BDN raw score, all three of these children are assigned a BDN raw score of 38, which is equivalent to a BDN Scaled Score of 10.

Note also that another child who earns a BD raw score of 38 but does so by completing only 10 items and earning 5 bonus points from items 9 and 10 only earns a BDN raw score of 34 and a BDN scaled score of 9. Thus, three different BD scaled scores (9, 10, 11) can produce the same BDN Scaled Score of 10, while two different BDN scores (9 and 10) can result from the same BD scale score (10). This score overlap produced by collapsing of the BD raw score point ranges to fit the restricted BDN raw score ranges is the source of score variability that reduces the correlation between BD and BDN scaled scores. The variability between the two sets of scores therefore is not due to any unknown source of error but rather to the collapsing of the Block Design score range in a meaningful way. The three children who completed BD items 9, 10, and 11 all receive the same score on BDN. For the child who earned no bonus points and a BD scaled score of 9, the BDN score of 10 accurately represents an upgrade in score when speed of performance is not a factor; for the child who earned the maximum number of time bonus points and a BD scaled score of 11, the BDN scaled score of 10 accurately represents a downgrade in score when speed of performance is not a factor. In the case of the two children earning the same BD raw score, one of these children correctly completed only 10 items but received time bonus points while the other child correctly completed 11 items but received no time bonus points. When only the number of items completed counts toward the raw score, the child who only completed 10 items earns lower BDN raw and scaled scores (34 and 9) than the child who completed 11 items (38 and 10), despite their identical BD raw and scaled scores of 38.

Because the variability in scores reflects only the variability in the factor intended to be represented by the score (absence of a time bonus), the reliability of the transformation, contrary to what the correlation coefficients in Table 8.7 seem to suggest, is perfect. A specific set of BD item raw scores will always produce a specific BD scaled score, and when transformed to a BDN raw score, this same set of BD item raw scores will always produce a specific BDN scaled score. Clinicians, therefore, need not look to a statistically derived value to determine if the difference obtained between a child's No Time Bonus scaled score and the parent subtest scaled score reflects a true difference due to the factor intended to be assessed, but rather can take the value obtained at face value. A scaled score difference of 0 means that, relative to the performance of same-age peers in the standardization sample, the child did not benefit from having the effect of a time bonus removed from the score. A difference of +1 or more means that the child did benefit from having the time bonus removed, and a difference of −1 or more means that the child was adversely affected by having the time bonus removed. The larger the difference between BD and BDN, the greater is the impact of processing speed, either negatively or positively, on the child's performance.

Degree of Unusualness of Scaled Score Discrepancies

The cumulative percentages (i.e., base rates) of the standardization sample obtaining scaled score discrepancies of a particular magnitude between various Perceptual Domain Subtests and selected subtests from the Verbal and Processing Speed Domains are shown in the following tables. Some of the base rate data tabled here appear in Appendix D, Table D.4 of the *WISC-IV Integrated Administration and Scoring Manual*. The additional base rates shown here were calculated by the author of this chapter using the WISC-IV Integrated standardization sample data.

Perceptual Domain Subtest Comparisons

Scaled Score Discrepancy	MR > BD	BD > MR	MR > PCn	PCn > MR	MR > PCm	PCm > MR	MR > EM	EM > MR
3	18.6	18.8	20.4	20.2	21.1	21.6	24.0	21.0
4	10.6	11.0	13.0	12.1	13.4	12.8	14.4	13.7
5	6.5	5.3	7.3	6.9	8.2	6.9	7.9	7.9
6	2.5	2.0	3.9	3.2	3.9	3.7	5.1	5.0
7	1.2	0.9	1.9	1.5	1.9	2.0	3.0	3.0

(continued)

Perceptual Domain Subtest Comparisons

Scaled Score Discrepancy	PCn > BD	BD > PCn	PCn > PCm	PCm > PCn	PCn > EM	EM > PCn	BD > PCm	PCm > BD
3	22.7	21.8	23.1	21.9	26.2	24.4	17.5	19.2
4	14.1	13.6	14.0	13.9	15.8	18.4	10.8	10.9
5	8.8	8.0	8.6	9.0	8.6	11.4	6.4	6.1
6	4.9	4.5	4.1	5.3	5.5	7.8	3.3	3.0
7	2.0	2.0	2.0	2.9	2.6	5.0	1.5	1.2

Perceptual Domain Subtest Comparisons

Scaled Score Discrepancy	BD > EM	EM > BD	BDMC > BD	BD > BDMC	EM > BDMC	BDMC > EM	EM > PCm	PCm > EM
3	21.0	21.7	16.9	17.8	23.0	23.5	22.1	21.3
4	13.3	13.5	9.6	10.3	14.9	14.7	14.4	13.7
5	6.8	7.6	5.4	5.0	8.3	9.3	8.4	8.4
6	3.3	4.1	2.3	2.2	4.0	5.1	5.0	4.1
7	1.5	1.7	0.6	1.1	2.1	2.6	2.8	2.6

Perceptual Domain Subtest versus Verbal Domain and Processing Speed Domain Comparisons

Scaled Score Discrepancy	PCn > SI	SI > PCn	BD > SS	SS > BD	EM > SS	SS > EM	EM > CAS	CAS > EM
3	20.7	19.5	21.0	21.2	25.2	22.7	30.9	24.5
4	13.2	13.0	13.0	13.3	14.3	3.7	21.1	16.5
5	7.6	7.7	6.7	7.5	8.1	8.7	16.2	11.7
6	4.3	4.5	4.0	4.1	4.9	4.9	9.9	7.5
7	1.7	2.3	2.0	2.1	2.0	2.7	5.4	4.0

Note from the previous table that the percentage of the standardization sample demonstrating scaled score discrepancies of 3 points or more is roughly equal for both comparison conditions (e.g. BD > EM and EM > BD). Also note that discrepancies of 5 scaled score points consistently represent differences demonstrated by 10% or less of the standardization sample and discrepancies of 6 scaled score points consistently represent differences demonstrated by 5% or less of the standardization sample. The only exceptions are the values for EM versus CAS, which are 1 point greater in each instance. Clinicians can feel comfortable using scaled score discrepancies of 5 and 6 points generally as the values representing differences demonstrated by less than 10% and less than 5% of the standardization sample, respectively.

When attempting to interpret the significance of scaled score discrepancies among Perceptual Domain Subtests and between Perceptual Domain and Verbal and Processing Speed Domain Subtests, clinicians using values of 5 or 6 scaled score points as the criteria for clinical significance for all comparisons will be assured of both statistical significance of the obtained discrepancy as well as a relatively high degree of unusualness of the occurrence of the difference within the standardization sample. Although somewhat more frequent in occurrence, a scaled score difference of 4 points might also be reasonably considered both statistically and clinically significant depending on the specific circumstances of the case and the number of significant subtest comparisons demonstrated by a child.

No Time Bonus Process Scores

The cumulative percentages (i.e., base rates) of the standardization sample obtaining scaled score discrepancies between Perceptual Domain Subtests and their No Time Bonus Process Score counterparts are provided in Appendix D, Table D.4 of the

(continued)

WISC-IV Integrated Administration and Scoring Manual. The range of values for subtest comparisons with No Time Bonus scores are summarized in the following table:

No Time Bonus Process Score Comparisons

Scaled Score Discrepancy	BDN > BD	BD > BDN	BDMCN > BDMC	BDMC > BDMCN	EMN > EM	EM > EMN
1	24.3	18.2	33.5	37.4	29.3	32.1
2	4.2	2.8	16.6	14.4	9.3	11.0
3	0.7	0.5	7.4	4.5	2.9	3.2
4	0	0.3	2.1	0.5	.8	1.4
5	0	0.1	0.8	0	0	0.5
6	0	0	0.3	0	0	0
7	0	0	0.3	0	0	0

*Note that these values represent a comparison between two Process Subtest scores.

Note from the previous table that the percentage of the standardization sample demonstrating scaled score discrepancies of 1 or more points is roughly equal for both comparison conditions (Process Score > Subtest Score and Subtest Score > Process Score). When comparing time bonus and subtest scores for BD and EM, a difference of 2 or more scaled score points is both significant (based on the discussion in the previous section) and unusual. In the case of BDMC versus BDMCN, a difference of 3 or more scaled score points is both significant and unusual.

The values tabled highlight the fact that, for the standardization sample, removing bonus points earned for speed had a minimal impact on most children's standing relative to same-age peers. There is little question of the clinical significance of a score difference greater than 1 scaled score point. The performance of a child who demonstrates a difference of 2 or more scaled score points between a subtest scaled score and the no time bonus counterpart has been affected by processing speed demands in a significant and unusual manner.

Perceptual Domain scaled score differences required for statistical significance at the .15 and .05 levels are located in Appendix D, Table D.3 and summarized in Rapid Reference 8.21, along with the additional values calculated for inclusion in this text. Given the range of the tabled values it is reasonable to use a rounded value of 3 scaled score points to signify a statistically significant difference for comparisons involving Perceptual Domain Subtests.

Cumulative percentages (i.e., base rates) of the standardization sample obtaining various scaled score discrepancies involving various Perceptual Domain Subtests are located in Appendix D, Table D.4 of the *WISC-IV Integrated Administration and Scoring Manual*. Additional Perceptual Domain discrepancy base rates were calculated for this chapter using the WISC-IV Integrated standardization sample data. A summary table showing base rate data from the WISC-IV Integrated manual and from the analyses completed for this text is provided in Rapid Reference 8.21.

Rapid Reference 8.21 also provides a discussion of guidelines for interpreting scaled score discrepancies and discrepancy comparison base rates, including a detailed discussion of the special case of No Time Bonus Process Scores. Tables 8.4 through 8.7 provide data that help to understand the discussion about the interpretation of No Time Bonus process scores provided in Rapid Reference 8.21.

Table 8.4 Relationship between BD and BDN Raw and Scaled Scores at Various Age Ranges

Age 6:4–6:7

Cumulative # Items Correct	BD Raw Score Range with Bonus Points	BDN Raw Score	BD SS	BDN SS	Max SS Gain	Max SS Loss
4	10	10	8	9	+1	—
5	14	14	10	10	0	0
6	18	18	11	11	0	0
7	22	22	13	12	—	−1
8	26	26	14	14	0	0
9	30–33	30	15	15	0	0
10	34–40	34	16–17	16	—	−1
11	38–47	38	16–18	17	+1	−1
12	42–54	42	17–19	19	+2	0
13	46–61	46	17–19	19	+2	0
14	50–68	50	17–19	19	+2	0

(continued)

Table 8.4 (Continued)

Age 9:4–9:7

Cumulative # Items Correct	BD Raw Score Range with Bonus Points	BDN Raw Score	BD SS	BDN SS	Max SS Gain	Max SS Loss
4	10	10	5	5	0	0
5	14	14	6	6	0	0
6	18	18	7	7	0	0
7	22	22	8	8	0	0
8	26	26	9	9	0	0
9	30–33	30	10–11	10	0	−1
10	34–40	34	11–13	12	+1	−1
11	38–47	38	12–15	13	+1	−2
12	42–54	42	13–16	14	+1	−2
13	46–61	46	14–19	16	+2	−3
14	50–68	50	15–19	19	+4	0

Age 12:4–12:7

Cumulative # Items Correct	BD Raw Score Range with Bonus Points	BDN Raw Score	BD SS	BDN SS	Max Gain	Max Loss
4	10	10	3	2	—	−1
5	14	14	4	4	0	0
6	18	18	5	5	0	0
7	22	22	6	6	0	0
8	26	26	7	7	0	0
9	30–33	30	8	8	0	0
10	34–40	34	9–10	9	0	−1
11	38–47	38	9–11	10	+1	−1
12	42–54	42	10–13	11	+1	−2
13	46–61	46	11–16	13	+2	−3
14	50–68	50	12–19	16	+4	−3

Age 16:4–16:7

Cumulative # Items Correct	BD Raw Score Range with Bonus Points	BDN Raw Score	BD SS	BDN SS	Max Gain	Max Loss
4	10	10	1	1	0	0
5	14	14	2	1	—	−1
6	18	18	3	2	—	−1
7	22	22	4	3	—	−1
8	26	26	5	4	—	−1
9	30–33	30	5–6	5	0	−1
10	34–40	34	6–7	6	0	−1
11	38–47	38	7–9	8	+1	−1
12	42–54	42	8–11	9	+1	−2
13	46–61	46	9–14	11	+2	−3
14	50–68	50	10–19	14	+4	−5

Table 8.5 Relationship between BDMC and BDMCN Raw and Scaled Scores for Various Age Ranges

Age 6:4–6:7

Cumulative # Items Correct	BDMC Raw Score Range with Bonus Points	BDMCN Raw Score	BDMC SS	BDMCN SS	Max Gain	Max Loss
1	1–2	1	4	5	+1	—
2	2–4	2	4–5	6	+2	—
3	3–6	3	5–6	7	+2	—
4	4–8	4	5–7	7	+2	0
5	5–10	5	6–8	8	+2	0
6	6–12	6	6–9	8	+2	−1
7	7–14	7	7–10	9	+2	−1
8	8–16	8	7–10	9	+2	−1
9	9–18	9	8–11	10	+2	−1
10	10–20	10	8–12	10	+2	−2
11	11–22	11	9–12	10	+1	−2

(continued)

Table 8.5 (Continued)

12	12–24	12	9–13	10	+1	−3
13	13–26	13	9–13	11	+2	−2
14	14–28	14	10–14	11	+1	−3
15	15–30	15	10–15	12	+2	−3
16	16–32	16	10–16	13	+3	−3
17	17–34	17	11–16	13	+2	−3
18	18–36	18	11–17	14	+3	−3
19	19–38	19	11–18	15	+4	−3
20	20–40	20	12–18	16	+4	−2
21	21–42	21	12–19	17	+5	−2
22	22–44	22	12–19	17	+5	−2
23	23–46	23	13–19	18	+5	−1
24	24–48	24	13–19	18	+5	−1
25	25–50	25	13–19	19	+6	0

Age 9:4–9:7

Cumulative # Items Correct	BDMC Raw Score Range with Bonus Points	BDMCN Raw Score	BDMC SS	BDMCN SS	Max Gain	Max Loss
1	1–2	1	1	1	0	0
2	2–4	2	1–2	1	0	−1
3	3–6	3	2–3	2	0	−1
4	4–8	4	2–4	3	+1	−1
5	5–10	5	2–5	4	+2	−1
6	6–12	6	3–6	4	+1	−2
7	7–14	7	3–6	5	+2	−1
8	8–16	8	4–7	5	+1	−2
9	9–18	9	4–8	6	+2	−2
10	10–20	10	5–8	6	+1	−2
11	11–22	11	5–9	7	+2	−2
12	12–24	12	6–9	7	+1	−2
13	13–26	13	6–10	8	+2	−2
14	14–28	14	6–10	8	+2	−2
15	15–30	15	7–11	9	+2	−2
16	16–32	16	7–11	9	+2	−2

Cumulative # Items Correct	BDMC Raw Score Range with Bonus Points	BDMCN Raw Score	BDMC SS	BDMCN SS	Max Gain	Max Loss
17	17–34	17	7–12	10	+3	−2
18	18–36	18	8–13	10	+2	−3
19	19–38	19	8–14	11	+3	−3
20	20–40	20	8–15	12	+4	−3
21	21–42	21	8–16	13	+5	−3
22	22–44	22	9–17	13	+4	−4
23	23–46	23	9–18	14	+5	−4
24	24–48	24	9–19	15	+6	−4
25	25–50	25	9–19	16	+7	−3

Age 12:4–12:7

Cumulative # Items Correct	BDMC Raw Score Range with Bonus Points	BDMCN Raw Score	BDMC SS	BDMCN SS	Max Gain	Max Loss
1	1–2	1	1	1	0	0
2	2–4	2	1	1	0	0
3	3–6	3	1	1	0	0
4	4–8	4	1–2	1	0	−1
5	5–10	5	1–3	1	0	−2
6	6–12	6	1–3	2	+1	0
7	7–14	7	2–4	3	+1	−1
8	8–16	8	2–5	3	+1	−2
9	9–18	9	2–5	4	+2	−1
10	10–20	10	3–6	4	+1	−2
11	11–22	11	3–7	5	+2	−2
12	12–24	12	3–7	5	+2	−2
13	13–26	13	4–8	6	+2	−2
14	14–28	14	4–8	6	+2	−2
15	15–30	15	4–9	7	+3	−2
16	16–32	16	5–9	7	+2	−2
17	17–34	17	5–10	8	+3	−2
18	18–36	18	5–10	9	+4	−1
19	19–38	19	6–11	10	+4	−1
20	20–40	20	6–11	10	+4	−1
21	21–42	21	6–12	11	+5	−1

(continued)

Table 8.5 (Continued)

22	22–44	22	7–13	12	+5	–1
23	23–46	23	7–15	12	+5	–3
24	24–48	24	7–17	13	+6	–4
25	25–50	25	7–19	14	+7	–5

Age 16:4–16:7

Cumulative # Items Correct	BDMC Raw Score Range with Bonus Points	BDMCN Raw Score	BDMC SS	BDMCN SS	Max Gain	Max Loss
1	1–2	1	1	1	0	0
2	2–4	2	1	1	0	0
3	3–6	3	1	1	0	0
4	4–8	4	1	1	0	0
5	5–10	5	1	1	0	0
6	6–12	6	1	1	0	0
7	7–14	7	1	1	0	0
8	8–16	8	1–2	1	0	–1
9	9–18	9	1–2	1	0	–1
10	10–20	10	1–3	2	+1	–1
11	11–22	11	1–3	2	+1	–1
12	12–24	12	1–4	3	+2	–1
13	13–26	13	1–4	4	+3	0
14	14–28	14	1–5	4	+3	–1
15	15–30	15	1–6	5	+4	–1
16	16–32	16	2–7	5	+3	–2
17	17–34	17	2–7	6	+4	–1
18	18–36	18	2–8	7	+5	–1
19	19–38	19	2–9	7	+5	–2
20	20–40	20	3–9	8	+5	–1
21	21–42	21	3–10	9	+6	–1
22	22–44	22	3–11	10	+7	–1
23	23–46	23	3–13	11	+8	–2
24	24–48	24	4–15	12	+8	–3
25	25–50	25	4–17	13	+9	–4

Table 8.6 Relationship between EM and EMN Raw and Scaled Scores for Various Age Ranges

Age 9:4–9:7

Cumulative # Items Correct	EM Raw Score Range with Bonus Points	EMN Raw Score	EM SS	EMN SS	Max Gain	Max Loss
1	4–8	4	5–6	5	0	−1
2	8–16	8	6–8	7	+1	−1
3	12–24	12	7–10	8	+1	−2
4	16–32	16	8–13	10	+2	−3
5	20–40	20	9–16	11	+2	−5
6	24–48	24	10–19	13	+3	−6
7	28–56	28	12–19	16	+4	−3

Age 12:4–12:7

Cumulative # Items Correct	EM Raw Score Range with Bonus Points	EMN Raw Score	EM SS	EMN SS	Max Gain	Max Loss
1	4–8	4	3–4	3	0	−1
2	8–16	8	4–6	5	+1	−1
3	12–24	12	5–8	6	+1	−2
4	16–32	16	6–10	7	+1	−3
5	20–40	20	7–13	9	+2	−4
6	24–48	24	8–17	11	+3	−6
7	28–56	28	9–19	14	+5	−5

Age 16:4–16:7

Cumulative # Items Correct	EM Raw Score Range with Bonus Points	EMN Raw Score	EM SS	EMN SS	Max Gain	Max Loss
1	4–8	4	1–2	1	0	−1
2	8–16	8	2–4	1	—	−3
3	12–24	12	3–6	3	0	−3
4	16–32	16	4–8	5	+1	−3
5	20–40	20	5–10	7	+2	−3
6	24–48	24	6–13	9	+3	−4
7	28–56	28	7–19	13	+6	−6

Table 8.7 Correlations between Subtest Scaled Scores and No Time Bonus Process Scaled Scores

Age	BD with BDN	BDMC with BDMCN	EM with EMN
6	.99	.95	—
7	.99	.86	—
8	.99	.92	.94
9	.97	.89	.95
10	.97	.88	.94
11	.97	.87	.94
12	.98	.87	.91
13	.95	.83	.87
14	.94	.86	.92
15	.94	.82	.85
16	.90	.79	.82

Figure 8.2 provides a worksheet to aid in the interpretation of Perceptual Domain tasks scaled score comparisons. Rapid Reference 8.22 provides a case study example that includes the use of the interpretive worksheet and illustrates the application of WISC-IV Integrated process-approach procedures in the interpretation of Perceptual Domain Subtest performance.

Working Memory Domain

The WISC-IV Integrated application of the process approach to the Working Memory Domain tasks is accomplished through the use of Process Subtests; Subtest Scaled Score discrepancy comparison tables indicating subtest scaled score significant discrepancy values and base rates for discrepancies; additional Process Scores and base rates for Core, Supplemental, and Process Subtests; and additional process-approach procedures. The WISC-IV Integrated includes six Working Memory Domain Process Subtests: Visual Digit Span (VDS), Spatial Span (SSp), Letter Span (LS), Letter-Number Sequencing Process Approach (LNPA), Arithmetic Process Approach (ARPA), and Written Arithmetic (WA). LNPA is a variant of the Letter-Number Sequencing Core Subtest. VDS, SSp, and LS are variants of the Core Subtest Digit Span. ARPA and WA are variations

| | Subtest 1 | | Subtest 2 | | Scaled Score Analyses | | |
Subtest Comparison	Raw Score	Scaled Score	Raw Score	Scaled Score	Scaled Score Diff (b–d)	Scaled Score Difference Significant?	Scaled Score Difference Unusual?
	a	b	c	d	e	e > 3 Y N	e = 5 e > = 6 Y < 10% Y < 5% N
MR vs. BD						Y N	Y < 10% Y < 5% N
MR vs. PCn						Y N	Y < 10% Y < 5% N
MR vs. PCm						Y N	Y < 10% Y < 5% N
MR vs. EM						Y N	Y < 10% Y < 5% N
PCn vs. BD						Y N	Y < 10% Y < 5% N
PCn vs. PCm						Y N	Y < 10% Y < 5% N
PCn vs. EM						Y N	Y < 10% Y < 5% N

Figure 8.2 Perceptual Domain Subtest and Process Score Comparison Worksheet

	No Time Bonus Process Scores	Subtest Scores			Scaled Score Analyses		
BD vs. PCm			Y	N	Y < 10%	Y < 5%	N
BD vs. EM			Y	N	Y < 10%	Y < 5%	N
BD vs. BDNC			Y	N	Y < 10%	Y < 5%	N
EM vs. BDMC			Y	N	Y < 10%	Y < 5%	N
EM vs. PCm			Y	N	Y < 10%	Y < 5%	N
PCn vs. SI			Y	N	Y < 10%	Y < 5%	N
BD vs. SS			Y	N	Y < 10%	Y < 5%	N
EM vs. SS			Y	N	Y < 10%	Y < 5%	N
EM vs. CAS			Y	N	Y < 10%	Y < 5%	N
BDN vs. BD			e > 1?	Y N	e = 2 Y < 10%	e > 2 Y < 5%	N
BDMCN vs. BDMC			e > 1?	Y N	e = 3 Y < 10%	e > = 4 Y < 5%	N
EMN vs. EM			e > 1?	Y N	e = 2 Y < 10%	e > = 3 Y < 5%	N

Figure 8.2 (Continued)

≡ Rapid Reference 8.22

Perceptual Domain Case Study

Ashley, Age 15-7, Grade 10

Ashley, a 10th grade student, is failing an Algebra course and barely passing an English course. Her parents are concerned about her increasingly negative attitude toward school and the increased number of absences due to "illness." Ashley has been receiving resource room assistance with reading and math since the early elementary grades, but she never received a formal assessment of her cognitive abilities. Although the school-based team did not see a need for conducting such an assessment at this point in time, Ashley's parents insisted that such an evaluation would be helpful to them. Honoring the request of the parents, Ashley was administered the WISC-IV and earned the following scores:

WISC-IV

Verbal Domain		Perceptual Domain	
Similarities	12	Block Design	6
Vocabulary	10	Picture Concepts	13
Comprehension	11	Matrix Reasoning	8
Verbal Comprehension Index	104	Perceptual Reasoning Index	94
Working Memory Domain		Processing Speed Domain	
Digit Span	12	Coding	10
Letter Number Sequencing	11	Symbol Search	12
Working Memory Index	107	Processing Speed Index	106
Full Scale IQ 104			

Ashley's performance produced average range scores for all 4 Indexes and relatively uniform subtest scores within the Verbal, Working Memory and Processing Speed domains. Interpretation at the Index level suggests that Ashley has average capacity for reasoning with and retrieving and expressing verbal information (VCI 104), average capacity for reasoning with visually presented nonverbal material (PRI 94), average capacity for registering and manipulating auditorily presented verbal information (WMI 107), and average capacity for quickly processing nonverbal visual information (PSI 106). The 7 point spread across the three scores of the Perceptual domain, however, did suggest a lack of homogeneity in performance that was deserving of greater scrutiny. To obtain a better understanding of Ashley's abilities, the Perceptual domain Supplemental and Process Subtests were administered, with the following results:

(continued)

Perceptual Domain Supplemental Subtest	
Picture Completion	14
Perceptual Domain Process Subtests and Scores	
Block Design No Time Bonus	6
Block Design Multiple Choice	9
Block Design Multiple Choice No Time Bonus	13
Elithorn Mazes	7
Elithorn Mazes No Time Bonus	11

The Processing Speed Domain Task Comparison Worksheet (see below) reflected several additional significant scaled score discrepancies that are relevant to understanding Ashley's cognitive profile. Ashley's performance with the additional Perceptual domain tasks greatly helped to clarify the picture in terms of specific cognitive strengths and weaknesses in this domain.

Of great assistance to the interpretation of Ashley's performance was the outspoken manner in which she announced her likes and dislikes as she passed judgment on each of the tasks with which she was presented. When introduced to the Picture Completion Subtest, Ashley remarked: "This should be fun!" And so it was; Ashley thoroughly enjoyed herself throughout her exceptional level performance (14), correctly identifying the missing element for 26 of the 29 items administered, but delivering many answers at the relatively slow rate of 10 seconds or more per item. Ashley's Picture Completion performance was much more similar to the attitude and level of proficiency she demonstrated with the Picture Concepts Subtest (13); with which she remarked: "OK, I see what you're getting at here." Her additional verbalizations of her modes of reasoning to arrive at correct responses reflected good use of organized approaches to hypothesis generation and testing punctuated by an occasional occurrence where she would "draw a blank" and offer no possible solutions followed with a terse "Don't know." With both the Picture Completion and Picture Concepts Subtests, Ashley demonstrated a high level of comfort with nonverbal visual tasks that involved concrete objects as the content for consideration.

In contrast to her outlook and performance with concrete visual tasks, Ashley was quite put off by the content and format of the Block Design (6) and Matrix Reasoning (8) Subtests, both tasks that predominantly utilize abstract visual elements. For the Matrix Reasoning Subtest, Ashley clearly grasped the rationale underlying successful performance, but she had little patience for items involving abstract visual design patterns that initially made no sense to her, offering comments such as "What is that?" and "That makes no sense!" or "Whatever" before delivering obviously ill-considered incorrect responses. When Ashley could sense quickly the underlying concept represented in an item (mostly those items using concrete objects, or clear design patterns), she would spend relatively long amounts of time (10-25 seconds) considering the relationships among elements before responding with a correct response.

For the Block Design Subtest, Ashley maintained a skeptical grimace throughout the task demonstration and her successful completion of items 3-7. As Ashley struggled with the placement of the diagonal blocks of Item 8, she remarked "Jeez, this is a pain!" and was not able to complete the design within the time limit. Although now visibly annoyed with the task, Ashley regrouped and completed the symmetrical pattern of Item 9, but again was thrown off balance with the diagonal blocks of Item 10 and ran out of time, exclaiming "That's crap!". Successful completion of the 9-block symmetrical pattern of Item 11 required nearly the entire allowed time of two minutes. When presented with the asymmetrical nine-block Item 12, Ashley exclaimed "Are you kidding? No way!" and floundered for 45 seconds before giving up. Similar less than appreciative comments and unsuccessful outcomes were obtained with the final two items.

Ashley's difficulties with Block Design appeared to be rooted more in difficulties related to figuring out how to orient diagonal blocks in asymmetrical designs in order to get her design to match the model rather than generally poor problem-solving ability or a lack of visual perceptual capacity. This hypothesis was strengthened by Ashley's performance with the Block Design Multiple Choice Subtest. Ashley correctly chose the design that matched the model for all 25 items of this subtest, earning a Block Design Multiple Choice No Time Bonus process score in the above average range (13). Although her work pace was not particularly slow, she tended to deliver most of her responses in the 6 to 10 second range, thereby losing the bonus point for quick responding with the result being a Block Design Multiple Choice (with time bonus) score toward the lower end of the average range (9). Although Ashley was very effective with the items of this subtest, her distaste for more work with block designs was apparent as she commented several times: "How many more of these are there?"

In a similar manner, administration of the Elithorn Mazes Subtest yielded results that reflected an effective approach to organizing and solving problems involving nonverbal visual materials (Elithorn Mazes No Time Bonus 11), but a work pace that was less than optimal resulting in loss of points for speed of performance (Elithorn Mazes 7).

An interview with Ashley that emphasized vocational interests and post-high school plans revealed that Ashley has a very strong interest in interior design and plans to pursue a career in this area. It was somewhat ironic, and very misleading, that Ashley earned her lowest scores in the area most closely related to her career aspirations. Although Ashley realizes the importance of understanding math, she also realizes that the aspects of math that will be most helpful to her career pursuits are not being emphasized in the Algebra course she is taking now and failing.

Summary

Administration of the Block Design Multiple Choice and the Elithorn Mazes Subtests revealed that Ashley's PRI score of 94 is not an accurate characterization of

(continued)

her ability to effectively process visual information and reason with visually presented nonverbal material. When speed of visual processing is not an emphasis and when the stimuli are more in line with her areas of interest, Ashley is able to demonstrate performance in the above average to superior range. When very quick responses are emphasized and abstract materials that are of little interest to Ashley are involved, her performance can deteriorate well into the below average range. Ashley is motivated to pursue a career in design, and she is beginning to experience a narrowing of interests that is not uncommon when vocational interests are well-known and are exerting a strong pull. Ashley's teachers were unaware of her career interests, so no attempt had been made to try to incorporate Ashley's career interests into the curriculum. At a meeting with Ashley's parents and teachers, it was agreed that Ashley's IEP would be amended to incorporate the findings from the assessment and emphasize vocational transition plans, including:

1. Incorporating Ashley's career interests into the reading and math curriculum as much as possible.

2. Emphasizing concrete applications of math skills to help Ashley maintain interest and performance.

3. Make arrangements for a 12th grade work-study placement in a setting where interior design is involved.

4. Help Ashley explore opportunities for advanced study or employment involving interior design.

Additionally, Ashley's parents agreed to allow her to enroll in an art course at a local institute held on Saturday mornings, with continued participation contingent on Ashley putting forth her best effort and earning passing grades in Algebra and English class and improving her daily attendance.

Ashley's case illustrates several points about the use of the WISC-IV Integrated tasks and features:

1. The content and format of the Block Design Subtest emphasize visual processing capacities that are not necessarily generalizable to how a child will perform with visual processing tasks involving other kinds of visual stimuli, i.e., a low score on Block Design does not necessarily suggest a general visual processing deficit.

2. Use of time bonus and no time bonus scores can be very helpful in testing hypotheses about a child's performance.

3. The concrete/abstract dimension of Perceptual domain task content can have a great influence on task performance levels and needs to be taken into account in interpretation efforts.

4. Low scores on subtests may be the results of ineffective use of cognitive capacities that are not the primary cognitive capacities intended to be assessed with the subtest.

5. Low scores on subtests may be the result of a lack of adequate engagement with a task rather than a lack of capacity.

6. The additional WISC-IV Integrated subtests used with Ashley required less than 15 minutes for administration, a small investment for the important additional information obtained in this case.

Perceptual Domain Subtest and Process Score Comparison Worksheet

Subtest Comparison	Subtest 1		Subtest 2		Scaled Score Analyses		
	Raw Score	Scaled Score	Raw Score	Scaled Score	Scaled Score Diff (b-d)	Scaled Score Difference Significant?	Scaled Score Difference Unusual?
	a	b	c	d	e	e > 3	e = 5 e >= 6
MR vs. BD	22	8	30	6	2	N	N
MR vs. PCn	22	8	23	13	−5	Y	Y < 10%
MR vs. PCm	22	8	35	14	−6	Y	Y < 5%
MR vs. EM	22	8	26	7	1	N	N
PCn vs. BD	23	13	30	6	7	Y	Y < 5%
PCn vs. PCm	23	13	35	14	−1	N	N
PCn vs. EM	23	13	26	7	6	Y	Y < 5%
BD vs. PCm	30	6	35	14	−8	Y	Y < 5%
BD vs. EM	30	6	26	7	−1	N	N
BD vs. BDMC	30	6	36	9	−3	Y	N
EM vs. BDMC	26	7	36	9	−2	N	N
EM vs. PCm	26	7	35	14	−7	Y	Y < 5%
	No Time Bonus Process Scores		Subtest Scores		Scaled Score Analyses		
BDN vs. BD	30	6	30	6	0	E > 1? N	e = 2 e > 2 N
BDMCN vs. BDMC	25	13	36	9	4	e > 1? Y	e = 3 e >= 4 Y < 5%
EMN vs. EM	26	11	26	7		e > 1? Y N	e = 2 e >= 3 Y < 5%

of the Supplemental Subtest Arithmetic. The additional process-approach procedures involve recording the longest span of stimuli with which the child responds correctly for specific memory process tasks.

As part of the application of the process approach, the tasks of the Working Memory Domain were organized according to the primary memory capacities likely to be involved in task performance. Tasks involving the immediate registration and brief holding of stimuli are referred to as *Registration* tasks. Tasks involving holding and manipulating information beyond the initial registration period are referred to as *Mental Manipulation* tasks. Rapid Reference 8.23 provides information about the administration and scoring of the Working Memory Domain Process Subtests.

Scaled Score equivalents for Working Memory Domain process tasks are located in the *WISC-IV Integrated Administration and Scoring Manual* in Appendix C, Table C.3. The scaled scores in Table C.3 are organized according to task processing demands (i.e., Registration and Mental Manipulation). The Working Memory Domain process-approach interpretation offers numerous tables for task scaled score discrepancy comparisons and base rates as outlined in Rapid Reference 8.24.

When to Use the Working Memory Domain Process Subtests

In many cases, the Working Memory Domain Process Subtests and additional Process Scores and observations will enable a clinician to see how a child's performance varies when item stimulus format is altered. In other cases, Working Memory Domain Process Subtests will offer children who find it difficult to produce adequate responses to the Supplemental Arithmetic Subtest a chance to demonstrate their abilities through several modified response formats (ARPA-A and ARPA-B and WA). The Working Memory Domain Process Subtests are not intended to be used with every child who is assessed. There are no set rules dictating the specifics of the use of any of the Process Subtests other than that administration of any of these subtests must occur after completion of the administration of the Core and Supplemental Subtests of the WISC-IV. Clinicians can select the specific subtests that are most likely to assist in understanding a particular child's test performance. The decision to use one or more Working Memory Domain Process Subtest may be based on information that is obtained prior to the administration of the WISC-IV Core and Supplemental Subtests, such as parent and/or teacher input or records review. After administration of the Core and Supplemental Subtests, the clinician may choose to administer one or more of the process subtests based on observations of the child's performance during the assessment or based on the scores earned by the child on one or more

≡ *Rapid Reference 8.23*

Administration and Scoring of the Working Memory Domain Process Subtests

While administration and scoring of the Working Memory Domain Registration and Mental Manipulation tasks is straightforward and easy to learn quickly for clinicians experienced with individually administered test directions, a few points will help clinicians to quickly get familiar with these tasks:

• Directions for Administering and Scoring of all of the Working Memory Domain Process Subtests and process procedures are located in the *WISC-IV Administration and Scoring Manual.*

• Start, Reverse, and Discontinue rules are printed on the Record Form for easy reference.

• When administering the Arithmetic Subtest, be sure to record the exact time of completion for all items administered in order to calculate the Arithmetic Time Bonus Process Score (ART).

• When administering the Arithmetic Process Approach Subtest Part A, be sure to record the exact time of completion for all items administered in order to calculate the ARPA-A Time Bonus Process Score. Also be sure to administer the subtest using the Start and Discontinue rules as stated in the manual and on the Record Form rather than only duplicating the items administered for the Arithmetic Subtest.

• When administering Arithmetic Process Approach Subtest Part B, be sure to allow the child to use a pencil and paper, and be sure to prompt him or her to use the pencil and paper if he or she is not doing so.

• The Visual Digit Span Subtest requires the use of Stimulus Booklet 3 and the Visual Digit Span Item Card and Sleeve. Make sure the item card is properly inserted into the Sleeve before administration. The exposure time for items varies depending on the number of digits to be viewed. Be sure to refer to the small window in the Sleeve for the exposure time for each item.

• The Spatial Span Subtest requires the use of the Spatial Span Board. The Spatial Span Board Blocks are all numbered on one side, which is the side that faces the examiner during administration of items. Clinicians will find it easier to follow a child's responses if they perfect the technique of *writing the numbers of the blocks touched by the child without looking at the response record when writing.* This enables the clinician to keep track of quick moves by the child and reduces the likelihood of missing any of the child's block touches. This technique can be mastered with practice.

• As indicated on the Record Form, only Trials 1 and 3 earn scores for each item of the Letter-Number Span Process Approach Subtest.

≣ *Rapid Reference 8.24*

Working Memory Domain Process Approach Scaled Score Interpretive Tables Available in the *WISC-IV Integrated Administration and Scoring Manual*

Process-Approach Element	Interpretive Table	Table Location
Registration Process Scaled Scores	Scaled Score Differences Required for Statistical Significance	Table D.10
Registration Process Scaled Scores	Discrepancy Comparison Base Rates	Table D.11
Mental Manipulation Process Scaled Scores	Scaled Score Differences Required for Statistical Significance	Table D.12
Mental Manipulation Process Scaled Scores	Discrepancy Comparison Base Rates	Table D.13
Registration versus Mental Manipulation Process Scaled Scores	Scaled Score Differences Required for Statistical Significance	Table D.14
Registration versus Mental Manipulation Process Scaled Scores	Discrepancy Comparison Base Rates	Table D.15
Registration and Mental Manipulation Process Observations	Longest Span Base Rates	Tables D.16–D.20
Registration and Mental Manipulation Process Observations	Longest Span Discrepancy Comparison Base Rates	Tables D.21–D.24

of the Core and/or Supplemental Subtests. Rapid Reference 8.25 lists conditions most likely to lead to the use of one or more Working Memory Domain Process Subtests. Whatever the reason for choosing to use Working Memory Domain Process Subtests, examiners must keep in mind that the administration of these subtests must occur after the administration of the WISC-IV Core and Supplemental Subtests. Administration of the standard WISC-IV subtests should not be interrupted in order to administer a process subtest.

≡ Rapid Reference 8.25

When to Use the Working Memory Domain Process Subtests

The decision to use one or more of the Working Memory Domain Process Subtests may occur prior to or after administration of the WISC-IV Core and Supplemental Subtests.

Prior to administration of the WISC-IV, information gathered from parents, teachers, and background records can inform the clinician about situations in which the use of Working Memory Domain Process Subtests might be warranted. These situations could include:

Background information indicating

- Child has delays in auditory perceptual or language development.
- Child has impoverished linguistic environment, present or past.
- Child is bilingual or parents speak a language other than English in the home.
- Child is receiving English as a Second Language services.
- Child has a Language Disorder, Auditory Processing Disorder (APD or CAPD), or other language-related disorder diagnosis.
- Child has a Learning Disability diagnosis, especially in Reading or Math.
- Child has reading problems.
- Child has math problems
- Child has memory problems
- Child has traumatic brain injury, including concussions.

Concerns expressed by parents or teachers

- Child has language difficulties, poor articulation, poor auditory discrimination, or other *hearing* problems despite no presence of hearing loss.
- Child displays inattentiveness to auditory stimuli.
- Child displays memory problems, such as forgetfulness, inability to retain information for short periods, or inability to follow multistep directions.

After administration of the WISC-IV, observations of how the child performed the Core and/or Supplemental Working Memory Domain Subtests and/or the scores earned on these subtests may lead to the decision to administer one or more of the Working Memory Domain Process Subtests. In the case of behavior observations, it may be the way in which the child performed the task rather than the score the child obtained that leads to the administration of one or more process subtests. Observations and scores leading to the use of process subtests could include:

(continued)

Observations during testing

- auditory discrimination difficulties
- frequent request for repetition of test directions and or items
- inattentiveness to auditory stimuli
- inconsistent on DS and LNS trials (e.g., frequently misses the first trial of an item but gets the second trial right or vice versa)
- frequent rescanning of visual stimuli and responses for Matrix Reasoning and/ or Picture Concepts

Scores earned on the WISC-IV Core and/or Supplemental Subtests

- when all Working Memory Domain Subtest scores are in the Below Average range or lower
- when one Working Memory Domain Subtest is significantly lower or higher than the others
- when the Arithmetic Subtest Score is Below Average or lower
- when the Word Reasoning Subtest Score is Below Average or lower or when the Word Reasoning Subtest score is significantly lower than the other Verbal Domain Subtest scores
- when a significant difference is observed between Digit Span Forward and Digit Span Backward raw and scaled scores or longest spans
- when the WMI score is significantly lower than the VCI, PRI, or PSI Index scores
- when the WMI score is low or lower than expected based on parent and/or teacher input about the child's abilities

Use and Interpretation of the Working Memory Domain Process Subtests
To effectively use and interpret the Working Memory Domain Process Subtests, it is necessary to have an understanding of the multifactorial nature of the Core and Supplemental Subtests in terms of the cognitive capacities they assess. Similarly, clinicians need to understand what cognitive capacities are assessed by the Working Memory Domain Process Subtests and how these can be used in concert with the Core and Supplemental Subtests to obtain a clearer picture of a child's cognitive strengths and weaknesses.

What Do Working Memory Domain Core, Supplemental,
and Process Subtests Measure?
The Working Memory Domain subtests were designed primarily to assess the capacities involved in the initial registration and holding of stimuli (sometimes

referred to as *short-term memory*) and the mental manipulation of information that is being held in mind (often referred to as *working memory*). All three of the core and supplemental Working Memory Domain Subtests assess these capacities using auditorily presented verbal and verbal-quantitative stimuli. Assessment of these capacities is the primary focus of interpretation of the Working Memory Index as well as the individual Working Memory Domain subtests. The roles of these primary cognitive capacities in task performance are described in detail in Rapid Reference 8.26.

☰ *Rapid Reference 8.26*

Cognitive Capacities Assessed with the Working Memory Domain Core and Supplemental Subtests

Primary Cognitive Capacities

Initial Registration of Auditorily Presented Verbal Information—This cognitive capacity is essential for effective performance on all of the items of the Digit Span, Letter-Number Sequencing, and Arithmetic Subtests. Before a child can respond to any of the items on these three subtests, he or she must effectively register the auditorily presented verbal information and hold it at least for 1 to 3 seconds.

Mental Manipulation of Auditorily Presented Verbal Information—This cognitive capacity is essential for effective performance on all of the items of the Digit Span Backward, Letter-Number Sequencing, and Arithmetic Subtests and can be very helpful, but not essential, in the performance of the Digit Span Forward items. Items requiring mental manipulation cannot be completed by a simple dumping of the information being held in the initial registration buffer. The information must be held for more than 1 to 3 seconds and manipulated in some way in order for a correct response to be constructed. The use of this capacity to mentally manipulate information after registration is usually referred to as *working memory*.

Although all three of the Core and Supplemental tasks except Digit Span Forward require the use of both initial registration and working memory, the contributions of these two capacities to task performance are distinct but not dissociable. A child with extremely poor initial registration capacity for a certain type of stimuli will not be able to perform effectively on a task that requires mental manipulation of that same type of stimuli (note that this is not the same as saying that a child who scores poorly on a task involving initial registration of stimuli also will score poorly on a task involving initial registration and working memory of the same stimuli, as discussed in the text of this chapter).

(continued)

Secondary Cognitive Capacities

Auditory Acuity—While listening to the directions and the individual test items spoken by the examiner, the child must have adequate auditory acuity. If the child cannot hear all of the speech sounds made by the examiner, directions may be misunderstood and/or items may not be heard accurately. Typically, a child's auditory acuity is assessed and verified to be within normal limits with or without the use of assistive devices prior to test administration so that this capacity should not be a factor in performance. If overlooked, however, a deficit in auditory acuity can significantly impact task performance with all verbal subtests.

Auditory Discrimination—Before responding to the items of each auditorily presented Working Memory Subtest, the child must be able to listen to and effectively process the language used by the examiner when directions and test items are being provided. If the child is prone to auditory discrimination errors when listening to others speaking, specific letters, numbers, or words may be misunderstood, resulting in incorrect responses or no response at all.

Attention to Auditory Stimuli—To perform auditorily presented Working Memory Domain tasks the child must have the capacity for focusing and sustaining attention for the auditory stimuli of each item.

Auditory Processing Speed—The speed with which a child can register auditory information can greatly affect the child's ability to register all the information that is presented in a short period of time. Although DS and LNS item stimuli are presented at the relatively slow rate of one stimulus unit per second, a child with extremely slow auditory processing speed may not be able to keep up with this rate of information delivery, thereby reducing the child's capacity for registering all of the stimuli. Similarly, although the Arithmetic Subtest items are read to the child at a normal conversational pace, a child with slow auditory processing speed may not be able to register all of the information provided in each word problem.

Mental Processing Speed—The speed with which a child can manipulate information while holding it in mind can greatly affect a child's performance with the Arithmetic Subtest. A child with slow mental processing speed may not be able to complete Arithmetic items within the 30-second time limit despite the ability to correctly solve the problem.

Retrieval of Verbal Information from Long-Term Storage—Both the Arithmetic and Letter-Number Sequencing Subtests require the retrieval of verbal information from long-term storage. The requirement for the retrieval of math facts, procedures, and/or problem-solving routines is fairly obvious as the child must have knowledge of mathematics in order to solve the auditorily presented math word problems. No matter how effective the child is at holding and manipulating information in mind, such holding and manipulating will not result in a correct response unless the child knows what to do to solve the word problem. Perhaps less obvious but no less critical to performance is the need for the child to be able to retrieve the correct sequence of the letters of the alphabet and the order of the numbers from 1 to 10 while holding and manipulating the specific series of number and letter stimuli for each item of the Letter-Number Sequencing Subtest.

Math Calculation and Problem-Solving Skills—Before engaging in the retrieval from long-term storage of knowledge about how to perform calculation and solve problems, a child must have learned how to perform the math calculations and have had some exposure to math problem-solving exercises. If the child has no math skills, effective performance of Arithmetic items is not possible.

Expressive Language Ability—All three of the Core and Supplemental Working Memory Domain Subtests require the child to orally respond to items. Although the expressive language response demands of these tasks appear to be minimal in nature, some children with language processing difficulties or limited English proficiency may find it difficult to produce an accurate response while attempting to hold and manipulate verbal information.

Executive Functions—As a class of cognitive capacities, executive functions are responsible for cueing and directing the use of other mental capacities that are used for the purposes of perceiving, feeling, thinking, and acting. As such, they are intricately involved in the performance of all the tasks of the WISC-IV. The degree of involvement of specific executive functions in the performance of specific subtests, however, is highly variable and dependent on many factors including the directions provided to the child about how to perform the task and the input, processing, and output demands of the task. In the case of the Working Memory Domain Subtests, it is important to understand the role of executive functions in cueing and directing the use of both primary and secondary cognitive capacities. For most subtests, demands for the use of executive functions are reduced greatly through the use of explicit directions and teaching examples that model how to perform a task and/or the kind of response that is desired. For some children however, even these executive function aids do not help to ameliorate the effects of their severe executive function deficits, and the effects of these deficits often can be observed in a child's efforts to perform tasks.

For the Working Memory Domain Subtests, accurate responding depends in part on the effective use of one or more of the following executive function capacities:

- cueing and directing efficient perception of auditory stimuli
- cueing the appropriate consideration of the cognitive demands of a task and the amount of mental effort required to effectively perform the task
- cueing the modulation of effort while performing tasks
- cueing and directing the focusing of attention to the auditory details of the stimuli being presented
- cueing and directing sustained attention to task

(continued)

- cueing and directing the use of initial registration capacities
- cueing and directing the use of mental manipulation (working memory) capacities
- cueing and directing the use of reasoning abilities (generating novel solutions or making associations with prior knowledge that lead to Arithmetic problem solutions)
- cueing and directing the flexible shifting of cognitive mindset to consider and respond to the specific demands of the task
- cueing and directing the organization of information
- cueing and directing the execution of sequencing routines
- cueing and directing auditory processing speed
- cueing and directing a shift to more extensive detail (local) processing rather than pattern (global) processing
- cueing and directing the retrieval of verbal information from long-term storage
- cueing and directing the monitoring of work and the correcting of errors
- cueing and directing the coordination of the use of multiple mental capacities simultaneously

Beyond the primary cognitive capacities targeted for assessment with the Working Memory Domain Subtests, the specific formats of each subtest make demands on the child that require the engagement of additional cognitive capacities in order to achieve success. While these capacities are required for effective subtest performance, they are not considered to be the primary target of the assessment (i.e., the intention of the subtest is not to quantitatively assess the child's use of these cognitive capacities). These secondary cognitive capacities include Auditory Acuity, Auditory Discrimination, Auditory Processing Speed, Attention to Auditorily Presented Verbal Information, Language Expression, and multiple executive functions applied to cue and direct the use of initial registration and working memory resources. The roles of these secondary cognitive capacities in subtest performance are described in detail in Rapid Reference 8.26.

With the addition of the Letter-Number Sequencing Subtest to the WISC-IV and the selection of the Digit Span and Letter-Number Sequencing Subtests to comprise the Working Memory Index, the WISC-IV Core battery offers a relatively narrow perspective on working memory capacities. The limitation of input format to audtiorily presented, relatively decontextual verbal information (i.e., randomly ordered digits and digit-and-letter sequences) greatly reduces the generalizability of Working Memory Index interpretation. Additionally, as mentioned in Chapter 5 of this text, the WMI is only a measure of initial registration capacities for many children under the age of 8 and older, low-functioning children. This is the case when a young or low-functioning child performs significantly better with Digit Span Forward than Digit Span Backward and earns all or most of his or her points on Letter-Number Sequencing by merely repeating the sequences as they were presented, thereby turning the task into an initial registration task similar to Digit Span Forward rather than a working memory task. In such cases, the WMI score is actually only a measure of the child's initial registration capacity rather than a measure of initial registration and working memory capacities combined. Attempting to assess a child's working memory capacities solely through the lens of the WMI Index has a number of drawbacks, as detailed in Rapid Reference 8.27. Interpretation can be strengthened considerably with the addition of the supplemental Arithmetic Subtest and possibly one or two additional Working Memory Process Subtests.

Without an understanding of the role that secondary cognitive capacities play in task performance, clinicians frequently will have difficulty effectively interpreting a child's performance. For example, it is a neuropsychological fact that stimuli must be effectively registered before they can be manipulated in mind (i.e., no manipulation of information can occur if the information was not initially registered and/or is no longer being held in mind). How then does a clinician explain the performance of a child who repeats only four digits forward but is able to repeat six digits in reverse? The former result suggests a capacity for initially registering and holding only four digits, but in order to perform Digit Span Backward, the child had to first register and hold six digits and then mentally manipulate those six digits to provide a correct response. In such cases, although the child has the capacity to initially register and hold six digits, difficulties in the use of one or more secondary capacities reduced the child's ability to demonstrate that capacity in a consistent manner.

When performance on a mental manipulation task is better than performance on the predecessor initial registration task, the most likely source of difficulty is the poor use of one or more of the executive function capacities needed to cue and direct efficient performance. Such paradoxical results most often involve poor use of one or more of the following executive function capacities:

- cueing the appropriate consideration of the cognitive demands of a task and the amount of mental effort required to effectively perform the task
- cueing the modulation of effort while performing tasks

≡ *Rapid Reference 8.27*

Index Score versus Process-Approach Interpretation of Working Memory Capacities

Clinicians should use great caution when interpreting the meaning of the Working Memory Index standard score. The WMI represents a very narrow perspective on worming memory capacities and often does not relate the most clinically meaningful information about a child's working memory strengths and weaknesses.

The limitations of the WMI as a measure of working memory are apparent when the two tasks comprising this Index score—Digit Span and Letter-Number Sequencing—are analyzed from a process-approach perspective:

- DS and LN only use orally presented verbal information.
- DS and LN require orally presented verbal responses.
- DS only uses series of numbers; LN only uses series of numbers and letters.
- DS only involves random presentation of decontextual (i.e., nonmeaningful) number series; LN only involves random presentation of minimally contextual (i.e., minimally meaningful) number and letter series.
- DS requires precise sequencing of the randomly presented, decontextual stimuli; LN requires precise sequencing of the randomly presented, minimally contextual stimuli.
- DS assesses working memory capacities with only one-half of the subtest (DSB); the other half (DSF) only assesses initial registration of stimuli; depending on patterns of performance with DSF and DSB, the DS subtest score might not be reflecting the child's working memory capacities at all, and in the best case scenario, DS will only be a partial reflection of the child's use of working memory capacities.
- LN does not always assess working memory capacities because of the manner in which items are scored. Because the child need not follow the desired order of numbers first and letters second when responding, points can be earned simply for repeating the number-letter sequence as it was presented, thereby making the item a measure of initial registration rather than working memory; depending on patterns of item performance, the LN score might not be reflecting the child's working memory capacities at all.

The narrow and potentially misleading focus of the WMI is best demonstrated when the Supplemental Arithmetic Subtest is administered and a subtest-level process approach to interpretation is employed. Consider the following two cases.

WM Task	Sean			Steven		
	Raw Score	Scaled Score	Percentile Rank	Raw Score	Scaled Score	Percentile Rank
Digit Span Forward	7	7	16	12	14	91
Digit Span Backward	6	8	25	7	10	50
Digit Span	13	7	16	19	12	75
Letter-Number Sequencing	17	9	37	17	10	50
Working Memory Index	16	88	21	22	104	61
Arithmetic	29	14	91	19	6	9

In these two cases, if the Arithmetic Subtest had not been administered and only the WMI standard scores of 88 for Sean and 104 for Steven were used for interpretation, a clinician would be led to the incorrect assumption that Steven's ability to perform tasks involving working memory capacities is signifi-cantly better than Sean's. The picture changes substantially, however, when the Supplemental Arithmetic Subtest and the Digit Span Forward and Backward Process scaled scores are considered and interpreted from a process-approach perspective.

The typical interpretation of Sean's WMI standard score of 88 is that he dem-onstrated Below Average working memory capacity. Note, however, that Sean earned a score in the Superior range with the Arithmetic Subtest (Scaled Score 14, 91st percentile)—a task that is more demanding than DS or LN in terms of the multiple cognitive capacities required for successful performance, including a heavy working memory demand. Note also the pattern of Sean's subtest per-formance: As the tasks increased in terms of complexity and working memory capacity demand, Sean performed more effectively. Although it could be hy-pothesized that the variability in Sean's subtest scores could be attributable to difficulties with a number of cognitive capacities listed in Rapid Reference 8.26, the steady increase in performance across these tasks is most consistent with variation in one factor: the steady increase in the meaningful context of the stimuli. Sean earned a score in the Below Average range (DS Scaled Score 7, 16th percentile) when the stimuli were randomly presented, decontextual number series (DSF and DSB; DS). His performance improved into the Aver-age range (LN Scaled Score 9, 37th percentile) when the stimuli were randomly presented but a minimally meaningful context was apparent in the requirements of the task—organization by numerical and alphabetical order. Sean's perfor-mance increased into the Superior range (AR Scaled Score 14, 91st percentile)

(continued)

when the items involved the meaningful contexts of everyday math problems. Sean's pattern of performance suggests that, while Sean was able to apply his well-developed working memory capacities to solve contextually meaningful math problems, he struggled to apply these working memory capacities to tasks that were randomly presented with little or no context for the application of working memory. This process-approach interpretation of Sean's performance was only possible with the administration of the *Supplemental* Arithmetic Subtest. If only the core battery Working Memory Domain Subtests had been administered to Sean, interpretation would have focused on the WMI standard score and/or the DS and LN Subtest scaled scores. The clinician would have underestimated Sean's working memory capacities, not realized the significant effect of context on Sean's use of working memory capacities or the extent of the variability of performance caused by varying the context of the information presented, and been left with no viable explanation for the seemingly paradoxical 2 scaled score point difference between LN and DS in favor of the more complex LN task except perhaps to attribute it to *error variance*, thereby reinforcing the idea that subtest-level performance is too unreliable to be meaningfully interpreted. In fact, observation of a paradoxical pattern of performance of DS > LN is one of the suggested triggers for administering one or more Working Memory Domain Process Subtests along with the Supplemental Arithmetic Subtest.

The typical interpretation of Steven's WMI standard score of 104 is that he demonstrated Average working memory capacity. Note, however, that Steven earned a score in the Low range with the Arithmetic Subtest (Scaled Score 6, 9th percentile)—a task that is more demanding than DS or LN in terms of the multiple cognitive capacities required for successful performance, including a heavy working memory demand. Note also the pattern of Steven's subtest performance: As the tasks increased in terms of complexity and working memory capacity demand, Steven performed less effectively. Although it could be hypothesized that the variability in Steven's subtest scores could be attributable to difficulties with a number of cognitive capacities listed in Rapid Reference 8.26, the steady decrease in performance across these tasks is most consistent with variation in one factor: the steady increase in the demand for the use of working memory capacities with more complex information. Steven performed very well (DSF Scaled Score 14, 91st percentile) when the stimuli were randomly presented, decontextual number series and only initial registration capacities were necessary for accurate responding. His performance decreased into the Average range when the stimuli were similar to the randomly presented series of DSF, but working memory involvement was required in order to reverse the order of the numbers before responding (DSB Scaled Score 10, 50th percentile) or to order the stimuli in numerical and alphabetical order before responding (LN Scaled Score 10, 50th percentile). When working memory demands were further increased for solving everyday math problems, Steven's performance decreased into the Low range (AR Scaled Score 6, 9th percentile). Steven's pattern of performance suggest that Steven was at his best when working memory demands were minimized and only rote initial registration of information was required, independent of contextual meaning. As working memory demands increased, Steven was unable to maintain effective performance; as a result, his scores dropped further with each increase in the demand for the use of working memory capacities. This process-approach interpretation of Steven's performance was only possible with the administration of the *Supplemental* Arithmetic Subtest and calculation of the Digit Span Process Scores of DSF and DSB. If only the core battery subtests had been administered to Steven, interpretation would have focused on the WMI standard score and/or the DS and LN Subtest scaled scores. The clinician would have overestimated Steven's working memory capacities, not realized the significant effect of increased working memory demands on Steven's level of performance or the extent of the variability of performance caused by varying working memory demands, and ignored the seemingly trivial 2 scaled score point difference between LN and DS predictably in favor of the less complex DS task except perhaps to attribute it to *error variance*, once again reinforcing the idea that subtest-level performance variability is too unreliable to be meaningfully interpreted. Steven's case is especially important in that it illustrates the danger of overestimation of working memory capacities that is possible when only the core battery Working Memory Domain Subtests are administered. Steven's results also provide a strong case for the routine administration of the Arithmetic Subtest and calculation of the DSF and DSB Process Scores even if no additional Working Memory Domain Process Subtests are included in the assessment.

From a clinical perspective and in contrast to the WMI scores, the data available for interpretation suggest that, although Sean earned the lower WMI score, concerns about Sean's working memory capacities or his ability to apply them are less than the concerns raised by Steven's decreasing effectiveness with increasing working memory demands and his low level of performance with the Arithmetic Subtest.

- cueing and directing efficient perception of auditory stimuli
- cueing and directing the focusing of attention to the auditory details of the stimuli being presented
- cueing and directing sustained attention to task
- cueing and directing the use of initial registration capacities

Although any of these six executive function capacities could be involved in paradoxical performance with Digit Span items, the likelihood that problems will only occur with DSF items and not DSB items is unlikely for the last four capacities listed. Some combination of the first two executive function capacities listed is highly likely to be the source of difficulty. Many children underestimate the difficulty involved in merely repeating digits forward but accurately perceive the difficult nature of repeating digits in reverse order; as a result, they do not cue the appropriate consideration of the cognitive demands of Digit Span Forward and/ or do not cue the appropriate level of mental effort needed to effectively perform DSF. These children underactivate resources for DSF then appropriately activate resources for DSB with the result being better performance on DSB than DSF. Similar performance paradoxes may be observed with any of the Process Subtest span tasks when they are used in an assessment.

When Working Memory Domain Subtest scores are interpreted either collectively using the WMI or individually, information such as that provided in Rapid References 8.26 and 8.27 usually is not applied effectively to enhance interpretation. It is typically assumed that the WMI and Core Working Memory Subtest score levels reflect a general level of working memory capacity. The secondary capacities required for effective performance are either ignored completely or assumed to be intact and functioning as expected to allow for the focus of interpretation to be on the primary capacities of initial registration and mental manipulation of stimuli. In addition, the narrow foci of the two subtests that comprise the WMI greatly limit what the WMI can reflect about a child's working memory capacity.

In many cases in which low performance is observed on one or both of the WMI core subtests, the generalized assumption of poor initial registration and/ or poor working memory capacities is not necessarily warranted. To know if the assumption about these primary capacities is valid, the role of the secondary cognitive capacities in task performance and the effect of input and response formats must be understood and explored in more detail. When not accessed, or when applied ineffectively, secondary cognitive capacities can interfere with task performance to a significant degree, making it inappropriate to focus subtest score interpretation exclusively on the primary capacities that are thought to be assessed. Additionally, without knowing how the child performs when input and response formats are varied, the clinician is in danger of overinterpreting the generalizability of the WMI score.

When low scores or scores that are not consistent with what is known about the child are obtained from one or both of the Core Working Memory Subtests, the Working Memory Domain Process Subtests can be used to test hypotheses about the sources of poor or unusual performance. As indicated in the previous discussion, poor performance on these tasks is thought to reflect a lack of initial registration and working memory resources. Clinicians who appreciate that a low score on one or both of the Working Memory Domain Subtests could be due to many different sources, or due to input or output format limitations, can draw on the Process Subtests and process-approach observations to help obtain a better understanding of why the child performed poorly and the educational implications of such poor performance.

The additional memory span subtests alter many of the cognitive demands of the Core Digit Span and Letter-Number Sequencing Subtests, as detailed in Rapid Reference 8.28. Although the ARPA-A and Arithmetic Process Approach and Written Arithmetic Process Subtest alterations greatly reduce working memory demands, the Written Arithmetic Subtest can also increase the need for the use of other cognitive capacities for some children. The specific ways that the Arithmetic Process Approach and the Written Arithmetic Process Subtest response formats may decrease or increase cognitive demands also are detailed in Rapid Reference 8.28.

Rapid Reference 8.28

How Working Memory Domain Process Subtests Alter Cognitive Demands

The formats of the Working Memory Domain Process Subtests alter many of the cognitive demands of the Core and Supplemental Subtests in ways that make it easier or harder for some children to demonstrate their capacity to handle item content. These include:

- altering the stimuli for initial registration and mental manipulation span items:
  - using visuospatial presentation of nonverbal, visual stimuli (i.e., block locations on a board—Spatial Span)
  - using visual presentation of numbers (Visual Digit Span)
  - using auditory presentation of nonrhyming or rhyming letters (Letter Span)
  - using sequences of letters that spell words as the letter stimuli in number-letter sequences (Letter-Number Sequencing Process Approach)

The use of different formats for stimuli will improve some children's ability to initially register and mentally manipulate series of stimuli. For other children, these altered formats will be more challenging and will reduce their ability to complete span items.

Note that the use of visual formats for the Spatial Span and Visual Digit Span Process Subtests introduces an entire set of secondary capacities that were not involved in the Core and Supplemental Subtests, including:

- Visual Perception and Discrimination
- Attention to Visual Stimuli
- Initial registration of visual stimuli
- Mental Manipulation of visual stimuli

- Visual processing speed
- Executive Function direction and cueing of the use of the visual capacities listed previously
- altering the presentation format of arithmetic word problems, presenting each word problem visually as well as auditorily, greatly reducing the demands for mental manipulation (Arithmetic Process Approach Part A and Part B)
- altering the response format of arithmetic word problems by allowing the child to use pencil and paper to do calculations, further reducing the working memory demands of the task (Arithmetic Process Approach Part B)
- altering the arithmetic presentation and response formats by changing all word problems to calculation problems with no words. This format change further reduces the need for working memory capacity but at the same time increases the demand for knowledge of how to perform calculations using formal notation for operations (e.g., the use of parentheses that indicate the order of operations in a multistep calculation problem).

It should be clear from the information provided in Rapid Reference 8.28 that the Process Subtest registration and mental manipulation task formats provide the clinician with a chance to see how the child performs with the same item content when different cognitive demands are present. While the Process Subtest task scaled scores are valuable indicators of how effective the child is with the use of these cognitive capacities, their value as an interpretive tool is enhanced when they are compared to the scores earned on other Core, Supplemental, and Process registration and mental manipulation tasks. Such comparisons enable the clinician to generate or further test hypotheses about the effects of altering task format and input, processing, and output demands.

As noted previously, there are instances when altering the formats of registration, working memory, and arithmetic problem items will reduce the child's effectiveness with item content. From a clinical perspective, knowing when an altered format reduces effectiveness is as important as knowing when an altered format increases effectiveness. Rapid Reference 8.29 provides an interpretive summary table that can be used to assist with the comparison of registration and mental manipulation tasks in terms of the cognitive capacities that may be involved in the performance of test items.

Meaningful interpretation of scaled score comparisons starts with the determination of whether a statistically significant and clinically meaningful difference exists between the scores earned on the subtest tasks being compared. The WISC-IV Integrated manual provides tables for statistically significant scaled

Rapid Reference 8.29

Cognitive Capacities Likely to Be Assessed by Working Memory Domain Tasks and Reflected in Scaled Score Values

Cognitive Capacity	Working Memory Domain Tasks														
	DSF	VDS	SSpF	LSN	LSR	DSB	SSpB	LNS	LNS PA	AR	ART	ARP A-A	ARPA- AT	AR PA-B	WA
Initial registration of stimuli	XXX	XXX	XXX	XXX	XXX	XXX	XXX	XXX	XXX	XXX	XXX	XXX	XXX	XXX	
Mental manipulation of stimuli						XXX	XXX	XXX	XXX	XXX	XXX	XX	XX	X	X
Auditory Discrimination	XX	XX		XX	XX	XX		XX	XX	XX	XX		XX	XX	
Visual Discrimination		XX	XX				XX			XX	XX	X	X	XX	XX
Attention to auditory stimuli	XX	XX		XX	XX	XX		XX	XX	XX	XX	XX	XX	XX	
Attention to visual stimuli			XX				XX								XX
Auditory Processing Speed	XX	XX		XX	XX	XX		XX	XX	XX	XX	XX	XX	XX	

(continued)

Working Memory Domain Tasks

Cognitive Capacity	DSF	VDS	SSpF	LSN	LSR	DSB	SSpB	LNS	LNS PA	AR	ART	ARP A-A	ARPA-AT	AR PA-B	WA
Visual Processing Speed			XX				XX					X	X	X	X
Mental Processing Speed										XX	XXX	XX	XXX	XX	
Retrieval of verbal information from long-term storage								XX	XX	XX	XX	XX	XX	XX	XX
Math skills									XX	XX	XX	XX	XX	XX	XX
Expressive Language Ability		XX		XX	XX			XX	XX	XX	XX	XX	XX	XX	
EF—Direct perception and registration of stimuli	XX	XX	XX	XX	XX	XX	XX	XX	XX	XX	XX	XX	XX	XX	
EF – Cueing appropriate consideration of the cognitive capacities and mental effort required to perform a task	XX	XX	XX	XX	XX	XX	XX			XX	XX	XX	XX	XX	XX

EF—Cueing the modulation of effort	XX	XX	XX	XX	XX	XX	XX	XX	XX	XX	XX	XX	XX	XX
EF—Direct mental manipulation	X	X	X	X	X	X	XX	X	XX	XX	XX	XX	X	X
EF—Direct attention to details of stimuli being presented	XX	XX	XX	XX	XX	XX	XX	XX	XX	XX	XX	XX	XX	XX
EF—Cueing the shift to an imbalanced emphasis on processing details over patterns	XX	XX	XX	XX	XX	XX	XX	XX	XX	XX			XX	XX
EF—Direct sustained attention to task	XX	XX	XX	XX	XX	XX	XX	XX	XX	XX	XX	XX	XX	XX
EF—Cueing the use of reasoning abilities								XX	XX	XX	XX	XX	XX	XX
EF—Cueing the flexible shifting of mindset to consider the stimuli							XX							

(continued)

Working Memory Domain Tasks

Cognitive Capacity	DSF	VDS	SSpF	LSN	LSR	DSB	SSpB	LNS	LNS PA	AR	ART	ARP A-A	ARPA- AT	AR PA-B	WA
EF—Cueing the organization of information								XX	XX	XX	XX	XX	XX	XX	XX
EF—Directing the retrieval of information from long-term storage								XX	XX	XXX	XXX	XXX	XXX	XXX	XXX
EF—Cueing the execution of sequencing routines	XX	XX	XX	XX	XX	XX	XX	XX	XX	XX	XX	XX	XX	XX	XX
EF—Cueing and directing auditory processing speed	XX	XX		XX	XX	XX		XX	XX	XX	XX	XX	XX	XX	
EF— Coordinate use of multiple capacities simultaneously	XX	XX	XX	XX	XX		XX	XX	XX	XX	XX	XX	XX	XX	XX

EF—Cueing the monitoring of responses and the correcting of errors	XX	XX	XX	XX	XX	XX	XX	XX	XX	XX	XX	XX	XX	XX
EF—Cueing and directing visual capacities (as specified in the EF list in Rapid Reference 8.20)		XX		XX						XX	XX	XX	XX	XX
Format														
Auditorily presented numbers	XXX				XXX									
Auditorily presented letters and numbers						XXX								
Auditorily presented rhyming letters			XXX											
Auditorily presented nonrhyming letters		XXX												

(continued)

Working Memory Domain Tasks

Cognitive Capacity	DSF	VDS	SSpF	LSN	LSR	DSB	SSpB	LNS	LNS PA	AR	ART	ARP A-A	ARPA-AT	AR PA-B	WA
Auditorily presented words as letter strings and numbers									XXX						
Visually presented visuospatial locations			XXX												
Visually presented numbers		XXX													
Auditorily presented math word problems										XXX	XXX	XXX	XXX	XXX	
Visually presented math word problems											XXX	XXX	XXX		
Visually presented math calculation problems															XXX
Decontextual, nonmeaningful stimuli	XXX	XXX	XXX	XXX	XXX	XXX	XXX	XX	XX						
Contextual, meaningful stimuli								X	X	XXX	XXX	XXX	XXX	XXX	XXX

XXX = Primary Capacity targeted for assessment with the task.

XX = Secondary Capacity highly likely to be impacting task performance.

X = Secondary Capacity possibly impacting task performance.

score discrepancies and for scaled score discrepancy base rates for the Working Memory Domain tasks. Additional comparison values were calculated using the same procedures as those outlined in the *WISC-IV Integrated Technical and Interpretive Manual* and are included in Rapid Reference 8.30. The values provided here and in the WISC-IV manual are based on the data obtained from the performance of the WISC-IV Integrated standardization sample of 730 children when comparisons involve Process Subtest tasks. Data for comparisons involving only Core and/or Supplemental Subtest tasks are based on the WISC-IV standardization sample of 2,200 children.

≣ Rapid Reference 8.30

Guidelines for Interpreting Comparisons Between Working Memory Domain Tasks

Determining a Significant Difference Between Task Scaled Scores

The scaled score values for significant differences between and among Core, Supplemental, and Process registration and mental manipulation tasks are provided in the following tables. Some of the comparisons tabled here appear in Appendix D, Tables D.10, D.12, and D.14 of the *WISC-IV Integrated Administration and Scoring Manual*. Additional comparison values were calculated using the same procedures as those outlined in the WISC-IV Integrated manuals.

Registration Task Comparisons

Significance Level	DSF vs. VDS	DSF vs. LSN	DSF vs. LSR	DSF vs. SSpF	LSN vs. LSR	LSN vs. SSpF	LSR vs. SSpF	VDS vs. SSpF	VDS vs. LSN	VDS vs. LSR
.15	2.53	2.81	3.07	2.67	3.31	2.95	3.19	2.67	2.81	3.07
.05	3.44	3.83	4.17	3.64	4.50	4.01	4.34	3.64	3.83	4.17

Mental Manipulation Task Comparisons

Significance Levels	DSB vs. LN	DSB vs. LNPA	DSB vs. SSpB	LN vs. SSpB	LN vs. AR*	LN vs. LNPA	LNPA vs. SSpB	AR vs. DSB*
.15	2.42	2.62	2.75	2.37	2.06	2.22	2.58	2.49
.05	3.29	3.57	3.74	3.23	2.80	3.02	3.51	3.38

*Indicates newly calculated values that do not appear in the WISC-IV Integrated manual.

(continued)

Mental Manipulation Task Comparisons

Significance Levels	AR vs. ARPA-A	AR vs. ARPA-B	AR vs. WA	ARPA-A vs. ARPA-B	ARPA-A vs. WA	ARPA-B vs. WA
.15	2.09	2.05	2.12	2.00	2.07	2.03
.05	2.84	2.79	2.88	2.72	2.81	2.76

Registration versus Mental Manipulation Task Comparisons

Significance Levels	DSF vs. DSB	DSF vs. LN*	DSF vs. AR	SSpF vs. SSpB	SSpF vs. LN*	SSpF vs. AR*
.15	2.66	2.27	2.22	2.76	2.43	2.50
.05	3.62	3.09	3.02	3.76	3.31	3.40

*Indicates newly calculated values that do not appear in the WISC-IV Integrated manual.

Based on the values in the previous table, clinicians can feel comfortable using a rounded value of 3 scaled score points to indicate a significant difference for any Working Memory Domain Subtest comparisons. In most cases, using a difference of 3 scaled score points is equivalent to using a value that is roughly halfway between the .15 and .05 levels.

Comparisons involving Time Bonus Process Scores represent a different kind of comparison than the subtest comparisons tabled here. ART and ARPA-AT are scores that are derived by applying an alternate scoring structure to their *parent* subtests AR and ARPA. Because they represent numerical transformations that assign different values to the same test performance, the only source of variance to account for in these transformed scores is due to differences in the amount of time taken to complete items (i.e., there is no source of error variance in these scores independent of the error variance already accounted for in the parent subtest). If you know how many items the child completed correctly, you can predict (i.e., calculate) with 100% accuracy the child's Time Bonus raw score.

It is therefore not really appropriate to calculate and use a standard error of measurement for these tasks to indicate the amount of possible variation in Time Bonus scores that is due to unaccounted for sources of variance on repeated administrations *of the parent task*. Likewise, differences between Time Bonus Process Scaled Scores and their parent Subtest Scaled Scores are not influenced equally by independent sources of error variance, making it inappropriate to average SEM values to obtain a statistically significant value for the reliability of a difference between these two scores, as the Time Bonus score is completely dependent on the parent subtest item scores and cannot vary independent of them.

The transformation of parent subtest scores into Time Bonus scores, how-ever, does not always produce a perfect correlation between the two sets of scores. This is because the Subtest raw score distribution has a more restricted range of values, and the less restricted set of values of the Time Bonus raw score distribution must be collapsed into ranges to fit the more restricted Subtest raw score range. A more detailed explanation of this effect is provided for the Perceptual Domain No Time Bonus Process Scores in Rapid Reference 8.21.

Because the variability in Time Bonus scores reflects only the variability in the factor intended to be represented by the score (i.e., a time bonus), the reliability of the transformation, contrary to what the correlation coefficients in the *WISC-IV Integrated Technical and Interpretive Manual* seem to suggest, is perfect. A specific set of AR item raw scores will always produce a specific AR scaled score; and when transformed to an ART raw score, this same set of AR item raw scores will always produce a specific ART scaled score. Clini-cians, therefore, need not look to a statistically derived value to determine if the difference obtained between a child's Time Bonus scaled score and the parent subtest scaled score reflects a true difference due to the factor intended to be assessed, but rather they can take the value obtained at face value. A scaled score difference of 0 means that, relative to the performance of same-age peers in the standardization sample, the child did not benefit from having the effect of a time bonus added to the score. A difference of +1 or more means that the child did benefit from having the time bonus added, and a difference of −1 or more means that the child was adversely affected by having the time bonus added. The larger the difference between AR and ART, the greater is the impact of processing speed, either negatively or posi-tively, on the child's performance.

Degree of Unusualness of Scaled Score Discrepancies

The cumulative percentages of the standardization sample (i.e., base rates) obtaining scaled score discrepancies of a particular magnitude between Core/Supplemental Subtests and their Process Subtest counterparts as provided in Appendix D, Table D.2 of the *WISC-IV Integrated Scoring and Ad-ministration Manual*. A subset of the values reflecting cumulative percentages of the standardization sample (i.e., base rates) obtaining scaled score dis-crepancies at or above the statistically significant difference of 3 scaled score points is summarized in the following tables for Working Memory Domain task comparisons. Some of the base rate data tabled here appear in Ap-pendix D, Tables D.10, D.12, and D.14 of the *WISC-IV Integrated Scoring and Administration Manual*. The additional base rates shown here were calculated by the author of this chapter using the WISC-IV Integrated standardization sample data.

(continued)

Registration Task Comparisons

Scaled Score Discrepancy	DSF > VDS	VDS > DSF	DSF > LSN	LSN > DSF	DSF > LSR	LSR > DSF	DSF > SSpF	SSpF > DSF
3	22.8	18.8	19.1	18.6	22.0	18.2	25.4	25.7
4	13.9	12.0	10.2	11.6	12.4	15.4	18.2	17.3
5	8.6	6.3	5.8	4.1	6.7	7.8	11.4	11.1
6	4.8	3.7	2.6	2.8	3.0	6.1	7.6	6.9
7	2.3	1.5	1.5	0.8	1.9	3.3	4.0	3.9

Registration Task Comparisons

Scaled Score Discrepancy	LSN > LSR	LSR > LSN	LSN > SSpF	SSpF > LSN	LSR > SSpF	SSpF > LSR	VDS > SSpF	SSpF > VDS
3	14.7	16.6	24.8	23.6	23.7	21.6	23.9	26.2
4	10.0	8.9	15.8	16.3	16.8	15.6	15.5	17.9
5	4.0	5.2	11.8	9.5	11.6	9.7	10.7	12.4
6	1.8	3.0	7.1	6.4	8.5	7.0	5.4	7.3
7	0.7	1.8	4.9	3.2	4.8	3.2	3.4	4.5

Registration Task Comparisons

Scaled Score Discrepancy	VDS > LSN	LSN > VDS	VDS > LSR	LSR > VDS
3	19.5	22.7	18.5	21.8
4	12.1	13.6	13.0	13.6
5	5.4	8.1	5.5	10.6
6	2.2	3.6	2.5	5.5
7	0.7	1.6	1.0	4.7

Mental Manipulation Task Comparisons

Scaled Score Discrepancy	DSB > LN	LN > DSB	DSB > LNPA	LNPA > DSB	DSB > SSpB	SSpB > DSB	LN > SSpB	SSpB > LN
3	18.5	22.4	19.5	20.0	25.4	24.3	21.7	23.9
4	11.1	12.7	10.7	12.0	15.8	16.1	13.3	15.6
5	6.5	6.3	7.2	6.4	10.3	11.3	8.1	9.6
6	4.4	3.0	4.0	2.9	7.2	6.5	5.1	6.1
7	2.8	1.4	2.2	0.8	4.1	4.1	2.6	3.6

Mental Manipulation Task Comparisons

Scaled Score Discrepancy	LN > AR	AR > LN	LN > LNPA	LNPA > LN	LNPA > SSpB	SSpB > LNPA	AR > DSB*	DSB > AR*
3	18.7	17.6	16.3	18.1	23.1	25.3	20.1	20.0
4	10.2	10.7	9.2	11.0	15.7	18.6	11.5	12.5
5	4.4	6.3	4.0	6.8	9.2	11.1	7.0	6.7
6	1.2	4.0	1.9	4.2	6.0	5.6	3.9	3.3
7	0.4	2.8	0.6	1.8	3.7	2.5	1.8	1.2

Mental Manipulation Task Comparisons

Scaled Score Discrepancy	AR > ART#	ART > AR#	AR > ARPA-A	ARPA-A > AR	AR > ARPA-B	ARPA-B > AR	AR > WA	WA > AR
3	6.8	4.0	6.1	10.1	8.6	10.3	13.7	12.4
4	3.4	2.2	1.7	5.1	2.1	5.3	6.7	5.5
5	2.1	1.3	0.8	2.1	0.6	2.5	3.8	1.5
6	1.5	0.8	0.6	1.3	0.2	1.0	1.3	1.0
7	0.9	0.3	0.4	0.4	0.2	0.2	0.6	0.4

Mental Manipulation Task Comparisons

Scaled Score Discrepancy	ARPA-A > ARPA-AT#	ARPA-AT > ARPA-A#	ARPA-A > ARPA-B	ARPA-B > ARPA-A	ARPA-A > WA	WA > ARPA-A	ARPA-B > WA	WA > ARPA-B
3	3.3	2.3	0.5	3.6	12.6	11.5	11.4	13.5
4	1.1	0.7	0.0	1.4	5.5	4.7	6.0	4.3
5	0.7	0.1	0.0	0.3	2.9	1.5	2.3	1.4
6	0.4	0.0	0.0	0.0	0.5	0.4	0.7	0.4
7	0.3	0.0	0.0	0.0	0.1	0.0	0.1	0.0

Registration versus Mental Manipulation Task Comparisons

Scaled Score Discrepancy	DSF > DSB	DSB > DSF	DSF > LN*	LN > DSF*	DSF > AR	AR > DSF	SSpF > SSpB	SSpB > SSpF
3	21.8	22.0	20.1	22.2	24.5	22.7	21.4	20.4
4	14.2	12.5	13.4	14.0	16.5	14.8	13.6	11.2
5	9.0	8.6	8.3	8.0	9.6	9.3	8.1	6.6
6	5.3	4.2	5.6	4.0	5.1	5.7	4.1	3.3
7	2.5	2.1	4.0	1.5	2.0	3.4	2.3	1.6

(continued)

Registration versus Mental Manipulation Task Comparisons

Scaled Score Discrepancy	SSpF > LN*	LN > SSpF*	SSpF > AR*	AR > SSpF*
3	22.7	22.1	23.4	22.5
4	14.3	13.6	17.4	15.1
5	9.5	7.9	9.6	8.5
6	7.4	3.5	4.9	4.9
7	4.9	1.4	2.3	2.8

*Note from the previous table that the percentage of the standardization sample demonstrating scaled score discrepancies of 3 points or more is roughly equal for both pair comparison conditions (e.g., DSF > SSpF; SSpF > DSF). Also note, however, that the size of the scaled score discrepancies representing differences demonstrated by less than 10%, or less than 5%, of the standardization sample vary widely depending on the tasks being compared.

When attempting to interpret the significance of scaled score discrepancies among Working Memory Domain tasks, clinicians are advised to use the worksheet presented in Figure 8.3. Using values of 5 or 6 scaled score points as the criteria for clinical significance for all comparisons, however, would assure both statistical significance of the obtained discrepancy as well as a high degree of unusualness of the occurrence of the differences within the standardization sample.

Working Memory Domain task scaled score differences required for statistical significance at the .15 and .05 levels are located in Appendix D, Tables D.10, D.12, and D.14 and are summarized in Rapid Reference 8.30 along with the additional values calculated for inclusion in this text. Given the range of the tabled values, it is reasonable to use a rounded value of 3 scaled score points to signify a statistically significant difference for comparisons involving Working Memory Domain Subtests.

Cumulative percentages of the standardization sample (base rates) obtaining various scaled score discrepancies involving various Working Memory Domain Subtest tasks are located in Appendix D, Tables D.11, D.13, and D.15 of the *WISC-IV Integrated Administration and Scoring Manual*. Additional Working Memory Domain discrepancy base rates were calculated by the author of this chapter using the WISC-IV Integrated standardization sample data. A summary table showing Working Memory Domain base rate data from the WISC-IV Integrated manual and base rate data from the analyses completed for this text is provided in Rapid Reference 8.30. Rapid Reference 8.30 also provides a discussion of guidelines for interpreting scaled score discrepancies and discrepancy comparison base rates.

Figure 8.3 provides a worksheet to aid in the interpretation of Working Memory Domain task scaled score comparisons. Rapid Reference 8.31 provides a case

Registration Task Comparison	Task 1 Raw Score (a)	Task 1 Scaled Score (b)	Task 2 Raw Score (c)	Task 2 Scaled Score (d)	Scaled Score Diff (b−d) (e)	Scaled Score Analyses Scaled Score Difference Significant? (e > 3)	Scaled Score Difference Unusual?		
DSF vs. VDS						Y N	$e = 5$ $Y < 10\%$	$e \geq 6$ $Y < 5\%$	N
DSF vs. LSN						Y N	$e = 5$ $Y < 10\%$	$e \geq 6$ $Y < 5\%$	N
DSF vs. LSR						Y N	$e = 5$ $Y < 10\%$	$e \geq 6$ $Y < 5\%$	N
DSF vs. SSpF						Y N	$e = 6$ $Y < 10\%$	$e \geq 7$ $Y < 5\%$	N
LSN vs. LSR						Y N	$e = 4$ $Y < 10\%$	$e \geq 5$ $Y < 5\%$	N
LSN vs. SSpF						Y N	$e = 5$ $Y < 10\%$	$e \geq 6$ $Y < 5\%$	N
LSR vs. SSpF						Y N	$e = 5$ $Y < 10\%$	$e \geq 6$ $Y < 5\%$	N
VDS vs. SSpF						Y N	$e = 5$ $Y < 10\%$	$e \geq 6$ $Y < 5\%$	N
VDS vs. LSN						Y N	$e = 5$ $Y < 10\%$	$e \geq 6$ $Y < 5\%$	N
VDS vs. LSR						Y N	$e = 5$ $Y < 10\%$	$e \geq 6$ $Y < 5\%$	N

Figure 8.3 Working Memory Domain Task Comparison Worksheet

Scaled Score Analyses

Mental Manipulation Task Comparison	Task 1 Raw Score (a)	Task 1 Scaled Score (b)	Task 2 Raw Score (c)	Task 2 Scaled Score (d)	Scaled Score Diff (b–d) (e)	Scaled Score Difference Significant? (e > 3)		Scaled Score Difference Unusual?		
DSB vs. LN						Y	N	e = 5 Y < 10%	e >= 6 Y < 5%	N
DSB vs. LNPA						Y	N	e = 5 Y < 10%	e >= 6 Y < 5%	N
DSB vs. SSpB						Y	N	e = 5 Y < 10%	e >= 6 Y < 5%	N
LN vs. SSpB						Y	N	e = 5 Y < 10%	e >= 6 Y < 5%	N
LN vs. AR						Y	N	e = 5 Y < 10%	e >= 6 Y < 5%	N
LN vs. LNPA						Y	N	e = 5 Y < 10%	e >= 6 Y < 5%	N
LNPA vs. SSpB						Y	N	e = 5 Y < 10%	e >= 6 Y < 5%	N
AR vs. DSB						Y	N	e = 5 Y < 10%	e >= 6 Y < 5%	N
AR vs. ARPA-A						Y	N	e = 3 Y < 10%	e >= 4 Y < 5%	N
AR vs. ARPA-B						Y	N	e = 3 Y < 10%	e >= 4 Y < 5%	N
AR vs. WA						Y	N	e = 4 Y < 10%	e >= 5 Y < 5%	N

Figure 8.3 (Continued)

Comparison					Scaled Score Difference Significant?	Scaled Score Difference Unusual?
ARPA-A vs. ARPA-B					Y N	e = 5 Y < 10% e >= 6 Y < 5% N
ARPA-A vs. WA					Y N	e = 5 Y < 10% e >= 6 Y < 5% N
ARPA-B vs. WA					Y N	e = 5 Y < 10% e >= 6 Y < 5% N

Scaled Score Analyses

Registration vs. Mental Manipulation Task Comparison	Task 1 Raw Score (a)	Task 1 Scaled Score (b)	Task 2 Raw Score (c)	Task 2 Scaled Score (d)	Scaled Score Diff (b–d) (e)	Scaled Score Difference Significant? e > ?	Scaled Score Difference Unusual? e >= ? e = ?
DSF vs. DSB						Y N	e = 5 Y < 10% e >= 6 Y < 5% N
DSF vs. LN						Y N	e = 5 Y < 10% e >= 6 Y < 5% N
DSF vs. AR						Y N	e = 5 Y < 10% e >= 6 Y < 5% N
SSpF vs. SSpB						Y N	e = 5 Y < 10% e >= 6 Y < 5% N
SSpF vs. LN						Y N	e = 5 Y < 10% e >= 6 Y < 5% N
SSpF vs. AR						Y N	e = 5 Y < 10% e >= 6 Y < 5% N

Figure 8.3 (Continued)

431

Mental Manipulation Task vs. Time Bonus Process Score	Time Bonus Process Scores		Subtest Scores		Scaled Score Analyses		
	Raw Score	Scaled Score	Raw Score	Scaled Score	Scaled Score Diff (b–d)	Scaled Score Difference Significant?	Scaled Score Difference Unusual?
	a	b	c	d	e	$e > ?$	$e \geq ?$ $e = ?$
AR vs. ART						$e > 1?$ Y N	$e = 3$ $e \geq 4$ Y < 10% Y < 5% N
ARPA-A vs. ARPA-AT						$e > 1?$ Y N	$e = 3$ $e \geq 4$ Y < 10% Y < 5% N

Figure 8.3 (Continued)

≡ Rapid Reference 8.31

Working Memory Domain Case Study

Kyle, Age 8-6, Grade 3

Kyle is a third grade student who has been receiving Tier II reading support since early first grade. Remedial instruction has focused on improving Kyle's reading comprehension, including more than 6 months of participation in a specially designed remedial reading instructional program that targets improvement of reading comprehension skills, with less than the expected results. Kyle's classroom teachers have consistently commented on his seeming lack of comprehension of what he is reading, one of the major reasons for the continued targeting of comprehension skills in remedial reading instruction. Although Kyle seemed to be making progress in the remedial instruction program when weekly assessments were completed in the second grade, he performed poorly on benchmark assessments completed each quarter. Now in his third year of Tier II remedial reading support, and with the pattern of weekly progress countered by lower than expected progress on quarterly assessments continuing, the team decided that a more comprehensive assessment was needed to help with further program decisions. Kyle was administered the WISC-IV and earned the following scores:

WISC-IV

Verbal Domain		Perceptual Domain	
Similarities	12	Block Design	11
Vocabulary	12	Picture Concepts	13
Comprehension	12	Matrix Reasoning	13
Verbal Comprehension Index	110	Perceptual Reasoning Index	115
Working Memory Domain		Processing Speed Domain	
Digit Span	11	Coding	10
Letter-Number Sequencing	8	Symbol Search	11
Working Memory Index	97	Processing Speed Index	103

Full Scale IQ   108

Kyle's performance produced average to above average range scores for all 4 Indexes and relatively uniform subtest scores within the Verbal, Perceptual and Processing Speed domains. Interpretation at the Index level suggests that

(continued)

Kyle has above average reasoning with visually presented nonverbal material (PRI 115), high average capacity for reasoning with and retrieving and expressing verbal information (VCI 110), average capacity for registering and manipulating auditorily presented verbal information (WMI 97), and average capacity for quickly processing nonverbal visual information (PSI 103). The significant but not unusual 3 point difference between Digit Span and Letter-Number Sequencing is the only apparent "crack" in what appears to be a solidly average or better Index score profile.

While scanning the completed record form, the psychologist quickly applied some elements of the process approach to item level interpretation, noting that Kyle was much more effective with digits forward items (raw score 9) than with digits backward items (raw score 5), and that for the Letter-Number Sequencing Subtest, Kyle typically repeated the string of letters and numbers verbatim rather than manipulating them into the requested order of numbers followed by letters. From the psychologist's perspective, these observations and the nature of Kyle's referral problems warranted closer examination using some of the Working Memory domain Supplemental and Process Subtests and Process scores. These yielded the following results:

Working Memory Domain Supplemental Subtest	
Arithmetic	6
Working Memory Domain Process Subtests and Scores	
Digit Span Forward	12
Digit Span Backward	8
Spatial Span Forward	12
Spatial Span Backward	6
Letter Span Nonrhyming	11
Letter Span Rhyming	6
Arithmetic with Time Bonus	6
Arithmetic Process Approach Part A	9
Arithmetic Process Approach Part B	9
Written Arithmetic	11

The Working Memory Domain Task Comparison Worksheet (see below) reflected several additional significant scaled score discrepancies that are relevant to understanding Kyle's cognitive profile.

Working Memory Domain Task Comparison Worksheet

Registration Task Comparison	Task 1 Raw Score	Task 1 Scaled Score	Task 2 Raw Score	Task 2 Scaled Score	Scaled Score Diff (b-d)	Scaled Score Difference Significant?	Scaled Score Difference Unusual?
	a	b	c	d	e	e > 3	e = 5 e >= 6
DSF vs. LSN	9	12	12	8	−3	Y	e = 5 e >= 6 N
DSF vs. LSR	9	12	3	6	6	Y	e = 5 e >= 6 Y < 5%
DSF vs. SSpF	9	12	7	12	0	N	e = 6 e >= 7 N
LSN vs. LSR	7	11	3	6	4	Y	e = 4 e >= 5 Y < 10%
LSN vs. SSpF	7	11	7	12	−1	N	e = 5 e >= 6 N
LSR vs. SSpF	3	6	7	12	−6	Y	e = 5 e >= 6 Y < 5%

Mental Manipulation Task Comparison	Task 1 Raw Score	Task 1 Scaled Score	Task 2 Raw Score	Task 2 Scaled Score	Scaled Score Diff (b-d)	Scaled Score Difference Significant?	Scaled Score Difference Unusual?
	a	b	c	d	e	e > 3	e = 5 e >= 6
DSB vs. LN	5	8	12	8	0	N	e = 5 e >= 6 N
DSB vs. SSpB	5	8	4	6	2	N	e = 5 e >= 6 N
LN vs. SSpB	12	8	4	6	2	N	N
LN vs. AR	12	8	14	6	2	N	e = 5 e >= 6 N
AR vs. DSB	14	6	5	8	=2	N	e = 5 e >= 6 N

(continued)

AR vs. ARPA-A	14	6	14*	9	−3	Y	e = 3 e >= 4 Y < 10%
AR vs. ARPA-B	14	6	15*	9	−3	Y	e = 3 e >= 4 Y < 10%
AR vs. WA	14	6	15*	11	−5	Y	e = 4 e >= 5 Y < 5%
ARPA-A vs. ARPA-B	14	9	15*	9	0	N	e = 5 e >= 6 N
ARPA-A vs. WA	14	9	15*	11	−2	N	e = 5 e >= 6 N
ARPA-B vs. WA	15	9	15*	11	−2	N	e = 5 e >= 6 N

Registration versus Mental Manipulation Task Comparison	Task 1		Task 2		Scaled Score Analyses		
	Raw Score	Scaled Score	Raw Score	Scaled Score	Scaled Score Diff (b-d)	Scaled Score Difference Significant?	Scaled Score Difference Unusual?
	a	b	c	d	e	e > 3	e >= ? e = ?
DSF vs. DSB	9	12	5	8	4	Y	e = 5 e >= 6 \N
DSF vs. LN	9	12	12	8	4	Y	e = 5 e >= 6 N
DSF vs. AR	9	12	14	6	6	Y	e = 5 e >= 6 Y < 5%
SSpF vs. SSpB	7	12	4	6	6	Y	e = 5 e >= 6 Y < 5%
SSpF vs. LN	7	12	12	8	4	Y	e = 5 e >= 6 N
SSpF vs. AR	7	12	14	9	3	Y	e = 5 e >= 6 N

Results from the additional Working Memory domain tasks and process scores revealed a very clear pattern of strengths and weaknesses in the performance of memory process tasks that provided great insight into Kyle's lack of academic progress in reading.

Kyle was significantly more effective with Digit Span Forward (12) than he was with Digit Span Backward (8), revealing a relative weakness with holding and manipulating series of digits despite adequate initial registration of digit series. This same weakness was observed in Kyle's Letter-Number Sequencing Subtest responses; Kyle had great difficulty with reorganizing the two and three digit items, typically repeating exactly what he heard. Manipulation of letters and numbers was only accomplished for three items involving a combination of three letters and numbers after the provision of a cue to do so. These results indicated a lack of working memory capacity despite average range scores for both of the Core Working Memory Domain Subtests.

Administration of the Spatial Span Subtest replicated the pattern of significant difference between forward and backward tasks (Spatial Span Forward 12; Spatial Span Backward 6). In terms of initial registration capacities, the finding that stood out most was the significant and unusual difference between Kyle's performance with the Letter Span Nonrhyming (11) and Letter Span Rhyming (6) tasks. Despite Kyle's demonstrated relative strength in initially registering and repeating number series and spatial locations and his ability to initially register and repeat individual series of phonemes (letter names) that sounded different from each other (e.g., x, l, q, h), he performed very poorly when required to initially register and repeat phoneme series that sounded very similar (e.g., z, d, p, b).

Significant working memory weaknesses also were apparent in Kyle's efforts with the Arithmetic Subtest (6), a finding that stood in contrast to Kyle's good class reports and test scores in math. Use of the Arithmetic Process Approach variations reflected improved performance into the average range when printed versions of the items remained in view, thereby reducing the working memory requirements of the Supplemental Arithmetic Subtest (ARPA-A, 9). When allowed to use a pencil and paper to attempt to complete the items he got wrong on the ARPA-A administration, Kyle was able to correctly answer an additional item, a performance consistent with the typical improvement observed in the standardization sample thereby resulting in an ARPA-B score (9) identical to his ARPA-A score (9) despite the additional improvement in performance. The results obtained with the ARPA-B procedure again supported the contention that working memory difficulties played a large role in Kyle's initial difficulties with the Arithmetic Subtest. Further support of the effect of working memory demands on mental arithmetic performance was evidenced by Kyle's significant improvement when using pencil and paper to perform the calculation equivalents of the Arithmetic Subtest mental arithmetic word problems (Written Arithmetic 11).

In the state where Kyle lives, comprehensive assessments are done collaboratively by a school psychologist and an educational evaluator. Based on the WISC-IV Integrated findings, the school psychologist consulted with the educational evaluator to ensure that Kyle would be administered measures of

(continued)

phonological awareness/processing, nonsense word decoding, and rapid naming along with the basic combination of word reading and reading comprehension tasks that often constituted a "full diagnostic reading profile" in this particular school district. The psychologist also asked the educational evaluator to note the number of times Kyle looked back at the passage when completing the reading comprehension task and the approximate length of these look-backs as well as the amount of time Kyle initially required to read each passage.

The educational evaluator's assessment produced the following scores:

KTEA-II Subtests	
Phonological Awareness	76
Naming Facility	100
Letter & Word Recognition	92
Nonsense Word Decoding	80
Word Recognition Fluency	85
Decoding Fluency	84
Reading Comprehension	109

Not surprisingly, Kyle performed very poorly when required to segment or blend the individual sounds in words (Phonological Processing 76) as well as when required to decode nonsense words, the reading skill that most heavily draws on an understanding of subword sound units and their relationship to letter and letter clusters (Nonsense Word Decoding 80). Kyle rapid naming capacity and word recognition skills were somewhat better developed, yielding score in the average range (Naming Facility 100, Letter & Word Recognition 92). When Kyle was required to apply his word reading and decoding skill quickly and efficiently, he earned scores that were at the below average-average range border (Word Recognition Fluency 85, Decoding Fluency, 84). The 15 point difference between Kyle's Naming Facility score (100) and his Word Recognition Fluency score (85), and the numerous word reading errors Kyle made on the latter task strongly suggested that his low Word Recognition Fluency score was due to problems with word reading skills rather than poor rapid naming capacities. Counter to the expectations of many, Kyle performed best with the reading comprehension task, earning a score in the upper end of the average range (Reading Comprehension 109). Although Kyle was able to answer many comprehension questions about the passages he read, he read each passage at a very slow rate and had to look back at the passage in order to "find" the answer to almost every question presented. These look-backs ranged in length from a few seconds to as much as 90 seconds depending on the type of question, the length of the passage, and the location of the relevant information in the passage.

Kyle's high average range score on the Reading Comprehension Subtest (109) came as a surprise to many members of the multidisciplinary team, especially in light of Kyle's teachers' observations related to his poor use of comprehension skills during both general education classroom reading. The school psychologist and the special education teacher, however, understood that Kyle's reading comprehension problems clearly were related to two factors: (1) his difficulties with holding and manipulating information in mind when reading and (2) his lack of decoding knowledge.

Kyle's relatively effective performance with the Letter & Word Recognition Subtest (94) reflected his capacity for rote memorization of word lists provided by his teachers as part of reading instruction since early first grade. This capacity for memorizing word lists was consistent with Kyle's average capacities for initial registration and recall of number and number-letter series, spatial locations and nonryhming phonemes. When Kyle encountered words he had not committed to sight recognition, however, he was unable to apply decoding rules and strategies to sound out these unknown words, tending to substitute words he knew for those he didn't know when reading real words, and substituting familiar real words for unfamiliar nonsense words. Kyle's decoding deficiencies were not a particular surprise to the special education teacher who knew that Kyle's remedial and classroom instruction had focused almost exclusively on reading comprehension, language enrichment, and vocabulary building. Decoding rules and strategies had not been introduced in any systematic, direct way in any of his remedial instruction, producing a state of instructional disability resulting from a lack of knowledge about these foundational skills that are so critical to the development of good independent reading. The special education teacher clearly understood how a lack of decoding knowledge was impacting Kyle's comprehension of text passages; if words in the text were not being decoded and identified correctly, the passages were not accessible to Kyle's effective comprehension skills. Additionally, the time and effort spent trying to recognize unknown words were disrupting the flow of text reading and drawing his minimal working memory resources away from his comprehension efforts.

Although Kyle's average reading comprehension score seems to contradict what is known about the effect of poor word decoding skills on comprehension, an understanding of the test development rationale typically used to construct individually-administered reading comprehension tasks such as the KTEA-II Reading Comprehension Subtest helps to dispel this seeming paradox. The reading passages of the KTEA-II Reading Comprehension Subtest are composed primarily of high frequency, easily read words (relative to a child's grade level) in order to emphasize assessment of comprehension of what was read rather than to assess the child's skill with decoding difficult, less familiar words. In this context, performance on the Reading Comprehension Subtest is often better thought of as an estimate of the child's potential for comprehending what is read when all, or most, of the words in the passage are recognizable to the child. The

(continued)

literature-based books being used in Kyle's classroom contained many words that were less familiar to Kyle, and these books were not being comprehended at the same level as the passages of the KTEA-II, resulting in a situation where the test score that Kyle earned was not consistent with the comprehension level observed in the classroom. What the KTEA-II Reading Comprehension score was best able to achieve for Kyle, however, was to indicate where Kyle's comprehension skills were likely to be if he were to learn how to effectively decode the words that were not recognizable to him.

The process-oriented observations gathered and reported by the educational evaluator, however, did reflect behaviors consistent with the processing weaknesses reflected in the results with WISC-IV Integrated tasks that required the use of working memory capacities. Kyle's difficulties with holding and manipulating information in mind were reflected in the number and length of look-backs Kyle had to use to extract meaning from the text he read. Although Kyle understands how to extract meaning from text, he had difficulties holding onto and actively processing the passages he read. As a result, he had to resort to rereadings of parts of passages cued by the context of a leading question in order to get the meaning from the text. Such working memory difficulties are compounding Kyle's comprehension problems caused by his inability to decode words.

It is also important to note that the school psychologist had the classroom and remedial reading teachers and Kyle's parents rate Kyle's self-regulation capacities with the Behavior Rating Inventory of Executive Functions (BRIEF). Results of the BRIEF reflected no concerns with self-regulation; rather, the ratings indicated that the use of many self-regulation capacities were a relative strength for Kyle. Kyle's effective use of executive functions in the classroom likely had a great deal to do with his ability to produce for his teachers on a daily basis and do well on the weekly assessments despite his relative inability to improve his reading comprehension skills as reflected on the quarterly assessments. While Kyle was willing and able to profit from instruction, the instruction that was being offered was not addressing his specific skill deficits, thereby having a minimal effect on his reading comprehension skill. Despite his working memory difficulties, Kyle has been able to use his well-developed self-regulation capacities to profit from the excellent math instruction he is receiving and the result is average to above average scores on tests of math achievement including quarterly and state-mandated assessments. Kyle's strong need for visual aids in learning math, however, must be duly noted by his math teachers. If the excellent use of visuals that is currently part of his math curriculum is removed in later years, Kyle is at risk of falling behind his peers in math skill development.

Summary

The findings of Kyle's assessment posed a dilemma for the team. Although the school psychologist and special education teacher provided a compelling argument for the nature of Kyle's reading problems and the need for the addition of direct, systematic decoding instruction to his remedial reading program, the only professional competently trained in the use of such decoding instruction strategies was the special education teacher. Fortunately for Kyle, the combination of his lack of response to intervention coupled with the significant discrepancy between his VCI score of 110 and his Nonsense Word Decoding score 80 provided a solid rationale for classifying Kyle as learning disabled, despite his lack of exposure to reading instruction in decoding skills. (It should be noted that one of the team's problems was the exclusive use of reading comprehension passage benchmarks for progress monitoring rather than a combination of measures of word reading, decoding, fluency, and comprehension). Of interest here is the fact that the education evaluator objected to the classification of Kyle using the Nonsense Word Decoding Subtest discrepancy, incorrectly referencing a section in a recently published authoritative text on learning disabilities (Fletcher, Lyon, Fuchs & Barnes, 2007, pages 76–77), and suggesting that the text indicated that the Letter & Word Recognition Subtest should be used for comparison rather than the Nonsense Word Decoding Subtest.

In the end, the team agreed to classify Kyle as a child with a reading disability and provided an IEP that addressed Kyle's need for systematic decoding skill instruction. Kyle's strengths in executive function capacities are likely to enable him to grasp the decoding skill instruction that he will be offered, and the outlook for increased reading comprehension is good.

Kyle's case illustrates several points about the use of the WISC-IV Integrated tasks and features:

1. In the hands of a psychologist that understands the relationship of abilities, processes, and skills involved in the development of reading capacities, the WISC-IV Integrated can be an extremely useful tool to assist in the proper identification of cognitive capacities that are likely to be having an impact on reading achievement.

2. Appropriate diagnosis of learning disabilities requires an adequate amount of diagnostic assessment. Had the school psychologist and the education evaluator followed the typical practices of this school district, only the WISC-IV Core Subtests and the KTEA-II Letter & Word Recognition and Reading Comprehension Subtests would have been used; Kyle's severe ability-achievement discrepancy would not have been recognized and the process and skill deficits affecting his reading achievement would not have been identified. Without a clear picture of Kyle's cognitive and academic strengths and weaknesses, appropriate instructional strategies might not have been identified and recommended for use with Kyle.

3. The absence of severe deficits in either Index or Subtest scores does not necessarily indicate the absence of clinically relevant ability or process deficits. Careful observation of how a child performs tasks can be critical to

(continued)

seeing the "chink in the armor" of a child who is effectively coping with existing deficits in the best way they know how, whether or not instructional practices are helping with such coping.

4. The presence of working memory deficits in a child's profile does not guarantee that skill deficiencies will be present. The critical role of executive functions in enabling a child to use the capacities they have as effectively as possible or to benefit from good instruction is important to acknowledge. With the right instruction provided, some children who effectively self-regulate will be able to overcome their working memory deficits and achieve at a level commensurate with, or better than, their grade placement.

5. Initial registration and working memory capacities are highly related, but they are also dissociable, that is, a child might have good initial registration capacities despite the presence of significant weaknesses in working memory capacities, or vice versa.

study example that includes the use of the interpretive worksheet and illustrates the application of WISC-IV Integrated process-approach procedures in the interpretations of Working Memory Domain task performance.

Processing Speed Domain

The WISC-IV Integrated application of the process approach to the Processing Speed Domain tasks is accomplished through the use of Process Subtests; subtest scaled score discrepancy comparison tables indicating subtest scaled score significant discrepancy values and base rates for discrepancies; additional Process Scores and base rates for Core, Supplemental, and Process Subtests; and process-approach observation base rates. The WISC-IV Integrated includes two Process Subtests based on the content of the Processing Speed Domain Coding subtest: Coding Copy (CDC) and Coding Recall (CDR). Coding Copy is a processing speed variant that reduces the cognitive demands of the Coding subtest. Although the Coding Recall Subtest is based on the content of the Coding Subtest, the process-approach procedures it employs generate measures of incidental recall rather than variants involving modification of processing speed demands. Process-approach procedures involve recording observations of completion strategy for the Cancellation Subtest items and the number of items completed during 30-second time intervals for the Core Coding Subtest (Form B) and the Coding Copy Process Subtest. Rapid Reference 8.32 provides information about the administration and scoring of the Processing Speed Domain Process Subtests and process-approach procedures.

≡ Rapid Reference 8.32

Administration and Scoring of the Processing Speed Domain Process Subtests

Administration and scoring of the Processing Speed Domain tasks is straightforward and easy to learn quickly for clinicians experienced with individually administered test directions. A few points will help clinicians to quickly get familiar with these tasks:

- Directions for administering and scoring all of the Processing Speed Process Subtests and process procedures are located in the *WISC-IV Integrated Administration and Scoring Manual*.
- Both the Coding Copy and the Coding Recall Subtests require the use of Response Booklet 3 for task administration.
- Unlike all other Process Subtests, *Coding Recall must be administered immediately after administration of the WISC-IV core battery Coding Subtest*. The Coding Recall Subtest cannot be validly administered after completion of the core battery.
- Process-approach procedures can be applied to the Core Subtests Coding and Symbol Search, the Supplemental Subtest Cancellation, and the Process Subtest Coding Copy. These procedures involve recording observations during the standard administration of these subtests.
- The Coding Copy Process Subtest is a timed, 2-minute task.

Scaled score equivalents for the Coding Copy Process Subtest and Cancellation Process Scores (Cancellation Random and Cancellation Structured) are located in the *WISC-IV Integrated Administration and Scoring Manual* in Appendix C, Table C.4. Scaled score differences required for statistical significance are provided in Table B.3 for Core and Supplemental Processing Speed Subtests and in Table D.25 for Process Subtests and Process Scores. Scaled score discrepancy comparison base rates are provided in Table B.4 for Processing Speed Domain Core and Supplemental Subtest comparisons and in Table D.26 for Process Subtests and Process scores. Table D.27 provides base rates for process-approach observations of Cancellation Subtest strategies, and Tables D.29 and D.30 provide base rates for time interval performance on Coding B and Coding Copy. Coding Recall raw score base rates for Cued Symbol Recall, Free Symbol Recall, and Cued Digit Recall are provided in Table D.28.

When to Use the Processing Speed Domain Process Subtests

In many cases, the Coding Copy Process Subtest will enable clinicians to gather information about a child's graphomotor capacities without the need for additional multitasking involving symbol coding. In other cases, the Process Subtests, Process Scores, and process procedures will enable a clinician to gain greater insight into how a child performs the Processing Speed Domain tasks and possible sources of cognitive strengths or weaknesses. The Processing Speed Domain Process Subtests and process-approach procedures are not intended to be used with every child who is assessed. There are no set rules dictating the specifics of the use of the Processing Speed Domain Process Subtests other than that (a) administration of the Coding Recall tasks must occur immediately after administration of the Coding Subtest *during the administration of the core battery*, and (b) administration of the Coding Copy Subtest must occur after completion of the administration of the Core and Supplemental Subtests of the WISC-IV.

Because most of the Processing Speed Domain process-approach procedures involve recording observations while administering Core and Supplemental Subtests, clinicians will need to make decisions about whether or not to use these procedures prior to administration of the Core and Supplemental Subtests. The decision to use one or more Processing Speed Domain process-approach procedures will therefore be based on information that is obtained prior to the administration of the WISC-IV Core and Supplemental Subtests, such as parent and/or teacher input, records review, or interactions with the child prior to the start of the WISC-IV.

After administration of the Core and Supplemental Subtests, the clinician may choose to administer Coding Copy based on observations of the child's performance or the score earned on the Coding Subtest or Coding Recall based on observations regarding difficulties with the memory process demands of various tasks. Rapid Reference 8.33 lists conditions most likely to lead to the use of the Processing Speed Domain process-approach procedures.

Use and Interpretation of the Processing Speed Domain Process Subtests

To effectively use and interpret the Processing Speed Domain Process Subtests, it is necessary to have an understanding of the multifactorial nature of the Processing Speed Core and Supplemental Subtests in terms of the cognitive capacities they assess. Similarly, clinicians need to understand what cognitive capacities are assessed by the Coding Copy and Coding Recall Process Subtests and how these can be used in concert with the Core and Supplemental Subtests to obtain a clearer picture of a child's cognitive strengths and weaknesses.

What Do Processing Speed Domain Core, Supplemental, and Process Subtests Measure?

The Processing Speed Domain Subtests were designed primarily to assess the use of processing speed with nonverbal, visual stimuli. Assessment of processing

≡ *Rapid Reference 8.33*

. . . .

When to Use the Processing Speed Domain Process Subtests and Procedures

Because of the preconditions for their use, the decision to employ Processing Speed Domain process-approach procedures needs to occur prior to the administration of the WISC-IV Core and Supplemental Subtests. Most of the process-approach procedures involve recording observations while the child performs the Processing Speed Core and Supplemental tasks. In addition, when Coding Recall is used, it must be administered immediately after administration of the Coding Subtest. The decision to use the Coding Copy Process Subtest, however, is often made after observing a child's performance with the core battery Coding Subtest.

Prior to administration of the WISC-IV, information gathered from parents, teachers, and background records can inform the clinician about situations in which the use of Processing Speed Domain Process Subtests and Procedures might be warranted. These situations could include:

Background information indicating

- delays in fine motor or graphomotor development
- slow processing speed or slow work pace
- poor handwriting, especially when a diagnosis of ADI ID is present
- traumatic brain injury, including concussions
- history of Occupational Therapy services

Concerns expressed by parents or teachers

- slow work pace, slow processing speed, difficulty with timed tasks
- poor graphomotor (handwriting) skills or poor pencil-handling skills
- poor use of visual-perceptual skills
- poor organization skills
- difficulty with sustained attention for basic tasks

After administration of the WISC-IV, observations of how the child performed the Core and/or Supplemental Processing Speed Domain Subtests and/or the scores earned on these subtests may lead to the decision to administer the Coding Copy Subtest, whereas difficulties with tasks involving memory processes may lead to the decision to administer the Coding Recall tasks. In the case of behavior observations, it may be the way in which the child performed the tasks rather than the scores the child obtained that leads to the administration of the process subtests. Observations and scores leading to the use of process subtests could include:

(continued)

Observations during testing

- poor graphomotor or pencil-handling skills (e.g., immature pencil grip, excessive pressure when recording symbols)
- slow or inconsistent work pace
- errors in Coding Subtest symbol recording

Scores earned on the WISC-IV Core and/or Supplemental Subtests

For Coding Copy use:

- when all Processing Speed Subtest scores are in the Below Average range or lower
- when the Coding Subtest score is in the Below Average range or lower

For Coding Recall use:

- when all Working Memory Subtest scores are in the Below Average range or lower

speed is the primary focus of interpretation of the Processing Speed Index as well as the individual Processing Speed Domain subtests. The role of processing speed in task performance is discussed in Rapid Reference 8.34.

Beyond the primary cognitive capacity targeted for assessment with the Processing Speed Domain Subtests, the specific formats of each subtest make demands on the child that require the engagement of additional cognitive capacities in order to achieve success. While these capacities typically are required for effective subtest performance, they are not considered to be the primary target of the assessment (i.e., the intention of the subtest is not to quantitatively assess the child's use of these cognitive capacities). These secondary cognitive capacities include Visual Discrimination, Graphomotor abilities/skills, Attention to Visually Presented Information, and multiple executive functions applied to cue and direct the use of visual processing and processing speed resources. The roles of these secondary cognitive capacities in subtest performance are described in detail in Rapid Reference 8.34.

The Processing Speed Index comprised of the Core battery Coding and Symbol Search Subtests offers a fairly limited measure of processing speed. Both of the PSI Subtests employ a visual presentation format that requires the processing of nonverbal visual stimuli and graphomotor responses. The subtests selected for inclusion in the PSI do not address processing speed directly applied to academic tasks such as the fluent reading or writing of words or the completion of

≡ Rapid Reference 8.34

Cognitive Capacities Assessed with the Processing Speed Domain Core and Supplemental Subtests

Primary Cognitive Capacities

Visual, Motor, and Visuomotor Processing Speed—As the name given to the composite of the Core Subtest implies, *processing speed* is the primary capacity intended to be assessed with the Core and Supplemental Processing Speed Subtests. Each of these subtests must be completed within a specified amount of time, and the tasks are relatively simple and clearly demonstrated so as to require little or no reasoning to *figure out* how to complete them. Slower processing speed with these tasks can be the result of slow speed of visual processing, slow speed of motor movement, or slow speed only when required to integrate visual processing with motor movement. The Symbol Search Subtest is likely to be affected the least by motor processing-speed problems. Factors other than processing speed, however, can influence performance on these tasks, as specified in the following.

Secondary Cognitive Capacities

Visual Acuity—While attempting to perform the Processing Speed Domain tasks, visual acuity is necessary to ensure that all of the visual elements of each task can be accurately viewed. If the child cannot see clearly all of the visual information provided for each task, poor performance marked by slow speed or incorrect responses may result. Typically, a child's visual acuity is assessed and verified to be within normal limits with or without the use of corrective lenses prior to test administration so that this capacity should not be a factor in performance. If overlooked, however, visual acuity problems can significantly impact task performance with any or all of the Processing Speed Domain Subtests.

Attention to Visual Stimuli—To perform Processing Speed Domain tasks, the child must have the capacity for focusing and sustaining attention for the visual stimuli of each task.

Visual Perception/Representation—To perform Processing Speed Domain tasks, the child must have the perceptual capacity to form relatively accurate visual representations of the stimuli presented. Some younger children and severely perceptually impaired older children might lack this capacity and have difficulty visually organizing the information being presented, especially the more abstract geometric representations of the Symbol Search Subtest.

Visual Discrimination—All of the Processing Speed Domain tasks require careful application of visual discrimination abilities (i.e., the ability to see visual similarities and differences in the visual stimuli being presented). As is the case with Visual Perception, some younger children and severely perceptually impaired older children might lack this capacity and have difficulty seeing the

(continued)

visual similarities and differences in the visual images being presented, especially the more abstract geometric representations of the Symbol Search Subtest.

Graphomotor Ability—The Coding Subtest requires the child to handle a pencil and transcribe code symbols into empty boxes continuously for a 2-minute period. While not as demanding on the motor system, the Symbol Search Subtest requires the child to draw a slash through the "yes" or "no" boxes to complete each item for a period of 2 minutes and the Cancellation Subtest requires the child to draw a slash through as many animal pictures as possible in 45 seconds. Children who may be lacking in motor coordination for a variety of reasons may find it difficult to transcribe the coding symbols at all or to continue the transcription process for 2 minutes. Slowed performance, poorly formed symbols, or coding errors may result from motor-coordination difficulties and/or motor fatigue. Such difficulties are most likely to be observed in Coding Subtest performance.

Visualization and Working Memory Applied to Visual Stimuli—There should be little doubt that being able to generate visual images "in the mind's eye" and hold and manipulate such visual images can enhance a child's performance with all of the Processing Speed Domain Subtests. For the Coding Subtest, movement can be reduced and time might be saved if the child can hold in mind the number-symbol associations. For the Symbol Search Subtest, being able to hold in mind the visual images of the target symbols while inspecting the symbols to the right of the targets can reduce the need for repeated back-and-forth scanning with each item. For all three of the Processing Speed Subtests, the child must hold in mind the directions for task completion for either 2 minutes (Coding and Symbol Search) or 45 seconds (Cancellation), but it could be argued that such holding of information does not require mental manipulation of the directions and the repetitious nature of the tasks continually reinforces the initial registration of the directions, thereby eliminating the necessity for working memory. Other than the possible minimal involvement in holding subtest directions, working memory capacities do not really need to be engaged in order for a child to perform well with any of the Processing Speed tasks. A child who is exceptionally fast can continually refer back to the code key when doing the Coding Subtest or update the visual images of the target and choice symbols by continually rescanning the stimuli of each Symbol Search item, thereby minimizing the need for any involvement of working memory capacities.

Language Representation of Visual Stimuli—A child may find it useful to verbally label the Coding Subtest symbols and symbol-number associations and recite these during performance of the task, to verbally describe visual features of the Symbol Search stimuli, or to verbally state the rule for the Cancellation tasks. Although such verbal mediation may enhance performance for children who choose to use it, it is by no means a necessity for successful performance.

Executive Functions—As a class of cognitive capacities, executive functions are responsible for cueing and directing the use of other mental capacities that are used for the purposes of perceiving, feeling, thinking, and acting. As such, they are intricately involved in the performance of all the tasks of the WISC-IV. The degree of involvement of specific executive functions in the performance of specific subtests, however, is highly variable and dependent on many factors including the directions provided to the child about how to perform the task and the input, processing, and output demands of the task. In the case of the Processing Speed Domain Subtests, it is important to understand the role of executive functions in cueing and directing the use of both primary and secondary cognitive capacities. For most subtests, demands for the use of executive functions are reduced to a great degree through the use of explicit directions and teaching examples that model how to perform a task and/or the kind of response that is desired. For some children however, even these executive function aids do not help to ameliorate the effects of their severe executive function deficits, and the effects of these deficits often can be observed in a child's efforts to perform tasks.

For the Processing Speed Domain subtests, accurate responding depends in part on the effective use of one or more of the following executive function capacities:

- cueing and directing efficient perception of visual stimuli
- cueing the appropriate consideration of the cognitive demands of a task and the amount of mental effort required to effectively perform the task
- cueing and directing the focusing of attention to visual details and task demands
- cueing and directing sustained attention to task
- cueing and directing the organization and/or planning of work strategies
- cueing and directing the execution of motor routines
- cueing and directing visual, motor, and visual-motor processing speed
- cueing and directing a work pace that can achieve the needed balance between speed and accuracy
- cueing and directing the monitoring of work and the correcting of errors
- cueing and directing the coordination of the use of multiple mental capacities simultaneously
- cueing and directing the inhibition of impulsive responding
- cueing and directing the use of working memory resources
- cueing and directing the generating of novel solutions or making associations with prior knowledge that lead to problem solutions (e.g., referring back to own work instead of looking up at the coding key)

math problems. As a result of this narrow focus of input, processing, and output demands, PSI scores have limited generalizability to academic settings. Clinicians who wish to know about a child's processing speed for reading cannot infer this from the PSI score or the individual Symbol Search or Coding Subtest scores. Such information needs to be obtained from one or more specific measures of reading speed. From a process-approach perspective, however, there is a link between performance on the Coding Subtest and written expression production. Because effective performance of both Coding and written expression tasks involves basic graphomotor ability or skills, a child who experiences extreme difficulties with graphomotor production on the Coding Subtest is likely to experience similar difficulties with the graphomotor demands of written expression tasks. Additionally, the multitasking demands of the Coding Subtest are similar to the multitasking demands of written expression tasks, and both require the effective use of executive function capacities to direct and coordinate such multitasking performance. When a child earns a low score on the Coding Subtest, performance with written expression production should be assessed. Use of the Coding Copy Process Subtests also can offer important insights into how a child responds to reduced graphomotor and multitasking demands. Because of the increased complexity involved in producing words and sentences in writing, however, a high score on the Coding Subtest is no guarantee that a child will not experience graphomotor or other kinds of difficulties with written expression tasks.

When Processing Speed Domain Subtest scores are interpreted, either collectively using the PSI or individually, it is typically assumed that score levels reflect the general level of processing speed. It is often the case that the secondary capacities required for effective performance are either ignored completely or assumed to be intact and functioning as expected to allow for the focus of interpretation to be on the primary capacities. For example, if a child earns a low score on the Coding Subtest, the assumption often is that the child's processing speed is slower than that of same-age peers. In many cases in which low performance is observed, such an assumption is not necessarily warranted. To know if the assumption about the primary capacity is valid, the role of the secondary cognitive capacities in task performance must be understood and explored in detail. When not accessed, or when applied ineffectively, these secondary cognitive capacities can interfere with task performance to a significant degree, making it inappropriate to focus subtest score interpretation exclusively on the primary capacities thought to be assessed.

When low scores or scores that are not consistent with what is known about the child are obtained with one or more of the Core or Supplemental Processing Speed Subtests, Coding Copy and the other process-approach procedures can be used to test hypotheses about the sources of poor or unusual performance. As indicated in the previous discussion, poor performance on these tasks is thought to reflect a lack of processing speed resources. Clinicians who appreciate that a low score on one or more of the Processing Speed Domain Subtests could be due to many different sources can draw on Coding Copy and Cancellation Process Scores and process-approach procedures to help obtain a better understanding of why the child performed poorly and the educational implications of such poor performance. Coding Copy alters many of the cognitive demands of the Coding Subtest, as detailed in Rapid Reference 8.35. The Cancellation Process Scores enable a clinician to understand variability in Cancellation item performance based on varying the organization and/or planning demands of the two items, as described in Rapid Reference 8.35.

≡ Rapid Reference 8.35

How Coding Copy Changes the Cognitive Demands of Coding

Coding Copy only requires the child to view rows of visual symbols and copy the symbols into empty boxes located directly below the symbols as quickly as possible. Although graphomotor abilities/skills and visual, motor, and visual-motor processing speeds are still required for task performance, this simplification of the task results in some reduction of cognitive demands, including:

- reduced need for multitasking of graphomotor abilities/skills with visual search and scanning and visual code matching
- reduced likelihood of involvement of working memory resources
- reduced likelihood of involvement of organization and/or planning abilities/skills
- reduced need for executive direction and coordination of multitasking
- reduced likelihood of executive function cueing of
  - the use of working memory
  - the use of organization and/or planning abilities/skills
  - the use of novel strategies to improve performance

How Cancellation Random and Cancellation Structured Differ in Terms of Cognitive Demands

The Cancellation Subtest is comprised of two separate timed visual search items. The first item—Cancellation Random (CAR)—involves locating and crossing out as many animal pictures as possible in 45 seconds on an 11 × 17 page full of pictures of animals and other objects randomly placed and spaced on the page. The second item—Cancellation Structured (CAS)—involves conducting a similar

(continued)

search of another 11 × 17 page full of objects to find only the animal pictures, but now the objects are arranged across the page in even rows. The altered visual format of CAS results in some reduction of cognitive demands, including:

- reduced need for organization and/or planning abilities/skills to conduct a search
- reduced need for executive function involvement to cue the use of an organized, self-directed search

Interpreting CAR versus CAS Scaled Score Discrepancies

As reflected in the raw score to scaled score conversion tables for CAR and CAS, a majority of children benefit from the format change from random placement to structured rows (i.e., it requires more raw score points on CAS in order to maintain the same scaled score as that earned on CAR).

Similar to the circumstances with comparing Verbal Domain Multiple Choice Process Subtests with their Core/Supplemental counterparts, the relationship between CAR and CAS scaled scores follow three distinct patterns:

CAR = CAS: When CAR and CAS scaled scores are identical, the child performed better with the CAS format in a manner that was consistent with the increases demonstrated by same-age children in the standardization sample earning CAR scaled scores of a similar magnitude.

CAS > CAR: When the CAS scaled score is greater than the CAR scaled score, the child performed even better with the CAS structured format than the increases typically demonstrated by same-age children in the standardization sample earning CAR scaled scores of a similar magnitude. When a child's CAS scaled score is significantly greater than the CAR scaled score, the gains from the use of the CAS structured format can be extremely large. As the size of the scaled score difference increases in favor of the CAS score, the larger the percent of raw score increase demonstrated by the child.

CAR > CAS: In many cases, when a CAS scaled score is less than the CAR scaled score, the child performed better with CAS structured format, but the increase demonstrated was less than the increases typically demonstrated by same-age children in the standardization sample earning CAR scaled scores of a similar magnitude. Only in a smaller number of cases does a CAS scaled score that is less than the CAR scaled score reflect poorer performance with the structured format. When a child's CAS scaled score is significantly lower than his or her CAR scaled scorer, the raw score change resulting from the structured format is more likely to be 0 and may even move into the negative range as the size of the discrepancy in favor of the CAR scaled score increases into the statistically unusual range of 4 scaled score points or more.

Interpreting Cancellation Process Observations

Clinicians have the option of carefully observing the child as he or she performs each Cancellation item and roughly tracing the child's search path as he or she works. After administration, the search paths can be coded into one of four categories as follows:

Code	Initial Approach	Later Approach
A	Started Organized	Remained Organized
B	Started Organized	Became Disorganized
C	Started Disorganized	Became Organized
D	Started Disorganized	Remained Disorganized

Base rates for each coded strategy are provided in Appendix D, Table D.27 of the *WISC-IV Integrated Administration and Scoring Manual*. Data from the base rate table support the contention that the structured format of CAS reduces the cognitive demands present with CAR by providing a strong prompt for the use of an organized search strategy. The base rate data indicate the following:

Consistent use of an organized strategy (A) increased with age for CAR but remained fairly stable across all ages for CAS.

Consistent use of an organized strategy (A) occurred more frequently for CAS than for CAR at all ages except age 16, when an organized strategy was used equally for both CAS and CAR by a majority of the children.

Consistent use of a disorganized strategy (D) decreased with age for CAS but not necessarily for CAR.

Consistent use of a disorganized strategy (D) was less likely to occur for CAS than for CAR at all ages.

Shifting from a disorganized to an organized strategy (C) occurred more often for CAS than for CAR at most ages.

Shifting from an organized to a disorganized (B) occurred more often for CAR than for CAS below the age of 12.

Clinicians who observe and record a child's search patterns for the CAR and CAS items can gain insight into the child's use, or lack of use, of organization abilities and executive function capacities by comparing the child's strategy selections to those of same-age peers in the standardization sample. Base rate data suggest that the older the child, the more likely it is that a consistent, organized strategy will be employed for both items.

The Coding Recall Process Subtest involves process tasks that reflect a child's incidental recall of the symbols and the symbol-number associations used in the Coding Subtest. As such, it is not a measure of processing speed but rather a measure of incidental memory processing.

It should be clear from the information provided in Rapid Reference 8.35 that Coding Copy and the Cancellation Process Scores and process observations can provide the clinician with a chance to see how specific cognitive demands can affect a child's performance. While the process scores are valuable indicators of how effective the child is with the use of select cognitive capacities, their value as an interpretive tool is enhanced when they are compared to the scores earned on other Processing Speed tasks. Such comparisons enable the clinician to generate or further test hypotheses about the effects of task format and input, processing, and output demands.

As noted previously, there are instances in which secondary cognitive capacity demands will reduce the child's effectiveness with task performance. From a clinical perspective, knowing when cognitive demands reduce effectiveness is as important as knowing when an altered format increases effectiveness. Rapid Reference 8.36 provides an interpretive summary table that can be used to assist with the comparison of Processing Speed Domain tasks in terms of the cognitive capacities that may be involved in the performance of each task.

≡ Rapid Reference 8.36

Cognitive Capacities Likely to Be Assessed by Processing Speed Domain Tasks and Reflected in Scaled Score Values

Cognitive Capacity	Processing Speed Domain Task					
	CD	CDC	SS	CAR	CAS	CDR
Visual Processing Speed	XXX	XXX	XXX	XXX	XXX	
Motor Processing Speed	XXX	XXX	XX	XX	XX	
Visual-Motor Processing Speed	XXX	XXX	XX	XX	XX	
Retrieval of incidentally stored information						XXX
Attention to Visual Details	XX	XX	XX	XX	XX	XX
Visual Perception	XX	XX	XX	XX	XX	XX
Visual Discrimination	XX	XX	XX	XX	XX	XX
Multitasking	XXX	XX				
Organization and/or Planning Ability/Skills	X			XX	X	

Cognitive Capacity	Processing Speed Domain Task					
	CD	CDC	SS	CAR	CAS	CDR
Graphomotor Ability/Skill	XX	XX	X	X	X	X
Visualization/Use of Working Memory with Visual Material	X		X			XX
Language Representation of Visual Stimuli	X		X	X	X	X
Executive Functions:						
EF—Cueing and directing efficient perception of visual stimuli	XX	XX	XX	XX	XX	XX
EF—Cueing the appropriate consideration of the cognitive demands of a task and the amount of mental effort required to effectively perform the task	XX	XX	XX	XX	XX	
EF—Cueing and directing the focusing of attention to visual details and task demands	XX	XX	XX	XX	XX	
EF—Cueing and directing sustained attention to task	XX	XX	XX	XX	XX	
EF—Cueing and directing the execution of motor routines	XX	XX	X	X	X	X
EF—Cueing and directing visual, motor, and visual-motor processing speed	XX	XX	XX	XX	XX	
EF—Cueing and directing a work pace that can achieve a balance between speed and accuracy	XX	XX	XX	XX	XX	
EF—Cueing and directing the monitoring of work and the correcting of errors	XX	XX	XX	XX	XX	XX
EF—Cueing and directing the coordination of the use of multiple mental capacities simultaneously	XX	XX	XX	XX	XX	XX

(continued)

Cognitive Capacity	Processing Speed Domain Task					
	CD	CDC	SS	CAR	CAS	CDR
EF—Cueing and directing the inhibition of impulsive responding			XX			
EF—Cueing and directing the use of working memory resources	X		X			X
EF—Cueing and directing the planning/organization of work strategies	X			XX	X	
EF—Cueing and directing the generating of novel solutions or retrieving associations to improve performance	X			XX	X	
EF—Cueing and directing retrieval of incidentally stored information						XX

XXX = Primary Capacity targeted for assessment with the task.
XX = Secondary Capacity highly likely to be impacting task performance.
X = Secondary Capacity possibly impacting task performance.

INTERPRETIVE SCORE COMPARISONS

Meaningful interpretation of scaled score comparisons starts with the determination of whether a statistically significant and clinically meaningful difference exists between the scores earned on the subtests being compared. The WISC-IV Integrated manual provides tables for statistically significant scaled score discrepancies and for scaled score discrepancy base rates for the Processing Speed Domain tasks. Additional comparison values were calculated using the same procedures as those outlined in the *WISC-IV Integrated Technical and Interpretive Manual* and are included in Rapid Reference 8.37. The values provided here and in the WISC-IV manual are based on the data obtained from the performance of the WISC-IV Integrated standardization sample of 730 children with the exception of the tables reporting Core and Supplemental Subtest values, which are based on the WISC-IV standardization sample of 2,200 children.

Processing Speed Domain scaled score differences required for statistical significance at the .15 and .05 levels are located in Appendix B, Table B.3 and Appendix D, Table D.25 and summarized in Rapid Reference 8.37, along with

≡ Rapid Reference 8.37

Guidelines for Interpreting Comparisons Involving Processing Speed Domain Subtests

Determining a Significant Difference Between Scaled Scores

The scaled score values for significant differences between various Processing Speed Domain Subtests are shown in the following table. Some of the comparisons tabled here appear in Appendix B, Table B.3 (Core and Supplemental Subtest comparisons) and in Appendix D, Table D.25 of the *WISC-IV Integrated Scoring and Administration Manual* (Core and Supplemental with Process Subtest comparisons). Additional comparison values were calculated using the same procedures as those outlined in the WISC-IV Integrated manuals.

Significance Level	CD vs. SS*	CD vs. CA*	SS vs. CA*	CDC vs. CD*	CDC vs. SS	CDC vs. CA*	CAR vs. CAS*	CAR vs. CD	CAR vs. SS	CAR vs. CDC
.15	2.61	2.63	2.79	2.45	2.62	2.64	3.23	2.95	3.09	2.96
.05	3.55	3.58	3.80	3.34	3.57	3.60	4.40	4.01	4.21	4.03

*Indicates values that appear in the WISC-IV Integrated manual.

Based on the values in the previous table, clinicians can feel comfortable using a rounded value of 3 scaled score points to indicate a significant difference for all of the various subtest comparisons. Using a difference of 3 scaled score points is equivalent to using a value that, in most cases, is roughly halfway between the .15 and .05 levels.

Degree of Unusualness of Scaled Score Discrepancies

The cumulative percentages (i.e., base rates) of the standardization sample obtaining scaled score discrepancies of a particular magnitude between various Processing Speed Domain tasks are shown in the following tables. Some of the base rate data tabled here appear in Appendix B, Table B.4 and in Appendix D, Table D.26 of the *WISC-IV Integrated Scoring and Administration Manual*. The additional base rates shown here were calculated by the author of this chapter using the WISC-IV Integrated standardization sample data.

Processing Speed Domain Core and Supplemental Subtest Comparisons

Scaled Score Discrepancy	CD > SS*	SS > CD*	CD > CA*	CA > CD*	SS > CA*	CA > SS*
3	17.3	19.1	22.5	21.9	22.9	21.8
4	10.5	9.7	14.2	13.6	15.6	14.5

(continued)

5	6.3	4.9	8.5	8.0	9.6	8.8
6	3.8	2.2	4.6	4.6	5.4	5.5
7	2.2	1.0	2.6	2.0	2.9	3.9

*Indicates values that appear in the WISC-IV Integrated manual.

Processing Speed Domain Core and Supplemental Subtest with Process Task Comparisons

Scaled Score Discrepancy	CDC > CD*	CD > CDC*	CDC > SS	SS > CDC	CDC > CA*	CA > CDC*	CAR > CAS*	CAS > CAR*
3	12.6	13.9	20.6	19.3	21.7	22.3	14.0	12.6
4	5.9	6.3	11.7	12.3	14.5	15.3	7.3	5.6
5	2.9	2.5	6.7	6.3	8.7	9.0	3.2	3.0
6	1.6	1.0	4.4	4.4	5.3	5.0	1.5	1.2
7	0.8	0.3	2.1	1.8	2.6	2.7	0.5	0.5

*Indicates values that appear in the WISC-IV Integrated manual.

Processing Speed Domain Supplemental Subtest with Process Task Comparisons

Scaled Score Discrepancy	CAR > CD	CD > CAR	CAR > SS	SS > CAR	CAR > CDC	CDC > CAR
3	24.8	21.5	22.9	21.1	25.2	23.1
4	15.1	14.2	15.2	13.7	15.3	14.9
5	9.5	8.1	9.9	8.6	9.7	10.2
6	5.3	4.5	6.5	5.2	6.0	6.5
7	2.1	2.1	3.7	3.0	3.4	4.1

Note from the previous table that the percentage of the standardization sample demonstrating scaled score discrepancies of 3 points or more is roughly equal for both comparison conditions (e.g., CD > SS and SS > CD). Also note that discrepancies of 5 scaled score points represent differences demonstrated by 10% or less of the standardization sample and discrepancies of 6 scaled score points represent differences demonstrated by 5% or less of the standardization sample. The only exceptions are the values for CDC versus CD and CDC versus CAR, which are 1 point lower in each instance. Clinicians can feel comfortable using scaled score discrepancies of 5 and 6 points generally as the values representing differences demonstrated by less than 10% and less than 5% of the standardization sample respectively.

When attempting to interpret the significance of scaled score discrepancies among Processing Speed Domain tasks, clinicians using values of 5 or 6 scaled score points as the criteria for clinical significance for all comparisons will be assured of both statistical significance of the obtained discrepancy as well as a relatively high degree of unusualness of the occurrence of the difference within the standardization sample. Although somewhat more frequent in occurrence, a scaled score difference of 4 points might also be reasonably considered both statistically and clinically significant depending on the tasks being compared, the specific circumstances of the case, and the number of significant subtest comparisons demonstrated by a child.

the additional values calculated for inclusion in this text. Given the range of the tabled values it is reasonable to use a rounded value of 3 scaled score points to signify a statistically significant difference for comparisons involving Processing Speed Domain Subtests.

Cumulative percentages (i.e., base rates) of the standardization sample obtaining various scaled score discrepancies involving various Processing Speed Domain Subtests are located in Appendix D, Table D.4 of the *WISC-IV Integrated Administration and Scoring Manual*. Additional Processing Speed Domain discrepancy base rates were calculated using the WISC-IV Integrated standardization sample data. A summary table showing base rate data from the WISC-IV Integrated manual and from the analyses completed for this text is provided in Rapid Reference 8.37.

Figure 8.4 provides a worksheet to aid in the interpretation of Processing Speed Domain task scaled score comparisons. Rapid Reference 8.38 provides a case study example that includes the use of the interpretive worksheet and illustrates the application of WISC-IV Integrated process-approach procedures in the interpretation of Processing Speed Domain task performance.

Comparison	Task 1 Raw Score (a)	Task 1 Scaled Score (b)	Task 2 Raw Score (c)	Task 2 Scaled Score (d)	Scaled Score Diff (b–d) (e)	Scaled Score Difference Significant? (e > 3)	Scaled Score Difference Unusual? (e = 5 / e > = 6)
CD vs. SS						Y N	e = 5 Y < 10% e > = 6 Y < 5% N
CD vs. CA						Y N	e = 5 Y < 10% e > = 6 Y < 5% N
SS vs. CA						Y N	e = 5 Y < 10% e > = 6 Y < 5% N
CDC vs. CD						Y N	e = 4 Y < 10% e > = 5 Y < 5% N
CDC vs. SS						Y N	e = 5 Y < 10% e > = 6 Y < 5% N
CDC vs. CA						Y N	e = 5 Y < 10% e > = 6 Y < 5% N
CAR vs. CAS						Y N	e = 4 Y < 10% e > = 5 Y < 5% N
CAR vs. CD						Y N	e = 5 Y < 10% e > = 6 Y < 5% N
CAR vs. SS						Y N	e = 5 Y < 10% e > = 6 Y < 5% N
CAR vs. CDC						Y N	e = 5 Y < 10% e > = 6 Y < 5% N

Figure 8.4 Processing Speed Domain Task Comparison Worksheet

≡ Rapid Reference 8.38

Processing Speed Case Study

Brendan, Age 10-4, Grade 5

Throughout grades K-4, Brendan was viewed as a bright but extremely active child who required much effort on the part of his teachers to help him stay focused and on task throughout the school days. Although difficult to manage in many ways, Brendan had always demonstrated good academic skills and performed adequately on state achievement tests. In 5th grade, Brendan's grades started to drop and while he was less disruptive to classroom routines (he tended to confine his fidgeting to in-seat behavior such as continually moving his legs or drumming on his desktop with his hands), he seemed unable to attend to classroom instruction for more than a few seconds at a time, and he could not get organized, or stay organized, without a great deal of assistance. Concerned about how the school year was going, Brendan's parents requested a psychoeducational evaluation. Brendan was administered the WISC-IV as part of the evaluation and earned the following scores:

WISC-IV

Verbal Domain		Perceptual Domain	
Similarities	14	Block Design	11
Vocabulary	13	Picture Concepts	12
Comprehension	14	Matrix Reasoning	7
Verbal Comprehension Index	121	Perceptual Reasoning Index	100
Working Memory Domain		Processing Speed Domain	
Digit Span	9	Coding	8
Letter-Number Sequencing	9	Symbol Search	13
Working Memory Index	94	Processing Speed Index	103
Full Scale IQ 108			

Brendan's performance produced relatively uniform Index scores across 3 of 4 domains and relatively uniform subtests scores within the Verbal and Working Memory domains. Interpretation at the Index level suggests that Brendan has a strength in reasoning with, and retrieving and expressing verbal information (VCI 121) and average capacities for reasoning with nonverbal visual material (PRI 100), registering and manipulating auditorily presented verbal information

(continued)

(WMI 94), and quickly processing nonverbal visual information (PSI 103). The 5 point scaled score differences between Picture Concepts (12) and Matrix Reasoning (7) and between Symbol Search (13) and Coding (8), however, reflected significant and unusual discrepancies. Considering the nature of Brendan's referral problems, the psychologist decided to expand the assessment in the Perceptual and Processing Speed domains and administered the Elithorn Mazes, Cancellation, and Coding Copy Subtests. The following results were obtained:

Perceptual Domain Process Subtest	
Elithorn Mazes	11
Processing Speed Domain Supplemental Subtest	
Cancellation	9
Processing Speed Domain Process Subtest and Process Scores	
Cancellation Random	7
Cancellation Structured	11
Coding Copy	11

The Processing Speed Domain Task Comparison Worksheet (see below) reflected additional significant scaled score discrepancies of the unusual magnitude such as that reflected in Brendan's Symbol Search-Coding contrast. Brendan's pattern of performance with all of the Processing Speed tasks is clinically relevant as discussed below.

Despite the expressed concerns with organization and planning, Brendan performed as effectively with the Elithorn Mazes Subtest (11) as he had done with the Block Design Subtest. While performing the items of the Elithorn Mazes Subtest, Brendan displayed effective latency periods during which he engaged motor planning strategies to guide his effective production of paths through the mazes of most items.

Brendan's performance with the Coding Copy Subtest (11) was significantly better than his performance with the Coding Subtest (8) and was more in line with his Symbol Search score (13). Although Brendan earned a Cancellation Subtest score (9) in the average range, the 4 point difference between Brendan's score on the Cancellation Random (7) and Cancellation Structured (11) tasks is of particular clinical interest. Brendan performed significantly better when provided with the organizational format of the Cancellation Structured task (11) than with the nonorganized format of the Cancellation Random task (7).

Process approach analysis of Brendan's performance with the Coding, Symbol Search, Coding Copy, Cancellation and Matrix Reasoning Subtests offered additional information that was very valuable in understanding Brendan's approach to tasks. For the Symbol Search and Coding Subtests, the number of items Brendan completed in each 30 second time interval was recorded during administration. For each Cancellation task, Brendan's search pattern was observed and recorded. For the Matrix Reasoning Subtests, Brendan's performance with each item was timed and carefully observed and incorrect response choices were analyzed.

Brendan earned a score in the lower end of the average range for the Coding Subtest (8) that resulted from his inability to maintain a consistent work pace for the entire two minute time period. Brendan copied 11 items in the first thirty-second interval then improved his output to 14 items in the second interval. After completing 4 items in the third interval, Brendan made a coding error but immediately realized his mistake. Rather than quickly copying over the error and moving on, Brendan stopped working to ponder the situation for nearly 20 seconds; finally, he corrected his error and moved on, but with this loss of focus Brendan was only able to complete 7 items in the third interval. Brendan never really regained his focus after the disruption caused by his coding error as he completed only 5 items in the final thirty-second interval.

Although Brendan earned a Symbol Search score in the above average range (13) and was able to complete 32 items in the allotted two minute period, he again was not able to maintain a consistent work pace for the entire task and made 4 response errors. After quickly completing 13 items in the first 30 seconds, Brendan's work pace slowed substantially as he completed only 7 items in the second thirty-second interval. Brendan's pace remained at a much slower rate as he completed only 6 items in each of the last two intervals. It is uncommon for children to make errors with the Symbol Search items; Brendan's four errors reflected a lack of consistent attention to the visual details of this task.

Despite the average range score for Coding Copy (11), a similar pattern of inconsistent effort was observed here as well. Brendan started at a brisk pace similar to his start with Symbol Search, copying 39 items in the first 30 second interval. As was the case with Symbol Search, however, he was unable to maintain his initial effort, copying 10 fewer items in the second interval (29). Brendan's momentum continued a downward slide as he copied only 17 symbols in the third interval and 16 in the fourth interval.

Although Brendan's efforts produced different scores for these three tasks, the way in which Brendan approached these three tasks produced a similar pattern of results. When given tasks requiring sustained attention and effort for a two minute time period, Brendan was unable to maintain a consistent work effort, with variable performance in the first half of each task followed by considerable deterioration of performance during the second half.

Inconsistent performance also was costly for Brendan in his efforts with the Matrix Reasoning Subtest (7). On the easier items of this subtest, Brendan

(continued)

adopted a very quick response style (4-6 seconds per item). As a result, he frequently overlooked subtle visual details that would enable him to distinguish the correct response choice from a very similar, but incorrect response choice. As the items became more difficult, Brendan sometimes slowed down and took longer to consider his response. When Brendan slowed down and considered items for longer periods of time (20-25 seconds per item) he was much more likely to provide a correct response even though these items were much more difficult than many of the items he got wrong. Employing his impulsive response style for most items, Brendan correctly responded to only 11 of the 25 items he attempted, resulting in a score in the below average range.

Summary

Brendan performed best with the Symbol Search Subtest (13), a task that required him to quickly perceive and discriminate abstract visual symbols, but that required a minimal motor response of marking yes or no for each item. In contrast, Brendan performed much less effectively with the Coding Subtest (8) that required him to engage in multitasking efforts to match and complete code items as quickly as possible. When the multitasking aspect of the Coding Subtest was reduced to simply copying the code items, Brendan's performance improved significantly (Coding Copy 11). Efforts with the Elithorn Mazes Subtest (11) were consistent with performance on the Block Design Subtest, indicating at least average ability to apply planning and organization to problem-solving efforts involving nonverbal visual materials.

Although Brendan was able to earn average to above average scores with many Perceptual and Processing Speed subtests, analysis of his performance using process approach procedures reflected difficulties with sustaining effort and attention for two minute work periods and an impulsive response style that limited his capacity to demonstrate his reasoning abilities as applied with nonverbal visual materials that required close attention to details. In a similar manner, Brendan earned average scores with tasks that modeled or shaped an organized approach to task performance (Block Design 11; Elithorn Mazes 11; Cancellation Structured 11) when these cues were absent and speed of performance was emphasized (Cancellation Random 7); Brendan was not able to self-generate an organization strategy to aid performance.

Coupled with the significant and unusually large difference between Brendan's capacity for reasoning with verbal material (VCI 121) and his relatively poorer capacity to register, hold, and manipulate auditorily presented verbal information (WMI 94), these findings were highly consistent with parent and teacher reports of Brendan's work habits at home and in school and with elevated Parent and Teacher ratings on the Inhibition, Working Memory, Planning/Organization, Organization of Materials, and Monitor Scales of the Behavior Rating Inventory of Executive Functions (BRIEF) and elevated Parent and Teacher scores on the Hyperactivity/Impulsivity and Inattention subscales of the ADHD-IV Rating

Scales. Brendan's profile of intellectual strengths and weaknesses as viewed from the WISC-IV Integrated perspective offered information that reinforced the need for the school-based multidisciplinary team to take action to provide accommodations to Brendan to assist in helping him improve his capacity to self-organize thinking and work strategies and increase his capacity for sustained attention and effort. Brendan's parents were also considering sharing the psychoeducational report with a pediatrician specializing in working with children with ADHD to determine if medical intervention should be considered.

Brendan's case illustrates several points about the use of the WISC-IV Integrated tasks and features:

1. Use of the process approach to task administration and task performance observation and interpretation allowed for a more detailed description of Brendan's cognitive capacities than that obtained from interpretation based solely on Index, or even subtest level, scores.

2. Average and above scores on subtests do not always mean that a child is performing a task effectively; in the case of the Symbol Search and Coding Copy Subtests, Brendan's efforts reflected the same inefficient approaches to task performance that were the cause of his difficulties with the Coding and Matrix Reasoning Subtests.

3. Low scores on subtests may be the results of ineffective use of cognitive capacities that are not the primary cognitive capacities intended to be assessed with the subtest.

4. Not all children who demonstrate difficulties with planning and organization score poorly on the Elithorn Mazes Subtest even though it is intended to measure organization and planning with nonverbal visual material.

5. Not all children who demonstrate difficulties with focusing and sustaining attention and effort with tasks earn low scores on tasks that assess sustained attention and effort. The difficulties observed with such tasks are often of a relative, rather than an absolute, nature.

6. Interpretation of the results of cognitive measures must occur in the context of the other information gathered in the evaluation.

7. The additional WISC-IV Integrated subtest administrations and process approach procedures used with Brendan required approximately 15 minutes, a small cost for the wealth of critically important additional information obtained in this case.

🪶 TESTYOURSELF 🪶

1. **All subtests of the WISC-IV Integrated must be administered in order to get clinically meaningful scores.**
   True or False?

2. **The integration of the process approach into the WISC-IV is realized through all of the following features except:**
   (a) process standard scores.
   (b) cumulative percentage base rates for process observation.
   (c) classification of WISC-IV subtests into one or more of Luria's three functional units (arousal, coding & storage, planning).
   (d) cumulative percentage base rates for subtest scaled score discrepancy comparisons.

3. **The process approach relative to the WISC-IV embodies all of the following conceptions except:**
   (a) The WISC-IV subtests are complex tasks, with each one requiring the use of multiple cognitive capacities for successful performance.
   (b) Variations in input, processing, and/or output demands can greatly affect performance on tasks involving similar contents.
   (c) Careful, systematic observation of task performance greatly enhances the understanding of task outcome.
   (d) Systematic categorization of each process score according to its psycho-metric properties.

4. **Which of the following Processing Subtests of the WISC-IV Integrated is NOT in the Verbal Domain?**
   (a) Similarities Multiple Choice
   (b) Written Arithmetic
   (c) Picture Vocabulary Multiple Choice
   (d) Information Multiple Choice

5. **Which of the following WISC-IV subtests is NOT directly addressed on the WISC-IV Integrated?**
   (a) Matrix Reasoning
   (b) Vocabulary
   (c) Block Design
   (d) Letter-Number Sequencing

6. **The decision to use process subtests may occur prior to or after administration of the WISC-IV Core and Supplemental Subtests.**
   True or False?

7. **Susan's teachers are concerned because she has poor coordination, takes a lot longer to complete tasks than her peers, and makes poor use of visual-perceptual skills. Which of the following subtests would be BEST to administer to Susan?**

   (a) Block Design Multiple Choice No Time Bonus and Elithorn Mazes

   (b) Vocabulary Multiple Choice and Similarities Multiple Choice

   (c) Coding Copy and Cancellation

   (d) Spatial Scan and Written Arithmetic

8. **In general, removing bonus points earned for speed on Block Design has a significant impact on most children's standing relative to same-age peers.**
   True or false?

9. **The cognitive demands of Coding Copy differ from that of Coding in that Coding Copy:**

   (a) eliminates the need of visuo-motor skills.

   (b) eliminates the need of graphomotor skills.

   (c) reduces the likelihood of involvement of working memory resources.

   (d) alters open-ended inductive reasoning demands to a demand for recognition of the effective application of inductive reasoning.

10. **Which of the following subtests of the Working Memory Domain does NOT require BOTH Initial Registration and Working Memory?**

    (a) Arithmetic

    (b) Digit Span Forward

    (c) Digit Span Backward

    (d) Letter-Number Sequencing

11. **Sam's teachers have been concerned because he has had particular difficulty following multistep directions. Which process subtests might be especially useful to better understand her problems?**

    (a) Verbal Domain

    (b) Perceptual Domain

    (c) Processing Speed Domain

    (d) Working Memory Domain

Answers:

1. False; 2. c; 3. d; 4. b; 5. a; 6. True; 7. a; 8. False; 9. c; 10. b; 11. d

Nine

ILLUSTRATIVE CASE REPORTS

This chapter presents case studies of three children who were referred for psychoeducational evaluations. The WISC-IV profile of Ryan, the first study, was included in Chapter 4 to exemplify how to utilize the CHC-based interpretive approach advocated in this book and to demonstrate the utility of the new automated *WISC-IV Data Management and Interpretive Assistant* (DMIA)

CAUTION

Common Errors to Avoid in Report Writing

- Including inappropriate or excessive detail
- Using unnecessary jargon or technical terms
- Using vague language
- Making abstract statements
- Not supporting hypotheses with sufficient data
- Making generalizations from isolated information, such as a single outlier scaled score
- Inserting value judgments
- Discussing the test itself rather than the child's abilities
- Using poor grammar
- Presenting behavior or test scores without interpreting them
- Failing to adequately address reasons for referral
- Failing to provide confidence intervals or otherwise denote that all obtained test scores have a band of error
- Giving test results prematurely (e.g., in the "Appearance and Behavioral Characteristics" section)

Source: From A. S. Kaufman & E. O. Lichtenberger, *Essentials of WISC-III and WPPSI-R Assessment. Copyright* © 2000 John Wiley & Sons, Inc. This material is used by permission of John Wiley & Sons, Inc.

included on the CD-ROM accompanying this book. The second case study describes the profile of a 14-year-old girl with HIV who was referred for evaluation of suspected learning disability and demonstrates how to integrate data from the KABC-II with the WISC-IV. The third case study describes the profile of an 11-year-old boy with working memory, processing speed, attention, and executive function difficulties and demonstrates how to interpret the WISC-IV within the context of the Cognitive Hypothesis Testing Model (Hale & Fiorello, 2004). For case examples using the WISC-IV Integrated, see Chapter 8 of this book.

The goal of this chapter is to bring all facets of this book together to show how the WISC-IV may be used as a core battery in assessment. The case studies demonstrate the cross-validation of hypotheses with behavioral observations, background information, and supplemental tests. Each report includes the following information about the child: reason for referral, background information, physical appearance of the child, and behavioral observations during the assessment, evaluation procedures, test results and interpretation, diagnostic impressions, and recommendations.

PSYCHOLOGICAL REPORT by Jennifer T. Mascolo, PsyD

Name: Ryan S.	DOB: 1/16/94
Age: 10	Grade: 5th
Date of Testing: 2/26/04	Date of Report: 3/01/04

DON'T FORGET
....
Pertinent Information to Include in Identifying Information Section

- Name
- Date of birth
- Age
- Grade in school (if applicable)
- Date(s) of testing
- Date of report

Source: From A. S. Kaufman & E. O. Lichtenberger, Essentials of WISC-III and WPPSI-R Assessment. Copyright © 2000 John Wiley & Sons, Inc. This material is used by permission of John Wiley & Sons, Inc.

Referral and Background Information

Ryan was referred for a psychoeducational evaluation by his elementary school's Building Intervention Team (BIT) due to academic difficulties, primarily in the area of reading. More specifically, his teacher noted that he is unable to recognize certain words that he is otherwise expected to know, and he exhibits difficulty decoding unfamiliar words. Additionally, Ryan's reading comprehension is not commensurate with that of his classmates. For instance, he often misses the main points to class reading assignments and fails to identify details accurately. Ryan's teacher further described Ryan's comprehension as "inconsistent" and stated that he seems to perform better when reading about familiar topics. In addition to reading difficulties, Ryan also demonstrates difficulties in the area of writing. That is, Ryan's teacher reported that although he has good ideas and can communicate them verbally, his written products generally contain spelling errors and are relatively bland and lack variety (e.g., he uses the same words repeatedly and includes minimal descriptive words in his writing). Finally, Ryan has recently begun experiencing difficulties in math, a subject in which he has historically performed average or better.

Information from Ryan's parents, Mr. and Mrs. S., revealed that Ryan, who was born via caesarean section, met developmental milestones within normal limits. Other than an asthma episode at age 5, Ryan's health history is unremarkable and he is currently reported to be in good health. Ryan's parents describe him as a "delightful, energetic, and well-behaved" child. Ryan attends school regularly and reportedly has a "good attitude" toward school. Parental concerns are consistent with teacher reports and center largely on Ryan's inability to decode words and comprehend written text consistently.

In terms of educational history, Ryan attended a preschool program that focused on teaching precursor skills thought to be necessary for kindergarten success (e.g., letter identification, development of basic concepts, and color and shape recognition). Ryan reportedly liked preschool and especially enjoyed the social opportunities afforded by this setting.

In kindergarten, Ryan's performance was described as "average," with specific areas of concern. Although he seemed to do well with number concepts and color and shape identification, he had difficulty in other areas, such as letter recognition and rhyming. These difficulties continued throughout Ryan's early elementary school years and, based on the results of a district-wide reading assessment in 3rd grade, Ryan was provided with remedial reading

DON'T FORGET

Pertinent Information to Include in Reason for Referral Section

A. Who referred the child
   1. List name and position of referral source.
   2. List questions and concerns of referral source.

B. Specific symptoms and concerns
   1. Summarize current behaviors and relevant past behaviors.
   2. List any separate concerns that the child has.

Source: From A. S. Kaufman & E. O. Lichtenberger, Essentials of WISC-III and WPPSI-R Assessment. Copyright © 2000 John Wiley & Sons, Inc. This material is used by permission of John Wiley & Sons, Inc.

services twice a week. These services focused primarily on developing Ryan's sight-word vocabulary and teaching him how to use context cues to obtain meaning from a passage.

In fourth grade, Ryan's reading difficulties became more pronounced. It was around this time that Mr. and Mrs. S. noted that Ryan was inconsistent in his completion of reading assignments, and generally only completed readings that focused on topics he enjoyed or was familiar with. Mr. and Mrs. S. also noticed that Ryan required more assistance to complete his homework. For example, they often had to read directions to him and assist him with decoding words in his content-area texts (e.g., science and social studies).

Presently, Ryan continues to receive remedial reading services, but Mr. and Mrs. S., along with Ryan's teacher, are concerned that Ryan's difficulties are not being sufficiently addressed. Their primary concern is that Ryan is not making gains that are commensurate with the type of intervention being offered. Additionally, Ryan's parents and teacher are concerned that if Ryan continues to experience frustration on academic tasks, his interest and positive attitude toward school will diminish.

DON'T FORGET

Pertinent Information to Include in Background Information Section

Present in paragraph form the information you have obtained from all sources, including referral source, child, family members, social worker, teachers, medical records, etc. State pertinent information only, not needless details.

The following information may be included:

- Current family situation (parents, siblings, etc.—*no gossip*)
- Current symptoms
- Medical history (including emotional disorders)
- Developmental history
- Educational history
- Previous treatment (educational or psychological)
- New or recent developments (including stressors)
- Review of collateral documents (past evaluations)

Source: From A. S. Kaufman & E. O. Lichtenberger, *Essentials of WISC-III and WPPSI-R Assessment.* Copyright © 2000 John Wiley & Sons, Inc. This material is used by permission of John Wiley & Sons, Inc.

Despite Ryan's parents' and teachers' concerns, information from a recent interview with Ryan revealed that he likes school but is having difficulty with reading and completing his class work on time. Ryan's favorite subjects are math and science. Ryan is particularly fond of math because he is "good at it." However, consistent with his teacher's report, he noted that math has recently become more difficult for him. Ryan's least favorite subjects are reading, spelling, and writing. Ryan stated that he does not like the books that he has to read in school, and thus he does not enjoy reading. Nevertheless, Ryan reported that when he is at home he enjoys reading "joke books" with his father and looking at comic books with his friends. Furthermore, Ryan reported that spelling and writing are difficult for him, but he also stated that he is able to do better with these tasks if his mother and father help him and if he can use the "spell check" feature on his parents' computer. Despite Ryan's difficulties, he does not describe school as stressful. When Ryan feels stress, however, he attempts to cope with it positively by seeking out his parents' support.

In terms of Ryan's social and emotional functioning as it relates to school, he feels that he is an integrated member of the school, and feels that others are nice to him. Ryan reports getting along with his peers, and having several close friends that he socializes with on a daily basis. Furthermore, he has no reservations about interacting with others and participating in classroom activities. For instance, he is comfortable asking and answering questions, and talking to his classmates.

Appearance and Behavioral Observations

Ryan was neatly groomed and presented as a well-mannered child. Rapport was easily established and was maintained throughout the evaluation process. Furthermore, Ryan communicated his ideas and feelings in a thoughtful and meaningful way. He was particularly conversant about video games and movies, and was quite good at summarizing the plots for some of his favorite, most-often-watched movies.

Ryan appeared engaged and motivated during most of the tasks administered. He liked to ask questions and discuss various topics that came up during the evaluation, and often brought up other topics that interested him. For instance, he tended to offer detailed explanations for how he knew certain things and often told stories about personal experiences that related to certain questions. Ryan was very persistent when working through the math-related tasks, and he often commented on how he enjoyed figuring out some of the more difficult items, while pointing out that he was glad that he did not have to read any of the word problems. Unlike Ryan's approach to math tasks, during the vocabulary-based tasks

DON'T FORGET

. . . .

Pertinent Information to Consider Including in Appearance and Behavioral Observations Section

- Talk about significant patterns or themes you see going on during testing.
- Sequence information in order of importance, rather than in order of occurrence. (Don't just make a chronological list.)
- Describe the behavioral referents to your hypotheses (and provide specific examples).
- Describe what makes this child unique. (Paint a picture for the reader.)
- Suggested areas to review (in addition to significant behavior):

Appearance

- Size: height and weight
- Facial characteristics
- Grooming and cleanliness
- Posture
- Clothing style
- Maturity: Does the person look his or her age?

Behavior

- Speech articulation, language patterns
- Activity level (foot wiggling, excessive talking, nail biting, tension, etc.)
- Attention span/distractibility
- Cooperativeness or resistance
- Interest in doing well
- How does the child go about solving problems?
- Does the child use a trial-and-error approach?
- Does the child work quickly or reflectively?
- Does the child check his or her answers?
- How does the child react to failure or challenge?
- Does the child continue to work until time is up?
- Does the child ask for direction or help?
- Did failure reduce interest in the task or lead to avoidance of other tasks?
- When frustrated, is the child aggressive or dependent?
- What is the child's attitude toward self?
- Does the child regard self with confidence, have a superior attitude, feel inadequate, or appear defeated?
- How did the child strive to get approval and respond to your praise of effort?

> *Validity of test results*
> - "On the basis of John's above behaviors, the results of this assessment are considered a valid indication of his current level of cognitive and academic ability."
> - Or if not, state why.
>
> Source: From A. S. Kaufman & E. O. Lichtenberger, *Essentials of WISC-III and WPPSI-R Assessment.* Copyright © 2000 John Wiley & Sons, Inc. This material is used by permission of John Wiley & Sons, Inc.

he appeared less enthusiastic. For instance, many of his answers on vocabulary items were brief. Finally, Ryan used a very slow and labor-intensive approach to processing speed tasks. Overall, the results of this assessment are considered a valid indication of Ryan's current level of cognitive and academic ability.

Evaluation Procedures

Wechsler Intelligence Scale for Children–Fourth Edition (WISC-IV)
Woodcock-Johnson Tests of Cognitive Abilities, Third Edition (WJ III),
  select subtests
Wechsler Individual Achievement Test–Second Edition (WIAT-II)
School observation—Reading class
Interview with teachers
Interview with parents
Interview with child

Reading Class Observation

Ryan was observed in his reading class in the morning. There were approximately 13 students in the classroom, and the desks were arranged in several rows facing the chalkboard. Ryan sits in the front row, close to where the teacher usually stands while presenting a lesson. On this day, the teacher was leading a discussion pertaining to a reading homework assignment concerning erosion. Upon starting the discussion, the teacher asked volunteers to read various passages from the text to the class. Ryan sat quietly while a majority of his classmates enthusiastically volunteered by raising their hands. Despite his silence, Ryan appeared to listen carefully to what his classmates were reading. A discussion followed about erosion and weathering, in which the teacher asked how the process of erosion takes place. At this point, Ryan was asked to read a passage pertaining to this topic. Ryan read slowly and in a labor-intensive manner. Furthermore, he made many mistakes that distorted the meaning of what he was reading. More specifically, he frequently omitted words and inserted words that were not in the text. Additionally, he altered word endings and switched words around. For instance, he changed "something" to "someone," and read "when the rain hits the rock" as "when the rock hits the rain." Ryan also demonstrated limited sight-word vocabulary in his reading repertoire, but demonstrated a rudimentary level of decoding skill to decipher simpler words. When Ryan encountered a more difficult word that he was unable to decode, he tended to skip it. At times Ryan lost his place and mistakenly read an entire sentence over again, and other times he skipped entire sentences. As a result, Ryan demonstrated very limited comprehension of what he read.

TEST RESULTS AND INTERPRETATION

Cognitive Performance

WISC-IV
The WISC-IV groups an individual's ability into four global areas: Verbal Comprehension Index (VCI), which measures verbal ability; Perceptual Reasoning Index (PRI), which involves the manipulation of concrete materials or processing of visual stimuli to solve problems nonverbally; Working Memory Index (WMI), which measures short-term memory; and Processing Speed Index (PSI), which measures cognitive processing efficiency.

On the WISC-IV, Ryan earned a Full Scale IQ (FSIQ) of 83, which ranks his overall ability at the 13th percentile and classifies his global IQ as falling Below Average/Normative Weakness. There is a 95% chance that his true FSIQ is between 79 and 88. However, this estimate of his general intellectual ability on the WISC-IV cannot be interpreted meaningfully and should be deemphasized because he displayed considerable variability among the four Indexes that constitute this full scale score. Ryan's Indexes ranged from 70 on the PSI (2nd percentile) to 98 on the VCI (45th percentile), suggesting that Ryan's intelligence is best understood by his performance on the separate WISC-IV Indexes, namely, Verbal Comprehension, Perceptual Reasoning, Working Memory, and Processing Speed. Table 9.1 on page 477 lists Ryan's cognitive performance on the WISC-IV.

Because Ryan's WISC-IV FSIQ could not be interpreted and his Verbal Comprehension (98) and Perceptual Reasoning (90) Indexes were similar, these Indexes were combined to yield a General Ability Index (GAI). The GAI differs from the FSIQ in that it is not influenced directly by Ryan's performance on working memory and processing speed tasks. Ryan earned a GAI of 94, classifying his general

DON'T FORGET

Pertinent Information to Include in Test Results and Interpretation Section

- Use paragraph form.
- Put numbers in this section, including IQs and Indexes with confidence intervals and percentile ranks. Do not include raw scores.
- Tie in behaviors with results to serve as logical explanations or reminders wherever appropriate.
- With more than one test, attempt to explain similarities in performances and differences (discrepancies) if you have sufficient information to do so.
- Support hypotheses with multiple sources of data, including observed behaviors.
- Do not contradict yourself.
- Be sure that you are describing the Indexes, not just naming them. Remember, the reader has no idea what "Perceptual Reasoning" means.
- Describe the underlying abilities that the Indexes are measuring.
- Talk about the child's abilities, not about the test.
- Be straightforward in your writing. Do not be too literary, and avoid writing in metaphors.

Source: From A. S. Kaufman & E. O. Lichtenberger, *Essentials of WISC-III and WPPSI-R Assessment.* Copyright © 2000 John Wiley & Sons, Inc. This material is used by permission of John Wiley & Sons, Inc.

level of intellectual ability as Average Range/Within Normal Limits. The chances are good (95%) that Ryan's true GAI is somewhere within the range of 89 to 100. His GAI is ranked at the 34th percentile, indicating that he scored higher than 34% of other children of the same age in the standardization sample.

Before discussing Ryan's Indexes on the four scales, one must first determine whether each Index is interpretable—that is, does it measure a reasonably unitary trait for Ryan, or do his scaled scores on the subtests that constitute the Index include substantial variability? Three of Ryan's WISC-IV Indexes are considered "interpretable." The largest discrepancy among his subtest scaled scores within an Index was 6 points (the difference between his scaled scores of 13 on Comprehension and 7 on Vocabulary for the VCI). To be considered *not* interpretable, discrepancies between the highest and lowest subtest scaled scores within an Index must be greater than or equal to 5 points. Discrepancies within the other three Indexes were 4 points (PRI), 0 points (WMI), and 1 point (PSI). Consequently, Ryan's PRI, WMI, and PSI are all considered to provide good estimates of his skill on the abilities measured by each scale.

Table 9.1 Ryan's WISC-IV Performance from the WISC-IV DMIA v1.0

Examinee Name:	Ryan		Date of Birth: 1/16/1994		
Date of Assessment:	3/1/2004		Age:	10 yr 1 mo	

Enter the scores in cells bordered in red with examinee's scores.
The program will automatically calculate the next steps for you.

Index/IQ Subtest	Score	95% CI	Percentile Rank	Descriptive Category	Is Index/IQ/Cluster Interpretable?
Verbal Comprehension	98	93-103	45	Average Range/Within Normal Limits	*No*
Similarities	9		37		
Vocabulary	7		16		
Comprehension	13		84		
(Information)	12		75	*Does not contribute to Index or IQ*	
(Word Reasoning)	6		9	*Does not contribute to Index or IQ*	
Perceptual Reasoning	90	85-95	25	Average Range/Within Normal Limits	*Yes*
Block Design	6		9		
Picture Concepts	10		50		
Matrix Reasoning	9		37		
(Picture Completion)	8		25	*Does not contribute to Index or IQ*	
Working Memory	83	78-88	13	Below Average/Normative Weakness	*Yes*
Digit Span	7		16		
Letter-Number Sequencing	7		16		
(Arithmetic)	11		63	*Does not contribute to Index or IQ*	
Processing Speed	70	65-75	2	Below Average/Normative Weakness	*Yes*
Coding	5		5		
Symbol Search	4		2		
(Cancellation)	5		5	*Does not contribute to Index or IQ*	
Full Scale IQ	83	78-88	13	Below Average/Normative Weakness	*No*
GAI	94	89-100	34	Average Range/Within Normal Limits	*Yes*
CPI	73	68-82	4	Below Average/Normative Weakness	*Yes*
Clinical Cluster *(roll cursor over the red triangle to see which subtests comprise each cluster)*					
Gf Cluster	100	92-108	50	Average Range/Within Normal Limits	Yes
Gv Cluster	83	74-92	13	Below Average/Normative Weakness	Yes
Gf-nonverbal Cluster	97	88-106	43	Average Range/Within Normal Limits	Yes
Gf-verbal Cluster	86	76-96	17	Average Range/Within Normal Limits	Yes
Gc-VL Cluster	81	72-90	11	Below Average/Normative Weakness	Yes
Gc-K0 Cluster	114	104-124	83	Average Range/Within Normal Limits	Yes
Gc-LTM Cluster	Not interpretable				No
Gsm-MW Cluster	83	75-91	13	Below Average/Normative Weakness	Yes

The PSI, a measure of Processing Speed *(Gs)*, represents Ryan's ability to perform simple, clerical-type tasks quickly. Ryan's *Gs* ability was assessed with two tasks—one required Ryan to quickly copy symbols that were paired with numbers according to a key (Coding), and the other required him to identify the presence or absence of a target symbol in a row of symbols (Symbol Search). The difference between Ryan's performances on these two tasks (Coding scaled score of 5 minus Symbol Search scaled score of 4 equals 1) was not significant (i.e., ≥ 5), indicating that his PSI is a good estimate of his processing speed. Ryan obtained a PSI of 70 (65–83), which is ranked at the 2nd percentile and is classified as Below Average/Normative Weakness. Ryan's processing speed is a significant weakness as compared to other individuals his age in the normative population. In addition, his ability in this area is significantly lower than his abilities in other areas. Overall, Ryan's processing speed is a notable weakness, a finding that should play an essential role for developing educational interventions.

The WMI, a measure of Short-Term Memory *(Gsm)*, represents Ryan's ability to apprehend and hold, or transform information in immediate awareness and then use it within a few seconds. Ryan's *Gsm* ability was assessed by two tasks— Digit Span, which required him to repeat a sequence of numbers in the same order as presented by the examiner (Digit Span Forward) and also in the reverse order (Digit Span Backward), and Letter-Number Sequencing, which required him to listen to a sequence of numbers and letters and recall the numbers in ascending order and the letters in alphabetical order. Ryan obtained a WMI *(Gsm)* of 83 (77–92), which is ranked at the 13th percentile and is classified as Below Average/Normative Weakness. Ryan's working memory is considered a significant weakness compared to other children his age in the normative population. Like processing speed, Ryan's working memory is a notable weakness, a finding that should play an essential role for developing educational interventions.

The PRI, a measure of Visual Processing and Fluid Reasoning *(Gv/Gf)*, represents Ryan's ability to analyze and synthesize visual stimuli as well as to reason with it. Ryan's *Gv/Gf* ability was assessed by tasks that required him to recreate a series of modeled or pictured designs using blocks (Block Design), identify the missing portion of an incomplete visual matrix from one of five response options (Matrix Reasoning), and select one picture from each of two or three rows of pictures to form a group with a common characteristic (Picture Concepts). Ryan obtained a PRI *(Gv/Gf)* of 90 (83–98), which is ranked at the 25th percentile and is classified as Average Range/Within Normal Limits.

The VCI, a measure of Crystallized Intelligence *(Gc)*, represents Ryan's ability to reason with previously learned information. One's *Gc* ability develops largely as a function of both formal and informal educational opportunities and experiences and is highly dependent on exposure to mainstream U.S. culture. Ryan's *Gc* was assessed by tasks that required him to define words (Vocabulary, scaled score = 7), draw conceptual similarities between words (Similarities, scaled score = 9), and answer questions involving knowledge of general principles and social situations (Comprehension, scaled score = 13). The variability among Ryan's performances on these tasks was significant (i.e., scaled score range was equal to or greater than 5 points), indicating that his overall *Gc* ability cannot be summarized in a single score (i.e., the VCI). Ryan's Crystallized Intelligence is discussed further below.

Clinical Comparisons

In addition to the 10 core-battery subtests of the WISC-IV, Ryan was administered five supplemental subtests. The administration of these supplemental subtests allowed for further examination of Ryan's cognitive abilities. Specifically, these supplemental subtests were combined into several clinical clusters. These clusters are also listed in Table 9.1. Similar to the WISC-IV Index analyses, Clinical Comparisons can be made using the clinical clusters only when the subtests constituting each cluster in the comparison are unitary (i.e., the difference between the highest and lowest subtest scaled scores in the cluster is less than 5). In Ryan's case, all clinical clusters were determined to be unitary, with the exception of the Gc-LTM Cluster. Therefore, four of the six possible Clinical Comparisons were conducted, the results of which appear next.

Gc-VL versus Gc-K0

The difference between Ryan's General Information (Gc-K0) Cluster of 114 (83rd percentile; Average Range/Within Normal Limits) and his Lexical Knowledge (Gc-VL) Cluster of 81 (11th percentile; Below Average/Normative Weakness) is unusually large (differences as large as Ryan's discrepancy of 33 points occur less than 10% of the time in the normative population). Higher standard scores on Gc-K0 than Gc-VL can occur for many reasons. For example, some children might have an adequate fund of information but lack a strong vocabulary knowledge base and therefore have difficulty reasoning with words. Not only is Ryan's lexical knowledge ability less well developed than his general information ability, it is also in the Below Average range of functioning relative to his age mates and, therefore, is a Normative Weakness.

Gf versus Gv

The difference between Ryan's Gf Cluster of 100 (50th percentile; Average Range/Within Normal Limits) and his Gv Cluster of 83 (13th percentile; Below Average/Normative Weakness) was not unusually large, indicating that it is not uncommon to find a difference of this magnitude in the normative population. Nevertheless, it is important to recognize that Ryan's ability to analyze and synthesize visual information fell within the Below Average range of functioning compared to his age mates and, therefore, represents a Normative Weakness.

WJ III Cognitive—Select Subtests

In addition to the WISC-IV, Ryan was administered select tests from the WJ III (see Table 9.2). These tests measured abilities that were not measured by the WISC-IV, namely, Auditory Processing (Ga) and Long-Term Retrieval (Glr).

Auditory Processing (Ga) involves the ability to discriminate, analyze, and synthesize auditory stimuli. Ryan's auditory processing was assessed through phonetic tasks that required him to listen to a series of separated syllables or

Table 9.2 Ryan's WISC-IV, WJ III, and WIAT-II Performance from the WISC-IV DMIA vl.0

Examinee Name: Ryan			
Date of Assessment: 2/26/2004			
Date of Birth: 1/16/1994			
Age: 10 yr 1 mo			
Cognitive Subtest or Index	**Score**	**Converted Score**	**Confidence Interval**
WISC-IV			
VERBAL COMPREHENSION INDEX (Gc)			
PERCEPTUAL REASONING INDEX (Gf/Gv)	90	90	85-95
WORKING MEMORY INDEX (Gsm)	83	83	78-88
PROCESSING SPEED INDEX (Gs)	70	70	65-75
Other Subtests, Clusters, or Indexes To Be Plotted	**Score**	**Converted Score**	**Confidence Interval**
Phonemic Awareness	76	76	71-81
Sound Blending	83	83	78-88
Incomplete Words	80	80	75-85
Long Term Retrieval (Glr)	88	88	83-93
Visual-Auditory Learning	93	93	88-98
Retrieval Fluency	85	85	80-90
Reading Composite	82	82	77-87
Math Composite	95	95	90-100
Written Language Composite	90	90	85-95
Spelling	87	87	82-92
Written Expression	96	96	91-101
Oral Langauge Composite	92	92	87-97
Total Achievement	87	87	82-92

phonemes (e.g., "m-oth-er") and blend the sounds into a complete word (e.g., "mother"; Sound Blending) and identify a complete word (e.g., "record") that was initially presented with one or more missing phonemes (e.g., "re_ord"; Incomplete Words). These tasks primarily measured Ryan's skill in synthesizing and analyzing speech sounds. Ryan obtained a Phonemic Awareness Cluster of 76 (71–81), which is ranked at the 5th percentile and is classified as Below Average/ Normative Weakness. Ryan's observed difficulty with phonetic coding has had a negative impact on his development of basic reading skills (e.g., decoding words). This weakness will likely become even more salient as Ryan's reading material progresses and he is presented with an increased number of unfamiliar (and multisyllabic) words.

Long-Term Retrieval (*Glr*) involves the ability to store information efficiently and retrieve it later through association. Ryan's *Glr* ability was assessed through tasks that required him to learn and recall a series of rebuses (i.e., pictographic representations of words; Visual-Auditory Learning) and name as many examples as possible from a series of three categories (i.e., things to eat or drink, first names of people, and animals) within a 1-minute time period (Retrieval Fluency). More specifically, these tasks assessed Ryan's ability to learn, store, and retrieve a series of associations as well as his ability to fluently retrieve information from stored knowledge.

Although Ryan's overall *Glr* performance suggests that his efficiency in transferring and storing information to be recalled later is adequate (SS = 88 [83–93]; 21st percentile; Average Range/Within Normal Limits), his Ideational Fluency performance as measured by the WJ III Retrieval Fluency test was at the lower end of the Average Range and was ranked at the 16th percentile, suggesting that he indeed had difficulty with this task. Ryan's observed difficulty with Ideational Fluency may be partly related to his weakness in processing speed given that the Retrieval Fluency test is timed. Children who have difficulty retrieving information quickly often have difficulty acquiring basic reading skills.

Achievement Assessment

In addition to an assessment of cognitive functioning, Ryan was administered tests from the WIAT-II (see Table 9.2). The WIAT-II comprises subtests that allow for the derivation of four domain-specific composite scores, namely, Reading, Writing, Mathematics, and Oral Language. In addition to these domain-specific composites, the WIAT-II provides a Total Achievement score, which is based on an aggregate of an individual's subtest scores that make up each domain-specific composite. Ryan obtained a Total Achievement Composite of 87 (82–92), which is ranked at the 19th percentile and is classified as Average Range/Within Normal Limits. Ryan's performances in math, writing, and oral language are within normal limits as compared to same-aged peers from the normative population. Conversely, Ryan's reading performance represents a significant normative weakness. A more complete description of Ryan's performance within each academic domain appears in the following sections.

Reading

Ryan's performance in the area of reading reflects his skill in identifying words presented in isolation (Word Reading, scaled score = 83), applying structural and phonic analysis to decode a series of nonsense words (Pseudoword Decoding, scaled score = 82), and reading and understanding connected text (Reading Comprehension, scaled score = 87). Ryan obtained a Reading Composite of 82 (77–87), which is ranked at the 12th percentile and is classified as Below Average/ Normative Weakness. Ryan's overall reading achievement is consistent with referral concerns. His basic reading skills as well as his ability to apply his knowledge to comprehend written discourse appear to be equally underdeveloped. His primary area of difficulty appears to be related to an inability to accurately decode words, which, in turn, negatively impacts his ability to obtain meaning from written text. For instance, an error analysis suggested that although Ryan could generally identify initial letter sounds, he did not consistently attend to medial or final sounds when attempting to read the word (e.g., he read "goal" as "go"). Moreover, when Ryan attended to initial and final sounds, he often confused medial sounds and either added sounds not in the initial word or omitted sounds (e.g., he read "during" as "doing"). Finally, although Ryan attempted to apply phonetic strategies to decode words, he often broke down each word into separate parts without fully blending the word after decoding those parts. For instance, when presented with the word "carefully," Ryan broke it down into two separate words, "careful" and "fully." While Ryan's reading decoding difficulties may be related to his weaknesses in working memory, processing speed, and fluency, his reading comprehension is likely most strongly impacted by his weakness in lexical knowledge, as evidenced by his performance on the Gc-VL Cluster (standard score = 81).

Mathematics

In the area of mathematics, Ryan was required to perform basic mathematical computations (e.g., addition, subtraction) to solve problems (Numerical Operations, standard score = 98), as well as solve more involved word problems *that were read to him* by the examiner (Math Reasoning, standard score = 95). Ryan's overall performance in math (Math Composite standard score = 95 [90–100]; 38th percentile) is consistent with his academic record review, which revealed generally average math performance. Although Ryan's teacher indicated that he has recently begun to struggle with specific math tasks, it is likely that this is a result of the nature of his present math instruction (e.g., the current curriculum is focused almost exclusively on word problems) and may also be related in part to his weaknesses in the areas of processing speed and working memory—abilities that have both demonstrated a consistent relationship to math achievement.

Written Language

Ryan's performance in the area of writing reflects his ability to accurately spell a series of isolated words that are presented orally by the examiner (Spelling, standard score = 87); and to write words fluently, combine words, and generate connected text using contextual cues (e.g., pictures) or verbal prompts (Written Expression, standard score = 96). Ryan obtained a Written Language Composite of 90 (85–95), which is ranked at the 25th percentile and is classified as Average Range/Within Normal Limits. Although Ryan performed Within Normal Limits on the spelling subtest, he demonstrated several noteworthy errors. That is, although Ryan's misspellings generally approximated the orally presented word, in that he wrote phonetic representations of the word, there were instances, similar to his reading performance, wherein Ryan either added sounds not presented in the original word or omitted sounds. Other errors resulted in approximations of only the initial sound of the word. Although the former errors likely will not detract from the content of Ryan's written work and will interfere only minimally with its readability, the latter types of errors, wherein Ryan spells only the initial letter-sound correctly, could exert more of an impact on the readability of Ryan's written work. A review of Ryan's classroom writing samples supports this finding. More specifically, although some of Ryan's work was easily read despite multiple spelling errors, when Ryan could not spell a word phonetically, he tended to write words using only their initial sounds (e.g., he wrote "destroy" as "distrude"), which seriously detracted from the readability of his work and disrupted the continuity of his writing.

Oral Language

Ryan's performance in the area of Oral Language reflects his ability to name words, generate stories, or provide directions when given visual or verbal cues (Oral Expression, standard score = 98), as well as generate words based on visual or verbal descriptions and select pictures that match a specific word or sentence (Listening Comprehension, standard score = 92). Ryan's expressive and receptive language skills are Average, as reflected by his obtained Oral Language Composite of 92 (87–97; 29th percentile). Although Ryan performed Within Normal Limits on both tasks that make up this domain, he demonstrated difficulty on specific aspects of each task. For instance, on the expressive language task, Ryan had difficulty when he was asked to quickly name words that were associated with specific semantic categories (similar to his difficulties on the WJ III Retrieval Fluency test). On the receptive language task, Ryan's difficulty centered on an inability to state single words that reflected a definition presented by the examiner. Ryan's difficulty on this specific task appears to be directly related to his weakness in lexical knowledge.

Diagnostic Impressions

Data obtained from the administration of the WISC-IV, WIAT-II, and select tests from the WJ III, coupled with information from select comparisons among

DON'T FORGET

Pertinent Information to Include in Summary and Diagnostic Impressions Section

- State summary information early in the body of the report.
- Include summary of referral, key background, or behavioral observation points.
- Summarize the most important interpretations of global scores and strengths and weaknesses.
- Defend your diagnosis, if one is made.

Source: From A. S. Kaufman & E. O. Lichtenberger, *Essentials of WISC-III and WPPSI-R Assessment.* Copyright © 2000 John Wiley & Sons, Inc. This material is used by permission of John Wiley & Sons, Inc.

Ryan's cognitive abilities, suggest that he demonstrates Below Average to Average Range functioning across the various cognitive and academic domains that were evaluated. Ryan's intact areas of functioning include his associative memory, general language development and reasoning abilities, and oral language ability. His overall global intellectual ability was classified as Average Range/Within Normal Limits. Ryan demonstrated specific cognitive weaknesses in processing speed, working memory, fluency, lexical knowledge, phonetic coding, and visual processing—all of which contribute to his reported academic difficulties, particularly in the areas of reading and writing. For instance, although Ryan appears to have a sufficient amount of information available to him (Gc-K0) to read and understand age-appropriate reading passages and compose written text, his inability to efficiently process (Gs) and retain information in immediate awareness long enough to encode or transform it (Gsm-WM), coupled with his weaknesses in Lexical Knowledge (Gc-VL), and specific aspects of Visual Processing (Gv) and Auditory Processing (Ga-PC) negatively impact his ability to decode specific words, consistently comprehend written text, and communicate his thoughts effectively in written form.

Although Ryan has good knowledge of factual information, he lacks facility with words and, therefore, has difficulty reasoning with words. This difficulty constrains his ability to communicate his thoughts effectively in writing, despite having adequate knowledge of a topic. Ryan's weak vocabulary also impacts his ability to comprehend what he reads. This finding is consistent with his teacher's description of his comprehension skills as "inconsistent."

Ryan's weakness in the areas of processing speed and retrieval fluency interfere with his ability to process information efficiently and is likely partly responsible for his self-reported difficulty with completing tasks on time. These weaknesses also impact his ability to read fluently, which leads to a deterioration in reading comprehension. Weaknesses in processing speed and fluency may also impact Ryan's written expression. For example, he may have difficulty generating ideas quickly, copying notes from the board, and taking notes during an oral presentation. As a result, Ryan may have difficulty keeping up with his classmates.

Ryan's performance on various measures of achievement is consistent with referral concerns, and is both consistent with and logically related to the outcomes found in the evaluation of his cognitive abilities. Ryan demonstrated weak word-attack and word-recognition skills. His spelling and reading comprehension skills, although not considered Normative Weaknesses, represent areas of difficulty for him. It is important to note that the tests administered to Ryan included many context cues. For instance, on the writing test, Ryan was sometimes provided with a picture that he needed to write about and/or was *provided with* sentences that he had to connect using specific words (e.g., conjunctions). Additionally, this writing test required Ryan to generate relatively short paragraphs rather than lengthy ones.

Similarly, the reading comprehension test that was administered to Ryan allowed him to refer back to the text when answering questions, which reduced the demands on Ryan's short-term memory. The demands of Ryan's current curriculum clearly exceed those that were required to complete the academic tests administered during this evaluation.

In summary, Ryan's pattern of related cognitive and academic weaknesses exist within an otherwise normal ability profile. This pattern of strengths and weaknesses is consistent with a specific learning disability in the area of reading (see Figure 9.1 for a graphic representation of Ryan's test performances). His performance suggests that he has a disorder in two psychological processes, namely processing speed and short-term memory, that interfere with his ability to read individual words in isolation. Ryan's weaknesses in vocabulary, retrieval fluency, and phonetic coding also contribute to his reading difficulties. It is likely that the same cognitive processes and abilities that contributed to Ryan's reading difficulty, as well as poor reading ability in and of itself, have contributed to the difficulties that Ryan demonstrates in other academic domains (e.g., spelling, written language). Hence, it is recommended that the current assessment results be presented before the Committee on Special Education to determine whether there is agreement that a disabling condition, as defined by the Individuals with Disabilities Education Act (IDEA), exists, and to discuss the appropriate supports and

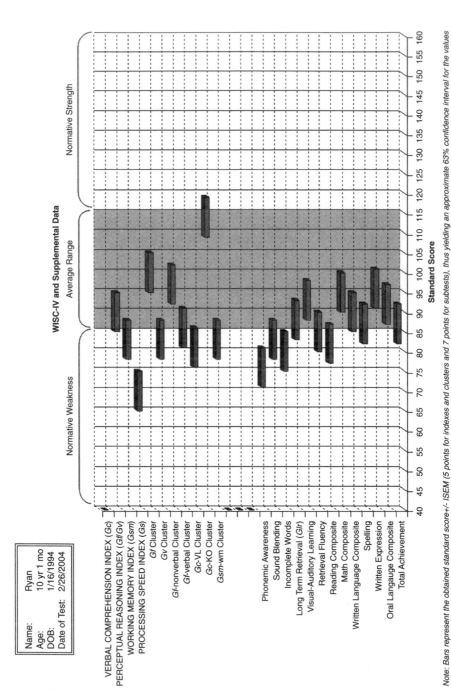

Name: Ryan
Age: 10 yr 1 mo
DOB: 1/16/1994
Date of Test: 2/26/2004

WISC-IV and Supplemental Data

Normative Weakness | Average Range | Normative Strength

Standard Score

VERBAL COMPREHENSION INDEX (Gc)
PERCEPTUAL REASONING INDEX (Gf/Gv)
WORKING MEMORY INDEX (Gsm)
PROCESSING SPEED INDEX (Gs)
Gf Cluster
Gv Cluster
Gf-nonverbal Cluster
Gf-verbal Cluster
Gc-VL Cluster
Gc-KO Cluster
Gsm-wm Cluster
Phonemic Awareness
Sound Blending
Incomplete Words
Long Term Retrieval (Glr)
Visual-Auditory Learning
Retrieval Fluency
Reading Composite
Math Composite
Written Language Composite
Spelling
Written Expression
Oral Language Composite
Total Achievement

Note: Bars represent the obtained standard score+/– ISEM (5 points for indexes and clusters and 7 points for subtests), thus yielding an approximate 63% confidence interval for the values

Figure 9.1 A Graphic Representation of Ryan's Test Performances from the WISC-IV DMIA v1.0

services that should be provided to Ryan in an effort to circumvent the impact that his Normative Weaknesses have on his ability to learn and achieve at a level commensurate with his same-age peers.

Recommendations

The primary purpose of psychoeducational assessment is not so much diagnostic as it is to generate data that may be used to develop effective interventions to resolve the issues that led to the referral in the first place. Because of the close relationship that exists between theory and assessment, the resulting data provide a significant foundation from which learning difficulties can be clearly understood and appropriate instructional interventions developed. Regardless of the types of interventions that are developed, ongoing evaluation of their effectiveness should remain a part of whatever plan is developed to ameliorate the observed academic difficulties and concerns. The integration of corroborative information from standardized tests, teacher and parent reports, and prereferral data provided the basis for the following recommendations for Ryan:

1. To address Ryan's identified difficulty in the area of word knowledge, it may be beneficial to provide specific supports that can be used during the completion of academic tasks. Such supports may include, but are not limited to, the following: (a) provide Ryan with a word bank for written expression tasks; (b) provide a glossary of terms that Ryan can refer to when completing reading assignments; (c) ensure that test questions do not include vocabulary terms that are unknown; (d) review or teach vocabulary words when Ryan is asked to read from content-area texts; (e) write key words and terms on the board when lecturing on new content areas; (f) ensure that instructions contain words that Ryan knows; (g) simplify instructions by extending upon unknown words with words that are familiar to Ryan, or define terms when initially presenting them (e.g., "the *composition* of igneous rock, that is, *what it is made up of,* is ...."); and (h) teach Ryan to use a thesaurus when completing writing tasks.
2. Ryan's short-term memory weaknesses are most appropriately addressed through specific instructional modifications and self-implemented strategies. For instance, Ryan's teachers should avoid the use of elaborate or multistep instructions whenever possible. Additionally, Ryan's teachers should sequence material from simple to

more complex. His teachers can also provide frequent opportunities for practice and review of newly learned material, including systematic review within a few hours of learning. In terms of self-implemented strategies, Ryan should be encouraged to request repetition of instructions or statements when necessary, and should be taught to use mnemonic aids and verbal mediation strategies (e.g., saying the information to be remembered while looking at it) that he can apply when trying to retain new information.

3. To address Ryan's visual processing difficulties, it may be beneficial to (a) avoid excessive reliance on visual models, diagrams, and demonstrations; (b) accompany visual demonstrations with oral explanations; and (c) break down spatial tasks into component parts (e.g., providing a set of verbal instructions to match each part). Additionally, because Ryan may have trouble forming a visual representation of a concept in his mind (e.g., a mental image), manipulatives or hands-on, concrete learning experiences may be beneficial when learning about an abstract concept that is visual in nature (e.g., the rotation of the planets in the solar system). Concrete or hands-on experiences should also be supplemented with verbal information.

4. Ryan's teacher can attempt to circumvent any adverse impact caused by his processing speed weakness in several ways, including (a) providing him with additional time to complete tasks; (b) shortening the length of in-class assignments; (c) allowing him to complete unfinished seatwork at home; (d) assisting Ryan in generating ideas and listing them prior to completing writing assignments; (e) utilizing a guided-notes (i.e., fill-in-the-blank) system that Ryan can use during classroom lectures or lessons.

5. Ryan's auditory processing weaknesses negatively impact his reading performance and can potentially interfere with his ability to accurately process orally presented information (e.g., instructions, class discussions). To address these difficulties, it may be beneficial to (a) encourage Ryan to physically orient himself toward the teacher during the provision of oral instructions ("seeing" what is being stated supports the processing of auditory information); (b) ensure that words are clearly enunciated during the presentation of oral information (e.g., dictation of spelling words); (c) check for understanding of orally presented directions by asking Ryan to paraphrase what he heard; and (d) provide Ryan with direct instruction regarding the use of word-attack skills and context cues to decode words.

PSYCHOLOGICAL REPORT by Nadeen L. Kaufman, EdD

Name: Cheryl J.   DOB: 4/15/89
Chronological age: 14 years, 11 months   Grade: 9
Date of Testing: 3/27/04   Date of Report: 4/2/04

Referral and Background Information

Cheryl was referred for evaluation by her parents, Mr. and Mrs. J., and by Dr. Ronald F., a hematologist. Dr. F. and Mr. and Mrs. J. would like to gain some insight into Cheryl's cognitive and achievement abilities and current level of functioning; they suspect that she might have a learning disability. Cheryl has been experiencing difficulty with her 9th-grade schoolwork and has a history of reading and spelling problems. Her school grades have been deteriorating, and she has been having more difficulty as the demands in school have become greater. In the recent past, Cheryl has been noncompliant in taking her medication for HIV; both her medical condition and her noncompliance have been great concerns to her parents, physicians, and therapist.

Cheryl, adopted at the age of 2 months, was diagnosed with an "unknown blood disorder" at age 6 months, and as being HIV-positive at age 18 months. Virtually nothing is known about her biological parents. A referral was made from Cheryl's therapist, Dr. Judy S., for psychological testing. Dr. S., Dr. F., and Cheryl's parents suspect that Cheryl may have a learning disability that is making school extraordinarily difficult for her and may be related to her noncompliance with her medications.

Cheryl lives at home with her brother and sister and both of her adoptive parents in San Bernardino, CA. She is the youngest of the three children, all of whom were adopted as infants. Her brother, Milton, is 19, and her sister, Candace, is 17; Cheryl is almost 15. Both parents, Milton, and Cheryl are Caucasian; Candace is African American.

Cheryl's birth history is unknown and her early developmental history is unremarkable. She reached all developmental milestones within a normal time frame. Since the diagnosis of HIV-positive at age 18 months, Cheryl has required close blood monitoring, with frequent visits to the doctor's office for blood tests. Based on occasional abnormalities revealed by the blood tests, she has had blood transfusions her whole life, sometimes several times a year. She has also had many medical "emergencies" throughout her life because every infection or cold is legitimate cause for concern. During the past two years, her failure to take prescribed medications has led to three visits to the emergency room at a nearby hospital. No other major illnesses or injuries were reported, but Cheryl's mother stated that Cheryl's health has been at the forefront of their parenting efforts since the diagnosis of her disease.

It is her parents' belief that Cheryl has just recently begun to take more responsibility for her own health care. Cheryl is also currently being seen by a health team that assists in taking care of her physical and emotional needs in relation to her HIV and health maintenance.

Cheryl attended preschool from age 2 to age 4½. Mrs. J. reported that Cheryl was very tearful when she first began school and that she cried often even though her older sister, Candace, was at school with her. When Cheryl went to kindergarten she reportedly enjoyed school more and did not cry when school began. Mrs. J. also reported that Cheryl was younger and less mature than the other children in the classroom "because of her late birthday." When Cheryl went into the first grade she experienced "stomach aches" and did not like school. Her parents then placed her in a kindergarten–first grade combination classroom at a private school for the second semester. The following autumn, Cheryl began the first grade again, at a new public school, and apparently did better and felt more comfortable.

Mrs. J. reported that Cheryl had difficulty with phonics at an early age and that she was eventually tested by a school psychologist when she was in second grade. Mrs. J. stated that the school psychologist said that Cheryl had a "high IQ" but that she was immature for her age.

Throughout Cheryl's education, she has had moderate difficulties with her schoolwork, but her health care, rather than her school difficulties, has typically been the focus of her problems. Recently, however, her schoolwork has become more demanding and difficult and has become a pressing concern to her; it has also assumed more importance to her parents. In the summer before the 9th grade, Cheryl expressed some doubt in her own ability to achieve academically. She was beginning to recognize that she was having problems completing assignments, especially writing and spelling. Cheryl agreed to this testing and expressed a desire to improve her schoolwork and obtain a better understanding of her academic and intellectual strengths and weaknesses.

Cheryl, Mrs. J., and several of Cheryl's teachers reported that she is a very social adolescent. Mrs. J. stated that there had been a change in her peer group to a "less academically oriented" group, with whom she spends a great deal of time. Her counselor and two teachers describe one of her strengths as her extremely personable nature and ability to get along well with others. Cheryl's math teacher stated that she "talks too much in class and is out of her seat a lot." In comparison, Cheryl's history teacher reported that Cheryl was "withdrawn" and "not socializing." The amount of time that Cheryl spends socializing in class may be related to the peers that are in each of her classes with whom she can socialize. Both Mrs. J. and Cheryl reported that outside of school, Cheryl's time is mostly spent on the phone with friends or going out with her friends. Cheryl also added that most of her friends are older than she. When asked why her friends were older she said that they just were and did not offer any further explanation.

At the beginning of the second (and final) testing session, the examiner asked Cheryl how she was doing in school and asked her if she had any questions. Cheryl reported that she was having great difficulty in school and that she spent 4–5 hours per night doing homework. Whereas she undoubtedly does not spend this amount of time on homework each night, it does suggest that Cheryl feels academically overwhelmed. She said that she just cannot keep up and that it takes her a lot longer to do her schoolwork than it does the other students. She reported that she did not feel that her social life interfered with her schoolwork; however, most adolescents would provide a similar response.

Appearance and Behavioral Observations

Cheryl is an attractive adolescent girl with brown eyes and straight, dark-blond hair cut bluntly above her shoulders. She was well groomed and dressed casually and she wore many earrings in her ears. Cheryl appeared her stated age of almost 15 and her overall presentation of herself was consistent with that of an independent adolescent. She made very little eye contact, her posture was poor, and she did not converse easily with the examiner. Cheryl seemed to feel relatively uncomfortable during most of the testing and even though she complied with all that was requested of her, it was apparent that she retained her sense of privacy and minimal social involvement with the examiner. At one point during the testing, Cheryl's pager went off and she asked if she could use the phone. When she was asked to wait, she did, and returned to the task without any difficulty. It should be noted that Cheryl's behavior is not unusual for an adolescent.

Cheryl arrived for her appointments on time and was cooperative and pleasant. She spoke softly and she often had her hands in front of her mouth while she was speaking. Although Cheryl seemed to be uninterested, especially during the first testing session, she appeared to be trying her best. Cheryl was a little anxious, as evidenced by her excessive psychomotor activity. She tapped her foot on the ground repeatedly, moved around in her seat, and engaged in a number of self-stimulating behaviors. For example, she continually engaged in the following behaviors: running her hands through her hair, playing with her necklace, playing with strings on her clothing, touching her face, touching her neck, and pulling or biting on her lips. These behaviors did not seem to distract her from what she was doing but rather seemed to soothe her emotionally and reduce her anxiety.

While solving problems and answering test questions, Cheryl continued to speak softly. The tone of her speech lacked confidence, as her answers were often stated in more of a questioning tone. Cheryl also bit her nails when she seemed unsure of herself. Despite her apparent lack of confidence, she was able to say when she did know an answer and would ask questions if she did not know something or did not understand what was being asked of her. In general, she responded well to feedback and encouragement from the examiner.

Evaluation Procedures

Wechsler Intelligence Scale for Children–Fourth Edition (WISC-IV)
Kaufman Assessment Battery for Children–Second Edition (KABC-II)
Kaufman Test of Educational Achievement–Second Edition, Comprehensive Form (KTEA-II, Form A)
Clinical interview with Mrs. J.
School observation
Interviews with teachers
Interview with school counselor
Interview with Dr. Judy S.
Home visit and observation

Test Results and Interpretation

During the first testing session, Cheryl was administered the core battery of the Wechsler Intelligence Scale for Children–Fourth Edition (WISC-IV), and about half of the Kaufman Test of Educational Achievement–Second Edition, Comprehensive Form (KTEA-II, Form A). At the second session, five days later, she was administered the remainder of the KTEA-II and the core battery of the Kaufman Assessment Battery for Children–Second Edition (KABC-II). The WISC-IV and KABC-II are each individually administered tests of a child's intellectual and processing ability, and each provides scales to identify the child's cognitive strengths and weaknesses. The KTEA-II measures school achievement in reading, math, oral language, and written language.

Cognitive Assessment

WISC-IV

The WISC-IV groups an individual's ability into four global areas: Verbal Comprehension Index (VCI), which measures verbal ability; Perceptual Reasoning Index (PRI), which involves the manipulation of concrete materials or processing of visual stimuli to solve nonverbal problems; Working Memory Index (WMI), which measures short-term memory; and Processing Speed Index (PSI), which measures cognitive processing efficiency.

On the WISC-IV, Cheryl earned a Full Scale IQ (FSIQ) of 114, which ranks her overall ability at the 82nd percentile and classifies her global IQ as falling within the Average Range. There is a 95% chance that her true FSIQ is between 109 and 119. However, this estimate of her general intellectual ability on the WISC-IV cannot be interpreted meaningfully and should be deemphasized because she displayed considerable variability in the four Indexes that constitute this full scale score. Her Indexes ranged from 88 on the WMI (21st percentile) to 119 on the VCI (90th percentile), suggesting that Cheryl's intelligence is best understood by her performance on the separate WISC-IV Indexes, namely, Verbal Comprehension, Perceptual Reasoning, Working Memory, and Processing Speed.

Before discussing Cheryl's Indexes on the four scales, one must first determine whether each Index is interpretable—that is, does it measure a reasonably unitary trait for Cheryl, or do her scaled scores on the subtests that make up the Index include substantial variability? In fact, all four of Cheryl's WISC-IV Indexes are considered "interpretable." The largest discrepancy among her subtest scaled scores was 4 points on the VCI (the difference between her scaled scores of 15 on Similarities and 11 on Vocabulary). Discrepancies on the other three Indexes were 3 points (PRI), 2 points (PSI), and 0 points (WMI). None of these values met or exceeded the critical value needed for each of these scales. Consequently, Cheryl's PRI, VCI, WMI, and PSI are all considered to provide good estimates of the abilities measured by each scale.

The PRI, a measure of Visual Processing and Fluid Reasoning *(Gv/Gf)*, represents Cheryl's ability to reason using visual stimuli. Cheryl's *Gv/Gf* ability was assessed by tasks that required her to recreate a series of modeled or pictured designs using blocks (Block Design), identify the missing portion of an incomplete visual matrix from one of five response options (Matrix Reasoning), and select one picture from each of two or three rows of pictures to form a group with a common characteristic (Picture Concepts). Cheryl obtained a PRI *(Gv/Gf)* of 117 (108–123), which ranks her at the 87th percentile and classifies her PRI as Above

Average/Normative Strength. Cheryl's perceptual reasoning ability is considered a significant strength compared to other individuals her age in the normal population. In addition, her ability in this area is significantly higher than her abilities in other areas. Therefore, Cheryl's perceptual reasoning ability is a notable integrity, a finding that may play an essential role in developing educational interventions.

The VCI, a measure of Crystallized Intelligence *(Gc)*, represents Cheryl's ability to reason with previously learned information. An individual's *Gc* ability develops largely as a function of formal and informal educational opportunities and experiences and is highly dependent on exposure to mainstream U.S. culture. Cheryl's *Gc* ability was assessed by tasks that required her to define words (Vocabulary), draw conceptual similarities between words (Similarities), and answer questions involving knowledge of general principles and social situations (Comprehension). Cheryl obtained a VCI *(Gc)* of 119 (111–125), which ranks her at the 90th percentile and classifies her VCI as Above Average/Normative Strength. Cheryl's crystallized intelligence is considered a significant strength compared to other individuals her age in the normal population. In addition, her ability in this area is significantly higher than her abilities in other areas. Therefore, Cheryl's crystallized intelligence is a notable integrity, a finding that may play an essential role in developing educational interventions.

The WMI, a measure of Short-Term Memory *(Gsm)*, represents Cheryl's ability to apprehend and hold, or transform, information in immediate awareness and then use it within a few seconds. Cheryl's *Gsm* ability was assessed by two tasks—Digit Span required Cheryl to repeat a sequence of numbers in the same order as presented by the examiner (Digit Span Forward) and also in the reverse order (Digit Span Backward), and Letter-Number Sequencing required her to listen to a sequence of numbers and letters and recall the numbers in ascending order and the letters in alphabetical order. Cheryl obtained a WMI *(Gsm)* of 88 (81–97), which ranks her at the 21st percentile and classifies her WMI as Average Range/Within Normal Limits. Cheryl's short-term memory is considered a significant weakness compared to her abilities in other areas. In fact, the difference between her short-term memory and her abilities in other areas is so large that it is not commonly found in the normal population of children her age. Therefore, Cheryl's short-term memory is a notable personal weakness, a finding that may play an essential role in developing educational interventions.

The PSI, a measure of Processing Speed *(Gs)*, represents Cheryl's ability to fluently and automatically perform cognitive tasks, especially when under pressure to maintain focused attention and concentration. Cheryl's *Gs* ability was assessed by two tasks—one required Cheryl to quickly copy symbols that were paired with numbers according to a key (Coding), and the other required her to identify the presence or absence of a target symbol in a row of symbols (Symbol Search). Cheryl obtained a PSI *(Gs)* of 112 (102–120), which ranks her at the 79th percentile and classifies her PSI as Average Range/Within Normal Limits.

As noted, Cheryl's WISC-IV FSIQ could not be interpreted because she demonstrated considerable variability in her performance across the four Indexes that make up this score, namely the Verbal Comprehension, Perceptual Reasoning, Working Memory, and Processing Speed Indexes. However, it is often useful to provide a global estimate of an individual's current level of functioning. Because Cheryl's performance on the Verbal Comprehension and Perceptual Reasoning Indexes was similar, these Indexes can be combined to yield a General Ability Index (GAI). The GAI differs from the FSIQ in that it is not influenced directly by Cheryl's performance on working memory and processing speed tasks.

Cheryl earned a GAI of 120, classifying her general level of intellectual ability as Above Average/Normative Strength. The chances are good (95%) that Cheryl's true GAI is somewhere within the range of 114 to 126. Her GAI is ranked at the 91st percentile, indicating that she scored higher than 91 percent of other children of the same age in the standardization sample. Table 9.3 summarizes Cheryl's performance on all tests administered.

KABC-II

The KABC-II, like the WISC-IV, provides a comprehensive measure of cognitive abilities. Ordinarily, examiners opt to administer a single measure of comprehensive cognitive ability to a child, and supplement that measure with selected tasks to enrich the breadth of the cognitive assessment. For Cheryl, a second comprehensive test was administered for several reasons: (1) as noted, Cheryl seemed to be uninterested in the testing, especially during the first session, so validation of the results was warranted; (2) the WISC-IV PRI combines *Gf* and *Gv* abilities—the KABC-II provides *separate* scales to measure *Gf* and *Gv,* which might offer additional insights; (3) the KABC-II measures Learning Ability *(Glr),* an important skill to assess for individuals with learning problems in school; and (4) the KABC-II is a new test—the best way for examiners to understand the clinical aspects of new instruments is to administer them alongside traditional tests such as Wechsler's.

The KABC-II is based on a double theoretical foundation: Luria's neuropsychological model and the Cattell-Horn-Carroll (CHC) psychometric theory. It offers five scales, each given a label that reflects both theoretical models: Sequential/ *Gsm,* Simultaneous/*Gv,* Learning/*Glr,* Planning/*Gf,* and Knowledge/*Gc.* Examiners who opt to administer the Luria model of the KABC-II give only four of

Table 9.3 Psychometric Summary for Cheryl J.

Wechsler Intelligence Scale for Children–Fourth Edition (WISC-IV)

Index/Subtest	Standard Score (mean = 100; SD = 15)	95% CI	Percentile Rank
Verbal Comprehension	119	[111–125]	90th
Similarities = 15			
Vocabulary = 11			
Comprehension = 14			
Perceptual Reasoning	117	[108–123]	87th
Block Design = 11			
Picture Concepts = 13			
Matrix Reasoning = 14			
Working Memory	88	[81–97]	21st
Digit Span = 8			
Letter-Number Sequencing = 8			
Processing Speed	112	[102–120]	79th
Coding = 13			
Symbol Search = 11			
Full Scale IQ	114	[109–119]	82nd
General Ability Index	121	[115–126]	92nd

(continued)

these scales (Knowledge/*Gc* is excluded when the Luria model is used because measures of language ability and acquired knowledge may not provide fair assessment of the cognitive abilities of some children—e.g., those from nonmainstream backgrounds or those with receptive/expressive language disorders). Cheryl was administered the CHC model of the KABC-II, which comprises all five areas of cognitive ability (with each area measured by two subtests). She earned a KABC-II Fluid-Crystallized Index (FCI) of 120, ranking her at the 91st percentile and classifying her overall cognitive ability as Above Average/Normative Strength.

Cheryl's KBAC-II FCI of 120 and WISC-IV GAI of 121 are virtually the same. However, like Cheryl's WISC-IV FSIQ, her FCI is not very meaningful in view of the considerable variability among Cheryl's Indexes on the KABC-II. Her range of Indexes on the KABC-II was greater than the 2-SD range on the WISC-IV, extending from 94 on Sequential/*Gsm* (34th percentile) to 135 on Planning/*Gf* (99th percentile). Quite clearly, the best understanding of Cheryl's strengths and

Table 9.3 (Continued)

Kaufman Assessment Battery for Children–Second Edition (KABC-II)
Cattell-Horn-Carroll (CHC) Model

Scale/Subtest	Standard Score (mean = 100; SD = 15)	95% CI	Percentile Rank
Sequential/*Gsm*	94	[85–103]	34th
Number Recall = 10			
Word Order = 8			
Simultaneous/*Gv*	106	[96–116]	66th
Rover = 13			
Block Counting = 9			
Learning/*Glr*	126	[117–133]	96th
Atlantis = 16			
Rebus = 13			
Planning/*Gf*	135	[120–144]	99th
Story Completion = 17			
Pattern Reasoning = 14			
Knowledge/*Gc*	115	[106–122]	84th
Verbal Knowledge = 11			
Riddles = 15			
Fluid-Crystallized Index	120	[115–125]	91st

weaknesses will come from an integration of her Indexes on both the WISC-IV and KABC-II.

On the KABC-II, four of Cheryl's five Indexes are considered "interpretable." That is to say, she performed with reasonable consistency on the subtests that constitute four of the KABC-II scales, but her scores were too variable on the fifth scale—Knowledge/*Gc*. The largest discrepancy in her scores was 4 points (the difference between her highest and lowest subtest scaled scores on a scale), and that discrepancy occurred twice—on the Simultaneous/*Gv* scale (where she earned 13 on Rover and 9 on Block Counting) and on the Knowledge/*Gc* scale (where she earned 11 on Verbal Knowledge and 15 on Riddles). The difference of 4 points on Simultaneous/*Gv* is smaller than the critical value of 6 points to determine "uninterpretability" for ages 13–18 years. However, for Knowledge/*Gc*, the critical value for ages 13–18 years is 4 points, exactly equal to Cheryl's subtest score variability on that scale. Consequently, all of Cheryl's scale Indexes—except Knowledge/

Table 9.3 (Continued)

Kaufman Test of Educational Achievement–Second Edition (KTEA-II), Comprehensive Form (Form A)

Composite/Subtest	Standard Score	Percentile Rank
Reading Composite	**105**	**63rd**
Letter and Word Recognition	89	23rd
Reading Comprehension	120	91st
(Nonsense Word Decoding)	(85)	(16th)
(Decoding Composite)	**(87)**	**(19th)**
Mathematics Composite	**112**	**79th**
Mathematics Concepts and Applications	112	79th
Mathematics Computation	111	77th
Oral Language Composite	**121**	**92nd**
Listening Comprehension	117	87th
Oral Expression	124	95th
Written Language Composite	**88**	**21st**
Written Expression	91	27th
Spelling	88	21st
Total Battery Composite	**108**	**70th**

Note: Tests appearing in parentheses are supplemental measures. CI = Confidence Interval.

Gc—are able to be interpreted. (The critical values for each scale denote subtest scaled score differences that are so large that they occurred less than 10% of the time in the normative sample; such differences render a scale Index uninterpretable.)[1]

On the KABC-II, Cheryl's Planning/*Gf* Index of 135 (120–144) ranks her performance at the 99th percentile relative to adolescents her age and classifies her ability as Upper Extreme/Normative Strength. To perform at this high level, Cheryl had to solve nonverbal problems rapidly where these problems require Fluid Reasoning *(Gf)*, executive functioning (generating and evaluating hypotheses), verbal mediation, and planning ability. One of these tasks required her to complete series of abstract patterns (Pattern Reasoning), and the other required her to complete a story told with pictures (Story Completion). Cheryl's strong *Gf* reflects both a Normative Strength (relative to others her age) and a Personal

[1]Note that the critical values for determining scale interpretability differ for the WISC-IV and KBAC-II.

Strength (relative to her own level of ability); furthermore, the difference between her Index of 135 and her own average Index is "uncommonly large" (i.e., differences that large occurred less than 10% of the time in the normative population). Therefore, Cheryl's *Gf* ability is a Key Asset for her, a finding that should play an essential role in developing educational interventions.

Cheryl's Learning/*Glr* Index of 126 (117–133) ranks her performance at the 96th percentile relative to adolescents her age and classifies her ability as Above Average/ Normative Strength. Cheryl demonstrated the ability to use her Long-Term Storage and Retrieval *(Glr)* to learn new material that is taught by the examiner in a standardized, structured manner (two paired-associate learning tasks—Atlantis required her to learn the nonsense names of fish, plants, and shells; Rebus Learning required her to "read" words that are paired with symbols). Her ability to learn new material *(Glr)* is both a Normative Strength and a Personal Strength for Cheryl, a finding that should play an essential role in developing educational interventions—especially since the ability to learn new material translates directly to the classroom.

Cheryl's Simultaneous/*Gv* Index of 106 (96–116) ranks her performance at the 66th percentile relative to adolescents her age and classifies her ability as Average Range/Within Normal Limits. Cheryl demonstrated the ability use her simultaneous and Visual Processing *(Gv)* on two tasks, one requiring her to use executive functioning and visualization to solve problems (getting "Rover" to a bone on a checkerboard-like grid using the shortest path), and the other (Block Counting) requiring her to count an array of blocks where some blocks are hidden or partially hidden. Though her *Gv* ability is in the Average Range relative to other adolescents her age, it represents a Personal Weakness for Cheryl, a finding that may play an essential role in developing educational interventions.

Cheryl's Sequential/*Gsm* Index of 94 (85–103) ranks her performance at the 34th percentile relative to adolescents her age and classifies her ability as within the Average Range/Within Normal Limits. Cheryl demonstrated her Short-Term Memory *(Gsm)* and sequential processing on Word Order, which required her to point in sequence to pictures named by the examiner, sometimes with an intervening interference task (color naming), and Number Recall (forward digit span). Although her *Gsm* ability is in the Average Range relative to other adolescents her age, it represents an "uncommon" Personal Weakness for Cheryl—i.e., her Index of 94 is below her Indexes on other KABC-II scales by an unusually large number of points (a magnitude that occurred less than 10% of the time in the normal population). This finding should play an essential role in developing educational interventions.

Integrating Test Scores from the WISC-IV and KABC-II

Cheryl's scores on the two comprehensive tests of cognitive abilities are basically quite consistent with one another. She displayed wide variability on both instruments, but her strengths and weaknesses on both tests combine to paint a fairly clear picture of Cheryl's cognitive strengths and weaknesses. Despite her apparent lack of interest in the assessment process during the first session (when the WISC-IV was given), her similar level of performance on the KABC-II, during the second session when interest level was more optimal, suggests that her WISC-IV profile provides a valid estimate of her functioning.

The WISC-IV PRI measures a blend of Gf and Gv, making the nature of Cheryl's Normative and Personal Strengths unclear. When viewed in the context of Cheryl's KABC-II profile, it is evident that Cheryl's PRI of 117 (87th percentile) is the approximate midpoint of her exceptional Gf ability (Planning/Gf Index = 135, 99th percentile) and her average Gv ability (Simultaneous/Gv = 106, 66th percentile). In fact, on the KABC-II, Cheryl had a *Personal Weakness* in her Gv ability. Examination of Cheryl's PRI subtest scaled scores indicates consistency with stronger Gf than Gv—she performed at the 91st and 84th percentiles on the two subtests that are primarily measures of Gf (Matrix Reasoning and Picture Concepts, respectively) compared to the 65th percentile on Block Design (primarily Gv). In fact, Cheryl's exceptional fluid reasoning ability was evident throughout the subtest profiles of-both the WISC-IV and KABC-II, most notably on the Gc scales. On the VCI, Cheryl performed better on Comprehension and Similarities (91st and 95th percentiles, respectively), both of which require Gf for successful performance, than on Vocabulary (65th percentile). Similarly, on the Knowledge/Gc scale, Cheryl scored higher on Riddles (95th percentile) than on Verbal Knowledge (65th percentile). Riddles requires Gf to integrate verbal clues to solve each "riddle"; Verbal Knowledge measures word knowledge and factual information, neither of which requires Gf. The Knowledge/Gc Index was not interpretable for Cheryl, undoubtedly because its component tasks differ in the amount of Gf each demands. Cheryl's strong Gf, evidenced on both comprehensive tests, has implications for Cheryl's educational intervention.

The WISC-IV and KABC-II also help document Cheryl's relative weakness in short-term memory, as she earned a WMI of 88 and a similar Sequential/Gsm Index of 94. Both of these Indexes are Within Normal Limits, but both are clear-cut weaknesses for Cheryl relative to her other cognitive abilities. This finding of a Gsm personal weakness on two different instruments has implications both diagnostically and for planning Cheryl's educational interventions.

In addition to the integration of test results on the WISC-IV and KABC-II to better understand her strengths and weaknesses on abilities measured by both tests, each test contributes information on a unique CHC ability. On the WISC-IV, Cheryl earned a PSI of 112, indicating that her processing speed was Average Range/Within Normal Limits. On the KABC-II, she displayed a Personal

Strength and Normative Strength on the Learning/*Glr* Scale (Index = 126), indicating that her learning ability and long-term storage and retrieval are areas of strength for her, important information for planning educational interventions.

Based on scores on both batteries, the following standard scores are the best estimates of her performance on six CHC abilities (*Gf, Glr,* and *Gv* are from KABC-II; *Gc* and *Gs* are from WISC-IV; *Gsm* is the average of her two pertinent Indexes).

CHC Broad Ability	Standard Score	Percentile Rank
Fluid Reasoning/*Gf*	135	99th
Long-Term Storage and Retrieval/*Glr*	126	96th
Crystallized Ability/*Gc*	115	84th
Processing Speed/*Gs*	112	79th
Visual Processing/*Gv*	106	66th
Short-Term Memory/*Gsm*	91	27th

Achievement Assessment

KTEA-II Comprehensive Form A

Cheryl's standard scores on the KTEA-II Form A (based on grade norms) were extremely varied. Her overall Test Battery Composite of 108 (70th percentile) was nothing more than a midpoint of her separate composite standard scores, which ranged from 88 to 121: Oral Language (121, 92nd percentile), Mathematics (112, 79th percentile), Reading (105, 63rd percentile), and Written Language (88, 21st percentile). Her Reading Composite of 105 suggests an average level of reading ability, but that standard score is misleading. Cheryl performed in the Above Average category on Reading Comprehension (120), but had great difficulty with basic reading fundamentals (89 on Letter and Word Recognition). Her phonetic abilities, in particular, are a significant weakness for her; she earned a standard score of 85 (16th percentile) on the supplementary Nonsense Word Decoding subtest, a task that required her to decode nonsense words by making use of principles of phonics. Her standard score of 87 (19th percentile) on the supplementary KTEA-II Decoding Composite (Letter and Word Recognition + Nonsense Word Decoding) provides an overview of this area of weakness.

Cheryl performed strikingly better in her Oral Language (121) than Written Language (88). She is notably better in expressing her ideas orally (124 on Oral

Expression) than via writing (91 on Written Expression). However, she is about equally able to comprehend information whether it is presented orally (117 in Listening Comprehension) or in printed form (120 in Reading Comprehension). Her performance on both of these "Comprehension" subtests was facilitated by the strong fluid reasoning that she displayed on the cognitive batteries.

Cheryl's performance in mathematics reveals intact functioning in the basic skills of computation and quantitative concepts (111) and also in the ability to apply mathematical principles to solve word problems (112).

The KTEA-II provides a systematic error analysis to help examiners identify specific academic areas of strength and weakness. Cheryl's responses on several subtests were further examined by this error-analysis procedure.

The KTEA-II error analysis for Spelling classifies spelling errors into 15 categories, and compares the number of errors that Cheryl made to the number made by other adolescents in Grade 9 who attempted the same number of items. Relative to her peers, Cheryl was classified as Weak in 7 of the 15 categories. The most noteworthy area of weakness, in which she made seven to eight errors (when the average person in her grade made two to four errors), were Suffixes and Word Endings, Long Vowels, Silent Letters, and Single and Double Consonants. For example, she spelled "construction" as "constructine," a problem with word endings; she spelled "while" as "whyle," a problem with long vowels; and she spelled "regretted" as "regretid," a problem with both long vowels and suffixes and word endings.

Further error analysis in the areas of Letter/Word Recognition and Nonsense Word Decoding revealed similar skill-weakness error patterns when Cheryl read words and nonsense words aloud. Again, the Weak skill areas included Suffixes and Word Endings, Long Vowels, and Silent Letters. For example, she pronounced the word "truth" with a short "u" sound; and "gigantic" with a short "i" sound in the first syllable, both examples of long vowel errors; she read "revolutionary" as "revolutinry," a problem with suffixes and word endings. In Nonsense Word Decoding, she pronounced "trame" with a short "a" sound as well as pronouncing the silent "e" as a long e sound, a problem with both long vowels and silent letters; "plewness" was read as "plewrest," a problem with suffixes and word endings.

The KTEA-II error analysis for Written Expression classifies writing errors into five categories: task, structure, word form, capitalization, and punctuation. When compared to her same-age peers, Cheryl made significantly more capitalization and punctuation errors (6 and 16, respectively) than her same-grade peers, who averaged only 0–2 errors in capitalization and 6–11 errors in punctuation.

Diagnostic Impressions

In view of Cheryl's extreme fluctuation in her performance on both cognitive batteries, it was difficult to find a "best estimate" of her current level of functioning. For the purposes of evaluating discrepancies between Cheryl's ability and achievement, her GAI of 121 on the WISC-IV, derived from her VCI and PRI, will be used. That score is significantly and substantially higher than her standard scores on the KTEA-II Decoding Composite (88), Written Language Composite (88), and both subtests that compose the Written Language Composite—Written Expression (91) and Spelling (88). These discrepancies are approximately 2 SDs, strongly supportive of a learning disorder. Based on these discrepancies, on a possible processing disorder in sequential processing or short-term memory, on the results of the error analysis, and on clear-cut areas of integrity in fluid reasoning, planning abilities, learning ability, and long-term storage and retrieval, Cheryl appears to demonstrate a learning disorder. This disorder appears to manifest in reading decoding, writing mechanics, written expression, and spelling, and is perhaps related to the sequential and memory Personal Weaknesses that she evidenced on the cognitive tests. This learning disorder undoubtedly explains many of the reading, writing, and spelling difficulties she has experienced in school, but it cannot explain all of her academic problems. For example, her mathematics ability is at the high end of the Average Range (which is consistent with her intellectual ability), and is evenly developed in different areas such as computational ability and math reasoning. The "D" that she is receiving after five weeks of class is probably related to the "bad citizenship" that was noted by her math teacher.

Cheryl's phonics problem and general difficulty with other basic reading skills are of less concern than her difficulties in written-language mechanics and spelling. She has compensated well for her reading-skill deficiencies, as attested by her Above Average performance on KTEA-II Reading Comprehension. The ability to understand what we read is quite dependent on reasoning ability. Cheryl has spontaneously been able to apply her exceptional reasoning and problem-solving abilities to gain understanding of material that she reads.

Although Cheryl's school and learning difficulties have been the focus of this assessment, it is important to address her emotional and social functioning and how it relates to her academic abilities and achievement. This assessment suggests that Cheryl is both anxious and oppositional. Her approach to many of the tasks and her interactions with the examiner, as well as some of her teachers reports, suggest that she is angry and that she does not relate to adults as well as she should. Cheryl's attitude and emotions significantly affect her school performance. Her relatively weak short-term memory likely makes school considerably more difficult for her than other students; however, she has compensated for her personal weaknesses well. Furthermore, Cheryl's poor citizenship grades and teacher reports about her socializing in class suggest that some of Cheryl's school problems stem from behavioral difficulties and her negative and angry attitude.

It is important to note that many of Cheryl's difficulties may also be related to her HIV status. That is, individuals infected with HIV, especially those who are perinatally exposed, often have cognitive, affective, and behavioral symptomatology directly resulting from the disease. Cognitive impairments generally include language deficits (especially expressive language), short-term memory impairments, visual-spatial processing difficulties, and phonological awareness deficits. These impairments in perinatally exposed children are due to the inability of the child's brain to make appropriate neuronal connections due to the introduction of the virus at a time when the brain is not fully developed. Although many children reach developmental milestones within normal limits, as Cheryl has, subtle cognitive difficulties can become evident over time due to the progressive nature of the disease. Although antiretroviral medications can delay, and sometimes reverse, the manifestation of these subclinical deficits, these deficits can still exert a negative impact on the child's functioning. Additionally, certain antiretroviral medications and protease inhibitors, which are commonly used to treat HIV-infected children and adolescents, can have negative effects over time. An unfortunate feature of these medications is that many are ototoxic. That is, they can impact a child's hearing and cause subtle hearing loss. This feature may partly explain Cheryl's reported history of difficulty with phonics as well as her observed weakness on phonologically based measures. Another common reason for phonological difficulties in HIV-infected children is the fact that these children often experience frequent colds and ear infections, which can compromise their hearing during sensitive periods of development. In essence, their frequent, and often lengthy, infections cause them to lose important linguistic information (e.g., subtle phonemic distinctions) and effectively delay appropriate development of phonological abilities.

In addition to the previously mentioned cognitive difficulties, affectively, HIV-infected individuals often manifest an increased level of anxiety and depression and, behaviorally, these individuals often have difficulties maintaining attention and are sometimes described as highly distractible.

Although Cheryl's cognitive *(Gsm)* and behavioral difficulties clearly have a negative impact on her academic functioning, the primary causes of her academic difficulties—that is, cognitive, behavioral, medical—cannot be determined. As such, Cheryl cannot be diagnosed as learning disabled under the Individuals with Disabilities Education Act (IDEA). That is, the exclusionary criteria that must be considered in learning-disability referrals requires the examiner to demonstrate that certain factors, such as a medical condition, are not the *primary* cause of the child's academic difficulties. Given that Cheryl's reported and observed difficulties are common consequences of HIV infection, it is difficult to rule out her health status as a primary cause of her current academic difficulties.

Because IDEA generally does not apply to individuals with communicable diseases, such as HIV, Cheryl may not meet criteria for classification of "Other Health Impaired" under IDEA because her physical condition appears to directly impact her ability to learn. Therefore, her health status cannot be ruled out as a *primary* cause for her learning difficulties. Nonetheless, individuals like Cheryl are protected under Section 504 of the Americans with Disabilities Act if there is evidence that the individual is "experiencing academic difficulty (below grade level performance), and it is suspected that the medical condition is or will adversely affect classroom functioning." Clearly, Cheryl meets this criterion. Thus, it is recommended that Cheryl receive a 504 accommodation plan to address her current academic difficulties through the provision of special education supports and services, as described in the next section.

Recommendations

The following recommendations have been made to assist both Cheryl and her parents with Cheryl's cognitive, academic, emotional, and behavioral difficulties. This assessment suggests that Cheryl's difficulties are the result of a complex set of variables and dynamics and, therefore, should be addressed from a multimodal approach.

1. Cheryl should receive remedial tutoring to help with her learning difficulties. The school system will probably not be capable of providing Cheryl with the amount of help that she needs. Cheryl needs to be tutored in spelling, grammar, written expression, and the mechanics of reading decoding and writing. The following local Learning Specialists will be able to provide the help that Cheryl needs: (a) Andrea P. and (b) Annabelle M. The following book also provides some useful suggestions for intervention that take into account Cheryl's strengths

in planning and reasoning ability and her weaknesses in short-term memory and sequential processing: Naglieri, J. A., & Pickering, E. B. (2003), *Helping children learn: Intervention handouts for use in school and at home,* Baltimore: Paul H. Brookes.

2. If the decision is made to send Cheryl to another school, it should be a school that has a low student-teacher ratio and provides a very structured environment. The school should also have teachers who are certified in teaching special education. We suggest that it is important for Mr. and Mrs. J. to verify credentials documenting both the school and the teaching staff.

3. Cheryl needs to be encouraged to take responsibility for her health care and her schoolwork. If she feels that she is being forced to do something because someone else wants her to do it, she is less likely to follow through. If Cheryl chooses not to follow through with taking care of her health and schoolwork she needs to experience the consequences herself. It will be very important for Cheryl to feel that she has the emotional support and structure that she will need from her parents because she will be dealing with new demands and responsibilities. The additional stress in the household will be best handled by Mr. and Mrs. J.'s setting firm limits for Cheryl with predetermined consequences, both positive and negative.

4. Cheryl's emotional and behavioral difficulties need to be addressed by a trained therapist such as Dr. S., who reported that Cheryl views therapy with her as a "punishment" for not adhering to her health care regimen. Dr. S.'s area of expertise in combining psychotherapy and HIV health care management is invaluable. Therefore, it is recommended that Cheryl continue seeing Dr. S. on a regular basis, but perhaps only once a month while Cheryl still views this as punishment. In addition, it is recommended that Cheryl work with an art therapist. Cheryl is a creative and artistic individual who would benefit from expressing herself though her artistic talent. Art therapy is often seen as a less threatening, less verbal, and more hands-on and creative form of therapy. Mr. Alex O., a local art therapist, may be helpful.

5. Cheryl's oppositional behavior can be both frustrating and overwhelming. Cheryl will need firm and consistent limits to be set by both parents in order to help her take responsibility and make the best use of learning remediation and therapy. Therefore, it is recommended that Mr. and Mrs. J. continue in family therapy with Dr. S. as well as attend a parenting support group.

PSYCHOLOGICAL REPORT by James B. Hale, PhD

Name: Jacob L.   DOB: 1/28/96
Age: 11   Grade: 6th
Date of Testing: 9/13/07   Date of Report: 9/18/07 (final sections on
                                 intervention were added 11/12/07)

Relevant Background Information

Jacob's gestation and delivery were unremarkable. Developmental milestones were said to be acquired within normal limits, but language difficulties led to a speech and language evaluation at age three. No services were required as a result of this evaluation. Except for seasonal allergies treated with Claritin as needed, Jacob had a healthy childhood. Hearing was reportedly within normal limits, but his nearsighted vision was corrected with lenses.

During his free time, Jacob enjoys a wide range of sports, and extracurricular activities. Jacob reported that his relationships with family (including stepfather) and peers were good, but he sometimes had conflicts with his two brothers, and he seldom had contact with his natural father. There was no known family history of learning or psychiatric disorder, but the father had "attention" and "learning problems" throughout school, and continued to have employment difficulties at the time of evaluation.

Academically, Jacob was described as an "active child" in preschool, and he struggled with competing work and mathematics during kindergarten. The teacher provided supplemental instruction using flashcards and moved his seat to the front of the room, but Jacob continued to struggle with "careless" errors. His reading and language had improved over time, but Jacob continued to struggle with math algorithm errors that seemed "random" to the teacher. Progress monitoring was conducted, but he did not seem to respond to intervention. In addition, he had difficulty with attention, organization, following directions, and being prepared for class. Written expression was limited, in part due to poor planning, organization, and handwriting skills.

Assessment Observations

Jacob presented as an 11 year, 7 month old boy with adequate health and hygiene. He was compliant and cooperative during testing, but became fatigued during testing sessions. Jacob struggled somewhat with receptive language, and asked to have directions repeated. Expressively, Jacob was quiet and had subtle articulation difficulties, but his oral language was otherwise adequate. Graphomotor skills were inconsistent, and increased task demands appeared to interfere with adequate processing speed. Jacob's attention, working memory, and executive functions were limited, as he had considerable difficulty maintaining his focus and effort on tasks. These difficulties also seemed to affect Jacob's performance on novel problem-solving tasks. His affect was appropriate and full range. Although impulsive at times, Jacob was not easily frustrated and responded well to encouragement and redirection, showing good persistence throughout the evaluation.

ASSESSMENT RESULTS AND CLINICAL IMPRESSIONS

Intellectual Screening

On the WISC-IV, Jacob obtained a Full Scale SS of 83, with 95% confidence that his true score fell between 79 and 88. However, he had significant subtest and factor variability, with scores ranging from average to deficient, suggesting the global Full Scale SS was not representative of his intellectual functioning. An examination of subcomponent scores suggested the General Ability Index (GAI) more accurately represented his level of intellectual functioning. His GAI SS of 96 was in the average range, and at the 39th percentile compared to his same age peers. However, given his variable profile, idiographic analysis of test data and cognitive hypothesis testing appeared to be warranted.

Jacob's WISC-IV profile was variable, with the Verbal Comprehension factor the highest stable score achieved during the evaluation; his VCI of 98 (44th percentile), classified as Average Range/Within Normal Limits, is significantly higher than his other WISC-IV Indexes. Jacob performed well on measures of verbal crystallized abilities, those skills acquired through formal and informal experiences and education. He had no difficulty with word knowledge and use, displaying adequate lexical-semantic knowledge and good convergent/concordant thought for tasks that required categorical thinking or common-sense problem solving. Receptive and expressive language skills appeared to be adequate, yet some minor inconsistencies with word retrieval and language formulation were noted.

Jacob's PRI of 94 was not interpretable because of the considerable variability in his performance on Perceptual Reasoning subtests (ranging from the 9th percentile on Matrix Analogies to 63rd percentile on Block Design). Jacob had no difficulty using bimanual motor skills when required to analyze and synthesize abstract block patterns, suggesting good part-whole relationships and visual-spatial processing. He also performed well on a task that required recognition of relationships among visually meaningful objects within an array of distracting pictures, suggesting again good understanding of convergent/concordant thought processes. However, on Matrix Reasoning, Jacob struggled with fluid reasoning or novel problem-solving skills when required to determine if a meaningful object or abstract shape completed a pattern, suggesting some difficulty with divergent/discordant thought and/or fluid reasoning. This pattern can also be related to difficulty with attention, working memory, executive function, and behavior regulation.

Consistent with this latter pattern, Jacob struggled with the Working Memory and Processing Speed subtests. His Indexes on both scales were interpretable and both were Normative Weaknesses. Notably, Jacob's WMI of 68 qualifies as a High-Priority Concern; it is not only a Lower Extreme/Normative Weakness, but it is also significantly lower than his other WISC-IV indexes by an "Uncommon" amount (i.e., differences as large as Jacob's occurred less than 10% of the time in the normal population). Jacob had little difficulty with recalling orally presented digits in forward sequence (SS = 8) but struggled with attention, sequencing, and working memory when asked to mentally manipulate sequences to produce the reverse order (SS = 4). Similarly, he struggled with mental manipulation of letters and numbers, often responding with an incorrect letter or order. This difficulty appeared to transcend auditory-verbal stimuli, as Jacob had difficulty with quick, efficient, graphomotor reproduction of symbols according to a number-symbol template, and determining if one of two target symbols were contained in a group of distracter shapes. His considerable problems with working memory and processing speed tasks are encapsulated by his Cognitive Proficiency Index (CPI) of 71 (3rd percentile), a new standard score that combines WMI and PSI. The 25-point difference between Jacob's global intelligence (GAI = 96) and CPI is both statistically significant and substantial. Differences of 25 points or more occur less than 5% of the time in the normal population.

Verbal Comprehension (SS = 98)	Scale Score	Perceptual Reasoning (SS = 94)	Scale Score
Similarities	9	Block Design	11
Vocabulary	9	Picture Concepts	10
Comprehension	11	Matrix Reasoning	6
Working Memory (SS = 68)	Scale Score	Processing Speed (SS = 78)	Scale Score
Digit Span	5	Coding	7
Letter-Number Sequencing	4	Symbol Search	5

Cognitive Hypothesis Testing

Based on the intellectual screening, several hypotheses regarding Jacob's cognitive strengths and weaknesses were developed and subsequently evaluated using NEP-SY-II, WJ III, and Dean-Woodcock Neuropsychological Battery subtests. Jacob's receptive and expressive language skills, as well as his visual-spatial perceptual analysis and synthesis skills appeared to be adequate. His convergent/concordant thought processes and crystallized abilities appeared to be better developed than his divergent/discordant thought or fluid reasoning, yet these results were inconsistent. Jacob appeared to struggle with attention, working memory, processing speed, and executive function, and these difficulties appeared to transcend auditory-verbal and visual-nonverbal domains. Subtle language formulation difficulties were noted, but did not appear to be significant, and likely secondary to executive control of oral expression. Although graphomotor skills were reportedly a problem, and processing speed was low, Jacob's spontaneous writing sample and Coding symbols were fairly well formed. Nonetheless, sensory-motor functions were further examined to rule out this possible problem.

Attention, Working Memory, Fluid Reasoning, and Executive Function

Jacob had difficulty with translating words to math equations for mental computation on the Arithmetic subtest, and the corresponding written WISC-IV Integrated task did not improve performance. However, algorithm errors were readily identifiable, and there was occasional poor attention to the math operand. Jacob also struggled with Integrated tasks designed to foster attention, such as the addition of a visual model before recall, or semantic information to aid storage. These findings provide further confirmation of auditory-verbal working memory deficits, and visual-motor working memory impairments were also substantiated. On the NEPSY-II, Jacob struggled with most sustained auditory and visual attention, working memory, inhibition/interference control, and executive function tasks. His basic auditory processing and attention for naming were adequate, but he struggled with auditory inhibition and flexibility when asked to provide a competing response, making many errors on this task. However, his speeded naming was slow, consistent with poor automaticity and processing speed. Jacob also struggled with novel problem solving, inductive and deductive reasoning, maintaining cognitive set, mental flexibility, and executive control processes on tasks that required analyzing patterns among abstract visual stimuli and developing alternative sorts of picture cards that had similar and different characteristics. He also had difficulty repeating and recalling unrelated word lists, and a series of oral instructions, likely due to difficulty with carrying out multiple steps or organizing steps into the correct sequence. In combination, these difficulties likely explain Jacob's considerable difficulty with carrying out multiple computation steps or following math algorithms.

Sensory-Motor Skills

According to the NEPSY-II and Dean-Woodcock Neuropsychological Battery results, Jacob did not appear to have significant difficulty with visual, visual-motor, or fine motor skills, so this could not account for his poor processing speed on the WISC-IV. Bimanual coordination does not appear to be difficult for Jacob, and since visual-spatial-motor skills appear to be adequate, Jacob's major difficulty appears to be processing visual symbolic information quickly and efficiently. He had some difficulty with repetitive tapping due to slow performance, but speeded visual-motor responding was adequate when graphomotor skills were required, as was his graphomotor reproduction of symbols on the WISC-IV Integrated component of Coding. Visual-spatial-holistic processes appeared to be intact, and he had little difficulty with somatosensory feedback to the motor system, suggesting processing speed skills were likely to be the source of his apparent constructional or graphomotor difficulties, because there were no signs of constructional apraxia.

Achievement Functioning

On the WIAT-II, Jacob had little difficulty with reading single words, decoding psuedowords, or reading comprehension, resulting in an average Reading Composite (SS = 101) score. He made meaningful substitutions on some words, suggesting a tendency to read words by sight, but on others he used phoneme-grapheme correspondence skills to decode words, suggesting adequate sound-symbol awareness. Although his automaticity appeared to be limited, reading comprehension was quite good, and he was able to infer correct responses in some cases, consistent with good understanding of part-whole relationships seen during cognitive/neuropsychological assessment. Although Written Language was adequate (SS = 90), Jacob struggled somewhat with orthographic representation during spelling, with errors largely being phonemic equivalents. Apparently, his relative difficulty with orthography does not appear to be related to visual-perceptual problems or visual memory given his cognitive/neuropsychological testing, but possibly due to difficulty with letter retrieval and/or automaticity. Jacob's writing sample was interesting and adequate overall, but he made some grammar and punctuation errors, which could be in part related to language formulation and word retrieval, and attention to detail.

In contrast with his adequate reading and written language skills, Jacob struggled with math computation and word problems. Although math computation skills were in the low average range, there was a mix of math computation, math algorithm, and math fact errors. For math reasoning, Jacob had no difficulty reading charts, and answering time and money items, but he struggled with multiple step word problems. On many of these he asked for repetition, and at times he would write down the wrong algorithm resulting in error responding. Interestingly, he did not make any computation errors on these simple word problems for which he had the wrong algorithm, suggesting his difficulty was in translating the verbal to written information for subsequent computation.

Reading Composite (SS = 101)	Standard Score
Word Reading	104
Reading Comprehension	106
Pseudoword Decoding	100
Mathematics Composite (SS = 77)	Standard Score
Numerical Operations	83
Math Reasoning	75
Written Language Composite (SS = 90)	Standard Score
Spelling	89
Written Expression	95

Recommendations

Several recommendations were offered to the team to address Jacob's difficulty with attention, working memory, impulse control, processing speed, and general executive function. Recommendations included direct, structured instruction, task analysis of complex tasks, extended time testing due to processing speed weaknesses, metacognitive instruction to improve executive control of behavior, limited use of multiple instructions/sequences and checking to ensure comprehension, fluency instruction to increase processing speed, notetaking/tape recorder services for lecture, daily assignment book for organization/work completion, drill and repetition in math facts using flashcards to gain automaticity, and a math checklist for carrying out multiple step math computations. Additional metacognitive strategies were offered to address written language difficulties, oral repeating after written expression to check grammar, and reduce latency of response/increase speeded performance. Although executive skills appeared to be somewhat impaired, behavior ratings and school reports only suggested minor behavioral disruption associated with these deficits, suggesting further monitoring of psychosocial status would be necessary. Although medication intervention for attention and executive deficits was considered, and an ADHD diagnosis was considered, the team and parents felt that instructional interventions would be sufficient at this time.

Team Decision and Intervention Development

Jacob qualified for special education services with a specific learning disability in the area of mathematics. During the follow-up consultation meeting with the teacher, we developed multiple intervention strategies, and hierarchically arranged them in order of importance. Although math and written language deficits were important to address, Jacob was to receive special education itinerant support for these difficulties. As a result, the general education teacher wanted to focus on Jacob's organizational problems, his lack of preparedness for class and poor work completion. We collaboratively defined six behaviors in preparation for the metacognitive intervention designed to improve class preparedness and work completion. These included Pencil Out, Paper Out, Folder Out, Homework In, Folder In and Homework Out. Jacob developed a self-monitoring sheet and computed his daily score for each item across his classes. He wrote PO, PO, FO, HI, FI, and HO on his sheet, and developed the sentence "2 Play Free Outside, bring the HI-FI from HOme. At the beginning of class, the teacher gave a general direction to students to "GET READY, GET SET, and then GO for class," which served as a discriminative stimulus for Jacob to complete the six items on the checklist. If he completed the checklist by the time the teacher said "GO," he received credit for completing the tasks checked. The teacher randomly checked the daily list, and weekly meetings with the consultant were scheduled to help Jacob chart the data.

Intervention Evaluation

As can be seen in Figure 9.2, Jacob responded well to the intervention, and readily completed the sheet following the teacher's classroom prompt. However, after some time, treatment integrity was somewhat compromised as neither Jacob nor the teacher consistently fulfilled their intervention obligations. When Jacob completed the checklist, he was typically successful on all six items. Upon discussion with Jacob and the teacher during Week 7, it was decided that the random checks would be completed by the teacher and consultant to support random checks of the data. In addition, Jacob was offered tangible reinforcers for weeks he exceeded 90% task completion averaged across the six domains. As can be seen, these changes resulted in Jacob achieving the criterion for successful performance during 4 of the 5 subsequent weeks. After a final consultation, Jacob was asked to generalize his performance to using an appointment book with the acronym copied on the top of each page, with periodic checks of homework completion and preparedness to ensure he was regularly completing the six tasks in his classes.

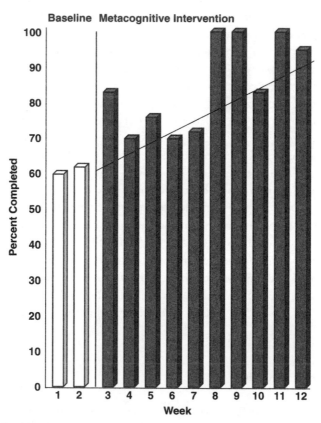

Figure 9.2 Jacob's Response-to-Intervention (RTI)

🐟 TEST YOURSELF 🐟

1. **List five topics to include in the "Background Information" section of the report.**

2. **Every single behavior that was noticed during the assessment session should be described in detail in the "Appearance and Behavioral Characteristics" section of the report.**
   True or False?

3. **Besides a description of the child's physical appearance and behavioral observations, what else should be mentioned in the "Appearance and Behavioral Characteristics" section of the report?**
   (a) Test scores
   (b) Referral question
   (c) A statement about the validity of the results
   (d) Brief recommendations

4. **The least meaningful type of score metric, and therefore the one that should not be used in case reports, is the**
   (a) raw score.
   (b) percentile rank.
   (c) standard score.
   (d) scaled score.

5. **If you forget to mention some of the test results in the "Test Results and Interpretation" section, there is no need to worry because you can simply write about them in the "Summary" section of the report.**
   True or False?

6. **Which of the following is highly recommended in writing your report?**
   (a) Using a lot of metaphors
   (b) Listing as many observed behaviors as possible
   (c) Using technical terms
   (d) Omitting confidence intervals, as they are too confusing
   (e) None of the above

Answers:

1. See Don't Forget box on page 471; 2. False; 3. c; 4. a; 5. False; 6. e

References

Ackerman, P. T., & Dykman, R. A. (1995). Reading-disabled students with and without comorbid arithmetic disability. *Developmental Neuropsychology, 11,* 351–371.

Aguera, F. (2006). How language and culture impact test performance on the Differential Abilities Scale in a pre-school population. Unpublished manuscript. St. John's University, NY.

Akamatsu, T., Mayer, C., & Hardy-Braz, S. T. (2008) Why considerations of verbal aptitude are important in educating deaf and hard-of-hearing students. In M. Marschark & P. Hauser (Eds.), *Deaf cognition: Foundations and outcomes* (pp. 131–169). New York: Oxford University Press.

Alfonso, V. C., Flanagan, D. P., & Radwan, S. (2005). The impact of Cattell-Horn-Carroll (CHC) theory on test development and the interpretation of cognitive and academic abilities. In D. P. Flanagan & P. L. Harrison (Eds.), *Contemporary intellectual assessment: Theories, tests, and issues,* 2nd ed. (pp. 185–202). New York: Guilford.

Alfonso, V. C., Oakland, T., LaRocca, R., & Spanakos, A. (2000). The course on individual cognitive assessment. *School Psychology Review, 29,* 52–64.

American Educational Research Association, American Psychological Association, & National Council on Measurement in Education. (1999). *Standards for educational and psychological testing.* Washington, DC: American Educational Research Association.

American Psychiatric Association. (1994). *Diagnostic and statistical manual of mental disorders* (4th ed.). Washington, DC: Author.

American Psychiatric Association. (2000). *Diagnostic and statistical manual of mental disorders* (4th ed., Text Rev.). Washington, DC: Author.

American Psychological Association. (1990). *Guidelines for providers of psychological services to ethnic, linguistic, and culturally diverse populations.* Washington DC: Author.

American Psychological Association. (2002). Ethical principles of psychologists and code of conduct. *American Psychologist, 57,* 1060–1073.

Anastasi, A. (1988). *Psychological testing* (6th ed.). New York: Macmillan.

Anastasi, A., & Urbina, S. (1997). *Psychological testing* (7th ed.). Upper Saddle River, NJ: Prentice Hall.

Attwood, T. (1998). *Asperger's Syndrome: A guide for parents and professionals.* Philadelphia: Jessica Kingsley.

Baddeley, A. (1986). *Working memory.* Oxford: Oxford University Press.

Baddeley, A. (1992). Is working memory working? The fifteenth Bartlett Lecture. *Quarterly Journal of Experimental Psychology, 44A,* 1–31.

Bannatyne, A. (1974). Diagnosis: A note on recategorization of the WISC scaled scores. *Journal of Learning Disabilities, 7,* 272–274.

Barnhill, G., Hagiwara, T., Myles, B. S., & Simpson, R. L. (2000). Asperger Syndrome: A study of 37 children and adolescents. *Focus on Autism and Other Developmental Disabilities, 15*(3), 146–153.

Binet, A. (1916). New methods for the diagnosis of the intellectual level of subnormals. In E. S. Kite (Trans.), *The development of intelligence in children.* Vineland, NJ: Publications of the Training School at Vineland. (Originally published 1905 in *L'Année Psychologique, 11,* 191–244).

Binet, A., & Simon, T. (1905). Méthodes nouvelles pour le diagnostique du niveau intellectuel des anormaux [New methods for the diagnosis of the intellectual level of abnormals]. *L'Année Psychologique, 11,* 191–244.

Binet, A., & Simon, T. (1908). Le développment de l'intelligence chez les enfants [The development of intelligence in children]. *L'Année Psychologique, 14,* 1–90.

Bolen, L. M. (1998). WISC-III score changes for EMR students. *Psychology in the Schools, 35*(4), 327–332.

Borsuk, E. R., Watkins, M. W., & Canivez, G. L. (2006). Long-term stability of membership in a WISC-III subtest core profile taxonomy. *Journal of Psychoeducational Assessment, 24,* 52–68.

Bower, A., & Hayes, A. (1995). Relations of scores on the Stanford-Binet Fourth Edition and Form L-M: Concurrent validation study with children who have Mental Retardation. *American Journal on Mental Retardation, 99*(5), 555–563.

Bracken, B. A., & McCallum, R. S. (1998) *The Universal Nonverbal Intelligence Test.* Chicago: Riverside Publishing Company.

Braden, J. P. (1994). *Deafness, deprivation, and IQ.* New York: Plenum Press.

Braden, J. P. (1995). Review of Wechsler Intelligence Scale for Children–Third Edition. In J. V. Mitchell (Ed.), *The tenth mental measurement yearbook* (vol. 1, pp. 1098–1103). Lincoln, NE: Buros Institute of Mental Measurement.

Braden, J. P. (2005). Hard of hearing and deaf clients: Using the WISC-IV with children who are hard of hearing or deaf. In A. Prifitera, D. H. Saklofske, & L. G Weiss (Eds.), *WISC-IV clinical use and interpretation: Scientist-practitioner perspectives* (pp. 351–380). San Diego, CA: Academic Press.

Braden, J. P., & Iribarren, J. A. (2007). Test Review: Wechsler, D. (2005). Wechsler Intelligence Scale for Children–Fourth edition Spanish. *Journal of Psychoeducational Assessment, 25,* 292–299.

Braden, J. P., & Niebling, B. C. (2005). Evaluating the validity evidence for intelligence tests using the joint test standards. In D. P. Flanagan & P. L. Harrison (Eds.), *Contemporary intellectual assessment: Theories, tests, and issues,* 2nd ed. (pp. 615–630). New York: Guilford.

Brauer, B. A., Braden, J. P., Pollard, R. Q., & Hardy-Braz, S. T. (1998). Deaf and hard of hearing people. In J. Sandoval, C. L. Frisby, K. F. Geisinger, J. D. Scheuneman, & J. R.. Grenier (Eds.), *Test interpretation and diversity: Achieving equity in assessment* (pp. 297–315). Washington, DC: American Psychological Association.

Brigham, C. C. (1923). *A study of American intelligence.* Princeton, NJ: Princeton University.

Brunnert, K., Naglieri, J., & Hardy-Braz, S. (2008). *Essentials of WNV assessment.* New York: Wiley.

Calhoun, S. L., & Mayes, S. D. (2005). Processing speed in children with clinical disorders. *Psychology in the Schools, 42*(2), 333–343.

Caltabiano, L., & Flanagan, D. P. (2004). Content validity of new and recently revised intelligence tests: Implications for interpretation. Manuscript in preparation.

Canivez, G. L., & Watkins, M. W. (2001). Long-term stability of the Wechsler Intelligence Scale for Children–Third Edition among students with disabilities. *School Psychology Review, 30*(2), 438–453.

Carroll, J. B. (1993). *Human cognitive abilities: A survey of factor-analytic studies.* Cambridge, England: Cambridge University Press.

Carroll, J. B. (1997). Commentary on Keith and Witta's hierarchical and cross-age confirmatory factor analysis of the WISC-III. *School Psychology Quarterly, 12,* 108–109.

Carroll, J. B. (1998). Foreword. In K. S. McGrew & D. P. Flanagan, *The intelligence test desk reference (ITDR): Gf-Gc cross-battery assessment* (pp. xi–xii). Boston: Allyn & Bacon.

Cathers-Schiffman, T. A., & Thompson, M. S. (2007). Assessment of English- and Spanish-speaking students with the WISC-III and Leiter-R. *Journal of Psychoeducational Assessment, 25,* 41–52.

Cohen, B. H. (1996). *Explaining psychological statistics*. Pacific Grove, CA: Brooks & Cole.

Cohen, J. (1952). A factor-analytically based rationale for the Wechsler-Bellevue. *Journal of Consulting Psychology, 16,* 272–277.

Cohen, J. (1959). The factorial structure of the WISC at ages 7-7, 10-6, and 13-6. *Journal of Consulting Psychology, 23,* 285–299.

Cohen, M. (1997). *Children's Memory Scale*. San Antonio, TX: The Psychological Corporation.

Crawford, J. R., Garthwaite, P. H., & Gault, C. B. (2007). Estimating the percentage of the population with abnormally low scores (or abnormally large score differences) on standardized neuropsychological test batteries: A generic method with applications. *Neuropsychology, 21,* 419–430.

Cummins, J. C. (1984). *Bilingual and special education: Issues in assessment and pedagogy*. Austin, TX: PRO-ED.

Daniel, M. H. (1997). Intelligence testing: Status and trends. *American Psychologist, 52*(10), 1038–1045.

Das, J. P., & Naglieri, J. A. (1997). *Cognitive Assessment System*. Itasca, IL: Riverside.

Diller, L., Ben-Yishay, Y., Gerstman, L. J., Goodkin, R., Gordon, W., & Weinberg, J. (1974). *Studies in cognitive and rehabilitation in hemiplegia*. Rehabilitation Monograph No. 50. New York: New York University Medical Center Institute of Rehabilitation Medicine.

Dumont, R., & Willis, J. (2001). Use of the Tellegen & Briggs formula to determine the Dumont-Willis Indexes (DWI-1 & DWI-2) for the WISC-IV. http://alpha.edu/psychology/.

Dynda, A. M. (2008). *The relation between language proficiency and IQ test performance*. Unpublished manuscript. St. John's University, NY.

Education for All Handicapped Children Act of 1975. Pub. L. No. 94-142. (1975).

Educational Amendment of 1978, Pub. L. No. 95-561 (1978).

Eisenmajer, R., Prior, M., Leekam, S., Wing, L., Gould, J. Welham, M., & Ong, B. (1996). Comparison of clinical symptoms in autism and Asperger's Disorder. *Journal of the American Academy of Child and Adolescent Psychiatry, 35,* 1523–1531.

Elliott, C. D. (1990). *Differential Ability Scales*. San Antonio, TX: The Psychological Corporation.

Elliott, C. D. (2007). Differential Ability Scales (2nd ed.) Administration and scoring manual. San Antonio, TX: The Psychological Corporation.

Evans, J. J., Floyd, R. G., McGrew, K. S., & Leforgee, M. H. (2002). The relations between measures of Cattell-Horn-Carroll (CHC) cognitive abilities and reading achievement during childhood and adolescence. *School Psychology Review, 31,* 246–262.

Falk, R. F., Silverman, L. K., & Moran, D. M. (2004). *Using two WISC-IV indices to identify the gifted*. http://www.gifteddevelopment.com/About_GDC/indices.htm.

Figueroa, R. A. (1990). Assessment of linguistic minority group children. In C. R. Reynolds & R. W. Kamphaus (Eds.), *Handbook of psychological and educational assessment of children: Vol. 1. Intelligence and achievement.* (pp. 135–152). New York: Guilford.

Figueroa, R. A., & Hernandez, S. (2000). *Testing Hispanic students in the United States: Technical and policy issues*. Report to the President's Advisory Commission on Educational Excellence for Hispanic Americans. Washington, DC: U.S. Department of Education, Office of Educational Research and Improvement (OERI).

Fiorello, C. A., Hale, J. B., Holdnack, J. A., Kavanagh, J. A., Terrell, J., & Long, L. (2007). Interpreting intelligence test results for children with disabilities. Is global intelligence relevant? *Applied Neuropsychology, 14,* 2–12.

Flanagan, D. P. (2000). Wechsler-based CHC cross-battery assessment and reading achievement: Strengthening the validity of interpretations drawn from Wechsler test scores. *School Psychology Quarterly, 15,* 295–329.

Flanagan, D. P., & Alfonso, V. C. (2000). Essentially, essential for WAIS-III users. *Contemporary Psychology, 45,* 528–539.

Flanagan, D. P., & Harrison, P. L. (Eds.). (2005). *Contemporary intellectual assessment: Theories, tests, and issues* (2nd ed.). New York: Guilford.

Flanagan, D. P., Harrison, P. L., & Genshaft, J. L. (Eds.). (1997). *Contemporary intellectual assessment: Theories, tests, and issues.* New York: Guilford.

Flanagan, D. P., & Kaufman, A. S. (2004). *Essentials of WISC-IV assessment.* New York: Wiley.

Flanagan, D. P., McGrew, K. S., & Ortiz, S. O. (2000). *The Wechsler intelligence scales and Gf-Gc theory: A contemporary approach to interpretation.* Boston: Allyn & Bacon.

Flanagan, D. P., & Ortiz, S. O. (2001). *Essentials of cross-battery assessment.* New York: Wiley.

Flanagan, D. P., & Ortiz, S. O. (2002a). Cross-battery assessment: A response to Watkins, Youngstrom, and Glutting (Part I). *Communique, 30*(7), 32–34.

Flanagan, D. P., & Ortiz, S. O. (2002b). Cross-battery assessment: A response to Watkins, Youngstrom, and Glutting (Part II). *Communique, 30*(8), 36–38.

Flanagan, D. P., Ortiz, S. O., & Alfonso, V.C. (2007). *Essentials of cross-battery assessment* (2nd ed.). New York: Wiley.

Flanagan, D. P., Ortiz, S. O., Alfonso, V. C., & Dynda, A. (2008). Best practices in cognitive assessment. In A. Thomas & J. Grimes (Eds.), *Best practices in school psychology,* 5th ed. (pp. 633–659). Washington DC: The National Association of School Psychologists.

Flanagan, D. P., Ortiz, S. O., Alfonso, V. C., & Mascolo, J. T. (2002). *The achievement test desk reference (ATDR): Comprehensive assessment and learning disabilities.* Boston: Allyn & Bacon.

Flanagan, D. P., Ortiz, S. O., Alfonso, V. C., & Mascolo, J. (2006). *The Achievement Test Desk Reference (ATDR)–second edition: A guide to learning disability identification.* New York: Wiley.

Floyd, R. G., Evans, J. J., & McGrew, K. S. (2003). Relations between measures of Cattell–Horn-Carroll (CHC) cognitive abilities and mathematics achievement across the school-age years. *Psychology in the Schools, 40*(2), 155–171.

Floyd, R. G., Keith, T. Z., Taub, G. E., & McGrew, K. S. (2007). Cattell–Horn–Carroll cognitive abilities and their effects on reading decoding skills: g has indirect effects, more specific abilities have direct effects. *School Psychology Quarterly, 22,* 200–233.

Flynn, J. R. (1987). Massive IQ gains in 14 nations: What IQ tests really measure. *Psychological Bulletin, 101,* 171–191.

Gagne, E. D. (1985). *The cognitive psychology of school learning.* Boston: Little, Brown.

Gallaudet Research Institute. (2003). *Regional and national summary report of data from the 2001–2002 annual Survey of Deaf and Hard of Hearing Children and Youth.* Washington, DC: GRI, Gallaudet University.

Gathercole, S. E., Hitch, G. J., Service, E., & Martin, A. J. (1997). Phonological short term memory and new word learning in children. *Developmental Psychology, 33*(6), 966–979.

Georgas, J., Weiss, L. G., Van de Vijver, F. J. R., & Saklofske, D. H. (Eds.). (2003). *Culture and children's intelligence: Cross-cultural analysis of the WISC-III.* San Diego, CA: Academic Press.

Ghaziuddin, M., & Mountain-Kimchi, K. (2004). Defining the intellectual profile of Asperger syndrome: Comparison with high-functioning autism. *Journal of Autism and Developmental Disorders, 34*(3), 279–284.

Ghaziuddin, M., Tsai, L. Y., & Ghaziuddin, N. (1992). Brief report: A comparison of the diagnostic criteria for Asperger Syndrome. *Journal of Autism and Developmental Disorders, 22,* 643–649.

Gilchrist, A., Green J., Cox, A., Burton, D., Rutter, M., & Le Couteur, A. (2001). Development and current functioning in adolescents with Asperger Syndrome: A comparative study. *Journal of Child Psychology and Psychiatry, 42*(2), 227–240.

Glutting, J. J., McDermott, P. A., & Konold, T. R. (1997). Ontology, structure, and diagnostic benefits of a normative subtest taxonomy from the WISC-III standardization sample. In D. P. Flanagan, J. L. Genshaft, & P. L. Harrison (Eds.), *Contemporary intellectual assessment: Theories, tests, and issues* (pp. 349–372). New York: Guilford.

Glutting, J. J., McDermott, P. A., Watkins, M. M., Kush, J. C., & Konold, T. R. (1997). The base rate problem and its consequences for interpreting children's ability profiles. *School Psychology Review, 26*(2), 176–188.

Glutting, J. J., Watkins, M. W., Konold, T. R., & McDermott, P. A. (2006). Distinctions without a difference: The utility of observed versus latent factors from the WISC-IV in estimating reading and math achievement on the WIAT-II. *The Journal of Special Education,* 103–114.

Goddard, H. H. (1913). The Binet tests in relation to immigration. *Journal of Psycho-Asthenics, 18,* 105–107.

Gold, J. M., Carpenter, C., Randolph, C., Goldberg, T. E., & Weinberger, D. R. (1997). Auditory working memory and Wisconsin Card Sorting Test performance in schizophrenia. *Archives of General Psychiatry, 54,* 159–165.

Goldstien, G., Allen, D., Minshew, N., Williams, D., Volkmar, F., Klin, A., & Schultz, R. (2008). The structure of intelligence in children and adults with high functioning autism. *Neuropsychology, 22*(3), 301–312.

Goldstein, G., Beers, S. R., Siegel, D. J., & Minshew, N. J. (2001). A comparison of WAIS-R profiles in adults with high-functioning autism or differing subtypes of learning disability. *Applied Neuropsychology, 8*(3), 148–154.

Goldstein, G., Minshew, N. J., Allen, D. N., & Seaton, B. E. (2002). High-functioning autism and schizophrenia: A comparison of an early and late onset neurodevelopmental disorder. *Archives of Clinical Neuropsychology, 17,* 461–475.

Gould, S. J. (1981). *The mismeasure of man.* New York: Norton.

Gustaffson, J. E., & Undheim, J. O. (1996). Individual differences in cognitive functions. In D. C. Berliner & R. C. Cabfee (Eds.), *Handbook of educational psychology* (pp. 186–242). New York: MacMillan.

Hale, J. B., & Fiorello, C. A. (2004). *School neuropsychology; A practitioner's handbook.* New York: Guilford.

Hale, J. B., Fiorello, C. A., Kavanagh, J. A., Hoeppner, J. B., & Gaither, R. A. (2001). WISC-III predictors of academic achievement for children with learning disabilities: Are global and factor scores comparable? *School Psychology Quarterly, 16,* 31–55.

Hale, R. L. (1979). The utility of the WISC-R subtest scores in discriminating among adequate and underacheiving children. *Multivariate Behavioral Research, 14,* 245–253.

Hale, R. L., & Landino, S. A. (1981). Utility of the WISC-R subtest analysis in discriminating among groups of conduct problem, withdrawn, mixed, and non-problem boys. *Journal of Consulting and Clinical Psychology, 41,* 91–95.

Hale, R. L., & Saxe, J. E. (1983). Profile analysis of the Wechsler Intelligence Scale for Children—Revised. *Journal of Psychoeducational Assessment, 1,* 155–162.

Hardy-Braz, S. T. (1999). *School psychologists working with students who are deaf: Who are they and what are they doing that is different?* Poster presentation at the convention of the National Association of School Psychologists, Las Vegas, NV.

Hardy-Braz, S. T. (2003a). Enhancing school-based psychological services: Assessments and interventions with students who are deaf or hard-of-hearing. Workshop presented at the meeting of the National Association of School Psychologists, Toronto, Canada.

Hardy-Braz, S. T. (2003b). Testing children who are deaf or hard of hearing. In D. Wechsler (Ed.), *WISC-IV Administration and scoring manual* (pp. 12–18). San Antonio, TX: The Psychological Corporation.

Harrington, R. G. (1982). Caution: Standardized testing may be hazardous to the educational programs of intellectually gifted children. *Education, 103,* 112–117.

Harris, J. G., & Llorente, A. M. (2005). Cultural considerations in the use of the Wechsler Intelligence Scale for Children—Fourth Edition. In A. Prifitera, D. H. Saklofske, & L. G. Weiss (Eds.), *WISC-IV clinical use and interpretation: Scientist-practitioner perspectives* (pp. 382–416). San Diego, CA: Academic Press.

Harrison, P. L. (1990). Mental Retardation: Adaptive behavior assessment and giftedness. In A. S. Kaufman, *Assessing adolescent and adult intelligence* (pp. 533–585). Needham Heights, MA: Allyn & Bacon.

Hebben, N., & Milberg, W. (2002). *Essentials of neuropsychological assessment.* New York: Wiley.

Holdnack, J. A., & Weiss, L. G. (2006). Essentials of WISC-IV Integrated interpretation. In L. Weiss, D. Saklofske, A. Prifitera, & J. Holdnack (Eds.), *WISC-IV advanced clinical interpretation* (pp. 181–199). San Diego, CA: Academic Press.

Horn, J. L. (1991). Measurement of intellectual capabilities: A review of theory. In K. S. McGrew, J. K. Werder, & R. W. Woodcock, *Woodcock-Johnson Technical Manual* (pp. 197–232). Chicago: Riverside.

Horn, J. L., & Noll, J. (1997). Human cognitive capabilities: *Gf-Gc* theory. In D. P. Flanagan, J. L. Genshaft, & P. L. Harrison (Eds.), *Contemporary intellectual assessment: Theories, tests, and issues* (pp. 53–91). New York: Guilford.

Individuals with Disabilities Education Act, Pub. L. No. 105-17. (1991).

Jacob K. Javits Gifted and Talented Students Education Act of 1988, Pub. L. No. 100-297. (1988).

Jensen, A. R. (1976). Construct validity and test bias. *Phi Delta Kappan, 58,* 340–346.

Jensen, A. R. (1980). *Bias in mental testing.* New York: Free Press.

Jensen, A. R. (1998). *The g factor: The science of mental ability.* Westport CT: Praeger Publishers.

Kail, R. (1991). Developmental changes in speed of processing during childhood and adolescence. *Psychological Bulletin, 109,* 490–501.

Kamphaus, R. W. (1993). *Clinical assessment of children's intelligence.* Boston: Allyn & Bacon.

Kamphaus, R. W., Petoskey, M. D., & Morgan, A. W. (1997). A history of intelligence test interpretation. In D. P. Flanagan, J. L. Genshaft, & P. L. Harrison (Eds.), *Contemporary intellectual assessment: Theories, tests, and issues* (pp. 32–51). New York: Guilford.

Kamphaus, R. W., Winsor, A. P., Rowe, E. W., & Kim, S. (2005). A history of intelligence test interpretation. In D. P. Flanagan, J. L. Genshaft, & P. L. Harrison (Eds.), *Contemporary intellectual assessment: Theories, tests, and issues,* 2nd ed. (pp. 23–38). New York: Guilford.

Kaplan, E. (1988). A process approach to neuropsychological assessment. In T. J. Boll & B. K. Bryant (Eds.), *Clinical neuropsychology and brain function: Research, measurement, and practice* (pp. 129–167). Washington, DC: American Psychological Association.

Kaplan, E., Fein D., Kramer, J., Delis, D., & Morris, R. (2004). *The Wechsler Intelligence Scale for Children–Fourth Edition (WISC-IV) Integrated.* San Antonio, TX: The Psychological Corporation.

Kaufman, A. S. (1975). Factor analysis of the WISC-R at 11 age levels between 6½ and 16½ years. *Journal of Consulting and Clinical Psychology, 43,* 135–147.

Kaufman, A. S. (1979). *Intelligent testing with the WISC-R.* New York: Wiley.

Kaufman, A. S.. (1983). Intelligence: Old concepts—new perspectives. In G. W. Hynd (Ed.), *The school psychologist: An introduction* (pp. 95–117). Syracuse, NY: Syracuse University Press.

Kaufman, A. S. (1990). *Assessing adolescent and adult intelligence.* Boston: Allyn & Bacon.

Kaufman, A. S. (1992). Evaluation of the WISC-III and WPPSI-R for gifted children. *Roeper Review, 14*(3), 154–158.

Kaufman, A. S. (1993). King WISC the Third assumes the throne. *Journal of School Psychology, 31,* 345–354.

Kaufman, A. S. (1994). *Intelligent testing with the WISC-III.* New York: Wiley.

Kaufman, A. S. (2000a). Foreword. In D. P. Flanagan, K. S. McGrew, & S. O. Ortiz, *The Wechsler intelligence scales and Gf-Gc theory: A contemporary approach to interpretation* (pp. xiii–xv). Boston: Allyn & Bacon.

Kaufman, A. S. (2000b). Tests of intelligence. In R. J. Sternberg (Ed.), *Handbook of intelligence* (pp. 445–476). New York: Cambridge University Press.

Kaufman, A. S. (2003). Foreword. In J. Georgas, L. G. Weiss, F. J. R. van de Vijver, & D. H. Saklofske (Eds.), *Culture and children's intelligence: Cross-cultural analysis of the WISC-III* (pp. xix–xxiv). San Diego, CA: Academic Press.

Kaufman, A. S. (2006). Foreword. In D. Wechsler & J. A. Naglieri, *Wechsler Nonverbal Scale of Ability administration and scoring manual* (pp. iii–iv). San Antonio, TX: The Psychological Corporation.

Kaufman, A. S., & Doppelt, J. E. (1976). Analysis of WISC-R standardization data in terms of the stratification variables. *Child Development*, 165–171.

Kaufman, A. S., Flanagan, D. P., Alfonso, V. C., & Mascolo, J. T. (2006). Test review: Wechsler Intelligence Scale for Children, Fourth Edition (WISC-IV). *Journal of Psychoeducational Assessment, 24*, 278–295.

Kaufman, A. S., & Harrison, P. L. (1986). Intelligence tests and gifted assessment: What are the positives? *Roeper Review, 8*, 154–159.

Kaufman, A. S., & Kaufman, N. L. (1990). *Kaufman Brief Intelligence Test (K-BIT)* Circle Pines, MN: American Guidance Service.

Kaufman, A. S., & Kaufman, N. L. (1993). *Manual for the Kaufman Adolescent and Adult Intelligence Test (KAIT)*. Circle Pines, MN: American Guidance Service.

Kaufman, A. S., & Kaufman, N. L. (2004a). *Kaufman Test of Educational Achievement—Second Edition (KTEA-II)*. Circle Pines, MN: American Guidance Service.

Kaufman, A. S., & Kaufman, N. L. (2004b). *Kaufman Assessment Battery for Children—Second Edition, Technical Manual*. Circle Pines, MN: American Guidance Service.

Kaufman, A. S., & Lichtenberger, E. O. (1999). *Essentials of WAIS-III assessment.* New York: Wiley.

Kaufman, A. S., & Lichtenberger, E. O. (2000). *Essentials of WISC-III and WPPSI-R assessment.* New York: Wiley.

Kaufman, A. S., & Lichtenberger, E. O. (2002). *Assessing adolescent and adult intelligence* (2nd ed.). Boston: Allyn & Bacon.

Kaufman, A. S., & Lichtenberger, E. O. (2006). *Assessing adolescent and adult intelligence* (3rd ed.). Hoboken, NJ: John Wiley & Sons.

Kaufman, A. S., Lichtenberger, E. O., Fletcher-Janzen, E., & Kaufman, N. L. (2005). *Essentials of KABC-II assessment.* New York: Wiley.

Kaufman, A. S., & Wang, J. (1992). Gender, race, and education differences on the K-BIT at ages 4 to 90 years. *Journal of Psychoeducational Assessment, 10*, 219–229.

Kaufman, J. C., Plucker, J. A., & Baer, J. (2008). *Essentials of creativity assessment.* New York: Wiley.

Kavale, K. A., & Forness, S. R. (1984). A meta-analysis of the validity of Wechsler scale profiles and recategorizations: Patterns and parodies. *Learning Disabilities Quarterly, 7*, 136–156.

Kavale, K. A., & Forness, S. R. (2000). What definitions of learning disability say and don't say: A critical analysis. *Journal of Learning Disabilities, 33*, 239–256.

Kavale, K. A., Holdnack, J. A., & Mostert, M. P. (2006). Responsiveness to intervention and the identification of Specific Learning Disability: A critique and alternative proposal. *Learning Disability Quarterly, 29*(2), 113–127.

Keith, T. Z. (1988). Research methods in school psychology: An overview. *School Psychology Review, 17*, 502–520.

Keith, T. Z. (1997). What does the WISC-III measure? A reply to Carroll and Kranzler. *School Psychology Quarterly, 12*, 117–118.

Keith, T. Z., Fine, J. G., Taub, G. E., Reynolds, M. R., & Kranzler, J. H. (2006). Hierarchical multi-sample, confirmatory factor analysis of the Wechsler Intelligence Scale for Children—Fourth Edition: What does it measure? *School Psychology Review*, 35, 108–127.

Kelley M. F., & Surbeck, E. (1991). History of preschool assessment. In B. A. Bracken (Ed.), *The psychoeducational assessment of preschool children* (2nd ed., pp. 1–17). Boston: Allyn & Bacon.

Kelly, M., & Braden, J. P. (1990). Criterion-related validity of the WISC-R Performance Scale with the Stanford Achievement Test–Hearing Impaired Edition. *Journal of School Psychology, 28,* 147–151.

Klausmeier, K. L., Mishra, S. P., & Maker, C. J. (1987). Identification of gifted learners: A national survey of assessment practices and training needs of school psychologists. *Gifted Child Quarterly, 31,* 135–137.

Klin, A. (1994). Asperger Syndrome. *Child and Adolescent Psychiatric Clinics of North America, 3,* 131–148.

Klin, A., Pauls, D., Shultz, R., & Volkmar, F. (2005). Three diagnostic approaches to Asperger Syndrome: Implications for research. *Journal of Autism and Developmental Disorders, 35*(2), 221–234.

Klin, A., Sparrow, S. S., Marans, W. D., Carter, A., & Volkmar, F. R. (2000). Assessment issues in children and adolescents with Asperger Syndrome. In A. Klin, F. R. Volkmar, & S. S. Sparrow (Eds.), *Asperger Syndrome* (pp. 309–339). New York: Guilford.

Klin, A., Volkmar, F. R., Sparrow, S. S., Cicchetti, D. V., & Rourke, B. D. (1995). Validity and neuropsychological characterization of Asperger's Syndrome: Convergence with Nonverbal Learning Disabilities Syndrome. *Journal of Child Psychology and Psychiatry, 36,* 1127–1140.

Kohs, S. C. (1923). *Intelligence measurement.* New York: Macmillan.

Koyoma, T., Tachimori, H., Osada, H., Takeda, T., & Kurita, H. (2006). Cognitive and symptom profiles in high-functioning pervasive developmental disorder not otherwise specified and attention-deficit/hyperactivity disorder. *Journal of Autism and Developmental Disorder, 36*(3), 373–380.

Koyoma, T., Tachimori, H., Osada, H., Takeda, T., & Kurita, H. (2007). Cognitive and symptom profiles in Asperger's syndrome and high-functioning autism. *Psychiatry and Clinical Neuroscience, 61,* 99–104.

Kramer, J. H. (1993). Interpretation of individual subtest scores on the WISC-III. *Psychological Assessment, 5,* 193–196.

Krouse, H. E. (2008) The reliability and validity of the WISC-IV with deaf and hard-of-hearing children. Unpublished master's thesis. North Carolina State University, Raleigh.

Larry P. v. Wilson Riles. 343 F. Supp. 1306 (N. D. Cal. 1972) affr 502 F . 2d 963 (9th Cir. 1974); 495 F. Supp. 926 (N. D. Cal. 1979); appeal docketed, No. 80-4027 (9th Cir., Jan. 17, 1980).

Launey, K. B., Carroll, J., & Van Horn, K. R. (2007). Concurrent validity of the WISC IV in eligibility decisions for students with educable mental disabilities. *Psychological Reports,* 1165–1170.

Leffard, S. A., Miller, J. A., Bernstein, J. , Demann, J. J., Mangis, H. A., & McCoy, E. L. B. (2006). Substantive validity of working memory measures in major cognitive functioning test batteries for children. *Applied Neuropsychology, 13,* 230–241.

Lincoln, A. J., Courchesne, E., Kilman, B. A Elmasian, R., & Allen, M. (1988). A study of intellectual abilities in high-functioning people with autism. *Journal of Autism and Developmental Disorders, 18,* 505–524.

Little, S. G. (1992). The WISC-III: Everything old is new again. *School Psychology Quarterly, 7*(2), 148–154.

Loe, S. A., Kadlubek, R. M. & Marks, W. J. (2007). Administration and scoring errors on the WISC-IV among graduate student examiners. *Journal of Psychoeducational Assessment, 25,* 237–247.

Logie, R. (1996). The seven ages of working memory. In J. Richardson, R. Engle, L. Hasher, R. Logie, E. Stoltzfus, & R. Zacks (Eds.), *Working memory and human cognition* (pp. 31–65). New York: Oxford.

LoGiudice, C., & LaQuay, K. (2005). *Spotlight on vocabulary: Roots, prefixes, and suffixes.* East Moline, IL: LinguiSystems.

Lohman, D. F. (1989). Human intelligence: An introduction to advances in theory and research. *Review of Educational Research, 59*(4), 333–373.

Lohman, D. F. (1994). Spatial ability. In R. J. Sternberg (Ed.), *Encyclopedia of human intelligence* (pp. 1000–1007). New York: Macmillan.

Luckasson, R., Borthwick-Duffy, S., Buntix, W. H. E., Coulter, D. L., Craig, E. M., Reeve, A., et al. (2002). *Mental retardation: Definition, classification, and systems of supports* (10th ed.). Washington, DC: American Association on Mental Retardation.

Maller, S. (1996). WISC-III Verbal item invariance across samples of deaf and hearing children of similar measured ability. *Journal of Psychoeducational Assessment, 14,* 152–165.

Maller, S. (2003). Intellectual assessment of deaf people: A critical review of core concepts and issues. In M. Marschark & P. E. Spencer (Eds.), *Oxford handbook of deaf studies, language, and education* (pp. 451–463). New York: Oxford University Press.

Manjiviona, J., & Prior, M. (1995). Comparison of Asperger Syndrome and high-functioning autistic children on a test of motor impairment. *Journal of Autism and Developmental Disorders, 25,* 23–39.

Marland, S. P. (1972). *Education of the gifted and talented: Vol. 1. Report to the Congress of the United States by the U.S. Commissioner of Education.* Washington, DC: U.S. GPO.

Mascolo, J. T. (2008, April). Data-based decision making: Using assessment to inform interventions. Invited presentation. Fordham University, Lincoln Center Campus. New York.

Matarazzo, J. D. (1972). *Wechsler's measurement and appraisal of adult intelligence* (5th and enlarged ed.). New York: Oxford University Press.

Mather, N., & Jaffe, L. (2002). *Woodcock-Johnson III: Reports, recommendations, and strategies.* New York: Wiley.

Mayes, S. D., & Calhoun, S. L. (2004). Similarities and differences in Wechsler Intelligence Scale for Children–Third Edition (WISC-III) profiles: Support for subtest analysis in clinical referrals. *Clinical Neuropsychologist, 18,* 559–572.

Mayes, S. D., & Calhoun, S. L. (2006). WISC-IV and WISC-III profiles in children with ADHD. *Journal of Attention Disorders, 9,* 486–493.

Mayes, S. D., & Calhoun, S. L. (2007). Wechsler Intelligence Scale for Children–Third and –Fourth Edition predictors of academic achievement in children with Attention-Deficit/Hyperactivity Disorder. *School Psychology Quarterly, 22,* 234–249.

Mayes, S. D., & Calhoun, S. L. (2008). WISC-IV and WIAT-II profiles in children with high-functioning autism. *Journal of Autism and Developmental Disorders, 38*(3), 428–439.

Mayes, S. D., Calhoun, S. L., & Crites, D. L. (2001). Does *DSM-IV* Asperger's Disorder exist? *Journal of Abnormal Child Psychology, 29*(3), 263–271.

McCoach, D. B., Kehle, T. J., Bray, M. A., & Siegle, D. (2001). Best practices in the identification of gifted students with learning disabilities. *Psychology in the Schools, 38,* 403–411.

McDermott, P. A., Fantuzzo, J. W., & Glutting, J. J. (1990). Just say no to subtest analysis: A critique on Wechsler theory and practice. *Journal of Psychoeducational Assessment, 8,* 290–302.

McDermott, P. A., Fantuzzo, J. W., Glutting, J. J., Watkins, M. W., & Baggaley, R. A. (1992). Illusions of meaning in the ipsative assessment of children's ability. *Journal of Special Education, 25,* 504–526.

McGrew, K. S. (1994). *Clinical interpretation of the Woodcock-Johnson Tests of Cognitive Ability—Revised.* Boston: Allyn & Bacon.

McGrew, K. S. (1997). Analysis of the major intelligence batteries according to a proposed comprehensive Gf-Gc framework. In D. P. Flanagan, J. L. Genshaft, & P. L. Harrison (Eds.), *Contemporary intellectual assessment: Theories, tests, and issues* (pp. 151–180). New York: Guilford.

McGrew, K. S. (2005). The Cattell-Horn-Carroll (CHC) theory of cognitive abilities: Past, present and future. In D. P. Flanagan & P. L. Harrison (Eds.), *Contemporary intellectual assessment: Theories, tests, and issues,* 2nd ed. (pp. 136–181). New York: Guilford.

McGrew, K. S., & Flanagan, D. P. (1996). The Wechsler Performance Scale debate: Fluid Intelligence *(Gf)* or Visual Processing *(Gv)*? *Communique, 24*(6), 14–16.

McGrew, K. S., & Flanagan, D. P. (1998). *The intelligence test desk reference (ITDR): Gf-Gc cross-battery assessment.* Needham Heights, MA: Allyn & Bacon.

McGrew, K. S., Flanagan, D. P., Keith, T. Z., & Vanderwood, M. (1997). Beyond *g:* The impact of *Gf-Gc* specific cognitive abilities research on the future use and interpretation of intelligence tests in the schools. *School Psychology Review, 26,* 177–189.

McGrew, K. S., Woodcock, R. W., & Werder, J. K. (1991). *Woodcock-Johnson Psycho-Educational Battery—Revised technical manual.* Chicago: Riverside.

McLaughlin-Cheng, E. (1998). Asperger Syndrome and autism: A literature review and meta-analysis. *Focus on Autism and Other Developmental Disabilities, 13*(4), 234–245.

Mercer, J. R. (1979). *The System of Multicultural Pluralistic Assessment: Technical manual.* New York: The Psychological Corporation.

Milberg, W. P., Hebben, N., & Kaplan, E. (1986). The Boston process approach to neuro-psychological assessment. In K. Adams & I. Grant (Eds.), *Neuropsychological assessment of neuropsychiatric disorders* (pp. 65–86). New York: Oxford University Press.

Milberg, W. P., Hebben, N., & Kaplan, E. (1996). The Boston process approach to neuro-psychological assessment. In K. Adams & I. Grant (Eds.), *Neuropsychological assessment of neuropsychiatric disorders* (2nd ed., pp. 58–80). New York: Oxford University Press.

Miller, J. N., & Ozonoff, S. (1997). Did Asperger's cases have Asperger Disorder? A research note. *Journal of Child Psychology and Psychiatry, 38,* 247–251.

Miller, J. N., & Ozonoff, S. (2000). The external validity of Asperger Disorder: Lack of evidence from the domain of neuropsychology. *Journal of Abnormal Psychology, 109*(2), 227–238.

Moran, J. L., & Mefford, R. B., Jr. (1959). Repetitive psychometric measures. *Psychological Reports, 5,* 269–275.

Morris, R. D., Stuebing, K. K., Fletcher, J. M., Shaywitz, S. E., Lyon, G. R., Shankweiler, D. P., et al. (1998). Subtypes of reading disability: Variability around a phonological core. *Journal of Educational Psychology, 90*(3), 347–373.

Mpofu, E., & Ortiz, S. O. (in press). Equitable assessment practices in diverse contexts. In E. L. Grigorenko (Ed.), *Assessment of abilities and competencies in the era of globalization.*

Mueller, H. H., Dennis, S. S., & Short, R. H. (1986). A meta-exploration of WISC-R factor score profiles as a function of diagnosis and intellectual level. *Canadian Journal of School Psychology, 2,* 21–43.

Myhr, G. (1998). Autism and other pervasive developmental disorders: Exploring the dimensional view. *Canadian Journal of Psychiatry, 43,* 589–595.

Naglieri, J. A., & Pickering, E. B. (2003). *Helping children learn: Intervention handouts for use in school and at home.* Baltimore: Paul H. Brookes.

National Association for Gifted Children. (2008). Position paper: Use of the WISC-IV for gifted identification. http://www.nagc.org

Nettlebeck, T. (1994). Speediness. In R. J. Sternberg (Ed.), *Encyclopedia of human intelligence* (pp. 1014–1019). New York: Macmillan.

Nicholson, C. L., Alcorn, C. L., & Erford, B. T. (2006). *Educational applications of the WISC-IV: A handbook of interpretive strategies and remedial recommendations.* Los Angeles: Western Psychological Services.

Nyden, A., Billstedt, E., Hjelmquist, E., & Gillberg, C. (2001). Neurocognitive stability in Asperger Syndrome, ADHD, and Reading and Writing Disorder: A pilot study. *Developmental Medicine and Child Neurology, 43,* 165–171.

Ochoa, S. H., Powell, M. P., & Robles-Piña, R. (1996). School psychologists' assessment practices with bilingual and limited-English-proficient students. *Journal of Psychoeducational Assessment, 14,* 250–275.

Oh, H. J., Glutting, J. J., Watkins, M. W., Youngstrom, E. A., & McDermott, P. A. (2004). Correct interpretation of latent versus observed abilities: Implications from structural equation modeling applied to the WISC-III and WIAT linking sample. *The Journal of Special Education, 38,* 159 –173.

Ortiz, S. O. (2001). Assessment of cognitive abilities in Hispanic children. *Seminars in Speech and Language, 22*(1), 17–37.

Ortiz, S. O. (2008). Best practices in nondiscriminatory assessment. In A. Thomas & J. Grimes (Eds.), *Best practices in school psychology V,* (pp. 661–678*).* Washington, DC: National Association of School Psychologists.

Ortiz, S. O., & Dynda, A. M. (in press). Diversity, fairness, utility and social issues. In E. Mpofu & T. Oakland (Eds.), *Assessment in rehabilitation and health.* Boston: Allyn & Bacon.

Ortiz, S. O., & Ochoa, S. H. (2005). Intellectual Assessment: A nondiscriminatory interpretive approach. In D. P. Flanagan & P. L. Harrison (Eds.), *Contemporary intellectual assessment* (2nd ed., pp. 234–250). New York: Guilford.

Ozonoff, S., Rogers, S. J., & Pennington, B. F. (1991). Asperger's Syndrome: Evidence of an empirical distinction from high-functioning autism. *Journal of Child Psychology and Psychiatry, 32,* 1107–1122.

Parker, F. (1981). Ideas that shaped American schools. *Phi Delta Kappan, 62,* 314–319.

Pfeiffer, S. I., & Jarosewich, T. (2003). *Gifted Rating Scales Manual.* San Antonio, TX: The Psychological Corporation

Prifitera, A., & Saklofske, D. H. (Eds.). (1998). *WISC-III clinical use and interpretation: Scientist-practitioner perspectives.* San Diego, CA: Academic Press.

Prifitera, A., Saklofske, D. H., Weiss, L. G., & Rolfhus, E. (Eds.). (2005). *WISC-IV clinical use and interpretation: Scientist-practitioner perspectives.* San Diego, CA: Academic Press.

Prifitera, A., Saklofske, D. H., Weiss, L. G., & Rolfhus, E., (2005). The WISC-IV in the clinical assessment context. In A. Prifitera, D. H., Saklofske, & L. G. Weiss (Eds.), *WISC-IV: Clinical use and interpretation* (pp. 3–32). San Diego, CA: Elsevier Science.

Prifitera, A., Weiss, L. G., & Saklofske, D. H. (1998). The WISC-III in context. In A. Prifitera & D. H. Saklofske (Eds.), *WISC-III clinical use and interpretation: Scientist-practitioner perspectives* (pp. 1–38). San Diego, CA: Academic Press.

Psychological Corporation, The. (2001). *Wechsler Individual Achievement Test—Second Edition.* San Antonio, TX: Author.

Psychological Corporation, The. (2002). *WPPSI-III technical and interpretive manual.* San Antonio, TX: Author.

Psychological Corporation, The. (2003). *WISC-IV technical and interpretive manual.* San Antonio, TX: Author.

Psychological Corporation, The. (2004). *WISC-IV Integrated technical and interpretive manual.* San Antonio, TX: Author

Raiford, S. E., Weiss, L. G., Rolfhus, E., & Coalson, D. (2005). *General Ability Index* (WISC-IV Technical Report No. 4). Retrieved May 25, 2008, from http://harcourtassessment.com/hai/Images/pdf/wisciv/WISCIVTechReport4.pdf.

Rapaport, D., Gill, M. M., & Schafer, R. (1945–46). *Diagnostic Psychological Testing* (2 vols.). Chicago: Yearbook Publishers.

Raven, J. C. (1938). *Progressive matrices: A perceptual test of intelligence.* San Antonio, TX: The Psychological Corporation.

Reeves, C. L. (2004). Differential ability antecedents of general and specific dimensions of declarative knowledge: More than *g. Intelligence, 32,* 621–652.

Reynolds, C. R. (2000). Methods for detecting and evaluating cultural bias in neuropsychological tests. In E. Fletcher-Janzen, T. Strickland, & C. R. Reynolds (Eds.), *Handbook of cross-cultural neuropsychology* (pp. 249–285). New York: Kluwer Academic/Plenum Publishers.

Reynolds, C. R. (2007). Introduction: Subtest level profile analysis of intelligence tests: Editior's remarks and introduction [Special issue on Profile Level Analysis of Intelligence Tests]. *Applied Neuropsychology, 14*(1).

Reynolds, C. R., & Kamphaus, R. W. (2003). *Reynolds Intellectual Assessment Scales (RIAS)*. Tampa, FL: Psychological Assessment Resources.

Rhodes, R., Ochoa, S. H., & Ortiz, S. O. (2005). *Assessment of Culturally and Linguistically Diverse Students: A practical guide*. New York: Guilford.

Richardson, J. (1996). Evolving concepts of working memory. In J. Richardson, R. Engle, L. Hasher, R. Logie, E. Stoltzfus, & R. Zacks (Eds.), *Working memory and human cognition* (pp. 3–30). New York: Oxford.

Rimm, S., Gilman, B., & Silverman, L. (2008). Nontraditional applications of traditional testing. In J. VanTassel-Baska (Ed.), *Critical issues in equity and excellence in gifted education series, Volume 2: Alternative assessment of gifted learners* (pp. 175–202)Waco, TX: Prufrock Press.

Robinson, B. R., & Harrison, P. L. (2005). WISC-III core profiles for students referred or found eligible for special education and gifted programs. *School Psychology Quarterly, 20*(1), 51–65.

Roid, G. H. (2003). *Stanford-Binet Intelligence Scales–Fifth Edition, Technical Manual*. Itasca, IL: Riverside.

Rumsey, J. M. (1992). Neuropsychological studies of high-level autism. In E. Schopler & G. B. Mcsibov (Eds.), *High-functioning individuals with autism* (pp. 41–64). New York: Plenum Press.

Saklofske, D. H., Weiss, L. G., Raiford, S. E., & Prifitera, A. (2006). Advanced clinical interpretation of WISC-IV index scores. In L. G. Weiss, D. H. Saklofske, A. Prifitera, & J. Holdnack (Eds.), *WISC-IV advanced clinical interpretation* (pp. 139–179). Amsterdam: Elsevier.

Saklofske, D. H., Weiss, L. G., Zhu, J., Rolfhus, E., Raiford, S. E., & Coalson, D. (2005). *General Ability Index Canadian norms* (WISC-IV Technical Report No. 4.1). Retrieved August 5, 2008, from http://pearsonassess.com/hai/Images/pdf/wisciv/WISC-IV_4.1_Re1.pdf.

Sanchez, G. I. (1934). Bilingualism and mental measures: A word of caution. *Journal of Applied Psychology, 18,* 765–772.

Sandoval, J. (1979). The WISC-R and internal evidence of test bias with minority groups. *Journal of Consulting and Clinical Psychology, 47,* 919–927.

Sandoval, J., Frisby, C. L., Geisinger, K. F., Scheuneman, J. D., & Grenier, J. R. (Eds.). (1998). *Test interpretation and diversity: Achieving equity in assessment*. Washington, DC: American Psychological Association.

Sattler, J. M. (1974). Assessment of children's intelligence (revised ed.). Philadelphia: Saunders.

Sattler, J. M. (1992). *Assessment of children* (Rev. and updated 3rd ed.). San Diego, CA: Author.

Sattler, J. M. (2001). *Assessment of children: Cognitive applications* (4th ed.). La Mesa, CA: Author.

Sattler, J. M. (2008). *Assessment of children: Cognitive foundations* (5th ed.). San Diego, CA: Author.

Sattler, J. M., & Dumont, R. (2004). *Assessment of children WISC-IV and WPPSI-III Supplement*. La Mesa, CA: Jerome M. Sattler.

Sattler, J. M., & Hardy-Braz, S. T. (2002). Hearing impairments. In J. M. Sattler (Ed.), *Assessment of children: Behavioral and clinical applications* (pp. 377–389). La Mesa, CA: Jerome M. Sattler.

Sattler, J. M., Hardy-Braz, S. T., & Willis, J. O. (2006). Hearing impairments. In J. M. Sattler & R. D. Hoge (Eds.), *Assessment of children: Behavioral and clinical applications* (5th ed., pp. 478–492). La Mesa, CA: Jerome M. Sattler.

Scarr, S. (1978). From evolution to Larry P., or what shall we do about IQ tests? *Intelligence, 2,* 325–342.

Schneider, W., & Shiffrin, R. M. (1977). Controlled and Automatic Human Information Processing: Detection, search, and attention. *Psychological Review, 84,* 1–66.

Schopler, E. (1996). Are autism and Asperger Syndrome (AS) different labels or different disabilities? *Journal of Autism and Developmental Disorders, 26,* 109–110.

Schwean, V. L., & Saklofske, D. H. (2005). Assessment of Attention-Deficit/Hyperactivity Disorder with the WISC-IV. In A. Prifitera, D. H. Saklofske, & L. G. Weiss (Eds.), *WISC-IV clinical use and interpretation: Scientist-practitioner perspectives* (pp. 235–280). San Diego, CA: Academic Press.

Shapiro, E. (1996). *Academic skills problems: Direct assessment and intervention* (2nd. ed.). New York: Guilford.

Shaw, S. E., Swerdlik, M. E., & Laurent, J. (1993). Review of the WISC-III [WISC-III Monograph]. *Journal of Psychoeducational Assessment,* 151–160.

Siegel, D. J., Minshew, N. J., & Goldstein, G. (1996). Wechsler IQ profiles in diagnosis of high-functioning autism. *Journal of Autism and Developmental Disabilities, 26,* 398–406.

Silverman, L. K. (in press). The measurement of giftedness. In L. Shavinina (Ed.). *The international handbook on giftedness.* Amsterdam: Springer Science.

Silverman, L. K., Gilman, B., & Falk, R. (2004). *Who are the gifted using the new WISC-IV?* Paper presented at the 51st Annual Convention of the National Association for Gifted Children, Salt Lake City, UT. Retrieved May 30, 2008, from http://www.gifteddevelopment.com/PDF_files/NewWISC.pdf.

Slate, J. R. (1995). Discrepancies between IQ and index scores for a clinical sample of students: Useful diagnostic indicators? *Psychology in the Schools, 32,* 103–108.

Sotelo-Dynega, M. (2007). *Cognitive performance and the development of English language proficiency.* Unpublished manuscript. St. John's University, New York.

Sparrow, S. S., & Gurland, S. T. (1998). Assessment of gifted children with the WISC-III. In A. Prifitera & D. Saklofske (Eds.), *WISC-III clinical use and interpretation: Scientist-practitioner perspectives* (pp. 59–72). San Diego, CA: Academic Press.

Sparrow, S. S., Pfeiffer, S. I., & Newman, T. M. (2005). Assessment of children who are gifted with the WISC-IV. In A. Prifitera, D. H. Saklofske, & L. G. Weiss (Eds.), *WISC-IV clinical use and interpretation* (pp. 282–298). San Diego, CA: Academic Press.

Spruill, J. (1998). Assessment of Mental Retardation with the WISC-III. In A. Prifitera & D. Saklofske (Eds.), *WISC-III clinical use and interpretation* (pp. 73–90). San Diego, CA: Academic Press.

Spruill, J., Oakland, T., & Harrison, P. (2005). Assessment of Mental Retardation. In A. Prifitera, D. H. Saklofske, & L. G Weiss (Eds.), *WISC-IV clinical use and interpretation: Scientist-practitioner perspectives* (pp. 289–331). San Diego, CA: Academic Press.

Stankov, L. (1994). Auditory abilities. In R. J. Sternberg (Ed.), *Encyclopedia of human intelligence* (pp. 157–162). New York: Macmillan.

Stankov, L., & Horn, J. L. (1980). Human abilities revealed through auditory tests. *Journal of Educational Psychology, 72*(1), 21–44.

Sternberg, R. J. (1982). Lies we live by: Misapplication of tests in identifying the gifted. *Gifted Child Quarterly, 26,* 157–161.

Sternberg, R. J. (1993). Procedures for identifying intellectual potential in the gifted: A perspective on alternative "metaphors of mind." In K. A. Heller, F. J. Monks, & A. H. Passow (Eds.), *International handbook of research and development of giftedness and talent* (pp. 185–207). New York: Pergamon.

Sternberg, R. J. (1995). What do we mean by giftedness?: A pentagonal implicit theory. *Gifted Child Quarterly, 39,* 88–94.

Sternberg, S. (1966). High-speed scanning in human memory. *Science, 153,* 652–654.

Stott, L., & Ball, R. (1965). Infant and preschool mental tests: Review and evaluation. *Monographs of the Society for Research in Child Development, 30,* 4–42.

Strauss, E., Sherman, E. M. S., & Spreen, O. (2006). A compendium of neuropsychological tests: Administration, norms, and commentary (3rd ed.). New York: Oxford University Press.

Swanson, H. L., & Howell, M. (2001). Working memory, short-term memory, and speech rate as predictors of children's reading performance at different ages. *Journal of Educational Psychology, 9*(4), 720–734.

Szatmari, P., Archer, L., Fisman, S., Streiner, D. L., & Wilson, F. (1995). Asperger's Syndrome and autism: Differences in behavior, cognition, and adaptive functioning. *Journal of the American Academy of Child and Adolescent Psychiatry, 34,* 1662–1671.

Talland, G. A., & Schwab, R. S. (1964). Performance with multiple sets in Parkinson's Disease. *Neuropsychologia, 2,* 45–57.

Taub, G. E., Keith, T. Z., Floyd, R. G., & Mcgrew, K. S. (2008). Effects of general and broad cognitive abilities on mathematics achievement. *School Psychology Quarterly, 23,* 187–198.

Tellegen, A., & Briggs, P. F. (1967). Old wine in new skins: Grouping Wechsler subtests into new scales. *Journal of Consulting Psychology, 31,* 499–506.

Terman, L. M. (1916). *The measurement of intelligence: An explanation of and a complete guide for the use of the Stanford revision and extension of the Binet-Simon intelligence scale.* Boston: Houghton Mifflin.

Terman, L. M., & Merrill, M. A. (1937). *Measuring intelligence.* Boston: Houghton Mifflin.

Terman, L. M., & Merrill, M, A. (1960). *Stanford-Binet Intelligence Scale: Manual for the third revision form L-M.* Boston: Houghton Mifflin.

Thompson, A. P. (1987). Methodological issues in the clinical evaluation of two- and four-subtest short forms of the WAIS-R. *Journal of Clinical Psychology, 43,* 142–144.

Thompson, A. P., Howard, D., & Anderson, J. (1986). Two- and four-subtest short forms of the WAIS-R: Validity in a psychiatric sample. *Canadian Journal of Behavioural Science, 26,* 492–504.

Tyerman, M. J. (1986). Gifted children and their identification: Learning ability not intelligence. *Gifted Education International, 4,* 81–84.

U.S. Congress. (1978). *Educational amendment of 1978 (P.L. 95-651).* Washington, DC: U.S. Government Printing Office.

U.S. Congress. (1988). *Jacob K. Javits gifted and talented students education act of 1988 (P.L.100-297).* Washington, DC: U.S. Government Printing Office.

U.S. Department of Health, Education, and Welfare. (1972). *Education of the gifted and talented, Vol. 1, report to the Congress of the United States by the U.S. Commissioner of Education.* Washington, DC: U.S. Government Printing Office.

Valdes, G., & Figueroa, R. A. (1994). *Bilingualism and testing: A special case of bias.* Norwood, NJ: Ablex.

Vanderwood, M. L., McGrew, K. S., Flanagan, D. P., & Keith, T. Z. (2002). The contribution of general and specific cognitive abilities to reading achievement. *Learning and Individual Differences, 13,* 159–188.

Vellutino, F. R., Scanlon, D. M., & Lyon, G. R. (2000). Differentiating between difficult-to-remediate and readily remediated poor readers. *Journal of Learning Disabilities, 33,* 223–238.

Vig, S., Kaminer, R. K., & Jedrysek, E. (1987). A later look at borderline and mentally retarded preschoolers. *Journal of Developmental and Behavioral Pediatrics, 8,* 12–17.

Volker, M. A., Lopata, C., & Cook-Cottone, C. (2006). Assessment of children with intellectual giftedness and reading disabilities. *Psychology in the Schools, 48,* 855–869.

Wagner, R. K., Torgesen, J. K., Laughton, P., Simmons, K., & Rashotte, C. A. (1993). Development of young readers' phonological processing abilities. *Journal of Educational Psychology, 85*(1), 83–103.

Watkins, M. W., Glutting, J. J., & Lei, P. (2007). Validity of the full-scale IQ when there is significant variability among WISC-III and WISC-IV factor scores. *Applied Neuropsychology, 14,* 13–20.

Watkins, M. W., & Kush, J. C. (1994). Wechsler subtest analysis: The right way, the wrong way, or no way? *School Psychology Review, 23,* 640–651.

Watkins, M. W., Youngstrom, E. A., & Glutting, J. J (2002). Some cautions concerning cross-battery assessment. *Communique, 30*(5), 16–19.

Wechsler, D. (1939). *The measurement of adult intelligence.* Baltimore: Williams & Wilkins.

Wechsler, D. (1944). *The measurement of adult intelligence* (3rd ed.). Baltimore: Williams & Wilkins.

Wechsler, D. (1949). *Manual for the Wechsler Intelligence Scale for Children.* San Antonio, TX: The Psychological Corporation.

Wechsler, D. (1955). *Manual for the Wechsler Adult Intelligence Scale.* San Antonio, TX: The Psychological Corporation.

Wechsler, D. (1958). *The measurement and appraisal of adult intelligence* (4th ed.). Baltimore: Williams & Wilkins.

Wechsler, D. (1974). *Manual for the Wechsler Preschool and Primary Scale of Intelligence.* San Antonio, TX: The Psychological Corporation.

Wechsler, D. (1991). *Manual for the Wechsler Intelligence Scale for Children—Third Edition (WISC-III).* San Antonio, TX: The Psychological Corporation.

Wechsler, D. (2003) *Wechsler Intelligence Scale for Children—Fourth Edition (WISC-IV) administration and scoring manual.* San Antonio, TX: The Psychological Corporation.

Wechsler, D., & Naglieri, J. A. (2006). *Wechsler Nonverbal Scale of Ability technical and interpretive manual.* San Antonio, TX: The Psychological Corporation.

Weiss, L. G. & Gabel, A. D. *Using the cognitive proficiency index in the psychoeducational assessment.* (WISC-IV Technical Report No. 6). Retrieved May 28, 2008 from, http://harcourtassessment.com/hai/Images/pdf/wisciv/WISCIVTechReport6.pdf.

Weiss, L. G., Harris, J. G., Prifitera, A., Courville, T., Rolfhus, E., Saklofske, D. H., et al. (2006). WISC-IV interpretation in societal context. In L. G Weiss, D. H. Saklofske, & J. Holdnack (Eds.), *WISC-IV advanced clinical interpretation* (pp. 1–57). Burlington, MA: Academic Press.

Weiss, L. G., Prifitera, A., Holdnack, J. A., Saklofske, D. H., Rolfhus, E., & Coalson, D. (2006). The essentials and beyond. In L. G Weiss, D. H. Saklofske, & J. Holdnack (Eds.), *WISC-IV advanced clinical interpretation* (pp. 59–97). Burlington, MA: Academic Press.

Weiss, L. G., Saklofske, D. H., Prifitera, A., & Holdnack, J. (Eds.). (2006). *WISC-IV advanced clinical interpretation.* Burlington, MA: Academic Press.

Weiss, L. G., Saklofske, D. H., Schwartz, D. M., Prifitera, A., & Courville, T. (2006). Advanced clinical interpretation of WISC-IV index scores. In L. G. Weiss, D. H. Saklofske, A. Prifitera, & J. Holdnack (Eds.), *WISC-IV advanced clinical interpretation* (pp. 99–138), San Diego, CA: Elsevier/Academic Press.

Werner, H., & Kaplan, E. (1950). Development of word meaning through verbal context: An experimental study. *Journal of Psychology, 29,* 251–257.

Whitworth, J. R., & Sutton, D. L. (2005). *WISC-IV compilation: What to do now that you know the score.* Novato, CA: Academic Therapy Publications.

Williams, P. E., Weiss, L. G., & Rolfhus, E. L. (2003). Wechsler intelligence scale for children–Fourth edition: Clinical validity technical report #3. San Antonio, TX: The Psychological Corporation.

Wing, L. (1998). The history of Asperger Syndrome. In E. Schopler, G. B. Mesibov, & L. J. Kunce (Eds.), *Asperger Syndrome or high-functioning autism?* (pp. 11–28). New York: Plenum.

Winner, E. (1997). Exceptionally high intelligence and schooling. *American Psychologist, 52*(10), 1070–1081.

Winner, E. (2000). The origins and ends of giftedness. *American Psychologist, 55*(1), 159–169.

Witt, J. C., & Gresham, F. M. (1985). Review of Wechsler Intelligence Scale for Children–Revised. In J. V. Mitchell (Ed.), *The ninth mental measurement yearbook* (vol. 2, pp. 1716–1719). Lincoln, NE: Buros Institute of Mental Measurement.

Wolf, M., & Bowers, P. (2000). The question of naming-speed deficits in developmental reading disability: An introduction to the Double-Deficit Hypothesis. *Journal of Learning Disabilities, 33,* 322–324. (Special issue on the Double-Deficit Hypothesis: Special Issue Editors: M. Wolf & P. Bowers).

Woodcock, R. W. (1993). An information processing view of *Gf-Gc* theory. *Journal of Psychoeducational Assessment* Monograph Series: WJ-R Monograph, 80–102.

Woodcock, R. W. (1994). Measures of fluid and crystallized intelligence. In R. J. Sternberg (Ed.), *The encyclopedia of human intelligence* (pp. 452–456). New York: Macmillan.

Woodcock, R. W., McGrew, K. S., & Mather, N. (2001). *Woodcock-Johnson III Tests of Achievement*. Itasca, IL: Riverside Publishing.

Yerkes, R. M. (1921). Psychological examining in the United States army. *Memoirs of the National Academy of Sciences, 15,* 1–89.

Yirmiya, N., & Sigman, M. (1991). High functioning individuals with autism: Diagnosis, empirical findings, and theoretical issues. *Clinical Psychology Review, 11,* 669–683.

Yopp, H. K. (1988). The validity and reliability of phonemic awareness tests. *Reading Research Quarterly, 23*(2), 159–177.

Zachary, R. A. (1990). Wechsler's intelligence scales: Theoretical and practical considerations. *Journal of Psychoeducational Assessment, 8,* 276–289.

Zhu, J., Cayton, T., Weiss, L., & Gabel, A. (2008). *WISC-IV extended norms* (WISC-IV Technical Report No. 7). Retrieved June 5, 2008, from http://harcourtassessment.com/hai/Images/pdf/wisciv/WISCIVTechReport7.pdf.

Annotated Bibliography

Flanagan, D. P., & Harrison, P. L. (Eds.). (2005). *Contemporary intellectual assessment: Theories, tests and issues* (2nd ed.). New York: Guilford.
A hard-cover edited book that includes chapters on all major intelligence tests, including the WISC-IV, as well as the prevailing theories of the structure of cognitive abilities and the nature of intelligence. In addition, a variety of new approaches to test interpretation are included alongside guidelines for using intelligence tests with different populations (e.g., preschool, learning disabled, gifted, culturally and linguistically diverse).

Flanagan, D. P., Ortiz, S. O., & Alfonso, V. C. (2007). *Essentials of cross-battery assessment* (2nd ed.). New York: Wiley.
Provides a comprehensive set of guidelines and procedures for organizing assessments based on contemporary CHC theory and research, integrating test results from different batteries in a psychometrically defensible way, and interpreting test results within the context of research on the relations between cognitive and academic abilities and processes. Also includes guidelines for assessing culturally and linguistically diverse populations and individuals suspected of having a specific learning disability. This book includes a CD-ROM containing three software programs for assisting in data management and interpretation, making decisions regarding specific learning disabilities, and discerning difference from disability in individuals whose cultural and linguistic backgrounds differ from the mainstream.

Flanagan, D. P., Ortiz, S. O., Alfonso, V. C., & Mascolo, J. T. (2006). *The achievement test desk reference (ATDR): A guide to learning disability identification* (2nd ed.). Boston: Allyn & Bacon.
Reviews comprehensive, brief, and special purpose tests of achievement, including the WIAT-II, KTEA-II, WJ III, specialized reading, math, and written language tests, and tests of auditory and phonological processing. Demonstrates how to integrate findings from achievement tests with findings from cognitive tests following CHC theory and its research base. Offers an operational definition of Specific Learning Disability and demonstrates how to incorporate this definition into everyday practice in the schools.

Kaufman, A. S., & Lichtenberger, E. O. (2006). *Assessing adolescent and adult intelligence* (3rd ed.). New York: Wiley.
Provides a thorough, theory-based, research-based, and clinically based interpretation of tests of adult intelligence. This book features the WAIS-III but also includes chapters on the KAIT, WJ III, and brief measures of adult intelligence.

Kaufman, A. S., Lichtenberger, E. O., Fletcher-Janzen, E., & Kaufman, N. L. (2005). *Essentials of KABC-II assessment.* New York: Wiley.
Covers thoroughly the interpretation of the KABC-II, including treatment of the integration of the KABC-II and WISC-IV. The case of Vanessa (age 11) integrates selected WISC-IV subtests and scales with the KABC-II. The interpretive system for the KABC-II (which is based on both Luria and CHC theories) parallels our WISC-IV interpretive system.

Lichtenberger, E. O., & Kaufman, A. S. (2004). *Essentials of WPPSI-III assessment.* New York: Wiley.
Interprets the WPPSI-III in a systematic, thorough fashion, including integration of the WPPSI-III with the WISC-III and WISC-IV.

Lichtenberger, E. O., Mather, N., Kaufman, N. L., & Kaufman, A. S. (2004). *Essentials of assessment report writing.* New York: Wiley.
Covers the basics of writing psychological assessment reports. Uses the WISC-IV throughout for illustrative purposes.

Prifitera, A., Saklofske, D. H., Weiss, L. G., & Rolfhus, E. (Eds.). (2005). *WISC-IV use and interpretation: Scientist-practitioner perspectives.* San Diego, CA: Elsevier/Academic Press.
A hard-cover edited book that includes chapters on a variety of topics pertinent to the WISC-IV, such as clinical applications, psychometric properties, gifted assessment, LD assessment, and neuropsychological assessment.

The Psychological Corporation. (2003). *WISC-IV technical and interpretive manual.* San Antonio, TX: Author.
Includes information about the reliability and validity of the WISC-IV as well as other important psychometric characteristics of the test.

Sattler, J. M. (2008). *Assessment of children: Cognitive foundations* (5th ed.). San Diego, CA: Author.
A hard-cover text that covers cognitive assessment historically, psychometrically, and theoretically in a thorough manner. It includes three chapters on the WISC-IV and its interpretation.

Wechsler, D. (2003). *WISC-IV administration and scoring manual.* San Antonio, TX: The Psychological Corporation.
Includes the administration and scoring procedures for the WISC-IV as well as norms and conversion tables.

Weiss, L. G., , Saklofske, D. H., Prifitera, A., & Holdnack. J. A. (Eds.). (2006). *WISC-IV: Advanced clinical interpretation.* San Diego, CA: Elsevier/Academic Press.
A hard-cover edited book that goes beyond the Prifitera and colleagues (2005) book by treating a variety of key topics pertinent to the WISC-IV at an advanced, in-depth level. Especially incisive are the chapters on (a) WISC-IV interpretation in a societal context (which exlores the issues of test bias and ethnic differences in an innovative, thorough manner) and (b) advanced clinical interpretation of WISC-IV index scores (which provides useful data and interpretation of the Cognitive Proficiency Index or CPI).

Index

Ability-achievement discrepancy (AAD), 218, 230
Achievement assessment
  KTEA-II Comprehensive Form A, 501–502
  mathematics performance, 482
  oral language performance, 483
  reading performance, 481–482
  written language performance, 482–483
Achievement functioning, 511–512
ADHD. *See* Attention-Deficit/Hyperactivity
  Disorder
ALDs. *See* Assistive listening devices
APD. *See* Auditory Processing Disorder
Application of theory
  defined, 13
  described, 13–15
Aptitude-achievement consistency, 289–290
Arithmetic (AR) subtest
  behaviors to note on, 95
  broad and narrow classifications for, 27
  (Rap. Ref. 1.3)
  common administration errors, 100
  cultural loading/linguistic demand of, 303
  (Fig. 7.2)
  and culture-language matrix, 305 (Fig. 7.3)
  description of, 30 (Table 1.2)
  discontinue rules, 66 (Table 2.3)
  keys for scoring, 125–126
  location of administration, 319 (Rap. Ref. 8.3)
  reverse rules for, 64 (Table 2.2)
  starting points/reverse rules of, 63 (Rap.
  Ref. 2.1)
Arithmetic Process Approach Part A (ARPA-A),
  314 (Rap. Ref. 8.2)
Arithmetic Process Approach Part A (ARPA-B),
  314 (Rap. Ref. 8.2)
Arithmetic Time Bonus Process Score (ART), 222,
  320 (Rap. Ref. 8.4), 401 (Rap. Ref. 8.23)
Army alpha/Army Beta, 4
Army Performance Scale Examination, 4
ART. *See* Arithmetic Time Bonus Process Score
Asperger's disorder
  clinical implications for testing populations,
  249–250
  cognitive performance patterns of individuals
  with, 244–247
  differences between autistic disorder and, 244
  (Table 6.1)

  highest/lowest mean WISC-IV, 221 (Rap.
  Ref. 6.1)
  mean WISC-IV composite scores for, 247
  (Fig. 6.1)
  WISC-IV findings for individuals with, 247–249
Assessment observations, 507–508
Assistive listening devices (ALDs), 257, 258
Attention-Deficit/Hyperactivity Disorder (ADHD),
  55, 216
  with/without learning disorders, 226–228
  highest/lowest mean WISC-IV subtest scaled
  scores of, 227 (Rap. Ref. 6.5)
  WISC-IV integrated process scores with largest
  effect size for discriminating samples of
  (from matched control), 228 (Rap. Ref. 6.6)
  See also Special group studies
Auditory Processing Disorder (APD), 403 (Rap.
  Ref. 8.25)
Auditory Processing (*Ga*), 229, 479–480
Auditory Processing speed, 331 (Rap. Ref. 8.9)
Autistic disorder
  clinical implications for testing populations,
  249–250
  cognitive performance patterns of individuals
  with, 244–247
  composite scores, mean WISC-IV, 247 (Fig. 6.1)
  differences between Asperger's disorder and,
  244 (Table 6.1)
  highest/lowest mean WISC-IV subtest scaled
  scores of, 221 (Rap. Ref. 6.1)
  WISC-IV findings for individuals with, 247–249
  See also Autistic-spectrum disorders; Special
  group studies
Autistic-spectrum disorders, 242–250
  See also Asperger's disorders; Autistic disorders

Basal, 63
Base rate <10% criterion, 146
BDMC. *See* Block Design Multiple Choice
Behavior Rating Inventory of Executive Functions
  (BRIEF), 440 (Rap. Ref. 8.31), 464
Bias, cultural or linguistic, 296–297
Bilingual assessment
  vs. assessment of bilinguals, 300–301
  See also Bilingual-multicultural assessment
Bilingual-multicultural assessment
  bias *vs.* fairness, 296–300

bilingual assessment *vs.* assessment of bilinguals, 300–301
CHC culture-language matrix and classifications, 302–308
conclusion, 308
fundamental objective in assessment, 301–302
Binet, Alfred, 3–4
Binet-Simon scale, 4
Block Design (BD) subtest
behaviors to note on, 73
broad and narrow classifications for, 26 (Rap. Ref. 1.3)
cognitive capacities, 376–377 (Rap. Ref. 8.20)
common administration errors, 98–99
cultural loading/linguistic demand of, 303 (Fig. 7.2)
and culture-language matrix, 305 (Fig. 7.3)
description, 29 (Table 1.2)
discontinue rules, 66 (Table 2.3)
highest standard score possible without time bonuses, 265 (Table 7.1)
keys for scoring, 115–116
location of administration, 318 (Rap. Ref. 8.3)
raw/scaled scores at various age ranges, relationship, 385–387 (Table 8.4)
reverse rules for, 64 (Table 2.2)
seating arrangement for, 71
starting points/reverse rules of, 62 (Rap. Ref. 2.1)
Block Design Multiple Choice (BDMC)
cognitive capacities, 376 (Rap. Ref. 8.20)
definition, 316 (Table 8.1)
location of administration, 319 (Rap. Ref. 8.3)
process approach, 313 (Rap. Ref. 8.2)
reducing/adding cognitive demand, 372–373 (Rap. Ref. 8.19)
relationship between raw and scaled scores for various age ranges, 387–390 (Table 8.5)
Block Design Multiple Choice No Time Bonus (BDMCN), 373
process scores, 320 (Rap. Ref. 8.4)
reducing cognitive demand, 373 (Rap. Ref. 8.19)
relationship between raw and scaled scores for various age ranges, 387–390 (Table 8.5)
Block Design No Time Bonus (BDN)
process scores, 320 (Rap. Ref. 8.4)
raw/scaled scores at various age ranges with BD, relationship of, 385–387 (Table 8.4)
reducing/adding cognitive demand, 372 (Rap. Ref. 8.19)
Block Design Process Approach (BDPA)
definition, 317 (Table 8.1)
description, 322, 361
location of the administration, 319 (Rap. Ref. 8.3)

process approach (perceptual domain), 313 (Rap. Ref. 8.2)
score tables, 375
Block Design Process Approach (BDPA) subtest 317 (Table 8.1), 322
Boston Process Approach. *See* Process Approach
BRIEF. *See* Behavior Rating Inventory of Executive Functions

Cancellation (CA) subtest
behaviors to note on, 92
broad and narrow classifications for, 27 (Rap. Ref. 1.3)
common administration errors, 101
cultural loading/linguistic demand of, 303 (Fig. 7.2)
and culture-language matrix, 305 (Fig. 7.3)
description of, 30 (Table 1.2)
discontinue rules, 66 (Table 2.3)
keys for scoring, 124–125
location of administration, 319 (Rap. Ref. 8.3)
reverse rules for, 64 (Table 2.2)
starting points/reverse rules of, 63 (Rap. Ref. 2.1)
Cancellation process observations, interpretation of, 452–453 (Rap. Ref. 8.35)
Cancellation Random (CAR), 315
vs. CAS scaled score discrepancies, 452 (Rap. Ref. 8.35)
clinical samples with notable differences between scaled scores on, 239 (Rap. Ref. 6.16)
process observations, 452–453 (Rap. Ref. 8.35)
Cancellation Structured (CAS), 315
vs. CAR scaled score discrepancies, 452 (Rap. Ref. 8.35)
clinical samples with notable differences between scaled scores on, 239 (Rap. Ref. 6.16)
process observations, 452–453 (Rap. Ref. 8.35)
Cattell-Horn-Carroll (CHC) abilities
relationship with academic achievement, 287–288 (Table 7.4)
Cattell-Horn-Carroll (CHC) Model, 497 (Table 9.3)
Cattell-Horn-Carroll (CHC) Theory, 6, 14, 19, 37, 134
Ceiling effect, 273, 276
CHC cognitive abilities
math achievement, 287–288 (Table 7.4)
reading achievement, 287–288 (Table 7.4)
relations between processes/academic achievement, 287 (Table 7.4)
writing achievement, 287–288 (Table 7.4)
Cheryl's indexes, 493, 496–497

Clinical applications, WISC-IV integrated verbal domain subtests
  administration and scoring of, 327
  how multiple-choice process subtests alter/ reduce cognitive demands, 335–336
  interpretive worksheet for comparing (process subtest and core/supplemental subtest raw and scaled scores, 349 (Fig. 8.1)
  use and interpretation of, 329–330
  what do it measure, 330–334
  when to use, 326, 328–329
Clinical clusters
  composition of, 169–172 (Rap. Ref. 4.12)
  definition, 133
  general information (Gc-K0), 187 (Rap. Ref. 4.14), 479
  hypotheses for observed differences between, 185–189 (Rap. Ref. 4.14)
  lexical knowledge (Gc-VL) cluster, 187–188 (Rap. Ref. 4.14)
  reliability coefficients and SEMS for, 173–174 (Table 4.4)
  size of difference between pairs needed to be considered unusually large or uncommon, 175 (Table 4.5)
Clinical comparisons, planned. See Planned clinical comparisons
Clinical information, 67
Clinical profile analysis
  criticism, 16 (Fig. 1.2)
  definition, 9
  intelligence test, 9–11, 16 (Fig. 1.2)
Coding (CD) subtest
  behaviors to note on, 81
  broad/narrow classifications for, 26 (Rap. Ref. 1.3)
  common administration errors, 100–101
  cultural loading/linguistic demand of, 303 (Fig. 7.2)
  and culture-language matrix, 305 (Fig. 7.3)
  description of, 29 (Table 1.2)
  discontinue rules, 66 (Table 2.3)
  keys for scoring, 119
  location of administration, 319 (Rap. Ref. 8.3)
  process-approach procedures by, 314 (Rap. Ref. 8.2)
  reverse rules for, 64 (Table 2.2)
  starting points/reverse rules of, 62 (Rap. Ref. 2.1)
Coding Copy (CDC), 222, 318 (Table 8.1)
  definition, 315 (Rap. Ref. 8.2), 442
Coding Recall (CDR), 315, 318 (Table 8.1)
  definition, 315 (Rap. Ref. 8.2)
  process subtest, 453–454
Cognitive ability analysis

CHC theory of, 133–134, 169 (Rap. Ref. 4.12)
  math achievement, 287–288 (Table 7.4)
  reading achievement, 287–288 (Table 7.4)
  relations between processes/academic achievement, 287 (Table 7.4)
  with the WISC-IV, 283–284
  writing achievement, 287–288 (Table 7.4)
KABC-II, 495–499
  integrating test scores from, 499–501
WISC-IV, 493–495
  integrating test scores from, 499–501
Cognitive Assessment System (CAS), 6
Cognitive demands
  how coding copy changes, 451 (Rap. Ref. 8.35)
  multiple-choice response format, 335–336 (Rap. Ref. 8.10)
Cognitive Hypothesis Testing, 469, 508, 510
Cognitive Processing, 193 (Rap. Ref. 4.15)
Cognitive Proficiency Index (CPI), 1, 133, 195–196
  computation, 199
  definition, 219
  vs. WMI, 219-220
Cohen, J., 11
Color blindness, 103 (Rap. Ref. 2.4)
Composite scales
  average reliability coefficients of, 33 (Rap. Ref. 1.5)
Composite scores
  defined, 106, 110
  mean WISC-IV, 247 (Fig. 6.1)
  selection of, 136–140, 139 (Fig. 4.2)
  See also Full scale IQ
Comprehension (CO) subtest
  behaviors to note on, 86
  broad and narrow classifications for, 27 (Rap. Ref. 1.3)
  common administration errors, 97–98
  cultural loading/linguistic demand of, 303 (Fig. 7.2)
  and culture-language matrix, 305 (Fig. 7.3)
  description of, 29 (Table 1.2)
  discontinue rules, 66 (Table 2.3)
  keys for scoring, 121–122
  location of the administration, 319 (Rap. Ref. 8.3)
  reverse rules for, 64 (Table 2.2)
  starting points/reverse rules of, 62 (Rap. Ref. 2.1)
Comprehension Multiple Choice (COMC), 313, 316 (Table 8.1)
  definition, 316 (Table 8.1)
  location of the administration, 319 (Rap. Ref. 8.3)
  process approach, 313 (Rap. Ref. 8.2)

Confirmatory factor analysis (CFA), 34, 209
(Rap. Ref. 8.3)
Core battery test
concept, 111
defined, 444
guidelines for substituting supplemental
subtests for, 110 (Table 3.1)
CPI. *See* Cognitive Proficiency Index
Cross-battery approach, 14
CHC, 302
defined, 14
Essentials of, 303
Crystallized Intelligence (Gc) cluster, 19
composition of, 169–170 (Rap. Ref. 4.12)

Deaf/hard-of-hearing
communication demands of the WISC-IV,
258–259
communication modalities/languages used by
examinees, 255 (Rap. Ref. 6.19)
examinee variables to consider in the
assessment of population in, 257–258
examiner qualifications, 260–261
historical overview, 253–254
points to remember when assessing children,
260 (Rap. Ref. 6.20)
use of WISC-IV perceptual reasoning subtests
with population in, 256–257
use of WISC-IV verbal subtests with
population, 255–256
variables to consider when assessing examinees,
255 (Rap. Ref. 6.18)
WISC-IV administration guidelines and caveats
for, 254
Dean Woodcock neuropsychological battery, 511
Descriptive categories
alternative (combined) type, 137
(Rap. Ref. 4.4)
normative, 136 (Rap. Ref. 4.3)
traditional, 136 (Rap. Ref. 4.2)
Diagnostic impressions, 503–505
Differential Abilities Scale (DAS), 5–6, 14, 256
Digits Backward
clinical samples with notable differences
between scaled scores on, 237–238, 238
(Rap. Ref. 6.15)
definition of, 36 (Rap. Ref. 1.8)
Digits Forward
clinical samples with notable differences
between scaled scores on, 237–238, 238
(Rap. Ref. 6.15)
definition of, 36 (Rap. Ref. 1.8)
Digit Span Backward (DSB) process score,
117, 314
Digit Span (DS) subtest
behaviors to note on, 78

broad and narrow classifications for, 26
(Rap. Ref. 1.3)
common administration errors, 100
cultural loading/linguistic demand of, 303
(Fig. 7.2)
and culture-language matrix, 305 (Fig. 7.3)
description of, 29 (Table 1.2)
discontinue rules, 66 (Table 2.3)
keys for scoring, 117–118
location of the administration, 319
(Rap. Ref. 8.3)
process-approach procedures by, 314
(Rap. Ref. 8.2)
reverse rules for, 64 (Table 2.2)
starting points/reverse rules of, 62
(Rap. Ref. 2.1)
Digit Span Forward (DSF) process score, 117, 314
Discontinue rules
chunking, 77
definition, 65
of subtest, 66 (Table 2.3)
See also Individual subtests
Double-deficit hypothesis, 21

Education for All Handicapped Children Act of
1975, 5
Elithorn Mazes (EM), 313, 317
administration of, 397 (Rap. Ref. 8.22)
cognitive capacities, 376 (Rap. Ref. 8.20)
definition, 317 (Table 8.1)
location of the administration, 319
(Rap. Ref. 8.3)
process approach, 313 (Rap. Ref. 8.2)
reducing cognitive demand, 373 (Rap. Ref. 8.19)
relationship between raw and scaled scores for
various age ranges, 391 (Table 8.6)
Elithorn Mazes No Time Bonus (EMN), 313, 373
process scores, 320 (Rap. Ref. 8.4)
reducing cognitive demand, 373 (Rap. Ref. 8.19)
relationship between raw and scaled scores for
various age ranges, 391 (Table 8.6)
English-language learners (ELLs), 299–300, 308
Examinee
abbreviations for recording responses in, 68
(Rap. Ref. 2.2)
administration considerations, 60–61
vs. another battery for 6- and 16-year-olds, 61
(Table 2.1)
keys to preparing to administer, 54
rules for starting and discontinuing subtests,
61–63
Examinee, behavior. *See* Chunking; *Individual
Subtests,* behavior to note on
Examiner
administration consideration, 60–61
qualifications

Examiner (*Cont.*)
  for assessing deaf or hard-of-hearing
    individuals, 259–260
  and bilingual-multicultural assessment, 299
  history of, 12
  selective testing table to identify WISC-IV, 40
    (Fig. 1.5)
Executive function, 332 (Rap. Ref. 8.9), 510
  of cognitive capacities, 369 (Rap. Ref. 8.18)
  demands of, 336 (Rap. Ref. 8.10)
Expressive language disorders, 222–223
  highest/lowest mean WISC-IV subtest scaled
    scores of, 222 (Rap. Ref. 6.2)
  WISC-IV integrated process scores with largest
    effect size for discriminating samples of, 224
    (Rap. Ref. 6.3)

Floor items, 112–113
Fluid Reasoning (G*f*) cluster, 19
  composition of, 169–170 (Rap. Ref. 4.12)
  CHC ability, 287 (Table 7.4)
  vs. Gv, 479
Flynn effect, 268
Freedom from Distractibility (FD) index, 12, 25
  (Rap. Ref. 1.2), 28, 204 (Rap. Ref. 5.1)
FSIQ. *See* Full scale IQ
Full-Scale IQ, 10, 11, 13, 25
  appropriate situations for calculating index
    scores and (raw score zero), 113
  calculating index score with zero raw scores, 113
  child's WISC-IV standard scores, 138 (Fig. 4.1)
  consequences of normalization and smoothing
    procedures, 268–269
  correlations with WIAT-II achievement
    composites, 44 (Rap. Ref. 1.11)
  correlation with WISC-IV, 41 (Rap. Ref. 1.9)
  definition, 106
  description, 110
  identification of gifted children, 263
  noninterpretability of, 143 (Rap. Ref. 4.7)
  obtaining, 108–110
  practice effects, 34 (Rap. Ref. 1.6)
  and raw score of zero, 113
  reliability coefficients of, 33 (Rap. Ref. 1.5)
  special considerations for calculating, 110–112
  subtests composing, 109
  WISC-IV and other Wechsler scales, correlation
    with, 41–42 (Rap. Ref. 1.9)

Galton, Sir Francis, 3
General Ability Index (GAI), 133
  determining interpretability of, 139 (Fig. 4.2), 144
    (Fig. 4.3)
  noninterpretability of, 143 (Rap. Ref. 4.7)
  psychological report, example of description in,
    142 (Rap. Ref. 4.6)

General information (G*c*-K0) Cluster, 171
  (Rap. Ref. 4.12), 193–194 (Rap. Ref. 4.15)
  composition of, 171 (Rap. Ref. 4.13)
  vs. Gc-VL, 479
Giftedness learning disabilities, 270–271
Gifted students, identification of
  alternative composites and subtest issues,
    271–273
  cultural bias, 266–267
  dealing with unconventional correct responses,
    274, 275 (Table 7.2)
  fluid reasoning, 267–268
  improved standard subtest ceilings and
    extended norms, 273–274
  and learning disabilities, 270–271
  national surveys, 263
  profiles on WISC-IV, 268–270
  speed of performance, 264–265, 266
  testing time, 264
  use of specific cutoff scores, 263
G-loading
  application of, 210 (Rap. Ref. 5.3)
  described, 32–34
  high/low, 42
Greenberg, Darielle, 242–253

Hale, James B., 507–514
Hard-of-hearing examinees
  communication modalities/languages used, 255
    (Rap. Ref. 6.19)
  points to remember when assessing children,
    260 (Rap. Ref. 6.20)
  variables to consider when assessing deaf, 255
    (Rap. Ref. 6.18)
Hardy-Braz, Steven T., 253–260
Hebben, Nancy, 216–242
High-Priority Concerns (HPC)
  definition, 164 (Rap. Ref. 4.10)
  interpretive steps, 160 (Fig. 4.11)

Index, defined, 164 (Rap. Ref. 4.10)
Indexes, WISC-IV
  correlations with WIAT-II achievement
    composites, 44 (Rap. Ref. 1.11)
  differences in mean standard scores
    (White minus African American), 47
    (Rap. Ref. 1.13)
  differences in mean standard scores (White
    minus Hispanic), 48 (Rap. Ref. 1.14)
  differences required for statistical significance,
    152–153 (Table 4.2)
  high-priority concern, 162–163
  needed to be considered unusually large or
    uncommon, 155 (Table 4.3)
  noninterpretable, 150 (*see also* Interpretation of
    WISC-IV index)

nonunitary description in psychological report, 149 (Rap. Ref. 4.9)
normative strengths/weaknesses, 151
personal strengths/weaknesses, 151–152
practice effects for, 34 (Rap. Ref. 1.6)
special considerations for calculating scores, 110–112
subtests composing, 109
Index profile analysis, WISC-IV
classification and interpretation of, 165–168 (Rap. Ref. 4.11)
clinical impressions/suggested (post hoc) clinical comparisons, 161
conduct clinical comparisons when supplemental WISC-IV subtests are administered, 164
determining best way to summarize overall intellectual ability, 137, 139–140, 142
determining normative strengths/normative weaknesses in, 151
determining personal strengths/personal weaknesses in, 151–152, 154
difference between the child's GAI/CPI, 195–196
interpretation fluctuations in the child's, 163
location of information in manual needed for score conversions, 135 (Rap. Ref. 4.1)
report child's WISC-IV standard scores/subtest scaled scores, 134–137
select clinical samples, 240–242
terms used to describe fluctuations in (child), 164 (Rap. Ref. 4.10)
Index scores
appropriate situations for calculating, 113
classified as strength, 165–166 (Rap. Ref. 4.11)
classified as weakness, 166–167 (Rap. Ref. 4.11)
description, 108–110
special considerations for calculating WISC-IV/FSIQ using supplemental subtests, 110–112
subtests making, 109
as unitary construct description, 167–168 (Rap. Ref. 4.11)
Individualized education program (IEP), 5
Individuals with Disabilities Education Act (IDEA), 1, 5, 279, 485, 505
definition, 280 (Rap. Ref. 7.1)
representation of academic abilities by, 280–281 (Rap. Ref. 7.1)
Individuals with Disabilities Education Improvement Act (IDEIA), 270
Information (IN) subtest
behaviors to note on, 94
broad and narrow classifications for, 27 (Rap. Ref. 1.3)
common administration errors, 98

cultural loading/linguistic demand of, 303 (Fig. 7.2)
and culture-language matrix, 305 (Fig. 7.3)
description of, 30 (Table 1.2)
discontinue rules, 66 (Table 2.3)
keys for scoring, 125
location of administration, 319 (Rap. Ref. 8.3)
reverse rules for, 64 (Table 2.2)
starting points/reverse rules of, 63 (Rap. Ref. 2.1)
Information Multiple Choice (INMC), 313
definition, 313 (Rap. Ref. 8.2), 316 (Table 8.1)
location of administration, 319 (Rap. Ref. 8.3)
process approach, 313 (Rap. Ref. 8.2)
Instruction/item repeating, 70–71
Intellectual ability, 137–142
Intellectual disability
concept, 250–251
defined, 216
finding subtests with adequate floors, 252–253
mean composite scores for children (mild/moderate), 252 (Fig. 6.2)
mean WISC-IV composite scores for children with mild/moderate, 252 (Fig. 6.2)
WISC-IV findings on, 251–252
Intellectual giftedness
cutoff scores for identifying, 263
definition of "gifted/talented", 262
"nontypical" profiles, 269
time needed for WISC-IV assessment, 264
WISC-IV score patterns for children with, 224 (Rap. Ref. 6.3)
See also Special group studies
Intellectually disabled, 223, 225–226
highest/lowest mean WISC-IV subtest scaled scores, 225 (Rap. Ref. 6.4)
See also Intellectual giftedness
Intellectually gifted. See Intellectually disabled
Intelligence
classification
David Wechsler's, 4
global IQ, 8
WISC-IV, 26–27 (Rap. Ref. 1.3)
defined, 8
g theory of (see G-loading)
quantification of general level, 8
Intelligence test
CHC abilities and processes measured by, 285 (Rap. Ref. 7.2)
development, 3–6
interpretation
application of theory, 13–15
clinical profile analysis, 9–11, 16 (Fig. 1.2)
psychometric profile analysis, 11–13, 16 (Fig. 1.2)

Intelligence test (*Cont.*)
    quantification of general level, 8, 17 (Fig. 1.2)
    theoretical wave test of, 13
Intelligence test interpretation
    first wave, 8, 16–17 (Fig. 1.2)
    fourth wave, 13–15, 16–17 (Fig. 1.2)
    second wave, 9–11, 16–17 (Fig. 1.2)
    technological development, 11
    third wave, 11–13, 16–17 (Fig. 1.2)
Interindividual cognitive ability analysis, 287–288
    (Table 7.4)
Interpretation of scores, 154
Interpretation, WISC-IV index
    fluctuations in the child's index profile, 163
    of indexes, 142–150
    normative strengths/normative weaknesses in
        the index profile, 151
    optional steps
        conduct clinical comparisons when
            supplemental subtests are administered,
            163–199
        determine whether the difference between
            the child's GAI/CPI is unusually large,
            195–199
    personal strengths/personal weaknesses,
        151–154
    quantitative/qualitative analysis of WISC-IV
        data, 134
    reporting of standard scores/subtest scaled
        scores, 134–137
    way to summarize overall intellectual ability,
        137, 139–140, 142
Intervention evaluation (Jacob), 513–514
Intraindividual analysis, 15, 19–22
    CHC theory of structure for, 19
    clusters that are used, 19–20
    effects of intervention, 20
    group-data methodology in, 21–22
    relative weakness test in, 20
Ipsative analysis. *See* Intraindividual analysis
IQ, performance. *See* Performance IQ (PIQ)
Item density. *See* Item gradients
Item gradients, 36
Items, reversal, 63

Kaufman, Nadeen L., 489–506
Kaufman Assessment Battery for Children
    (K-ABC), 5, 245
Kaufman Assessment Battery for Children-
    Second Edition (KABC-II)
    CHC abilities, 285–286 (Rap. Ref. 7.2)
    integrating test scores from, 499–501
    psychometric summary, 497 (Table 9.3)
Kaufman Brief Intelligence Test (K-BIT), 48
Kaufman Test of Educational Achievement
    (KABC-II) CHC Model, 497 (Table 9.3)

    (KTEA-II), Comprehensive Form (Form A),
        498 (Table 9.3)
    negative reviews of, 21–22
Kaufman Test of Educational Achievement-
    Second Edition (KTEA-II)
    comprehensive Form A, 501–502
    error analysis, 502
    psychometric summary, 498 (Table 9.3)
Key Assets (KA)
    definition, 164 (Rap. Ref. 4.10)
    high-priority concerns (HPC), 162–163
    normtive (Post Hoc) clinical comparisons, 160
        (Fig. 4.1)
    personal strength/personal weakness,
        151–154

Language disorders
    expressive
        highest/lowest mean WISC-IV subtest scaled
            scores of, 222 (Rap. Ref. 6.2)
        WISC-IV integrated process scores with
            largest effect size for discriminating
            samples of (from matched controls), 224
            (Rap. Ref. 6.3)
    mixed receptive-expressive, 222–223
    scaled process scores producing largest effect
        sizes when children with, 224 (Rap. Ref. 6.3)
    See also Special group studies
Learning disability
    assessing individuals with WISC-IV/WIAT-II,
        277
    assessment flowchart, 294 (Fig. 7.1)
    definition, 299
    operational definition of, 278 (Table 7.3), 278
        (Table 7.3)
Letter-Number Sequencing (LN) subtest
    behaviors to note on, 84
    broad and narrow classifications for, 26
        (Rap. Ref. 1.3)
    common administration errors, 100
    cultural loading/linguistic demand of, 303
        (Fig. 7.2)
    and culture-language matrix, 305 (Fig. 7.3)
    description of, 29 (Table 1.2)
    discontinue rules, 66 (Table 2.3)
    keys for scoring, 121
    location of the administration, 319
        (Rap. Ref. 8.3)
    process approach procedures, 314
        (Rap. Ref. 8.2)
    reverse rules for, 64 (Table 2.2)
    starting points/reverse rules of, 62
        (Rap. Ref. 2.1)
Letter-Number Sequencing Process Approach
    (LNPA), 314, 392
    definition, 317 (Table 8.1)

location of the administration, 319
(Rap. Ref. 8.3)
process approach, 312–314 (Rap. Ref. 8.2)
Letter Span (LS)
defined, 317 (Table 8.1)
as process subtest, 314 (Rap. Ref. 8.2)
Lexical Knowledge (Gc-VL) Cluster
composition of, 171 (Rap. Ref. 4.12)
size difference for clinical clusters and, 175
(Table 4.5)
vs. Gc-K0, 479
websites, 193–194 (Rap. Ref. 4.15)
Lichtenberger, Elizabeth O., 242–253
Longest Digit Span Backward (LDSB) process
scores, 118, 208 (Rap. Ref. 5.2)
Longest Digit Span Forward (LDSF) process
score, 118, 208 (Rap. Ref. 5.2)
Longest Visual Digit Span (LVDVS) process
scores, 320 (Rap. Ref. 8.4)
Long-Term Memory (Gc-LTM) Cluster
definition of, 171–172 (Rap. Ref. 4.12)
internal consistency reliability coefficients and
SEMs, 173–174 (Table 4.4)
Long-Term memory (Glr) cluster, 19
composition of, 171–172 (Rap. Ref. 4.13)
defined, 19
size difference for clinical clusters and, 175
(Table 4.5)
vs. Gsm, 499

Mascolo, Jennifer T., 276–295, 469–488
Mathematics disorder
highest/lowest mean WISC-IV subtest scaled
scores of, 229 (Rap. Ref. 6.7)
WISC-IV integrated process scores with largest
effect size for discriminating samples of, 231
(Rap. Ref. 6.9)
Matrix Reasoning (MR) subtest
behaviors to note on, 85
broad and narrow classifications for, 26
(Rap. Ref. 1.3)
cognitive capacities, 376–377 (Rap. Ref. 8.20)
common administration errors, 99
cultural loading/linguistic demand of, 303
(Fig. 7.2)
and culture-language matrix, 305 (Fig. 7.3)
description, 29 (Table 1.2)
discontinue rules, 66 (Table 2.3)
keys for scoring, 121
location of administration, 319 (Rap. Ref. 8.3)
reverse rules for, 64 (Table 2.2)
starting points/reverse rules of, 62
(Rap. Ref. 2.1)
McCloskey, George, 310
Measurement error, 371
Mental manipulation, 242

of auditorily presented verbal information, 405
(Rap. Ref. 8.26)
Mental manipulation tasks
comparison, 423–424 (Rap. Ref. 8.30)
defined, 400
registration task vs., 427–428 (Rap. Ref. 8.30)
Mental retardation, 216
Metacognitive intervention, 513, 514 (Fig. 9.2)
Mixed Receptive-Expressive Language Disorder,
222–223
Motor impairment, 218
described, 232–234
index score differences, 233 (Rap. Ref. 6.11)

National Association of Gifted Children (NAGC),
269, 272
Noninterpretable Index, 149
GAI/FSIQ, 143 (Rap. Ref. 4.7)
strength/weakness, 155
Nontypical profiles, 269
Nonverbal Fluid Reasoning (Gf-nonverbal) Cluster
composition of, 170 (Rap. Ref. 4.12)
internal consistency reliability coefficients and
SEMs, 173–174 (Table 4.4)
sampling of educational strategies, 192–193
(Rap. Ref. 4.15)
Nonverbal reasoning, 370
Normtive analysis
vs. ipsitive analysis, 133–134
See also Intraindividual analysis
Normative Strength (NS), 164 (Rap. Ref. 4.10)
Normative Weakness (NW), 164 (Rap. Ref. 4.10),
279
Notable discrepancy, 235, 236
No Time Bonus Process Scaled Scores
correlations between subtest scaled scores, 392
(Table 8.7)
correlations between subtest scaled scores and,
392 (Table 8.7)
guidelines for interpreting, 383–384
(Rap. Ref. 8.21)

Organization, WISC-IV, 31 (Fig. 1.3)
Ortiz, Samuel O., 295–308

Perceptual domain process subtests
administration and scoring of, 362
(Rap. Ref. 8.16)
case study, 395–399 (Rap. Ref. 8.22)
guidelines for interpreting comparisons,
378–384 (Rap. Ref. 8.21)
use and interpretation of, 363
what do core, supplemental measure (process
subtests), 365–374
when to use, 364 (Rap. Ref. 8.17)

Perceptual Organization Index (POI), 25
(Rap. Ref. 1.2)
Perceptual Reasoning Index (PRI), 7, 43, 149
composite scores of VCI and, 235
(Rap. Ref. 6.13)
composite scores relative to the combined mean
of VCI, PRI, and WMI, 236 (Rap. Ref. 6.14)
determining interpretability of, 144 (Fig. 4.3)
index score calculation with zero raw scale, 113
VCI compared with, 234–235
Performance IQ (PIQ), 10, 28
and autistic-spectrum disorders, 245–246
and bilingual-multicultural assessment, 297
and hard-of-hearing children, 253–254
and the intellectually gifted, 264
Personal strength (PS)
definition, 164 (Rap. Ref. 4.10)
determine whether uncommon, 157 (Fig. 4.9)
identifying statistically significant differences
between index and mean of indexes, 155
(Table 4.3)
in index profile, 151–152
personal weakness (PW) vs., 164 (Rap. Ref. 4.10)
Phonetic coding (PC), 288 (Table 7.4)
Phonological awareness/processing, 504
Picture Completion (PCm) subtest
behaviors to note on, 91
broad and narrow classifications for, 27
(Rap. Ref. 1.3)
cognitive capacities, 376–377 (Rap. Ref. 8.20)
common administration errors, 99–100
cultural loading/linguistic demand of, 303
(Fig. 7.2)
and culture-language matrix, 305 (Fig. 7.3)
description of, 30 (Table 1.2)
discontinue rules, 66 (Table 2.3)
keys for scoring, 123–124
location of the administration, 319
(Rap. Ref. 8.3)
reverse rules for, 64 (Table 2.2)
starting points/reverse rules of, 63
(Rap. Ref. 2.1)
Picture Concepts (PCn) subtest
behaviors to note on, 79
broad and narrow classifications for, 26
(Rap. Ref. 1.3)
cognitive capacities, 376–377 (Rap. Ref. 8.20)
common administration errors, 99
cultural loading/linguistic demand of, 303
(Fig. 7.2)
and culture-language matrix, 305 (Fig. 7.3)
description of, 29 (Table 1.2)
discontinue rules, 66 (Table 2.3)
keys for scoring, 118–119
reverse rules for, 64 (Table 2.2)

starting points/reverse rules of, 62
(Rap. Ref. 2.1)
Picture Vocabulary Multiple Choice (PVMC)
definition, 316 (Table 8.1)
location of the administration, 319
(Rap. Ref. 8.3)
process approach, 313 (Rap. Ref. 8.2)
PIQ. See Performance IQ
Planned clinical comparisons
definition of, 168
examples of interpretive statements used in,
176–178 (Rap. Ref. 4.13)
POI. See Perceptual Organization Index
Post Hoc clinical comparison, 176–178
(Rap. Ref. 4.13)
clinical impression of, 160 (Rap. Ref. 4.11)
definition of, 168
description of findings in psychological report,
176–178 (Rap. Ref. 4.13)
PRI. See Perceptual Reasoning Index
Primary cognitive capacities, 330–331, 366–367
(Rap. Ref. 8.8), 405 (Rap. Ref. 8.25), 447
(Rap. Ref. 8.33)
Process Approach
ADHD, 226–228
case example 1, 351–356 (Rap. Ref. 8.14)
case example 2, 357–360 (Rap. Ref. 8.15)
children who are intellectually gifted/
intellectually disabled, 223, 225–226
children with autistic disorder and Asperger's
disorder, 220–222
children with expressive language disorders/
mixed receptive-expressive language
disorders, 222–223
children with reading/mathematics/written
expression disorders, 229–231
definition of, 237
index score vs. interpretation of
working memory capacities, 410–413
(Rap. Ref. 8.27)
integration of, 310
profile analysis, 217–220
scaled score, interpretive, 402 (Rap. Ref. 8.24)
special group studies, 216–217
TBI and motor impairment, 232–234
utility of the process approach, 236–237
VCI compared with PRI, 234–235
WISC-IV integrated administration/scoring
procedures
to administer coding, 315
perceptual domain, 313
processing speed domain, 315
process subtests, 318–319
verbal domain, 312–313 (Rap. Ref. 8.2)
working memory domain, 314

WISC-IV integrated base rates for, 323–325 (Rap. Ref. 8.5)
Process Approach interpretation
index score *vs.*, 410–413 (Rap. Ref. 8.27)
verbal domain, 351–356 (Rap. Ref. 8.14), 357–360 (Rap. Ref. 8.15)
Processing speed domain
administration and scoring of, 443 (Rap. Ref. 8.32)
case study, 461 (Rap. Ref. 8.38)
cognitive capacities, 447 (Rap. Ref. 8.34)
reflected in scaled score values, cognitive capacities likely to be assessed by, 454–456 (Rap. Ref. 8.36)
tasks
cognitive capacities, 454 (Rap. Ref. 8.36)
interpretation of, 460 (Fig. 8.4)
use and interpretation of, 444
when to use, 443–444
WISC-IV Integrated, 318 (Table 8.32)
Processing Speed Index (PSI), 7, 28
administration and scoring of, 443 (Rap. Ref. 8.32)
case study, 461–465 (Rap. Ref. 8.38)
guidelines for interpreting comparisons involving, 457–459 (Rap. Ref. 8.37)
index score calculation with zero raw scale, 113
interpretability of, 147 (Fig. 4.5)
low scores on, 236 (Rap. Ref. 6.14)
when to use, 445–446 (Rap. Ref. 8.33)
Process score
clinical perspective, 375
guidelines for interpreting comparisons, 378–384 (Rap. Ref. 8.21)
cognitive capacities, 376 (Rap. Ref. 8.20)
comparison worksheet, 393–394 (Fig. 8.2)
defined, 115
Digit Span Backward (DSB)/Digit Span Forward (DSF), 117, 314
how to reduce or add cognitive demands, 372–373 (Rap. Ref. 8.19)
LDSB/LDSF, 118
Process subtests, WISC-IV
definition, 316
perceptual domain
administration and scoring of, 362
how to reduce or add cognitive demands, 372–373 (Rap. Ref. 8.19)
use and interpretation of, 363–365
when to use, 363
processing speed domain
administration and scoring of, 443 (Rap. Ref. 8.32)
use and interpretation of, 444
what it does, 444–446

when to use, 443–444, 445–446 (Rap. Ref. 8.33)
supplemental measure, 365–374
working memory domain
administration and scoring of, 401 (Rap. Ref. 8.23)
to alter cognitive demands, 415–416
cognitive capacities assessed with, 405–408 (Rap. Ref. 8.26)
description, 392
use and interpretation of, 404
what it does, 404–405
when to use, 400, 402, 403 (Rap. Ref. 8.25)
Process subtests, WISC-IV integrated
overview of domains, 326
perceptual domain, 316–317 (Table 8.1)
processing speed domain, 318 (Table 8.1)
verbal domain, 316 (Table 8.1)
administration and scoring of, 327
how multiple-choice process subtests alter/reduce cognitive demands, 335–336
use and interpretation of, 329–330
what do it measure, 330
when to use, 326, 328–329
verbal domain subtest interpretive worksheet for comparison of core/supplemental subtest raw and scaled scores, 349 (Fig. 8.1)
working memory domain, 317 (Table 8.1)
Profile analyses
classification/interpretation of index fluctuations, 165–168 (Rap. Ref. 4.11)
operational steps, optional, 163–199
conducting clinical comparisons, 163–199
largeness of GAI and CPI, 195–199
qualitative *vs.* quantitative, 134
required steps
interpreting fluctuations, 163
intellectual ability, summarizing, 137–142
interpretability determination, 142–150
normative strengths/normative weaknesses, 151
personal strengths/personal weaknesses in, 151–163
reporting standard scores/subtest scaled scores, 134–137
Prompting
on LN subtest, 128 (Rap. Ref. 3.2)
See also Querying
Prorating, WISC-IV, 114
Psychological report, example of
academic performance/achievement, 480 (Table 9.2)
achievement functioning, 511–512
appearance and behavioral observation, 472–474, 491–492

Psychological report, example of (*Cont.*)
assessment observations, 507–508
cognitive hypothesis testing, 510
cognitive performance, 475–478
to describe an interpretable FSIQ in, 140
(Rap. Ref. 4.5)
to describe a nonunitary index in, 149
(Rap. Ref. 4.9)
to describe findings of planned/Post Hoc
clinical comparisons in, 176–178
(Rap. Ref. 4.13)
to describe the GAI in a, 142 (Rap. Ref. 4.6)
diagnostic impressions, 483–486, 503–505
evaluation procedures, 474, 492
finding of noninterpretable FSIQ/GAI, 143
(Rap. Ref. 4.7)
intellectual screening, 508–509
to interpret unitary index in, 148 (Rap. Ref. 4.8)
KABC-II performance, 495–499, 497
(Table 9.3)
KTEA-II performance, 498 (Table 9.3),
501–502
mathematics performance, 482
oral language performance, 483
planned clinical comparisons, 478–479
reading class observation, 474–475
reading performance, 481–482
recommendations for, 487–489, 505–506,
512–513
referral and background information,
469–472, 489–491, 507
sensory-motor skills, 511
team decision/intervention development,
513–514
test results and interpretation, 475–488, 492
test scores from, 499–501
WIAT-II performance, 480 (Table 9.2)
test scores from, 499–501
WISC-IV performance, 475–478, 477 (Table
9.1), 480 (Table 9.2), 493–495, 496 (Table 9.3)
WJ III cognitive-select subtests, 479–481, 480
(Table 9.2)
written language performance, 482–483
Psychological reports
common errors to avoid in writing, 468
information to include "appearance and
behavioral observations," 473–474
information to include "background
information," 471
information to include in "identifying
information section," 469
information to include in "summary and
diagnostic impressions section," 484
information to include "reason for referral
section," 470

information to include "test results and
interpretation," 476
unitary index interpretation in, 148
(Rap. Ref. 4.8)
Psychometric Profile Analysis, 11–13, 16 (Fig. 1.2)
PVMC. *See* Picture Vocabulary Multiple Choice

Querying
and verbal subtest, 114–115
similarity subtest, 97
See also Prompting

Rapport with examinee
appropriate feedback and encouragement, 57
establishing rapport, 54–56
keys to establishing positive, 56
maintaining, 56
Raw score
common errors in calculating, 108
defined, 106
description, 107
and scaled scores (at various age ranges)
relationship between BD/BDN, 385–387
(Table 8.4)
relationship between BDMC/BDMCN,
387–390 (Table 8.5)
relationship between EM/EMN, 391
(Table 8.6)
of zero
appropriate situations for calculating, 113
special considerations, 113
Reading disorder
highest/lowest mean WISC-IV subtest scaled
scores of, 229 (Rap. Ref. 6.7)
WISC-IV integrated process scores with largest
effect size for discriminating samples of, 231
(Rap. Ref. 6.9)
Reading expression disorders
highest and lowest mean WISC-IV subtest
scaled scores of, 230 (Rap. Ref. 6.8)
WISC-IV integrated process scores with the
largest effect size for discriminating samples
of, 232 (Rap. Ref. 6.10)
Registration tasks
comparisons, 423–424 (Rap. Ref. 8.30), 426
(Rap. Ref. 8.30)
defined, 400
mental task *vs.*, 427–428 (Rap. Ref. 8.30)
Relative weakness, 20
Reversal items, 63
Reynolds Intellectual Ability Scale (RIAS), 6

Scaled scores
cognitive capacities likely to be assessed by
verbal domain tasks and reflected in, 337–338
(Rap. Ref. 8.11)
defined, 106

degree of unusualness of discrepancies,
    425–428 (Rap. Ref. 8.30)
described, 107–108
determining a significant difference between,
    423–425 (Rap. Ref. 8.30)
errors in obtaining, 109
and raw score (at various age ranges)
    relationship between BD/BDN, 385–387
        (Table 8.4)
    relationship between BDMC/BDMCN,
        387–390 (Table 8.5)
    relationship between EM/EMN, 391
        (Table 8.6)
Score differences
    average percent process subtest raw score gain
        when core/supplemental and process subtest
        scaled scores are equal, 348 (Table 8.3)
    average raw score gain percentages
        corresponding to process subtest minus core,
        345–347 (Table 8.2)
Scores
    comparisons involving processing speed
        domain subtests, 457–459 (Rap. Ref. 8.37)
    definition, 107
    description, 107–108
    determining a significant difference between,
        378–382 (Rap. Ref. 8.21)
    errors in obtaining, 109
    guidelines for interpreting comparisons
        between, 339–341
    how to reduce/add cognitive demands, 372–373
        (Rap. Ref. 8.19)
    interpretation of, 154
    location of information needed for converting,
        135 (Rap. Ref. 4.1)
    prorating on, 114
    reporting, 138 (Fig. 4.1), 321–322
    scaled, 107–108
    stability of over time, 20
    standard (see Standard scores)
    types of, 106
Scores, composite. See Composite scores
Scoring
    errors
        most frequently observed administration
            and, 65
        frequently asked questions, 127–130
            (Rap. Ref. 3.2)
    keys for individual subtests, 115–127
    location of information in, 135 (Rap. Ref. 4.1)
    subtests requiring judgment, 114–115
Secondary cognitive capacities, 331–332, 367–367
    (Rap. Ref. 8.8), 405–408 (Rap. Ref. 8.25),
    447–449 (Rap.
    Ref. 8.33)
Sensory-Motor Skills, 511

Short-Term Memory (Gsm) factor, 269
Short-Term Memory (Gsm-WM) Cluster, 19, 172
    (Rap. Ref. 4.12)
    composition of, 172 (Rap. Ref. 4.13)
Short-Term Memory (Gsm-WM) Cluster
    internal consistency reliability coefficients and
        SEMs, 173–174 (Table 4.4)
    Verbal Fluid Reasoning (Gf-verbal) Cluster, 172
        (Rap. Ref. 4.12)
Similarities Multiple Choice (SIMC), 316
    (Table 8.1)
    definition, 316 (Table 8.1)
    location of the administration, 319
        (Rap. Ref. 8.3)
    process approach, 312 (Rap. Ref. 8.2)
Similarities (SI) subtest
    behaviors to note on, 75
    broad and narrow classifications for, 26
        (Rap. Ref. 1.3)
    common administration errors, 97
    cultural loading/linguistic demand of, 303
        (Fig. 7.2)
    and culture-language matrix, 305 (Fig. 7.3)
    description of, 29 (Table 1.2)
    discontinue rules, 66 (Table 2.3)
    keys for scoring, 116–117
    location of the administration, 318
        (Rap. Ref. 8.3)
    reverse rules for, 64 (Table 2.2)
    starting points/reverse rules of, 62
        (Rap. Ref. 2.1)
SLD assessment, defined, 291
Smerbeck, Audrey M., 262–276
Spatial Span (SSp), 314 (Rap. Ref. 8.2), 317
    (Table 8.1)
Spearman's g theory, 8
Special group studies
    Asperger's disorder
        highest/lowest mean scaled score of
            WISC-IV, 221 (Rap. Ref. 6.1)
        verbal perceptual discrepancies, 235
            (Rap. Ref. 6.13)
    attention-deficit/hyperactivity disorder
        (ADHD), 227 (Rap. Ref. 6.5)
    autistic disorder
        highest/lowest mean scaled score of
            WISC-IV, 221 (Rap. Ref. 6.1)
        verbal-perceptual discrepancies, 235
            (Rap. Ref. 6.13)
    and differential performance on digits forward/
        backward, 238 (Rap. Ref. 6.15)
    expressive language disorders
        highest/lowest mean scaled score of
            WISC-IV, 222 (Rap. Ref. 6.2)
        verbal-perceptual discrepancies, 235
            (Rap. Ref. 6.13)

Special group studies (*Cont.*)
  integrated process scores with ADHD, 228
    (Rap. Ref. 6.6)
  math disorder
    highest/lowest mean scaled score of
      WISC-IV, 229 (Rap. Ref. 6.7)
    verbal-perceptual discrepancies, 235
      (Rap. Ref. 6.13)
  motor impairment, 233 (Rap. Ref. 6.11)
  reading disorder, 229 (Rap. Ref. 6.7)
    highest/lowest mean scaled score of
      WISC-IV, 229 (Rap. Ref. 6.7)
    verbal-perceptual discrepancies, 235
      (Rap. Ref. 6.13)
  reading mathematics disorders (for
    discriminating samples), 231 (Rap. Ref. 6.9)
  reading/written expression disorders
    highest/lowest mean scaled score of
      WISC-IV, 230 (Rap. Ref. 6.8)
    index score differences, 232 (Rap. Ref. 6.10)
    verbal-perceptual discrepancies, 235 (Rap.
      Ref. 6.13)
  traumatic brain injury (TBI), 233
    (Rap. Ref. 6.11)
    and index score differences, 234
      (Rap. Ref. 6.12)
    verbal-perceptual discrepancies, 235
      (Rap. Ref. 6.13)
Specific learning disability (SLD)
  assessing individuals referred with the WISC-IV
    and WIAT-II, 277–279
  assessment defined, 291
  assessment flowchart, 294 (Fig. 7.1)
  cognitive ability analysis with WISC-IV,
    283–284
  comprehensive framework for determination,
    291–293
  evaluation of exclusionary factors, 282–283
  guiding questions implied by operational
    definition, 292 (Rap. Ref. 7.3)
  integrated ability analysis with the WISC-IV and
    WIAT-II, 289–290
  interindividual academic ability analysis with the
    WIAT-II, 279–282
  interindividual cognitive ability analysis with the
    WISC-IV, 283–284
  operational definition of, 278 (Table 7.3)
  reevaluation of exclusionary factors, 289
  summary of operational definition of, 290–291,
    292 (Rap. Ref. 7.3)
  WIAT-II, 280 (Rap. Ref. 7.1)
  WISC-IV and WIAT-II, operational definition
    of, 293, 295
Standard scores
  definition of, 106

  metrics for, 107 (Rap. Ref. 3.1)
  See also Scores, reporting
Stanford-Binet tasks, 4
Strengths/weaknesses
  administration and scoring, 206–208
    (Rap. Ref. 5.2)
  interpretation, 212–213 (Rap. Ref. 5.4)
  overview, 202–203
  reliability and validity, 209–211 (Rap. Ref. 5.3)
  standardization of, 214 (Rap. Ref. 5.5)
  test development/content, 203–205
    (Rap. Ref. 5.1)
Subtest administration
  frequently asked question, 102–103
    (Rap. Ref. 2.4)
  modifying standardized procedures, 60
  starting points/reverse rules, 62–63
    (Rap. Ref. 6.2)
  timing of, 69, 69 (Rap. Ref. 2.3)
Subtests, WISC-IV
  abbreviation for recording responses, 68, 69
  administration, FAQs for, 101–103
  administration by modifying standardized
    procedures, 60
  administration rules
    arithmetic, 93–96, 100
    behaviors to note on (BD), 73
    block design (BD), 71–75, 98–99
    cancellation (CA), 91–92, 101
    coding, 79–81, 100–101
    common errors in administration (in
      WISC-IV), 97–101
    comprehension, 86–88, 97–98
    digit span, 76–78, 100
    information (in), 92–93, 98
    letter-number sequencing, 83–85, 100
    matrix reasoning, 85, 99
    picture completion, 89–91
    picture concepts, 78–79, 99
    similarities, 75–76, 97
    symbol search, 88–89, 101
    vocabulary, 81–83, 97
    word reasoning, 96–97, 98
  average reliability coefficients of, 33
    (Rap. Ref. 1.5)
  best/worst predictors of WIAT-II achievement
    composites, 46 (Rap. Ref. 1.12)
  common errors in administration, 97–101
  discontinue rules, 66 (Table 2.3)
  feedback and encouragement (*see* rapport)
  important points to remember when using a
    stopwatch for timed test, 69 (Rap. Ref. 2.3)
  list of timed test, 69
  querying, 70
  repeating items, 70–71

reverse rules in, 64 (Table 2.2)
rules for starting points/reverse, 61–63, 62–63
    (Rap. Ref. 2.1)
scoring judgment in, 114–115
scoring keys for, 115
starting points/reverse rules, 62–63
    (Rap. Ref. 6.2)
as substitutions for core battery subtests, 110
    (Table 3.1)
supplemental
    rules of administration, 89–101
    as substitutions for core battery subtests, 110
        (Table 3.1)
testing conditions
    environment, 53–54
    materials, 54
testing individuals with special needs
    modifying standardized procedures, 60
timing, 69
Supplemental subtest
average percent process subtest raw score
    gain when subtest scaled scores are equal,
    348–349 (Table 8.3)
cognitive capacities assessed with verbal
    domain core and, 330–332 (Rap. Ref. 8.9)
interpreting differences between scores for
    core and, 342–344 (Rap. Ref. 8.13)
perceptual domain
    primary cognitive capacities, 366
        (Rap. Ref. 8.18)
    secondary cognitive capacities, 367
        (Rap. Ref. 8.18)
scaled score differences, average raw score
    gain percentages corresponding to process
    subtest minus core, 345–347 (Table 8.2)
working domain
    primary cognitive capacities, 405
        (Rap. Ref. 8.26)
    secondary cognitive capacities, 406–408
Symbol Search (SS) subtest
behaviors to note on, 89
broad and narrow classifications for, 27
    (Rap. Ref. 1.3)
common administration errors, 101
cultural loading/linguistic demand of, 303
    (Fig. 7.2)
and culture-language matrix, 305 (Fig. 7.3)
definition, 29 (Table 1.2)
discontinue rules, 66 (Table 2.3)
keys for scoring, 122–123
location of the administration, 319
    (Rap. Ref. 8.3)
reverse rules for, 64 (Table 2.2)
starting points/reverse rules of, 62
    (Rap. Ref. 2.1)

Terman, Lewis, 4
Testing conditions, WISC-IV
    environment, 53–54
    materials, 54
Testing individuals with special needs
    modifications in, 59–60
    modifying standardized procedures, 60
Testing the limits, 266
Timed Test
    important points to remember when using a
        stopwatch, 69 (Rap. Ref. 2.3)
Traumatic Brain Injury (TBI) children, 232–234
    highest and lowest mean WISC-IV subtest
        scaled scores of, 233 (Rap. Ref. 6.10)
    WISC-IV integrated process scores with the
        largest effect size for discriminating samples
        of (from matched controls), 234 (Rap. Ref.
        6.12)

Unitary Ability
    concept, 168
    definition of, 143
    how to interpret in (psychological report), 148
        (Rap. Ref. 4.8)
    summary of, 144 (Fig. 4.3)
Universal Nonverbal Intelligence Test (UNIT), 6

Verbal ability, 333
Verbal Comprehension Index (VCI), 7, 43,
    106, 139
    index score calculation with zero raw scale, 113
    interpretability of, 147 (Fig. 4.5)
Verbal domain tasks
    cognitive capacities likely to be assessed, 337–
        338 (Rap. Ref. 8.11)
Verbal IQ (VIQ), 10, 28
Verbal-Performance dichotomy, 9
Verbal-Performance discrepancy, 245
Visual Digit Span (VDS), 314, 317 (Table 8.1)
    definition, 314 (Rap. Ref. 8.2)
    as process-approach, 314 (Rap. Ref. 8.2)
Visual Processing (Gv) cluster
    composition of, 170 (Rap. Ref. 4.13)
    definition, 37
    vs. Gf cluster, 479
Vocabulary Multiple Choice (VCMC), 312, 316
    (Table 8.1)
    definition, 316 (Table 8.1)
    location of the administration, 319
        (Rap. Ref. 8.3)
    process approach, 312 (Rap. Ref. 8.2)
Vocabulary (VC) subtest
    behaviors to note on, 82
    broad and narrow classifications for, 26
        (Rap. Ref. 1.3)

Vocabulary (VC) subtest (*Cont.*)
common administration errors, 97
cultural loading/linguistic demand of, 303
(Fig. 7.2)
and culture-language matrix, 305 (Fig. 7.3)
description, 29 (Table 1.2)
discontinue rules, 66 (Table 2.3)
keys for scoring, 119–120
location of the administration, 319
(Rap. Ref. 8.3)
reverse rules for, 64 (Table 2.2)
starting points/reverse rules of, 62
(Rap. Ref. 2.1)
Volker, Martin A., 262

WAIS-IV, 41, (Rap. Ref. 1.5), 43 (Rap. Ref. 1.10),
63 (Table 2.1), 210 (Rap. Ref. 5.3)
WAIS-R as Neuropsychological Instrument
(WAIS-R, NI), 310
Wechsler, David
scale, 3
test, 14
Wechsler Adult Intelligence Scale-Third Edition
(WAIS-III), 5
Wechsler Adult Intelligence Scale (WAIS), 11
Wechsler-Bellevue Intelligence Scale
Form II (W-B II), 9, 16 (Fig. 1.2)
Form I (W-B I), 9
history of, 9–11
Wechsler Individual Achievement Test-Second
Edition (WIAT-II), 276
academic abilities by SLD area, 280–281
(Rap. Ref. 7.1)
achievement composites, 46 (Rap. Ref. 1.12)
intraindividual analysis, 279–282
Wechsler Intelligence Scale For Children–Fourth
Edition (WISC-IV)
administration changes from WISC-III
Arithmetic (AR) subtest administration
procedures, 95 (Table 2.13)
Arithmetic (AR) subtest scoring procedures,
126 (Table 3.10)
Block Design (BD) subtest administration
procedures, 72 (Table 2.4)
Block Design (BD) subtest scoring
procedures, 116 (Table 3.2)
Coding (CD) subtest administration
procedures, 80 (Table 2.7)
Comprehension (CO) subtest administration
procedures, 87 (Table 2.9)
Comprehension (CO) subtest scoring
procedure, 122 (Table 3.6)
Digit Span (DS) subtest administration
procedures, 77 (Table 2.6)
Digit Span (DS) subtest scoring procedures,
118 (Table 3.4)

Information (IN) subtest administration
procedures, 93 (Table 2.11)
Information (IN) subtest scoring procedures,
126 (Table 3.9)
Picture Completion (PCm) subtest
administration procedures, 90 (Table 2.11)
Picture Completion (PCm) subtest scoring
procedures, 124 (Table 3.8)
Similarities (SI) subtest administration
procedures, 76 (Table 2.5)
Similarities (SI) subtest scoring procedures,
117 (Table 3.3)
Symbol Search (SS) subtest administration
procedures, 88 (Table 2.10)
Symbol Search (SS) subtest scoring
procedures, 123 (Table 3.7)
Vocabulary (VC) subtest administration
procedures, 83 (Table 2.8)
Vocabulary (VC) subtest scoring procedures,
120 (Table 3.5)
alternative composites, 271–273
alternative descriptive system for, 137
(Rap. Ref. 4.4)
average reliability coefficients of subtests, 33
(Rap. Ref. 1.5)
best/worst predictors, 46 (Rap. Ref. 1.12)
broad and narrow classifications of, 26–27
(Rap. Ref. 1.3)
changes from the WISC-III to, 25
(Rap. Ref. 1.2)
CHC abilities, 285–286 (Rap. Ref. 7.2)
CHC classifications, psychological
corporation's, 28 (Rap. Ref. 1.4)
CHC structure of, 38 (Fig. 1.4)
classifications of, 26–27 (Rap. Ref. 1.3)
common administration errors, 97–101
composite measure, 23 (Table 1.1)
controlling for SES and other background
variables, 48 (Rap. Ref. 1.14)
convergent-discriminant validity coefficients in,
42, 43 (Rap. Ref. 1.10), 44
correlation of full scale IQS of, 41–42, 41
(Rap. Ref. 1.9)
cultural bias, 266–267
culture-language interpretive matrix (C-LIM)
incorporating data of, 305 (Fig. 7.3)
culture-language test classifications (C-LTC) for
subtests, 303 (Fig. 7.2)
dealing with unconventional correct responses,
274–276
description of, 22
difference in mean standard scores for Whites
vs. Hispanics, 47 (Rap. Ref. 1.13)
ethnic differences on, 45–49
FAQs for administration, 101–103
floors, ceilings, and item gradients, 34

fluid reasoning, 268
fundamental objective in assessment of,
   301–302
gifted profiles, 268–270
gifted profiles on, 270
g-loadings, 32
graph of culture-language interpretive matrix
   (C-LIM) incorporating hypothetical data, 306
   (Fig. 7.4)
individuals with special needs, testing, 58–60
information, general, 23 (Table 1.1)
integrating test scores from, 499–501
interesting facts about, 241 (6.17)
interesting facts about one-month practice
   effects, 36 (Rap. Ref. 1.8)
interpretive worksheet, 138(Fig. 4.1), 139
   (Fig. 4.2), 144(Fig. 4.3), 151(Fig. 4.7),
   156–157(Fig. 4.9), 179–181 (Fig. 4.13), 198
   (Fig. 4.16)
Jacob's profile, 508–509
key features listed in, 24 (Rap. Ref. 1.1)
normative descriptive system, 136(Rap. Ref. 4.3)
norming information, 24(Table 1.1)
organization of, 31(Fig. 1.3)
perceptual domain case study, 395–399
   (Rap. Ref. 8.22)
practice effects for separate scaled scores,
   35(Rap. Ref. 1.7)
practice effects of indexes/FSIQ, 34
   (Rap. Ref. 1.6)
profiles of select clinical samples, 240–242
psychometric summary, 496(Table 9.3)
quantitative/qualitative characteristics, other,
   49–50
recommendation, Jacob's difficulty, 512–513
recording responses, abbreviations for, 68
   (Rap. Ref. 2.2)
relationship to other Wechsler scales, 39
reliability coefficients and SEMS for clinical
   clusters of, 173–174 (Table 4.4)
relationship to WIAT-II, 44–45
selective testing table for combinations of, 40
   (Fig. 1.5)
score information, 23 (Table 1.1)
speed of performance, 264–266
structural validity, 37–39
structure of, 22
subtests
   definitions, 29–30 (Table 1.2)
   relationship to other Wechsler scales, 39
   standardization of, 30–32
terms used to describe fluctuations in a child's
   index profile, 164 (Rap. Ref. 4.11)
testing environment, 53–54
testing materials, 54
testing time, 264

traditional descriptive system for, 136
   (Rap. Ref. 4.2)
understanding bias vs. fairness, 296
WISC-IV interpretive worksheet, 138 (Fig. 4.1)
Wechsler Intelligence Scale for Children-Revised
   (WISC-R), 12
Wechsler Nonverbal Scale of Ability (WNV),
   41–44
Wechsler Preschool and Primary Scale of
   Intelligence (WPPSI), 5
Wechsler scales
   development, 3–6
   historical/contemporary views, 2–3, 6 (Fig. 1.1)
   interpretation steps (for iq)
      application of theory, 13–15
      clinical profile analysis, 9–11, 16 (Fig. 1.2)
      psychometric profile analysis, 11–13, 16
         (Fig. 1.2)
      quantification of general level, 8, 17 (Fig. 1.2)
   interpretive methods, 16–17 (Fig. 1.2)
   timeline of, 16–17 (Fig. 1.2)
Wechsler test interpretation, 15, 133
Wechsler Verbal vs. Nonverbal Performance,
   245–246
WISC-IV indexes. See Indexes, WISC-IV
WISC-IV integrated
   base rates for, 323–325
   clinical applications of verbal domain, 325–327
   cumulative percentages (base rates) for process
      observations, 323–325
   process-approach administration/scoring
      procedures, 312–316
   process score, 320–321
   process subtests, 316–319
      verbal domain, 316 (Table 8.1)
      perceptual domain, 316–317 (Table 8.1)
      processing speed domain, 318 (Table 8.1)
      working memory domain, 317 (Table 8.1)
   subtest scaled score discrepancy comparisons,
      321–323
   keys to preparing to administer, 54
   material changes and additions made to
      WISC-IV, 311 (Rap. Ref. 8.1)
   origin of subtests, 7
   process-approach administration scoring
      location of directions for various process
         subtests, 318–319 (Rap. Ref. 8.3)
      perceptual domain, 313 (Rap. Ref. 8.2)
      processing speed domain, 315 (Rap. Ref. 8.2)
      verbal domain, 312–313 (Rap. Ref. 8.2)
      working memory domain, 314 (Rap. Ref. 8.)
   subtest administration, 102–103 (Rap. Ref. 2.4)
Within Normal Limits (WNL)
   definition, 164 (Rap. Ref. 4.10)
   See also Descriptive categories, normative

WJ III COG, 479–481
  CHC abilities, 285–286 (Rap. Ref. 7.2)
Woodcock-Johnson Tests of Achievement-Third
  Edition (WJ III ACH), 279
Word Reasoning (WR) subtest
  behaviors to note on, 96
  broad and narrow classifications for, 27
    (Rap. Ref. 1.3)
  common administration errors, 98
  cultural loading/linguistic demand of, 303
    (Fig. 7.2)
  and culture-language matrix, 305 (Fig. 7.3)
  definition, 30 (Table 1.2)
  description of, 30 (Table 1.2)
  discontinue rules, 66 (Table 2.3)
  keys for scoring, 126–127
  location of the administration, 319
    (Rap. Ref. 8.3)
  reverse rules for, 64 (Table 2.2)
  starting points/reverse rules of, 63
    (Rap. Ref. 2.1)
Working memory domain
  Arithmetic Process Approach (ARPA), 314
  to assess capacities, 404–405
  case study, 433–442 (Rap. Ref. 8.31)
  cognitive capacities assessed with, 405–408
    (Rap. Ref. 8.26)
  description, 392
  how to alter cognitive demands, 415–416
    (Rap. Ref. 8.28)
  index score *vs.* process-approach interpretation
    of, 410–413 (Rap. Ref. 8.27)
  letter-number sequencing process approach
    (LNPA), 314
  letter span (LS), 314
  Spatial Span (SSp), 317 (Table 8.1)
  task
    cognitive capacities to be assessed, 417–422
    (Rap. Ref. 8.29)

comparison worksheet, 429–432 (Fig. 8.3),
    435 (Rap. Ref. 8.31)
  guidelines for interpreting comparisons
    between, 423–428 (Rap. Ref. 8.30)
  use/interpretation of, 404
  Visual Digit Span (VDS), 314, 317 (Table 8.1)
  when to use process subtests, 400–404
  WMI index, 409
  written arithmetic (WA) index, 314
    (Rap. Ref. 8.2)
Working memory domain tasks
  case study, 433–442 (Rap. Ref. 8.31)
  cognitive capacities likely to be, 417–422
    (Rap. Ref. 8.29)
  guidelines for interpreting comparisons
    between, 423–428 (Rap. Ref. 8.30)
  worksheet, 429–432 (Fig. 8.3)
Working Memory Index (WMI), 7, 28
  administration and scoring of, 401
    (Rap. Ref. 8.23)
  broad/narrow classifications of, 26–27
    (Rap. Ref. 1.3)
  CHC classifications, psychological
    corporation's, 28 (Rap. Ref. 1.4)
  definition, 150
  index score calculation with zero raw scale of
    zero, 113
  interpretability of, 147 (Fig. 4.5)
Written/reading expression disorders, 229–232
  highest and lowest mean WISC-IV subtest
    scaled scores of, 230 (Rap. Ref. 6.8)
  WISC-IV integrated process scores with the
    largest effect size for discriminating samples
    of, 232 (Rap. Ref. 6.10)
  See also Special group studies

Zero score. *See* Raw scores, of zero

ABOUT THE CD-ROM

INTRODUCTION

This appendix provides you with information on the contents of the CD that accompanies this book. For the latest information, please refer to the ReadMe file located at the root of the CD.

System Requirements

A computer with a processor running at 120 Mhz or faster

- At least 32 MB of total RAM installed on your computer; for best performance, we recommend at least 64 MB
- A CD-ROM drive

NOTE: Many popular spreadsheet programs are capable of reading Microsoft Excel files. However, users should be aware that a slight amount of formatting might be lost when using a program other than Microsoft Excel.

Using the CD

To install the items from the CD to your hard drive, follow these steps.

1. Insert the CD into your computer's CD-ROM drive.
   The license agreement appears.
   Note to Windows users: The interface won't launch if you have autorun disabled. In that case, choose Start@@—>Run. (For Windows Vista, choose Start@@—>All Programs@@—> Accessories@@—>Run.) In the dialog box that appears, type *D*:**Start.exe.** (Replace *D* with the proper letter if your CD drive uses a different letter. If you don't know the letter, see how your CD drive is listed under My Computer.) Click OK.

   Note for Mac Users: When the CD icon appears on your desktop, double-click the icon to open the CD and double-click the Start icon.

2. Read through the license agreement and then click the Accept button if you want to use the CD.

The CD interface appears. The interface allows you to browse the contents and install the programs with just a click of a button (or two).

What's on the CD

The following sections provide a summary of the software and other materials you'll find on the CD.

Content

This CD-ROM consists of worksheet files written and programmed in Microsoft Excel that allow readers to enter WISC-IV data along with other specific test data and have it analyzed following the steps outlined in Chapter 4 of this book. The Excel program called, *WISC-IV Data Management and Interpretive Assistant* (or WISC-IV DMIA v1.0) was programmed in collaboration with Elizabeth O. Lichtenberger. Note that the WISC-IV steps from Chapter 4 may be completed by hand, following the WISC-IV Interpretive Worksheet included in Appendix E (found in the "Contents" folder), or may be performed automatically using the WISC-IV DMIA v1.0.

Examples of the Excel worksheets on this CD are presented as figures in the book. These automated worksheets are provided on the CD for your convenience in using, applying and understanding the interpretive method described in this book. The WISC-IV DMIA v1.0 is meant to expedite analysis and interpretation of WISC IV data.

It is important to note that the WISC-IV DMIA v1.0 does not convert WISC-IV *raw scores* to any metric. Users of this program are responsible for following the test publisher's administration and scoring guidelines. That is, all WISC-IV scores entered into this program must be derived from the norms and procedures provided by the test publisher. Note that the WISC-IV Clinical Clusters created by Dawn Flanagan and Alan Kaufman are automatically computed by the WISC-IV DMIA v1.0 based on actual norms provided to them by the test publisher. See Chapter 4 for details.

Also included on this CD-ROM are all the appendices mentioned throughout the book. These appendices may be found in a folder marked "Content". The following 10 appendices are included in the Content folder:

Appendix A Definitions of CHC Abilities and Processes

Appendix B CHC Abilities and Processes Measured by Major Intelligence Tests

Appendix C WISC-IV Subtest *g*-Loadings, by Age Group and Overall Sample

Appendix D   Psychometric, Theoretical, and Qualitative Characteristics of the WISC-IV

Appendix E   WISC-IV Interpretive Worksheet

Appendix F1 General Ability Index (GAI) Conversion Table: U.S. and Canadian Norms

Appendix F2 Cognitive Proficiency Index (CPI) Conversion Table

Appendix G   Summary of Analyses of WISC-IV Indexes

Appendix H   Norms Tables for Clinical Clusters

Appendix I   Linking WISC-IV Assessment Results to Educational Strategies and Instructional Supports

Applications

The following applications are on the CD:

Adobe Reader

Adobe Reader is a freeware application for viewing files in the Adobe Portable Document format.

OpenOffice.org

OpenOffice.org is a free multi-platform office productivity suite. It is similar to Microsoft Office or Lotus SmartSuite, but OpenOffice.org is absolutely free. It includes word processing, spreadsheet, presentation, and drawing applications that enable you to create professional documents, newsletters, reports, and presentations. It supports most file formats of other office software. You should be able to edit and view any files created with other office solutions.

Shareware programs are fully functional, trial versions of copyrighted programs. If you like particular programs, register with their authors for a nominal fee and receive licenses, enhanced versions, and technical support.

Freeware programs are copyrighted games, applications, and utilities that are free for personal use. Unlike shareware, these programs do not require a fee or provide technical support.

GNU software is governed by its own license, which is included inside the folder of the GNU product. See the GNU license for more details.

Trial, demo, or evaluation versions are usually limited either by time or functionality (such as being unable to save projects). Some trial versions are very sensitive to system date changes. If you alter your computer's date, the programs will "time out" and no longer be functional.

CUSTOMER CARE

If you have trouble with the CD-ROM, please call the Wiley Product Technical Support phone number at (800) 762-2974. Outside the United States, call 1(317) 572-3994. You can also contact Wiley Product Technical Support at **http://support.wiley.com**. John Wiley & Sons will provide technical support only for installation and other general quality control items. For technical support on the applications themselves, consult the program's vendor or author.

To place additional orders or to request information about other Wiley products, please call (877) 762-2974.